To Our Children and Their Children
and
To Their Caregivers and Teachers

Preface

Welcome to the fourth edition of *The Young Child*. This text is written to provide you, the student of child development, the most important tool possessed by those who interact with, care for, and provide educational experiences for young children and their families. This tool is a knowledge base of current theory and research in the field of early growth, development, and learning and its translation into practice in the daily lives of very young children. Indeed, optimal child development depends on parents, caregivers, and educators who provide for and interact with children from a knowledgeable and growth-promoting perspective.

You may find it fascinating that today's scholars have very different views of how best to support human growth and development than many scholars of the past. You may even experience challenges to your long-held assumptions and views on childhood and perhaps your childhood experiences. You may also find comfort in learning about the "tried and true," those theories and research studies now considered classic, that continue to guide and support the study of child development and inspire continued research. As you study and follow growth and development from prenatal development through the early school-age years, you will be introduced to contemporary insights on such topics as the following:

- The impact and long-term consequences of early biological and psychological experiences on brain growth and neurological development
- The importance of, and potential impediments to, optimal prenatal development
- Increasing scholarly interest in the mental health of infants and young children
- Cultural diversity and the positive potential of varying developmental pathways
- How growth and development of children with challenges is supported
- Contemporary health, safety, and well-being issues of children and families
- How children learn and become literate
- The evolution of childhood social and moral competence
- The changing American family and the ecological systems surrounding and influencing families and children
- The changing dynamics and structures in child care and early education and their impact on childhood and individual child well-being

ORGANIZATION OF THE TEXT

This text is divided into six parts. Part One, *An Overview of Early Childhood Development*, outlines historical viewpoints and the evolution of the study of early childhood. It presents both classic and contemporary theories of early childhood development and emphasizes the importance of this information to our understanding of growth, development, and learning, and to the practices of parents and early childhood professionals. Through this discussion, the reader is introduced to contemporary issues associated with childhood and family life today and emerging research areas in the early childhood care and education profession.

Part Two, *The Child's Life Begins*, discusses the family before birth, with attention to educational, sociocultural, and economic considerations in the decision to parent. It describes prenatal development with an emphasis on health, nutrition, and medical supervision of pregnancy. Childbirth and family dynamics surrounding the newborn are also examined.

Parts Three through Six trace physical and motor, psychosocial, and cognitive, language, and literacy development during the following stages: infancy, ages 1 through 3, ages 4 through 5, and ages 6 through 8. This organization facilitates either chronological or topical discussion and study.

The chapters include charts and boxed material to amplify concepts and to give prominence to specific issues. Margin notes are provided to define new or unfamiliar terms. At the end of each chapter are Review Strategies and Activities, which include relevant, hands-on suggestions, field experiences, and reflective exercises. In addition, Further Readings are suggested along with relevant Websites and other print or electronic resources. A full Glossary is included at the end of the text along with helpful Appendixes.

ANGELA AND JEREMY

Two young children, Angela and Jeremy, are introduced in Chapter 2, and subsequent chapters follow their development and relationships. These vignettes illustrate the uniqueness of children's experiences and their growth and developmental pathways. Angela and Jeremy are composites of many children the authors have known and are not representative of any particular racial or ethnic group. We caution the reader to avoid viewing these children in a stereotypical or prejudicial manner. While both children and their families experience adversity to varying degrees, the vignettes attempt to illustrate the power of resiliency and potential for learning and development in all individuals and in all types of family contexts.

ACKNOWLEDGMENTS

As with previous editions of this text, we extend our appreciation to the early childhood education students at Texas State University–San Marcos, who have so capably provided the authors with ongoing feedback through their thoughtful written critiques of prior editions of this text. Many changes in each edition are based on these students' suggestions and comments. We are especially grateful to our many colleagues in the universities and teacher training programs in which we teach, and in the schools and child care programs with whom we collaborate, whose interest and support for this project continually provide inspiration and content suggestions. To our many friends and colleagues around the country whose support and interest have always exemplified the caring of the early childhood professional, we say a hearty thank you.

We would like to acknowledge the reviewers of this edition: Teresa Buchanan, Louisiana State University; Christy T. Corbin, University of Maryland; Donna Gray, Middlesex Community College; and Janet F. McLanahan, North Shore Community College.

To our colleagues at Merrill/Prentice Hall and The GTS Companies—Kevin Davis, Autumn Benson, Amanda King (Editorial Assistant), Mary Harlan (Production Editor), Carol Sykes, Kathy Kirtland, Karen Ettinger, and Philip Koplin (Copyeditor)—whose expertise in preparing a manuscript for publication is without equal, and whose skill and patience deftly guided this fourth edition of *The Young Child* to its final form, we extend genuine appreciation. We'd also like to thank Janette Wetsel for her hard work in preparing the content for the Instructor's Manual and Companion Website.

And of course, to our families, who tolerated our long and tedious hours of book and online time, we extend profound appreciation. It is hard to imagine pursuing this type of task without the support and encouragement of family and friends.

Margaret B. Puckett, Ed.D.

Janet K. Black, Ph.D.

Discover the Companion Website Accompanying This Book

THE PRENTICE HALL COMPANION WEBSITE: A VIRTUAL LEARNING ENVIRONMENT

Technology is a constantly growing and changing aspect of our field that is creating a need for content and resources. To address this emerging need, Prentice Hall has developed an online learning environment for students and professors alike—Companion Websites—to support our textbooks.

In creating a Companion Website, our goal is to build on and enhance what the textbook already offers. For this reason, the content for each user-friendly Website is organized by topic and provides the professor and student with a variety of meaningful resources. Common features of a Companion Website include:

FOR THE PROFESSOR—

Every Companion Website integrates **Syllabus Manager**™, an online syllabus creation and management utility.

- **Syllabus Manager**™ provides you, the instructor, with an easy, step-by-step process to create and revise syllabi, with direct links into Companion Website and other online content without having to learn HTML.
- Students may logon to your syllabus during any study session. All they need to know is the web address for the Companion Website and the password you've assigned to your syllabus.
- After you have created a syllabus using **Syllabus Manager**™, students may enter the syllabus for their course section from any point in the Companion Website.

- Clicking on a date, the student is shown the list of activities for the assignment. The activities for each assignment are linked directly to actual content, saving time for students.
- Adding assignments consists of clicking on the desired due date, then filling in the details of the assignment—name of the assignment, instructions, and whether it is a one-time or repeating assignment.
- In addition, links to other activities can be created easily. If the activity is on-line, a URL can be entered in the space provided, and it will be linked automatically in the final syllabus.
- Your completed syllabus is hosted on our servers, allowing convenient updates from any computer on the Internet. Changes you make to your syllabus are immediately available to your students at their next logon.

FOR THE STUDENT—

- **Topic Overviews**—outline key concepts in topic areas
- **Electronic Bluebook**—send homework or essays directly to your instructor's email with this paperless form
- **Message Board**—serves as a virtual bulletin board to post—or respond to—questions or comments to/from a national audience
- **Chat**—real-time chat with anyone who is using the text anywhere in the country—ideal for discussion and study groups, class projects, etc.
- **Web Destinations**—links to www sites that relate to each topic area
- **Professional Organizations**—links to organizations that relate to topic areas
- **Additional Resources**—access to topic-specific content that enhances material found in the text

To take advantage of these and other resources, please visit the Companion Website for *The Young Child: Development from Prebirth Through Age Eight,* Fourth Edition, at

www.prenhall.com/puckett

Brief Contents

xi

Contents

Note: Every effort has been made to provide accurate and current Internet information in this book. However, the Internet and information posted on it are constantly changing, so it is inevitable that some of the Internet addresses listed in this textbook will change.

An Overview of Early Childhood Development

CHAPTER ONE

The What and Why of Early Childhood Development

There are two last-ing bequests we can hope to give our chil-dren—one is roots; the other is wings.

HODDING CARTER

After studying this chapter, you will demonstrate comprehension by:

▶ Reflecting on personal goals as a developing early childhood professional.

▶ Defining early childhood development.

▶ Describing the importance of understanding early childhood development.

▶ Outlining historical perspectives on childhood.

▶ Describing the evolution of the study of early childhood development.

▶ Identifying current theories and research emphases in the study of early childhood development.

▶ Listing emerging issues in the field of early childhood development.

Have you ever found yourself wondering about the types of childhood experiences people have had—the famous, the infamous, the notorious, the obscure? Do you find yourself observing children in various contexts and marveling at their robust energy, outward-bound personalities, unbridled curiosity? . . . or contemplating their reticence, timidity, or apparent discomfort, maybe sadness? Are people just born the way they are? Do children come into the world with personalities and behaviors over which they or those around them will have little influence? When childhood segues into adulthood, what could—should—might—growth, development, and learning outcomes be? These are important reflections for the student of child growth and development and for parents and early childhood educators, who play important roles in the lives of children. We all benefit from knowledge of child growth and development. Such knowledge enhances self-understanding and acceptance, informs relationships with others, lays the most important foundation for parenting, and establishes informed rationale for the types of child care and education policies and programs provided for children and their families. Importantly, professionals who work with children and families have an ethical responsibility to make the study of child growth and development a career-long pursuit.

CHILD STUDY IN CONTEMPORARY CONTEXTS

The study of child growth and development throughout history has provided both stable and evolving perspectives on the biological characteristics of human beings, the origins of human behavior, and the outcomes of human experience. However, few eras have demanded a greater need for knowledge about child growth and development than the current one, as the information in Figure 1.1 suggests. Read a newspaper or magazine, notice the contents of "infotainment" programs on television, surf the Internet, and scan the tables of

FIGURE 1.1

Source: The State of Children in America's Union (Washington, D.C.: Children's Defense Fund, 2002). With permission.

21 Key Facts about American Children

3 in 5	preschoolers have mothers in the labor force.
2 in 5	preschoolers eligible for Head Start do not participate in the program.
1 in 3	is born to unmarried parents.
1 in 3	will be poor at some point in childhood.
1 in 3	is behind a year or more in school.
1 in 4	lives with only one parent.
1 in 5	is born to a mother who did not graduate from high school.
1 in 5	children under 3 is poor now.
1 in 6	is born to a mother who did not receive prenatal care in the first three months of pregnancy.
1 in 7	children eligible for federal child care assistance through the Child Care and Development Block Grant receives it.
1 in 8	has no health insurance.
1 in 8	never graduates from high school.
1 in 8	is born to a teenage mother.
1 in 8	lives in a family receiving food stamps.
1 in 12	has a disability.
1 in 13	was born at low birthweight.
1 in 16	lives in *extreme* poverty.
1 in 24	lives with neither parent.
1 in 60	sees their parents divorce in any year.
1 in 141	will die before their first birthday.
1 in 1,056	will be killed by firearms before age 20.

contents of a variety of professional journals and you will soon notice an array of reports about the status and concerns of contemporary families and the needs of children. Accurate knowledge about how children grow and develop, how they learn, and the long-term consequences of early experiences is as critical to a healthy society as it has ever been. Who needs knowledge about child growth and development, and what should they do with that information? Think about the following questions:

1. As young adults become parents, frequently without the benefit of extended family support systems, what do they need to know to ensure the best possible outcomes for their children?

2. With greater numbers of children at younger and younger ages receiving non-parental care, what concerns should we have about childhood health, safety, personality development, and early learning?

3. As public schools get into the business of caring for and educating younger and younger children, what changes must they make to meet the unique needs of their youngest students? . . . of young children with special needs? . . . of young children of different cultures and languages? What are the long-term effects of earliest education experiences?

4. What are the effects and long-term consequences of violence and other asocial events experienced either firsthand or vicariously through toys, movies, television, video and computer games, and the Internet?

5. How can early childhood professionals help children and families meet the challenges posed by threats of terrorism?

6. Politicians who have made child care, education, and welfare issues part of their platforms exert considerable power over the types of home and out-of-home experiences that children have. How can early childhood professionals help families to access quality resources to enhance life for themselves and their children? How can early childhood professionals protect infants and young children from policies that may be deleterious?

7. Various interest groups frequently exert influence on policy makers, educators, directors of child care programs, and other professionals to enforce schooling, child care, and family life agendas that may not be appropriately generalized to all children and families. How will these decision makers know how to respond to requests that do not serve the best interests of all children? In short, how might individual families make distinctions between what is best for their children and what is clearly not in their children's best growth and development interests or the best interests of their families?

Yes, knowledge of child growth and development is important in numerous aspects of our lives and in many sectors of society, for every minute of every day, children are affected by whether parents, educators, policy makers, the media, and all who interact with them can make sound judgments based on our best understanding about how children grow and develop. How do we determine what serves their best long-term developmental interests? Again, as in no time before, all of us must become students of child development.

Information abounds. Some of it is reliable, some is not. Hence, scholars and practitioners in the field of early childhood development take a discerning look at both classic and emerging research within the field and from a number of allied disciplines. The study of early childhood development draws knowledge from research and practice in many fields: the biological and neurological sciences, medicine, psychology, sociology, anthropology, education, and political science. Thus, the study of child growth and development is an interdisciplinary one, as is illustrated in Figure 1.2.

Research from many disciplines is bringing about new perspectives on growth and development and the human experience. As you read this text, you will see that childhood is quite different today from what you experienced. Contemporary researchers are interested in learning more about not just the sequences and patterns of growth, development, and learning, but also how various and numerous influences in many different contexts (home, school, neighborhood, social networks, and other contexts) affect individual developmental pathways and outcomes. Our knowledge base is expanding rapidly and altering many long-held assumptions about children. It isn't always true that what worked in the past (even the recent past) is appropriate or best for today's child. Hence, the study of child growth and development gives parents and practitioners necessary information to make wise decisions about what children need and how to relate to them.

FIGURE 1.2
The Interdisciplinary Nature of Child Study

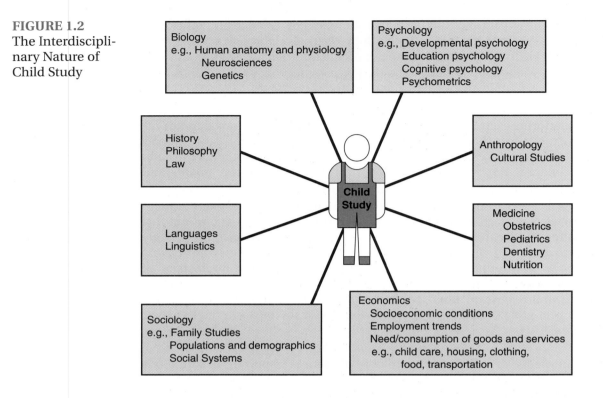

THE EARLY CHILDHOOD DEVELOPMENT PROFESSION

professionals:
individuals who have internalized the evolving knowledge base of their particular fields and use this knowledge to improve practices that have an impact on the lives of children and families

Professionals learn the knowledge base of their particular field. This knowledge base, coupled with practice in the field, facilitates the development of competent practitioners. Becoming a competent early childhood professional begins with learning about growth and development of young children. Professionalism entails continuously learning about young children and their families throughout one's career.

The study of children had its beginnings in the late 1700s during a period when children as young as 3 years of age could be found working in factories, and formal schooling was reserved for well-to-do boys, who were expected to sit quietly in adult-size furnishings and memorize curricula derived primarily from religious and moral beliefs. The scholarly journey from the 1700s to the 21st century has focused our attention more and more on what best serves the long-term well-being of children in families, schools, communities, and societies. Within the last century, a substantial body of knowledge has evolved to inform parenting and child care practices, education philosophy and pedagogy, and public policy. Research increasingly illustrates that while similarities exist among all children in various aspects of human growth and development, there is a need to learn about and respect variations in the backgrounds and experiences of young children and their families (Lally, Lerner, and Lurie-Hurvitz, 2001). Because the body of knowledge about child growth, development, and learning is continually changing and enlarging, professionals who work with young children and their families also continually evolve in their understanding of the types of relationships and experiences that maximize opportunities for optimal growth and development. In the field of early childhood education, this perspective is referred to as a **developmentally appropriate** one; that is, interactions with and expectations of children are based on current knowledge about age and individuality. Integral to understanding individuality is the knowledge that various contexts and interrelationships a child experiences as he or she grows, develops, and learns are often particular to the child's cultural heritage and milieu.

Today, most of the 50 states require teachers of young children to have specialized training in early childhood development and related areas. In 1982, the National Association for the Education of Young Children (NAEYC) developed guidelines for training professionals who work with young children. These Early Childhood Teacher Education Guidelines were subsequently adopted by the National Council for the Accreditation of Teacher Education (NCATE). Considerable research began in 1992 when NAEYC's National Institute for Early Childhood Professional Development launched a nationwide review process seeking professional input. From this effort, a national professional consensus was established, and the 1982 guidelines were revised and published as the *NAEYC Guidelines for Preparation of Early Childhood Professionals* (National Association for the Education of Young Children, 1996). In addition to NCATE's endorsement in September 1994, these revised guidelines were endorsed by the Division of Early Childhood of the Council for Exceptional Children. More recently, the National Association for the Education of Young Children and the National Council for Accreditation of Teacher Education (2001) have collaborated to develop and publish standards for early childhood professional preparation (Box 1.1). These provide an example of the standards that specifically address knowledge about child growth and development.

These efforts to define standards for professional development reflect two important federal laws: the Individuals with Disabilities Education Act, passed in 1991, and the Americans with Disabilities Act, passed in 1992. These laws mandate that individuals with disabilities are entitled to equal rights in (1) public accommodations such as child care centers, family child care homes, preschools, and public schools; (2) state and local services; and (3) employment. Specifically, all early childhood programs must provide services to young children with developmental delays or disabilities and to those who are at risk for developmental delays.

developmentally appropriate: pertains to (1) age appropriateness, the universal and predictable patterns of growth and development that occur in children from birth through age 8, and (2) individual appropriateness, the individual rates and patterns of physical/ motor, psychosocial, cognitive, language and literacy development, personality and learning style, and family and cultural background of each child

---

BOX 1.1

Tomorrow's teachers should know and be able to promote child development and learning, which includes

- understanding what young children are like;
- understanding what influences children's development;
- using this understanding to create environments where children can thrive.

Excerpt from National Association for the Education of Young Children & National Council for Accreditation of Teacher Education (2001).

inclusion:
the education model that includes children with developmental challenges in general education settings

Implicit in these laws is the concept of **inclusion**. Inclusion refers to procedures and curricular means for ensuring that all children are fully accepted members of the child care and learning communities in which they participate. The practice of inclusion benefits all children and families. Inclusion helps children to appreciate and accept individual differences while developing caring attitudes and a recognition of our human interdependence.

The ever-changing perspectives on human growth and development, and, most recently, the growing emphasis on the genesis of many anomalies that can be traced to early brain and neurological growth and development and the types of pre- and postnatal experiences that promote or impede optimal development in children, have quickened the profession's desire for knowledgeable and well-prepared early childhood care and education personnel. Contemporary studies offer hope for continuing revelations, preventive measures, and potential treatments for children with special needs. Hence, it is appropriate that professional development guidelines emphasize that early childhood and elementary education personnel

- have knowledge of and respect for wide variations in children and the uniqueness of each;
- understand the importance of full inclusion of children with special needs and developmental challenges;
- relate appropriately to individuals and their families;
- provide developmentally appropriate experiences and set challenging, yet achievable goals for individual children;
- apply sound and ethical principles in screening, diagnosis, and ongoing assessments of all children;
- learn about and access appropriate resources to facilitate and enhance the developmental outcomes for each child (National Council for the Education of Young Children & National Council for Accreditation of Teacher Education, 2001; Sandall, McLean, & Smith, 2000).

Another effort to provide training and credentialing for those who work with young children is the Child Development Associate (CDA) National Credentialing Program. This program was initiated in 1971 for the purpose of enhancing "the quality of child care by defining, evaluating and recognizing the competence of child care providers and home visitors" (Council for Early Childhood Professional Recognition, 1992, p. 1). A person who is awarded a CDA credential has demonstrated competency in working with young children and their families by successfully completing the CDA training and assessment process.

More recently, Congress mandated that half of the teachers in center-based Head Start programs have or obtain at least an associate degree in early childhood education or a related field by the year 2003. A report in May 2003 revealed that this goal was exceeded, and the percentage of front-line practitioners with associate or higher degrees is anticipated to increase (Schumacher & Irish, 2003).

Head Start and Early Head Start are federally funded programs designed to provide early childhood education along with comprehensive services (developmental health and well-being screening, monitoring, and intervention;

psychological services; and others) and family involvement and support for children living in poverty.

The recognition of the importance of training for those who work with young children arises from the results of longitudinal studies on various early childhood programs for both **at-risk** and **low-risk** children that traced long-term outcomes for school performance and life adjustments (Campbell & Ramey, 1994; Larsen & Robinson, 1989; Lazar & Darlington, 1982; Schweinhart, Barnes, & Weikart, 1993; Schweinhart & Weikart, 1997). Emphasis on professional development of early childhood educators emerged from studies that revealed the effects of various types of parenting practices and early care and education programs on children's physical/motor development, social and emotional development, and cognitive, language, and literacy outcomes (Barnett, 1995; Dunn & Kontos, 1997; Karoly et al., 1998; Kontos & Wilcox-Herzog, 1997; Melmed, 1997).

Increasing emphasis on the importance of the early years in growth and development and a concurrent trend of mounting need for nonparental child care for infants, toddlers, very young children, and before- and after-school care for school-age children has evoked concerns and prompted studies of the quality, accessibility, and affordability of child care (Helburn, 1995; Helburn & Bergmann, 2002; Kagan & Neuman, 1997). Because of the increasing demand for early childhood programs, professionally prepared teachers are needed. Unfortunately, at times, young children are in settings that are **developmentally inappropriate** because the adults who are working with them are unaware of information about how children grow, develop, and learn or of the nuances of developmental, socioeconomic, and cultural diversity. Concurrent with this lack of knowledge is often a failure to recognize the effects that their own interactions with and expectations of children can have on behaviors and development.

The growing recognition of the unique nature of early growth, development, and learning and of the importance of the early years for lifelong well-being and productivity has created a demand for professionally trained and knowledgeable early childhood educators. The goal of this text is to provide students with the background information needed to develop into competent early childhood professionals. Such competency requires the perspective that learning about young children and their families is an ongoing, career-long process.

at-risk: infants and children who are subject to any of a number of risk factors (such as poverty, drug exposure, genetic and/or developmental anomalies, and family dynamics) that make them vulnerable to compromised growth and development

low-risk: infants and children whose risk factors are minimal or absent

developmentally inappropriate: expectations or practices that fail to acknowledge age and individual characteristics and needs

DEFINITION OF EARLY CHILDHOOD DEVELOPMENT

The study of early childhood development is about how children from prebirth through age eight grow and develop in the physical/motor, psychosocial, cognitive, language, and literacy domains. For convenience, this book will discuss the various domains separately. Nevertheless, it should be noted that all development is interrelated, interactive, and mutually dependent; development in one area or domain influences or is dependent on development or behavior in other areas. For example, children's sense of trust (psychosocial development) influences the extent to which they will explore their surroundings for new information (cognitive development), and hearing acuity (physical development) influences the development of speech and language (cognitive, language, and literacy development). The uniqueness of the individual child is emphasized throughout this text, as are the many forms of diversity, including developmental, cultural, gender, and

The student of child development is both a scholar and a practitioner who gains knowledge and skills from professional literature and observation and interactions with children.

socioeconomic diversity, and the interdependence and interplay among various contexts in which children live, play, and are educated.

THE IMPORTANCE OF UNDERSTANDING EARLY CHILDHOOD DEVELOPMENT

It is important to know about early childhood development for several reasons. First, knowledge of early childhood development helps parents and professionals to facilitate optimal growth and learning in young children. Second, a knowledge of growth and development in the early years can facilitate self-understanding. Knowledgeable parents and educators relate and interact appropriately with children and conscientiously provide the **essential experiences** that are now associated with earliest brain growth and neurological development and are linked to long-term developmental and behavioral outcomes (Nelson & Luciana, 2001; Shonkoff & Phillips, 2000; Shore, 1997; Sylwester, 2000). Early childhood educators who understand child development are better prepared to interface individual developmental characteristics with appropriately challenging expectations and education practices and to provide the emotional support and social interactions that lead to optimal development.

essential experiences: experiences deemed critical at certain times during early growth and development, which have growth-inducing influence on the brain's neurological structures

EVOLUTION OF CHILD STUDY

John Locke (1632–1704) was one of the earliest scholars or philosophers to advocate humane treatment of young children. He also was one of the first to suggest that the child's environmental experience may influence the development of the child's knowledge. Locke described the newborn's mind as a *tabula rasa,* an "empty slate," on which knowledge is written that is based on the child's sensory experiences in his or her environment.

Jean Jacques Rousseau (1712–1778) was instrumental in dispelling the prevalent view of his era that children were simply miniature adults. He believed that children are born innately good and that growth and development follow the laws of nature. He suggested that there are distinct stages in growth and development: birth to age 5, age 5 to 12, age 12 to 15, age 15 to 20, and age 20 and over. He believed that development unfolds according to this set schedule. He published his beliefs about child development and education in his book *Émile* (1762), a story of an imaginary child who was reared with special motherly care complemented by a tutor. Rousseau stressed that education must begin at birth.

In 1774, Johann Pestalozzi (1746–1827) published a study of his son that also gave serious attention to the nature of development during the early years of growth and development. He emphasized that children's development physically, mentally, and morally depends on experience, which must include sensory stimulation.

Nearly a century later, Charles Darwin (1809–1882) published a day-to-day record of the development of his young son. Furthermore, Darwin's publication of *On The Origin of Species* (1859) had far-reaching effects on many aspects of scientific knowledge, including the study of children. As a biologist, Darwin took a trip to the Galapagos Islands in the South Pacific, where he collected birds and animals that were virtually unknown and, therefore, had not been classified according to any designated species. Darwin used these birds and animals to disprove the idea of a fixed nature of species. His conceptualization that the world is dynamic, not static, set the stage for the scientific study of children.

Darwin's theory that animals adapt to their particular environments over time led biologists, psychologists, and others to begin studying the adaptive characteristics of humans. One of these psychologists, G. Stanley Hall (1846–1924), was instrumental in implementing the scientific method to study change and development in children. In 1893, Hall published *The Contents of Children's Minds.* This book was one of the first texts to be used in colleges and universities for training students who wanted to learn about young children. Another of Hall's important contributions to the study of child development was the establishment of the first child development research journal, the *Journal of Genetic Psychology.* Some of Hall's more illustrious students included Arnold Gesell, who later developed **norms** regarding the physical maturation of children; John Dewey, whose democratic ideas about the learning process created major educational reform; and Lewis Terman, who developed the idea of the intelligence quotient (IQ). Hall's international reputation and influence enabled him to convince Sigmund Freud to come to Clark University to lecture on psychoanalysis.

norms: the average ages of the emergence of certain behaviors or average scores on tests that are based on large representative samples of a population

After World War I, Lawrence K. Frank (1890–1968) was influential in obtaining foundation monies to establish various institutes to study child development. The Society for Research in Child Development was founded in 1933. During World War II, child development research and study declined. The conclusion of World War II, however, brought a substantial increase in the number of investigations into the nature of children. This intense interest in learning about young children continues today on many fronts, as is illustrated in Figure 1.2.

THE NATURE OF A THEORY

theories:
bodies of principles
used to interpret a
set of circumstances
or facts

Scholars have proposed ideas or **theories** that attempt to explain in an organized or systematic manner how young children develop and learn. The backgrounds of these theorists, as well as political and sociological events, often influence the development of ideas and the nature of research. At times, radical thinkers propose such new ideas that they change previously accepted theories. Thus, as knowledge evolves, a theory may change. If research and practice continue to support a theory, it will continue to be instructive, but if new information does not support it, the theory will be modified or discounted.

THEORIES OF EARLY CHILDHOOD DEVELOPMENT

A number of theories attempt to explain early childhood development. These include psychoanalytic, behaviorist, maturationist, cognitive, and ecological systems. Some of these theories attempt to explain only one aspect of development; others are more comprehensive. All theories can help to provide information about the development of children. The following sections provide an overview of the various theories that have contributed to our understanding of growth, development, and learning.

psychoanalytic
theory:
a theory that attempts to explain the inner thoughts and feelings, at both the conscious and subconscious levels, that influence behavior

Psychoanalytic Theory

Psychoanalytic theory attempts to explain the inner thoughts and feelings, at both the conscious and subconscious levels, that influence behavior (Freud, 1938). Sigmund Freud (1856–1939) laid the foundations for psychoanalysis through his **psychosexual theory**. As a physician in Vienna specializing in nervous or mental conditions, he became intrigued with adults' problems that seemed to have begun in childhood. Freud developed a stage theory that suggested that certain drives and instincts emerge at various periods of development through biological systems, primarily the mouth, the anus, and the sex organs, as outlined in Table 1.1. This theory is currently viewed as simplistic and overly focused on

psychosexual
theory:
a theory that suggests that sexual drives play an important role in personality development

TABLE 1.1   A Comparison of Freud's Psychosexual and Erikson's Psychosocial Stages of Development

Freud's Five Stages and Related Conflicts		Approximate Ages	Erikson's Eight Stages
Oral	Weaning	Birth–1½ years	Basic trust versus mistrust
Anal	Toilet learning	1½–3 years	Autonomy versus shame/doubt
Phallic	Oedipal and Electra	3–5 years	Initiative versus guilt
Latency	—	5½–12 years	Industry versus inferiority
Genital	—	Adolescence	Identity versus role confusion
—	—	Young adulthood	Intimacy versus isolation
—	—	Middle adulthood	Generativity versus stagnation
—	—	Late adulthood	Ego integrity versus despair

Source: Erikson (1963) and Freud (1938).

sexual feelings and erogenous zones. However, Freud's basic premise that children's early experiences can influence their later lives has persisted through the years and into present-day perspectives.

Erik Erikson (1902–1994), who studied with Freud's daughter, Anna, built on Freud's theories and believed that Freud's exploration of sexuality as the main explanation for behavior was too limiting. He focused on the broader social contexts of the child and family, theorizing that relationships within these contexts influence behavior in positive and/or negative ways. Thus, he proposed a **psychosocial theory** of personality development (Erikson, 1963). Erikson's theory was characterized by stages that extended from birth to later adulthood, as illustrated in Table 1.1.

Two contemporary theorists whose ideas are rooted in the theories of Freud and Erikson are Carl Rogers and Abraham Maslow. However, unlike Freud, these scholars did not view growth and development as determined by negative early events, but believed that individuals could change or be influenced by the choices that they make. Rogers's theory suggests that individuals have the capacity for openness to their experiences and are capable of becoming fully functioning individuals, relatively free of ego defense mechanisms (Rogers, 1962). Such individuals are "unified" within themselves, where distinctions are made between the "role self" and the "real self," between a defensive facade and real feelings (p. 29). Such individuals are psychologically free to be themselves, to be creative, and to express themselves in unique ways. Rogers uses Einstein to illustrate this theory:

> Einstein seems to have been unusually oblivious to the fact that good physicists did not think his kind of thoughts. Rather than drawing back because of his inadequate academic preparation in physics, he simply moved toward being Einstein, toward thinking his own thoughts, toward being as truly and deeply himself as he could. This is not a phenomenon which occurs only in the artist or the genius. Time and again in my clients, I have seen simple people become significant and creative in their own spheres, as they have developed more trust of the processes going on within themselves, and have dared to feel their own feelings, live by values which they discover within, and express themselves in their own unique ways. (p. 30)

Maslow proposed a concept of **self-actualization**, the process of growing toward self-acceptance and authentic relationships that lead ultimately to a sense of personal fulfillment. Maslow suggested that feelings and aspirations must be considered if one is to understand behavior (Maslow, 1962, 1970). Self-actualized individuals are continually in the process of becoming, are in touch with and accepting of reality, are confident yet aware of their limitations, and have a commitment to a meaningful project or goal. Maslow suggested that for self-actualization to occur, certain needs must be met. These needs appear in hierarchical order, beginning with very basic physiological needs for food, hydration, rest, and freedom from disease, moving upward as needs are consistently and adequately met, through safety needs, the need to be loved and to belong, the need for self-esteem, the desire for knowledge and aesthetic appreciation, and ultimately to self-actualizing behaviors.

The theories of Rogers and Maslow are classified as humanistic theories. The humanistic perspective is an outgrowth of clinical and counseling psychology. The primary focus of humanistic theories is on inner feelings, thoughts, perceptions, and the emotional and social needs of individuals. Much of the emphasis in

psychosocial theory:
a theory that argues that social interactions are more important than sexual drives in personality development

self-actualization:
the process of having basic physical and social/emotional needs met so that outcomes for the individual lead to positive self-regard and a creative, contributing member of society

humanistic perspectives is on the development of communication and problem-solving abilities.

Behavioral Theories

behavioral theory: a theory that emphasizes that learning is the acquisition of specific responses provoked by specific stimuli

Proponents of **behavioral theory** concentrate on attending to observable, overt behavior rather than examining and explaining the internal processes of behavior. They do not classify behavior into stages but suggest that learning is a gradual and continuous process. Experience is considered most important. Behavioral theory is generally classified into three types: classical conditioning, operant conditioning, and social learning theory. A technique for changing behaviors called **behavior modification** comes from this school of thought.

behavior modification: a system of techniques employing positive and/or negative reinforcers to change behavior

Classical Conditioning Theory. The principles of **classical conditioning theory** were developed by Russian Ivan P. Pavlov (1849–1936). Pavlov paired two events, the placing of meat powder on a dog's tongue and the ringing of a bell, to create a conditioned stimulus. Over a period of time, these repeated events produced a conditioned response of salivation. The stimulus of the sound of the bell alone caused the dog to salivate even if no meat powder was present. The dog's association of the meat powder with the sound of the bell stimulated a response.

classical conditioning theory: a theory according to which, when an unconditioned neutral stimulus and an unconditioned response are paired repeatedly, a conditioned response is the result

In the United States, E. L. Thorndike conducted numerous animal experiments and is considered the father of behaviorism. However, John B. Watson (1878–1958) was responsible for implementing the ideas of classical conditioning. Watson's famous experiment with an 11-month-old infant, Albert, was used to justify the notion that certain behavioral responses can be created through conditioning. Watson believed he could take a baby at random and produce "any type of specialist I might select—doctor, lawyer, artist, merchant-chief, and yes beggarman and thief, regardless of his talents, penchants, tendencies, abilities, vocations and race of his ancestors" (Watson, 1928, p. 104).

In Watson's experiment (Watson & Rayner, 1920), Albert was shown a white rat at the same time a loud noise was made. Initially, Albert was not afraid of the rat but was distressed at the loud noise. Eventually, Albert's association of the loud noise with the rat produced a fear of many white furry objects, such as his mother's muff, rabbits, and Santa's beard. Unfortunately, Albert left the hospital where this experiment was conducted before Watson could **extinguish** his fear.

extinguish: stopping a behavior or response by not reinforcing it over a period of time

Watson's notions on child rearing were widespread and are still evident in some parenting practices today. Watson suggested that showing affection for young children would spoil them. He advocated feeding infants every four hours, advised parents against rocking their children, and suggested that a handshake was more appropriate than a goodnight hug and kiss (Watson, 1928).

operant conditioning theory: a theory in which behavior is changed or modified through the positive or negative consequences that follow the behavior

Operant Conditioning Theory. A later proponent of behaviorism was Harvard psychologist B. F. Skinner. Skinner explained Watson's views in a well-known book, *Walden Two* (1948). Skinner's philosophy and experiments expanded on classical conditioning theory and evolved into the **operant conditioning theory**, in which the operant is the action on the part of an individual as a response to environmental stimuli. Desired behavior is reinforced by using positive or negative reinforcers.

Positive reinforcement involves providing pleasant or satisfying consequences such as praise, food, a special privilege, a good grade, and so on after the appropriate behavior has occurred. Negative reinforcement occurs when behaviors are encouraged by the removal of a threatening or an aversive stimulus; for example, a child who is scolded for eating with his or her fingers may remove the aversive stimulus (scolding) by attempting to use a spoon. Both positive and negative reinforcement result in learning of new behaviors or in strengthening of existing behaviors. Punishment is used to decrease the frequency of undesirable behavior. However, sometimes punishment results in reinforcement. For example, a child who is frequently blamed for mishaps may learn to lie (deny complicity) if it helps to escape the unpleasantness of being punished when the child does cause a mishap. Skinner believed that punishment is generally an ineffective way to control undesirable behavior. Instead, he suggested extinguishing behavior or ceasing to reinforce the behavior until it stops. Skinner and his wife decided to try this technique on their 5-year-old daughter Julie (Skinner, 1979). Skinner reported that it took a month or two to accomplish. At first, Julie behaved in ways that in the past would have brought her punishment, and she watched her parents closely for their reactions. In time, the desired behaviors emerged. Skinner indicated that he and his wife found various reinforcement techniques more effective than punishment (Skinner, 1979, p. 279).

Social Learning Theory

Social learning theory is another adaptation of classical and operant conditioning. This theory emphasizes the importance of role models and significant adults in children's lives. Social learning theorists propose that children learn and imitate behaviors from people who are important to them, and that children do not always need reinforcement to learn. This theory was introduced in 1941 by Neil Miller and John Dollard in *Social Learning and Imitation*. Albert Bandura is a contemporary proponent of social learning theory. His research (1977, 1986, 1997) demonstrated that children learn behavior from observation. Bandura proposed that learning does not depend solely on direct instruction. In his classic research, two different groups of children observed two versions of a film in which a large plastic inflatable doll called a Bobo doll was hit by an adult model. In one version, the model's behavior was rewarded with adult praise, candy, and soft drinks. The second version concluded with another adult model hitting the first model with a rolled-up newspaper. After viewing the films, the children who saw the version with the reward were more likely to imitate aggressive behavior than were the children who viewed the version in which the model was punished. Bandura concluded that children learn from observing others.

social learning theory: a theory that argues that learning occurs through observing others, and emphasizes the influencing role of behavioral models

Maturational Theory

Maturational theory asserts that growth and development are characterized by an "unfolding" or maturing of genetically preprogramed traits and abilities. Development is thought to be a progressive reconstructing of old behaviors into new behaviors that results from physiological maturational changes. Growth and

maturational theory: a theory that holds that growth and development are predetermined by inheritance and largely unaffected by the environment

development are thought to proceed according to predetermined orderly and predictable patterns, though it is recognized that not all children proceed through these sequences at the same rate.

This perspective evolved from the early scientific studies in embryology. With the development of the microscope, scientists were able to microscopically examine the sperm and the ovum; they discovered that there was no fully formed organism in either, but that the embryo developed in a series of predictable stages. This discovery led to interest in the way the organism evolved not only prenatally, but also from birth on. Arnold Gesell (1880–1961), a Yale University professor, is best known for his studies of this progression in infants and young children. Gesell's studies set forth a number of principles of development and sequences for the unfolding of characteristics and capabilities that in the maturationist view is only slightly influenced by the environment.

Cognitive Theory

cognitive theory: a theory that explains the development of learning in terms of how children think and process information

schemata: mental concepts or categories; plural for schema

assimilation: the process of incorporating new motor or conceptual learning into existing schemata

accommodation: the cognitive process by which patterns of thought (schemata) and related behaviors are modified to conform to new information or experience

equilibration: the attempt to restore cognitive balance by modifying existing cognitive structures when confronted with new information

Cognitive theory attempts to explain how young children think and process information. Jean Piaget (1896–1980) developed a major theory of cognition in child development. Piaget's theory achieved widespread recognition in the United States during the 1960s for several reasons. First, the insistence of the behaviorists on quantifiable research with large populations was beginning to be questioned. Second, Piaget's theory on the nature of how young children learn came into acceptance during a time of great interest in the development of cognitively oriented experiences for young children. Finally, Piaget's theory readily explained what perceptive parents and teachers of young children had already observed: that the manner in which young children process information and relate to new knowledge differs distinctly from that of older children and adults.

Piaget worked in France to establish norms for Binet's Intelligence Test. In that process, he observed that many young children gave similar incorrect answers. Piaget began to wonder whether the development of cognition proceeded in stages. Using the clinical interview, Piaget questioned children to determine their thought processes. This approach, coupled with the detailed observations of his own three children, provided the basis for Piaget's theory (Piaget, 1952).

Piaget suggested that thinking develops sequentially in four stages: sensorimotor, preoperational, concrete operations, and formal operations. The first three stages will be discussed more thoroughly in later chapters on cognitive, language, and literacy development.

Piaget grew up around Lake Neuchatel in Switzerland and became intrigued with the differences in behavior in mollusks at various locations around the lake. This fascination created a lifelong interest in the effects of the environment on living organisms' subsequent adaptations to the environment.

Piaget proposed that children order their interactions with the environment and then adapt to or change this order if they have new insights or information. Ways of ordering thought were termed **schemata**. **Assimilation** represents the child's attempts to fit new ideas and concepts into existing schemata. **Accommodation** is the change in schemata that a child makes as a result of new information. As children grow older and have more experiences with their environment, their **equilibration**, or balance in thinking, is often disturbed. Piaget said that this dissatisfaction or **disequilibrium** with present ideas motivates the child to accommodate new information and change schemata.

While Piaget claimed that cognitive development influences language development, another theorist, Lev Vygotsky (1899–1934), a Russian psychologist, suggested that thought and language eventually converge into meaning, particularly in cultures in which verbal interaction is important and verbal language is used for problem solving (Vygotsky, 1962).

Recently, the work of Vygotsky has received considerable attention in the United States. Vygotsky produced some major works during a relatively short life. Two of his books, *Thought and Language* (1962) and *Mind in Society* (1978), have been translated into English. Many refer to Vygotsky's theory as a sociocultural approach to understanding child growth and development (Berk & Winsler, 1995). Vygotsky emphasized that cultures differ in the activities that they emphasize, stressing that child development takes place on both natural (biological/physiological) and cultural planes.

Vygotsky believed that cognition is not just in the mind, but also in the social experiences in which the individual is engaged. Social experiences, then, are thought to shape the ways individuals perceive and interpret the world around them. Because language supports social interaction, and because language is a primary form of communication, it also serves as a critical tool for thinking. Vygotsky determined that when children are provided with words, they are better able to form concepts than when they are not provided with words. The relationships between language and thought are central to Vygotsky's theory. In his view, language is the cultural tool through which higher-order thinking and self-regulatory thought occur.

Ecological Systems Theory

In the past, much of child development research focused on parent–child interactions or intrafamilial processes. Urie Bronfenbrenner (1979, 1986) argued that the factors influencing development are much more complex in that **intrafamilial** processes are affected by **extrafamilial** forces. The **ecological systems theory** defines four interacting and interdependent systems, represented by concentric circles in Figure 1.3. The interactions between and among the systems influence the course of a child's growth, development, and learning. An ecological systems theory emphasizes the multiplicity of relationships between and among the systems. When the linkages between the systems are characterized by harmony and positive interactions, healthy development can result. On the other hand, when there is disharmony or conflict between or among the systems, child growth and development can be negatively affected.

The child is at the core of the four systems. This system is typically depicted as a series of ever-widening circles of influence. The system closest to the child (the system containing the child) is called the microsystem; it includes all of the settings where the child spends a significant amount of time (home, child care setting, school, neighborhood, and so on). The microsystem focuses on the roles, relationships, and experiences in the child's immediate environment. The mesosystem pertains to the linkages and relationships between and among the different ecosystems, and is illustrated by the arrows pointing in either direction between the circles in Figure 1.3. The exosystem consists of three main interactive

disequilibrium:
an imbalance in thinking that leads the thinker to assimilate or accommodate

intrafamilial:
actions and behaviors occurring within the immediate family

extrafamilial:
actions and behaviors occurring outside the immediate family

ecological systems theory:
a theory that argues that a variety of social systems influence the development of children

FIGURE 1.3
An Ecological Systems Perspective

Bronfenbrenner's ecological systems theory is illustrated in a series of concentric circles, each representing wider spheres of influence and interacting relationships (Bronfenbrenner, 1979).

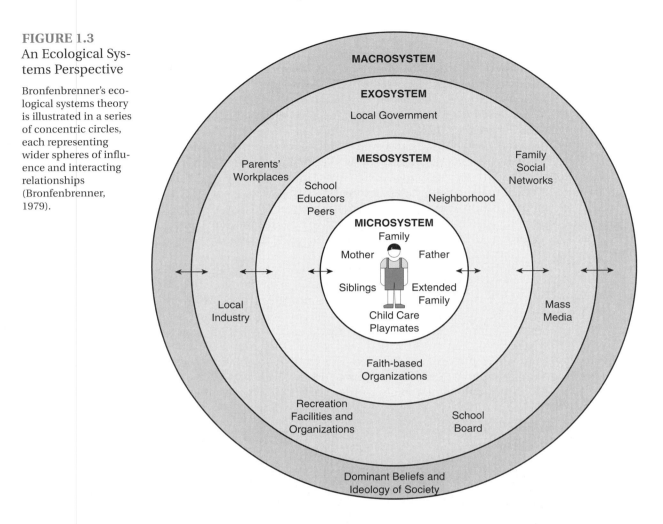

contexts: the parents' workplace, the parents' social networks, and the community influences on family functioning (Bronfenbrenner, 1986). Parental employment or unemployment characteristics, including the parents' education levels and the types of employment they can secure, along with their attitudes and feelings associated with work and employment, affect both the quantity and the quality of relationships and the types of child-rearing practices that take place within the family.

By the same token, social networks such as the presence or absence (and the characteristics of) kinship groups, faith-related affiliations, neighbors, and other friendships are believed to influence family processes and their developmental effects on children. Community entities and characteristics are also influential; these include whether a child is living in a rural, urban, or suburban community and the types of opportunities and resources available to children and families in the community. The fourth system, the macrosystem, involves the attitudes, values, customs, laws, regulations, and rules of the culture at large that influence all other systems and ultimately the family and the child.

TRENDS IN EARLY CHILDHOOD STUDY

Topics of research about young children and their families continue to reflect society's concerns on a variety of issues. Some of these concerns are as follows:

- The translation of research from the fields of biology and the neurosciences about early brain growth and neurological development into appropriate and healthy experiences for infants and young children.
- The translation of research from the biogenetics fields into appropriate education and counseling for families, and ethical and effective preventive or intervention measures to promote healthy child development outcomes.
- A contemporary concern for the physical safety and mental health of children growing up in a society in which the threat of violence, terrorism, and homeland war are present, and concomitantly, the care and nurturing of children who have experienced atrocities.
- The need for a well-trained, highly educated, eminently qualified early childhood workforce, and the identification of the knowledge and skills essential for providing services to children and their families in many different contexts (e.g., schools, child care settings, social service agencies, foster care, health care services, and family counseling).
- The recognition that research must incorporate the influences of contexts (nationality, race, culture, region, family configuration, and socioeconomic factors) on the developmental trajectories (or pathways) of child growth and development.
- The nature of contemporary family life, the multiple roles mothers and fathers play in sustaining family and child well-being, and how best to provide knowledge, skills, and support systems to families.
- Continued study of the long-term benefits and/or consequences of varying types of child care and family services, because of the growing number of infants and children in nonparental care for major portions of each day.
- A need for continuing study on how to assure that child care for infants and children is of highest quality and readily available to families who need it.
- Exploration of developmentally appropriate, relevant, mind-engaging early child care and schooling experiences in the context of a changing society in which education and family services and support systems have become increasingly politicized, often circumventing the child development knowledge base and threatening efforts toward the best interests of children.

We hope you have discovered that early childhood development is an interesting, important, and complex field of study. The next chapter will provide additional information on how researchers study children.

Did you notice the quote at the beginning of this chapter? It says, "There are two lasting bequests we can hope to give our children—one is roots; the other is wings." A knowledge of how young children develop and learn helps parents and early childhood development professionals to provide the conditions in which young children can develop deep roots and strong wings—two prerequisites for leading happy, productive lives. We hope the following chapters will help you learn how to provide both the roots and the wings to facilitate optimal development in young children.

KEY TERMS

accommodation
assimilation
at-risk
behavior modification
behavioral theory
classical conditioning
    theory
cognitive theory
developmentally
    appropriate
developmentally
    inappropriate

disequilibrium
ecological systems
    theory
equilibration
essential experiences
extinguish
extrafamilial
inclusion
intrafamilial
low-risk
maturational theory
norms

operant conditioning
    theory
professionals
psychoanalytic theory
psychosexual theory
psychosocial theory
schemata
self-actualization
social learning theory
theories

REVIEW STRATEGIES AND ACTIVITIES

1. Review the key terms individually or with a classmate.

2. Begin a journal to record and track your supplementary readings for this course. Start your journal by jotting down your initial responses to the seven questions posed at the beginning of this chapter. When you have completed this text, return to these questions and consider whether you would change your initial answers and, if so, how.

3. Think back to your early childhood years through age eight. Try to recall your earliest memory. At what age did it occur? What other recollections do you have from your early childhood years?

   a. Chart a life line. State how old you were at the time of your earliest recollection. Describe that recollection and others that took place during that period of time. Continue this process up through age eight or to your current age.

   b. Discuss these recollections with other students in your early childhood development class. Your classmates have probably had similar experiences, or their recollections will help you to remember some events you have forgotten.

   c. Relate events in your life to the various developmental theories.

   d. Identify personal cultural influences within your life from childhood to the present.

4. Why do you wish to become an early childhood professional?

   a. List the people or events that have encouraged your interest in the profession.

   b. What are your concerns about becoming an early childhood professional?

   c. What are your short- and long-term professional goals?

   d. Discuss your responses with students in your class.

FURTHER READINGS

Bredekamp, S., & Copple, C. (Eds.). (1997). *Developmentally appropriate practice in early childhood programs* (rev. ed.). Washington, DC: National Association for the Education of Young Children.

Children's Defense Fund. (2001). *The state of America's children*. Washington, DC: Author. [Updated editions of this report are published annually.]

Helburn, S., & Bergman, B. (2002). *America's child care problem: The way out.* New York: Palgrave for St. Martin's Press.

National Association for the Education of Young Children & National Council for Accreditation of Teacher Education. (2001). *NAEYC standards for early childhood professional preparation.* Washington, DC: Author.

Shonkoff, J. P., & Phillips, D. A. (Eds.). (2001). *From neurons to neighborhoods: The science of early childhood development.* Washington, DC: National Academy Press.

OTHER RESOURCES

The Benton Foundation Connect for Kids Weekly
http://www.connectforkids.org

National Center for Early Development and Learning
http://www.fpg.unc.edu/ncedl/ncedl.html

CHAPTER TWO

The Where, When, and How of Early Childhood Study and Assessment

*M*ore often teachers find as they study children, they themselves change. Thus (through child study), we often gain insight and understanding not only of the children but of ourselves as well. . . . But "understanding" alone, whether of the children or of ourselves, is not enough. The crucial question is whether such understanding improves the teacher's ability to help children learn, whether it facilitates provision of the experiences children need.

MILLIE ALMY AND CELIA GENISHI

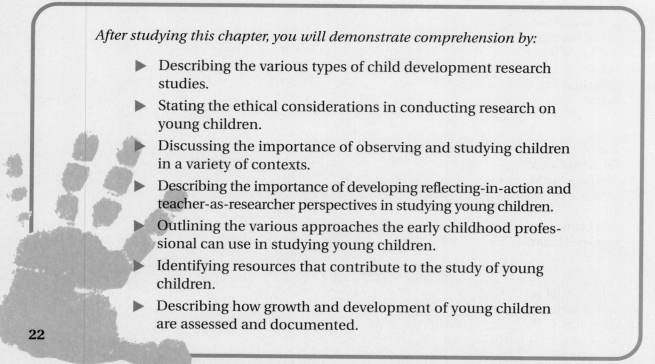

After studying this chapter, you will demonstrate comprehension by:

▶ Describing the various types of child development research studies.

▶ Stating the ethical considerations in conducting research on young children.

▶ Discussing the importance of observing and studying children in a variety of contexts.

▶ Describing the importance of developing reflecting-in-action and teacher-as-researcher perspectives in studying young children.

▶ Outlining the various approaches the early childhood professional can use in studying young children.

▶ Identifying resources that contribute to the study of young children.

▶ Describing how growth and development of young children are assessed and documented.

It is the first day of kindergarten, and Cathleen seems upset at having her mother leave her at the classroom door. Ms. Schwartz, Cathleen's teacher, invites her mother to stay awhile. This relieves Cathleen's anxiety, and she eventually begins to participate in the sociodramatic (pretend play) area of the classroom. She returns to her mother periodically but soon rejoins other children in the sociodramatic center. Eventually, Cathleen's mother tells Cathleen that she has some errands to run and will be back at 11:30 to pick her up. Cathleen seems to accept her mother's departure. This pattern is repeated for 3 days, with Cathleen's mother spending less and less time in the classroom. On the fourth day, Cathleen enters the classroom without hesitation and gives her mother a confident "goodbye." Later, Ms. Schwartz observes Cathleen in the sociodramatic area. Ms. Schwartz suggests that she "call" her mother on the toy phone and tell her what she is doing.

Juan is 18 months old. His mother is planning to return to her job as a buyer for a large department store. She has enrolled Juan in a child care center. The director, Mr. Hubbard, has encouraged Juan's parents to visit the center with Juan several times a few days before Juan is to begin attending. Mr. Hubbard also suggests that Juan's parents send Juan's favorite stuffed toy and blanket every day. A picture of Juan's mother and father is posted on a low-level bulletin board, along with pictures of the other toddlers' parents.

What would you have done had you been Cathleen's or Juan's teacher? Often, responses include telling Cathleen's mother to leave her and not allowing favorite blankets and stuffed animals to be brought into the child care center. Why did Ms. Schwartz and Mr. Hubbard act in the ways they did?

THE CONTRIBUTION OF RESEARCH LITERATURE TO THE DEVELOPMENT OF THE EARLY CHILDHOOD PROFESSIONAL

Ms. Schwartz and Mr. Hubbard acted on their knowledge of child growth and development research. Their training included many opportunities to read the professional early childhood development research and literature. Their training also provided them with opportunities to observe and study young children's behavior, as well as the responses and behavior of teachers of young children. In addition, their experience with children and families from diverse backgrounds helped them to become more appreciative and responsive to the uniqueness of all children and their families.

Through their reading and study of young children and observation of other early childhood professionals, Ms. Schwartz and Mr. Hubbard learned that a major developmental task of young children is to separate from parents and move into other social settings. Both Ms. Schwartz and Mr. Hubbard are familiar with the research on attachment (Chapters 6 and 9). They observed the techniques and strategies that early childhood professionals use to facilitate young children's adjustment to a new setting. Therefore, they make appropriate decisions about what to do to help children form additional attachments and assist them in separating from their parents.

Early childhood professionals learn about young children at both **preservice** and **inservice** levels by reading the studies and reports of researchers in the area of early childhood development. This is why you are reading this book. Early childhood professionals also learn about young children through observation and study of young children and their family backgrounds. Firsthand experiences with young children reinforce previously read child development information and facilitate further reading about the nature of behavior in young children. This chapter provides information about the study of children revealed through professional research literature on early childhood development.

TYPES OF CHILD DEVELOPMENT RESEARCH STUDIES

Scholars of child development may be affiliated with colleges or universities, research centers, public schools, other public agencies, or private research organizations. They often have hunches, or **hypotheses**, about the development of young children. They design research studies to determine whether their hunches are correct. The results of these studies may be published in theses, dissertations, professional journals, and scholarly books or presented in papers that are read at professional conferences and seminars. Often research findings are reported in the media.

Professionals in all fields are discerning consumers of research information. Four criteria are used in evaluating the quality of a research study: objectivity, reliability, validity, and replicability. **Objectivity** refers to the researcher's ability to pursue and report the research in such a manner that personal feelings, values, assumptions, or other biases are avoided. **Reliability** refers to the accuracy of the study; that is, scholars must ask, "To what extent does the test or instrument used in the study provide the same or consistent, noncontradictory results when the same or different forms of the test are administered to the same subjects?"

preservice:
individuals who are in training to teach or serve young children

inservice:
individuals who have completed professional training programs and are employed in the early childhood profession

hypothesis:
a hunch or supposition that one wants to verify or prove

objectivity:
the ability to observe and draw inferences about child development that are free of observer bias

reliability:
the consistency with which various research methods produce the same or similar results for each individual from one assessment to the next

Validity refers to the soundness of the test or instrument used in the study. In assessing validity of a study, scholars ask, "What does the test or instrument measure?," "Does the test or instrument, in fact, measure exactly what it proposes to measure?," and "How comprehensively and how accurately does the test measure what it is supposed to measure?" There are statistical formulas that can be used to determine reliability and validity. **Replicability** refers to the likelihood that other researchers can, using the same research procedures, obtain the same results. When more than one researcher obtains the same findings, the credibility of the research is greater.

Assessing objectivity, reliability, validity, and replicability of studies prevents the dissemination of inaccurate or untrue information that can result from such research pitfalls as poor research design, researcher bias, inappropriate or inaccurate use of statistical methods, insufficient size of population studied, or inadequate or unclear instructions and procedures for research subjects.

A brief overview of some of the more common types of research in child development is instructive. Some of the common types of research in child development are descriptive, cross-sectional, longitudinal, correlational, experimental, and ethnographic research. Although these types are presented separately for purposes of discussion, many research projects employ combinations of research methods. For example, correlational techniques can be used with longitudinal, cross-sectional, and descriptive studies.

Descriptive Studies

Descriptive studies generally attempt to describe behavior without attempting to determine cause and effect. Many early studies in child development, particularly the maturational theory studies, were descriptive. During the 1920s through the 1940s, Arnold Gesell and his colleagues at the Yale University Child Study Clinic observed a number of children at various ages in selected areas of development—physical and motor development, adaptive behaviors, language development, and personal–social behavior—and described specific commonalities among children of the same age. This information about common characteristics was then converted into *norms*, or averages, whereby teachers, parents, and physicians could determine the extent to which a particular child was developing "normally," or in similar fashion as other children the same age. For example, research of this nature described the average age at which infants should sit, stand, walk, talk, and so on (Gesell & Amatruda, 1941). This maturational approach to studying child development later led to the development of readiness tests to determine a child's developmental age and readiness for specific new experiences, such as admission to kindergarten or readiness for reading instruction. Gesell's studies focused attention on the biological unfolding of growth and development characteristics and provided sets of benchmarks and principles of development that continue to influence child study today. However, today, researchers recognize that these early developmental studies were conducted primarily on children from white, middle-class families, and therefore the findings are not easily generalizable to all children.

Cross-sectional and Longitudinal Studies

A **cross-sectional study** looks at an aspect of development or behavior at various ages or stages at the same time. For example, a **representative sample** of children at ages 2 to 18 had their heights and weights recorded at the same time.

validity:
the degree to which an instrument or a procedure measures what it is intended to measure

replicability:
the likelihood that a research procedure can be followed by another person with the same or similar results

descriptive study:
research collected by observing and recording behavior and providing a description of the observed behavior

cross-sectional study:
research that studies subjects of different ages at the same time

representative sample:
a sample of subjects who are representative of the larger population of individuals about whom the researcher wants to draw conclusions

This information was converted into charts that pediatricians use to predict young children's weight and height at later ages. Cross-sectional research can provide information about certain types of development, such as height and weight, within a relatively short time. However, this type of study cannot determine exactly when an individual changes.

longitudinal study:
research that collects information about the same subjects at different ages over a period of time

One way to study change in the development of individuals is the **longitudinal study**. This type of study looks at the same individuals over a period of time. An important example of this type of study is the research conducted on a number of young children in low-income families who were enrolled in early childhood education programs in the 1960s when the federal Head Start program was being launched (Barnett, 1995; Berrueta-Clement, Schweinhart, Barnett, Epstein, & Weikart, 1984; Lazar & Darlington, 1982; Schweinhart, Barnes, & Weikart, 1993; Schweinhart & Weikart, 1997). For example, in one of the programs studied, the Perry Preschool Program at Ypsilanti, Michigan (Schweinhart et al., 1993; Schweinhart & Weikart, 1997), subjects from ages 4 through 23 years were tested and interviewed over the years to determine whether their participation in early childhood programs had long-term effects. They were then compared with children who had not attended a preschool program. Generally, these studies indicated that at-risk **preprimary** children who were in high-quality early childhood programs were better students and more productive as young adults than were children of similar circumstance who were not enrolled in early childhood programs. Figure 2.1 contrasts cross-sectional and longitudinal studies.

preprimary:
the time in young children's lives before they enter the primary (first, second, and third) grades

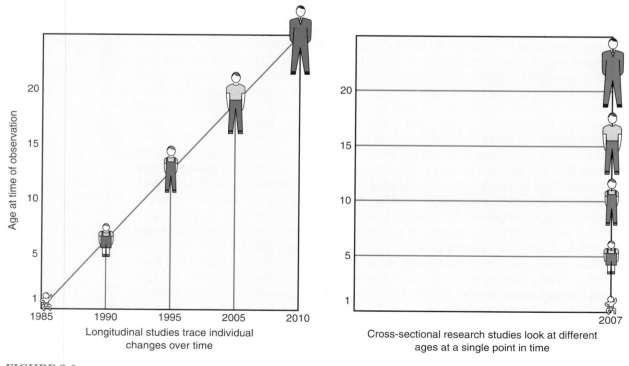

FIGURE 2.1
Comparison of Longitudinal and Cross-Sectional Research

Correlational Studies

Correlational studies look at the nature of the relationship between two sets of measurements. For example, in a study of the effects of a training course on caregivers' behavior and children's development, Rhodes and Hennessy (2001) found a relationship between the resulting change in adult interactions with children that was associated with significant gains among the children in social and cognitive development.

Correlational studies indicate only relationships, not causes. Thus it cannot be said that a specific type of caregiver training causes specific types of social or cognitive behaviors in children. It can be said only that there is a positive relationship between caregiver training and gains in social and cognitive development in children.

correlational study: research that attempts to determine a relationship between two or more sets of measurements

Experimental Studies

In an **experimental study**, the researcher usually divides the population under study into two groups by **random selection**. One group is designated as the *experimental group* and receives some special treatment, such a particular type of teaching methodology or special coaching on a particular concept or skill; the second group is called the *control group* and usually does not receive this treatment. The control group is the baseline group to which changes in the experimental group are compared. Sometimes, the two groups receive two different types of treatment or experiences. In some experimental designs, subjects are given pretests and posttests to measure the influence of the treatment or experiences after the subjects have been exposed to it. The researcher then employs statistical analyses to determine if the differences between the groups (or within the same group after a particular treatment) were significant (that is, the differences were not simply due to chance), and the same results would therefore likely occur with another similar group of subjects.

experimental study: research that involves treating each of two or more groups in different ways to determine cause-and-effect relationships

random selection: a procedure for assigning subjects to an experimental or control group so that each person has the same chance of being selected for either group

Ethnographic Studies

More intimate than the previous types of research in child study is a form of research known as ethnographic research. Ethnographic research entails systematic observation in the child's natural setting. Like Bronfenbrenner's ecological perspective, ethnography requires the researcher to consider the relative and reciprocal influence of all aspects of the child's environment: biological, racial, ethnic, socioeconomic, sociocultural, psychological, and cognitive (Norton, 1996). The researcher is interested in observing and assessing the individual child's responses and interactions within her or his natural environment.

This type of research is intensive and time consuming because it requires the researcher to become a participant in the life and experiences of the research subject (child and/or family). As such, the researcher employs what is known as **participant–observer** techniques (Freel, 1996). Because this type of research is open ended, research questions often evolve during the study. Unlike most studies, where questions, assumptions, and hypotheses are framed at the outset and the study is designed to corroborate, prove, or disprove them, ethnographic studies can lead the researcher to unforeseen points of interest and inquiry. Thus, ethnography becomes a theory-generating rather than a theory-testing form of research (Casper, 1996).

participant–observer: a researcher who participates in the daily lives of the subjects of the study

Interactions with the subjects of the study are generally unstructured and spontaneous, allowing participants to behave in context in their own unique and individualistic ways. The researcher may ask questions such as, "What do/did you think about that?," "What do/did you do when she said that to you?," "What did others do?," "What do you think happened when...?," "If it happens again, what will you do?," "Tell me how you learned to do that," and so on. Open-ended questions allow the research subjects to describe their thinking, behaviors, and intentions in their own words and from their own perspectives. Consider this account of a home visit given by an ethnographic scholar:

> The first time I visited one of our participants in her home, I noticed that her large apartment building looked almost deserted, even in comparison with the surrounding, equally shabby housing. The perception of abandonment deepened when I entered the building. I felt that the mother's apartment, up a winding flight of stairs and at the end of a long hall, was the only inhabited one. Once the video-taping began I heard squeals coming from somewhere in the small apartment. These were definitely animal sounds and were definitely not coming from a cat, dog, or mouse. I'm sure my attention was on the floor for much of that visit, looking out for rats. Later in the visit, when the mother and I had talked a bit and gotten to know each other a little, she told me that she had a crib for her baby but she preferred he sleep with her so she could keep watch over him. She was afraid that rats would bite her baby. I had an immediate, visceral understanding of this mother's fear and more empathy for her plight than I ever could have gained had she related her concern in a rat-free office. (Happily, by the time of the next visit six weeks later, the mother had moved to a building with no rats. I later learned that her former building had been condemned.) (Freel, 1996, p. 6).

Ethnographic studies utilize open-ended interviews-in-context, home visits, video and audio taping, and copious notes, which record verbatim the words, phrases, and sentences of the observed and in strict chronological order. Written narrative accounts are recorded immediately so as not to lose essential facts, impressions, or circumstantial data. The researcher is not focused just on the dramatic, but more importantly on the everyday, often mundane behaviors and events. Because this type of research project can yield an enormous amount of data, the researcher must analyze the data carefully for patterns, similarities, and discrepancies. The questions behind this process are, "What are we seeing?," "What did it mean?," and "How significant for child development were the behaviors that were observed?" (Freel, 1996).

Social Indicators

Social indicators are statistical markers that provide information on the well-being of specific populations. For example, the health care profession is very interested in tracking the evolution and spread of disease. The SARS epidemic in China in 2003 was followed through statistical tracking. Hence, policy makers could respond with intervention and prevention policies and scientists could focus their efforts on determining the cause, spread, treatment, and perhaps cure for the disease.

Social indicators do not determine cause and effect. Statistics can tell us that poverty is on the rise, or that more 2-year-olds in a certain year are fully immunized than 2-year-olds were in a previous year, or that there is an increase in stay-at-home fathers over previous accounts, but this information answers no questions about why these changes occurred. Social indicators often reveal a need to accelerate scientific efforts and often generate further research specifically focused on improving our lives.

Ethical use of social indicators can lead to socially responsible outcomes, such as identifying populations in need of supportive or health-promoting interventions, improving the conditions and experiences of children in public education, and improved quality of child care. State and local economic conditions can be projected and planning initiated for such needs as transportation, housing, food supplies, and employment opportunities. Unethical use of social indicators misleads by over- or underplaying selected findings (sometimes out of context) to arouse individual or public concern, to garner support for political issues, or to simply argue one's point of view. Professionals in early childhood education and family development learn to be discerning consumers of statistical information and to recognize its misapplication. Furthermore, professionals in all fields interpret and share valid statistical information in accurate and honest ways, and use this information to serve the best interest of children and families.

ETHICS OF CHILD DEVELOPMENT RESEARCH

Because of the increasing awareness regarding the rights and feelings of young children and their families, careful attention must be given to ensure that neither physiological nor psychological harm occurs to children during or as a result of a

Opportunities to interact with children in home and preschool settings provide students important insights into child growth, development, and learning.

research process. Both the American Psychological Association (2002) and the Society for Research in Child Development, Committee on Ethical Standards for Research with Children (1990–1991) have developed procedures for conducting research with human subjects. These standards outline the rights of children and the responsibilities of researchers, and stipulate that parental or guardian permission must be obtained before any research can begin.

Another area of ethics involves the honesty of the researcher in reporting the study. Most researchers plan well-designed studies. However, the unpredictable nature of children and other complications sometimes prevent the researcher from completing the study as originally intended. It is the responsibility of the researcher to acknowledge all limitations to the study when conducting or reporting the research and its findings. At times, pilot studies or smaller preliminary studies can help to identify potential problems with a research design before it is carried out on a full scale and its findings published or otherwise reported.

SOCIOCULTURAL PERSPECTIVES IN STUDYING YOUNG CHILDREN

Often, early child development research information comes from studies conducted by researchers who have the same economic and sociocultural backgrounds as the children they have studied, as with the Gesell studies mentioned above. Therefore, the application of the research to other groups or to the general population of children is inappropriate. Researchers must include children from a variety of socioeconomic, cultural, and gender groups before attempts at universal application. If the group studied does not represent different populations (i.e., age, grade, socioeconomic level, race, ethnicity, gender, ableness), then the researcher must accurately describe the population that made up the research sample population and generalize the findings to members of that particular population only. For instance, if the study included only low-income children, then its findings cannot accurately be said to be true of children in families with higher incomes. Researchers acknowledge an array of diverse characteristics and influences among children associated with age, grade, socioeconomic background, race, ethnicity, gender, ableness, and contexts in which the studies are conducted when attempting to design research or interpret findings. Sensitivity to cultural behaviors, values, beliefs, and expectations and to the effects of the research design on individuals prevents bias and accurately portrays the subjects of the study. Sensitivity to sociocultural perspectives facilitates accurate interpretation of findings.

YOUNG CHILDREN WITH DISABILITIES AND THE STUDY OF CHILD DEVELOPMENT

The science of early childhood development has begun to take shape through recent studies and revelations about variations in developmental trajectories and the projection of developmental outcomes. Recognizing that there are wide ranges in what might be considered challenges or strengths in individuals, today's perspective on children with special needs is far more promising than historical perspectives. Historical perspectives tended to focus on children with disabilities as somehow deficient, or as facing limitations in their potential developmental outcomes.

In this context, the most helpful and perhaps enlightened view of child growth and development is the one that states that "child development [is] a continuous process influenced by reciprocal transactions between children and their caregivers, caregivers and the caregiving environment, and an array of external systems. The cumulative effects of these transactions over time [are] seen to contribute to the complexity of human development and the poor predictability of individual developmental pathways" (Shonkoff, Phillips, & Keilty, 2000, p. 3). This view acknowledges the difficulty of predicting developmental outcomes for both "typically" developing and "atypically" developing children. The influencing factors are many and the degree of variation and levels of challenge are multiple. This requires that distinctions be made among concepts of persistent disabilities, maturational delays, and individual difference in development and behavior.

It is also important to recognize that for every child there are challenges and strengths, any of which can be met along the developmental pathway with obstacles or interference to adaptions and optimal growth and development or supports and buffers. Some children and families have greater knowledge and resources, while others may be limited in their information and support systems. Some children (and family members) are more resilient and adaptive, and cope in more positive and constructive, growth-promoting ways than others.

This adaptability is exemplified by a young boy who lived on a farm in the Midwest who lost both his arms in a piece of farm equipment as he was helping his grandfather put crops in storage. The boy was fitted with prostheses for both arms and received extensive physical therapy. Eventually, he became very adept at using his feet and toes to draw, write, and do his homework. In fact, he could write and draw even more skillfully using his feet and toes than a number of his classmates could using their fingers and hands. This story demonstrates that a wide range of resilient and adaptive behaviors exists within each individual. These considerations guide screening, assessment, intervention, and inclusion practices. It is important for early childhood professionals to take a broad view of child development, particularly when engaging all children in inclusive ways in play groups, classrooms, and other groups.

YOUR STUDY AND OBSERVATION OF YOUNG CHILDREN

Your study of young children can help you to develop a knowledge base regarding the unique nature of child development and behavior. This knowledge fosters an awareness of the enormous diversity in development and behavior among children. It can help you to select materials and instructional strategies for working with young children. Informed study can also help one to avoid bias and become more objective in looking at children. This study involves exploring topics of interest in the professional literature and observing children in many contexts. Studies have shown that teacher training relating to appropriate interactions and expectations resulted in more positive relationships and less detachment behaviors in their interactions with children, and their students exhibited significant gains in complex social and cognitive play (Rhodes & Hennessy, 2001).

However, it is important to acknowledge biases and to realize that early childhood professionals bring their own backgrounds, experiences, belief systems, and values to the interpretation of children's behavior. At times, it may be helpful to have other professionals use the same procedures and tools to verify your information and ensure objectivity.

Four behaviors are important for the developing early childhood professional to acquire: perspective-taking, reflecting-in-action, teacher-as-learner, and teacher-as-researcher.

Perspective-taking is the ability to view and understand a situation from another's point of view. This skill is a particularly important one for individuals who interact with children and their families on a day-to-day basis. The development of focused perspective-taking begins with reflecting on one's notions, assumptions, and perspectives of children, parents, culture, ableness, teaching and learning, and how one thinks adults are "supposed" to interact with children, parents, and colleagues.

Generally, teachers' perspectives on children are influenced by the following factors (see Blosch, Tabachnick, & Espinosa-Dulanto, 1994, p. 225):

- The teacher's personal and professional experiences and beliefs.
- The teacher's and the school's beliefs about assessment as it relates to children's age, developmental level, cultural and class background, and beliefs and policies promulgated at the national, state, school district, and individual school setting or campus levels.
- The teacher's awareness or lack of awareness of children's competencies and broader social issues that relate to the teacher's attitudes toward children as being "different" with respect to ethnicity, gender, race, language, and class group identities or membership.

A second behavior the developing early childhood professional must acquire is **reflecting-in-action**. From the outset of their field-based experiences, early childhood professionals need to reflect on their behaviors and how those behaviors affect children and their families. Time can be set aside in both preservice and inservice settings for early childhood professionals to engage in reflection, both individually and in collaboration with colleagues.

Such opportunities assist the early childhood professional in developing habits of reflecting. These experiences cast the professional in the role of **teacher-as-learner**, one who learns continually from children, their families, and other professionals and from the changing professional research and literature. Reflection entails frequently revisiting one's image of the child, information gained about child growth, development, and learning obtained through observation, and one's image of self as a professional educator (Trepanier-Street, Hong, & Donegan, 2001). Teachers reflect on many aspects of their work, including

- their own perceptions, perspectives, and preferences;
- their observations of individual and group behaviors and developmental progress;
- how best to facilitate growth, development, and learning;
- creative ways to problem solve;
- how best to interact with challenging children, parents, or colleagues;
- ethical issues and sound decision making;
- their own continuing need to know.

perspective-taking: the ability to understand one's own or another's viewpoint and be aware of the coordinated and interrelated sets of ideas and actions that are reflected in behavior

reflecting-in-action: an ongoing process in which educators think about and critically analyze their own and their students' performance to review, assess, and modify interactions, expectations, and instructional strategies

teacher-as-learner: the process by which educators continue to learn from children, parents, other professionals, and the changing professional research and literature throughout their careers

The process of acquiring new ideas, values, and practices leads teachers to enhance their personal and professional knowledge and skills.

Children, parents, and teachers learn from one another. In this process, new hypotheses about development and practice emerge. These hypotheses often lead to investigations into behaviors, teaching strategies, and approaches to assessment of learning and development. The result is often new understandings or perspectives about children, families, early childhood development behavior and learning, instructional methods, and oneself as a professional and as a person.

From this process emerges an expanded perspective: **teacher-as-researcher**. Early childhood professionals, through perspective-taking and reflecting-in-action, continuously learn about themselves and the children they teach, thereby acquiring and demonstrating the behaviors of a researcher. If this process is internalized, the early childhood professional becomes a skilled observer who views children and families from objective and empathic perspectives. For example, rather than viewing a child whose vocabulary is limited as having a language or an intellectual deficit, the teacher-as-researcher views the child from a developmental perspective that looks for causes and solutions. Awareness of the background experiences that may have deterred vocabulary development helps the educator to relate in appropriate and helpful ways to the child's parents or caregivers to further the child's vocabulary development. From this perspective, the early childhood professional assumes a proactive role in identifying and providing the types of experiences that help children progress.

As professionals adopt these behaviors, child study comes to focus on what children can do—their strengths and competencies—rather than on their differences from the so-called norm or their alleged deficiencies. This frame of mind and this level of professionalism are essential in child care and education settings as these programs are increasingly characterized by greater diversity among children in culture, socioeconomic backgrounds, ableness, and knowledge and experience.

teacher-as-researcher: the process by which early childhood professionals, through their perspective-taking and reflecting-in-action, acquire and demonstrate the behaviors of a researcher

ONGOING STUDY OF CHILDREN IN MANY CONTEXTS

Competent early childhood professionals realize the importance of day-to-day observation and study of children in a variety of situations, including settings within the classroom, in outdoor learning areas, at mealtimes, and during rest and quiet times, as well as in the wider context of family and community. Complete understanding of young children involves study of their behavior in a variety of contexts over an extended period of time, as children's behavior may vary from one setting to another. The nature of the setting, the people, the time of day, the child's personality, and many other factors influence the way children behave. In addition, contrived, unfamiliar, or laboratory-type environments can convey misleading information about children, their behaviors, and their competencies (Bronfenbrenner and Ceci, 1994).

Studying children in a variety of settings over a period of time helps the early childhood professional to see the common characteristics of young children as well as individual behaviors. The study of young children can also help the early childhood professional to provide specific examples of children's behavior when in conference with parents. The study of young children can also serve as a means of documenting that the program goals for facilitating young children's development and learning are being accomplished. Appropriate, reliable, and valid strategies for studying young children are becoming increasingly important because many early childhood programs depend on private, state, or federal funding and often require documentation of performance or achievement of goals and objectives.

AUTHENTIC ASSESSMENT OF THE DEVELOPMENT OF YOUNG CHILDREN

Sociologists and psychologists emphasize that the competencies needed to function effectively in the 21st century include problem-solving skills; the ability to communicate orally, through writing, and through technology; the capacity to work with others in cooperative, collaborative ways; and the ability to view events from a changing and global perspective. The explosion of knowledge that characterizes the contemporary world suggests that children (and adults) need to know how to access information; develop skills in discerning, selecting, sorting, and classifying information; and develop skills in determining what information they need and can use.

These projections have been the impetus for the school reform movement that began in the 1980s and continues today. However, the school reform movement has been increasingly marked by greater emphasis on standards and required content in each of the subject matter disciplines. This has been coupled with accountability measures to ensure that the standards are being met and that curriculum content is adequately covered. Such emphasis has resulted in curricular designs that do not develop many of the skills and attributes citizens of the twenty-first century need. The reform movement thus has come to be characterized by more and more testing of children, mostly through the use of standardized tests that employ paper-and-pencil tasks with multiple-choice questions. Many people in the field of child development and early education find this emphasis on testing and limited curricula to be deleterious. Increasing concern about excessive and inappropriate use of standardized tests in early childhood and elementary programs has precipitated the need to find new ways to evaluate learning.

One such approach is referred to as **authentic assessment**. Authentic assessment is the process of observing and documenting children's learning and behavior and using the information to make educational decisions that promote their learning and development. It is continuous, context bound, and qualitative in nature. Essentially authentic assessment (Puckett & Black, 2000) is developmentally appropriate and

authentic assessment: the ongoing, continuous, context-based observation and documentation of children's learning behaviors

- celebrates development and learning;
- emphasizes emerging development;
- capitalizes on the strengths of the learner;
- is based on real-life events;
- is performance based;
- is related to instruction;
- focuses on purposeful learning;
- is ongoing in all contexts;
- provides a broad and general picture of student learning and capabilities;
- is collaborative among parents, teachers, students, and other professionals as needed.

Clearly, skilled and focused observation is integral to authentic assessment. The student of child development employs a variety of techniques to record and assemble observational information. This information combined with more structural/formal approaches can provide an informative profile of a child or a group of children.

APPROACHES TO STUDYING YOUNG CHILDREN

A variety of tools and techniques are available to the early childhood professional in the study of young children. Generally, these tools and techniques are classified as formal or informal approaches to assessment (Table 2.1).

Formal Approaches to Assessment

Formal assessment generally includes the use of various types of **standardized tests**, including the following:

Achievement tests, which measure *past* learning or what knowledge and/or skills a student has learned or achieved from instruction.

Intelligence tests, which measure what an individual ostensibly *could* learn, establish an intelligence level rating (e.g., intelligence quotient, [IQ]), and measure abilities associated with vocabulary and word meaning, concepts, and selected nonverbal tasks.

Readiness tests, which assess skills that are thought to be prerequisites for success in formal instructional settings. Generally, these tests assess language development (e.g., speaking in complete sentences, number of words in vocabulary, listening to and recalling what was said or heard); large and small motor coordination and development; visual–perceptual development (ability to distinguish size, shape, color, and other attributes); reading readiness (recognizing and naming letters, attaching sounds to specific letters); number

formal assessment: information gathered about young children, usually through standardized tests

standardized test: a test that is administered and scored according to set procedures and whose scores can be interpreted according to predetermined statistical measures

achievement test: a test that measures what children have learned as a result of instruction

intelligence test: a standardized measure used to establish an intelligence level rating (i.e., intelligence quotient [IQ]) by measuring a child's ability to perform various selected mental tasks

---

TABLE 2.1   Formal and Informal Approaches to Studying Young Children

Formal	Informal
Achievement tests	Narrative observations; running records, specimen records, anecdotal records
Readiness tests	
Developmental screening tests	Checklists
Diagnostic tests	Rating scales
Intelligence tests	Time sampling
	Event sampling
	Interviews/conferences: child, parents, support staff, resource persons, peers
	Children's products: art, writings, class work, projects

readiness test:
a test that measures capabilities needed for certain new experiences or types of curriculum

developmental screening test:
an initial procedure for identifying individuals who may need formal diagnostic tests

diagnostic test:
a process of compiling and assessing characteristics and symptoms (physiological, emotional, or social) to identify needs and establish treatment and/or intervention strategies

readiness (ability to count using one-to-one correspondence and understanding of a variety of mathematically related concepts such as "small" and "large," "more than" and "less than," "first" and "last," and so on); and social–emotional development (or adaptive behaviors), which can include, but is not limited to, how children interact with and relate to others, separate from their parents, and regard themselves and their own abilities.

Developmental screening tests, which are used to identify heretofore unrecognized disease or disability. Results from these tests are used to determine whether a child needs more extensive evaluation and more precise diagnosis.

Diagnostic tests, which are individually administered by trained professionals for the purpose of determining the extent and identification of specific anomalies followed by intervention strategies and treatment.

As mentioned earlier, various professional disciplines have attempted to write sets of standards that state what children at each grade level should know and be able to do. The standards movement, as it has come to be called, has precipitated overreliance on scores from standardized tests to determine the extent to which children have "risen to the standard." This information is typically used to hold schools and school districts accountable. Unfortunately, young children do not do well on formal types of group administered tests and have been shown to exhibit undue stress behaviors when taking them (Fleege, Charlesworth, Burts, & Hart, 1992). Consequently, the scores from such tests are of dubious value, and professionals have long decried subjecting young children to them.

Difficulties for young children in taking formal tests arise from the following:

- Discomfort, fear, or stress inherent in most formal testing situations
- Lack of familiarity and/or rapport with the person administering the test
- Insufficient fine motor control to manage the artifacts of formal tests (e.g., some types of manipulatives, pencils, test booklets, and bubble-in answer sheets)
- Insufficient language and vocabulary development to understand and follow oral instructions
- Limited listening skills
- Short attention span
- Distractibility

Further, early childhood development is rapid. Skills and knowledge are increasing at a pace that precludes the ability to draw conclusions or inferences that would remain stable over any appreciable length of time as descriptors or characterizations of a particular child's abilities or achievements.

Testing puts stress on young children, even those who perform well on tests. A study by Fleege et al. (1992) documented the stress behaviors of both able and less competent learners in a kindergarten classroom during the administration of a standardized test. This study indicates that kindergarten teachers may respond to the stress observed in their students by using a variety of techniques that violate standardized testing procedures, further rendering scores of dubious accuracy or usefulness.

Group standard-ized testing often causes undue stress in young children.

During the 1980s, when concern over the uses and misuses of standardized tests with young children was mounting among professionals in the early childhood development field, the National Association for the Education of Young Children published a widely disseminated position statement on testing. According to this statement, the increased use of standardized testing with young children is indicative of the escalating trend toward curricula that are inappropriate for children's age and developmental level (National Association for the Education of Young Children, 1988). Unfortunately, many contemporary kindergartens continue to mimic upper grades, with limited opportunities for appropriate developmental experiences, in spite of the fact that there is no research to indicate that this is the way young children learn or that their developmental needs have changed.

The result of curriculum escalation is increased school failure among young children. Raising the legal age for school entry, beginning school a year later for children whose birth dates fall well into the school year, and using standardized tests to place children more accurately in the hope of preventing school failure are some of the inappropriate attempts to solve this problem (Bredekamp & Shepard, 1989; Charlesworth, 1989, 1998). Testing narrows the curriculum as teachers begin to focus on specific test items. More often than not, teachers "teach to the test." With increasing emphasis on school and teacher accountability, this practice is increasing, and scholars continue to oppose the trend (Adcock & Patton, 2001).

Standardized testing encourages instructional strategies that require rote learning and memorization of bits of information that are mostly removed from their meaningful context. For example, learning to spell words from a unit of study or a familiar story or book places the words in a meaningful context, unlike having the learner simply memorize a certain number of spelling words from a predeveloped list. Reading for information, composing stories, problem solving, and creative thinking are not emphasized when preparation for the test becomes the curriculum. Yet these are the skills that children need to learn if they are to be knowledgeable and competent citizens of the 21st century.

Unfortunately, excessive testing of children remains a characteristic of education practice throughout the United States, in spite of professional best judgment and research on its deleterious effects. Professionals in early childhood and elementary education have an ethical responsibility to avoid practices that are potentially harmful to young children in child care and school settings.

The preceding discussion indicates that formal methods of studying young children in educational settings need to be used judiciously and with caution. While formal approaches are helpful in identifying children who may have special developmental or educational needs and do provide information that, when combined with other types of assessment and sources of information, can provide a comprehensive profile of a particular child, informal approaches tend to be a more appropriate technique for general classroom use and professional development child study. Informal approaches provide more comprehensive and immediate information about current performance that can easily be translated into educational experiences for individual children.

Informal Approaches to Assessment

informal assessment: information gathered about young children through approaches other than standardized tests

Informal assessments assess emerging development in all developmental domains and focus on what children do and how they do it. Informal assessments can focus on *performance* (what children do and how they demonstrate their capabilities), *processes* (what strategies children use to pursue information, acquire skills, or solve problems), and *products* (the types of constructions, such as blocks, clay, manipulatives, drawings, and writings, that children create and produce). As such, informal approaches, particularly in classroom settings, are said to be *performance based*.

Regardless of the techniques used, it is important to study and be aware of a child's total development and behavior. This study of the whole child includes focusing on *physical/motor development* (health, hygiene, posture, movement, visual and hearing acuity, attention span, management of clothes and personal needs, coordination in using learning materials and play apparatus, and so on); *emotional/social development* (awareness and modulation of emotions, self-awareness, self-regard, self-confidence, interaction styles and social competence, prosocial behaviors, moral competence, and so on), *speech and language development* (ability to speak clearly, use of language, vocabulary, communication strategies, etc.), *cognitive development* (concepts, misconcepts, perceptions, reasoning, use of logic, perspective-taking ability, types of intelligences, and learning in the content areas, such as literacy, mathematics, science, social studies, and the arts). The following are informal ways of studying young children.

narrative observation: a written observation of behavior

Narrative Observations.   **Narrative observations** are records of behaviors as they occur. The period of time may vary from several minutes to hours at a time. Notepads and a pencil and keen observational skills are all that is needed. Running records, specimen records, and anecdotal records are three techniques for obtaining and recording narrative information.

running record: a type of narrative observation that records all behaviors in sequential order as they occur

Running records are accounts of *all* behaviors as they occur during a specified time span. Figure 2.2 provides an example of a running record. These observations describe the sequence of behaviors as well as the setting and events surrounding the behavior. Running records provide a rich source of information. If there is only one teacher in the classroom with no aide, running records may not be practical, for they require focused attention on an individual for a sustained period of time.

FIGURE 2.2
A Running Record

Child's Name: Daniel		Age 3½	Date: 3/10
Observer: Veronica		Place: Lab	Time: 9:36

Observations	**Comments**
Daniel is sitting at a table in the classroom rolling out clay. He is making primarily flat shapes with a rolling pin.	Daniel has excellent arm strength and good coordination of his movements.
He stands while rolling out the clay and sits to cut the shapes.	The table is evidently too high for Daniel because he had to stand while rolling out the clay.
After rolling out each piece of clay completely, he takes a cookie cutter and cuts circles out of the clay.	Daniel is cutting out circles exclusively, because no other shapes are available. Other children working with clay are using other cutters.
Taking two of the cut-out circles, he places them over his eyes and says, "I have new glasses, like my daddy."	Daniel has used the objects he created to move into fantasy and socialize with the other children.
Teacher asks, "What can you see with your new glasses?"	
Daniel: "Dark."	
Teacher: "No, what can you see?"	(Teacher is attempting to draw language from Daniel. His response indicates that he may not be certain of the teacher's intent or the actual meaning of the question.)
Daniel: "I can't see anything with my new glasses, it's just dark...they're just *pretend* glasses!"	

However, using parent volunteers or planning for a time when the children are involved in independent activity can give the classroom teacher some time to conduct running records. Procedures for using running records include the following:

1. Description of the setting, including the time the observation begins and the activity that is taking place.
2. Recording information in a detailed, sequential, and unbiased manner. Information must be factual and objective, recording only what actually happened.
3. Comments and analyses: drawing inferences and conclusions that evidence accurate child development descriptions.

Specimen Records.   **Specimen records** are narrative observations that are more detailed than running records. Specimen records usually focus on a particular time of day, setting, or child. Specimen records provide detailed information about such observations as the effects of scheduling, the influence of certain curricular or guidance techniques, and specific children and their behavior. The format used for

specimen record:
a type of narrative observation that provides detailed information about a particular event, child, or time of day

FIGURE 2.3
A Specimen
Record

A group of pre-school-age boys were beginning an outdoor play activity. There was a disagreement about who was going to enact the more desirable characters. Their language characterizes the overt organizational behaviors of the fantasy theme among the frustrated subjects.

John (M1):	There will be three Lukes today.
All:	I want to be Luke today! (competing for the role)
Jim (M6):	I'll be Luke.
Bruce (M4):	There can't be all Lukes. (frustrated)
Kevin (M3):	I'll be Chewy.
Paul (M5):	Who else is Luke?
Chuck (M2):	He is. (points to Bruce)
Dan (M7):	What?
Bruce (M4):	We got our whole game mixed up!
Kevin (M3):	Right, I'm Chewy.
Bruce (M4):	Two people are Lukes, all right?
Jim (M6):	No, I'm Luke!
Chuck(M2):	I wanna...
Bruce (M4):	All right!
Jim (M6):	Let's have a converse (conference?), let's hold hands. Let's hold hands...we are having a converse, right? (looking for agreement among the play group members)
Paul (M5):	Right now?
Bruce (M4):	Hold onto my sleeve. (to Paul)
John (M1):	The game's mixed up. (directed to the adult observer)
Adult:	The game's mixed up? (responding to John's statement)
Bruce (M4):	Yeah, we get it mixed up all of the time.

The boys formed a circle and held hands during the "converse"(conference). The discussion developed out of frustration and lack of cooperation at the outset of the play activity. This specimen of linguistic behavior provides a source of information regarding play theme management and status hierarchies in play groups.

running records can be used for specimen records. If needed and practical, audiotapes, recorders, or videocameras may provide more complete and detailed information. Parental permission is required to tape or photograph children. Figure 2.3 provides an example of a specimen record.

Anecdotal Records. **Anecdotal records** differ from running and specimen records in that they are usually written after the incident occurs. They are brief and describe only one incident at a time that the observer believes is significant. Anecdotal records are cumulative and describe in an objective and factual manner what happened, how it happened, when and where it happened, and what was said and done. Commentaries can be written in the margin or at the conclusion of the anecdote. Anecdotal records can be particularly helpful to the busy classroom teacher who finds it somewhat difficult to do the more time-consuming running

anecdotal record: a type of narrative observation that describes an incident in detail

Date: February 19
Observer: Schwartz
Child: Ann S.
Time: 8:38 a.m. During center time this morning, Ann was playing in the dramatic play center with a rag doll. While sitting on the floor, Ann began to repeatedly beat the floor with the head and upper torso of the doll while holding on to the doll's legs and feet. At first she hit the floor lightly and sporadically. Then the intensity and frequency of the activity increased to the extent that the doll's arm began to tear away. I intervened at this point and redirected Ann to another activity with the teacher assistant.
Time: 9:20 a.m. During the transition from centers to story time, Ann walked past the block area and knocked down Daniel's tower of blocks, which he had built during today's center time. Daniel screamed as the tower fell, and Ann watched passively as he called for me. Ann was unable to verbalize what had happened, but did manage to apologize to Daniel for this "accident."
Time: 10:30 a.m. On the playground, I observed Ann push her way past children on three separate occasions. Twice she pushed past children to gain access to the slide and once she pushed a child from behind to get a tricycle. The latter incident caused the child to skin her knee, requiring a trip to the school nurse. Ann was unable to verbalize what had happened and denied any responsibility for the incident.
Time: 11:15 a.m. As the children were washing their hands and getting drinks of water, I saw Ann purposefully tear her painting as it was hanging on the drying rack. Her expression was passive, a blank stare, as she tore the wet painting in two pieces. As both halves hung on the rack, she had no explanation for how the "accident" occurred.
Summary: While observing Ann throughout this morning, it was clear that something was bothering her. The aggressive incidents were uncharacteristic of Ann and appeared to occur without provocation. Despite efforts by the classroom teaching team to involve Ann in guided group activities this morning, she tended to lose interest and find solitary activities. Typically, when she was working or playing independently this morning, she had difficulty or acted aggressively. Further attention must be given to these behaviors for the next several days. A closer observation may be warranted. If this continues, I may need to contact Ann's parents.

FIGURE 2.4
An Anecdotal Record

record and the more detailed specimen record, as illustrated in Figure 2.4. Ms. Schwartz, a kindergarten teacher, became concerned about 5-year-old Ann's periodic aggressive behavior. Ms. Schwartz began to keep anecdotal records after these episodes occurred. These notes were then analyzed according to time, activity, and children involved. Ms. Schwartz was better able to determine what provoked Ann's aggressive behavior and then plan guidance strategies to assist Ann in managing her anger and frustrations.

Observation with Predefined Instruments.   Predefined instruments used in studying young children include checklists, rating scales, time sampling, event sampling, and interviews. As with narrative observations, these techniques have advantages and disadvantages.

A **checklist** is a list of developmental behaviors that have been identified as important to look for in young children. They are helpful tools in studying children when many easily specified behaviors need to be observed and recorded. Checklists are usually used with one child at a time and are prepared in an objective manner that is cognizant of widely held expectations for age and individual differences. Figure 2.5 illustrates a checklist.

Rating scales are similar to checklists in that they include large numbers of traits or behaviors to observe. They provide more detailed information about the quality of traits or behaviors than checklists. However, the use of rating scales is dependent on the observer's judgment, so objectivity is critical. Figure 2.6 provides an example of a rating scale.

Two other techniques that are used to observe and record behavior in young children are time sampling and event sampling. Time sampling and event sampling entail observing predetermined behaviors or categories of behavior at specific points in time or within a predetermined time interval. **Time sampling** is fairly simple and does not entail large amounts of time to do. However, time sampling does not provide information about the context or sequential nature of a behavior or event. Figure 2.7 illustrates time sampling.

In **event sampling** (Figure 2.8), the observer has a particular focus (event or behavior) in mind, such as a recurring problem of distraction or off-task behaviors. Event sampling records how often these behaviors occur over a period of several days. Such observation techniques help to identify the causes of the problem. Information can be used to plan alternatives or to modify situations that cause the targeted behavior.

Other Methods of Gathering Information about Young Children. At times, **interviews** can be helpful in obtaining information about young children. During an interview, an adult enters into a one-to-one dialogue with the child, either free-flowing or using predetermined questions, depending on the intended focus of the interview. The purpose of an interview is usually to find out how and what children think and the way they are processing and using information. It is important for a successful interview that the interviewer spend time establishing rapport with the child. If the interview is to provide useful information, the following are essential:

1. Children must be able to express themselves verbally and feel psychologically safe in doing so.

2. Children must be physically comfortable, neither tired nor sleepy, hungry, thirsty, or in need of a rest room break.

3. The interview dialogue must in no way coax or probe for information that threatens the child or seeks information that should be held private or has no bearing on the assessment itself.

4. Children must trust and feel comfortable with the interviewer.

5. The interviewer must be sensitive to the child's psychological comfort level and to the child's receptive language and cognitive development, as some responses may represent appropriate and effective thinking but provide an incorrect answer (e.g., "What color is an apple?" The child's answer could be "red," "yellow," or "green," though the scoring instructions may require a "correct" answer of "red").

6. Interviews are best conducted in a familiar, child-friendly setting that is free of distractions.

Pretend Play Behaviors	Frequently	Sometimes	Seldom
Engages in imitative behaviors without props			
Engages in imitative behaviors using props			
Imitates actions and behaviors of adults			
Imitates actions and behaviors of playmates			
Verbally describes imitative actions			
Engages in sociodramatic play alone			
Engages in sociodramatic play with one or two playmates			
Engages in sociodramatic play with more than two playmates			
Communicates own perspectives and preferences			
Demonstrates ability to take the perspective of another			
Demonstrates willingness to cooperate			
Demonstrates a sense of fairness			
Uses language effectively to communicate during play			
Engages contextualized voice inflections, facial expressions, gesture, and other body language to convey meaning and intent			
Uses props effectively to support play themes			
Uses props creatively to support play themes			
Becomes actively engaged in the play theme			
Engages in prosocial play themes			
Accepts the gain or loss of players during a sociodramatic scenario without serious disruption			
Demonstrates ability to resolve conflicts			
Assumes leadership role			
Assumes follower role			
Appears to find satisfaction in sociodramatic play			

FIGURE 2.5
Checklist

FIGURE 2.6
Rating Scale

Infant Language Behaviors	Frequently	Sometimes	Never
1. Searches for and attends to another's voice			
2. Cues recognition of familiar voice			
3. Plays with voice: coos and makes gurgling and other mouth sounds			
4. Coos, smiles, makes eye contact with familiar person			
5. Cues a desire for interaction			
6. Cues a desire to cease interaction			
7. Responsive to singing voice			
8. Babbles			
9. Repeats one sound over and over (echolalia)			
10. Points and gestures			

FIGURE 2.7
Time Sampling

Behavior: Biting other children
Subject(s):   Jimmy (2 years, 6 months)
Observer: Ms. Gilliam
Observation Begins: 8:00 a.m.
Observation Ends: 4:00 p.m.
Date: 6/7

Hour of the Day	Time of Incident	Observer Notes
8:00		Observation begins
	8:09	
	8:35	
9:00		Morning snack
		Group time
10:00		Centers
	10:32	
11:00		Begin lunch routine
12:00		
1:00		Nap time begins 12:30
		Nap time
2:00		Nap time
		Child awake: 2:36 p.m.
3:00	3:02	Selected centers
	3:48	
4:00		Observation ends

Findings: 5 biting incidents during observation period

FIGURE 2.8
Event Sampling

Behavior:	Biting other children	
Subject(s):	Jimmy (2 years, 6 months)	
Observer:	Ms. Koth	
Observation Begins:	8:00 a.m.	
Observation Ends:	4:00 p.m.	
Date:	6/7	

Time	Observed Behavior	Observer Comments
8:09 a.m.	Jimmy and Josh are pulling on a large unit block. Both are kneeling facing each other. Each is using two hands to hold on to the block. Jimmy has lowered his head as a wedge between Josh's body and the block. After a brief pause, Josh screams, releases the block, and grasps his left forearm. Josh runs to the classroom teacher, still grasping his arm, crying, and unable to speak.	The physical behavior of biting appears to be Jimmy's strategy for gaining materials and objects that are held or claimed by other children. No audible language was observed during the confrontation.
8:35 a.m	Jimmy repeats a similar conflict with Kenneth over a pair of headphones in listening center. Same physical posture and strategy to gain control of a disputed object.	Similar circumstances—no language observed, physical posture was similar, confrontation was brief with no amiable solution.

Sometimes, teachers find that engaging in group dialogue sessions provides information about various group dynamics and their effects on individual children. Group dialogues provide an opportunity for teachers to observe how children are faring in a group context. During these dialogue sessions, the teacher may discover how one child's behavior affects another, how children interact in guided discussions, what kinds of perceptions or misperceptions seem to be common among many or all of the students, what kinds of behaviors are occurring that interfere with learning or positive social interactions among the children, and so on.

Other methods of gathering information about a young child include samples of the child's products, such as artistic creations, writings, and daily class work; informal and formal meetings, including conferences and home visits with the child's family; school records, if objective and factual; and other teachers, **support staff**, **resource persons**, and **peers**.

Technology can be helpful in recording various types of information. Audiotapes can help teachers to study children's oral language, including participation in singing, chanting, language games, or oral reading. Videotapes can be helpful

support staff:
other people within the educational setting who support the learning and development of young children, such as nurses, social workers, diagnosticians, psychologists, secretaries, and food service and housekeeping personnel

resource persons:
people outside the educational setting, usually from health-related fields, who can provide information about young children's development and learning

peers:
other children who are the same age as a particular child

in documenting and analyzing a wide range of behaviors. Videotapes can also be used to aid discussion about a child with parents and other support personnel who find it difficult to observe the child on a regular basis. A parent's written permission is required to audiotape, videotape, or photograph children. Computers can be useful for storing and quickly retrieving information about children. Figure 2.9 provides guidelines for conducting observations.

DOCUMENTING AND RECORDING CHILD BEHAVIOR AND DEVELOPMENT

All high-quality early childhood programs have some record-keeping procedures to document the development of young children. All approaches, including those developed by the early childhood professional, need to be evaluated for (1) developmental appropriateness, (2) objectivity, and (3) usefulness to early childhood professionals and parents in helping them to understand and facilitate a child's growth, development, and learning.

Early childhood professionals continue their child study and hone their observation skills. At times, early childhood professionals may need to revise or eliminate the use of certain assessment or reporting techniques that are not developmentally appropriate or do not meet standards for professional practice. Additional methods of studying and documenting children's behavior and development may need to be designed and used. In recent years, the use of **portfolio** systems for documenting student performance, processes, and products has proven successful in portraying ongoing growth, development, and learning in individual children (Puckett & Black, 2000; Puckett & Diffily, 2004).

Early childhood professionals are very busy, and not all have an aide or a teaching team. Consequently, they may need to be creative in devising ways that help them learn more about children in their own environment. As this chapter has briefly illustrated, there are a variety of ways to study individual children and child development. The following are some guidelines for early childhood professionals to facilitate their child study and observation:

portfolio:
an assemblage of information derived from various assessment strategies, including representative samples of the child's play creations and academic products

1. Become well acquainted with widely held age-related expectations for growth, development, and learning.

2. Identify times when focused observations might be conducted, and also practice observing on the run.

3. Become familiar with the various techniques for observing and recording child behaviors and characteristics.

4. Practice objectivity. Ask yourself often, "What *actually* happened? Are my descriptions of the event colored by my own feelings or biases? Would all others observing this event agree with my description?"

5. Determine whether additional personnel are needed to carry out observations and assessments. Parent volunteers, student teachers, or child development students can assist in either supervising children or completing checklists, time sampling, or event sampling forms. Where professional judgment (not just counting or determining whether an objective characteristic exists or not) is required, the professional early childhood educator should carry out the task. The

FIGURE 2.9
Effectively
Observing Young
Children

Skilled observation of young children requires certain characteristics of the observer and a naturalistic setting in which children can be observed doing and behaving in a typical manner. While many observations do indeed occur in contrived or laboratory-type situations, any plan for observation must be clear about what it is that is to be observed and what inferences about child development or individual children can be accurately drawn from the observations in a particular context. To be an effective observer of child behavior and learning, the observer must:

1. Be quite clear about what it is that is to be observed, identifying not only the developmental domain (motor development, language development, social interaction behaviors) but also, more specifically, what aspect(s) of a particular developmental domain (e.g., balance beam skill) will be observed and in what contexts (the classroom, the playground, the gymnasium) the behaviors will be observed.

2. Be clear about how and for what purposes observational information will be used.

3. Have a plan for recording observations (e.g., checklist, time sampling, anecdotal record, running record).

4. Prepare in advance for the observation by reading and learning about the behaviors that will be observed.

5. Determine the most appropriate time of day for a particular observation. (Using the balance beam example, perhaps earlier rather than later in the day or after a rest time would provide more accurate information, as fatigue would not have to be considered as an influencing factor.)

6. Establish the best location for the observation to take place, and determine the most unobtrusive location for an observer to be positioned if it is not an observation that requires the observer to follow about and interact with the child or children being observed.

7. Have all materials assembled and in place (clipboard, pen or pencil, observation forms or other recording instruments, laptop or hand-held computer, or equipment such as tape recorder, video camera, or other electronic recording devices).

8. Be as unobtrusive and inconspicuous as possible. In some instances, this means becoming an on-the-run or participant–observer, which entails observing while engaged in a particular activity with a child or group of children. Other times, observations may occur from a particular vantage point. In either case, children who become aware that they are being observed do not behave naturally.

9. Develop the art and skill of empathic objectivity. This sounds like an oxymoron, but it implies the sensitivity to accept individuality in children and sufficient objectivity to draw accurate and meaningful inferences from what is observed.

10. Test your inferences. Would others draw the same conclusions from the same observation situation? Do these behaviors consistently and predictably occur in other situations?

11. Be aware of your own biases, assumptions, knowledge level, and physical or psychological state at the time of the observation.

12. Adhere to a code of ethics that protects the privacy and the integrity of children and their families. Information obtained from child study is never appropriate casual conversation material.

educator must ensure that the integrity of the observation or assessment technique is not compromised and that the privacy of the student is maintained.

6. Clothing with pockets is helpful so that small notepads or index cards and a pencil are readily available for recording information as it occurs.

7. Keep all information about children and their families confidential, never talk to others about the children in their presence, and never share information with anyone who does not have a professional and legitimate reason to have the information.

Remember the quote at the beginning of this chapter? Take a look at it again. More than any other factor, your ability to study young children will be the key to understanding their behavior as well as your own and will make the difference between becoming a skilled early childhood professional or not. Child study is not to be looked upon lightly. Child study coupled with knowledge of child development provides the essential foundation for the developing early childhood professional.

KEY TERMS

achievement test
anecdotal record
authentic assessment
checklist
correlational study
cross-sectional study
descriptive study
developmental screening
    test
diagnostic test
event sampling
experimental study
formal assessment
hypothesis
informal assessment

inservice
intelligence test
interview
longitudinal study
narrative observation
objectivity
participant–observer
peers
portfolio
perspective-taking
preprimary
preservice
random selection
rating scale
readiness test

reflecting-in-action
reliability
replicability
representative sample
resource persons
running record
specimen record
standardized test
support staff
teacher-as-learner
teacher-as-researcher
time sampling
validity

REVIEW STRATEGIES AND ACTIVITIES

1. Review the key terms individually or with a classmate.

2. Select a child to observe during the semester. Keep a journal of your observations. Experiment with several of the observation techniques described in this chapter. (See below for other resources on how to observe and record child behavior.)

3. Read a child development research study in one of the research journals listed in this chapter.

    a. How would you describe this study: descriptive, longitudinal, correlational, or experimental?

    b. What research techniques or strategies did the researcher use?

    c. What were the limitations of the study?

    d. Describe the population studied.

    e. Did the researcher suggest a need for other related studies? What were the topics?

    f. How can you use the information from the study?

A number of other resources can be helpful in studying young children. These include the following:

1. Child development research journals such as *Early Childhood Research Quarterly, Journal of Research in Childhood Education, Child Development, Child Study Journal, Journal of Infant Behavior and Development, Merrill-Palmer Quarterly, Developmental Psychology, Journal of Applied Developmental Psychology, Society for Research in Child Development Monographs, Journal of the American Academy of Pediatrics, Journal of Child Language, Cognitive Development, American Educational Research Journal, Research in the Teaching of English, Journal of Experimental Child Psychology,* and *Zero to Three Bulletin.*

2. Journals from professional organizations and related groups such as *Young Children, Childhood Education, Dimensions of Early Childhood, The Reading Teacher, Language Arts, Science and Children, Mathematics Teacher, Arithmetic Teacher, Teaching Exceptional Children, Journal of Special Education, Gifted Child Quarterly, Elementary School Journal, Journal of Negro Education, Journal of Ethnic Studies, Journal of Children in Contemporary Society, Phi Delta Kappan, Educational Leadership,* and *Journal of Teacher Education.*

3. Professional magazines such as *Pediatrics for Parents, Child Health Alert, Day Care and Early Education, Child Care Information Exchange, Learning, Instructor, Prekindergarten, Early Years,* and *School-Age Notes.*

FIGURE 2.10
Related Resources that Help in the Study of Young Children

FURTHER READINGS

Beaty, J. J. (2002). *Observing development of the young child.* (5th ed.). Upper Saddle River, NJ: Merrill/Prentice Hall.

Feeney, S., & Freeman, N. K. (1999). *Ethics and the early childhood educator: Using the NAEYC Code.* Washington, DC: National Association for the Education of Young Children.

Leonard, A. M. (1997). *I spy something!: A practical guide to classroom observations of young children.* Little Rock, AR: Southern Early Childhood Association.

Odom, S. L., Hanson, M. J., Blackman, J. A., & Kaul, S. (2003). *Early intervention practices around the world.* Baltimore: Brookes.

Puckett, M. B., & Black, J. K. (2000). *Authentic assessment of the young child: Celebrating development and learning* (2nd ed.). Upper Saddle River, NJ: Merrill/Prentice Hall.

Small, M. F. (2001). *Kids: How biology and culture shape the way we raise our children.* New York: Doubleday.

Tertell, E. A., Klein, S. M., & Jewett, J. L. (Eds.). (1998). *When teachers reflect: Journeys toward effective inclusive practice.* Washington, DC: National Association for the Education of Young Children.

PART TWO

The Child's Life Begins

CHAPTER THREE

The Family Before Birth

A parent has the potential to gain what is without a doubt the highest satisfaction a human being can enjoy—the gratification of nurturing the development of a child into an emotionally stable and mature young man or woman. There is no greater reward for the adult; there is no greater gift to the child.

RICHARD A. GARDNER

After studying this chapter, you will demonstrate comprehension by:

▶ Discussing the implications of the presence or absence of choice for parenting.

▶ Discussing sociocultural and economic factors associated with decisions to become parents.

▶ Discussing emotional and psychological aspects of preparing for parenting.

▶ Describing the stages of prenatal development.

▶ Describing optimal prenatal care.

▶ Identifying sociocultural influences in prenatal care.

▶ Describing education for childbirth and parenting.

▶ Explaining the importance of preparing other children for the birth of a sibling.

The decision to have children needs the firm conviction that we are committed to family life and values. We need to be clear that family requires sacrifice, responsibility and hard work. Fathers need to show their children how a man nurtures.

JONATHON W. GOULD AND ROBERT E. GUNTER

However one chooses to conceptualize the term, it seems reasonable to assume that optimal mothering contributes to the optimal development of children.

TOMMIE J. HAMNER AND PAULINE H. TURNER

UNDERSTANDING THE ROLES AND PERSPECTIVES OF PARENTS

Throughout this text, much attention is given to the roles and perspectives of parents in the development of young children. It is important that early childhood professionals be aware of this information for several reasons. First, the behaviors and attitudes of parents directly influence the development of the young child and can do so even before birth, as in cases of poor nutrition, prenatal drug abuse, and maternal depression. To the extent that parents have knowledge, skills, and resources to guide their choices, decision making, and relationships with their children, growth and development can be supported. On the other hand, parental lack of knowledge, skills, and support systems, and presence of attitudes that work against healthy parenting, predispose children to less than optimal developmental outcomes.

Second, there are wide variations in family configurations, cultural values and attitudes toward children and parenting, and socioeconomic circumstances that influence decisions to have children and subsequent child-rearing practices. Cognizance of the uniqueness of each family helps educators to relate appropriately and to establish mutually supportive relationships, leading to the third benefit of understanding parental roles and perspectives: that of sharing information. Parents' knowledge of their young child can be helpful to early childhood professionals. In the early childhood profession, collaborating with parents is an important process, which cultivates mutual understanding and respect. For collaborations to be effective, early childhood professionals must have an empathic understanding of the challenges and demands of parenting. For instance, third-grade teacher Sharon Smith was upset with Joe's mother for not helping him learn his multiplication tables. Through talking with the school counselor, Ms. Smith learned that Joe's mother was a single parent working at two jobs, including one during the evening hours. There were five children in the family, and they lived in a two-room apartment. An awareness of the demands on Joe's mother helped Ms. Smith to adopt a more empathic attitude toward her. Tutoring by a sixth-grade student during school and help from an older brother provided support for Joe and his learning needs.

Early childhood professionals can help parents to understand the development of their children and learn appropriate parenting techniques. Remember from Chapter 2 how Mr. Hubbard helped Juan's parents to become aware of the importance of their behavior in helping Juan adjust to the child care center. Mr. Hubbard encouraged the parents to bring Juan to the center and stay with him for several short periods before he began to attend full time, and to bring Juan's favorite toy or blanket every day. An increased understanding of parental roles and perspectives can also benefit early childhood professionals in their own parenting roles. Finally, a broad awareness of how modern-day families are faring enhances the early childhood professional's understanding of the many circumstances affecting family life and child development.

THE STATUS OF FAMILIES IN THE UNITED STATES

Through social indicators often reported in popular literature and dramatized in the media, all of us are aware of the changing definitions and configurations of this institution we call "family." For some time now, the family has been undergoing changes in composition, gender roles, and parenting responsibilities. Children today are members of families that are described variously by the following characteristics:

Striving, two-wage-earner families

Single-parent families (mother only, father only)

Blended families and stepparented families

Teen parenting

Unmarried parenting and shared custody

Coparenting families

Delayed or older **primagravida**

Grandparents raising grandchildren

Coparenting by same-sex parents

primagravida:
a woman who is pregnant for the first time

> ## BOX 3.1   Childhood Living Arrangements
>
> According to the 2002 U.S. Census,
>
> 69% of children live with two parents
>
> 23% live with only their mother
>
> 5% live with only their father
>
> 4% live with neither parent
>
> 8% live in a household with a grandparent present

Immigrant families

Homeless families

Children living with neither parent in kinship care or foster care homes

There are wide variations in the living arrangement of children and who holds primary responsibility for their care and well-being, as illustrated in Box 3.1. Furthermore, there are wide variations among families in what is known and understood about child growth and development (Zero to Three National Center for Infants, Toddlers, and Families, 2000), and wide ranges in parental (or guardian) dispositions and abilities to relate to and access community resources and opportunities for children that promote and facilitate positive developmental outcomes. These characteristics influence parenting and child-rearing practices and the course of growth and development in individual children.

Data from the Federal Interagency Forum on Child and Family Statistics (2003) provide a number of indicators of child and family well-being in the United States. Based on information from the statistical studies of 20 federal agencies, a number of key national indicators are listed and described. Indicators of children's well-being center on such topics as

- *economic security,* which includes family income and secure parental employment, child poverty, housing, food security and quality of diet, and access to health care;
- *health,* which includes general health status, limitations to activity due to disabilities or chronic health conditions, childhood immunizations, low birth weight, infant and child mortality, adolescent mortality, and adolescent births;
- *behavior and social environment,* which includes psychological safety and well-being, family risk behaviors such as cigarette, alcohol, and illicit drug use, and youth victims or perpetrators of violent crimes;
- *education,* which includes family literacy, early childhood care and education, mathematics and reading achievement, high school completion, youth who are neither enrolled in school nor working, and enrollment in higher education.

Chief among the concerns emanating from these social indicators are the effects of poverty on the well-being of children and families. Social indicators also suggest trends that are similar for poor and nonpoor families, trends that, although not universally deleterious, often pose challenges for families and their children. Primary among these trends is the increasing need for nonparental child care.

Poverty and Child Development

Although poverty must not be viewed as harmful to all who experience it, children living in poverty are at higher risk for interferences to optimal growth development, and sometimes for long-term deleterious effects of certain experiences associated with poverty.

Infants born to mothers who are poor are more likely to be born prematurely and/or to have a low birth weight, often because of poor prenatal nutrition and inadequate prenatal health care. Mortality rates among births to poor mothers are higher. Incomplete **gestation** or **prematurity** and **low birth weight**, as we discuss later, carry a number of risks to healthy child development.

Inadequate, unsafe, or unsanitary housing; poor nutrition; limited health care often resulting in incomplete, and sometimes no immunization history; higher rates of avoidable accidents and treatable, but unattended diseases; and inadequate child care and supervision place children in these situations at risk for compromised health. Families living in poverty are faced with challenges associated with low education levels, employability and employment stability, transportation, health insurance, knowledge of and access to community resources, and maintenance of court-imposed child support decisions (Behrman, 1997).

Nonparental Child Care

Among contemporary child life trends is the increasing need for nonparental child care. United States Census reports indicate that in 2002, 62 percent of America's 72 million children (18 years old and younger) were living in families with both parents in the labor force. The percentages of employed parents rises for children living in mother- or father-only families. Figure 3.1 illustrates the nonparental child care arrangements that families make. Families needing nonparental child care are often confronted with issues associated with accessability, affordability, and assurances of the quality of care their children receive.

Stay-at-Home Parents

A concept taken for granted in generations past is now a separate topic in child well-being literature. The concept of the "stay-at-home parent" is now receiving census, often followed by opportunistic media attention. This term generally describes a family in which the father or mother chooses to stay home to care for children while the other spouse works.

Although it is more common in two-parent families for mothers than fathers to stay at home, it is reported that in 2002, there were 336,000 fathers who were not in the labor force primarily so they could provide care for their children younger than age 15 years. This is an example of how views about gender roles within the family are changing in contemporary culture.

Additionally, the U.S. Congress and state legislatures are taking a more sympathetic approach to the need for family leave time without penalty of loss of job

gestation:
the length of an average pregnancy of 280 days, or 40 weeks, from the first day of the last menstrual period; can range from 37 to 42 weeks

prematurity:
a preterm delivery that occurs prior to 37 completed weeks of gestation

low birth weight:
a newborn weight of less than 2,500 grams, or 5½ pounds

FIGURE 3.1
Child Care
Arrangements
of Preschool
Children

In 1999 the majority of children, 60%, ages 3 to 5 were enrolled in a center-based program. Relatives cared for 23% of children and nonrelatives cared for 16% of children.

*Child care arrangements of preschool children by age, race/ethnicity,
and type of child care arrangement: 1999[a]*

	Percentage in nonparental arrangements			Percentage with parental care only
	Relative care	Nonrelative care	Center-based program[b]	
Total	22.8	16.1	59.7	23.1
Age (years)				
Three	24.4	16.2	45.7	30.8
Four	22.0	15.9	69.6	17.7
Five	20.2	16.1	76.5	13.5
Race/ethnicity				
White, non-Hispanic	18.8	19.4	60.0	23.2
Black, non-Hispanic	33.4	7.4	73.2	13.7
Hispanic	26.5	12.7	44.2	33.4
Other	30.2	10.4	66.1	16.6

[a]Columns do not add up to total because some children participated in more than one type of nonparental arrangement.
[b]Center-based programs include day care centers, nursery schools, prekindergarten, preschools, and Head Start programs.

Source: Digest of Education Statistics (Table 45), U.S. Department of Education, National Center for Education Statistics, 2003, Washington, DC: Author.

or employment benefits. The Family and Medical Leave Act of 1993 (FMLA) was the first national policy designed to help working people attend to their work and family responsibilities. Its provisions include unpaid leave to care for a newborn or newly adopted child or a seriously ill family member, or to recover from their own serious health conditions, without loss of job security. Because this law provides for *un*paid leave, many employees are unable to benefit from it. However, a number of states are establishing policies that provide for paid family leave time through temporary disability insurance programs and other strategies that cover certain circumstances such as temporary medical disabilities including pregnancy and childbirth. Innovative and family-friendly policy strategies are being conceptualized and implemented in states around the country. This trend reveals a growing awareness of the importance of both mothers *and* fathers to the well-being of their children.

Kith and Kin

Through employment demands and increased job-related mobility, families experience geographic separations and sometimes isolation from extended families, friends, and community life. Frequent moves associated with employment or other family needs often suppress the development of a sense of membership in a community. Some families have greater skill and adaptability in making new friends, locating support systems, and navigating changes in their lives. Others find it difficult to identify and access the resources of a new community and may be less eager to forge new relationships.

Whether one is raising children in a community in which one has resided for some time or in a new and unfamiliar community, babysitting and child care issues can be a challenge. As the discussions above reveal, children receive child care in many settings. Many families utilize formal settings such as licensed child care centers, preschools, and licensed family child care homes. However, quite a number of children receive child care in unlicensed or unregulated informal situations, often referred to as "kith and kin" care. This includes care provided by grandmothers, aunts, uncles, and other relatives, as well as care provided by friends and neighbors. This type of care is the oldest form of child care, is often the most trusted by children's parents, yet can be the least reliable in situations where routine or daily care is required, or employment schedules entail nontraditional or odd hours. Studies of kith and kin care reveal the following:

- Its use is in part related to the educational level of parents, their income and employment status, work schedule, number of children, and ethnicity.
- Parental values, concepts of quality child care, age of children, cost of care, and constraints to accessing other types of care influence parental decisions to use kith and kin.
- As incomes rise, parents are more likely to use regulated child care settings.
- Typically, informal care providers have less education than other providers, less extensive experience caring for children, and different reasons for providing care than do formal settings (National Center for Children in Poverty, Columbia University School of Public Health, 2001).

A Welcome Child

In addition to these indicators of child well-being, it has been estimated that half of the babies born in the United States were unplanned and that, though the rate of teen pregnancies has declined in recent years (Federal Interagency Forum on Child and Family Statistics, 2003), eight in ten teenage pregnancies are unintended (Alan Guttmacher Institute, 1999). Unplanned pregnancies are not associated only with adolescence or poverty, however, but occur in all types of families to mothers of all childbearing ages and at all levels of the socioeconomic scale.

According to one report, women of age 20 years and older account for more than two-thirds of all children born to unmarried mothers. This report attributes this statistic to the fact that many couples cohabit, that is, they share the same residence and live as a couple, but do not marry (Child Trends, 2001). Furthermore, nearly 1 million married women in the United States experience an unintended pregnancy each year (Alan Guttmacher Institute, 2003). Although most families enthusiastically welcome their unplanned babies, risk factors rise when children are both unplanned and undesired. These children are at greater risk for psychological and/or physical abuse and neglect.

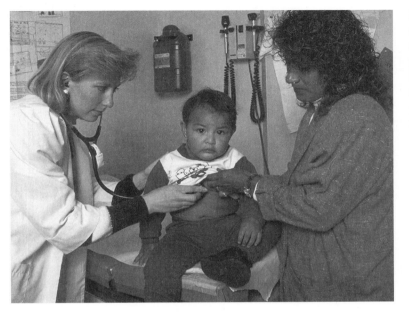

For collaboration to be effective, early childhood professionals must have an empathic view of the challenges contemporary families face.

Because of work demands and greater mobility, families are experiencing increased isolation from extended families, friends, and community life. Furthermore, violence has become commonplace in many neighborhoods and now infiltrates formerly safe areas of the community including the place that was once safest for children: their schools. Very young children either experience violence directly or witness violence against others in the home, the neighborhood, or the media.

*Meet Jeremy**—Ann and Bill Johnson live in a large metropolitan area in the South. Ann is a technical illustrator for a publisher, and Bill is an accountant. Bill grew up in a suburban area, where his father was an accountant and his mother was a child development specialist. Both parents were active in community affairs. Bill feels fortunate to have grown up with loving parents.

Ann's parents divorced when she was 7. Although her relationship with her father was close, he was transferred to another company on the West Coast. As a result, she saw him only a few times each year. Ann's mother was a somewhat distant person, and Ann never felt emotionally close to her.

After college graduation, Ann and Bill married. They worked hard to establish themselves in their respective careers. They traveled, saved their money, and eventually bought a house in the suburbs. When several of their friends began to start their families, Bill and Ann felt privileged to share in the discussions about pregnancy, childbirth, and becoming parents. They began to talk about having children of their own. Bill wanted several children, but Ann was not so sure. Her

*The vignettes of the childhoods of Jeremy and Angela that lace through this text are intended to illustrate the uniqueness of growth and development in children growing up in different contexts. Angela and Jeremy represent dichotomous family circumstances and are composites of many children the authors have known. Their stories are not representative of any socioeconomic, racial, or ethnic group. The reader is cautioned against applying stereotypical or prejudicial perspectives to their life stories.

own unhappy childhood made her question her ability to be a good parent. Eventually, Ann went to a counselor to work through her feelings. During this time, she and Bill read many books about pregnancy, childbirth, and parenting. This process helped Ann to resolve her fears, and she decided that she could provide a safe and secure childhood for her children.

Bill and Ann analyzed their family finances. Between them, they had a comfortable income. Ann's company provided paid maternity leave, and Bill's accounting firm would grant him parental leave. Ann and Bill began to investigate possible types of child care for infants. About this time, Bill's firm, along with several other businesses, decided to establish a child care center, which included an infant room.

Ann and Bill had always been health conscious. They exercised regularly and paid attention to their diets. Neither smoked or abused drugs or alcohol. Both had annual checkups. They consulted with their family physician and told her they would like to begin their family. The physician asked for a brief family history and inquired about possible genetic defects. Ann and Bill requested the names of several obstetricians whose practice focused on family-centered maternity care.

Three months later, Ann missed her menstrual period. She made an appointment with one of the recommended obstetricians, Dr. Susan Windle. Bill went with Ann to see Dr. Windle. They were ecstatic when Dr. Windle confirmed that Ann was pregnant. Dr. Windle took a detailed medical history of both Bill and Ann and shared information with them about the early stages of pregnancy. She described the care she would be providing for Ann and asked for questions. Dr. Windle also discussed various fees and hospital procedures and encouraged Ann and Bill to visit the birthing center. She told them about two childbirth classes, the first on general information regarding pregnancy and the development of the baby and the second on Lamaze-prepared childbirth, to be taken near the end of Ann's pregnancy. As they left Dr. Windle's office, Ann and Bill were given a number of brochures and booklets to read. They celebrated at one of their favorite restaurants. Over a candlelit dinner, they decided to name the baby Jeremy if it was a boy. They were not quite sure about a girl's name. Bill liked Elizabeth, while Ann liked Julia, the name of a favorite aunt.

During the beginning of her pregnancy, Ann's moods varied from elation to mild depression. At times, these mood swings were difficult for Bill to understand. At their first future parents' class, they found that other couples were experiencing similar problems. Jane, the instructor, explained that these mood swings were caused by the hormonal changes of pregnancy. Ann, like some of the other women, also reported increased fatigue and nausea. Jane told the class that usually by the end of the first three months, most of these discomforting but normal effects of pregnancy would subside.

Bill and Ann made regular trips to Dr. Windle throughout the pregnancy. Ann ate nutritious and well-balanced meals; increased her intake of fruits, vegetables, and dairy products; and took no medication without the approval of Dr. Windle. Bill and Ann attended childbirth classes, visited the hospital, bought furniture and clothes for the baby, and compromised on a girl's name, Julia Elizabeth. They enjoyed talking with other new parents and reading books about parenting, finding that this helped relieve some of their normal feelings of anxiety. They followed the development of their baby with **ultrasound** tests, which indicated that the fetus was developing normally and would probably be a boy—Jeremy.

Bill and Ann finalized their plans for the baby's care after Ann returned to work. They discussed their parental leaves with their employers. Bill wanted to take at least a week off after the baby was born. Ann decided to return to work when the baby was 6 weeks old. But as the baby's birth drew near, Ann decided that she did not want to leave her young baby in a group care situation, even

ultrasound:
a technique using sound frequencies that can detect structural characteristics of the fetus and the approximate week of pregnancy

though Bill's firm had implemented an excellent program for infants and toddlers. Ann and Bill felt more comfortable having someone care for their baby in their home. Ann contacted an agency that provided trained nannies. After several interviews, Ann and Bill chose Phyllis. She was 23, had worked for several other families, who provided excellent references; had knowledge of young children's development; and demonstrated a love of young children. Ann and Bill prepared a bedroom and bath in another wing of their home for Phyllis. Since Phyllis was completing her position with another family, she would be able to join the Johnsons about 2 weeks before Ann was to return to work.

Ann's mother wanted to come to help. Bill and Ann had learned from their parenting classes that each couple has to decide whether they want family help with their new baby. Some people can be a great help to new parents, giving them information about babies' habits as well as helping with household chores. However, some extended families are not very supportive and take control at a time when the new parents should be in charge. Ann finally decided that, given the somewhat tense relationship she had with her mother, it would be best to invite her mother for a visit after the new Johnson family had a week or two together. Bill and Ann had taken the time to prepare for the optimal development of their baby and to inform themselves about pregnancy and parenting. Now all they had to do was practice the exercises they had learned in the childbirth classes and wait.

Meet Angela—Cheryl Monroe is 15 years old. She lives in an urban area with her mother and four brothers and sisters. Her grades are barely passing, and she has considered dropping out of school, but her mother tells her that it is important to get an education. Every afternoon, Cheryl's mother takes the bus downtown, where she works until midnight cleaning business offices. Cheryl does not know who her father is.

Cheryl's dream is to be a movie star or a singer with a rock group. Like most adolescent girls, she is very interested in boys, and has been seeing James for about 7 months. They have been sexually active and spend most evenings watching TV, listening to music, and snacking.

It has been four months since Cheryl has had a menstrual period, and her changing body is now reinforcing the idea that she is indeed pregnant. Finally, she shares her suspicions with several of her teenage friends. They generally respond that she is lucky because she will have a cute baby to love her. Eventually, Cheryl tells her mother she is going to have a baby. Her mother reacts with concern, anger, and disappointment. She fears that this will probably mean an end to Cheryl's high school education. She doubts that James will be able to support Cheryl and believes that Cheryl's baby will be another mouth to feed in their already economically stressed household. James is proud of his impending fatherhood and brags about it to his friends. He does care for Cheryl and intends to help support the baby from his occasional part-time work.

One day, Cheryl's mother shares her concern about her daughter with one of the women in their church, Linnie Hudson. Ms. Hudson tells her that it is important for Cheryl to receive prenatal care as soon as possible. She tells her to talk to their minister about getting Cheryl into a clinic that provides care and services for unwed mothers. Cheryl's mother gets the information from Reverend Brown and schedules an appointment for Cheryl at the clinic.

During her first visit to the prenatal clinic, an examination reveals that Cheryl is 6 to 7 months pregnant. She is counseled on nutrition; told how to sign up for WIC (Women, Infants, and Children), a federally funded program that provides dairy and other food products for pregnant and nursing women and their young children; and scheduled for follow-up visits.

Cheryl spends the last 2 to 3 months of her pregnancy working on her studies at home, watching TV, helping out around the apartment, seeing James and her other friends, and visiting the clinic for prenatal checkups. Medical personnel feel encouraged from their exams that the baby seems to be developing normally. Ultrasound tests indicate the baby will probably be a girl. Cheryl convinces James to name their daughter Angela. Cheryl and James await Angela's birth.

These two vignettes describe two very different situations into which infants are born. One is planned and potentially optimal. The other is unplanned and potentially at risk. Planning for a family, good health in both parents, and good-quality prenatal care throughout the pregnancy promote optimal development.

THE PRESENCE OR ABSENCE OF CHOICE IN PARENTING

During the 1960s, several events stimulated a great deal of research on the early years of life. The translation of Piaget's (1952) work indicated that the early years are critical in the development of intelligence. Benjamin Bloom's (1964) research on human intelligence revealed that the capacity for the development of intellectual potential is greatest during the first 4 years. The studies of J. McVicker Hunt (1961) documented the importance of environments and early experience in the development of intelligence. Concurrent with the many studies on the intellectual development of infants and young children was an increasing amount of research on the social and emotional development of children. Erikson's (1963) studies of healthy personality, Thomas and Chess's (1977) studies on inborn patterns of behavior or temperament in young children, Ainsworth's (1973) and Bowlby's (1969, 1973, 2000) studies on infant attachment, and many others gave rise to interest in early growth and development and the experiences that enhance or impede development.

Today, prominent in the professional literature is the research emanating from the biological sciences and neurosciences regarding the earliest developments in the human brain and how environmental influences affect the brain's neurological "wiring." This neurological wiring is said to be most profound during the first 3 to 10 years of life and results in behavior patterns that remain, for the most part, constant into adolescence and adulthood (Perry, 1999; Shonkoff, Phillips, & Keilty, 2000). Professionals in early childhood development, including the pediatric community, are particularly interested in this new emphasis in human growth and development. We will be referring to the literature on this topic throughout this text.

Widely disseminated information about the importance of early development and its consequences for later life relationships and achievements has resulted in increased interest among the childbearing/child-rearing population. Many adults consider the choice of having a child a serious decision, one that entails education and preparation before the baby is born and even before conception. Increased recognition of the long-term emotional and financial commitment to child rearing; the availability of natural and artificial methods of birth control; and the growing social acceptance of small, one-child, or no-child families have provided many options for family planning. Ideally, the prospective mother and father will decide that they want to become parents because they (1) enjoy children, (2) want to share their love and lives with children as they continue to grow and mature, and (3) are committed to providing opportunities for their children to become well-adjusted and productive members of society (Earls & Carlson, 1993).

Unfortunately, many children are conceived under less than desirable circumstances. The relationship between the mother and father may be casual or unstable rather than based on a loving, supportive commitment. Many people do not realize the extent of responsibility involved in parenting. Others have children in an attempt to satisfy their own emotional needs, to please parents, or in response to pressure from friends. People who fail to take parenting seriously or to examine their motives for becoming parents are often frustrated and disconcerted by the expense and the loss of flexibility, privacy, and freedom that responsibility for children brings into their lives. If their lives are already stressful, a child adds to the pressure. The result is unhappy parents with children whose feelings of love and acceptance are jeopardized. These circumstances set the stage for at-risk children and children who fail to develop and learn in optimal ways.

Conversations with parents who are considered competent mothers and fathers indicate that while they believe that parenting brings many joys, it is also the most challenging and demanding job in the world. Competent parenting requires commitment and education. For the most part, good parents do not just happen, and the decision to have a child is not made lightly. Competent parents-to-be recognize that having a child is a long-term commitment requiring emotional maturity and adequate financial resources. Prospective parents benefit from deliberate efforts to plan and space childbearing, professional prenatal health care, family and community support systems, and education for parenting. Children also benefit.

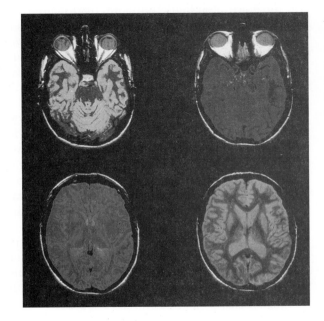

Advances in technology have made it possible to examine images of the brain's structure and neurological activity.

SOCIOCULTURAL AND ECONOMIC FACTORS

A number of sociocultural and economic factors affect the quality of life for children and their families. Some of these include the parents' age, the number and spacing of children in the family, cultural differences in prenatal care, and family income. These factors are common to all cultural and economic groups.

Age of Parents

The decision to become a parent is as related to the desire to love and nurture as it is to important considerations about what the addition of a child means in terms of life changes for both mother and father. Rossi (2002), in her well-known article "Transition to Parenthood," originally published in 1968, suggested that in addition to questions about the desire and ability to meet the dependency and nurturing needs of the child, serious reflection on the lifestyle changes and sacrifices that are required of parents should also be addressed. Rossi suggested that these questions be asked: "What does maternity deprive the mother of?" and "Are the intrinsic gratifications of maternity sufficient to compensate for shelving or reducing a woman's involvement in nonfamily interests and social roles?" (Rossi, 1992, p. 332). These questions are as important today as they were when Rossi originally proposed them. However, the social and cultural context in which these questions are asked has changed considerably. Many more families have women who are employed; women are pursuing educational opportunities and careers not always open to them in the past; contemporary employers strive to establish "family-friendly" policies including parental leave for fathers and mothers, flexible work hours, on-site or assisted child care arrangements, and other benefits. Contraception and birth control advances have facilitated choice, timing, and spacing of pregnancies, and fathers have become more involved in childbearing and child-rearing decisions. Further, contemporary fathers are involved in the direct care and nurturing of their children and the sharing of daily home life responsibilities. (In the 1960s, the concept of paternity leave might have thrown many an employer into distress; indeed, while this concept has been gaining acceptance, it still meets with some resistance in our society.) With this contemporary family life and social context, we would add to Rossi's questions, "What impact will parenting have on both the mother and the father?" All of these considerations relate to the age at which having children takes place.

Decisions before pregnancy about whether to complete education, prepare for a specific craft or career, become established in a relationship with one's partner, become economically self-sufficient, and prepare physiologically and psychologically for childbearing and child rearing influence the age at which a family begins or additional children are planned. Two concurrent trends regarding age of first pregnancy are evident in contemporary family life: an increasing tendency for women to postpone first pregnancies until their 30s and a high incidence of teen pregnancies.

The highest rates for first births have generally been, and continue to be, among women ages 20 to 24 years. Research conducted by the Alan Guttmacher Institute reveals that approximately one half of all births involve men and women in their 20s. Age at the birth of their first child is slightly younger for women than men. In their 30s, women are more likely to have had children—82% of women compared to 67% of men. But by their 40s, the difference is less dramatic—85% of men and 87% of women have children (Alan Guttmacher Institute, 2002a). According to the National Center for Health Statistics, increasingly, women age 35 and older are becoming pregnant for the first time. This trend has been generally attributed to women choosing to complete their educations and launch careers before beginning their families.

Most women age 35 and older have successful pregnancies and healthy infants. As a rule, older parents have more education and greater economic security. Their desire for children and their maturity motivate them to seek professional prepregnancy and **prenatal** guidance and health care. Such motivations set the stage for conscientious care and nurturing of their offspring. Concerns associated with postponed childbearing center on **fertility**, or the capability of conceiving a child. Generally, fertility peaks for women in their mid-20s, then gradually declines until age 30, after which it begins to drop more rapidly. Fertility in men gradually decreases from their teenage years and begins to decline significantly after age 40. Certain types of chromosomal abnormalities have been associated with age of the mother and father. For instance, Down syndrome, a condition due to a chromosomal abnormality resulting in mild to severe retardation, has been associated with parents (both mother's and father's ages) who were either quite young or older than age 35.

prenatal:
the time from conception until birth, an average of 266 days, or 38 weeks

fertility:
the capability of conceiving a child

The standard age/risk figures for Down syndrome births and other serious conditions resulting from chromosome anomalies are estimated to be as follows (Sussman & Levitt, 1989):

1 in 1,500 chance when the mother is under age 30

1 in 300 chance when the mother is 35

1 in 100 chance when the mother is 40

1 in 30 chance when the mother is 45

In recent years, news reports of women bearing children in their late 40s and 50s and even beyond have been sensationalized in the media. Studies reveal that women in their 40s and beyond are more likely to suffer from physical conditions that are less conducive to healthy childbearing than younger women. These include **hypertension**, **gestational diabetes**, anemia, and poor nutrition, which can lead to premature births and low-birth-weight babies, as well as depletion of physical and psychological resources associated with prior childbearing and child rearing. The average infant mortality rate among women giving birth in their 40s is 94 per 1,000 live births. This is higher than the rate among women in their 20s and 30s, and almost as high as the rate among teenage mothers. This is true for women around the world and at every income level (Alan Guttmacher Institute, 2002b).

hypertension:
high blood pressure

gestational diabetes:
diabetes that develops after a woman becomes pregnant

An interesting phenomenon associated with **fertility rate** is the fact that whereas births among women in their 30s have increased, there has been a steady decline in the rates of births to teenagers. According to a recent report, the birth rate for teenagers in 2001 was 45.3 births per 1,000 women of age 15 to 19 years. Birth rates have been declining steadily since the 1991 rate of 61.8 per 1,000. In spite of this promising decline during the past decade, the United States continues to have the highest rates of unintended and teenage pregnancies among Western nations (Henshaw, 2003).

fertility rate:
the number of births per 1,000 women of age 15 to 44 years

anorexia:
a severe disorder, usually seen in adolescent girls, characterized by self-starvation

bulimia:
a severe disorder, usually seen in adolescent girls, characterized by binging and then self-induced vomiting

Many of the concerns associated with later pregnancies hold for teen pregnancies as well. Some pregnancies occur to children as young as 12 years old, compounding the risk factors for both child and mother. Many teenagers fail to recognize the early symptoms of pregnancy and/or acknowledge the pregnancy until they are beyond the earliest stages, and hence do not obtain timely diagnosis and ongoing professional prenatal health care. They may be ill-informed and fearful of pregnancy, have little or no knowledge of available resources, and have limited family support systems and financial resources. Issues with body image and poor prenatal nutrition pose additional risks to both child and mother. (Nutritional and diet disorders such as **anorexia** and **bulimia** are not uncommon among adolescent girls and young women.) Immature physiology combined with ongoing poor nutrition increases their risk of obstetric complications.

Although not true of all teenagers, some are inclined to engage in risk behaviors such as the abuse of tobacco, alcohol, and other substances, and these individuals are at high risk for sexually transmitted diseases (STD), particularly when sexual activity involves multiple partners. Sexually transmitted diseases can be carried into pregnancy and result in insult and injury to the developing child.

Many children are born to unmarried couples in all age ranges. Single parents face many problems raising children alone, coparenting them with an absent spouse, or coraising them with other family members. Some teenage girls want a baby to provide them with the love they feel they have not received from their parents or others who are important to them. They may not realize, however, how challenging single parenting can be or how profoundly dependent their infant will be on them for love and nurturing.

The unmarried father may want to be involved with his child, but a number of barriers can hinder his involvement, including his employment hours and responsibilities, his desire and need to continue schooling, the distance between his and the child's mother's places of residence, and perhaps relationship issues with the child's mother and her family.

Typically, unmarried teenage mothers must rely on their parents or other members of the family for social and economic support. Sometimes the parents of teenage girls feel imposed upon and resent having to sacrifice their time, financial resources, and jobs to help care for their grandchildren. These grandparents may also be caring for the teen mother's siblings and/or their own aging parents. Because of these problems, many teenage mothers and their children come to rely on public assistance.

Reducing the rate of teen pregnancies remains a high social priority. The recent downward trend in rates of teen pregnancies has been attributed to greater emphasis through education, peer groups, and adult mentors on delaying sexual activity; more conservative attitudes among teenagers about casual sex and out-of-wedlock childbearing; fear of sexually transmitted diseases, which now includes the much–publicized AIDS disease; and the availability of long-lasting contraceptive methods accompanied by more consistent and/or correct use of contraceptive methods.

It is to everyone's advantage to help teen parents complete their educations. Research suggests that teenage mothers who stay in school, limit the number of additional children, and have a successful marriage are similar to mothers who had their first child in their 20s or later (Alan Guttmacher Institute, 2002b). Professionals in many fields (e.g., education, social services, pediatrics, public health) are involved in helping teenagers to delay parenting, which so often reduces choices and opportunities for them. Teenagers can be helped to understand the quality-of-life issues related to adolescent pregnancy, and that delaying parenthood by completing schooling and seeking job training provides long-term benefits. In the event of pregnancy, teenagers need accurate information about the importance of good prenatal care and competent parenting.

In an effort to help teen parents stay in school, some school districts provide on-campus or near-campus child care. Where this is not feasible, counselors may assist needy teen parents in accessing community resources such as federal or state financial assistance and child care and food subsidies. Many secondary schools offer child development courses.

Some communities provide **home visitor** and **doula** programs to support prospective parents (Abramson, Altfeld, & Tiebloom-Mishkin, 2000; Behrman, 1999). Depending on the sponsoring agency, these programs have varying goals including the promotion of healthy child development, school readiness, prevention of child abuse and neglect, moral support and guidance for the first-time mother, assisting families with education and employment issues, and assessing and assisting with other family needs. Examples of home visiting programs include the Parents as Teachers Program (PAT), the Home Instruction Program for Preschool Youngsters (HIPPY), and the Comprehensive Child Development Program (CCDP).

The doula is a paraprofessional who provides emotional and physical support to mothers beginning sometime during pregnancy and continuing through labor, delivery, and the first weeks after the infant is born. Depending on the philosophy and resources of the sponsoring community-based agency, doulas are trained to provide education, guidance, and physical and psychological support to expectant families. To encourage mutual trust and close relationships, home visitors and doulas should be selected for their cultural and background similarity with the families whom they help. Studies have shown benefits of doula support that include shorter duration of labor, fewer labor and delivery complications, and lower cesarean rates (Klaus, Kennell, & Klaus, 1993).

Prospective Fathers

Infrequently addressed in scholarly and popular literature is the health and reproductive behaviors of prospective fathers as well as the fathers' roles and desires to be a part of their children's lives. Few health professionals are specifically trained to provide men with reproductive health education and services, and there appears to be a tendency of many men not to seek routine check-ups or to pursue professional support systems and guidance regarding reproductive issues and health (Alan Guttmacher Institute, 2003). Box 3.2 identifies issues associated with the reproductive health education and support system needs of men, listing only some of the findings from a recent study.

The concept of fatherhood as limited to breadwinner and weekend family participant is changing to one that views fathers and mothers as equal partners in

home visitor:
a trained nurse or paraprofessional who provides in-home education and support services to pregnant women and families with young children

doula:
a Greek word for a female servant who provides assistance and support during childbirth.

BOX 3.2   Reproductive Health Needs and Education of American Men

Ages 15–19   Initiating Sexual Relationships

There are wide variations in when and how safely teenage men transition to sexual activity.

Fewer than 1 in 4 teenage men is sexually experienced by age 15.

Nine in 10 have had intercourse before their 20th birthday.

Very few adolescent men are married.

Three percent of adolescent men are fathers.

Seven percent of births each year involve teenage men.

Ages 20–29   Settling Down

Twenty-seven percent of men in their early 20s are married or cohabiting, a number that doubles by the late 20s.

One-fourth of men have fathered a child by age 25, and nearly one half have done so by age 30.

Minority men and men with low incomes and less education are more likely to become fathers in their 20s.

Approximately 8 in 10 births involve men in their early 20s, and half of those involving men in their late 20s are nonmarital.

Ages 30–49   Forming Families

Most men in their 30s and 40s have married and become fathers; however, many men who have had children are not living with them due to separation, divorce, nonmarital childbearing, and children's starting to leave home.

By age 49, the average man has had about two children.

Many men are fathers to stepchildren, adopted children, or foster children.

In their 30s and 40s, men living in poverty are the least likely to be married and the most likely to be separated or divorced.

The number of men who father children after age 49 is very small.

Source: Reproduced with the permission of The Alan Guttmacher Institute from: The Alan Guttmacher Institute (AGI), *In their own right: addressing the sexual and reproductive health needs of American men.* New York: AGI, 2002. Executive Summary. With permission.

---

child rearing. Fathers are more engaged in learning about and participating in the health care and psychological support of their expectant partners. In contrast to generations past, today's fathers may attend prenatal classes and participate in the delivery process, take paternal leave to care for and bond with their newborns, actively participate in the routine care of their infants and children, take an active role in their learning experiences, and provide them emotional support and social interaction.

In unmarried situations and divided families due to divorce or separation, this dynamic is more difficult to achieve. Emotional bonding between the infant or child and the absent parent is compromised, and the detrimental effects are exacerbated when parents are unable to negotiate constructive coparenting strategies. This, psychologists believe, has enormous implications for the mental health of young children. Scholars refer to a "caregiving system" that surrounds infants and children through their mothers and fathers (Solomon & George, 1996). This system becomes disorganized when coparenting is unsuccessful. Mothers and fathers in such situations may begin to question their own ability to provide for and protect the child and may engage in gatekeeping behaviors that exclude the other parent. Each parent may hold gender biases that influence the role they seek in the relationship and the amount of participation and involvement they believe they or the other parent should have (Solomon, 2003). Achieving harmonious coparenting partnerships entails "painful, difficult psychological work" (Solomon, 2003, p. 34), and may require professional counseling to assure healthy outcomes for both the parents and their children.

Size of Family

Another consideration is the number of children already in the family and their ages relative to the anticipated baby. Some child development experts suggest a spacing of three years between children as optimal for effective parenting and child rearing. Studies of birth and mortality rates around the world have found that when births are separated by less than 2 years, the infant mortality rate is 45% higher than it is when births are 2 to 3 years apart, and 60% higher than when births are 4 or more years apart (Alan Guttmacher Institute, 2002b). Closely spaced pregnancies may also result in low birth weight and prematurity.

There are other benefits to spacing, including time and opportunity for the mother's hormonal and physical condition to return to its prepregnancy state and to obtain optimal weight and the physical and psychological stamina to meet the needs of a growing family. It is beneficial to all family members when spacing provides time to adapt family routines and work schedules to a new family configuration and to learn to manage or realign additional home life responsibilities with existing family needs and ongoing commitments.

Couples need time to refocus their psychological energies in ways that meet their own needs, as well as their children's needs. While achieving a stable and harmonious marital relationship is a prerequisite to childbearing, studies indicate that the more harmonious a marriage is, the higher is the quality of parent–child relationships. Lower-quality marital relationships have been linked to lower-quality parent–child relationships and later behavior problems in children (King & Heard, 1999). This is often referred to as the "spillover effect," in which the effects from one relationship have an impact on another relationship (Susman-Stillman, Appleyard, & Siebenbruner, 2003).

Further, studies suggest that where the mother and a nonresident father maintain a positive relationship, father involvement is greater and child development outcomes more positive than where relationships between unmarried or divorced parents are discordant. It appears that in all types of marital arrangements, whether parents are married, single, or coparenting, the mother–father relationship can be more or less supportive for father's involvement (Susman-Stillman, Appleyard, & Siebenbruner, 2003). It is noted, however, that in divided families, mothers (or the custodial parent) may need to make decisions about whether an absent parent or unrelated mother or father figure (as in cohabiting situations) will be a person who contributes to the well-being of their children and the stability of the family (Roy & Burton, 2003).

Children may also benefit from well-spaced pregnancies. The nurturing interactions of parents (mother and father) with infants and siblings can be more focused and extended, providing time for parents and their very young children to successfully form intimate and mutually loving and supportive relationships. Older siblings, as we shall see in later chapters, may benefit from having experienced a longer period of parent–child focus prior to having to learn to share their parents' time and affections with another child. The infant can benefit from the types of age-appropriate playful and loving interactions and care that siblings can provide.

Attitudes and Support from Important Others

The attitudes of members of the extended family and of friends and associates often affect prospective parents through words and interactions that are supportive and helpful or nonsupportive and unsettling. The reactions of family members to the pregnancy can influence the perceptions and feelings about childbearing and child rearing that the prospective parents form. Recall the ecological systems theory described in Chapter 1. The concept of circles of influence is typified here, where influences flow reciprocally between the person(s) at the center (prospective parents, in this case) and members of various familial and social systems surrounding them. Parents who will become grandparents, siblings who will become aunts and uncles, friends who may become part of an emotional and social support system that exists beyond the biological family, and colleagues at the work place who may assist in assuring family-friendly work expectations all will have their own feelings, needs, concerns, and joys regarding the prospects. Moving outward into the wider circles of influence, the availability and role of the health care professions become important contributors to family and child well-being, as do other social services and education institutions. All of these ecological influences affect the parents' ability to develop positive, secure feelings about the decision to parent, and, hence, help them to prepare for and build positive and secure relationships with their infants (Susman-Stillman, Appleyard, & Siebenbruner, 2003).

Economic Considerations in Having a Child

Seldom do we consider the long-term costs of raising a child. When we do, it can be daunting when viewed in the aggregate, as Figure 3.2 illustrates. However, perhaps Figure 3.3 can help to clarify the types of expenditures involved in child rearing. Many parents probably believe that they are less financially secure than they would like to be, but the cost of adequately clothing and feeding a child should be considered in making a decision about having a baby. Can the family's financial resources realistically support the child, or will the addition of a child create an undue economic hardship? Ideally, these questions should be considered in family planning. Families that are too large for the financial resources available can

A Husband–Wife Family	
making	will spend
less than $38,000 a year	$121,230
$38,000–$64,000 a year	$165,630
more than $64,000 a year	$241,770
A Single-Parent Family	
making	will spend
less than $38,000 a year	$115,140
$38,000 or more a year	$242,910

FIGURE 3.2
What Does It Cost to Raise a Child to Age 18 Years?

lead to stress and resentment in parents, and the children come to feel that they are not wanted and are a burden to their parents.

In addition, lack of adequate economic resources can adversely affect the prenatal health care of the mother and the developing child. Unfortunately, within U.S. society, many families lack access to adequate nutrition and prenatal care. Although some programs, such as the federally funded Supplemental Nutrition Program for Women, Infants, and Children (WIC), provide milk and other essential foods to low-income pregnant women and new mothers, their infants, and their young children, they do not serve all eligible people. People are often unaware of medical services, and the services that are available may be underfunded and understaffed.

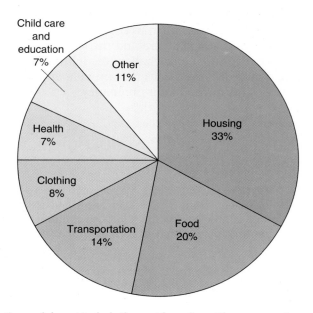

FIGURE 3.3
Types of Costs Involved in Rearing a Child

These percentages do not allow for inflation and do not include the cost for college. They represent amounts for a husband–wife family with a yearly income under $38,000.

Source: Expenditures on Children by Families: 2000 Annual Report, U.S. Department of Agriculture Center for Nutrition Policy and Promotion, 2000, Washington, DC: Author.

Prospective parents anticipate both the joys and the challenges and demands of raising healthy, well adjusted children.

The consequences of poor nutrition and poor prenatal care are reflected in infants who have low birth weight. If these at-risk infants survive, the financial cost of extended hospital care and the social cost of long-term developmental problems constitute major challenges. Solutions to these problems include establishing a network of services that provide appropriate education and health care to families during and after pregnancy.

EMOTIONAL AND PSYCHOLOGICAL ASPECTS OF PREPARING FOR PARENTHOOD

> Parenting is a stage in life, a personal choice, a psychological transition, a psychobiological condition, a cultural creation, a necessity for the species, a political icon, a state of mind. For some, the word conjures up memories of the past; for others, the anticipated and desired; and for many, an idealization. (Mayes, 2002, p. 4)

This summary description of prospective parenting by pediatrics and psychobiology professor Linda C. Mayes expresses well the physical, psychological, and intellectual milieu associated with decisions to bring children into the world. The transition to parenting (or to the addition of children to the family) is receiving scholarly attention (Zero to Three National Center for Infants, Toddlers, and Families 2002). This transition is a time of anticipation, marked by concerns for the health and well-being of the mother and child and the parents' abilities to meet the physical and psychological needs of another person. It is a time when prospective parents begin to change their mental focus to one that encompasses all that they can imagine parenting might be or require of them. For some, this transition can be unsettling, conjuring anxious, perhaps negative feelings, even resentment. For others, there may be curiosity, joy, and preoccupation in anticipating events to come as the pregnancy progresses. Mixed emotions are not uncommon. It stands to reason that the couple's sense of well-being, both emotional and economic, and their attitudes toward the pregnancy affect their own well-being and both the prenatal and postnatal well-being of their child.

Ideally, the newborn child has a mother and a father whose relationship is stable, mature, and based on mutual love and support. In reality, not all couples are so fortunate, and the idea that a baby can help a troubled relationship is a myth. The demands of adjusting to another family member may only add to an already stressful situation. Couples who have an unstable relationship are wise to seek professional counseling before they decide to become parents.

Reaction of the Prospective Mother

From the discovery that a pregnancy is in progress to the birth of a baby is a time of enormous change in the life of a woman. Over the ensuing weeks, her physique and physiology undergo changes, as will her emotional state. Hormonal changes can precipitate mood swings and feelings of sleepiness, irritability, or mild depression. Family and social support systems become important to her feelings of confidence and well-being.

During the course of pregnancy, the mother begins to form a psychological relationship with her unborn child; she is just beginning to develop a sense of herself as parent to *this* baby (Slade, 2002). Both mothers and fathers must make "room in their minds" for a new person in their lives (Mayes, 2002). Studies seeking to understand how parents make the transition into parenthood have found that toward the end of pregnancy and in the early postpartum period, the fetus and then the infant becomes an increasingly exclusive focus of thought and action, particularly in the mother (Leckman & Mayes, 1999). Preoccupation with the infant's cues and characteristics before and after its birth is common, and, indeed, biologically driven through numerous **neurobiological agents** such as estrogen, prolactin, oxytocin, dopamine, and others along with specific genes acting in the brain to promote maternal behavior (Mayes, 2002).

Because becoming a parent (whether biological or through adoption, foster care, or stepparenting) involves understanding the needs of those who are dependent on others for their care and protection, psychologists today are interested in the extent to which parental **perinatal** mental health is conducive to positive parenting and healthy child outcomes. There is considerable evidence demonstrating that strong spousal or partner support plays a critical role in reducing the intensity and impact of maternal anxiety and depression (Cardone, 2002). Interest in perinatal mental health and its accompanying research is encouraging the development of strategies for prevention and intervention with couples who may be at risk for poor outcomes (Slade, 2002).

Reaction of the Prospective Father

Concerns for perinatal mental health (or how well prospective parents make room for their new infant) extend to fathers as well as mothers. As with the mother-to-be, and with similar intensity, the father-to-be spends a great deal of time thinking

neurobiological agents: hormones and chemicals that facilitate the transmission of information throughout the nervous system

perinatal: the period encompassing the weeks before a birth, the birth, and the few weeks thereafter

about the pregnancy and about the child who will soon enter his life. The research of Leckman and Mayes (1999) included interviews with couples at selected points in time during the perinatal period, and found that men think about becoming fathers, sexual intimacy, their potency and virility, as well as how they will care for their pregnant partner. The findings of these studies also reveal that father-to-be may wonder about how others will view him as a person who has fathered a baby; how he will manage the delivery process, including whether to be present or not; what types of support are required of him; how he will handle the waiting; whether the baby will be healthy; and how well he will be able to provide for and meet the needs of his partner and their infant (Mayes, 2002). Sharing his feelings and concerns with his spouse and with their health care professionals as needed can provide a father assurances and emotional support as he makes the transition into parenting. Fathers, then, just as mothers do, benefit from supportive and helpful health care professionals, relatives, friends, and family-friendly employers.

PRENATAL DEVELOPMENT

Human uniqueness and individuality are due to the fact that everyone has a different set of inherited characteristics. In addition to **heredity**, everyone has a different **environment**, that is, different relationships, physical settings, and interactional educational experiences. Even within the same family, each member has a different set of inherited characteristics as well as different experiences. Children are born in different order, and as new family members are added, relationships change and developmental outcomes are unique for each individual child.

For many decades, people have debated the relative influences of heredity and environment on the development of an individual. In certain situations, the influence of heredity or environment may be obvious, but more often behavior is best explained by the interaction of both heredity and environment. In any case, optimal development of an individual depends on both healthy genetic traits and a healthy environment.

Chromosomes and Genes

At conception, the sperm from the father penetrates the mother's egg, or ovum. There is a period of about 24 hours approximately every 28 days during which an ovum is in the position to be fertilized by a sperm. At the point of fertilization, the **chromosomes** of the mother and father unite. Chromosomes are located in the nucleus of a cell and contain an estimated 80,000 **genes**. This combination of genes from the mother and the father determines a person's genetic potential, or **genotype**. Genotype also includes **recessive genes**. These genes are not evident if they are paired with dominant genes. Genes are composed of deoxyribonucleic acid (**DNA**), a molecule that contains the chemically coded information that causes the development of tissues, organs, and physiological functions; it is the blueprint for genetic inheritance.

Congenital Anomalies

At times, numerical or structural abnormalities of chromosomes can result in incomplete or imperfect cell formation. Many of these abnormalities result in

heredity:
the inherited characteristics of humans encoded by genes

environment:
the experiences, conditions, objects, and people that directly or indirectly influence the development and behavior of a child

chromosomes:
ordered groups of genes within the nucleus of a cell

genes:
molecules of DNA that encode and transmit the characteristics of past generations

genotype:
the combination of genes inherited from both parents and their ancestors

recessive gene:
a gene that carries a trait that may not appear unless a gene for the same trait is inherited from both parents

DNA:
deoxyribonucleic acid, the molecule containing the information that causes the formation of proteins that stimulate the development of tissues and organs and affect other genes and physiological functions

spontaneous **abortion** early in the pregnancy. If the baby is born, these defective chromosomes can result in **congenital anomalies** including malformations and/or mental retardation. Some anomalies may be obvious at birth; others may be internal and not immediately observable, but become expressed at a later age. Examples of diseases or conditions with genetic origins include cystic fibrosis, diabetes mellitus (juvenile diabetes), Down syndrome, and hemophilia. These disorders occur when both parents' chromosomes carry the gene for them and the infant receives a gene for the anomaly from both parents.

Some congenital anomalies result when two or more combinations of abnormal genes and environmental agents cause a defect. Spina bifida (an opening in the spinal column), anencephaly (a defect in the development of the neural tube during embryonic development that leads to an absent forebrain and an incompletely developed skull), cleft lip and palate, congenital heart disease, and dislocation of the hips are some of the disorders caused by a combination of genetic and environmental factors.

Another condition that can cause congenital malformation and sometimes stillbirth is the Rh factor, or Rh incompatibility. The **Rh factor** (detected in the rhesus monkey, after which this condition is named) is caused when the **fetus** of a mother who has Rh-negative blood inherits Rh-positive blood from the father. The mother forms antibodies against the fetus as if it were a foreign body. Usually, this condition does not harm the first baby because the formation of antibodies takes time. However, with subsequent pregnancies, the antibodies present in the mother's bloodstream can cross the placenta and attack the blood cells of the fetus. A simple blood test can determine a woman's blood type and Rh factor; further blood testing and antibody screening can determine whether an Rh-negative woman has developed antibodies to Rh-positive blood. Treatments are available to prevent an Rh-negative person's antibody response to Rh-positive blood cells.

Genetic Counseling and Testing

Genetic counseling can be helpful to a couple whose family histories indicate possible genetic defects or whose fetus has been diagnosed as at risk. As indicated, problems can occur if a child is born to parents who each carries the same harmful trait. Genetic counselors cannot accurately predict whether a child will be born with a disorder, but they can provide information to couples, who can then decide whether to have a child. When conception has already occurred, various tests can provide information about the condition of the fetus. Although this information cannot always predict the extent of the disorder, it may be helpful to parents in making the very difficult decision about whether to complete or terminate the pregnancy (American Academy of Pediatrics Committee on Genetics, 1994; American College of Obstetricians and Gynecologists, 1999).

There are several techniques for determining genetic defects. Testing the blood of the prospective parents can help to determine several possible problems. The gene for sickle-cell anemia is present in 8% of African Americans. Tay-Sachs disease, an enzyme deficiency that is seen more commonly in descendants of Ashkenazi Jews, causes neurological degeneration and early death. Maternal serum screening can determine the presence of both sickle-cell anemia and Tay-Sachs disease. The **alphafetoprotein test**, for example, is used to detect disorders in the brain or spinal column. Another procedure, **amniocentesis**, can aid in identifying all chromosomal disorders and more than 100 biochemical disorders. This

abortion:
the ending of a pregnancy

congenital anomalies:
skeletal or body system abnormalities caused by defective genes within the chromosomes, which usually affect the developing embryo during the first eight weeks of pregnancy

Rh factor:
a condition in the mother that produces antibodies that destroy the red blood cells of her second baby and subsequent babies

fetus:
the developing human from nine weeks after conception to birth

genetic counseling:
information provided to parents or prospective parents about the possibility and nature of genetic disorders in their offspring

alphafetoprotein test (AFP):
a blood test that can identify disorders in the brain or spinal column in the fetus

amniocentesis:
a technique that involves extracting amniotic fluid for the purpose of detecting all chromosomal and more than 100 biomedical disorders

procedure involves analysis of the fetal cells in the amniotic fluid. Amniocentesis is recommended when the mother is of advanced age or the family history indicates that the fetus may be at risk. It is usually done approximately 15 to 18 weeks into the pregnancy, when sufficient amniotic fluid surrounds the fetus. It is used to look for Down syndrome or neural tube defects.

A third method of determining chromosomal disorders is the **chorionic villus test (CVT)**. A sample of cells is taken from the hairlike projections (villi) on tissue (chorion) in the placenta. The CVT has some advantages over amniocentesis, as it can be done as early as the 9th week of pregnancy, and the results are usually available in several days.

A fourth technique that is helpful in determining possible problems with the fetus is ultrasound. Ultrasound exams are often used to confirm results of the tests just described. The uterus is scanned with high-frequency sound waves to create an image of the fetus.

The Human Genome

The Human Genome Project is an international research effort begun in 1991 by the U.S. Department of Energy and the National Institutes of Health and coordinated with research institutes in other countries. The initial completion goal was for the year 2003, to mark the 50th anniversary of the discovery of the double-helix structure of DNA by James Watson, Francis Crick, and their colleagues. It was completed, at least in rough draft form, ahead of schedule in 2000. It has constructed detailed genetic maps of the human **genome** (the single set of chromosomes characteristic of sex cells, or gametes) and other organisms to localize an estimated 50,000 to 80,000 genes. The outcome of this research is providing detailed information about the structure, organization, and function of human DNA. The information gleaned from this research allows scrutiny of embryonic development for a wider range of physical conditions from rare, inherited ailments to more familiar diseases such as cancer. This process involves the identification of a gene in the cell of a preembryo through a technique called **polymerase chain reaction (PCR)**. If the PCR of a single cell from the eight-cell preembryo results in many copies of a target DNA sequence, the preembryo has the disease-causing gene. This process is very expensive and sometimes has to be repeated before a definitive diagnosis can be made.

The Human Genome Project has become one of the most important projects in biology and biomedical science in history, providing information about genetic variation in humans and the identification and measures of risk in individuals for any of a number of diseases, which has the potential for dramatically altering the manner in which diseases are prevented and treated. Also, as a result of the Human Genome Project, a variety of techniques for gene treatments for some genetic disorders are being developed so rapidly that PCR may become obsolete. Nevertheless, PCR can provide information to prospective parents to help them make the decision to avoid passing on a genetically based disease.

Although these techniques can help to detect problems, a number of disorders cannot be determined before birth. Nevertheless, recent medical advances provide new intervention procedures for some conditions. Blood transfusions, special diets, fetal surgery, and other treatments before and after birth can greatly reduce the severity of some conditions. Advances in genetics and genetic programming will continue to provide more information and improved treatments for these and other disorders.

---

chorionic villus test (CVT): a test that analyzes samples of the hairlike projections (chorionic villi) of tissue in the placenta to determine chromosomal disorders (can be done earlier than amniocentesis)

genome: the sum total of gene types possessed by a particular species

polymerase chain reaction (PCR): a procedure used to identify disease-causing genes in an eight-cell embryo

Stages of Prenatal Development

Implantation Stage: Conception to Week Three of Pregnancy.   The fertilized cell of a developing human is called a **zygote**. The **gender** of the zygote is determined at conception by the sperm type. If the sperm cell carries an X chromosome, the zygote will develop into a female; if the sperm cell carries a Y chromosome, the zygote will develop into a male.

During the week after fertilization, the zygote travels to one of the Fallopian tubes, where cell division begins. By about the 5th or 6th day, cell division creates two different parts. Inside is the cell mass that gradually develops into a human being. The complex outside cell mass becomes the **placenta**. The placenta transmits nutrients from the mother's bloodstream to the developing embryo and fetus. The placenta also filters out waste from the fetus through the mother's bloodstream. By the end of the 2nd week, the zygote has moved through the Fallopian tube and has become implanted in the uterus.

Sometimes a zygote divides into two identical halves that develop separately, creating **identical twins**. These monozygotic, or one-zygote, twins will look alike, since they have the same genetic code. If two ova (eggs) are fertilized by two sperm, the result is **fraternal twins** (dizygotic, or two zygotes). These twins do not share the same genetic code.

Embryonic Stage: Weeks Three to Eight.   The **embryonic stage** is critical to the healthy development of the fetus. It is during the first 8 weeks that the major organ systems develop. Exposure to **teratogens**, such as chemical substances, viruses, alcohol, drugs, or other environmental factors, can cause congenital malformations.

Fetal Stage: Week Nine to Conclusion of Pregnancy.   By week 9, the embryo has a humanlike appearance and is now a fetus. The **fetal stage** continues until birth. During the fetal stage, growth and differentiation in organs and tissues take place. In addition, the weight and size of the fetus increase considerably. Figure 3.4 illustrates critical periods during fetal growth.

PRENATAL CARE

It is important that the expectant mother seek professional prenatal health care as soon as she suspects that she is pregnant. Signs of pregnancy include one or several of the following symptoms: a missed menstrual period, drowsiness and a need for more rest, nausea, and swollen, sensitive breasts. The first eight weeks of pregnancy are critical to the developing fetus, since this is the time that all major organ systems develop. Early prevention or detection of problems is important in ensuring the development of a healthy infant.

At the first prenatal visit, medical personnel will run one of several available tests to determine pregnancy. An examination provides basic information about the overall health of the mother-to-be. Blood tests are done to determine whether the prospective mother is anemic or has had **rubella**, or whether there could be Rh blood factor. The initial examination may also include blood tests for the hepatitis B virus, urine tests to provide information on blood sugar and protein levels or any current infections, and a Pap test to check for changes of the cervix indicative of

zygote:
the first cell resulting from the fertilization of the ovum by the sperm

gender:
the maleness or femaleness of the zygote as determined by the kind of sperm fertilizing the ovum (Y sperm: genetically male; X sperm: genetically female)

placenta:
an organ attached to the wall of the uterus, which transmits nutrients from the mother to the embryo/fetus and filters wastes from the embryo/fetus to the mother

identical twins:
twins whose development began when the zygote split into two identical halves, thus ensuring that both twins have the identical genetic code

fraternal twins:
twins whose development began by the fertilization of two ova (eggs) by two sperm, causing each twin to have a different genetic code

embryonic stage:
weeks three through eight of pregnancy, during which the major organ systems are formed

Prenatal Age	Significant Developments	Trimester	Significant Developments	Brain and Neurological Growth
Conception to 3–4 weeks	Fertilized egg travels through Fallopian tube; cell division begins; implantation occurs; placenta forms. Central nervous system (CNS) begins to evolve.	F i r s t t r i m e s t e r	Cell division and differentiation create neural plate, which folds inward to form neural tube out of which the embryonic brain forms three major sections: forebrain, midbrain, and hindbrain, which evolve into separate lobes or regions.	First 40 days
4–8 weeks	Embryo is approximately 1/4 inch long. All major organs are forming; heart begins to beat; bones form. Buds for arms, legs, fingers, and toes appear. Eyes, ears, nose form.		Neurons develop within the neural plate and multiply rapidly.	
2–3 months 	Brain formation results in disproportionately large head; 20 buds for teeth appear. Liver, spleen, bone marrow produce blood cells; circulatory system is completed. Major organs are maturing in size and function. Fine hair covers the skin. Primitive reflexes move arms and legs.	S e c o n d	Neurons migrate to predetermined destinations, growing axons and dendrites and making first synaptic contact.

At 7–9 weeks the brain is about the size of the eraser end of a pencil. | 7–9 weeks |
| 3–4 months 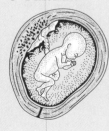 | Fetus is about 4 inches long and weighs 1 ounce. Sex differentiation has occurred. Fingers and toes are evident. Facial features are distinct; eyelids closed. | t r i m e s t e r | At four months the brain has doubled in size. All neurons of the cerebral cortex have been generated, though their axons are yet to be insulated with myelin, which helps signals to travel. | 4–5 months |

FIGURE 3.4
Prenatal Growth and Development

5–6 months	Fetal movement is felt. Heart beat is audible. Eyebrows and fingernails appear. Vernix caeosa covers the delicate, wrinkled skin.	S e c o n d		
	Sucking reflex emerges; fetus can hear mother's internal sounds and voice. Movements become more deliberate and coordinated.	t r i m e s t e r	Neurons developing at a rate of 250,000 per minute from conception to birth; each will ultimately become connected to 5,000–15,000 other neurons.	
7 months	Kidneys have formed and begin to secrete urine; fetus moves, stretches, swallows, sleeps, wakes, and can hear and is growing to 11–14 inches and 2½ pounds. Thumb sucking may occur. Is approaching age of viability and has a likelihood of survival if born.	T h i r d t r i m e s	More neurons have been generated than will ultimately be needed. Pruning (elimination) of overproduced neurons begins and continues into childhood.	
8 months	Eyelids open; fingerprints are established; active movement; hiccup and other reflexes are emerging. Fetus is increasing in length and weight; living quarters are becoming cramped and restricting movement. Fetus is gaining weight at a rate of ½ lb/week.	t e r	Major accumulation of synapse in the prefrontal cortex continues for several months postnatally. Infant brain is one-third of its adult size, but its gross anatomy is very similar to the adult brain.	8 months
9 months	Fine hair disappearing from skin; bones are ossifying; bones in head remain soft and flexible for delivery. Fetus is getting in position for delivery and is 17–21 inches long and weighs 6 to 9 pounds.		Synaptic activity is very active at birth. Environmental stimuli increase synaptic and pruning activity as the infant experiences, responds, and adapts.	9 months and first weeks after birth

teratogens:
environmental factors, such as viruses and chemical substances, that can cause abnormalities in the developing embryo or fetus

fetal stage:
the stage that begins after the first eight weeks of pregnancy and continues until birth

rubella:
a viral disease that can cause birth disorders if the mother contracts it during the first three months of pregnancy (also known as German measles)

acquired immunodeficiency syndrome (AIDS):
a disease that attacks the immune system, causing death from illnesses that the immune system cannot ward off

human immunodeficiency virus (HIV):
the virus that causes AIDS; it can be transmitted from an infected mother to the fetus or embryo via the placenta or delivery fluids

cancer. Tests are offered for sexually transmitted diseases including **acquired immunodeficiency syndrome (AIDS)** [caused by **human immunodeficiency virus (HIV)**]. Physicians may alert prospective mothers to the dangers of **toxoplasmosis**, a potentially teratogenic parasitic infection caused by contact with cat droppings and raw or undercooked meat. Questions about the prospective mother's and father's medical history, family history, and personal health habits attempt to identify nutritional state, possible substance abuse, and the need for genetic screening. Prospective mothers are counseled about the importance of proper diet and avoiding drugs and radiation, and are advised to check with their physicians before taking any medication. It is important that prospective mothers have medical checkups at regular intervals throughout pregnancy as prescribed by a health care professional, to monitor for **toxemia** and other potential problems.

Nutrition

The importance to the health and development of the fetus and the health and well-being of the mother of a balanced and nutritious diet during pregnancy is well documented and widely discussed. Because nutrients are passed from the mother to the fetus through the placenta, it is important for her to maintain a nutrient-rich diet. It is recommended that a woman of normal weight before pregnancy should gain 25 to 35 pounds, though this can vary for individuals (American College of Obstetricians and Gynecologists, 1999). Women who are underweight or overweight (or carrying twins) may be advised to gain more or less than these amounts, respectively. The physician or other prenatal health care professional plans with the prospective mother an appropriate diet and weight gain regime. The mother may be cautioned against consuming caffeine, alcohol, or calorie-rich/nutrient-poor snacks and junk foods. The appropriate calorie intake per day is determined, and adhering to these instructions helps to assure a healthy pregnancy.

Both under- and overnutrition can interfere with the healthy development of the fetus. Throughout prenatal development there are **critical periods** during which organs are forming and are particularly vulnerable to insult. Dietary deficiencies can compromise the development and normal functions of developing bodily systems. Further, dietary deficiencies can result in poor health outcomes for the expectant mother.

There appear to be generational effects of poor nutrition during pregnancy. An interesting study of grandchildren of Dutch women who were starved during World War II indicates that the effects of malnutrition during the third trimester of pregnancy led to small babies. When these babies became adults, their offspring were of normal expected size. However, when the offspring babies matured into women, they produced underweight infants. Surprisingly, the grandmothers' malnutrition was programmed in utero, affecting the grandchildren. This research suggests that long-term effects of malnutrition may appear over several generations or more (Diamond, 1990).

Teratogens

A teratogen is any agent capable of disrupting fetal growth and producing malformations. Just as nutrients and most medications pass from the mother through the placenta to the developing fetus, so do many other substances, with varying types and severity of consequences. The impact of a particular teratogen depends on its strength or amount and the time it is introduced into the pregnancy. Pregnancy is divided into the first **trimester** (0 to 14 weeks), the second trimester (14 to 28 weeks), and the third trimester (28 to 40 weeks), with dynamic and characteristic growth and development accomplishments in each. This is illustrated in Figure 3.4. Some effects are more profound during one or the other of these trimesters, and some effects are equally damaging throughout the pregnancy. Effects also are related to the affinity of a particular teratogen for a specific type of tissue; for example, lead appears to have its greatest harmful effects on brain and nerve tissue.

   Though not exhaustive, Table 3.1 lists types of conditions and teratogens that affect the developing fetus. Consultation with health care professionals helps pregnant women and fathers-to-be to assess their lifestyles and take necessary precautions to avoid toxic or developmentally disruptive fetal development resulting from known insults. Although it may appear that almost anything can have an effect on the fetus or expectant mother, it is not always clear that effects are inevitable for all pregnancies. Little is known about what protects one fetus from a particular teratogen, whereas another might be severely damaged by it. The best precautions include early and continuing professional prenatal care and sensible health habits. Avoiding potentially harmful substances and activities becomes the highest priority. This may mean changing existing habits or lifestyles.

PRENATAL LEARNING

What the fetus experiences in utero intrigues us all. Research in recent years suggests that some learning does take place at the sensory level as the central nervous system evolves out of the neural tube, and axons and dendrites begin their initial migrations and synaptic activities. Although the information gleaned from in utero experience is sketchy and unrefined, when born, the **neonate** exhibits some remarkable behaviors—following the voice of the mother and sometimes the father, relaxing and sleeping readily to the familiar sound of the mother's heart rhythm, and calming to the scent of her presence. By studying variations in infants' sucking patterns in response to recordings of their mothers' voices, DeCasper and Fifer (1980) found that neonates prefer their mother's voice over that of others. In another study, mothers read *The Cat in the Hat* to their fetuses twice a day for the 6 weeks preceding the due date. After birth, the infants were read both *The Cat in the Hat* and *The King, the Mice, and the Cheese.* The infants demonstrated through their sucking that they preferred *The Cat in the Hat* (DeCasper & Spence, 1986). This study and others suggest that prenatal auditory experiences influence postnatal auditory preferences. Although psychologists have not begun to encourage specific types of extrauterine activities to encourage in utero learning, as we explore the quickly emerging capabilities of the newborn in the next chapter, it will become apparent that the capacity for adapting to various postnatal sensory experiences may well be related to certain sensed prenatal experiences.

EDUCATION FOR CHILDBIRTH AND PARENTING

In the past, women often had control over where they gave birth and who assisted them. With the increased use of anesthetics to relieve pain, physicians began to play the dominant role in directing the birth process, and fathers were usually relegated to the waiting room. Over a period of time, many parents became frustrated over their lack of involvement in one of the most important events in their

toxoplasmosis:
a viral infection that can be transmitted from cat droppings or raw meat to the mother and from her to the fetus or embryo via the placenta, causing birth disorders

toxemia:
a disease of unknown cause that occurs in the last trimester and can cause death to both mother and child

critical period:
a time of physiological and/or psychological sensitivity during which the normal development of a major organ or structural system is vulnerable to insult or injury

trimester:
the first, second, or third three months of pregnancy

neonate:
the newborn from birth to 4 weeks

TABLE 3.1   Conditions That Affect the Developing Fetus

Essential	Contribution	Detrimental	Potential Effects	Prevention
Prepregnancy check-up.	Establishes relationship with physician of choice. Assesses health history. Recommends and assists with genetic counseling as needed. Assists in planning and spacing of childbearing.	Delayed professional health care.	Ill-timed and/or unintended pregnancy. Failure to diagnose and respond to existing health needs. Lost opportunity to receive recommended prepregnancy immunizations and timely genetic counseling.	Talk with family physician. Seek recommendations. Interview two or more recommended American College of Obstetrics and Gynecology Board-certified physicians, licensed general practitioners, or certified nurse–midwives. Visit hospital/birthing center to learn about each one's procedures and expectations. Attend prenatal classes. Select best care.
Prenatal professional health care supervision including early and regularly scheduled examinations.	Early diagnosis and consultation provides an essential health care regime. Anticipates needs, and answers questions. Estimates due date; plans for delivery and perinatal and postnatal care.		Delayed diagnosis and treatment deprives fetus of essential health care during the critical first-trimester development of major body organs and systems and ongoing growth and health oversight.	
Optimal weight gain and maintenance.	Minimizes complications associated with an over- or underweight pregnancy.	Under- or overnutrition.	Deprives fetus of essential nutrients for growth. Compromises all types of fetal growth and development, notably fetal brain growth and neurological development, bone and teeth formation, and risks anemia and low birth weight. Compromised maternal health, and risks pregnancy, labor, and	Learn about and follow recommended nutritional guidelines for pregnancy and lactation, weight control, and exercise routines. Consume fresh natural foods and whole-grain products. Consult with physician about food additives, diet foods, and food and beverages to avoid.
Nutrient-rich diet: protein, carbohydrates, appropriate fats, folic acid, vitamins, and minerals including iron and zinc.	Provides the essential body-building and health-maintaining nutrients to sustain growth and health of both mother and fetus.			

			delivery complications. Obesity increases risk of gestational diabetes with risk of overweight baby with associated heart and kidney diseases and other abnormalities.	
Rest, relaxation, sleep.	Optimal state for the secretion of growth hormones necessary to build new body cells.			
Moderate daily exercise.	Improves circulation; oxygenates the blood, and increases blood supply to the fetus.			Avoid strenuous lifting, pulling, and climbing; not a good time to take up a new sport.
Adequate water and fluid intake.	Maintains body hydration and temperature, assists in elimination of body wastes.			
Dental hygiene.	Contributes to overall health of mother and fetus.	Gum disease.	Associated with preterm and low birth weight.	Regular dental examinations. Dental hygiene.
		Prolonged or excessive maternal stress.	Engages the psycho-physiological fight/flight response, increasing maternal heart rate, constricting blood vessels, and sometimes gastro-intestinal disturbances and other symptoms, which in turn may interfere with blood supply to fetus, and less than optimal uterine existence.	Follow sensible, healthy daily practices. Enlist spouse or other family members in sharing responsibilities and removing stressors. Assess need for consultation with employer; perhaps a change in hours, workload, or types of responsibilities. Share concerns with physician or health care professional. Seek counseling.
		Certain communicable diseases, e.g., influenza,	Variously associated with many anomalies	Seek prepregnancy immunizations as

(continued)

TABLE 3.1 Conditions That Affect the Developing Fetus (*continued*)

Essential	Contribution	Detrimental	Potential Effects	Prevention
		rubella, rubeola, chicken pox, mumps, viral hepatitis, poliomyelitis, and other viral and bacterial infections.	including mental retardation, deafness, blindness, and heart defects.	recommended. Consult with physician about preventive measures. Wash hands often; practice good hygiene. Seek immediate medical attention if exposed.
		Caffeine.	A maternal central nervous system stimulant that increases heart rate, urine production, and stomach acid. Associated with low birth weight.	Avoid foods containing caffeine; e.g., coffee, tea, soft drinks, chocolate. Read food and beverage labels.
		Artificial sweeteners.	Fetus has difficulty eliminating by-products of saccharine.	Use only on advice of physician. Read food and beverage labels.
		Over-the-counter medications, vitamin supplements, and herbal remedies.	Variously associated with spontaneous abortion, kidney problems, severe birth defects.	During first visit, tell physician what medications and supplements have been taken. Take only physician-prescribed medications and vitamins, which are essential for, and particular to, your pregnancy.
		Smoking tobacco or marijuana (first or second hand; either occasional or frequent; either partner)	Lowers fertility in men and women, potential damage to sperm, preterm delivery, prematurity, perinatal	Both parents should stop smoking. Seek professional help to do so if necessary. Avoid second-hand smoke.

	and neonatal deaths, low birth weight, sudden infant death syndrome. Newborn neurobehavioral symptoms, e.g., excitability, difficulty calming, nicotine withdrawal symptoms. Later behavioral disturbances, attentional and cognitive difficulties in childhood.	
Alcohol.	Fetal alcohol syndrome and other alcohol-related neurodevelopmental disorders, including low birth weight, neurological damage, craniofacial deformity, developmental delay, impaired cognitive abilities (attention, memory, problem solving, abstract thinking), mental retardation, hyperactivity, later behavioral difficulties in childhood.	No alcohol during pregnancy or during fertility efforts.
Cocaine, opiates, other illicit drugs or polydrug (multiple drug) use.	Neurological damage, low birth weight, prematurity, neonatal low-arousal states, deficient motor and reflexive activity, higher excitability, abnormal crying behaviors, neonatal addiction and withdrawal symptoms.	No illicit drugs during pregnancy or during fertility efforts.

(continued)

TABLE 3.1   Conditions That Affect the Developing Fetus (*continued*)

Essential	Contribution	Detrimental	Potential Effects	Prevention
		Other toxins, e.g., lead, mercury, pesticides, household cleaners, fertilizers and other agricultural products, industrial wastes and emissions, animal droppings, certain insect bites.	Neurological damage, low birth weight, visual impairments, other birth defects, developmental delays in cognitive and language abilities.	Consult with physician about particular exposures and how to avoid known toxins.
		Radiation.	Damage to growing cells, miscarriage, malformations, childhood cancers, gene mutations.	X-rays on advice of physician and administered under strict protective guidelines including lead apron shield. Consult with physician about sources of radiation and appropriate precautions.
		Sexually transmitted diseases (STDs)	Spontaneous abortion, prematurity, growth retardation, low birth weight, hearing and vision impairments, and other possible birth defects. Some STDs can be transmitted to the infant during pregnancy, labor, and delivery.	Practice safe sex, using condoms and spermicide. Advise physician if exposure is suspected. Both partners may need to be treated.

Sources: Fetal Alcohol Syndrome: Diagnosis, Epidemiology, Prevention, and Treatment, by K. Stratton, C. Howe, and F. Battaglia (Eds.), 1996, Washington, DC: National Academy Press.

"Level of Prenatal Cocaine Exposure and Scores on the Bayley Scales of Infant Development: Modifying Effects of Caregiver, Early Intervention, and Birth Weight," by D. Frank, R. R. Jacobs, M. Beeghy, M. Augustyn, D. Bellinger, H. Cabral, and T. Heeren, 2002, *Pediatrics, 110*(6), pp. 1143–1152.

"Maternal Cigarette Smoking and Child Psychiatric Morbidity: A Longitudinal Study," by G. M. Williams, M. O'Callahan, J. M. Najman, W. Bor, M. J. Anderson, D. Richards, and U. Chinlyn, 1998, *Pediatrics, 102*(1), p. e11. Retrieved October 7, 2002, from http://www.pediatrics.org

"The Maternal Lifestyle Study: Effects of Substance Exposure During Pregnancy on Neurodevelopmental Outcome in One-Month-Old-Infants," by M. Lester, E. Tronick, L. Lagasse, R. Seifer, C. R. Bauer, S. Shankaran, H. S. Bada, L. Wright, V. L. Smeriglio, L. Ju, L. P. Finnegan, and P. L. Maza, 2002, *Pediatrics, 110*(6), pp. 1182–1192.

Planning Your Pregnancy, by the American College of Obstetricians and Gynecologists, 2000, Washington, DC: Author.

Pregnancy: You and Your Baby: Prenatal Care, Labor and Delivery, and Postpartum Care, by the American College of Obstetricians and Gynecologists, 1999, Washington, DC: Author.

"Prenatal Alcohol Exposure and Childhood Behavior at Age 6 to 7 years: I. Dose–Response Effect," by B. Sood, V. Delaney-Black, C. Covington, B. Nordstrom-Klee, J. Ager, T. Templin, J. Janisse, S. Martier, and R. J. Sokol, 2003, *Pediatrics, 108*(2), p. e34. Retrieved June 30, 2003, from http://pediatrics. aappublications.org/e

"Tagum Study II: Follow-Up Study at Two Years of Age After Prenatal Exposure to Mercury," by G. B. Ramirez, O. Pagulayan, H. Akagi, A. F. Rivera, L. V. Lee, A. Berroya, C. V. Cruz, and D. Casintahan, 2003, *Pediatrics, 111*(3), pp. e289–e295. Retrieved June 30, 2003, from http://pediatrics.aappublications.org/e

Women and Smoking: A Report of the Surgeon General, by the Centers for Disease Control and Prevention, 2002, *MMWR, 51* (RR12), pp. 1–30.

lives. In addition, the increasing number of research studies documenting the negative effects of medication during labor and delivery caused increasing concern among many health care professionals (Sepkoski, 1985; Wilson, 1977). Over time, parents and health care professionals became advocates for educated childbirth and for more active involvement of the parents in the pregnancy, delivery, and care of the newborn in the hospital setting.

Lamaze method: a method developed by Fernand Lamaze, which involves training the prospective mother and a partner/coach in breathing and relaxation techniques to be used during labor

One of the better-known educated childbirth approaches is the **Lamaze method** (Karmel, 1959). The Lamaze technique instructs the mother-to-be and her coach, usually the father-to-be, in breathing patterns that help to control pain and discomfort during the different stages of labor. The prospective mother and her coach practice these techniques during the last months of pregnancy.

Prospective parents are given information about the various types of medication and their effects on the fetus and the mother. They are encouraged to discuss their preferred medications with their physicians in advance of delivery. Many Lamaze classes are preceded by a course dealing with general pregnancy and childbirth information. These classes usually occur earlier in the pregnancy and inform the prospective parents about physiological and psychological aspects of pregnancy, childbirth, and parenting.

Some parents-to-be choose to deliver their babies at home with the assistance of a physician or certified nurse–midwife. While home births provide the prospective parents with more control over the birthing process and can involve family or friends, some risks are involved. If complications arise, hospital equipment and trained specialists are not immediately available.

Many hospitals now provide birthing rooms that allow the mother to remain in one room throughout labor and delivery, with husband and family members often present. Birthing rooms are usually furnished with a homelike decor, yet provide all of the necessary medical support services.

Ideally, prospective parents select their obstetrician and hospital with care. An obstetrician who is comfortable with the father's active involvement throughout the pregnancy and who recognizes the value of educated childbirth provides valuable support to the prospective parents. Likewise, a hospital that offers family-involved birthing experiences; allows the father, other children, and close relatives extended visitation privileges; permits the baby to "room in" with the mother; and has classes for new parents on the care and feeding of the newborn provides helpful services to new parents. Such experiences help parents to learn about and get to know their baby and begin to develop confidence in their parenting abilities.

Some of the health services described in this chapter are not available to all socioeconomic groups. The provision of more extensive coverage to all segments of the population is a concern to child development professionals. As services expand to meet the needs of an increasingly diverse population, programs must be sensitive to the cultural backgrounds of various groups that will use them.

THE IMPORTANCE OF PREPARING SIBLINGS FOR THE BIRTH

Preparing brothers and sisters for the arrival of a new baby helps create positive sibling relationships from the beginning. Less jealousy and decreased sibling rivalry later on are the benefits of thoughtful attention to the needs of other children within the family.

For children younger than 3 years of age, parents need to plan some special activities or time spent alone with them after the birth of a new brother or sister. Thinking about how and when this will occur can prevent the children from feeling neglected. A doll and various accessories used in the care of young babies can help during times when parents are busy with the newborn. An older brother or sister can feed, bathe, and change the baby just as mother or father does. Siblings can help in preparing the baby's room or bed, gathering clothes, and choosing the baby's name.

Some hospitals have special programs for siblings. Prospective brothers and sisters can visit the hospital to see where their mother and the new baby will stay. Hospital staff members talk to the children about what babies are like and what their care entails. Discussion of the range of feelings about being a brother or sister can also help children deal with their emotions.

Careful thought must be given to who will care for the siblings during the mother's hospital stay. Those who care for them need to be nurturant and understanding of their expressions of distress at separation from their mother and other anxieties. Careful planning for siblings can reduce stress for the entire family and promote positive sibling relationships.

ANTICIPATING OPTIMAL OUTCOMES

This chapter has addressed a number of issues regarding optimal conditions preceding the birth of a child. Nevertheless, not all children born to advantaged families have advantaged circumstances during childhood and as adults. Likewise, not all children born into less than desirable settings remain disadvantaged. Studies indicate that the forces that create inequality in families are complex and interact in a synergistic process (Garrett, Ferron, Ng'Andu, Bryant, & Harbin, 1994). Werner and Smith (1982) studied adolescents who were classified as resilient. These children seemed to have been protected by the following factors: good temperament, small family size, positive parenting patterns, a relationship with a caring adult other than a parent, low levels of family conflict, fewer stressful experiences, and access to counseling and remediation services. Werner (1989) found that early responsibility in caring for a sibling, grandparent, or an ill or incompetent parent was another factor in the lives of resilient adolescents. In his transcultural study of individual competence, Heath (1977) identified a core set of behaviors including (1) an ability to anticipate consequences; (2) calm and clear thinking; (3) potential fulfillment; (4) orderly, organized approaches to life's problems; (5) predictability; (6) purposefulness; (7) realism; (8) reflectiveness; (9) strong convictions; and (10) implacability. Finally, self-esteem, coupled with the perception of the individual as one who can cope successfully by the family and others in the culture, was important.

Ann and Bill Johnson, like Cheryl Monroe and James, are awaiting the births of their babies. These babies will have been affected by very different sets of circumstances before their births. Chapter 4 will show how these circumstances influence the development of the babies and their family contexts at birth and soon afterward.

> ### ROLE OF THE EARLY CHILDHOOD PROFESSIONAL
>
> 1. Understand how cultural background and parental behaviors and attitudes directly influence the development of children even before birth.
> 2. Understand that behaviors and attitudes of parents influence development and learning during prenatal development and after birth, and throughout the early childhood years.
> 3. Appreciate the challenges associated with family planning and child rearing.
> 4. Provide information and opportunities for parents to acquire child development knowledge.
> 5. Understand that parents are valuable sources of information about their children and that early childhood professionals must work in partnership with parents if optimal development and learning are to occur in young children.

KEY TERMS

abortion
acquired
   immunodeficiency
   syndrome (AIDS)
alphafetoprotein test (AFP)
amniocentesis
anorexia
bulimia
chorionic villus test (CVT)
chromosomes
congenital anomalies
critical period
DNA
doula
embryonic stage
environment
fertility
fertility rate

fetal stage
fetus
fraternal twins
gender
genes
genetic counseling
genome
genotype
gestation
gestational diabetes
heredity
home visitor
human immunodeficiency
   virus (HIV)
hypertension
identical twins
Lamaze method
low birth weight

neonate
neurobiological agents
perinatal
placenta
polymerase chain reaction
   (PCR)
primagravida
prematurity
prenatal
recessive gene
Rh factor
rubella
teratogens
toxemia
toxoplasmosis
trimester
ultrasound
zygote

REVIEW STRATEGIES AND ACTIVITIES

1. Review the key terms individually or with a classmate.
2. Interview your classmates who are parents. Ask them to share with you some of the following:
   a. Their reactions on finding out they were going to be a parent.
   b. Their feelings and reactions as the pregnancy progressed.
   c. Reactions of the baby's other parent and of family and friends.

    d. The nature of their prenatal care.

    e. The types of care and interactions their children required at various times: birth, toddlerhood, two to eight years of age.

    f. A typical day as a parent.

    g. The joys and challenges of becoming a parent.

    h. How becoming a parent has changed their lives.

3. Develop a resource file of support services your community provides to prospective parents (e.g., local hospitals, public health centers, prenatal clinics, prenatal and parenting classes, related support groups).

4. Write a research paper on cultural perspectives and practices associated with pregnancy, birth, and parenting.

5. Describe how you think heredity and environment influenced your development. Share with your classmates in small discussion groups.

6. Invite the following speakers to your class:

    a. A genetic counselor to describe and discuss genetic counseling.

    b. A Lamaze instructor to describe and discuss the Lamaze method.

    c. A LaLeche League representative to discuss their perspectives on breast-feeding.

    d. A pharmacist to discuss the effects of drugs during pregnancy.

FURTHER READINGS

American College of Obstetricians and Gynecologists. (2000). *Planning your pregnancy.* Washington, DC: Author.

Centers for Disease Control and Prevention. (2002). *Safe motherhood: Promoting health for women before, during, and after pregnancy 2002.* Available at www.cdc.gov/nccdphp/drh

Dickerson, M. L. (2000). *Small victories: Conversations about prematurity, disability, vision loss, and success.* New York: American Foundation for the Blind.

Herschkowitz, N., & Herschkowitz, E. C. (2002). *A good start in life: Understanding your child's brain and behavior.* Washington, DC: Joseph Henry Press.

Klass, C. S. (2003). *The home visitor's guidebook: Promoting optimal parent and child development* (2nd ed.). Baltimore: Brookes.

Weisberger, E. (2001). *Letters from Nin: Wisdom, advice, and encouragement for a first-time mother.* Santa Barbara, CA: Fithian Press.

OTHER RESOURCES

Local chapters of the March of Dimes provide pamphlets on genetic counseling, prenatal development, and ways to prevent birth defects.

4

The Child and Family at Birth

To be a child is to know the fun of living. To have a child is to know the beauty of life.

AUTHOR UNKNOWN

After studying this chapter, you will demonstrate comprehension by:

▶ Describing the stages of labor.

▶ Identifying the various types of deliveries.

▶ Describing the assessment and care of newborns.

▶ Outlining the change in family dynamics at birth, including bonding and reactions of the newborn, parents, siblings, and extended family.

▶ Describing the care of infants with special needs and their families.

The birth of a child is one of nature's profound miracles. Even though hundreds of infants are born each day, each new life heightens our sense of wonder. For families, few words or phrases adequately describe the emotions that surround the anticipation, delivery, and first glimpse at their newborn. To the extent that the parents have experienced optimal prepregnancy and prenatal planning and health care, this event is enhanced for them. The nature and health of the pregnancy have been critical to the nature and health of the delivery process and the overall well-being of the newborn. Let us begin this chapter with a description of the delivery process.

STAGES OF LABOR

The average gestation period is 280 days, but can be shorter or longer by as many as 14 days. Most infants are born between 266 and 294 days. At the end of the gestation period, the fetus has reached full term and is positioned for the birth process. The process, generally referred to as **labor**, is divided into three stages.

The first stage of labor, **dilation**, progresses in three phases:

1. The earliest phase, in which a blood-tinged mucous is discharged from the vagina, and the **cervix** begins the dramatic process of enlarging or dilating to make way for easy passage of the baby. Mild **contractions** begin, occurring every 15 to 20 minutes, gradually becoming more regular until they are less than 5 minutes apart.

2. The active phase, in which the cervix continues dilating to up to 5 to 8 centimeters, the mucous membranes rupture, releasing amniotic fluids, and contractions become stronger and begin to occur about 3 minutes apart, lasting about 30 to 45 seconds.

labor:
the three stages of the birth process: dilation, birth of the baby, and discharge of the placenta

dilation:
the gradual opening of the cervix, which occurs in the first stage of labor

cervix:
the opening of the uterus

contraction:
the movement of the muscles of the uterus that pushes the baby through the cervical opening and into the birth canal

93

3. The transition phase, in which the cervix dilates to 8 to 10 centimeters and contractions occur 2 to 3 minutes apart and last about 1 minute.

The second stage of labor commences when the cervix is fully dilated and contractions become regular and stronger with noticeable rest periods between them. This phase ends with the birth of the baby. The third stage involves light, rhythmic contractions that assist in the expulsion of the placenta. The following vignettes about Ann and Bill and Cheryl and James illustrate these processes.

Stage 1: Dilation to Delivery

It is 6:25 in the morning. Ann Johnson feels a slight snap in her abdominal area. Amniotic fluid empties from her uterine cavity and soaks the bed linen. Ann realizes that she is in labor and Jeremy's birth will soon be a reality. Dilation actually began 2 days earlier, when Ann's check-up with Dr. Windle indicated that her cervix was dilated 3 centimeters. By the time her baby is born, Ann's cervix will have dilated to about 10 centimeters (4 inches). This opening is usually wide enough to allow most babies to be born.

Bill and Ann have learned from their childbirth education classes that each labor and delivery is unique. Nevertheless, one or more of the following signs usually indicates that labor is in process: lower backache, indigestion, diarrhea, abdominal cramps, the expulsion of the mucous plug, and the discharge of amniotic fluid.

Ann awakens Bill and tells him what has happened. He excitedly phones Dr. Windle. She tells Bill that since Ann's water has broken, it is best that they go to the hospital immediately. Dr. Windle says that she will meet them there in about 45 minutes. Ann and Bill dress, gather their bags (which have been packed for several weeks), and drive to the hospital.

Ann's contractions have been relatively short, lasting about 30 to 45 seconds, and have occurred about every 15 to 20 minutes. During the drive, she uses some of the Lamaze breathing exercises and records the time and duration of each contraction. Ann and Bill are greeted at the hospital by obstetrical nurse Maria Lopez. She helps Ann into a wheelchair and takes her to the birthing room, while Bill checks Ann into the hospital. Maria is familiar with Lamaze techniques, so she temporarily takes over as Ann's coach as the contractions occur.

The birthing room looks very much like a bedroom, attractively furnished in soothing colors. In addition to the birthing bed are a sofa, several comfortable chairs, and a table with four chairs. Unlike the traditional hospital setting, in which mothers are moved to the delivery room before the birth, Ann will remain in the birthing room for both labor and delivery and for a brief period thereafter. She is free to move around and to take refreshments as needed and permissible. Friends and family can visit, according to Ann and Bill's wishes. Dr. Windle and Maria will be on hand to help Bill and Ann and provide specialized medical assistance.

The birthing bed is very different from the traditional delivery table on which women lie down with their feet in stirrups. It allows Ann to recline slightly, and there is a place to rest her legs to help in pushing during the final stage of labor. The position of the birthing bed will relieve pressure on Ann's back and allow the force of gravity to assist in the birth process.

Dr. Windle soon arrives. She checks Ann and confirms that she is comfortable, looks over the birthing room and determines that everything is in a state of readiness, and briefs Ann on the initial procedures that will be taking place. She instructs Maria to set up an intravenous catheter (IV), a very thin, flexible tube placed in an arm vein, through which fluids to prevent dehydration can be administered as needed. The IV is also used to provide medications when necessary to control blood pressure, curtail contractions when labor is premature, augment or induce labor, or provide pain relief medication. This is a common procedure, though it is not routine practice in all hospitals. Bill enters the birthing room and resumes coaching Ann and timing her contractions. During this first stage of labor, Ann's contractions become more frequent and intense. Ann adapts her Lamaze breathing patterns to the intensity of contractions. She walks around the room or sits in the birthing bed, depending on what feels more comfortable. Since she seems to be experiencing intense pain in her lower back, Bill rubs her back to relieve the pressure. Throughout labor, Dr. Windle and Maria check in on Bill and Ann. At each visit and just after Ann has experienced a contraction, Dr. Windle places a stethoscope on Ann's abdomen and listens and records the fetal heart rate. On one or more of these visits, she asks whether Bill and Ann would like to listen. Then she places a handheld ultrasound instrument on Ann's abdomen, and they all listen with awe to the healthy, rhythmic beat of the fetal heart. Dr. Windle assures Ann and Bill that labor is progressing normally and that she will return shortly to check on them again.

It is now 10:00 a.m., and Ann has been in labor at least 4 hours—possibly longer, since she was asleep when her water broke. Jeremy is on his way into this world.

Now, let's see what is happening to Cheryl Monroe and James. It is four weeks before Cheryl Monroe's due date. She and James are watching television. Cheryl does not feel well; she has indigestion and diarrhea. While she is in the bathroom, she notices a mucus-like, blood-tinged discharge on her undergarments. The social worker who has been helping Cheryl had told her about the signs of labor. Cheryl walks to the living room and tells James and her sister that she thinks the baby is coming.

Cheryl's sister calls the emergency room to tell them of Cheryl's condition. Because it is 1 month before Cheryl's estimated due date, the emergency room nurse says that Cheryl needs to come to the hospital as soon as possible. James goes to a neighbor who has a car to ask him to drive them to the hospital.

Shortly after midnight, Cheryl's mother arrives home from her evening job to find the household in an uproar. She quickly gathers clothes and cosmetics into a bag for Cheryl. Cheryl is anxious, and her mother does her best to calm her while they walk to the neighbor's car for the short drive to the hospital. "After all," she says, "millions of women for all time have been having babies; Cheryl can do it too, and she will be all right." Cheryl's mother and James help her into the large hospital complex, which also has a medical school. Preliminary paperwork about Cheryl has been forwarded by the social worker. It is pulled from the file, and various forms are completed while Cheryl is placed in a wheelchair and taken to an examining room. The examination indicates that labor is well under way. Cheryl is then wheeled to a large room, where she is prepared for labor and delivery. The nurses are kind and efficient, and talk reassuringly to her.

Because of Cheryl's limited financial resources and the available facilities of her hospital of choice, she does not have access to a private birthing room. Cheryl will share a room and medical personnel with a number of other pregnant women. Because of staff limitations and concern and respect for the other expectant mothers, Cheryl's family and friends are allowed very brief visits in the labor room and no admittance to the delivery room. Cheryl's mother, James, and the neighbor are asked to make themselves comfortable in the waiting room. A nurse tells them that he will keep them informed of Cheryl's progress.

electronic fetal monitor:
a device used during labor, which is attached to the abdomen of the pregnant woman or the scalp of the fetus to determine the fetal heart rate

cesarean delivery:
a surgical procedure during which an incision is made through the abdominal and uterine walls of the mother to deliver the baby

preterm:
infants born several weeks before the full term (38 weeks) of pregnancy

isolette:
a small crib, which provides a controlled environment for newborns

episiotomy:
an incision made in the opening of the vulva to prevent it from tearing during delivery

A specialist comes in to assess the condition of the fetus. She uses an internal **electronic fetal monitor**, a device that entails inserting through the cervix an electrode, which is carefully attached to the scalp of the fetus to monitor fetal heart rate, and a catheter, which will measure the strength of Cheryl's contractions as labor progresses. The monitor indicates that the fetus is in stress. The specialist calls to the delivery room and tells them to prepare immediately for a **cesarean delivery**. Since Cheryl's baby will be **preterm** (a birth that occurs 3 weeks or more before the due date), the doctor orders an **isolette** to be brought to the delivery room. An isolette is a small crib, which provides a warm, controlled environment for the newborn. It includes attachments that monitor body temperature, heart rate, respiratory rate, arterial blood pressure, and inspired oxygen levels, providing an ongoing assessment of the physiological condition of the infant. Fluids and nutrition as needed can also be given through alternative means when the infant is unable to ingest food through the mouth and intestinal tract.

Stage 2: Birth

Stage 2 of labor begins when the cervix has dilated to 10 centimeters and the head of the fetus pushes through the cervical opening into the vagina. After some time, Ann Johnson has the urge to push. However, Lamaze training has prepared Ann to know what to do during this part of labor. She begins a Lamaze breathing technique to help her control the urge to expel the baby. The pains from the contractions become intense, and Ann mentions to Bill that she would like some medication. In their Lamaze class, Bill and Ann learned that at times, medication can be necessary and helpful in the birth process. However, it can also have some negative effects, the extent of which is determined by the type of medication, the amount given, and the stage of labor during which it is administered. Discussion with Dr. Windle and Maria reminds Ann that the most difficult part of labor is almost over and the baby will soon be born. Along with Bill, they encourage her to continue without any medication because the fetal head has already numbed the vaginal opening. Medication at this point might reduce Ann's contractions and make her awareness less effective in pushing during the final part of delivery. Bill also reminds her that continuing without medication will help the baby to be more alert not only at birth, but also for some time afterward (Emory, Schlackman, & Fiano, 1996). Buoyed by their encouragement, Ann decides to proceed without medication.

Ann's last ultrasound had indicated that the baby might be large, 8 to 9 pounds. For this reason, Dr. Windle decides to do an **episiotomy**. An episiotomy is a small incision that helps to prevent the opening of the vulva from tearing during the final stages of birth.

It is now close to 3:00 p.m., and it is time for Maria's nursing shift to end. She decides to stay longer, since it is almost time for Ann to give birth. The intense contractions are about 1 minute apart and last for almost 60 seconds. Dr. Windle and Maria now tell Ann to push. As she squeezes Bill's hand, Ann pushes, and the baby's head begins to appear. Shortly, with another push, the head emerges. Dr. Windle gently suctions the mucus from the baby's nose and mouth. From the mirror above the birthing bed, Bill and Ann have their first look at Jeremy. With the next contraction, Ann gives another big push, and Jeremy's full body appears. He begins to cry softly. (The stages of labor are illustrated in Figure 4.1.)

The birthing room has been kept a comfortable 78 °F, with soothing music playing in the background. This atmosphere provides a calm setting for Jeremy's

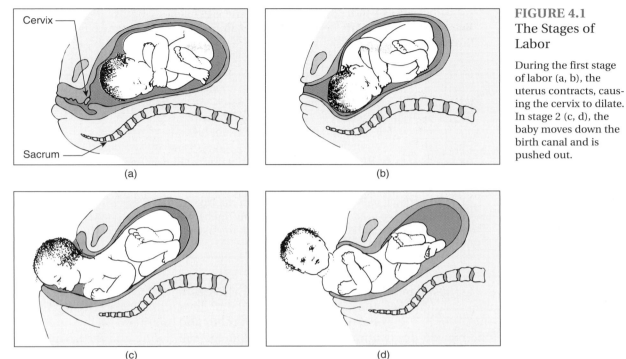

FIGURE 4.1
The Stages of Labor

During the first stage of labor (a, b), the uterus contracts, causing the cervix to dilate. In stage 2 (c, d), the baby moves down the birth canal and is pushed out.

transition from the comfort and safety of his **in utero** environment to a more demanding **extrauterine** one. Dr. Windle and Maria quickly evaluate Jeremy for any signs of complications. He appears fine, and is gently dried off and placed on Ann's abdomen. Ann and Bill speak softly and tenderly to their newborn and begin cuddling him. He has dark hair like Ann's father. Jeremy stops crying and looks directly into his mother's eyes. Ann and Bill are truly in awe of this little miracle. They look him over from head to toe, touching each little finger as Ann gently cups her hand around a tiny foot, caressing it as she visually explores Jeremy's delicate facial features. Bill decides that he looks like one of his brothers. After a while, the blood in the blood vessels in the umbilical cord stops throbbing, and Dr. Windle cuts the umbilical cord.

Guided by Maria, Bill takes Jeremy and places him on a warmer, a special infant bed equipped with a heat lamp, oxygen, instruments for removing fluid and mucus from the infant's airways, and other equipment and medications needed to attend to the needs of the newborn. Jeremy will be given a warm bath when his vital signs have stabilized, and will then be swaddled snugly to maintain body temperature and provide a sense of security.

in utero:
the environment in which the fetus grows within the uterus

extrauterine:
the environment outside of the uterus

Stage 3: Expulsion of the Placenta

The third stage of labor involves the expulsion of the placenta and umbilical cord (sometimes referred to as the afterbirth) through the cervix. When Ann's placenta and remaining umbilical cord appear, Dr. Windle and Maria examine them to be sure everything has been completely discharged from the uterus. A very calm and relaxed Jeremy has been enjoying his first bath. Jeremy is dried, then weighed and measured. He weighs 8 pounds, 2 ounces and is 21 inches long. An identification bracelet matching Ann's bracelet is placed around his wrist. Jeremy has arrived! What about Angela?

Cheryl is prepared for surgery. Because of her anxiety, the anesthesiologist administers medication to help her relax while preparations are hurriedly completed to begin surgery. A general anesthetic is administered, which puts her to sleep; hence, Cheryl will feel no pain and will not be aware of her child's birth. The physician makes an incision and pulls away layers of skin and abdominal muscle. As Angela is lifted from the uterine cavity, the physician discovers that the umbilical cord is wrapped around her neck, depriving her of oxygen. Angela does not begin breathing on her own. Quickly, a team of pediatric specialists, including a **neonatologist**, is called. Angela is placed in the isolette and taken immediately to the neonatal care unit. Cheryl and her family must wait to see their newborn while physicians and health care personnel work to ensure Angela's successful adaptation to extrauterine life.

neonatologist:
a physician who specializes in the care and treatment of the neonate, or newborn infant, during the first 4 to 6 weeks

anemia:
a condition caused by a lack of red blood cells

Oxygen deprivation can occur in other circumstances, for example, when the placenta detaches too soon during prenatal development, or if the mother smokes or has **anemia**, or in cases where mother and infant are Rh incompatible. Mild oxygen deprivation can destroy or damage cell tissue, and in the neonate, brain cell damage is a serious concern. The severity of the effects on the infant depend on the timing and duration of the oxygen deprivation, with outcomes that range from mild to severe seizures, mild to severe motor control abnormalities, and feeding, sleeping, and waking difficulties; to weak and uncoordinated motor controls; to stupor, coma, respiratory arrest, and sometimes death.

The long-term outcomes from oxygen deprivation in infants who survive depend on the extent of neurological damage. Physical/motor and learning disabilities, social and emotional difficulties, and mental retardation are common outcomes of early neurological damage (though not all such problems originate with oxygen deprivation during fetal development and delivery). Electronic fetal monitoring devices, along with other procedures for sampling fetal blood and assessing neonatal neurological signs, are used to assess and prevent or minimize the effects of oxygen deprivation.

There are a number of reasons for the performance of cesarean deliveries in addition to complications resulting in oxygen deprivation. Sometimes, the fetus's head is too large to pass safely through the mother's pelvis, or perhaps the fetus is not positioned to make a safe and expeditious journey; the buttocks, feet, shoulder, or other body part may be resting over the cervix, complicating or deterring the delivery process. This is referred to as abnormal presentation or **breech position delivery**. Additional reasons for cesarean deliveries include placenta or cord disturbances, such as premature delivery of the placenta or a prolapsed cord (the umbilical cord descends into the cervix or vagina, competing with the fetus for travel space and impairing blood flow to the fetus), concerns associated with maternal blood pressure or hemorrhaging, prolonged nonprogressive labor, the need to avoid the spread of sexually transmitted disease, and others.

breech position delivery:
a birth in which a body part other than the head presents itself for delivery first, usually the buttocks, feet, or in some cases the umbilical cord

Approximately 20% to 25% of births today are cesarean section deliveries. Many people in the medical and allied health professions have begun to question the feasibility and need for an increasing number of cesarean deliveries. Ostensibly, cesarean sections have been prescribed for reasons beyond those just listed: to protect physicians and health care personnel from the threat of lawsuits should the fetus be at risk, and convenience for the family and/or the obstetrician. Since this procedure is considered major surgery and entails a longer recovery period it is important to select wisely and conscientiously one's health care professionals and engage in serious conversation about their practices and preferences. Certainly, cesarian section deliveries can be life saving for mother or child or both should an emergency arise. The advantages of being in a hospital where immediate response is possible are obvious in such cases. Since prediction of emergencies is impossible, expectant parents are wise to be informed about all procedures that their health care professionals recommend. It can be emphasized, however, that the greatest majority of deliveries proceed normally and without incident.

Studies indicate that there are few long-term cognitive and neurological effects on cesarean-delivered infants (Entwisle & Alexander, 1987). While initial mother–child interaction may be affected by anesthetics and the mother's recovery from surgery, fathers often take a more active role in caring for their cesarean-delivered babies than fathers of traditionally delivered infants (Pederson, Zaslow, Cain, & Anderson, 1981).

Forceps may be used to facilitate delivery when there is risk to the fetus. In a forceps delivery, the physician fits forceps around the fetus's head and carefully and gently pulls the fetus through the vagina. This procedure is used only during the second stage of labor and with great skill and caution to prevent injury to the head.

forceps:
a surgical instrument, similar to tongs, that is applied to the head of the fetus to facilitate delivery

Apgar score:
a score that rates the physical condition of newborns in the areas of *a*ppearance, *p*ulse, *g*rimace, *a*ctivity, and *r*espiration

ASSESSMENT AND CARE OF NEWBORNS

Dr. Virginia Apgar (1953) developed a process to evaluate the ability of newborns to cope with the stress of delivery and adjust to breathing independently. The **Apgar score** (Table 4.1) is usually obtained by observing the newborn at 1, 5, and

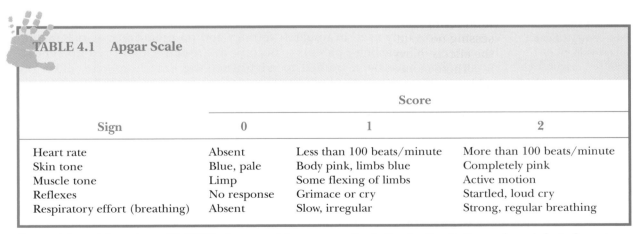

TABLE 4.1   Apgar Scale

	Score		
Sign	0	1	2
Heart rate	Absent	Less than 100 beats/minute	More than 100 beats/minute
Skin tone	Blue, pale	Body pink, limbs blue	Completely pink
Muscle tone	Limp	Some flexing of limbs	Active motion
Reflexes	No response	Grimace or cry	Startled, loud cry
Respiratory effort (breathing)	Absent	Slow, irregular	Strong, regular breathing

Sources: Adapted from Apgar, V. (1953). A proposal for a new method of evaluation in the newborn infant. *Current Research in Anesthesia and Analgesia, 32,* 260–267. Also Berman, R. E., & Vaughn, V. C., III. (1987). Evaluation of the newborn infant (Table 8-3, p. 363). *Nelson Textbook of Pediatrics,* 13th ed. With permission of W.B. Saunders Company.

The newborn is assessed and monitored closely during the first hours following delivery.

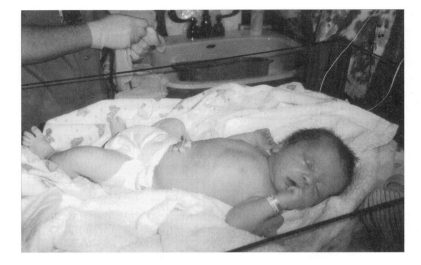

sometimes 15 minutes after birth. Five areas of appearance or performance are evaluated: the *a*ppearance (skin color), *p*ulse (heart rate), *g*rimace (reaction to slight pain), *a*ctivity (motor responsiveness and tone), and *r*espiration (breathing adequacy). The initials of these five categories spell APGAR, which helps to make them easy to remember. Each category receives 0, 1, or 2 points. Generally a score of 7 or above indicates that the newborn is doing well. If the newborn's score is between 5 and 7, there is usually a need for some type of additional care. Infants with a score of 4 or below require immediate medical attention, as such a score indicates a life-threatening situation.

Another evaluation procedure used to examine a variety of behaviors in newborns was developed by pediatrician T. Berry Brazelton in 1973. The **Brazelton Neonatal Behavioral Assessment Scale** (NBAS) assesses 26 behavioral items and 16 reflexes that newborns possess. This assessment technique requires training, since it tries to elicit the infant's highest level of performance and is most commonly used in research settings and on preterm or at-risk infants. The Brazelton Scale helps parents to become aware of the infant's competencies. Parents who have been trained to administer the Brazelton were, after four weeks, more knowledgeable about their infants, had more confidence in handling the infants, and had more satisfactory interactions with their infants than parents who had not learned the Brazelton assessment techniques (Myers, 1982). Further, fathers who learned how to administer the Brazelton Assessment Scale were more actively involved with their infants than fathers who had not received the training.

The NBAS also helps to identify infants who are not able to control or regulate the various states, ranging from deep sleep to crying. Ill or premature infants and those with immature central nervous systems may cry often, lack the ability to settle themselves, and resist cuddling. Such behaviors can be upsetting and frustrating to new parents. These parents can be provided with continued professional assistance in coping with their infants.

Newborns are routinely tested for phenylketonuria (PKU), an inborn error of metabolism in which abnormal levels of the enzyme phenylalanine form in the

Brazelton Neonatal Behavioral Assessment Scale: an assessment of 16 reflexes, responsiveness, state changes, and ability to self-calm in the newborn

blood. The test involves a simple heel prick to obtain a blood sample and is administered after the infant has consumed a sufficient number of formula or breast feedings for the test to accurately detect PKU presence. If untreated, PKU leads to mental retardation and other abnormalities. When detected and treated within the first 3 weeks after birth with a specialized diet, developmental outcomes are better than when the diet is started later. Other screening may also take place for suspected inheritable illnesses and abnormalities, such as sickle-cell anemia or thyroid disease. The American Academy of Pediatrics recommends testing for HIV (the AIDS virus) in newborns whose mothers' HIV status is undetermined. This is an important precaution, since AIDS (acquired immunodeficiency syndrome) can be transmitted to the fetus during pregnancy, labor, or delivery, and is carried in breast milk.

Jeremy's Apgar scores were 9 and 9 on his first assessment. A third evaluation was not needed, since he was doing well. Angela scored 3, 4, and 5 and required immediate attention, owing to her lack of ability to breathe independently and need for ventilation. Dr. Jones, Angela's neonatologist, will return to the neonatal care unit later in the day to determine if Angela's condition has stabilized. That afternoon, he reads her charts and examines her. After several days, Dr. Jones and the neonatal staff decide to conduct the NBAS, as he notes that Angela seems to have difficulty calming herself when she is in a fussy state. Dr. Jones thinks that he may have to provide Cheryl with some techniques for helping Angela settle into more predictable sleep/wake cycles and eventually to self-comfort with a blanket or soft toy. He will discuss with Cheryl her need to learn to cope effectively with what will most likely be a fussy baby for the first few weeks and an infant who will need frequent small feedings. Cheryl may need additional support from James or members of her family. He can arrange a professional home visitor to assist for a time if she thinks that would be helpful (Gomby, Culross, & Behrman, 1999).

The length of postpartum hospital stay in uncomplicated deliveries has decreased appreciably over the years, from 8 to 10 days in the 1950s to 48 hours or less today. Many very low-income women do not have medical insurance or the financial resources to remain in the hospital beyond the most minimal amount of time. Horror stories are told of women in labor "toughing it out" in their automobiles on the hospital parking lot until the last minute and then checking themselves into the hospital to deliver, only to be released within hours of the delivery. Concern over the welfare of mothers and their newborns when hospital stays are inadequate has prompted considerable discussion and debate about how best to educate families of the need for appropriate care and how to provide financial assistance to obtain it. Where hospital stays have been limited by managed care organizations, these concerns have resulted in federal laws that mandate that insurers cover 48-hour hospitalization in uncomplicated deliveries. The American Academy of Pediatrics, responding to concerns about the well-being of infants and mothers, has recommended that all infants dismissed after only a short stay be examined within 48 hours of discharge (Maisels & Kring, 1997). Some managed care programs and/or hospitals provide professional or paraprofessional postpartum home visitors or doulas to assist mothers, particularly first-time breast-feeding mothers, mothers with high-risk infants, and other mothers whose circumstances warrant additional support and follow-up.

INFANTS WITH SPECIAL NEEDS

In addition to genetic and chromosomal anomalies (Boxes 4.1 and 4.2), gestational age, birth weight, general health condition, and presence of disease or injury are markers for determining potential neonatal complications and projecting growth and development challenges facing the newborn. Most infants are born at a gestational age of 40 weeks (give or take 2 weeks on either side of this age). However, **viability** and integrity of the human organism is compromised at both younger (preterm) and older (postterm) gestational ages.

viability:
the capability of sustaining extrauterine survival

Most full-term infants are expected to weigh in the range from 5.5 to 7.5 pounds. Preterm infants bring low weight and underdeveloped body systems to the challenges in helping them meet the demands of extrauterine living. Postterm infants are larger, with large head circumferences, and are more difficult to deliver, and often must be delivered by cesarean section.

With the expertise, technology, and other resources available to today's medical profession, infants weighing less than 2 pounds have been helped to survive. While medical science has established means by which very low weight infants can be given a chance for healthy survival, many of these fragile infants face serious health and development challenges. Consider all the systems that need to be in place and functioning in a coordinated manner in the newborn: respiratory, cardiovascular, neurological, endocrine, digestive/gastrointestinal, urinary, and immune. Concurrently, the bones and skeletal system should have taken form and shape with initial **ossification**, and the skin should be sufficiently mature to carry out its functions of temperature regulation by preventing heat and water loss, and protection from infections. The skin is more efficient when fatty **subcutaneous tissue** has formed. In preterm and low-birth-weight infants, most, if not all, of these systems are underdeveloped and may fail to function properly.

ossification:
the conversion of the softer cartilage of the skeletal system into bone

subcutaneous tissue:
tissue that forms beneath the skin

Though not inevitable, when compared with full-term, normal-weight children, low-birthweight and preterm infants have higher rates of cerebral palsy, psychomotor problems, mental retardation, blindness, deafness, developmental delays, health issues, and learning difficulties (Hack, Klein, & Taylor, 1995). Some infants (full, pre-, and postterm) have inherited traits or predispositions to diseases in which a single gene or combination of genes is responsible. They might

---

BOX 4.1   Examples of Genetic Disorders

Albinism

Color blindness

Cystic fibrosis

Muscular dystrophy

Hemophilia

Huntington disease

Phenylketonuria (PKU)

Sickle-cell disease

Tay-Sachs disease

> **BOX 4.2   Examples of Chromosomal Abnormalities**
>
> Down syndrome
>
> Fragile X syndrome
>
> Trisomies (e.g., trisomy 13 refers to an extra chromosome 13)
>
> Turner syndrome
>
> Klinefelter syndrome

have a chromosome abnormality in which whole chromosomes or chromosome segments are altered in some way. For example, there may be an extra chromosome, extra chromosome material, a missing chromosome, or missing or altered chromosome material. Infants displaying unusual physiological characteristics or behaviors or who score differently on neonatal assessments require further comprehensive assessment and diagnosis, close perinatal monitoring, and timely treatments. Not all anomalies are evident at birth, and many do not appear until an age when a particular function or ability should emerge (Boxes 4.1 and 4.2).

FAMILY DYNAMICS: A NEW SOCIAL SYSTEM

The birth of a baby into a family unit establishes a new social system as different relationships and roles are created. Applying Bronfenbrenner's ecological systems theory (1979, 1986), we note that reactions on the parts of all members of this new social system vary depending on the nature of the pregnancy and birth experience; the size and nature of the family unit; the baby's position in the family unit; family values, attitudes, expectations, and traditions; the health status of family members; and the nature of support from the health care profession and other community services.

For the developing infant, there are expanding circles of influence that gradually enlarge his or her experience and influence developmental outcomes in positive or negative ways. These ecological influences on the infant's growth and development are addressed throughout this text. As we study the numerous influences on human growth, development, and learning, it becomes increasingly difficult to deny the importance of many in the lives of infants and children in modern-day society. Indeed, as the African proverb states, it does take a village to raise a child.

Bonding

Marshall H. Klaus and John H. Kennell are two pediatricians who have conducted research on bonding. They define **bonding** as the establishment of a complex psychobiological connection between parent and infant (Klaus & Kennel, 1982). The bonding process begins to occur perhaps during pregnancy, but most profoundly during those first few moments when the newborn is placed into the arms of eager and emotionally ready parents and the early days and weeks of the infant's introduction into their lives. The bond between child and parent grows and deepens over time, and additional bonds established between children and other family

bonding:
a complex psychobiological connection between parent and infant

members, close friends, and nonparental caregivers provide emotional nourishment to developing infants and children. (The connection from infant to parent is called *attachment* and grows over time to be expressed vociferously during the latter months of the first year.) In recent years, the importance of early bonding and attachment has been reemphasized as revelations about early brain growth and neurological development have been published (Gunnar, 1996, 1998; Kemp, 1999). Its influences on healthy psychosocial development and cognitive outcomes are now being documented. As we will see in the chapters on infancy and on psychosocial development, bonding and attachment are critical to early brain and neurological development, which sets the stage for long-term healthy psychosocial and cognitive outcomes.

Reactions of the Newborn

Reactions of newborns vary according to the quality of their prenatal existence and the extent to which optimal development was achieved, the labor and delivery experience, the nature of their parents' responses to them, and the infant's personality and temperament. Heretofore, the uterus has provided a comfortable and consistent temperature and constant nourishment. The infant has grown accustomed to the rhythm of the mother's heartbeat, which is considered one of the most important sensory cues during prenatal development (Perry, 1998); the sounds of mother's voice (DeCasper & Spence, 1986; Fifer & Moon, 1995); and the ebb and flow of her daily activities of rest, sleep, work, and play. After the arduous birth process, the infant must adjust to breathing independently; take an active role in the feeding process; adapt to variable room temperatures; become efficient in the use of all of the senses to see, feel, smell, taste, and hear; and begin the long, exciting journey of self-discovery and learning. Fortunately, most infants are resilient and possess many capabilities that help them to adjust and embark on the growth journey. Good-quality prenatal care, a normal labor and delivery process, warm and positive interaction with parents, and good-quality care from the medical profession are critical ingredients for the newborn's optimal adjustment.

These elements are particularly necessary in the case of preterm and low-birth-weight infants, who may have a different set of experiences from those of full-term, healthy infants. Many of these infants are born seriously ill and needing immediate treatment or intervention. Immature lungs and associated breathing difficulties are common, as are lack of competence in sucking, swallowing, and taking in and digesting nourishment. The infants' abrupt entry into the extrauterine environment can result in sensory overload from the cacophony of sounds, sights, touch, and activity surrounding them. They may need immediate and sometimes invasive medical procedures. Because of their need for intensive care, their first experiences may not be in the arms of their mothers or fathers, but in the warmth of an isolette or other infant conveyance to quickly be placed in a life-saving mode of care and attention by neonatal intensive care professionals.

In efforts to make this experience positive and supportive for both infants and family members, most modern-day hospital neonatal intensive care units are structured to

- provide consistency of care by a team of highly trained medical personnel who work closely with one another and with the family to determine an individualized care plan;

- provide a unique and individualized schedule of treatment and interactions that are sensitive to the infant's sleep–wake cycles, levels of alertness, medical needs, and feeding capabilities;

- provide supportive, comforting introductions to and interactions with a primary caregiver who assists parents in becoming engaged and interactive with their newborn (this medical professional coaches parents on how and when to caress, talk soothingly or sing softly, hold a finger, offer a pacifier, feed, rock, diaper, monitor baby cues, and provide other caregiving interactions, thus providing the infant with the comfort and security of his or her family);

- include parents during special examinations or assessments so that they may be a comfort to their infant during necessary diagnostic procedures;

- provide a calm and soothing physical environment that controls light, sound, and movements in and about the neonatal intensive care unit;

- provide comfortable family-friendly space and amenities (chair, blanket, drinking water, space for personal items) near the infant, making it possible for family to interact with their infant and converse when appropriate with medical care personnel;

- provide professional counseling and coaching for siblings as needed, and, later, guidance and support to the family in making the transition with their infant from hospital to home upon dismissal (Als & Gilkerson, 1995).

This type of neonatal intensive care is referred to as *developmental care* because of its concern for not only the infant's medical needs, but, importantly, also the emotional well-being of both infant and family. Such care acknowledges the strong bond between infants and their parents, which began to form long before the baby was born, and acknowledges parents and other family members as critical to the well-being of the infant. It is believed that this family-friendly developmentally supportive care during the earliest hours and days of extrauterine life and adjustment significantly improves both short- and long-term outcomes for fragile babies (Johnson, 1995).

Reactions of the Mother

Good-quality prenatal care, educational preparation for childbirth and parenting, a successful labor and delivery, and a supportive family all help the mother to adjust to her new role. However, even new mothers who enjoy optimal pregnancy and delivery conditions can feel overwhelmed, tired, and depressed.

In most instances, giving birth is a very rigorous event demanding a great deal of physical and emotional energy. After delivery, the mother's body begins to undergo dramatic hormonal adjustments as it returns to its nonpregnant state. Fluctuations in hormone levels can create mood swings and depression. In addition, caring for a newborn who needs to be fed every few hours around the clock can be tiring for some mothers and fathers.

The need to deal with the realities and responsibilities of parenting following the emotional high of anticipation of the baby's birth can be overwhelming. In addition, many mothers think that they should feel instant maternal love for their babies. If they do not, they feel confused or guilty. Some find that they do not bond immediately with their infants, sometimes taking several days or weeks to recover from pregnancy and birth and turn their thoughts and emotions from inward concerns (characteristic of pregnancy) to an outward focus on their infant's needs.

New mothers often have many questions about their babies' behavior, particularly eating and crying behaviors. A recent study of parents' views of early childhood development found that of three developmental domains—emotional, social, and intellectual—parents thought that they would have the greatest influence over their children's emotional development in spite of the fact that one in four reported having the least information about how children develop emotionally (Melmed, 1997). Books and advice from family, friends, and the medical profession can be helpful. At times, however, the mother's reading of her baby and her "maternal instinct" may be the best guides to responding to her infant.

The nurses at the hospital advised Ann to bathe Jeremy when he awakened from his afternoon nap and then feed him after his bath. Hungry, Jeremy cried more and more intensely during his bath. Ann became fearful that Jeremy would come to dislike bathtime. On her own, Ann decided to feed Jeremy first. She could see Jeremy relax as his tummy became full. After a time for burping and cuddling, Ann gave a relaxed and happy Jeremy his bath.

After several days in the neonatal care unit, Angela seems to be breathing more easily. Her skin tone has improved, and the usual weight loss after birth has not been as great as the doctors feared. Angela weighed less than 5 pounds at birth and was 14 inches long. The doctors tell Cheryl that they want to keep Angela in the neonatal care unit for a week or two just to be sure she is breathing independently and gaining weight.

At Dr. Jones's direction, Cheryl and James have been visiting Angela in the neonatal care unit several times a day. Angela cries frequently, which can be expected in preterm babies with her complications. The nurses tell Cheryl that it is important to respond to Angela's cries, since she is trying to communicate hunger, discomfort, or boredom. Cheryl replies that one of her hospital roommates told her that picking up crying babies can spoil them. The nurses reassure Cheryl that this is not the case. Cheryl feels confused. She has noticed that when she visits Angela and Angela has been crying, touching her and talking to her in a soothing voice do seem to calm her. Maybe the nurses are right.

Cheryl and James have felt extremely stressed by Angela's special needs. Visiting the neonatal care unit has been a bewildering experience for them. Cheryl wonders whether Angela will cry as much when she comes home. She is glad she will be at home without Angela for awhile, but these thoughts make her feel guilty. The nurses tell her that she can visit Angela during the week or two that the baby needs to remain in the neonatal care unit. Cheryl wonders how she will get there, since her family has no car and little money for public transportation. Cheryl's minister talks with her social worker to try to work out some times when neighbors and friends can take Cheryl and James to visit Angela. Cheryl notices that she, too, feels like crying much of the time and often feels the need to withdraw from the company of others. Her mother is concerned about her and wonders how they will manage when Angela leaves the neonatal care unit.

---

postpartum depression: a period of depression that affects most mothers for a few days and in some cases for weeks and months after childbirth

postpartum psychosis: a psychological condition associated with severe depression following childbirth in which there is a loss of insight, good judgment, and coping strength; sometimes there is a loss of touch with reality

Depending on the study, it is estimated that between 26 and 85 percent of childbearing mothers experience the "baby blues," or **postpartum depression** (O'Hara, 1994). Postpartum depression can range in character from very mild to major depression to **postpartum psychosis**. Typically, symptoms of mild depression begin to occur 4 to 5 days after delivery and last from several hours to 2 to 3 days (Epperson, 2002). However, some women (approximately 10%) experience postpartum major depression, which can persist for several weeks or months and may require medical attention and/or psychotherapy. In rare cases, postpartum psychosis occurs, in which the mother's moods, delusions, and bizarre behaviors make her a danger to herself and others, including her children. This is considered a psychiatric emergency, and hospitalization and medical attention are required.

While hormones play an important role in reproduction, they also affect brain chemistry in ways that can alter moods and behaviors. Chemical changes in the brain can cause postpartum depression symptoms of emotionality, sleep, and eating disturbances and altered energy levels (Epperson, 2002). In the great majority of cases, as hormonal levels and body shape return to their prepregnancy states, energy level increases as does confidence in mothering. Hormonal changes, medications, fatigue and loss of stamina, preexisting anxieties exasperated by infant care responsibilities, unresolved emotional conflicts, lack of support from the father or other family members, and economic or work-related issues are some of the possible contributors to postpartum depression. Sometimes, postpartum depression may be a continuation of depression occurring during pregnancy, which may or may not be related to the pregnancy itself. Depending on the extent and duration of the depression during pregnancy, there is some evidence that infants born to depressed mothers can be developmentally affected, demonstrating lower scores on the NBAS and exhibiting other neurological symptoms (Jones et al., 1998; Murray and Cooper, 1996). Friends, relatives, and the medical profession need to be sensitive to depression both during pregnancy and postpartum, and provide guidance, support, or treatment as needed.

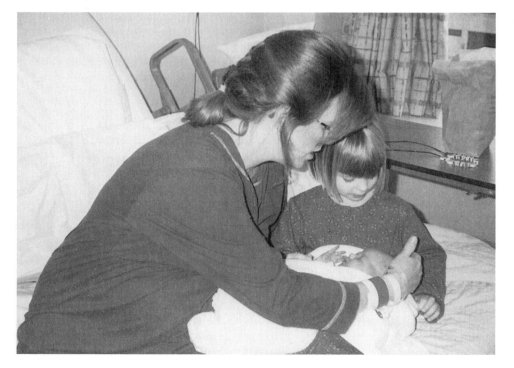

Parents can help their older children adjust to a new brother or sister by talking with them about the needs of the baby.

Reactions of the Father

Recently, more attention has been given to the reactions of prospective fathers. They worry about whether they will be good fathers, whether they will please their wives, the added financial responsibility, possible changes in their relationship with their wives, and lack of freedom. If there are siblings, fathers wonder how they will respond to and meet the needs of the new brother or sister. The increasing need for two incomes to support a family and family-centered maternity care have encouraged many fathers to become more involved in the birth and care of their children. The mother's perception of the father's role influences the types of interactions and responsibilities that she encourages.

Further, it is evident that positive mother–father relationships influence the extent to which fathers become engaged in the care and nurturing of their infants. Distressed parental relationships impede both parents' abilities to meet the needs of their children (Susman-Stillman, Appleyard, & Siebenbruner, 2003).

In the case of the nonresident father, the stereotype of avoidance of parental responsibilities appears to be inaccurate. Studies reveal that most fathers choose to be involved with their infants at birth and intend to stay connected and involved (Teitler, 2001), and where there is intent to marry the child's mother, the father is particularly engaged in the care of their infant (Carlson & McLanahan, 2002). Studies indicate that a father's participation in the preparation for the birth, delivery, and early care of the baby leads to later positive interaction patterns with his child (Klaus & Kennell, 1982; Parke & Sawin, 1981).

As Bill watches Ann breast-feed Jeremy in the hospital, he sometimes feels left out. In some ways, he wishes that Ann had not decided to nurse Jeremy. He knows that breast-fed babies have more immunity to illness and that a mother's milk is more suited to infants' immature digestive systems than formula, but if Jeremy were bottle fed, Bill could take part in feeding him.

Bill mentions these feelings to Ann. They discuss the fact that after a few weeks of initial breast-feeding, she will be able to express milk (manually or with a breast pump) from time to time for bottle feedings. She will discuss this option with her physician.

Reactions of Siblings

Even though parents prepare children for the birth of a new brother or sister, many adjustments must be made. Stewart and colleagues (1987) studied middle-class families with a firstborn child of 2, 3, or 4 years of age over a 15-month period. Findings indicated that these firstborns spent much time trying to get their mothers' full attention and that their strategies followed similar patterns regardless of age (Stewart, Mobley, Van Tuyl, & Salvador, 1987).

During the first 4 months after the birth of a brother or sister, the firstborns engaged in such behaviors as baby talk, using baby table manners, demanding a bottle or pacifier, and regressing in toileting behaviors. Other acting-out behaviors included verbal and physical confrontations with the parents, infant, and even inanimate objects. At times, the firstborn children were whiny, withdrawn, and clingy and had a need for a security blanket or toy. By the 4th month after the birth of the baby, displays of imitation or confrontation usually disappeared. Anxiety behaviors continued, however. Four months later, when new brother or sister was around 8 months old, the older siblings again used confrontational strategies. According to the researchers, these behaviors were explained by the baby's increasing mobility and responsiveness.

The brothers and sisters said that they helped to care for the new baby. Ninety-five percent of the mothers confirmed this behavior. Over half the siblings said they liked to cuddle the new baby. During the last visit, when the new baby was just more than 1 year old, 63% of the firstborns said that they were ready for a new baby.

Siblings of the same gender were reported to show a higher incidence of all types of behaviors. Fathers seemed to help out and give the firstborns needed attention. By the end of the study, the fathers were talking and playing with their firstborns as much as the mothers were. This study indicates that at least in some middle-class families, the attention-getting behaviors of firstborns are normal, that fathers can help to meet their need for attention, and that in spite of the obvious negative feelings of firstborns, they also have positive attitudes toward the new baby.

Parents can help their older children to adjust to a new brother or sister if they talk about the baby's needs and involve the older sibling in making decisions regarding the infant. Explaining the infant's behaviors and pointing out his or her interest in the older sibling can also facilitate positive interactions.

Reactions of Extended Family

Reactions of extended family can vary and also affect the immediate family of the newborn. Grandparents are usually thrilled. However, comments sometimes suggest mixed or negative feelings about the birth of a grandchild. Grandparents often view the birth of a grandchild as a sign that they are getting older. Adjusting to the aging process can be difficult for some. At times, feelings of failure or inadequacy that the grandparents experienced as parents can surface and create tension.

Ann's mother had not been successful at breast-feeding, and she kept telling Ann that Ann's breasts were too small to feed Jeremy. Fortunately, Ann's childbirth classes had given her background information about the physiological process of nursing. She calmly responded to her mother's concerns, explaining that the glands and not the size of the breasts stimulated milk production. Ann also pointed out that the baby's sucking increased the supply of milk. This information seemed to relieve Ann's mother.

Because many prospective parents today attend childbirth classes, they have up-to-date information. At times, this may contradict some of the ideas about parenting held by grandparents. Grandparents may feel unsure about what they should do. This insecurity may be viewed as a lack of interest in the grandchild or the new parents. In addition, some grandparents find it difficult to allow their children to become parents. The grandparents have been in control in their role as parents, and they feel a need to stay in control rather than allowing their child to take charge of his or her new family.

At times, the new parents' siblings may feel jealous at all the attention the new parents are receiving. Becoming an aunt or uncle also involves adjusting to a new role. If there has been a great deal of competition between the new parent and his or her siblings, old feelings of rivalry can surface and persist even when the sibling becomes a parent, and cousins can be pitted against one another.

Nevertheless, many extended family members can provide information, needed support, and encouragement to the new parents. The reactions of the extended family add to the complexity of relationships surrounding the birth of a baby. An awareness of some of these feelings and their possible causes can help new parents to better understand and cope with these behaviors and feelings.

We hope that this chapter has made you more aware of the complex set of circumstances that affect newborns and their families. An awareness of these factors and dynamics can facilitate a more complete understanding of young children and their families. A positive birth experience and adjustment of all family members to the newborn can pave the way for a child to "know the joy of living" and for the parents to enjoy and celebrate "the beauty of life" (see the quote at the beginning of this chapter).

ROLE OF THE EARLY CHILDHOOD PROFESSIONAL

Working with Families with Newborns

1. Become knowledgeable about factors that influence optimal prenatal development and successful deliveries.

2. Respond to parents' interests and desires for information about early growth and development; help parents to become aware of the critical development that occurs during the first 3 years.

3. Help parents to understand and respond appropriately to the reactions of siblings to a new baby. Provide suggestions for preparing siblings for a new baby and helping them to adjust to a new member of the family.

4. Respond in empathic and helpful ways to changes in classroom behavior in young children during the weeks after the birth of a sibling.

5. Become knowledgeable about community resources that are available to families with infants, and be prepared to share information with families when appropriate.

6. Become knowledgeable about community resources that are available to families with infants with special needs, and be prepared to share information with families when appropriate.

Bill, Ann, and Jeremy Johnson have had optimal circumstances for beginning their lives as a family. Cheryl Monroe, James, and Angela have not been as fortunate. The following chapters continue the story of the growth and development of Jeremy and Angela.

KEY TERMS

anemia	contraction	ossification
Apgar score	dilation	neonatologist
bonding	electronic fetal monitor	postpartum depression
Brazelton Neonatal	episiotomy	postpartum psychosis
Behavioral Assessment	extrauterine	preterm
Scale	forceps	subcutaneous tissue
breech position delivery	in utero	viability
cervix	isolette	
cesarean delivery	labor	

REVIEW STRATEGIES AND ACTIVITIES

1. Review the key terms individually or with a classmate.

2. Interview several parents of newborns. Ask them to share with you:

   a. The delivery and hospital experience.

   b. Opportunities for and experiences with bonding after delivery.

   c. The challenges they experienced and the adjustments they needed to make during the first two months after the baby's birth.

   d. Reactions of immediate and extended family to the baby's birth.

3. Invite an obstetrical or pediatric nurse to your class to discuss:

   a. The care of a newborn infant.

   b. The care of an at-risk infant.

   c. The care of the mother.

   d. Support for the family.

   e. Evaluation of the newborn, including the Apgar and Brazelton scales and other assessment tools.

   f. Follow-up support.

4. Discuss the short-term and long-term implications of good-quality prenatal and neonatal care.

FURTHER READINGS

American College of Obstetricians and Gynecologists. (1999). *Pregnancy: You and your baby: Prenatal care, labor and delivery, and postpartum care.* Washington, DC: Author.

American College of Obstetricians and Gynecologists. (2000). *Planning your pregnancy.* Washington, DC: Author.

Catlett, C., Winton, P., & Mitchell, A. (2002). Resources within reason: Supporting infants and toddlers in intensive care units (ICUs) and their families. *Young Exceptional Children, 6*(2), 28.

Klaus, M. H., Klaus, P. H., & Kennell, J. H. (2002). *The doula book: How a trained labor companion can help you have a shorter, easier, and healthier birth*. New York: Perseus.

Lamb, M. E. (1997). *The role of the father in child development* (3rd ed.). New York: Wiley.

McLean, M., Wolery, M., & Bailey, D. B. (2003). *Assessing infants and preschoolers with special needs*. Upper Saddle River, NJ: Pearson.

Nilson, L. (1990). *A child is born*. New York: Delacorte Press/Seymour Lawrence.

OTHER RESOURCES

Parke, M. (2003). Are married parents really better for children? Center for Law and Policy policy brief. Couples and Marriage Series. Brief No. 3. Available at http://www.clasp.org/DMS/Documents/1052841451.72

Infancy

CHAPTER FIVE

Infancy conforms to nobody—all conform to it.

RALPH WALDO EMERSON

Physical and Motor Development of the Infant

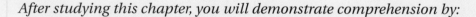

After studying this chapter, you will demonstrate comprehension by:

▶ Outlining principles of development related to the physical and motor development of infants from birth to the end of the first year.

▶ Discussing sociocultural influences on prenatal and infant growth and development.

▶ Describing earliest brain growth and neurological development.

▶ Describing major physiological competencies of the infant.

▶ Identifying expected patterns of physical and motor development during the first year.

▶ Discussing major factors influencing physical and motor development.

▶ Discussing contemporary infant health and well-being issues.

▶ Suggesting strategies for promoting and enhancing physical and motor development during the first year.

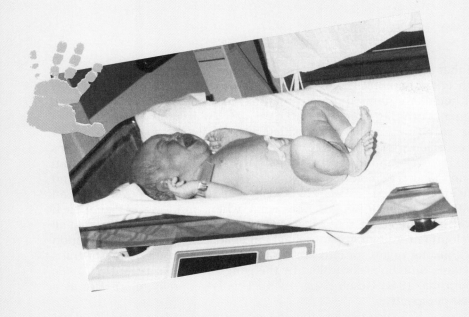

To make room for incoming expectant mothers in the prenatal care unit, Cheryl has been moved to a semiprivate room down the hall. Between school and work schedules, James has tried to be with Cheryl as much as possible. Today, members of her large extended family and one or two of her close friends have gathered eagerly around Cheryl in the hospital room to share in the joy of Angela's birth. Since Angela is receiving special attention in the neonatal intensive care unit, they are also concerned for her well-being. Family and friends stroll quietly into and out of Cheryl's room, returning from viewing the newborn through a window to the neonatal intensive care unit. They share their observations and excitement: "She's so beautiful, so tiny." "She was awake and squirming. I believe she has James's eyes; I always thought James and his brother had those same beautiful eyes." "She seems a little upset with all those nurses fussing over her." "Cheryl was a calm and easy baby," muses her mother. "I remember Cheryl being a crybaby when she was little," chirps one of her siblings. "No, you were the crybaby, not me," quips Cheryl in characteristic sibling retort. Happy banter continues among Cheryl and her friends and family: "Will Angela have musical ability and like to sing like Cheryl always did?" "Cheryl, are you going to sing to your baby?" "Will she have James's personality and charm, his energy, or his skills in games and sports?" "She is so tiny, will she be normal and healthy?"

PRINCIPLES OF GROWTH, DEVELOPMENT, AND BEHAVIOR

These observations and conversations about a newborn child are typical and suggest curiosity about what gives each child his or her unique characteristics and traits. They illustrate an old debate over the relative importance of heredity and environment in a child's uniqueness. For instance, we can all agree that eye color is genetically determined and is not altered by environmental influences. But can we all agree that an infant's motor skills are genetically determined and unalterable through environmental influences? What do we know about the relative influence of heredity and environment (nature and nurture), and what are we learning from modern-day science?

Over the years, theorists have provided a variety of perspectives on how growth proceeds and why it follows certain pathways in individuals, what causes individuals to behave in unique and idiosyncratic ways, and how and why certain capabilities and talents emerge. On one side is the point of view that growth and development are controlled primarily by nature (heredity) and are governed by an inborn, unalterable blueprint that defines what, when, and to what extent each aspect of growth and development will occur. This point of view proposes that all growth, development, thinking, and behavioral changes result from maturation occurring within the organism and are characterized by an unfolding of traits along predictable time lines controlled by the genes (Anastasi, 1958; Hall, 1893; Gesell & Amatruda, 1941; Gesell & Ilg, 1949). This is generally referred to as a **maturationist perspective**.

On the other side is the assertion that the environment is the more critical determinant of the outcomes of growth and development. This theory suggests that the human being is quite malleable and therefore growth and development are facilitated or impeded by influences in the individual's environment (Bandura, 1977, 1986; Bijou & Baer, 1961; Skinner, 1974; Watson, 1924). This **behaviorist perspective** asserts that the environment shapes developmental outcomes regardless of genetic makeup. Consequently, where the environment provides appropriate experiences (i.e., instruction, educational opportunities, praise, punishment, reinforcement, support, neglect), the outcomes for the individual can be externally influenced.

Piaget's (1952) **developmental interactionist perspective** on cognitive development challenged both notions that growth and development are at the mercy of the individual's genes and that growth, development, and learning are acquired primarily through experience and reinforcement techniques. Rather, he hypothesized that children are born with certain abilities that can flourish when supported by a rich and engaging environment. The individual is thought to construct knowledge within his or her mind as a consequence of physical and mental interactions with objects, situations, and people. Piaget's theory suggests that environments that provide limited stimulation and mental engagement impede optimal growth and learning.

Still others propose a **transactional perspective** in which one's inherited attributes and environmental experiences influence one another through an ongoing interplay between heredity and environment (Sameroff, 1983; Sameroff & Chandler, 1975). The transactional perspective says that inherited characteristics are shaped by experience and that experience is shaped by inherited traits. The interplay and interdependence between nature and nurture proceed in a mutual give-and-take manner throughout the life span of the individual. This perspective has made a major contribution to the study of human growth and development, for it suggests that as development proceeds, new characteristics or traits that are not present in the original fertilized egg may well emerge as a result of transactions between heredity and environment. For example, a child who is, by nature, slow to warm up to others may encounter an environment in which caregivers are sensitive and supportive, increasing the child's ability to trust and relate more readily to others. Slowly, over time, this inherent trait, while still present, may be mediated by relationships that facilitate interactions with others.

maturationist perspective: the point of view that growth and development are primarily governed by an individual's genetic makeup

behaviorist perspective: the point of view that growth and development are primarily governed by external influences in the individual's environment

developmental interactionist perspective: the point of view that growth and development result from an individual's actions and interactions within and upon the environment

transactional perspective: the point of view that growth and development are an outgrowth of the interplay between an individual's heredity and environment

This law of developmental direction applies not only to body proportions, but also to other forms of development. It is most obvious in the development and coordination of large and small muscles. Coordination of the large muscles of the upper body, including the neck, shoulders, upper trunk, and upper arms, generally precedes coordination of the smaller muscles in those body regions. Also, throughout infancy and early childhood, the muscles of the upper body become more mature and coordinated than those of the lower regions of the body, with the large muscles of the hips and upper legs developing before the smaller muscles of the lower legs, ankles, and feet.

3. *Most children follow similar developmental patterns.* As a rule, one stage of the pattern paves the way for the next. In motor development, for instance, a predictable sequence of development precedes walking. Infants lift and turn their heads before they turn over, and are able to move their arms and legs before grasping an object.

4. *There are critical or sensitive periods during growth and development in which the child is physically and psychologically more sensitive and vulnerable to environmental influences and social/emotional interactions.* During these periods, the child is susceptible to both positive and negative experiences, which can either enhance or impede the growth process. Indeed, contemporary studies of neurological development and brain growth emphasize the fact that there are prime time periods during which certain experiences have their greatest positive or negative effect on the central nervous system.

5. *There are individual rates of growth and development.* While the patterns or sequences for growth and development are similar among children, the rates at which individual children reach specific developmental milestones vary. For example, one child may begin walking unassisted at 9 months; another may begin at 15 months. For most children, physiological growth occurs in spurts, but for some, growth appears to occur in steady increments. A significant example of variance in individual rates of growth is in the manner in which children become literate. Contrary to prevalent assumptions that literacy must be taught at a certain age and through certain methodologies, literacy development has its origins in infancy and emerges through varied processes and at different rates among children of the same chronological age.

6. *Rates of development are not uniform among developmental domains in individual children.* For instance, a child's intellectual development may outpace his or her emotional or social development. Another child may show precocious motor skills but less sophisticated skill in the use of language.

7. *Throughout the life span, an individual's growth, development, learning, and behaviors are influenced by cultural and societal contexts.* The cultural and societal contexts in which individuals grow and develop encompass numerous elements, which influence and determine unique developmental pathways and outcomes: availability of nutritious foods and family food preferences and meal patterns; health care practices; faith-based rituals and belief systems; family composition, goals, values, and priorities; daily routines and responsibilities; family and community economic resources; access to educational opportunities; education level of family members; community characteristics, which include adequate and comfortable housing, recreational facilities, employment, and family enrichment opportunities; and the prevailing political climate of the community and the nation.

SOCIOCULTURAL PERSPECTIVES ON INFANCY

Anthropologists note that around the world, infants and children experience quite different types of caregiving. Yet most achieve the developmental goals essential for survival and participation in their particular and unique contexts and cultures (Small, 2001). Following are some examples of ways in which cultures around the world vary in their child development beliefs and practices.

The Birthing Process

Birthing procedures range from no or limited assistance from family and friends to high-technology hospitals with professional health care personnel who have had specialized training and where preparation classes for parents-to-be are accompanied by philosophies and policies that encourage spouse and family support during the birthing process. An example of minimal assistance is found among the Siriono of South America. The mother lies in a hammock, delivers the baby unassisted, and allows the newborn to fall from the hammock to the ground, a procedure that is thought to stimulate the birth cry. Although many of the women in the community gather around to keep the birth mother company, they make no attempt to assist her. This practice differs appreciably from hospital or at-home deliveries assisted by a certified nurse–midwife or possibly a nonprofessional midwife and other family members. Home deliveries are popular in a number of countries, such as England, the Netherlands, and Sweden.

Carrying, Cuddling, and Transporting the Infant

In the cultures of Africa, Asia, South America, and some other places, infants are carried about all day on their mothers' backs or in a sling or pouch at their mothers' sides while the mothers go about their daily chores. Infant and mother are virtually inseparable, and the infant is breast-fed on demand throughout the day. Some babies are carried this way until the age of 2, 3, or 4, when the arrival of a sibling usually necessitates the separation (Small, 2001).

In contrast, in Western cultures, babies are carried upright, peering over the shoulders of their parents or caregivers, and are often transported in a variety of devices such as strollers, baby carriages, and carrying seats of various types, such as pouches strapped across the shoulders and around the waist of the adult.

Infant Crying

In some cultures, infants' cries are perceived as distress signals and are responded to readily with food, a pacifier, patting, or holding. In others, such as that of the United States, adults often take a wait-and-see approach to determine the extent of the infant's distress and whether the baby is able to self-comfort and return to sleep. Japanese mothers often let their babies nestle in bed with them and cuddle and hold them until they fall back to sleep.

Cosleeping

In cultures where family interdependence and mutual support are valued (e.g., Asia, Africa, Latin America), children routinely sleep with one or both parents or siblings. Many children around the world sleep in the same room with their parents even when other rooms are available. In the United States, where independence is encouraged, infants and young children are less likely to cosleep with parents, though the trend to cosleeping appears to be increasing among some sectors of the population (Shonkoff & Phillips, 2000).

Nonparental Child Care

North Americans and Europeans in the mid-20th century believed that mothers should not work, but should devote their time and energies to child rearing. Yet for many cultures today, particularly in industrialized and technologically advanced countries, child care and employed mothers are the norm. Nonmaternal child care is provided by the grandmother or another older female in the extended family for Chinese infants, whose mothers return to work soon after the first month. Home care is preferred during the first year (Chance, 1984).

In some Native American tribes, all members of the family are expected to contribute to the maintenance and well-being of the family or group, regardless of the absence or presence of the mother. Grandmothers, aunts, male relatives, and other children may share responsibility for infants. Sometimes very young children (four and five years old) are expected to care for babies and toddlers (Locust, 1988). In the United States, Latino families are less likely to place their children in preschools, relying more frequently on family and friends when child care is needed (Fuller, Eggers-Pierola, Holloway, Liang, & Rambaud, 1995).

These examples illustrate varying views about infants and children and how best to care for them. Around the world and in our own communities, different views and assumptions about infancy and childhood presuppose children to a wide variety of experiences and age-associated expectations. Cultural differences in expectations are for the most part context specific, that is, whether by conscious design or intuition, adults tend to "prepare" their young for the types of capabilities they believe will be necessary for survival in a particular society or geographic location.

Given wide variations among cultures in child-rearing and education practices, scholars ask, "What are the goals of child growth and development?," or stated differently, "What outcomes are essential for survival and satisfying, constructive, productive living?" While these questions may seem at first rhetorical, reflecting on them helps parents, caregivers, and educators to assess their own assumptions, perspectives, and expectations. Knowledge of the importance of cultural contexts to individual child growth, development, and learning helps us to appreciate the many pathways children traverse toward mature forms of behaving, learning, and living. Contemporary scholars emphasize the following important goals (Shonkoff & Phillips, 2000):

- Learning to self-regulate emotions, behaviors, and attention
- Developing language, reasoning, and problem-solving abilities
- Learning to relate to others and to form and maintain friendships

We would add an additional goal:

- Achieving and maintaining healthy bodies and assuming increasing responsibility for one's own health and safety.

While this text draws attention to what the authors believe to be reasonable expectations for a given age of a child based on an ever-increasing amount of enlightening research, these goals for child growth and development are implicit in the suggested developmental milestones and age-related characteristics described herein.

BEGINNINGS: PHYSICAL AND MOTOR COMPETENCE OF THE NEWBORN

The newborn enters the world with impressive abilities. In making the transition from intrauterine to extrauterine life, the newborn must make a number of physiological adjustments, including breathing, taking in nourishment, and eliminating body wastes. The newborn makes adjustments from being surrounded by the warm amniotic fluid of the uterine environment to being surrounded by air, which is dry and cool and fluctuates in temperature. The newborn also adjusts from an environment of limited sensory stimulation to an environment of many complex and varied stimuli that quicken all of the sensory mechanisms of sight, sound, smell, touch, taste, and **kinesthesis**. Despite seemingly overwhelming demands on the heretofore profoundly dependent organism, the infant emerges as a remarkably competent individual. Let's begin our discussion of the infant's competencies and potential with a description of early brain growth and neurological development.

Recent advances in technology, neuroscience, and medicine have made it possible to study with amazing precision the neurological system and the brain. Imaging technology such as *high-resolution ultrasound recordings,* a noninvasive technique that creates a sonogram picture of the fetus using sound waves, are used quite frequently now. *Computed axial tomography* (CT or CAT scan) is a noninvasive procedure that uses computers to provide multiple-angle pictures of the brain, giving information about its structure. *Magnetic resonance imaging* (MRI), also a noninvasive technique, employs magnetic fields, radio frequencies, and computer technology to produce high-contrast images that allow scientists to examine various anatomical features of the brain. *Functional MRI* (fMRI) combines imaging of activity in the brain with MRI images of the brain's structure. *Positron emission tomography* (PET scan) uses radioactive dye, either injected or ingested, to view not only the structures of the brain, as with the CAT scan, but also complex neurological activity as it takes place in various parts of the brain. *Video-enhanced microscopy* combines microscopic images with video technology to examine the characteristics and activity of minute particles in living tissue. In addition to these remarkable imaging techniques, scientists now have methods to analyze the electrical and chemical activity in the brain and the neurological system. For example, by analyzing levels of the hormone cortisol in saliva, the impact of adverse and stressful experiences on the brain can be estimated. Cortisol levels rise when stress increases, and we now know that persistent high levels of cortisol can be damaging to brain cells and have been associated with some developmental delays and neurological impairments (Gazzaniga, 1988; Vincent, 1990). Specialized studies such as these are yielding important information for the study of child development.

Earliest Brain Growth and Neurological Development

During the first weeks of prenatal development, the **neural tube** (which will develop into the spinal column and brain) emerges out of the **embryonic cell mass**.

---

kinesthesis:
the perception of body presence, position, and movement

neural tube:
the rudimentary beginning of the brain and spinal cord

embryonic cell mass:
the developing fertilized ovum during the first 3 months of pregnancy when cells are dividing rapidly to form the fetus

Specific cells along the length of the tube develop into specific types of **neurons**, or nerve cells. During prenatal development, neurons are forming at a startling rate of 250,000 per minute. Neurons are tiny; it is estimated that 30,000 of them can fit into a space the size of a pinhead. The spinal column, brain, and a spectacular network of nerve cells make up the nervous system. The nervous system has three interrelated functions: "to receive and interpret information about the internal and external environment of the body, to make decisions about this information, and to organize and carry out action" based on this information (Delcomyn, 1998, p. 7).

The human organism has sophisticated capabilities for receiving and interpreting information about its internal and external environments through the *sensory system,* which includes all of the sense organs of the body and sensory neurons, which transport information from the sense organs to other parts of the nervous system. The *motor system* includes the muscles, certain glands of the body, and the motor neurons, which are needed to activate the muscles and glands. There is a third system in our sophisticated neurological makeup in which the complex task of taking information from the sensory system, accessing memory of previous experiences, and then making decisions about prior information stored in memory and the new information takes place. This system is referred to as the *integrating system* because it must coordinate and integrate many sources of information and many different parts of the nervous system. This activity is carried out by nerve cells called interneurons (Delcomyn, 1998).

During the embryonic period, neural cells that will form the parts of the nervous system grow from germ cells, which divide repeatedly, generating new cells. This process of generating new cells ceases before an infant's birth. Hence, infants are born with a lifetime supply of nerve cells, or neurons—more than 100 billion, which have already formed more than 50 trillion connections. No new cells will ever develop, but these cell bodies will continue to grow **axons** (usually a single long fiber), which convey information *away* from the cell body, and **dendrites**, branches that convey information *toward* the cell body, which will travel in designated pathways to connect at **synapses** to form a very dense and complex system of connections. Neurons communicate through these synapses either through certain chemicals known as **neurotransmitters** or by the transmission of electrical currents from one neuron to another. During infancy and the first year of development, these connections are bursting forth at an astounding rate. By the end of the infant's first year, the brain is two-thirds of its adult size, and by the end of the second year, it is about four-fifths of its adult size. Environmental sensory stimuli cause the brain to develop its own unique circuitry and determine which connections will last (or become "hard wired") and which connections will be so weak that they **atrophy** and die. Connections that are not used frequently enough are pruned away or sometimes rerouted to another compensating or perhaps less appropriate or debilitating connection. Studies of infants and young children who have not received healthy, consistent, predictable, repetitive sensory experiences during this critical period of growth and development have shown that they have significantly smaller brains and abnormal brain development (Perry, 1998).

During the early growth of nerve cells, **myelin**, which is a fatty tissue made up of **glial** membrane, begins to wrap around the axon and dendrites. Myelin promotes the efficient transmission of messages along the neurons and strengthens

neuron:
a type of cell that conveys information; a nerve cell

axon:
a branchlike projection from the neuron that carries information away from the cell body

dendrites:
branches from the neuron that carry information toward the cell body; a neuron can have several dendrites

synapse:
the point of contact between nerve fibers

neurotransmitter:
a chemical that facilitates the transmission of information through the synapse

atrophy:
waste away, diminish in size and/or function

myelin:
a fatty substance surrounding the axons and dendrites of some neurons, which speeds the conduction of nerve impulses

glial cells:
supporting cells, which serve to protect and insulate (as in myelin) cells in the nervous system

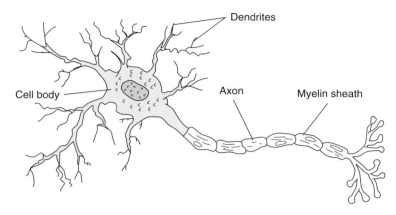

synapses (Figure 5.3). Its growth coincides with the development of vision and hearing systems, motor development, language, certain cognitive processes, and the expression and control of emotions. All experiences (or sensory input that the child receives) affect neurological development by strengthening the synapses. Over the life span of an individual, many nerve cells die as a consequence of the prenatal production of more cells than are actually needed or than can survive to adulthood and through lack of use. Consequently, reduction of the number of neurons present at birth occurs throughout development, resulting at adulthood in half the original number of cells. Figure 5.4 outlines the sequence of neuron development.

Of special interest to child developmentalists is the concept of *windows of opportunity*, which are identified periods during growth and development when certain synaptic activity can be strengthened if infants and young children are provided appropriate experiences. From recent studies of prenatal and infant

FIGURE 5.4
Sequence of Neu-
ron Development

1. Fertilization (ovum/sperm)
2. Cell division
3. Formation of neural plate
4. Evolution of neural tube
5. Cell proliferation (rapid formation of nerve cells called neurons)
6. Migration of primitive neurons
7. Cell differentiation into
   a. ectoderm, which evolves into outer surface of the skin, nails, teeth, lens of the eye, inner ear, brain, spinal cord, and nerves
   b. endoderm, which evolves into digestive system and lungs
   c. mesoderm, which evolves into bones, muscles, circulatory system, skeleton, gastrointestinal track, and inner layers of the skin
8. Growth of axons and dendrites
9. Myelination of axons
10. Synaptogenesis (formation of chemical and electrical contacts between nerve cells)
11. Neuronal and synaptic death (or pruning of redundant nerve connections)

TABLE 5.1	Windows of Opportunity in Early Brain Growth and Neurological Development

Age	Developmental Domain
Birth to 2 years	Social attachment, ability to cope with stress
Birth to 3 years	Regulation of emotions
Birth to 2 years	Visual and auditory acuity
Birth to 3 years	Vocabulary
Birth to 5 years	Motor development and coordinations
Birth to 10 years	First- and second-language development
1 year to 5 years	Mathematical and logical thinking
3 years to 10 years	Music appreciation and learning

neurological development and brain growth, it is evident that the first three years are critical, particularly for the neurological development that is associated with attachment, control of emotions, ability to cope with stress, vision, and motor development. Table 5.1 illustrates these windows of opportunity.

The concept of windows of opportunity is frequently misunderstood as implying that after a given age, the opportunity for specific types of neuronal development or learning is lost if certain types of experiences have not occurred (the window closes, so to speak). While there are prime times for certain types of neuronal growth, as we describe in later discussions, there are windows of opportunity for various types of growth and development throughout the life span. Missed prime times or opportunities, for the most part, are ameliorated by timely interventions that include consistent and appropriately challenging, nurturing, and enriching experiences.

After this brief synopsis of early neurological development and brain growth, we are now prepared to look more specifically at the present and emerging capabilities of the newborn.

The Neonate

The *neonatal period* is usually defined as the first four weeks of life, and is a critical period in infant development. Many physiological adjustments required for extrauterine existence are taking place. During this period, all of the child's bodily functions and psychological states are monitored to ensure it has a healthy beginning.

Physically, the newborn may be a frightful sight, though the infant's parents may disagree with this generalization. The skin is wrinkled, red, and covered with a cheeselike, greasy substance called **vernix caseosa**, which protects the skin during uterine development. In addition, the head is large in proportion to the rest of the body; the chest circumference is smaller than that of the infant's head. Sometimes, the neonate's head has become temporarily misshapen during a lengthy delivery. Following the struggle to enter the world, some infants fall into a deep sleep, and for the first day or so may even have difficulty staying awake long enough to nurse.

vernix caseosa: an oily covering that protects the skin of the fetus

Reflexes

reflex:
an unlearned, involuntary response to stimuli

subcortical:
refers to the portion of the brain just below the cerebral cortex, which is responsible for controlling unlearned and reflexive behavior

cerebral cortex:
the outer layer of the cerebral hemisphere, which is mostly responsible for higher mental functions, sensory processing, and motor control

survival reflexes:
reflexes essential to sustaining life

The full-term neonate is quite prepared for life and is equipped with a number of inborn movement patterns that help it adapt to new surroundings and new demands. These movement patterns, many of which are present prior to birth, are reflexes. **Reflexes** are unlearned, automatic responses to stimuli resulting from earliest neuromuscular development. Both Jeremy and Angela display the infant rooting and sucking reflexes. For the most part, these early reflexes are a function of **subcortical** (brain stem and spinal cord) mechanisms, though some cortical control is evident. The **cerebral cortex** is the part of the brain that is responsible for perception, memory, and thinking. Figure 5.5 illustrates the regions of the brain and their respective responsibilities.

Some reflexes are called **survival reflexes** because they are necessary for the infant to sustain life. An obvious example is breathing. The birth cry, which sometimes occurs before the infant is fully delivered, sets the respiratory mechanisms in motion, oxygenating the red blood cells and expelling carbon dioxide from the lungs. Gagging, sneezing, and hiccuping reflexes are present before and after birth.

Most subcortical or **primitive reflexes** gradually disappear as the cerebral cortex matures and begins to direct and control bodily movements and behaviors. Some reflexes such as breathing and other involuntary functions, such as bladder and bowel control, may continue to have elements of both subcortical and cortical control. The developmental course of the individual reflexes varies; some disappear in the first few days, others vanish within the first 12 to 18 months, and still others persist throughout life, becoming more precise and organized.

In preterm infants, subcortical reflexes are frequently not evident at birth, but will appear soon thereafter. Premature infants often exhibit weak rooting and

FIGURE 5.5
Regions of the Brain and Their Functions

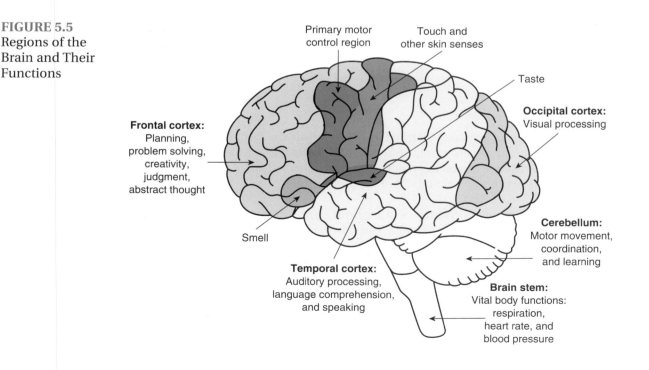

TABLE 5.2   Major Reflexes Present in Infancy

Reflex	Description
Survival Reflexes	
Breathing reflex	Inhales/exhales, oxygenating the red blood cells and expelling carbon dioxide.
Rooting reflex	Turns in the direction of a touch on the cheek as though searching for a nipple. Serves to orient the infant to the breast or the bottle.
Sucking and swallowing reflex	Stimulated by a nipple placed in the mouth; allows the infant to take in nourishment.
Eyeblink and pupillary reflex	Eyes close or blink; pupils dilate or constrict to protect the eyes.
Primitive Reflexes	
Grasping reflex	Holds firmly to an object touching the palm of the hand. Disappearance around the fourth month signals advancing neurological development.
Moro reflex	Often referred to as the *startle reflex;* a loud noise or sudden jolt will cause the arms to thrust outward, then return to an embrace-like position. Disappearance around the fifth or sixth month signals advancing neurological development.
Babinski reflex	Toes fan outward, then curl when the bottom of the foot is stroked. Disappearance by the end of the first year signals advancing neurological development.
Tonic neck reflex	A "fencing pose," often assumed when sleeping—head turned to one side, arm extended on the same side, and opposite arm and leg flexed at the elbow and knee. Disappearance around seven months signals advancing neurological development.

sucking responses. Continued absence or weakness of these early reflexes suggests delayed development or dysfunction in the central nervous system. In premature infants, these early reflexes disappear somewhat more slowly than they do in full-term infants. Table 5.2 lists some major reflexes observed in early infancy.

In addition to an impressive array of reflexes, there are other early behaviors of special interest. They are infant psychological states and activity levels, sensory capabilities, and expected growth and development patterns.

primitive reflexes: reflexes controlled by subcortical structures in the brain, which gradually disappear during the first year

Psychological States, Temperament, and Activity Levels

Jeremy, now 48 hours old, is cradled in his mother's arms and sleeping quite soundly. His face is scrunched into a tight expression—eyes tightly closed, mouth puckered into an overbite position, chin almost buried in his chest. He is swaddled snugly under the soft baby wrap, arms folded comfortably against his chest, knees bent slightly upward, and toes pointed inward.

Ann attempts to rouse her sleeping baby by gently rubbing her fingers across his soft cheek. He squirms slightly, stretching his legs and turning his head toward the touch; his mouth opens slightly, but he resists waking and returns to his previous comfortable sleeping state. His mouth makes faint sucking movements briefly before he lapses into a fairly deep sleep.

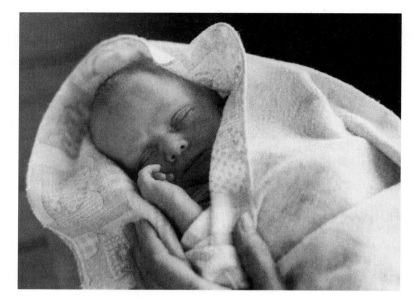

Angela, now 2 weeks old and home from the neonatal care unit, is crying vigorously. Her legs stretch stiffly, and her arms and hands flail in the air. Her blanket is in disarray, and her mother is hurriedly preparing a bottle to feed her. As the nipple of the bottle brushes against her lips, Angela frantically and clumsily searches and struggles to grasp it. Her sucking response is somewhat weak, and she whimpers until she succeeds in securing the nipple and the hunger pains begin to subside. The warmth and comfort of nourishment calm and soothe her.

psychological state:
pertains to conditions of arousal and alertness in infancy

Psychologists use the term **psychological state** when describing the infant's relationship to the outside world. States are characterized in terms of the degree of arousal and alertness the infant exhibits.

Sleep Behavior.   An eagerly awaited milestone in infant development is the ability to sleep through the night. Sleeping patterns of infants are often the subject of conversation with proud (or tired) parents. Researchers also are interested in infant sleep patterns. Patterns, characteristics, and problems of sleep in young children make up a large body of literature and a broad field of study.

Sleep patterns change as infants mature. Newborn infants usually sleep approximately 16 of 24 hours. By 6 months, sleep duration among infants averages 14.2 hours, with decreasing daytime sleep and increasing nighttime sleep (Iglowstein, Jenni, Molinari, & Largo, 2003). The longest period of sleep may be 4 to 4½ hours during the first days. By 4 to 6 weeks of age, the infant may be sleeping 12 to 14 hours a day, taking as many as seven "naps" during a 24-hour period.

Some infants sleep a 6-hour night by the 4th week after birth, but some will not sleep through the night until they are 7 or 8 months old. Some infants sleep more during the day and others sleep more at night, though most infants seem to sleep for longer periods at night. There is great variation in both the amount and

---

TABLE 5.3   Classification of Infant States

State	Characteristics
Regular sleep	Little body movement; regular breathing; no response to mild stimulation.
Irregular sleep	Increased body movements; irregular breathing; more easily aroused by external stimuli.
Periodic sleep	Occurs between regular and irregular sleep and is accompanied by muscle movements and rapid breathing, then short periods of calm inactivity.
Drowsiness	Little motor activity, yet sensitive to external stimuli.
Alert inactivity	Visually and/or auditorially scans the environment; large motor activity (head, trunk, arms and legs), alert and relaxed.
Waking activity	More intense motor activity may signal physiological need.
Crying	Motor activity passes into a whimpering, crying state, becoming louder as distress increases. Thrashing; twisting of torso and kicking vigorously.

Source: Reprinted from: Wolff, P. H. (1966). "Classification of infant states," in *Causes, controls, and organization of behavior in the neonate.* Madison, CT: International Universities Press. By permission of International Universities Press, Inc. Copyright © 1966 by International Universities Press, Inc.

type of sleep exhibited in infancy. In his study of states of arousal in infancy, Wolff (1966) identified seven states, summarized in Table 5.3.

By observing eye movements beneath the eyelid during sleep, the infant's sleep phase can be determined. There are two sleep phases, *rapid eye movement (REM)* and *non-rapid eye movement (NREM)* sleep. REM sleep is characterized by closed eyes; uneven respiration; limp muscle tone; intermittent smiles, grimaces, sighs, and sucking movements; and rapid eye movement beneath the eyelids as though the infant is dreaming. NREM sleep ranges from eyes partially open or still closed and a very light activity level with mild startles, to alertness but minimal motor activity, to eyes open with increased motor activity and reactions to external stimuli, to crying, sometimes quite intense.

Sleep researchers believe that REM sleep is vital to growth of the central nervous system. Observations of infant sleep states and patterns help physicians to identify central nervous system abnormalities. For instance, preterm infants generally display a greater amount of REM sleep. There is some evidence that infants suffering from brain injury or birth trauma may exhibit disturbed REM/NREM sleep patterns.

Jeremy, now 4 months old, is usually quite content at bedtime. His mother usually holds him in her lap for awhile after the evening feeding while he drifts into drowsiness and then into irregular sleep. Her soft voice hums to him while he drowses in her arms. Sensing his readiness for the crib, she carries him to his room. Placing him quietly in his crib, she continues to hum. She rubs his back softly and then leaves the room after observing that he will soon fall soundly to sleep.

However, on this particular evening, Jeremy resists sleep. His eyes are open and scanning his surroundings, though he appears tired and cries sporadically. Tonight, he is what most parents would call "fussy." His mother, also tired, wishes that some magic formula would soothe him and help him to rest. Nevertheless, after determining that Jeremy is not hungry, his diaper does not need changing, and his clothing is comfortable, she follows her established routine with him, sustaining each phase slightly longer. After being placed in his crib, he rouses somewhat and cries resistively while Ann strokes his back gently. Though he has not fallen into sound sleep, she leaves the room.

Predictable, unhurried bedtimes with regular routines help the reluctant infant to separate from the family and fall asleep more readily. Routines may include a relaxed bathtime during which the interaction between parent and child is enjoyable, followed by being held in the parent's lap, rocked, and sung to softly. Cuddling a soft stuffed toy while being held focuses attention away from more stimulating activities occurring around the infant. This routine is followed by being placed in bed with a moment of slow caresses and a kiss on the cheek, a whispered "good night," and then departure from the room. The American Academy of Pediatrics recommends that infants be placed on their backs (supine position) to sleep or on their sides (lateral position), making certain the lower arm is forward to prevent rolling over onto the stomach (Figure 5.6). This position for sleep has been widely publicized through the National Institute of Child Health and Human Development and the American Academy of Pediatrics Back to Sleep campaign, which was launched in 1994 to reduce the risk of sudden infant death syndrome (SIDS) (Malloy, 1998). SIDS is discussed later in this chapter.

A study of night waking among 9-month-old infants found that infants whose parent or caregiver routinely remained present with them at bedtime until they fell asleep were more likely to wake during the night (Adair, Baucher, Philipp, Levenson, & Zuckerman, 1991). This finding suggests that putting infants to bed when they are at least partially awake elicits their own internal devices for falling asleep. If the infant wakes during the night, barring problems such as hunger, discomfort, or impending illness, he or she can learn to employ the same internal devices rather than soliciting parental assistance. While this study did not establish actual cause and effect, the researchers suggested that infant temperament may be a factor, but parental difficulty in separating from the infant may also interfere with infant sustained sleep patterns. Other reasons for night waking include being too cold or too warm and needing appropriate clothing or bed covers, colic, an unfamiliar bed or new surroundings, disturbing sensory stimuli such as loud or startling noises, and distracting lights. Some infants signal that they are awake; others do not unless they are in some form of distress such as hunger or uncomfortable clothing. Infants generally sleep through the night by age 3 months, typically from 5 to 8 hours.

Sleep routines vary from family to family and in child care settings, and though sleep patterns are enhanced by predictable and reassuring rituals, the household need not be abnormally quiet, as infants generally adjust to reasonable and typical noises in their environments. Nor should siblings be expected to be particularly quiet—though rowdy play, of course, disturbs anyone's rest. Some infants may actually be soothed by usual household noises, which often provide an auditory sense of the permanence of people and the predictability of routines.

Similar routines in out-of-home child care arrangements facilitate naptime for infants and reassure them of the support of their caregivers. As with noise levels at home, rest times away from home can be scheduled during periods of the day when noise levels are at a minimum; however, there is no need to expect that all noise can be curtailed during group care naptimes.

Best Sleep Position

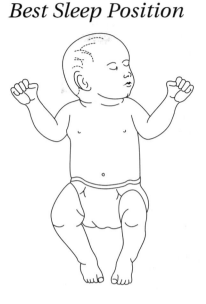

FIGURE 5.6
Recommended
Sleep Positions
for Infants

Alternative Sleep Position

Temperament.   **Temperament** is an individual's biologically based behavior style, which helps us to describe an individual's responses (Chess, 1967; Thomas & Chess, 1977; Thomas, Chess, & Birch, 1968). This aspect of infant development will be discussed more fully in Chapter 6; it is mentioned here as one of the psychological states in infancy. Chess and Thomas (1987) identified several dimensions of temperament, including activity level, rhythms, approach and withdrawal behaviors, adaptability, responsiveness, intensity of reaction, quality of mood, distractibility, and attention span and persistence. Using these activity

temperament:
an individual's
behavior style, which
is both biologically
and environmentally
derived

classifications, the researchers delineated three basic temperament patterns: *easy, difficult,* and *slow to warm up.* These behavior styles influence the reciprocal interactions between infants and their caregivers. There are wide variations in temperament among infants. Some infants are less able to calm themselves than others; some are easily comforted by their caregivers.

Angela is less easily soothed than Jeremy. At bedtime, she is quite fretful and restless. Inferring from the usual afternoon and evening family routines that bedtime is drawing near, she begins to whimper and cry and will not sustain her grasp on a soft toy offered to her. She resists being held or comforted.

Since birth, Angela has had a variety of caregivers, from hospital neonatal care nursing staff in her first 2 weeks to a home with extended family, including her grandmother and her own mother's siblings—some young children and some teenagers. Each has taken turns caring for and feeding her. Thus, Angela's care has been neither predictable nor consistent.

Angela's grandmother, sensing a difficult bedtime, intervenes. She carries Angela on her shoulder as she walks around the house giving clean-up and bedtime instructions to the other children. Patting a fretful Angela, she continues to walk, talk, and hush the baby. When this proves unsuccessful, she proceeds to a back bedroom, where, separated from the rest of the family, she places Angela across her lap and begins to sing and talk softly to her. For a time, Angela still wiggles, lifts her head and frets, and is easily distracted by the sound of children playing inside the house. Her grandmother continues to sing and talk or hum until at last Angela begins to rest and finally dozes.

Temperament is readily observable in infancy, expressing itself through various behaviors such as the ability to delay gratification or modulate emotions. In the preceding vignette, Angela seems unable to deal with the distractions around her and to self-calm, and she becomes more agitated as others try to comfort her.

While individual styles of behaving endure over time, the behavior itself is expressed in age-related forms. For instance, Angela's resistance to adult efforts to comfort her may at a later age emerge into self-comforting strategies such as thumb sucking, singing, talking to herself, or seeking a certain person, place, chair, pillow, or blanket that is associated with calmness and rest.

The activity levels of neonates have been positively correlated with activity levels at ages 4 and 8 (Korner et al., 1985). Activity levels have also been associated with birth order (Eaton, Chipperfield, & Singbell, 1989). A study of 7,000 children ranging in age from 4 days to 7 years, including first- through sixth-born children, found that earlier-born children were more active than later-born children.

Sensory Capabilities in Infancy

During the prenatal period, neurological development emerges intrinsically as a result of the properly timed activation of genes, which is not dependent on external input or neural activity (Delcomyn, 1998). However, during later prenatal development and the early months and years of infancy and early childhood, external input is critical to neurological development. Environmental input stimulates electrical activity in neurons, resulting in the process of circuitry building, or "wiring," of the neurological system as nerve cells grow axons and dendrites, which navigate toward their targets, forming important connections for the relay of messages throughout the body. The fact that the nervous system can be shaped by neural activity aroused by environmental stimuli is evidence of the brain's **plasticity**, which is most apparent when neuron connections are forming. This means that an individual's brain has the remarkable ability to change and compensate for problems if intervention is timely and intensive. However, inappropriate or negative experiences, as with child abuse and neglect, have been found to interfere with normal wiring of the brain, resulting in adverse developmental outcomes (Chugani, 1997; Perry, 1993a, 1993b). These early environmental stimuli have important implications for the development and integrity of the sensory and motor systems.

plasticity:
the ability of some parts of the nervous system to alter their functional characteristics

The infant's sensory equipment is remarkably operative at birth. Neonates are capable of seeing, hearing, tasting, smelling, and responding to touch. The neonate takes in and processes information to a much greater extent than we might expect. Development of **perception** begins as the infant seeks and receives information through the senses.

perception:
the physiological process by which sensory input is interpreted

Touch.   Scientists believe the sense of touch emerges between 7½ and 14 weeks of embryonic development. Skin, muscular, and inner ear (vestibular) senses are more mature at birth than are the other senses (Gottfried, 1984). The sense of touch, particularly around the mouth area, is especially acute and facilitates infant rooting and nursing. Certain other parts of the body are sensitive to touch. These include the nose, skin of the forehead, soles of the feet, and genitals. Most of the reflexes listed in Table 5.1 are stimulated by touch. In addition to touch, the skin is sensitive to temperature, pressure, vibration, tickle, and pain.

For obvious ethical reasons, little research exists on sensitivity to pain. Contrary to the previous notion that neonates do not experience great pain, we now know they do. Recent studies of pain associated with infant circumcision procedures have helped to advance knowledge about infant pain. By analyzing the recorded vocalizations of newborn males during circumcision, researchers identified significant differences in vocalizations as each step of the procedure

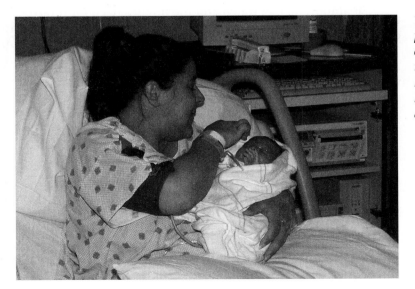

The newborn's parents are typically curious and intrigued by his or her physical and behavioral characteristics.

became more invasive (Porter, Miller, & Marshall, 1986). Some surgical procedures that were previously thought to be painless for newborns are now accompanied by analgesia or anesthesia whenever possible (American Academy of Family Physicians, 1996; American Academy of Pediatrics and American College of Obstetricians and Gynecologists, 1992; Ryan & Finer, 1994). Recognizing that infants do indeed experience pain with various medical procedures, research continues to identify safe methods for reducing pain. For instance, it has been found that giving newborns a drink of a sucrose solution moments before the routine heel prick to test a blood sample for the presence of PKU appears to reduce the pain of the procedure (Blass & Shah, 1995).

kangaroo care: the practice of holding an infant next to the mother's or father's skin to comfort and nurture it

Studies of preterm infants have found that touch plays a very significant role in their development. Skin-to-skin holding (or **kangaroo care**) has been shown to increase respiratory stability and more restful sleep in newborns (Als & Gilkerson, 1995). Further, mothers were shown to exhibit more positive adaptation to infant cues, and their infants were more inclined to hold their gaze on them, during skin-to-skin contact. In one study, it was found that when their infants were 3 months of age, both mothers and fathers who engaged in kangaroo care exhibited more sensitivity and a more nurturing home environment, and their infants scored higher on the Bayley Mental Developmental Index, than did the control group who did not engage in such care during the infants' first days and weeks (Feldman, Eidelman, Sirota, & Weller, 2002). Feldman et al. speculated that along with its effect on improving parental mood and interactions with the infant, there is a direct influence on infant development by contributing to neurophysiological organization. Many neonatal care units encourage parents of preterm infants in particular to gently hold and caress them (when the infant's physical condition permits). When the infant cannot be held, gently caressing the infant in the isolette is encouraged. In some hospitals, volunteers hold, rock, and softly stroke these small and vulnerable babies. A study by T. M. Field and her colleagues (1986) found that preterm infants who were gently touched and caressed several times each day gained weight faster than preterm infants who did not receive this regular stimulation. These infants also exhibited advanced mental and motor development at the end of the first year compared to the control group infants.

The importance of touch and the infant's need for it have been of interest to researchers for years. Lack of soothing tactile sensations during infancy has been associated with delays in cognitive and affective development (Ainsworth, 1962; Yarrow, 1961). Thus, in addition to the sheer pleasure experienced by both infant and caregiver that hugging, rocking, caressing, and patting bring, these experiences provide the infant with the tactile stimulation that is essential to perceptual and sensory development.

Vision.   The neonate's vision functions well at birth, though visual acuity is imperfect, with a tendency toward nearsightedness (Cornell & McDonnell, 1986). Neonates can follow a moving light and fixate on an object at a distance of about 9 inches. In his pioneering studies of infant visual preferences, Fantz (1961) found that infants prefer human faces, enjoy bold patterns such as checkerboards or bull's-eye patterns, and tend to look at the edges of the designs or at the point where two contrasts come together. While bold patterns appear to hold the infant's attention, research has also demonstrated that infants exhibit interest through fixed gazes in color, showing a preference for blue and green objects over red ones (Adams, Mauer, & Davis, 1986). Bornstein (1984, 1985) also found that infants respond to differences in colors and suggested that later ability to categorize by color, thought to be a result of cognitive development, has its origins in the earliest visual perceptual processes. Other researchers have found that infants watch more intently a face that is active, smiling, talking, blinking, or laughing (Haith, 1966; Samuels, 1985). Others have found that infants attend longer to a face that imitates their own facial movements and expressions (Winnicott, 1971). Whereas vision improves rapidly over the first few months of life, mature 20/20 vision is not achieved until about age 5 (Bornstein, 1988). Pediatric and ophthalmologic experts recommend that beginning in the newborn period, the eyes be examined regularly for disorders or abnormalities such as cataract, drooping eyelid (ptosis), or unusual discolorations (American Academy of Pediatrics, Committee on Practice and Ambulatory Medicine, Section on Ophthalmology, 2002).

Hearing.   Though the passages of the ear (eustachian tubes and external canal) may still contain amniotic fluids for the first few days after birth, the newborn hears fairly well. After the fluids are absorbed, the neonate responds vigorously to various sounds in the environment. The infant is startled by loud noises and soothed by soft sounds. It has been suggested that neonates can discriminate between loud and soft sounds but do not respond to variations in pitch (Bench, 1978). Researchers have also demonstrated that neonates are capable of discriminating among sounds that differ in duration, direction, and frequency as well as loudness (Bower, 1982).

Neonates seem particularly responsive to the human voice (Caron, Caron, & MacLean, 1988). The neonate will often stop crying when spoken to, visually scan for the source of the voice, and attempt to vocalize (Rosenthal, 1982). Could it be that human infants are genetically programmed to react to human speech?

It has been estimated that about 1 in 1,000 otherwise healthy infants has bilateral (both sides) congenital hearing loss, and among infants in neonatal intensive care, the incidence was found to be 5 in 1,000 (Mason & Herrmann, 1998). The American Academy of Pediatrics (APA, 2002) notes that 1 in 650 newborns is born with hearing loss. Because hearing loss in infants, if left undetected and untreated, can lead to speech and language delays, learning difficulties, and social and emotional problems, the medical profession makes every effort to screen infants before they are 6 months old. The AAP and other health care organizations have launched a campaign to assure that newborns are screened for hearing loss before they leave the hospital so that timely comprehensive evaluation and intervention services can be provided. However, requirements for newborn screening for hearing loss and other physical anomalies vary from state to state (U.S. General Accounting Office, 2003).

Taste.   Newborns are very responsive to variations in taste. The taste of milk seems to elicit a reaction of satisfaction in infants. Infants prefer sweet tastes and usually react negatively to sour, bitter, or salty tastes (Steiner, 1979). Since flavors from the mother's diet are carried in the amniotic fluids and swallowed by the fetus, and breast milk also carries flavors from the mother's diet, the question could be asked whether the fetus develops an affinity for certain tastes. In an experiment in which expectant mothers were asked to include carrot juice in their diets 4 days per week for the last trimester of their pregnancies and during the early weeks of breast-feeding, it was noted that compared to infants whose mothers did not drink carrot juice during this same period, when infants were old enough to be introduced to solid foods, they favored carrots. This study leads us to suspect that flavors from the mother's typical diet during pregnancy and lactation influence the infant's acceptance and enjoyment of similar foods when the infant is weaned to solid foods. Foods consumed by different cultures in their typical diets, then, are more likely to be favored by children as they are introduced to solid foods (Meanella, Jagnow, & Beauchamp, 2001).

Smell. Infants sense a variety of scents and will turn away from noxious odors such as vinegar or alcohol. Interestingly, they seem able to recognize the scent of their mothers within the first few days of extrauterine life (MacFarlane, 1977; Makin & Porter, 1989) and will turn away from an unused breast pad or the breast pad of another mother. Musick and Householder (1986) suggested that the early bonding process might be facilitated if the mother left her breast pad or another small article of her clothing in the bassinet to reinforce the infant's sensory attachment to her.

PHYSICAL AND MOTOR DEVELOPMENT DURING THE FIRST YEAR

Growth and development during this first year are both dramatic and significant. According to Sandra Anselmo, "In no other one-year period until puberty are there so many physical changes. The changes in infancy are measured in terms of days and weeks rather than in terms of months and years" (1987, p. 148).

Physical Characteristics

Birth weight and birth length are always of interest to parents, grandparents, and health care professionals. While birth weight and birth length often make for proud conversation, physical measurements are quite significant in the context of infant health and developmental outcomes. Low birth weight, for instance, has serious implications for survival and for subsequent normal development.

The average birth weight for full-term infants is 7½ pounds, with a range from 5½ to 10 pounds. Boys usually are slightly heavier than girls at birth. Birth length ranges from 18 to 22 inches, with an average of 20 inches. The neonate frequently loses weight in the first few days due to loss of body fluids and the inability to adequately take in nourishment, but will gain at a rate of 6 to 8 ounces per week, and by 5 to 6 months may have doubled the birth weight. The infant's length also will have increased, by 6 to 7 inches.

During the second half of the first year, gains in weight and length decelerate somewhat, though growth continues at a rapid pace. Weight may increase by 4 to 6 ounces weekly and height by 3 to 4 inches. By the first birthday, infants may have tripled in weight and grown 10 to 12 inches since birth. If growth were to proceed at such pace, an 18-year-old would measure more than 15 feet tall and weigh several tons! Fortunately, growth slows appreciably after the first 2 years.

Weight and height are observable characteristics. While this outward growth is readily observable, significant internal growth is taking place as the central nervous system matures and bones and muscles increase in weight, length, and coordination.

The soft bones of early infancy gradually *ossify* as calcium and other minerals harden them. The bones are soft and pliable and are difficult to break. They do not support the infant's weight in sitting or standing positions. The skull bones are separated by **fontanelles** (often called "soft spots"), which may compress to facilitate passage through the birth canal. These fontanelles tend to shrink after 6 months and may close between 9 and 18 months.

Interestingly, the bones of the skull and wrists ossify earliest, and the wrists and ankles develop more bones as the child matures. Girls may be several weeks ahead of boys in bone development at birth. Physicians may use X-rays of the wrists to determine the **skeletal age** of a child. Such X-rays reveal the number of bones in the wrist along with the extent of ossification. This information assists in assessing expected growth progress and diagnosing growth disorders and disease.

Though infants are born with all the muscle cells they will ever have (Tanner, 1989), there is a large amount of water in muscle tissue. Gradually, as protein and other nutrients replace this cellular fluid, the strength of the muscles increases.

Since neurological development and brain growth are rapid during prenatal development and the 1st year, head circumference measures provide a useful means for evaluating the status of the central nervous system in infants and young children. Small-for-age head circumference measurements at 8 months to 2 years of age may indicate central nervous system anomalies that are associated with developmental delay. As is true of other organs, not all parts of the brain develop at the same rate. At birth, the brain stem and the midbrain are the most highly developed. These areas of the brain control consciousness, inborn reflexes, digestion, respiration, and elimination.

The cerebrum and the cerebral cortex surround the midbrain and are significant in the development of primary motor and sensory responses. Following the law of developmental direction, the nerve cells that control the upper trunk and arms mature before those that control the lower trunk and legs. Observation of infant motor activity reveals a growing number of skills that use the muscles of the neck, arms, and hands, skills that precede the abilities to turn over, sit up, or crawl. By 6 months of age, the cerebral cortex has matured sufficiently to control most of the infant's physical activity. At this point in growth and development, many of the reflexes of early infancy should be fading, signaling maturation of the neurological system.

fontanelles: membranous spaces between the cranial bones of the fetus and infant

skeletal age: a measure of physical development based on examination of skeletal X-rays

Expected Patterns and Developmental Milestones

Recall the examples of cross-cultural variations in child growth and development. Both timing and sequence of development can vary among and within cultures and racial groups. As we described earlier in this chapter, current thinking about expected patterns of growth and development calls for a consideration of geographic, cultural, and socioeconomic factors that facilitate (or in some cases impede) growth and development. Parental goals and expectations influence growth and development through the types and timing of educational or enrichment opportunities that they provide, the quality and quantity of play that they encourage, and the behaviors that they elicit through their interactions with their children (Bronfenbrenner, 1986; Garrett et al., 1994; Ogbu, 1981). Therefore, in studying Table 5.4, consider the ages as approximations and recognize that the sequence may indeed vary. For instance, some children scoot in a seated position rather than crawl. This represents a variation, but not a developmental abnormality.

TABLE 5.4   Developmental Milestones in Motor Control during the First Year

Age	Motor Development
Birth–3 months	Supports head when in prone position
	Lifts head
	Supports weight on elbows
	Hands relax from the grasping reflex
	Visually follows a moving object
	Pushes with feet against lap when held upright
	Makes reflexive stepping movements when held in a standing position
	Sits with support
	Turns from side to back
3–6 months	Slaps at bath water
	Kicks feet when prone
	Plays with toes
	Reaches but misses dangling object
	Shakes and stares at toy placed in hand
	Head self-supported when held at shoulder
	Turns from back to side
	Sits with props
	Makes effort to sit alone
	Exhibits crawling behaviors
	Rocks on all fours
	Draws knees up and falls forward
6–9 months	Rolls from back to stomach
	Crawls using both hands and feet
	Sits alone steadily
	Pulls to standing position in crib
	Raises self to sitting posture
	Successfully reaches and grasps toy
	Transfers object from one hand to the other
	Stands up by furniture
	Cruises along crib rail
	Makes stepping movements around furniture
9–12 months	Exhibits "mature" crawling
	Cruises holding on to furniture
	Walks with two hands held
	Sits without falling
	Stands alone
	May walk alone
	Attempts to crawl up stairs
	Grasps object with thumb and forefinger

Infants with Special Needs

Infants whose prenatal development was less than optimal owing to the challenges of poverty, maternal health complications, inadequate nutrition, or teratogenic disturbances to fetal development or those who experienced prematurity or other birth trauma are most often infants identified as being *at risk*. Their growth and development is expected to be fraught with challenges that may require specialized care, treatment, and educational practices. Infants who are at risk for poor or delayed development or who have disabling conditions require assessment and identification that lead to timely diagnosis and intervention. The Apgar Scale, the Brazelton Neonatal Behavioral Assessment Scale, the Bayley Scales of Infant Development, and the Bayley Infant Neurodevelopmental Screener are examples of tests that are frequently used to provide initial and diagnostic information.

In addition to earliest possible intervention, infants with special needs require knowledge and special sensitivity on the part of their caregivers. Sometimes, the challenges of caring for an infant with special needs can be daunting for parents, family members, and nonparental caregivers. Today, Part C (formerly Part H): Early Intervention Program for Infants and Toddlers with Disabilities (Birth through age two) of the Individuals with Disabilities Education Act (IDEA) provides federal funds to states for services specifically for birth through age 2 and provides funds to develop, establish, and maintain a statewide system that offers early intervention services. The law provides for the following groups of children:

1. Infants and children who have a measurable developmental delay in one or more of the following developmental domains: cognitive, physical, language/communication, social, emotional, and adaptive, or self-help behavior.

2. Children who have a diagnosed physical or mental condition that could result in a developmental delay (e.g., Down syndrome, multiple sclerosis, sensory impairments, cerebral palsy, autism).

3. Children who are at risk of experiencing developmental delay, as determined by the state, if intervention is not provided.

Relationship of Physical and Motor Development to Psychosocial Development

Increasing physical and motor abilities during the first year expand the infant's psychosocial horizons. By communicating hunger, pain, and happiness cues through crying, cooing, and other vocalizations, infants learn that they can draw others into interactions with them. When these interactions are positive and supportive, infants learn to trust parents and caregivers and themselves to meet their needs. Each new developmental milestone brings with it new sets of behaviors and new types of interactions between infant and caregivers. For most infants, each new ability elicits encouragement, praise, and joy, supporting an emerging sense of self. As motor abilities increase, parents, siblings, and caregivers often begin to perceive the infant as more "grown up" and may unwittingly attribute greater self-sufficiency to the infant than is really the case. Misattributions—for example, expecting the infant to hold her own bottle for feeding, judge the depth of a stair step, or manage playthings designed for older children—compromise the infant's safety and deflates an emerging sense of confidence.

As a rule, motor development proceeds from the upper region of the body to the lower.

As the infant becomes more mobile, safety becomes a real and immediate concern. Concerns about safety bring about new forms of communicating, which include facial expressions, voice tone and pitch, and verbal cautions and commands. Keeping children safe while encouraging the types of activities that enhance motor development requires both vigilance and understanding. Undue restraint and excessive restrictions, particularly if delivered in impatience and anger, frighten and confuse the infant. Such interactions can reduce children's emerging self-confidence and willingness to explore, learn, and express themselves (Comer & Poussaint, 1992). While it may be necessary to say "no" and "don't touch" often, overuse of such restrictions can cause infants to associate negative and disapproving responses with the people who mean the most to them. Attempts to explore and investigate and to try out emerging skills are thus hindered, as is the confidence and independence that new skills bring. It is better to establish safe, "child-friendly" environments with supervision that offers substitutes and distractions than to impose constant verbal restrictions (Meyerhoff, 1994).

Relationship of Physical and Motor Development to Cognition

Motor experiences in infancy form the basis of meaning in earliest cognitive development. At first, movements are unintentional (as with many reflexes); later, most of them become purposeful. Piaget's (1952) stages of cognitive development begin with the *sensorimotor* stage, from birth to age 2. This sensorimotor stage of cognitive development follows a pattern from random, involuntary reflex activity, in which cognition is dominated by sensory input, to anticipatory and intentional behaviors, which are facilitated by increasing large and fine motor controls and mobility.

An environment that is rich in sensory input—sights, sounds, tastes, aromas, textures, and movement—has been shown to enhance brain growth and neurological development in infants (Shore, 1997). Talking, singing, sharing books, and interacting socially with the infant provide needed input for a rapidly developing mind. An environment that encourages social interactions and freedom to explore is essential to a well-integrated neurological and cognitive system.

FACTORS INFLUENCING PHYSICAL AND MOTOR DEVELOPMENT

Genetic Makeup

Each infant is a unique individual with a special genetic endowment. This genetic endowment is observable in physical features such as eye, hair, and skin color; shape and size of facial features; body build; activity levels; and so on. It is also related to mental and psychosocial characteristics such as temperament, some forms of mental retardation, and certain psychological disorders. Research in genetics is beginning to pinpoint the influence of heredity on less observable characteristics such as size and functioning of the internal organs, susceptibility to disease, psychological strengths and disorders, and numerous other facets of human individuality. Gene mapping research holds promise for identifying genetic anomalies and perhaps gene therapy to alleviate or minimize the influence of certain genes on developmental outcomes. Screening tests during pregnancy to detect genetic abnormalities allow for early identification and consideration of appropriate intervention strategies.

Integrity of Prenatal Development

Chapter 3 described very rapid development during the prenatal period. To the extent that this critical period in growth and development is protected from hazard, the integrity of the fetus is ensured. As reviewed in Chapter 3, studies of the vulnerability of the fetus during various prenatal stages indicate that there are both immediate and long-term effects of unhealthy intrauterine environments. Infants who benefit from a healthy prenatal journey—one that is free of drugs, toxins, poor nutrition, maternal stress, and other environmental hazards—are less likely to experience the myriad and sometimes devastating health, growth, and developmental outcomes associated with poor or inadequate intrauterine environments.

Birth Weight

Both low and high birth weights are associated with growth and development anomalies. Prematurity is measured by gestational age, which ranges from 23 weeks or less to a full term of 38 to 42 weeks. Gestational age is an important predictor of survival and developmental outcomes. Infants born at full term but weighing less than expected for a full-term baby are considered small for gestational age (SGA). Usually, these infants are healthy, but they are immature and small and have insufficient body fat to assist in regulation of body temperature. Weight gain is usually their primary challenge; however, there may be other, more serious reasons for the infant's failure to gain sufficient weight in utero.

A study of pregnant women exposed to air pollution from the World Trade Center attacks found that their infants at birth were up to ½ pound smaller than infants born to women who were not exposed. Keeping in mind that the exposure was extremely high though of short duration, this study suggests that exposure to air pollution may restrict intrauterine growth (Berkowitz et al., 2003). **Low birth weight** (LBW) infants range from 3.5 to 5.5 pounds. Infants in this birth weight range not only must build fat stores, but, perhaps more critical, may face respiratory distress syndrome (RDS) because of immature lungs and breathing mechanisms. While the

low birth weight:
a weight at birth of less than 5½ pounds, or 2,500 grams

majority of LBW infants have normal outcomes, they are at higher risk for mild to severe problems in cognition, cerebral palsy, convulsions, delayed speech, and visual and auditory impairments.

Very low birth weight (VLBW) infants weigh less than 3 pounds. These infants are extremely immature and need intensive neonatal care to help them survive. VLBW infants account for only 1.2% of births, but account for 46% of infant deaths (National Center for Health Statistics, 1994). They are at higher risk of dying in the first 28 days—some estimate 40 times more likely—than mature newborns (Brecht, 1989). Sometimes, their care requires lengthy and costly hospitalization. There is some evidence that very low birth weight infants may remain shorter and lighter in weight into adulthood and may be subject to adult health issues relating to metabolic and/or cardiac risks (Hack et al., 2003). While advances in neonatal medicine have resulted in increased survival prospects for these tiny babies, they are at extreme risk for long-term health problems and disabilities (Table 5.5).

TABLE 5.5   When to Worry about At-Risk Infants and Toddlers

Age	Phase	Primary Tasks	Warning Signs
0–3 months	Taking in	Crying for basic needs, developing attention, calming when needs met	Poor head control, no social smile, no visual/auditory responses, feeding problems, difficult to soothe, not attentive to faces
4–8 months	Reaching out	Attachment to adult, expanding interest in toys and people	No sitting, no mobility, no vocalizations, not seeking attention, not interested in toys/objects, feeding and sleeping problems
9–14 months	Moving out	Exploration, communication	Not moving from one position to another, asymmetric movement, no imitation, rigid play routines, no gestural or verbal communication
14–20 months	Speaking up	Learning by imitation, seeking independence	Not walking, not talking, not understanding directions, not using objects for intended purposes
21–30 months	Speaking out	Imagination, communication	Few words, no word combinations, no constructive or imaginative play, persistent withdrawn or aggressive behaviors
30–42 months	Playing alone	Independence, peer relations	Does not attend to age-appropriate tasks to completion, withdrawn or repetitive behaviors that cannot be interrupted, unintelligible speech, tantrums, lack of independence in self-help skills

Source: "When to worry about infants and toddlers 'at risk,'" by C. Andrew, 1998, *ACEI Focus on Infants and Toddlers, 11,* p. 2. Copyright 1998 by the Association for Childhood Education International, Olney, MD. Reprinted with permission.

An infant is considered large for gestational age if the birth weight is above the 90th **percentile** on intrauterine growth chart measures. These infants appear quite mature and healthy, but require immediate diagnosis and treatment. Women with gestational diabetes, women who have had multiple pregnancies, and an overproduction of growth hormone during fetal development are some possible risk factors for large-for-gestational-age infants. The birthing process may be particularly difficult for these infants, and many are delivered through cesarean section.

Preventing premature, low-birth-weight, and large-for-gestational-age neonates is a complex and challenging task, which involves addressing a number of issues: poverty; at-risk lifestyles; poor nutrition; inadequate health care; mother's age and health; number and character of prior pregnancies; genetics; in utero medical treatment; modern medical discoveries, ethics; and education.

percentile: a rank reflecting an individual's position relative to others, indicating the percentage of others falling below the noted rank or percentile

Socioeconomic Circumstances

Infant and family well-being depend on adequate food, shelter, clothing, transportation, and preventive and medical health care. The extent to which these family needs are met is dependent on income and available resources both within the family and in the community. Knowledge about, eligibility, and willingness to access local, state, and federal assistance programs such as the U.S. Special Supplemental Nutrition Program for Women, Infants, and Children (WIC) and the State Children's Health Insurance Program (SCHIP) also contribute to infant and family well-being. Population studies for the year 2002 reveal that 16% of U.S. children lived in families with incomes below the poverty line, and 6% of U.S. children lived in extreme poverty (Federal Interagency Forum of Child and Family Statistics, 2003).

Poverty has both immediate and long-term effects on child growth, development, and learning. Children living in poverty are more likely to experience food insecurity, leading to poor or inappropriate diets and malnutrition, and limited or neglected health care, including failure to immunize; have dental assessments; have timely treatment for diseases, infections, and injuries; and they have limited or no attention to psychological needs. Families whose energies are taxed by overwhelming economic issues may have little to share with children for nurturing, playful interactions, and enriching learning opportunities. Families receiving welfare assistance or making transitions to the workforce or work training may find the cost of child care for infants prohibitive, and thus make alternative arrangements that may or may not be in the child's best interest.*

GENERAL HEALTH AND FREEDOM FROM DISEASE

Regular Health Check-ups and Immunizations

Regular visits to the pediatrician or family health care specialist are necessary to monitor the infant's progress in growth and development; assess nutritional needs; treat infections, allergies, and illness; and administer disease-preventing

---

*Infant child care costs are always higher than the costs for older children due primarily to the need for a smaller adult-to-child ratio required by most state licensing standards. Other issues associated with nonparental infant care are discussed later in this chapter.

immunizations. The American Academy of Pediatrics recommends preventive health care visits for healthy infants and children at 1, 2, 4, 6, 9, 12, 15, and 18 months, then annually from ages 2 through 6, and then every 2 years through adolescence. More frequent visits may be necessary for children with special needs and between regular check-ups as the need arises. Newborns are routinely tested for phenylketonuria (PKU), an inborn error of metabolism in which abnormal levels of the enzyme phenylalanine form in the blood; if untreated, PKU leads to mental retardation and other abnormalities. When detected and treated within the first three weeks after birth with a specialized diet, developmental outcomes are better than when the diet is started later. In addition to checking growth progress through weight, height, and head circumference measurements, the physician and parent have an opportunity to discuss the child's growth and development, preventive health care measures, individual nutritional requirements, treatment of allergies, and other health and developmental concerns.

Fortunately, immunizations now prevent many life-threatening diseases in infants and children, and promising new vaccines are on the horizon. Infants and young children receive a standard series of immunizations against hepatitis B, diphtheria, tetanus, pertussis (whooping cough), Haemophilus influenzae type B, polio, measles, mumps, and rubella. All of these immunizations need to be given to children before they are two years old to protect them during their most vulnerable early months and years. Recommended vaccination schedules are updated annually and published every January. The American Academy of Pediatrics, in collaboration with the U.S. Centers for Disease Control and Prevention and the American Association of Family Physicians, develops the schedule, and through their practices, doctors (and local health departments) advise parents of any revisions or additions to the immunization schedule. They will also provide information about new or improved immunizations and alternative methods for administering them (e.g., nasal sprays, skin patches, time-release pills, genetically engineered food products). Additional vaccines are also available and administered when advisable, including chicken pox and rotavirus vaccines. (Rotavirus is responsible for the most common cause of diarrhea in infants and young children. Untreated diarrhea is a serious childhood infection, and can be

Preventive health care is provided through regular check-ups and immunizations.

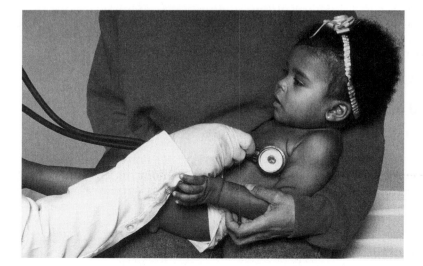

life threatening.) On the horizon are many new and improved vaccines including vaccines for ear infections, asthma, strep throat, juvenile diabetes, multiple sclerosis, AIDS, and some forms of cancer. Advances in genetics and immunology research are truly ushering in a new generation of vaccines and disease prevention and treatment practices.

The National Childhood Vaccine Injury Act (42 U.S.C. §300 aa-26) requires that physicians provide to a child's parent or legal representative before vaccination information about the vaccine that has been published by the Centers for Disease Control and Prevention. The physician or health care professional administering the vaccine must ensure that the person authorizing the vaccine reads and understands the vaccine information materials. The risks and benefits of immunization are discussed further in Chapter 8.

Dental Health

The first teeth begin to erupt between 5 and 9 months of age. The first teeth to erupt are usually the 2 lower middle incisors, followed in a few months by the 4 upper middle incisors. By the end of the first year, most infants have these 6 teeth. The complete set of 20 teeth does not erupt until around 2½ years. Pain associated with the eruption of teeth varies among infants. Some infants cry, are sleepy and fretful, seem to want to chew something, and drool considerably. Others appear to feel no pain or discomfort and may, to the surprise of their parents, present a "toothed" smile.

Care of teeth during the first year includes cleaning the infant's gums, tooth pads, and first teeth with gauze, and beginning the use of a very soft infant toothbrush after several teeth have erupted. This is not too early to get established with a dentist for assessment of dental needs and guidance on how to care for infant teeth and prevent caries.

Nutrition

The role of nutrition in ensuring optimal growth and developmental outcomes is paramount during prenatal development and infancy. During this period of very rapid growth, brain growth is particularly dramatic. Studies have linked impaired functioning of the central nervous system to poor nutrition in the early months of life (Dobbing, 1984; Galler, Ramsey, & Solimano, 1984) and to later cognitive and behavioral outcomes in childhood and adolescence (Galler, Ramsey, & Solimaso, 1985; Lucas, Morley, & Coles, 1998). Adequate nutrition helps to prevent illnesses and ensures the developmental integrity of the individual.

A major task of the newborn is that of learning to take in nourishment. This task is a complex one in which sensory–motor physiological capabilities, sleep/wake state, and focus of attention must all be coordinated. The reflex sucking system comes into play as the infant learns to coordinate sucking, swallowing, and breathing efficiently during the nursing process.

While most infants have little difficulty orally grasping the nipple of the breast or the bottle, sucking, swallowing, gagging, burping, and digesting, premature and small-for-gestational-age infants may have greater difficulty. Some of these fragile or ill infants may require **gavage feeding**. Newborns are always observed and assessed for feeding readiness and competence.

gavage feeding: introducing fluids or foods through a tube passed orally or through a nasal passage into the stomach

colostrum: the first fluid secreted by the mammary glands soon after childbirth, before true milk is formed

Breast-Feeding. Because of its biochemical composition, breast milk is uniquely suited to the infant's immature digestive system. It provides initial advantages through **colostrum**, the milk that precedes mature breast milk in the first several days after delivery. Colostrom provides immunity to a number of infections when the mother carries the immunities and is rich in the nutrients a newborn needs. Mature breast milk is secreted between the 3rd and 6th day after childbirth and changes over time (as long as breast-feeding takes place) to match the changing needs of the growing infant. Generally, for the first 6 months, breast milk provides all the fluids and nutrients an infant needs to be healthy. After 6 months, a pediatrician may prescribe supplements such as fluoride, vitamin C, and vitamin D if there is a need for them and may begin the introduction of selected solid foods. Health care professionals are encouraging mothers who choose to breast-feed to do so at least during the earliest months up to 5 to 6 months, but advise that continuing to breast-feed for 12 months results in more long-term benefits (American Academy of Pediatrics Work Group on Breastfeeding, 1997; U.S. Department of Health and Human Services, 1990a). Continuation beyond 12 months becomes a matter of mutual desirability.

Research documenting the benefits of breast-feeding to both infant and mother is compelling (American Academy of Pediatrics Work Group on Breast-feeding, 1997). For the infant, the following short- and long-term outcomes have been identified in numerous research studies in the United States, Canada, and other developed countries in Europe and elsewhere:

- Decreased risk for a number of acute and chronic diseases, including diarrhea, lower respiratory infection, otitis media (infection of the middle ear canal), bacterial meningitis, urinary tract infection, and allergies such as eczema, asthma, rhinitis, and food allergies.
- Possible protection against sudden infant death syndrome (SIDS), insulin-dependent diabetes mellitus, ulcerative colitis, Crohn's disease, lymphoma, and chronic digestive diseases.
- Possible lowering of low-density lipoproteins, or "bad" cholesterol, in an infant's blood.
- Improved oral facial development, preventing later poorly aligned teeth and potential for speech impediments (Davis & Bell, 1991).
- Possible enhancement of cognitive development and visual acuity (Jorgensen, Hernell, Lund, Hilmer, & Michaelsen, 1996).
- Positive association between duration of breast feeding and adult intelligence (Mortensen, Michaelsen, Sanders, & Reinisch, 2002).

For mothers, the benefits of breast-feeding are equally impressive:

- Increases in the level of oxytocin (a hormone that facilitates the excretion of milk through the milk ducts), which lessens postpartum bleeding and helps the uterus to return to its prepregnancy size and position.
- Burning of more calories, resulting in earlier return to prepregnancy weight.
- Building of bone strength.
- Contribution to family planning (child spacing) by suppressing ovulation.

BOX 5.1   Mother-Friendly Employers

Many mothers juggle their parenting responsibilities and working outside the home. Women who return to work and choose to continue breast-feeding their infants benefit from business practices that are mother friendly. Businesses, as well, benefit through reduced absenteeism, reduced employee turnover, shorter maternity leaves, increased productivity, recruitment incentive, fewer health insurance claims, and a positive image in the community. A number of states have enacted laws or policies that recognize businesses that are mother friendly. Such policies include:

A workplace atmosphere that supports a woman's choice to breast-feed her infant

Work schedule flexibility that provides timely breaks for lactating mothers to breast-feed their infants or to express breast milk

A private lactation room that is equipped with a sink and a clean, safe water source for hand washing and for rinsing breast pump equipment, comfortable furnishings, an electrical outlet, a phone, and a locking door or an appropriate "reserved" sign

Access to hygienic storage (e.g., refrigerator, ice chest) where breast milk can be kept cool, safe, and free from contamination

A procedure for informing employees of the employer's mother-friendly policy

Mother-friendly businesses may also provide:

Prenatal or postpartum classes on breast-feeding and infant nutrition through their wellness programs

The services of a lactation consultant

Literature and other resources on infant feeding and nutrition

- Reduction of the risk of ovarian cancer and, in premenopausal women, the incidence of breast cancer.
- Convenience, as the breast milk has been "properly stored," comes already prepared, and is ready to serve at the appropriate temperature. It can be pumped and stored for feedings when mother must be away or when other members of the family wish to participate in feeding the infant. (See Box 5.1.)

There are certain foods and substances to be avoided if the mother chooses to breast-feed. Some foods ingested by the mother may alter the content and character of the milk and may also disagree with the infant's delicate digestion and absorption system. Some medications can be dangerous for the infant, though some are not. Both prescription and nonprescription drugs should be used only on the advice of a physician. Illicit drugs, alcohol, and caffeine have all been shown to have dangerous adverse effects on the nursing infant. Certainly, smoking while breast-feeding should be avoided, for the effects of secondhand smoke are now well documented. Indeed, secondhand smoke has been shown to increase the incidence of asthma, wheezing, and chronic bronchitis and the risk of SIDS (American Academy of Pediatrics, 1998b; Gergen, Fowler, Maurer, Davis, & Overpeck, 1998).

Human Milk Banks.   Few health care professionals today would not encourage breast-feeding. However, some mothers may be unable to breast-feed for various reasons (infant's health status and hospitalization needs, mother's health, medications, disabilities, employment, adoption) or may simply choose not to do so. For some of these mothers and infants, there is the option to provide human milk provided by human milk donor banks, wherein human milk is obtained from well-screened donors, pasteurized, and made available to eligible applicants. There are six regional human milk banks in North America, five of which are members of the Human Milk Banking Association of North America (HMBANA). HMBANA member banks must follow stringent guidelines based on recommendations from the U.S. Centers for Disease Control and Prevention and updated yearly, and take additional precautions to protect against the transmission of infectious diseases (Arnold & Tully, 1996).

Formula Feeding.   The decision to provide formula is best guided by a pediatrician or pediatric health care specialist to ensure the most suitable product for the infant. Research to improve the nutritional content, quality, and digestibility of commercial formulas has evolved over many decades and is ongoing. The U.S. Food and Drug Administration bases its regulations of infant formula on standards for infant formulas developed by the American Academy of Pediatrics Committee on Nutrition. Today's formulas are designed to simulate human milk and provide essential proteins, fats, carbohydrates, vitamins, and minerals. Thus, the choice to provide formula instead of human milk during the first months is certainly a viable option. Formula can also be used as a supplement for breast milk when the mother must be away or chooses to omit a feeding or when the mother's breast milk is inadequate. In addition, there are special-purpose formulas for specific nutritional or medical needs.

To ensure optimal benefit from formula feeding, formula must be mixed according to the directions supplied by the manufacturer and prescribed by the infant's pediatrician. Overdiluted formula has less nutritional value and may fill the infant's stomach but not satisfy the infant's hunger; thus, it may fail to provide enough nutrients and calories to sustain growth. Overdilution is often a problem in economically disadvantaged families, who dilute the formula to make it last longer and thus reduce its cost. In addition to failing to meet the infant's nutritional needs, overdiluting can lead to **water intoxication**, a very serious condition that can cause brain swelling and convulsions in infants. Underdiluted formula may also cause problems. Because of water loss through urine, feces, regurgitation, fever, or vomiting, underdiluted formula can fail to meet the infant's need for fluid intake, leading to dehydration and other complications.

Other precautions need to be taken in feeding an infant. Bottle-fed infants must be held in a comfortable position during feeding. The bottle should never be propped. Because the infant lacks the motor skills necessary to move the propped bottle, there is a high risk for choking and asphyxiation. Propping the bottle has other risks as well. When the infant is lying down while bottle feeding, bacteria

water intoxication: a dangerous, potentially life-threatening physiological condition caused by overconsumption of water apart from or in overdiluted formula or juices

grow in the pooled liquid in the mouth and cheeks, then make their way to the eustachian tubes, resulting in painful and potentially damaging inner ear infections. Tooth decay in older infants can also occur when formula stays in the mouth too long, coating the teeth with sugars.

Infants' psychological need to be held when being fed is also important. Whether breast- or bottle-fed, infants experience both physical and emotional closeness to their parent or caregiver while being held and cuddled during feeding. Calm, unhurried feeding times contribute to the infant's sense of well-being and trust and enhance the bond between infant and caregiver.

Satiety.   Sensitivity to the infant's hunger and **satiety** cues also enhances infants' trust in both themselves and their caregivers. Overfeeding or underfeeding results when adults fail to recognize these cues. Turning the head away from a nipple, facial expressions of distaste, and other bodily attempts to refuse food are the infant's way of communicating satiety. Allowing infants to eat what they need without insisting on further intake helps infants to recognize their own feelings of hunger or fullness. Adults must also avoid giving food indiscriminately in an attempt to curtail crying. Not all crying is hunger related. Providing food or drink every time the child cries establishes a pattern of satisfying discomforts, regardless of what they are, by eating. The obvious outcome of this misguided behavior is obesity and poor physical and psychosocial health.

satiety: the feeling of having consumed sufficient food to satisfy hunger

For most healthy infants, feeding schedules break into 4-hour intervals. Some infants may need to be fed every three hours; smaller infants will need food every 2 hours. Caregivers soon learn to adjust to these rhythms, knowing that as the infant grows and matures, the schedule will become more predictable.

Solid Foods.   Taking in solid foods is a different developmental task than sucking and swallowing liquids. Now the infant must mouth or chew the food to soften it, experience its texture as well as its taste, move it to the back of the mouth, and successfully swallow it. This task is not always well coordinated, as is demonstrated by the infant's need for a bib.

Contrary to a somewhat common belief, early introduction of solid foods does not assist the infant in sleeping through the night. Hunger does awaken infants in the night, but nutritionists advise that the decision to introduce solid foods must be based on the infant's need for the nutrients provided by solid foods and on the infant's physiological readiness to handle solid foods, which usually emerges between 5 and 6 months of age.

The introduction of solid foods usually begins with iron-fortified cereals. New foods are introduced one at a time, and usually once a week, to accustom the infant to this new experience and to detect any allergic reaction to specific foods. As the intake of solid foods increases, the need for milk or formula decreases. Neither sugar nor salt should be added to foods given to infants; their immature digestive systems do not handle added seasonings well.

As the infant grows and learns to eat a variety of foods, care must be given to providing a balanced diet consisting of foods selected from the vegetable, fruit, meat, grain, and cereal groups. Foods selected for the youngest eaters should be appealing in color, flavor, texture, and shape. Self-feeding foods, foods that can be held in the hand or grasped from a tray, must be easy to chew and swallow. Mealtimes should be unhurried and pleasant.

*Clostridium
botulinum:*
the bacterium that
causes botulism

botulism:
a potentially fatal
form of food
poisoning

Food Safety.   In providing solid foods to an infant, several precautions must be taken. Foremost is avoiding food contamination. Foods should be fresh and properly stored. Adults must observe scrupulously hygienic procedures for preparing and serving baby meals: washed hands; clean utensils; foods kept at appropriate hot or cold temperatures; and covered, sanitary, and refrigerated storage of unused portions. It is best not to reheat leftover baby food, since illness is caused by microorganisms that grow in foods at room temperature.

Some foods cause particular problems for infants and young children. For instance, honey and corn syrup have been found to contain ***Clostridium botulinum***, the organism responsible for **botulism**. In infants less than 1 year old, the immature gastrointestinal tract allows this organism to become active and potentially lethal (Christian & Gregor, 1993). Foods that have caused choking in infants and young children include hot dogs and other chunks of meat, peanuts, grapes, raisins, hard or chewy candy, carrots, popcorn, fruit gel snacks, and chewing gum. Selection of nutritional substitutes for these foods and close supervision as the infant learns to handle new foods are imperative. Infants and small children should not be given foods to eat in a moving vehicle or as they are toddling about, as this increases the risk of choking.

Calorie Needs.   Concerns about obesity, cholesterol, and other diet-related health problems have led some parents to mistakenly believe that reducing fat and calories in the infant's diet is necessary. Quite the contrary is true. Body size, proportions, and composition are in a period of very rapid change. The infant's calorie needs per unit of body weight far exceed those of older children and adults to maintain their rapid growth. In the absence of teeth, infants depend on consuming sufficient amounts of breast milk or formula to meet their increased caloric needs. In addition, during the last trimester of prenatal development and during the first few years of postnatal development, myelination of nerve fibers takes place. Fat is a major component of myelin (the tissue that surrounds the nerves as they mature) and, as such, is an essential part of the infant's diet if optimal neurological integrity is to be obtained. The American Academy of Pediatrics (1998a) advises against practices that limit the diets of infants.

Colic.   *Colic* is abdominal discomfort that occurs in infants two weeks to three months of age. It is characterized by irritability, fussing, or crying sometimes for more than 3 hours per day and occurring as often as 3 days per week. It can be quite painful for the infant and distressing to parents. Why colic begins to appear at this age is unclear. Some suggested causes are swallowed air, high-carbohydrate foods, overfeeding, intolerance for cow's milk, intestinal allergy, a stressful environment, or impending illness (Pillitteri, 1992). Some infants seem more prone to colic than others, and no universal treatment exists, since the causes vary. Physical examination by a pediatrician may be needed to determine whether more serious problems exist.

Some preventive measures can be taken to reduce the incidence of colic. These include feeding in an unhurried and calm manner, burping at regular intervals during feeding, avoiding either overfeeding or underfeeding, and, with a physician's help, identifying possible food allergies. When colic occurs, holding the infant upright or lying the infant prone across the lap may be helpful. Sometimes, changing caregivers helps. A tired and frustrated parent or caregiver whose attempts to soothe the infant have met with failure may, if these efforts continue, exacerbate the tensions in both the infant and the caregiver.

Safety

The infant's growing mobility and inclination to put things in the mouth lead to a number of health and safety issues. The most common safety concerns during the first year are automobile accidents, falls, burns, choking or suffocation, poisonings, and drowning. Adult failure to recognize the infant's changing abilities and curiosities is often the reason infants get injured.

Infant Spaces and Furnishings.   The infant's surroundings must be sanitary and frequently examined for potential dangers: objects on the floor that could scratch, cut, or go into the mouth (e.g., balloons, coins, marbles, small toy parts, buttons, safety pins); exposed electrical outlets and electrical wires that could be pulled or mouthed; furnishings that topple easily; toxic substances within easy reach (e.g., medicines, cosmetics, household cleaning and gardening supplies, arts and crafts products); poisonous plants; swimming pools, bathtubs, and other bodies of water; hot water faucets and unsanitary toilet bowls; and many others.

All baby equipment and clothing should be selected according to current safety standards. These standards apply to bassinets, cribs, car seats, carriages, swings, playpens, walkers, jogging strollers, pacifiers, toys, and all other baby supplies and equipment. The Consumer Products Safety Commission regularly publishes information about safe products for children and items that have been recalled because of the hazards they pose. Parents and caregivers can avail themselves of this information at no cost, a responsible thing to do to prevent

Proper use of approved infant safety seats helps to prevent serious injuries or death.

unnecessary (and sometimes lethal) injuries to infants and children. (See the Further Readings and Resources at the end of this chapter.)

Transportation.   Beginning in infancy, automobile child safety seats must be consistently used in transporting an infant or a young child in a motor vehicle. Responding to the fact that more children are killed and injured in automobile accidents than from any other type of injury, every state now requires that infants and children be properly restrained when riding in a vehicle. Proper use of infant safety seats helps to prevent death and injury. The Federal Motor Vehicle Safety Standard Act 213 mandates that passenger safety seats manufactured after January 1981 must meet certain standards for design and use. However, this law did not prohibit the sale of infant passenger seats manufactured before this date. Consequently, some unsafe infant passenger seats may still be on the market through hand-me-downs, garage sales, and thrift shops. Since September 1, 1995, the National Highway Traffic Safety Administration has required that all manual safety belts have a lockable feature to lock them securely around child safety seats and that they be properly tethered to the adult seat back. Many automobile manufacturers now have integrated safety seats for children and other automobile child safety features.

The safest place for children of all ages to ride is in the back seat of a vehicle (National Safety Council, 2002). Infants should never be placed in the front seat of a vehicle that has a passenger air bag. Infants should ride facing the back of the car until they are 1 year old and weigh at least 20 pounds. Belt-positioning booster seats with lap/shoulder belt securing can be used for older and larger babies. Car seat manufacturer's instructions should be conscientiously followed, since incorrectly installed and secured car seats place children at risk in the event of a sudden stop or accident. Begin consistent (never wavering) use of car seats and restraints in infancy, and as children get older, the use of appropriate vehicle safety restraints will become an established habit.

Toys.   Wise selection of toys for infants involves choosing toys that are constructed of pieces too large to swallow, are lightweight and easily grasped, and are free of sharp edges, projectiles, batteries, or small removable parts. They should be made of washable, nontoxic materials and should be sturdy enough to withstand vigorous play. Toys should be selected for their sensory appeal and should be age appropriate for the infant who will play with them.

Opportunities to Interact, Explore, and Play

Each new motor skill extends the infant's ability to interact with people and objects in the environment. Infants enjoy looking at colorful objects in the environment. They enjoy listening to the human voice and to recordings of pleasing or familiar sounds and music and experiencing different textures such as soft toys, bedding, carpeting, and so on. Toys and focused interactions in which infant and parent or caregiver talk, laugh, imitate each other, play peek-a-boo and pat-a-cake, explore the surroundings, label objects and events, and share pictures and cloth or board books all provide opportunities to play, learn, and develop social competence. Play is essential to all facets of growth and development:

physical/motor, psychosocial, cognitive, language, and literacy. We will discuss play and play behaviors in the context of these developmental areas throughout the text.

HEALTH AND WELL-BEING ISSUES IN INFANT DEVELOPMENT

Infant Mortality Rates and Risks

Infant mortality rates (deaths during the first year of life) in the United States appear to be decreasing but remain alarmingly high for a modern industrialized and technologically advanced nation. Despite great strides in medical and child health protection over the years, in 1999 the infant mortality rate for all races was 7.0 deaths per 1,000 live births (Federal Interagency Forum on Child and Family Statistics, 2003). In the United States, an African-American infant is more than twice as likely to die during the first year as an Anglo infant (Children's Defense Fund, 2002). The causes of neonatal and infant deaths among all races relate to poor prenatal and newborn care, prematurity and low birth weight, congenital malformations and diseases, and complications associated with certain **syndromes**, including fetal alcohol syndrome, fetal tobacco syndrome, fetal marijuana syndrome, chemical withdrawal syndrome, and sudden infant death syndrome (SIDS). The damaging effects of alcohol, tobacco, and drugs have been discussed in previous chapters. However, a brief discussion of SIDS at this point might be helpful.

syndrome: a group of combined symptoms that characterizes a physiological or psychological disorder

Sudden infant death syndrome is the sudden and unexpected death of an apparently healthy infant during the first year. It is the most common cause of death between 1 and 6 months of age, peaking between 2 and 4 months of age. It is estimated that 90% of SIDS deaths occur before the age of 6 months (American Academy of Pediatrics, Committee on Child Abuse and Neglect, 2001).

In the past, it was thought that infants who died in their cribs had smothered in their covers (thus the term *crib death*). However, since its identification as a syndrome in the 1960s, this perplexing phenomenon has commanded considerable research, and its actual cause or causes are still difficult to pinpoint.

In a rigorous yet elusive search for causes over the past three decades, scientists have identified a number of factors associated with SIDS. While these factors are not causes in themselves, they have helped researchers to identify high-risk populations. The following factors have been associated with SIDS: late or no prenatal care; prematurity; low birth weight; low APGAR scores; male gender; **apnea**; sleeping in prone position; sleeping on soft surfaces; maternal age younger than 20 at first pregnancy or younger than 25 during subsequent pregnancies and an interval of less than 12 months since the preceding pregnancy; multiple births; maternal history of smoking, drug abuse, or anemia; and sibling(s) who died of SIDS (American Academy of Pediatrics, Committee on Child Abuse and Neglect, 2001; American Academy of Pediatrics Task Force on Infant Sleep Position and Sudden Infant Death Syndrome, 2000; Jeffrey, Megevand, & Page, 1999; Schoendorf & Kiely, 1992). In a small proportion of SIDS cases, child abuse is suspected (American Academy of Pediatrics, Committee on Child Abuse and Neglect, 2001).

apnea: absence of breathing for a period of up to 20 seconds

metabolic: pertains to the body's complex chemical conversion of food into substances and energy necessary for maintenance of life

A number of theories have attempted to explain SIDS. Some have implicated heredity; others have suggested upper respiratory viruses or a bacterium such as *C. botulinum*; still others have proposed **metabolic** disorders, allergies, **hyperthermia**

hyperthermia: a very high body temperature

hypothermia:
a below-normal body
temperature

and **hypothermia**, and central nervous system abnormalities. One popular explanation relates to the infant's cardiovascular system. Studies have found, in a number of cases, an abnormality in the way the brain regulates breathing and heart rate (Hunt & Brouillette, 1987). Subsequent studies suggest that SIDS may be due to abnormalities in the brainstem, which can be associated with delayed development of arousal along with immature cardiovascular and cardiorespiratory control. During sleep, the infant may not arouse sufficiently enough to breathe efficiently (American Academy of Pediatrics, Committee on Child Abuse and Neglect, 2001). However, not all infants studied exhibited this abnormality, so this theory awaits additional research. In spite of years of research, scientists are still unable to identify a specific cause or causes.

The incidence of SIDS appears to have decreased in recent years, owing in part to a *Back to Sleep* campaign. The Back to Sleep campaign has attempted to educate parents and child care personnel about SIDS and the importance of placing infants on their sides (with a rolled blanket for a prop, if necessary) or on their backs to sleep, as a preventive strategy, rather than on their stomachs. This practice is now widespread, and the reduction in the incidence of SIDS has been attributed to it.

Abuse and Neglect

Legally, abuse and neglect are defined in the United States as "the physical or mental injury, sexual abuse, negligent treatment, or maltreatment of a child under the age of eighteen by a person who is responsible for the child's welfare under circumstances which indicate that the child's health or welfare is harmed or threatened thereby" (Child Abuse Prevention and Treatment Act of 1975, 42 U.S. Code 5101).

Abuse takes many forms: physical, in which bodily injury is inflicted; psychological, in which a child is cursed, berated, ignored, or rejected; and sexual abuse, which ranges from exposure and fondling to incest and rape. The victims of sexual abuse are sometimes infants. Studies have found that infants and children under age three are particularly susceptible to child abuse (Mayhall & Norgard, 1983). Frustrations over infant crying, colic, diaper soiling, eating, sleeping, and other stresses, as well as maternal depression, family stress, and lack of knowledge about child development, may provoke an abusive adult. A common form of infant abuse is known as **shaken baby syndrome** and appears mostly in infants younger than six months of age. Shaking an infant or small child can cause serious physical and mental damage and even death.

**shaken baby
syndrome:**
head (intracranial)
or long bone injury
caused by forceful
shaking or jerking of
an infant; may result
in serious injuries
(including blindness), and often
death

Failure to thrive in infancy due to maternal deprivation or neglect has been documented. Studies have shown that some children who are raised in impoverished or neglectful conditions during the first year of life show signs of severe developmental retardation (Province & Lipton, 1962) and impaired neurological development (Perry, 1998). These infants exhibit delayed physical growth and skeletal development, resulting in heights and weights far below those expected for their ages. Neglected children are more susceptible to disease, have more gastrointestinal upsets, and are particularly emotionally vulnerable.

failure to thrive:
a condition in which
an apparently
healthy infant fails to
grow normally

Neglect may take different forms, such as inadequate dietary practices, which impede growth, and failure to provide other necessities such as clothing, shelter, supervision, and protection. Sometimes neglect includes denial of medical attention. Intellectual stimulation and emotional support may also be absent. Some infants are simply abandoned.

Abuse and neglect occur at all socioeconomic levels, in all ethnic groups, and in all types of families: one-parent, two-parent, extended, large, and small families. The incidence of abuse and neglect in families can be cyclical. Children who have been abused may become abusive adults (Gelles & Edfeldt, 1990), though intervention such as counseling and therapy, education, support groups for families, and subsequent positive life experiences may break the cycle. In some cases, children need to be removed from situations of neglect or abuse. All states have child-abuse-reporting laws under which suspected child abuse must be reported to appropriate authorities.

Recognizing the importance of the family in the child's development, the law provides for services to help families through counseling and other services and mandates that intervention services be provided in the types of settings in which infants and toddlers with disabilities could participate. This means that child care programs, nursery schools, public schools, and family care settings must make provisions to successfully integrate infants and toddlers with special needs into their programs. This includes providing additional and sometimes specialized training for adults who are responsible for the children, developing appropriate communicative and interactive skills, adapting physical environments, integrating remediation and intervention strategies into a developmentally appropriate curriculum, and working effectively with parents.

Nonparental Infant Care

Nonparental child care is a necessity for millions of U.S. families. It is estimated that each day, 13 million children spend a part or all of their day in nonparental care, and many of these children have been enrolled by 11 weeks of age (Children's Defense Fund, 2001). Because the early years of life are critical ones and because parents are increasingly depending on child care, it is essential that nonparental care be of the highest quality. High-quality child care is expensive and, as noted earlier, is more expensive for infants and toddlers than for older children. Wise selection of child care for infants and toddlers involves seeking well-trained, knowledgeable, and sensitive adults who have the personal qualities a parent determines will be good for their child. Adult-to-child ratios in group programs serving infants and toddlers ideally should be no more than one adult to three children. The home or center should meet health and safety standards, and the daily routines should be warm, supportive, infant friendly, stimulating, and satisfying. High-quality nonparental child care can be an enormous source of comfort to parents who need it. However, many families lack knowledge about how to choose high-quality child care, and the cost of such care often exceeds the family's ability to pay for it.

Those who provide infant care have a moral and ethical responsibility to be knowledgeable about infants' needs and the critical nature of early neurological and physiological development and the essential experiences needed to foster optimal growth and development. Through state licensing laws and standards, accreditation standards of the National Association for the Education of Young Children, and standards such as those set by the joint efforts of the American Public Health Association and American Academy of Pediatrics (2002), providers can assess their facilities, programs, and interactive environments and make continuous efforts to improve and enrich their programs so that parents who enlist their services can be confident in the choices they have made and the children they serve can benefit.

ROLE OF THE EARLY CHILDHOOD PROFESSIONAL

Facilitating Physical and Motor Development in Infants

1. Advocate for adequate and appropriate food, clothing, and shelter for families.

2. Encourage (and assist where possible) families to access professional medical and health care supervision.

3. Be ever vigilant for infants who may need early identification and assessment of special needs and timely intervention.

4. Provide sanitary and safe surroundings for infants.

5. Provide sensorimotor stimulation through engaging interactions, sensory-rich environments, and opportunities to explore.

6. Provide an encouraging, supportive, and predictable atmosphere of love, acceptance, and socially and emotionally satisfying interactions.

7. Provide guidance that is positive and instructive in helping the increasingly mobile infant to discover his or her capabilities in an atmosphere of both physical and psychological protection and safety.

8. Establish collaborative and supportive relationships with parents of infants.

9. Stay abreast of health and safety alerts, regulations, and laws to protect infants and young children.

10. Become aware of community resources that address the needs of infants and their families.

KEY TERMS

apnea
atrophy
axon
behaviorist perspective
botulism
cephalocaudal
cerebral cortex
Clostridium botulinum
colostrum
dendrites
developmental
   interactionist perspective
embryonic cell mass
failure to thrive
fontanelles
gavage feeding

glial cells
hyperthermia
hypothermia
kangaroo care
kinesthesis
low birth weight
maturationist perspective
metabolic
myelin
neural tube
neuron
neurotransmitter
percentile
perception
plasticity
primitive reflexes

proximodistal
psychological state
reflex
satiety
shaken baby syndrome
skeletal age
subcortical
survival reflexes
synapse
syndrome
systems perspective
temperament
transactional perspective
vernix caseosa
water intoxication

REVIEW STRATEGIES AND ACTIVITIES

1. Review the key terms individually or with a classmate.

2. Compare infant formulas and baby foods that are available at your local supermarket. What nutrients are listed on the labels and in what proportions? How do these foods differ? How are they alike? What considerations are essential in the selection of a formula or a solid food for individual infants?

3. Invite a child protective services professional from your state or regional health and human resources department to talk to the class about child abuse and neglect. What is the responsibility of the early childhood professional in dealing with abuse and neglect of young children?

4. Visit an accredited child care center or a family day care home that cares primarily for infants. Make a list of health and safety precautions practiced by the child caregivers and staff in these settings.

5. Identify and investigate support services and infant care programs for infants with special needs and their families.

6. Discuss with your classmates the issues surrounding infant health and safety and identify ways the early childhood professional can address these issues.

FURTHER READINGS

American Academy of Pediatrics, American Public Health Association, & U.S. Department of Health and Human Services. (2002). *Caring for our children* (2nd ed.). Elk Grove Village, IL: Author.

Cryer, D., & Harms, T. (Eds.). (2000). *Infants and toddlers in out-of-home care*. Baltimore: Brookes.

Dickerson, M. L. (2000). *Small victories: Conversations about prematurity, disability, vision loss, and success*. New York: American Foundation for the Blind.

Dietz, W. H., & Stern, L. (Eds.). (1999). *Guide to your child's nutrition*. Elk Grove Village, IL: American Academy of Pediatrics.

Gandini, L., & Edwards, C. P. (Eds.). (2001). *Bambini: The Italian approach to infant/toddler care*. New York: Teachers College Press.

Rogoff, B. (2003). *The cultural nature of human development*. New York: Oxford University Press.

Schiff, D., & Shelov, S. P. (1997). *Guide to your child's symptoms: Birth through adolescence*. Elk Grove Village, IL: American Academy of Pediatrics.

Shevlov, S. P. (1998). *Your baby's first year*. Elk Grove Village, IL: American Academy of Pediatrics.

Shonkoff, J. P., & Meisels, S. J. (Eds.). (2000). *Handbook of early childhood intervention* (2nd ed.). New York: Cambridge University Press.

Small, M. F. (2001). *Kids: How biology and culture shape the way we raise our children*. New York: Doubleday.

OTHER RESOURCES

American Academy of Pediatrics
    http://www.aap.org
Better Baby Care
    http://www.betterbabycare.org

Consumer Product Safety Commission
    4340 East West Highway, Suite 502, Bethesda, MD 20814-4408
    http://www.cpsc.gov/
    Hotline: 1-800-638-2772
Focus on Infants and Toddlers, 0 to 3, Newsletter
    Association for Childhood Education International
    17904 Georgia Ave., Ste. 215
    Olney, MD 20832
National Child Care Information Center (NCCIC)
    http://nccic.org
Pediatrics for Parents Newsletter
    P. O. Box 1069
    Bangor, ME 04402-1069
Zero to Three, Brain Wonders: Helping Babies and Toddlers Grow and Develop
    http://www.zerotothree.org/brainwonders

CHAPTER SIX

Psychosocial Development of the Infant

The first cry of a newborn baby in Chicago or Zamboango, in Amsterdam or Rangoon, has the same pitch and key, each saying, I am! I have come through! I belong! I am a member of the Family!

CARL SANDBURG

After studying this chapter, you will demonstrate comprehension by:

▶ Identifying important theories associated with psychosocial development.

▶ Describing the potential effects of earliest psychosocial experiences on brain growth and early neurological development.

▶ Relating the concept of essential experiences to psychosocial development during the first year.

▶ Identifying major social and emotional milestones in infancy.

▶ Describing factors that influence psychosocial development.

▶ Describing the role of adults in facilitating healthy psychosocial development in the infant.

Unlike the more visible physical characteristics and motor skills of infancy and early childhood, social and emotional development is less easily discerned. Infants' ways of expressing emotions and needs and of signaling their desire for social interaction are uniquely "infantile." At first, the infant is limited to crying and using body language to communicate needs. Crying and using body language convey many meanings and elicit varying responses from caregivers, depending on how these infant's cues are interpreted. Gradually, infants gain greater competence in communicating emotional and social needs as they interpret and adapt to the rhythms and behaviors of their caregivers, begin to trust their own ability to summons, begin to modulate their emotions, and begin to acquire language. The infant's caregivers, in tandem with this unfolding growth and development, are themselves developing caregiver–infant communicative styles and learning to interpret and adapt to the rhythms and behaviors of the infant. Psychosocial development during infancy depends on the ability of caregivers to understand and respond appropriately to infants' expressions of emotion and their very human desire for social interaction. This chapter explores the processes involved in the earliest stages of psychosocial development and emphasizes the importance of earliest interactions to personality development and mental health outcomes.

THEORIES OF PSYCHOSOCIAL DEVELOPMENT

The study of psychology in general and of psychosocial development in particular is concerned with how the human being behaves and what underlying and unseen mental processes shape and direct individual behaviors. In the past, and to a great extent today, research in psychology has relied on careful observation of infants and children in *naturalistic* settings (home and family contexts, laboratory nursery schools, play therapy settings, and other child care contexts). These

161

studies of the social and emotional actions, reactions, and interactions of infants and young children as they grow, develop, and learn in these varying contexts have yielded invaluable insights. Parenting and child care practices rely heavily on insights and continuing research of this nature. Complementing naturalistic studies and focusing them toward biological origins has been the research of neurobiologists. Today, through sophisticated imaging technologies, the biology of psychology has begun to further enlighten scholars and early childhood practitioners about the neurological origins of specific behavioral traits. Studies of early brain growth and neurological development are beginning to provide precise data on how and when certain behaviors emerge, what types of experiences enhance or thwart healthy neurological development, and how healthy psychosocial behaviors are promoted.

The study of psychosocial development examines the theoretical perspectives on behavior along with the biology of behavior. Let us begin this discussion by reviewing a few of the major theories that continue to guide thought and practice in early care and education and juxtapose them against emerging brain development research.

Freud's Psychoanalytic Psychology

Sigmund Freud (1933) was the first to propose a theory of personality based on underlying psychological structures and needs. Freud believed that behaviors were governed by unconscious desires and hidden motives. He was among the first to propose that personality development proceeded through a series of stages during which certain conflicts must be successfully resolved before the individual progressed to the next stage. Successful resolution of stage-related conflicts over time should lead to healthy development. Freud advanced the concept of **fixation**, which suggests that individual psychological behaviors can cease to move beyond a particular point in development, carrying immature forms of behaving forward into later stages and resulting in less than healthy psychological growth. Freud believed that early experiences determined the course and nature of later development and behavior. Further, he proposed that individuals are born with psychosexual instincts that change over the years from infancy to maturity. The focus of psychosexual energy relating to these instincts shifts from one part of the body to another as the individual matures. Development is characterized as a series of five stages revealing the shift in psychosexual energy. Table 6.1 describes this sequence. Many psychologists who studied Freud's works argue that he placed too much emphasis on the notion that sexual drives influence personality development. Nevertheless, Freud's work continues to influence child development theory and practice.

fixation: in psychoanalytic theory, a point in development that becomes fixed, failing to move forward to more mature forms

Erikson's Theory of Psychosocial Development

The psychoanalytic perspective advanced by Freud provides a template for understanding Erik Erikson's theory of personality development. Like Freud, Erikson believed that development progressed through a series of identifiable stages; also like Freud, he explored the emotional and social interactions between children and their caregivers. He, too, emphasized the relationship of early experiences to later personality development. But Erikson was interested in the larger cultural

TABLE 6.1 Freud's Psychosexual Stages of Development

Oral stage (1st year)	The primary focus of stimulation is the mouth and the oral cavity, and the primary sources of gratification are eating, sucking, and biting. The mother (or primary caregiver) is the source of satisfaction of the basic needs of this period.
Anal stage (2nd to 4th year)	Elimination and retention of fecal material become the focus of the child's attentions and energies. The child must learn the appropriate time and place for elimination. This is the time when the child first learns to conform to social expectations.
Phallic stage (4th to 6th year)	Psychic energy is focused on the genital organs and pleasure received through organ manipulation. The realization that one is biologically and psychologically separate from others occurs, and the resolution of conflicts relating to appropriate sex roles becomes an issue. Children are said to develop incestuous desires for the parent of the other sex during this stage.
Latency stage (middle childhood)	Energy formerly directed toward sexual concerns becomes channeled in other directions, mainly that of forming affectional and social relationships with parents and other children (usually same-sex friends).
Genital stage (adolescence)	Physical sexual changes and development become the center of attention. Sex-role identity becomes a major issue.

Source: Freud (1933).

and societal context in which psychosocial development occurs. By expanding on Freudian theory, Erikson identified eight stages of psychosocial development, each representing stage-related psychological conflicts to be resolved in order for the individual to proceed successfully to the next and subsequent stages leading to healthy personality development. His eight stages represent a life span perspective that not only includes developmental changes in infants and children, but also follows psychosocial development through childhood, adolescence, and adulthood.

The eight stages of personality development Erikson proposed are characterized by basic life conflicts to be resolved. These conflicts result from an individual's biological maturation and expectations imposed on the individual by society.

According to Erikson's theory, the first year of life is a critical period for the development of a sense of trust. The conflict for the infant involves striking a balance between trust and mistrust. This primary psychosocial task of infancy provides a developmental foundation from which later stages of personality development can emerge. It is represented in Figure 6.1 as the first stage in Erikson's eight-stage theory. Resolution of the trust/mistrust conflict is manifest in a mature personality by behaviors that basically exhibit trust (of oneself and others) but maintain a healthy amount of skepticism.

Infants learn to trust when their caregiving is characterized by nurturing and warm interactions and predictable routines. Needs for food, comfort, and satisfying interactions are met through a responsive and protective environment. The infant's first experiences of being fed when hungry, held and stroked soothingly when fretful, changed when clothing is soiled, protected from injury, and played

FIGURE 6.1
Erikson's Eight
Psychosocial
Stages

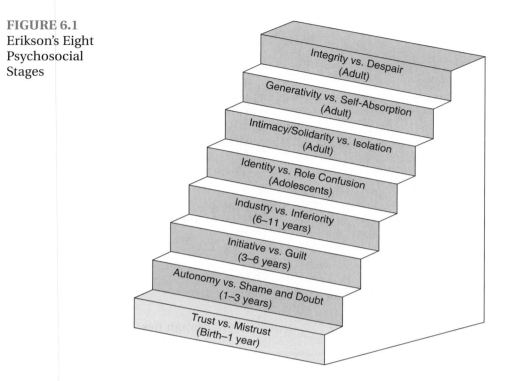

with when bored establish the basis for a developing sense of trust. Infants depend on their caregivers to come when beckoned; to interact with them in warm, supportive, and affectionate ways; and to respond appropriately to their many physiological, social, and emotional needs. When caregiving is responsive to infant cues, infants learn to trust their own ability to signal needs and to elicit caregiver attention. This helps to establish not only trust in others, but also trust in oneself. The infant who establishes a healthy sense of trust is better equipped for the next stage, developing a sense of autonomy. Autonomy builds upon a basic sense of trust and emerges during the toddler period of development described in Chapter 9.

Mistrust arises when the infant's caregivers fail to adequately respond to cues of hunger, discomfort, boredom, and other needs or do so in inconsistent and unpredictable ways. Infants who are subjected to neglect, rejection, or inappropriate expectations or infants who are repeatedly left to "cry it out" learn that other people cannot be trusted. Equally detrimental is the failure to learn to trust oneself and to gain a sense of self from positive and responsive interactions with others achieved by one's own efforts. Failure to develop a sturdy sense of trust undermines the ability to succeed in resolving the psychosocial challenge of autonomy versus shame and doubt during the toddler period.

During this first year, the infant comes to realize that persons and objects exist even though they may not be present. Piaget (1952) considered this a major milestone in cognitive development and termed it *object permanence.* The infant's appreciation of object permanence helps him or her to realize that parents or caregivers exist even when they cannot be seen and that they can be trusted to return when summoned.

Attachment Theory

The subject of infant bonding and **attachment** has received considerable attention in both the professional and the popular press in recent years. Recall from Chapter 4 that *bonding* (Klaus, Klaus, & Kennell, 1982; 2002) refers to the strong emotional tie between the mother or father (or caregiver) and the infant, usually thought to occur in the early days or weeks after delivery. Attachment emerges gradually during the first year and may be an outgrowth of the parent–infant bond. It is based on the quality of the interactions between the child and the parent or primary caregiver.

During the 1950s and early 1960s, John Bowlby, a psychiatrist and pioneer in the study of attachment, published a series of papers based on extensive research on mother–child attachments and separations. These papers, later enlarged and refined, were published in three volumes (Bowlby, 1969/2000, 1973, 1980) and have provided the impetus for continuing scholarly research.

Studying children who had been raised in institutions, Bowlby focused on their inability to form lasting relationships with others. Bowlby attributed this inability to the lack of opportunity to form an attachment to a mother or mother figure during infancy. He also studied children who, after experiencing strong infant–mother attachments, were separated from their mothers for extended periods of time. He observed that these children developed resistance to close human ties. Bowlby was convinced that to understand these behaviors, one should examine infant–mother attachments.

In the institutions in which the subjects of Bowlby's studies lived, staff members tended adequately to their custodial responsibilities of feeding, clothing, bathing, and overseeing the infants' safety. They did not necessarily respond to the infants in affectionate and nurturing ways. Staff members did not respond to infants' cries or return their smiles, nor did they coo and babble with them or carry them about. Even though their physical needs were being met, infants in these settings failed or were severely impaired in their ability to relate to caregivers. Studies of attachment highlight the critical need to form these attachments

attachment:
a strong emotional relationship between two people, characterized by mutual affection and a desire to maintain proximity

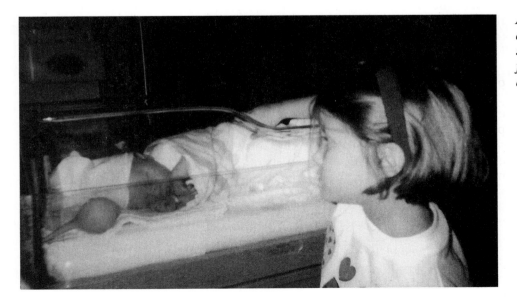

As with parents and their infants, siblings also form loving attachments.

during the early months and years and suggest that failure to do so may have a lifelong effect on healthy social and emotional development (Ainsworth, 1973; Bowlby, 1973; Bretherton & Walters, 1985; Zeanah, Mammen, & Lieberman, 1993).

Bowlby (1969/2000) proposed a sequence for the development of attachment between the infant and others. The sequence is divided into four phases:

Phase 1 (birth to 8 to 12 weeks):   Indiscriminate responsiveness to humans. During this phase, infants orient to people in their environment, visually tracking them, grasping and reaching for them, and smiling and babbling. The infant often stops crying on seeing a face or hearing a voice. These behaviors sustain the attentions of others and thus their proximity to the infant, which is the infant's goal.

Phase 2 (3 to 6 months): Focusing on familiar people.   The infant's behaviors toward others remain virtually the same except that they are more marked in relation to the mother or perhaps the father. Social responses begin to become more selective; however, the social smile is reserved for familiar people, while strangers receive a long, intent stare. Cooing, babbling, and gurgling are more readily elicited by familiar people. A principal attachment figure begins to emerge; this is usually the mother.

Phase 3 (6 months to 3 years): Active proximity seeking. Infants show greater discrimination in their interactions with people. They become deeply concerned

FIGURE 6.2
A Sensitive Response to Separation Anxiety

- Recognize that new experiences present new challenges for the infant; some of these challenges can be quite unsettling, maybe even alarming.
- Provide predictable, unhurried schedules, particularly when introducing the infant to new experiences.
- Begin to accustom the infant to short separations at home by:
  - maintaining visual and auditory contact by leaving the infant's door open at nap and bedtimes;
  - maintaining voice contact across rooms and, when departing the room of a protesting infant, providing softly spoken verbal assurances.
- Ritualize bedtimes and naptimes; e.g., provide a slower pace, soften volume on TV, give a bath and a change of clothing, brush teeth, read a story, rock and sing, kiss goodnight, and tuck in bed.
- Provide prior opportunities for the infant to become familiar with a new babysitter or child care arrangement.
- Select caregivers on the basis of their ability to respond to the infant's unique rhythms and temperament.
- Familiarize the caregiver with the infant's routines and preferences.
- Have available for the infant any special blanket, stuffed toy, or other object from which the infant gains comfort.
- Ritualize departure time: hug, kiss, spoken good-byes, wave, and so on. Never slip away when the child is not looking; rather, let the infant develop confidence in the arrangement.
- Anticipate the new experience with pleasure.
- Be dependable. First separations should be brief, and reunions should be unwaveringly predictable.

for the attachment person's presence, and cry when that person starts to leave. Infants will monitor the attachment person's movements, calling out to the person or using whatever means of locomotion they have to maintain proximity to the person. The attachment person serves as a base from which to explore and is followed when departing and greeted warmly upon return. Certain other people may become subsidiary attachment figures; however, strangers are now treated with caution and will soon evoke emotions of alarm and withdrawal.

During phase 3, two very predictable fears emerge. **Separation anxiety** occurs as the relationship between the infant and the attachment person becomes more intense and exclusive. The infant cries, sometimes quite vociferously, on the departure of the attachment person and exhibits intense joy on reunion. Although this phase can be disconcerting for parents and primary caregivers, it is nevertheless, a healthy aspect of psychosocial development. To the extent that adults respond to separation anxiety in supportive and empathic ways, the child can gain trust and confidence in their caregivers and in their own self-comforting strategies. Figure 6.2 offers suggestions for caregivers during this difficult phase.

separation anxiety: fear of being separated from the attachment person

Stranger anxiety is another characteristic fear of phase 3. Occurring around 7 to 8 months of age, the infant's stranger anxiety is characterized by intense or lengthy stares and crying at the sight of an unfamiliar person. Alarmed, the infant will cling tightly to the attachment person and resist letting go. Stranger anxiety, like separation anxiety, signals maturing cognitive and psychosocial development and can lead to healthy trust and mistrust when responded to in supportive and helpful ways. Figure 6.3 includes suggestions for dealing with stranger anxiety.

stranger anxiety: fear of strangers, characterized by avoidance, crying, or other distress signals

Phase 4 (3 years to the end of childhood): Partnership behavior. Before this phase, the child is unable to consider the attachment person's intentions. For instance, the suggestion that "I will be right back" is meaningless to the child,

FIGURE 6.3
A Sensitive Response to Stranger Anxiety

Learning to distinguish mother and father from others is an important task in infancy, and for many of today's infants, adapting to a nonparental caregiver may be an added task. The parent or caregiver must recognize that fears in the first year relate to new learnings and limited experiences.

- Discourage an unfamiliar person from attempting to hold the infant.
- Provide ample time for the infant to assess the stranger and sense your reaction to him or her.
- When introducing the infant to a new caregiver, invite the person to visit. Spend time together, allowing the infant time to accept this new person into his or her world.
- During this session, let yourself serve as the secure base from which the infant can venture forth to make friendly overtures with the new acquaintance.
- Allow the infant to "control" the encounter, deciding when to approach and when to retreat.
- Provide the infant with familiar and comforting objects to hold.
- The confidence of older siblings who are already familiar with the "stranger" may encourage the infant's comfort and acceptance.

who will insist on going along anyway. By age 3, the child has developed a greater understanding of parental intent and can envision the parent's behavior while separated. The child is now more willing and able to let go and can be more flexible. (From *Attachment and Loss, Volume I: Attachment* by John Bowlby. Copyright © 1969 by Tavistock Institute of Human Relations. Reprinted by permission of Basic Books, a member of Perseus Books, L.L.C.)

Mary Ainsworth has studied differences in attachment behaviors (Ainsworth, 1967, 1973; Ainsworth, Bell, & Stayton, 1974; Ainsworth & Wittig, 1969). Using her *Strange Situation* test, Ainsworth and her colleagues attempted to delineate individual differences in the quality of attachments that infants form. She devised a series of eight episodes designed to induce increasing anxiety in the infant. The episodes, lasting 30 seconds to 3 minutes or less, created eight pairing situations that included the mother with the infant, the mother and infant with a stranger, the infant alone with a stranger, and the infant being united with the mother. She recorded and analyzed exploratory behaviors, reactions to strangers, reactions to separation, and infant behaviors on reuniting with the mother after separation.

From her studies, Ainsworth identified three categories of attachment:

1. Insecure attachment: anxious and avoidant
2. Secure attachment
3. Insecure attachment: anxious and resistant

Securely attached infants were found to be visibly upset upon separation from the mother, and greeted her heartily and sought close physical contact with her on reunion. In their mother's presence, these infants more willingly explored their environments and were friendly with the stranger.

Insecurely attached, anxious/avoidant infants showed little distress when the mother departed and no great joy upon her return, generally avoiding contact with her. With strangers, they behaved similarly, tending to avoid or ignore them.

Insecurely attached, anxious/resistant infants were less likely to explore when the mother was present and were distressed when she departed. The reunion was strained, as the infant maintained proximity but resisted the mother's efforts at physical contact, displaying apparent anger at her absence. These infants were quite wary of strangers, even with the mother present.

Another classification of attachment, described by Main and Solomon (1990) as "disorganized," suggests that disorganization or conflicted feelings and behaviors expressing stress or anxiety can occur in any of Ainsworth's three categories of attachment. Risk factors associated with disorganized attachment include maladaptive parental behavior, abuse, neglect, maternal mental health, poverty, and absence of or failure to access intervention services (Sameroff, 1999). Expressions of these disorganized attachment behaviors increase in frequency as the severity of the risk factors increases. Some researchers believe that disorganization of attachment patterns may foretell later hostile behaviors in children (Lyons-Ruth, Alpern, & Repacholi, 1993). Avoidant attachments are also thought to predict later antisocial behaviors (Fagot & Kavanagh, 1990).

On the positive side, a large body of research found that securely attached infants

- formed early attachments between one and four months of age as a result of their mothers' sensitive responses to their cues;

- exhibited trust in their mothers' availability;
- progressed toward autonomous behaviors more easily;
- exhibited more confidence in exploratory behaviors;
- played with toys and other objects more than insecurely attached infants;
- enjoyed greater involvement and success in peer interactions as they got older (Cassidy & Berlin, 1994; Isabella, 1993).

What did these infants experience that their less successfully attached agemates did not? Do certain parental characteristics facilitate the attachment process? A number of researchers suggest that the mothers (or primary caregivers) of these infants exhibited more sensitive and responsive behaviors toward them. These mothers

- were more involved with their infants;
- were sensitive to their infants' behavioral cues;
- were readily accessible;
- were predictable;
- responded to their infants in developmentally appropriate ways;
- generally exhibited more positive behaviors and interactions and expressions of affection;
- enjoyed close physical contact with their infants;
- encouraged exploratory play and timed their interactions strategically so as not to intrude in their infants' play;
- had a sense of when to interact (Ainsworth, Bell, & Stayton, 1974; Cassidy & Berlin, 1994; Grossmann, Grossmann, Spangler, Suess, & Unzner, 1985; Isabella, 1993; Isabella, Belsky, & von Eye, 1989).

Many scholars view the security or insecurity of the infant–mother attachment as influencing the quality of all other relationships. However, Main and Weston (1981) determined that infants can form independent attachments to both mothers *and* fathers resulting from the types of interactions they have with each. Moreover, these scholars found that infants who have established secure attachments with both parents are more empathic during the toddler years to an adult in distress. Recent researchers have determined that while infants are capable of becoming closely attached to more than one caregiver, they tend to place these attachment people in an internal hierarchy or preference order (Lieberman & Zeanah, 1995). Other studies have found that when infant–mother attachments were insecure, secure infant–father attachments did not necessarily buffer the effects (Easterbrooks and Goldberg, 1990). However, this may be due to the fact that fathers in this particular study (and era) did not spend as much time with their infants and were not as engaged as the mothers in the infant's daily care routines. While Belsky and Rovine (1988) found that infants in nonmaternal care for more than 20 hours per week were at risk of developing insecure attachments with their mothers, this did not occur among infants who were cared for by their fathers in their mothers' absence. Hence, it appears that fathers can play a critical role in healthy attachment behaviors. Fike (1993) provided suggestions for both meeting fathers' needs for interaction with their children and fostering the very important relationships that develop between infants and fathers. Fathers should

1. understand the importance of setting positive expectations for their infants and practice a mental attitude of expecting positive relationships to develop;
2. appreciate the importance of holding, cuddling, and playing with their infants;
3. become involved in the daily lives of their infants through routines such as feeding, changing, bedtime and playtime routines, and so on;
4. become aware of the day-to-day events unfolding in their infants' lives;
5. communicate verbally with their infants in tones of approval and acceptance;
6. nurture their infants through attitudes, deeds, and actions that communicate the infants' unique worth.

Longitudinal studies have documented the long-term results of secure and insecure attachments. Many researchers have found that personality development is either positively or negatively affected by these early secure or insecure attachments. This expanding area of research has been enormously helpful to the early childhood professional by

- emphasizing the importance of the first year for the development of parent–child bonds;
- affirming the ameliorative potential for other attachments (family members, child care providers) when parental (or primary caregiver) attachments are insecure;
- affirming the importance of nonparental caregivers in complementing and supporting parent–child attachments;
- supporting the need for professional intervention when parent–child relationships are dysfunctional

Social smiling emerges as infants recognize the face and voice of a responsive caregiver.

Social Learning Theory

Recall from Chapter 1 that behavioristic theories place considerable emphasis on external events and environmental influences in shaping children's learning and personalities. As we discuss psychosocial development in infancy, Bandura's social cognitive theory comes into play. Bandura advanced the importance of observation and imitation in childhood behavior and first illustrated his theory through his famous Bobo doll experiment (see Chapter 1). He brought into focus the importance of role models in shaping the behaviors of children. Bandura proposed that human beings are not simply passive recipients of information and experience, but use sophisticated cognitive abilities to draw on past experiences to think about the consequences of their behavior and anticipate future possibilities. Bandura furthered the concept of **reciprocal determinism**. As infants and children undergo **socialization** within their families and cultural groups, their own unique characteristics, behaviors, and levels of understanding affect the manner in which they respond to people and events. But equally influential is the fact that the unique characteristics of the infant's social environment also affect the infant. Unlike age/stage theories, social learning theory suggests that the course of development for any individual depends on the kinds of reciprocal social learning experiences encountered. The individual's responses and interactions change over time as the individual matures and his or her social experiences expand.

reciprocal determinism: a socialization process through which the individual both influences and is influenced by the environment

Bandura's perspective brings us to the concept of context where we must recall contextualistic theories such as those of Bronfrenbrenner and Gottlieb. Again the reader is referred to Chapter 1 for a description of these theories. In terms of psychosocial development of the infant, it is important to note that during the first year, a microsystem (Bronfrenbrenner, 1986) surrounds the infant exerting primary influence through the home and family and through nonparental caregivers and the settings in which this occurs. As infants grow and change, their needs and capabilities change, resulting in changes in both their physical and interactive environments. For instance, when infants begin to roll over and sit alone, they can be provided greater space for movement, and a different array of toys than they previously experienced to support their emerging motor activity, and are more comfortable in a high chair for feeding. These abilities change appreciably the types of safety protections imposed on the infant and the types of interactions between the infant and objects and people in their environment. These supports and interactions then produce more changes in the growing infant, and as circles of influence enlarge, this type of reciprocal influence becomes a continuous process. The growing child affects his or her environment and the environment affects the growing child (Gottlieb, 1991; Sameroff, 1999).

socialization: the process by which individuals acquire the accepted behaviors and values of their families and society

Social Cognition

From the foregoing, we are directed toward a discussion of how children develop understanding of behavior and behavioral expectations. **Social cognition** is the ability to understand the needs, feelings, motives, thoughts, intentions, and behaviors of oneself and others. As infants develop a basic sense of trust, they learn to associate certain behaviors with the solicitation of certain responses from their caregivers. This awareness marks the beginning of the development of social cognition.

social cognition: the ability to understand the thoughts, intentions, and behaviors of oneself and others

From their experiences during the first year of life, infants become aware of the rhythms, sights, and sounds of the household or child care setting and the unique ways in which different adults or siblings hold and care for them. They learn to anticipate certain responses to their various cues; recognize the unique aromas of their mothers, fathers, and other caregivers; and perhaps sense the moods of these individuals by the manner in which they respond to them. In adult–infant interactions, the adult typically imitates the infant's facial expressions and vocalizations. As the infant experiences these pleasant interactions, the imitation becomes reciprocal, with the infant imitating the gestures, facial expressions, and vocalizations of the parent or caregivers. Infants' responses to facial expressions indicate that they look to others, usually attachment people, for clues in understanding the sights and sounds around them (Tronick, Cohn, & Shea, 1986).

Imitative behaviors become a means of both social cognition and interpersonal communication. Imitations seen in games of pat-a-cake and peek-a-boo and in learning to kiss or wave are behaviors indicative of emerging social cognition. As the infant experiences these social interactions and finds them pleasurable, the motivation to repeat them emerges. These and other forms of infant interpersonal communications contribute to social cognition and competence, and have implications for later language and cognitive development (Clyman, Emde, Kempe, & Harmon, 1986).

THE NEUROBIOLOGY OF PSYCHOSOCIAL DEVELOPMENT

The Relationship of Long-Held Theories to Emerging Research on Brain Growth

Revelations about early brain growth and neurological development support many theoretical perspectives on child development. Among them, the notion that there are periods during growth and development in which experiences seem to have greater or lesser effect on the changing organism holds sway across the spectrum from theory to hard data from the biological and neuroscientific fields. Whether we are talking about "stages" or "windows of opportunity," the concept of periods of vulnerability in which certain experiences enhance or thwart emerging development is an important one. The long-term effects of early experiences are also supported through neurobiological studies. Even though one can always learn new ways of thinking and behaving, the fact that neurological development is in a period of profound growth during the first three to ten years suggests the critical need for appropriate experiences. Thus, for example, the long-held theoretical perspective on the importance of early bonding and attachments is affirmed through contemporary neurobiological discoveries. (As we will see in later chapters, numerous long-held theories now enjoy contemporary support and amplification from research in the biological sciences.) Further, while genetics remains the determinant of many traits and characteristics, the human organism remains dependent on its environment for the opportunity to develop optimally—a perspective that is reinforced through scientific data on how the human brain becomes neurologically wired.

Psychosocial Development: A Neurological Perspective

Recall from Chapter 5 that the human organism has sophisticated capabilities for receiving and interpreting information about its internal and external environment through the sensory system. The human brain controls sensations, thinking,

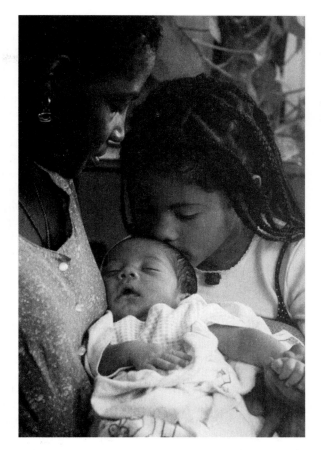

"Goodness of fit" between infants and the personalities and expectations of their caregivers supports psychosocial development.

feeling, behaving, and emotions. It controls the expressions of joy, love, hate, friendship, curiosity, fear, sadness, shyness, anxiety, and many other responses. Throughout the early childhood years, information derived through the senses and interactions with others stimulates the growth of a complex network of neural connections as axons grow and dendrites proliferate to communicate through synaptic activity, which comes to control these expressions. Not only the types of earliest experiences, but the timing of experiences influences the extent to which synaptic activity occurs and results in positive growth-enhancing outcomes.

While a great deal of genetically driven neurological development has taken place prenatally, external stimuli come importantly into play at birth and exert further influence on the formation of the brain's neurological circuitry. This neurological wiring is forming during the first three years for some developmental achievements and continues up to seven to ten years for others. Indeed, the brain continues to change its "wiring diagram" throughout life, overproducing and pruning synapses during childhood and adding synapses as new learning is achieved during adult life (Greenough, Gunnar, Emde, Massinga, & Shonkoff, 2001).

Environmental sensory stimuli cause the brain to develop its own unique circuitry and influences which connections will last and which will atrophy or be pruned away for lack of use, and, in some instances, which connections will be rerouted in response to injury, insult, or neglect. All of the sensory input that the child receives affects neurological development by strengthening synapses.

Hence, two concepts are of critical importance in this discussion: the concept of windows of opportunity and the concept of essential experiences.

As defined in Chapter 5, a *window of opportunity* is a period during growth and development when experiences are thought to have their greatest impact on the brain's formation of intricate neurological connections (see Table 5.1). During these periods, there is heightened sensitivity to environmental influences. Environmental influences, then, must be considered for their positive or negative effects.

During these windows of opportunity, certain *essential experiences* strengthen specific synaptic activity. Deprivation, neglect, or abuse, while harmful at any point, can, if they occur during these identified windows of opportunity, have particularly long-lasting deleterious neurological effects (Perry, 1996; Perry, Polland, Blakley, Baker, & Vigilante, 1995; Shonkoff & Phillips, 2000). Essential experiences are those needed to stimulate and enhance synaptic activity during early growth and development. They are the experiences and interactions that are provided by nurturing and supportive caregivers and lead to positive outcomes for memory and learning, expression and control of emotions, and social interactive behaviors. Box 6.1 gives examples of the types of essential experiences believed to support healthy brain growth and neurological development.

Of particular interest in our discussion of psychosocial development are the windows of opportunity for developing social attachment (birth to age 2 years), learning to control or modulate emotions, and developing the capacity to cope with stress (birth to age 3 years), and the essential experiences supportive of these developments.

It appears that strong, secure attachment to a nurturing caregiver can provide a protective biological structure that functions to buffer an infant against the later effects of stress or trauma (Gunnar, 1996). Gunnar and her associates at the University of Minnesota studied levels of a steroid hormone known as cortisol in children's reactions to stress. Cortisol is present in saliva, and its level increases when a person experiences physiological or psychological stress or trauma. Cortisol is only one of many chemicals that function as important neurotransmitters during synaptic activity. However, elevated cortisol affects metabolism, has been associated with depression and circulatory and heart disease, can suppress the immune system, and, when chronic, can lead to destruction of neurons that are associated with learning and memory (Dienstbier, 1989; Vincent, 1990).

Neuroscientists now caution that stressful or traumatic experiences in infancy and early childhood, when prolonged and uninterrupted by successful intervention strategies, can undermine neurological development and impair brain function. Children who suffer chronically high levels of cortisol have been shown to exhibit more developmental delays in cognitive, motor, and social development than other children (Gunnar, 1996). Earliest nurturing experiences and strong parent–child bonds during the first year appear to build inner strength (both biological and psychological) against the deleterious effects of stress and trauma, a strength that remains evident as children get older. School-age children who have enjoyed secure attachment dynamics during infancy and early childhood exhibit fewer behavior problems when stress or trauma confronts them.

Further, it is believed that the ability to express and control emotions has biological origins derived from the types of care, nurturing, and supportive interactions that stimulate specific neurological connections (Perry, 1996; Perry et al., 1995; Shonkoff & Phillips, 2000). Early experiences quite literally shape the biological

BOX 6.1   Essential Experiences in Infancy

Developmental Domain	Esssential Experiences
Social attachment and the ability to cope with stress	Consistent care that is predictable, warm, and nurturing. Gentle, loving, and dependable relationships with primary caregivers. Immediate attention to physiological needs for nourishment, elimination, cleanliness, warmth, exercise, and symptoms of illness. Satisfying and enjoyable social interactions, playful experiences, and engaging infant toys.
Regulation and control of emotions	Empathic adult responses and unconditional acceptance of the child's unique characteristics and personality traits. Adult expectations that are appropriate for the age and the individual. Guidance that is instructive and helps the child to learn about emotions and that suggests appropriate ways and contexts for the expressions of emotions. Relationships that are psychologically safe, that is, free of threat, coercion, teasing, or physical or psychological neglect or abuse. Opportunities to engage in socially and emotionally satisfying play.
Vision and auditory acuity	Regular vision and hearing examinations by health care professionals. Interesting and varied visual and auditory fields accompanied by verbal interactions that label and describe. Personal belongings, toys, and baby books that enlist interest in color, shape, texture, size, pattern, sound, pitch, rhythm, and movement. Experience with many forms of music, song, and dance.
Motor development and coordination	Opportunities and encouragement to use emerging muscle coordinations in safe and interesting surroundings. Supportive and positive interactions for effort. Play space, equipment, and toys that facilitate both large and small motor coordinations.
Vocabulary and language development	Rich verbal interactions that respond to the infant's efforts to communicate. Engaging the infant in talking, chanting, singing, sharing, picture books, telling stories, and sharing poems and rhymes. Toys and props that encourage pretend play. Conversations characterized by varied topics, interesting vocabulary, and engaging facial expressions and voice inflections. Interesting and enlightening firsthand experiences. Focused and responsive interactions in both native and second languages. Opportunities to converse and sing in either language.
Cognitive development	Toys and learning materials that encourage manipulations and constructions, dumping and pouring, pushing and pulling, dropping and retrieving, and hiding and finding. Toys and props that encourage and support pretend play. Social interactions that facilitate explorations and play. Baby books that introduce familiar objects, labels, and simple stories. Selected recorded music, or pleasing instrumental music and singing.

systems (neurological "wiring" and chemical characteristics) that underly expressions of emotions. Children who have been abused, abandoned, neglected, and otherwise emotionally maltreated suffer impaired ability to regulate their emotional responses due to abnormal migrations of neurons and synaptic activity (Perry, 1996; Perry et al., 1995). As we learn more about the timing and intensity of these insults to brain growth and neurological development, we will be better able to identify risk factors and to develop timely intervention strategies to prevent or correct the effects of injurious environments and enhance subsequent developmental outcomes (Puckett, Marshall, & Davis, 1999).

DIMENSIONS OF PSYCHOSOCIAL DEVELOPMENT IN INFANCY

Infant Temperament

From birth, infants display distinctive personality characteristics, the study of which has intrigued parents and researchers alike. Quite often, discussions of personality center on temperament, a characteristic that is believed to be at least in part influenced by genetic endowment (Plomin, 1987). Researchers have focused on various dimensions of temperament, such as emotionality (the extent to which events can be upsetting), activity (types and pace of behaviors), and sociability (the desire for social proximity and interaction versus shyness or withdrawal) (Buss & Plomin, 1984; Kagan, 1997; Kagan, Snidman, & Arcus, 1992). In studying individuality in children, Stella Chess and Alexander Thomas (1987; 1996) identified a number of dimensions of behavior that are associated with temperament. The components of temperament that they studied include activity level, rhythmicity (regularity or predictability of biological functions such as wake/sleep patterns and eating), approach and withdrawal behaviors, adaptability, sensory threshold, intensity of response, quality of mood, distractibility, persistence, and attention span. By gathering information about these behaviors in large numbers of children, Chess and Thomas were able to delineate three main types of temperament:

1. *The easy temperament.* The child is usually easygoing, even tempered, tolerant of change, playful, responsive, and adaptable. The child eats and sleeps with some regularity, is easily comforted when upset, and generally displays a positive mood.
2. *The difficult temperament.* The child is slower to develop regular eating and sleeping routines, is more irritable, derives less pleasure from playtime activities, has difficulty adjusting to changes in routines, and tends to cry louder and longer than more easily soothed children.
3. *The slow-to-warm-up temperament.* The child displays only mild positive or negative reactions, resists new situations and people, and is moody and slow to adapt. The slow-to-warm-up child may resist close interactions such as cuddling.

The easy child's behaviors provide positive feedback and reinforcement to caregivers and, in so doing, influence the kinds and amounts of attention the child will receive throughout early development. More often than not, these children experience what Chess and Thomas (1987; 1996) called a "goodness of fit" between themselves and the personalities and expectations of their caregivers. *Goodness of fit* is defined as a principle of interaction in which

> the organism's capacities, motivations and styles of behaving and the demands and expectations of the environment are in accord. Such consonance between organism and environment potentiates optimal positive development. Should there be dissonance between the capacities and characteristics of the organism on the one hand and the environment opportunities and demands on the other hand, there is poorness of fit, which leads to maladaptive functioning and distorted development. (Chess & Thomas, 1987, pp. 20–21)

Infants who are described as temperamentally difficult may fail to elicit appropriate nurturing and support from their caregivers. Adults who find this temperament hard to respond to may become punitive, overly demanding, or perhaps inconsistent and appeasing in their interactions. They may be vague or unclear with their child about their expectations, or perhaps their acceptance of them. The adults may feel inadequate to their task, helpless, and confused. Poorly prepared to deal with a difficult temperament, these adults may engage in power struggles for control. Obviously, a "poorness of fit" emerges in these situations and holds potential for ineffective and negative relationships and childhood behavior disorders that can persist into adulthood.

The slow-to-warm-up child generally does not present substantial difficulties in the adult–child relationship. However, this child, being slower to adapt and reticent with new acquaintances and situations, may not receive persistent efforts on the part of caregivers to maintain positive interactions.

Not all children fall neatly into these categories; easy children are not always easy, difficult children are not always difficult, and slow-to-warm-up children are not always reticent. However, these descriptions help us to appreciate wide variations in infant and child personalities. Recognizing and appreciating individual differences helps adults to respond appropriately to these behaviors. Adults must be cautious in applying these categories, however. Self-fulfilling prophecies may occur in which the child behaves according to adult expectations. If adults ascribe labels and misunderstand the infant's cues, they may fail to support the infant's needs for positive and nurturing interactions, regardless of temperament or personality type. If there is goodness of fit between infants and their environments, there are positive outcomes that carry over into later development.

Infant Emotions

In addition to the readily observable emotional states of contentment and distress, the infant displays an array of emotions, including affection, joy, surprise, anger, fear, disgust, interest, and even sadness. The newborn shows interest and surprise when something catches her or his attention, and smiles at a pleasing sound or when hunger has been satisfied. A sudden jolt or loud noise may evoke surprise and distress. The infant may show anger or even rage at being restrained or uncomfortable.

A number of scholars have suggested sequences for the emergence of discrete emotions (e.g., Brazelton, 1992; Denham, 1998; Izard, 1991; Stroufe, 1996). For instance, it is believed that distress, disgust, and surprise are expressed by newborns, while anger and joy emerge during the first 4 months and fear and shyness emerge between ages 6 months and 1 year.

While most emotions seem to be present from birth, differences in emotional responses occur as the infant gets older. The most significant changes in emotional and social responses in infants occur during the period from 6 to 12 months, owing primarily to significant emerging cognitive development. The abilities to recall the past, sense discrepancies, and attend to expressions of emotion in caregivers contribute to these differences (Lamb, Morrison, & Malkin, 1987). Thus, the emergence of fear of strangers and separation anxiety described earlier is understandable.

Crying: An Essential Mode of Communication

Infants are competent communicators, and first communicate their needs through crying. The first infant cries are reflexive, perhaps survival reactions to physiological needs for nourishment, warmth, movement, touch, or relief from discomfort. Infants have no control over their crying and will not be able to stop crying until a need has been met or they have exhausted themselves. As the infant gets older, the causes of crying change from internal to external stimuli and may be provoked by such things as loud noises, physical restraint, uncomfortable clothing, frustration with toys, or, as described earlier in this chapter, fear of strangers and of separation.

Infant crying frequently has different tones, rhythms, and intensities. Parents soon learn the nature and the message of their infant's various cries and respond according to various acoustical differences (Green, Jones, & Gustafson, 1987). Shaffer (1971) identified three distinct patterns of crying: the basic cry usually associated with hunger, an angry cry, and a pain cry.

Crying is sometimes unsettling to parents and caregivers, particularly when they are unable to determine the infant's needs. Learning to distinguish the accoustical variations in an infant's cries and what each means is one of the tasks of parenting and infant caregiving. Bell and Ainsworth (1972) found that infants whose parents responded promptly to their cries and other signals cried less often. When the infants did cry, the crying was of shorter duration. Further, infants who cried and fussed the most after 3 months of age were the ones whose parents did not respond readily to their cries. Another study found that infants who were held and carried about during the day cried less during the night (Hunziker & Barr, 1986).

As with older children and adults, infants experience boredom, loneliness, and a need for personal contact. Sometimes crying simply signals a need for companionship, the sound of a familiar voice, and the sensation of a familiar touch. When bored, infants may cry for a change of position or place or for the nearness and interaction of others. Certain music or recorded soothing sounds or perhaps selected visual stimuli that engage the child's attention may help to meet the child's needs. Brazelton described infant nursing behaviors as having feeding bursts and pauses in which the pause appears to be intentional to capture social stimuli (Brazelton, 1992). He emphasized the importance of interaction, talking, and quietly playing with an infant during feeding time. On the other hand, when infants are difficult to console, adults must find the just right interaction to comfort. Rocking the infant; holding the infant to one's shoulder to provide opportunities for visual scanning; talking in soft, soothing tones; gentle caresses; and directing the infant's attention to objects, toys, and other children are usually successful ways to calm a fussy infant.

Other Modes of Infant Communication

Parents and other caregivers who are cognizant of the infant's various means of communicating, such as whimpering, facial expressions, wiggling, vocalizing, and turning away from stimuli, are better able to respond and interact appropriately with their infants. These adults take cues from infant behaviors recognizing signals of contentment, discomfort, distress, or frustration. Infants whose caregivers respond to these noncrying signals soon learn to communicate without crying, unless, of course, there is pain, fear, frustration, or exhaustion. These infants will grow in their sense of trust in their caregivers and in themselves as communicators.

Cheryl's mother finds it difficult to work as a housekeeper and help to care for Angela. Cheryl goes to school and feels pressured to find other child care arrangements. The older siblings in the family have been called on to help with baby-sitting, but that has not always worked out, owing to their own childhood needs for play and socialization and desires to succeed in school.

James has tried to be helpful, but his visits to his infant daughter are becoming less and less frequent. His need to work and his desire to stay in school consume his time and energies. His feelings for both Cheryl and their baby are becoming ambivalent and confused, and he sometimes feels depressed. He isn't sure what his role should be.

Cheryl has experienced mixed feelings as the realities of constantly having to meet an infant's needs become more apparent. She isn't sure of James anymore and anticipates that they will probably split up soon. She feels sad, though she does not blame him. She is tired most of the time, since she has returned to school and her classes have become quite demanding. Sometimes she feels like a failure at school and at mothering, and her baby seems cranky much of the time.

Cheryl's mother frequently shares her frustrations with a friend at her church, including the difficulties of making a living and raising a two-generation family. Her friend tells her that some high schools in the area provide on-site child care for teenage mothers. Through a number of inquiries, Cheryl's mother is able to identify one such high school. It isn't the high school in which Cheryl is currently enrolled and will necessitate a family move if Cheryl chooses to take advantage of the child care program.

After several weeks of searching, Cheryl's family locates a small house within walking distance of the new high school. Cheryl doesn't want to move, yet she feels that she has no choice. She will miss James and her other friends. James offers to help; he will borrow his brother's pickup truck and will help them to prepare the new house for occupancy. Cheryl is pleased at this show of caring and thinks that maybe her relationship with James can continue.

Meanwhile, Angela has experienced a constant turnover in caregivers. At age 8 months, her sleeping patterns are still irregular and unpredictable. She is hungry at odd hours and is a finicky eater. She cries easily and often, continuously demands the company of others, and vigorously resists being put to bed. She can be quite playful, however, and enjoys the attention of her school-age aunts and uncles. She responds readily to Cheryl, but her relationship with her grandmother seems more comforting. She watches the comings and goings of all the family members and frets or cries when left in her playpen as others leave the room. Both Cheryl and her mother care deeply for Angela and want her to be a happy, cheerful baby.

Jeremy's experiences have been quite different. His psychosocial world has included his mother, his father, Phyllis (his baby-sitter), and an occasional visit from grandparents and trips to the church nursery. Except for his bouts with colic, Jeremy's routines of sleeping and eating are generally without incident. Bathing, dressing, playing, and interacting with Phyllis and his parents are, for the most part, relaxed, predictable, and enjoyable.

Ann, now back at work, is making every effort to maintain a sense of order in their lives, though meeting Jeremy's needs has at times overwhelmed her. Ann and Bill talk frequently and frankly about the dramatic change in their lifestyle, daily schedules, social life, and physical stamina.

Bill feels a need and a desire to nurture Jeremy and misses the child when he is at work. Jeremy has become his "buddy," and Bill cherishes the smiles, the reaching toward Daddy's face when being held, and the pounding at his legs with uncoordinated hands to get attention or to be held. Dinnertimes are not always serene, nor are bedtimes, yet Bill and Ann both savor the changes they are observing in their growing baby. Indeed, Jeremy has a distinct personality. Does he take after Bill's side of the family or Ann's? Together, they anticipate Jeremy's changing looks, behaviors, and interactions with each of them.

Since Jeremy's routines have been mostly predictable and pleasurable, with the adults in his world responding to his cues in focused ways, his sense of trust is emerging, and he has learned which cues result in which responses from others. At 8 months, however, he is beginning to fret on separation from his parents and sometimes from Phyllis. He is especially wary of strangers and seems to need more close physical contact than usual. He also cries more frequently than he used to and is especially difficult in the mornings when Ann and Bill are scurrying to dress and leave for work.

Self-Awareness

It is believed that to become a participant in the give-and-take of a relationship, the infant must first develop a sense of self as distinct and apart from others (Lewis, 1987; Lewis & Brooks-Gunn, 1979). Emotions such as love, hate, jealousy, and guilt—the types of complex emotions that are evoked through relationships with others—are related to an individual's sense of self. Five periods in the development of self–other differentiation were identified by Lewis (1987):

Period 1 (0 to 3 months) is characterized by reflexive interactions between the infant and caregivers and objects.

Period 2 (3 to 8 months) is a period in which the infant, through increasing numbers of experiences with others, progresses toward greater distinction between self and others, though the child may not make these distinctions in all situations.

Period 3 (8 to 12 months) is a period in which self–other differentiation appears to be accomplished; the infant evidences awareness of self as different and permanent in time and space.

Period 4 (12 to 18 months) is a period in which self-conscious emotions such as embarrassment and separation anxiety begin to emerge, as does the ability to recognize oneself in a mirror or photo image.

Period 5 (18 to 30 months) is a period in which self-definition begins to emerge, in which the infant can refer through language to his or her age, gender, and other defining characteristics.

The emergence of self-awareness depends on cognitive development—the ability to make mental "like me"/"not like me" distinctions. Self-awareness is also dependent on social experiences. Infants develop their understanding of self and subsequently a self-concept through their social interactive experiences with others: how others respond to them. As we will see in later chapters, self-concepts are continually being modified as new abilities emerge and social interactions expand beyond primary caregivers.

Social Smiling and Facial Expressions

Smiles observed in the neonate are thought to be triggered by internal stimuli associated with the immature central nervous system. There seems to be a developmental pattern for smiling (Campos & Stenberg, 1981; Emde & Harmon, 1972) that proceeds from internal stimuli to external elicitations.

At first, infants smile at faces regardless of facial expression. Then, from three to seven months, they begin to notice and respond to differences in facial expressions. In the latter part of the first year, infants not only can discriminate differences in facial expressions, but also may respond to each expression in a different emotional way (Campos & Stenberg, 1981). Researchers have also determined that infants from birth are capable of producing almost all of the muscle movements involved in facial expressions that display basic emotions (Oster & Ekman, 1977) and that emotions such as sadness, anger, fear, joy, interest, surprise, and disgust can be observed in facial expressions of infants as early as one month of age (Izard, Huebner, Risser, McGinness, & Dougherty, 1980). Whether these outward observable expressions can be linked conclusively to internal states or feelings is unclear.

Infants have also been shown to respond to positive and negative affect in the human voice, smiling more to sounds of approval than to sounds of disapproval (Fernald, 1993), and to information in facial and bodily cues of their caregivers (Klinnert, Campos, Sorce, Emde, & Svejda, 1983). By 6 to 8 months, infants use a process referred to as **social referencing** whereby they observe their familiar caregivers for affective cues to comfort or guide them in unfamiliar or frightening situations (Klinnert et al., 1983). As infants get older, they become more skilled at social referencing, looking to parents or caregivers more quickly, more frequently, and more intently, and then using these affective cues to guide their own behaviors.

social referencing: a behavior in which the emotional/social reactions of others are observed and used to guide one's own behavior in unfamiliar situations

True social smiling is thought to occur at approximately 6 to 8 weeks. It is believed that when the infant can remember and recognize the face and perhaps the voice of the primary caregiver, smiling becomes more social (Kagan, 1971; Wolff, 1963). As infants get older, they become more discerning in their smiling behavior, choosing to smile at familiar faces, voices, and interactions over unfamiliar ones. Yet the frequency of smiling increases with age. Cognition seems to play a major role in the emergence of smiling that is triggered by external stimuli.

Infant Interaction Patterns and Play Behaviors

In the first few weeks of life, the neonate's interaction patterns relate primarily to survival needs, signaling those needs to parents and caregivers through crying, squirming, and fretting. As the infant becomes more alert and begins to study the faces and responses of parents and to distinguish his or her primary caregivers from others, the infant's responsiveness increases. As experiences with others expand during the first year to include siblings, grandparents, nonparental caregivers, and in some cases other infants and young children, interactive strategies emerge and become more complex.

Infants' efforts to interact are characterized by gazing for some time at a face, reaching toward it, imitating facial expressions, and visually and auditorially tracking a person. Socially, the infant enjoys being gently tickled and jostled; responses include cooing, gurgling, babbling, kicking, and wiggling. Such behaviors elicit playfulness, attention, and encouragement from others.

Around age 5 months, interest in other children and siblings increases. The infant engages in prolonged onlooker behavior when placed in the same room with other children. Some consider this to be an early stage of social play development. Observing others is entertaining in and of itself, and infants derive considerable pleasure from simply being near the action.

Interest in siblings is particularly profound during the latter half of the first year. It is generally thought that playful and responsive siblings increase infant sociability. Some scholars believe that the infant's sociability itself influences the amount of attention received from siblings (Lamb, 1978). In any event, infants can be extremely interested in their siblings, following them around, imitating them, actively seeking their attention, and exploring their toys and other belongings. Siblings can be taught to respond to the infant in gentle and playful ways. Around 6 to 8 months, the infant will participate in games such as peek-a-boo and pat-a-cake and infant-initiated reciprocal activities, such as repeatedly dropping a toy to be retrieved, handed back to the infant, and dropped again.

How infants respond to other infants has been the focus of a number of studies (Adamson & Bakeman, 1985; Field, 1979; Fogel, 1979; Hay, Nash, & Petersen, 1983). Infants will react to the sound of another infant's cry and show an awareness of the presence of another infant. At 6 months of age, the infant will reach toward another infant, watch intently, and perhaps smile and make friendly sounds. At this age, infants have been shown to respond positively to one another in groups of two and generally to find other infants intriguing. An infant may crawl

Siblings may need to be coached on how to safely interact with the infant.

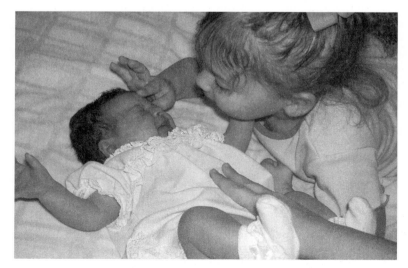

into or fall on another infant in clumsy efforts to interact; yet infant–infant inter-action is seen to be positive despite its awkwardness.

FACTORS INFLUENCING PSYCHOSOCIAL DEVELOPMENT IN INFANTS

From the foregoing, we are now able to list a number of factors that influence psy-chosocial development during infancy. They include the following.

The Quality and Consistency of Care

Among the most important qualities of infant care in terms of healthy psychoso-cial development are *consistency, predictability*, and *continuity* of care. Though personalities and adult responses to infants vary greatly, infants need their differ-ent caregivers (mother, father, siblings, nonparent caregivers) to respond to their cues in relatively similar and nurturing ways. Also, the infant needs to trust that certain events will occur in reasonable order and with some predictability. Earli-est experiences that are marked by predictability of routines, hunger satisfaction, comforting closeness, and reliable and prompt response to bids for attention and expression of need build a sense of trust that is critical to healthy psychosocial development.

Success and Quality of Bonding and Attachments

Success and quality of attachment behaviors have been shown to affect the man-ner in which the brain processes social and emotional information and becomes wired for positive affect. This has long-term implications for social and emotional development and the development of social and moral competence during later childhood.

Essential Experiences

Essential experiences occurring during opportune periods of brain growth and neurological development are simple, inexpensive, and usually come naturally but can be enhanced through conscientious effort on the part of infant caregivers. Early experiences that promote optimal early brain growth and neurological de-velopment establish a biological buffer against later stresses and enhance the ability to learn.

Sociocultural Experiences and Relationships within the Microsystem

Since the first sphere of influence on child growth and development occurs within the microsystem that includes the infant, the family, and other caregivers, the child's cultural heritage comes strongly into play.

Cultural contexts influence psychosocial development through the perceptions, values, goals, and expectations associated with child rearing held by the child's par-ticular cultural group. Expressions of emotions, expectations, and encouragement of infant responses; tolerance for infant behaviors; and perceived parental roles vary among and within cultures. Attitudes toward feeding, crying, holding, and clothing, the nature and amount of language to which the infant is exposed, and attitudes toward sickness and health, medicine and social services, religious belief systems, and many other issues provide the cultural contexts through which infant psychosocial development emerges (Casper, Cooper, Finn, & Stott, 2003; Garcia-Coll, 1990).

Socioeconomic status also plays a role in the family dynamics surrounding children and child rearing. Of particular concern are families of very low socioeconomic means. For some (though certainly not all) families of low socioeconomic status, survival needs often supersede the social and emotional needs of children and the physiological needs for adequate food, health care, and medication. The difficulties of surviving may be so overwhelming that they interfere with healthy parent–parent and parent–child interactions. Children in such families may be hungry and/or cold, suffer more illnesses, and even be neglected or abused. Parental efforts to provide food, clothing, shelter, and transportation for the family may be thwarted. Attending to the psychosocial needs of children is precluded by fatigue, frustration, anxiety, and sometimes resentment or a sense of futility. Personality development of infants in these situations can be at risk.

For such families, high-quality child care can provide a much needed support system. The professionals involved may provide access to needed social and health care services, job counseling, and parenting education. Along with a full day of good-quality nurturing and psychosocially sound interactions, the infant is given an improved chance at healthy development. The relief from the stress associated with child rearing and the assurance that the infant is well cared for during a number of hours of the day (or night) should provide some relief for the parents in these potentially unhealthy situations.

Within the child's microsystem the integrity of all of the entities within that system is important. Family health and freedom from discord or dysfunction, economic security, and overall psychological and social well-being are important contributors to psychosocial development and its manifestation in later years.

Interactions That Promote Social Cognition

Social interactions that provide opportunities to observe, imitate, and reference positive and supportive behaviors of others in their family and cultural groups help infants to develop social cognition. Learning to read facial expressions, body language, and other cues in their social interactions helps infants to begin to notice and regulate their own feelings and behaviors. Positive and supportive social interactions with others promote self-awareness and positive feelings.

Goodness of Fit with Caregivers

The child's personality, which includes characteristic temperament, influences the frequency and types of interactions with others that the child receives. The extent to which adults who care for infants can respond appropriately to different temperament profiles determines the extent to which there can be goodness of fit between infant and caregiver leading to positive personality outcomes. Since temperament is genetically influenced to some extent, it falls on the adult to make appropriate adaptations to the infant's expressions of need, while encouraging and modeling socially acceptable behaviors and providing unconditional acceptance of the child's uniqueness.

Continuity of Care

Continuity of care refers to caregivers' developmental expectations for the infant and knowledge and acceptance of the infant's individual temperament, rhythms, interaction patterns, and other characteristics that make the infant unique. While many infants are cared for by nonparental caregivers during their parents' working hours, continuity is maintained when the infant experiences a minimum number of caregivers during the course of a day or a week. Many child care centers today provide a **primary caregiver** to infants in an effort to reduce the number of adults to whom the infant must adapt. This practice enhances the infant's sense of order and facilitates opportunities to form positive relationships and, perhaps, healthy attachments between infant and nonparental caregivers.

primary caregiver: the person primarily responsible for the care and nurturing of a child

The vignettes about Angela and Jeremy earlier in this chapter reveal two very different situations in the quality and consistency of care each infant is receiving. Angela's routines are less predictable; so are her caregivers, as they change frequently. The quality of care she is receiving is not optimal, and the opportunity for her to develop stable, trusting relationships is tenuous.

Jeremy, on the other hand, is experiencing daily schedules and routines that are neither rigid nor inflexible yet are predictable to him. His caregivers are limited in number, and each responds effectively to his cues for attention and other needs. In both cases, the infants are being provided with nonparental care while their parents are away at school or work.

Nonparental Child Care

An increasing number of infants are receiving nonparental child care. Many enter nonparental child care arrangements as early as 6 weeks of age. These arrangements include care by a member of the child's extended family (grandparent, aunt, uncle, cousin, older sibling), neighbor, in-home baby-sitter, family day home, and child care centers. The quality of infant care programs is always a major concern, and parents need to be discerning in their choices of individuals who will care for their infants.

Recent studies have noted varying adjustment patterns among infants receiving nonparental child care. One study noted that initially, infants showed inhibited behaviors and less positive affect similar to those expected of older children challenged by a new environment. These behaviors, however, were found to diminish over the next 6 months, after which the children showed more positive affect and positive peer interactions later on (Fein, Gariboldi, & Boni, 1993). This study also found that caregivers were most responsive and comforting to infants at entry and that over the next 6 months, the infants' distress behavior diminished. This study also suggested that it takes 3 to 6 months for infants to feel comfortable in child care settings. We can assume that with poor-quality care, the adjustment period could well be longer. However, we would not wish to wait 6 months to determine infants' adjustment if there is any reason to believe the care is less than optimal.

While some studies propose that long hours (20 or more) in nonparental child care can impede the development of secure attachments between infants and their mothers (Belsky, 1988; Belsky & Rovine, 1988), other studies do not support this perspective. One study (Burchinal, Bryant, Lee, & Ramey, 1992) found that nonmaternal care had no detrimental effects on the development and maintenance of infant–mother attachments at age 1 year if the age of entry was less than 7 months, before attachment patterns begin to emerge, and the quality of the child care arrangement was exemplary. This study also noted that children who received extensive nonmaternal care beginning in early infancy were as likely to develop normal infant–mother attachments as their home-raised peers. The important point here is the quality of the child care arrangement. Quality of infant care programs is usually defined in terms of involved and developmentally appropriate caregiving, low infant-to-caregiver/teacher ratios, and small groups (the younger the child, the smaller the group should be).

Earlier in this chapter, we discussed the importance of the mother's and father's sensitivity and responsiveness to their infant's signals. It follows that the infant's nonparental caregivers must also be sensitive and responsive. Stressing the importance of high-quality child care programs, Raikes (1993) focused on how the amount of time an infant spends in the care of a "high-ability" teacher affects infant–teacher attachment. Since a secure attachment with a caring and nurturing caregiver can buffer the stress of parental separation, such an attachment can prove to be quite important. It is also thought that such child–caregiver attachments may even compensate for insecure parental attachments. Raikes's study was based on the following premises:

- High-ability caregivers/teachers support and facilitate the infant's developing sense of trust, predictability, and control.
- Experience with infants allows teachers to become fully acquainted with infants' personalities, that is, what upsets, excites, amuses, and bores infants.
- History in a relationship is required for secure attachments to develop.
- Infants' cognitive, social, emotional, and language development depend on quality relationships.

Raikes found that at least 9 months with the same caregiver/teacher provides the best opportunity for the infant to form a secure attachment. She proposed that rather than "promoting" infants at age 6 or 7 months, as is quite common in child care programs, a "new standard for excellence" in the field would keep infants and high-ability teachers together beyond 1 year of age.

Communication between parents and caregivers is also important in nonparental child care. The accreditation standards of the National Association for the Education of Young Children (NAEYC, 2004) and other standards set by funding entitles encourage frequent interactions and mutual support. The amount of parent–caregiver interaction varies appreciably among child care settings, yet frequent and meaningful communication is predictive of the quality of the child care program (Ghazvini & Readdick, 1994).

Parents need to assess their infants' responses and well-being on an ongoing basis. Are positive and nurturing relationships developing among all who share in the care and nurturing of the infant? Does the infant need the routine at home to be more like that of the infant care program, or vice versa? Is the infant overtired or overstimulated from the day's experiences? What is the parent doing to ensure consistency, predictability, and continuity in the infant's life at home? Are the

1. Trained, knowledgeable, nurturing, and committed caregivers
2. Safe, sanitary, healthy environment for infants and children
3. Low adult–child ratios, with emphasis on providing primary caregivers to individual infants over extended periods of time
4. Cognitively and linguistically enriching, socially stimulating, emotionally supportive environment and caregivers
5. Sensitive, appropriate, antibias interactions and activities for all children
6. Sensitivity to parental needs, goals, and concerns
7. Exceeds local and/or state licensing standards
8. Accredited through the National Association for the Education of Young Children or other nationally recognized accrediting agency.

FIGURE 6.4
Characteristics of High-Quality Child Care

infant's health and safety paramount to all caregivers? Is the infant exhibiting a basic sense of trust, secure attachments, healthy emotional development, and enjoyment of parents and other caregivers? Qualities to assess in seeking appropriate infant care are listed in Figure 6.4. Parents should make informed choices for themselves and their infants, choosing according to the infant's unique developmental needs and the caregiver's ability to meet those needs adequately and appropriately.

Overall Health, Safety, and Freedom from Stress

Certainly, we can assume that healthy infants are better equipped to deal emotionally and socially with their environments than less healthy infants. Obstetric and pediatric supervision during prenatal development and infancy provides preventive and corrective measures to facilitate healthy development. Proper nutrition and socially and emotionally satisfying interactions are essential to this health.

Infant Mental Health

There is no question that healthy early childhood development lays the foundation for adult mental health. With this assumption in place, many scholars are increasingly turning their attention to infant and early childhood mental health (Jellinek, Patel, & Froehle, 2002; Zeanah, 1999). Both the context in which infants are growing and being nurtured and the infant's physiological and psychological characteristics contribute to infant mental health. Mental health in childhood and adolescence is defined "by the achievement of expected developmental cognitive, social, and emotional milestones and by secure attachments, satisfying social relationships, and effective coping skills" (U.S. Surgeon General, 2000).

In infancy, success with such developmental psychosocial tasks as developing a sense of trust in self and others; forming secure attachments; modulating or regulating emotions; summoning the attention and interaction of others; communicating discomfort, distress, contentment, joy, and other emotions; accepting the nurturing and comforting efforts of caregivers; and becoming a competent communicator are necessary contributors to infant mental health. This process, however, is supported by a context (family, home, nonparental settings, community) and relationships that facilitate and nurture the infant's psychosocial development. It depends on caregivers who are responsive and empathic, who accurately interpret infant cues and behaviors, and who recognize when behaviors may be cause for concern. When concern arises, professional evaluation and guidance is sought.

Psychopathology in infants and early childhood is difficult to identify, since many troubling behaviors (e.g., fretfulness, temper tantrums, oppositional behaviors, inability to be soothed) represent normal, expected patterns, are usually transient, changing as the child matures or needs are met, may be sustained or exacerbated due to inappropriate adult–child interactions, and are observed without benefit of causal explanation.

While few events can be said to "cause" mental disorders, risk factors have been studied. These risks include prenatal damage from exposure to alcohol, illegal drugs, and tobacco; low birth weight; difficult temperament; inherited predisposition to a mental disorder; poverty; deprivation, abuse, and neglect; unsatisfactory relationships; parental mental health disorder; and exposure to traumatic events (Kraemer et al., 1997). These risk factors encompass dysfunctional family behaviors, such as severe parental discord, mental illness or criminal behavior in the parent, overcrowded living conditions or large family size, maladaptive sibling relationships, and exposure to acts of violence, which all contribute to stress-related mental health issues. Economic hardships increase the risk of child abuse. Poor caregiving from a mother suffering from depression is also considered a risk (U.S. Surgeon General, 2000).

Why a risk factor may have adverse effects on one child but not on another depends on individual differences in children, the age at which the child is confronted with the risk(s) or trauma, its intensity and the extent to which the risk or trauma persists over time, and the nature and timeliness of intervention. As with other developmental issues and challenges, suspected mental disorder should be diagnosed early and intervention provided in a consistent and timely way. Treatments vary and can include family counseling and support programs, psychotherapy, medications, and specialized residential treatment programs.

Infants who experience chronic illnesses, birth defects, injury, violence, emotionally unstable caregivers, or inconsistent or contradictory child-rearing practices are most likely to develop negative emotionality and psychosocial problems later. Manifestation of these problems in infants depends on factors such as age, temperament, past experiences, and bonding and attachment success. Factors relating to the intensity and duration of the problems the infant encounters, including the temperaments and coping abilities of various family members and the willingness and/or ability of the family to seek and benefit from professional help, also influence developmental outcomes.

Infants tend to exhibit signs of stress through physiological functions, such as changes in sleeping and waking patterns, feeding disturbances, heightened emotionality, frantic or unrelenting crying, depressive behaviors, withdrawing, and avoidant behaviors. When these behaviors are evident, parents and professionals might examine the family or child caregiving situation to determine causes and look for solutions. Again, professional counseling may be needed to help the family cope with their difficulties and respond appropriately to the infant.

ROLE OF THE EARLY CHILDHOOD PROFESSIONAL

Promoting Psychosocial Development in Infants

1. Provide warm, loving, supportive, predictable, consistent, and continuous care.
2. Respond readily to the infant's cues for food, comfort, rest, play, and social interaction.
3. Recognize that crying is the infant's way of communicating needs.
4. Be aware of sensitive periods relating to attachment behaviors, separation, and stranger anxiety, and respond in supportive/empathic ways.
5. Be aware of windows of opportunity and the need for certain essential experiences to promote optimal brain growth and neurological development.
6. Provide stimulating and satisfying social and emotional interactions.
7. Respond readily to the infant's playful overtures.
8. Recognize and accept the infant's unique temperament and ways of interacting with others.
9. Recognize and respond in accepting and supporting ways to the infant's various emotional displays.

KEY TERMS

attachment	reciprocal determinism	socialization
fixation	separation anxiety	social referencing
primary caregiver	social cognition	stranger anxiety

REVIEW STRATEGIES AND ACTIVITIES

1. Review the key terms independently or with a classmate.
2. Discuss with classmates the differences in the early lives of Angela and Jeremy. In terms of psychosocial development, what kinds of experiences are these infants having? What are the characteristics of the environmental contexts in which each child is developing? What suggestions can you make to enhance the psychosocial development of each child?
3. Review the qualities of a good infant care center. Visit an NAEYC-accredited or other high-quality child care center in which infants are enrolled.
   a. Describe the frequency and nature of the interactions between adults and infants:
      (i) What strategies do infants use to summon attention to their needs?
      (ii) What self-comforting strategies do infants employ?
      (iii) What adult behaviors elicit and help infants develop a sense of trust?
      (iv) How do adults respond to infants who are difficult to console?
      (v) How is infant attachment behavior displayed?
      (vi) How is playfulness displayed? Encouraged?

b. Observe the infants' reactions to other infants. What behaviors do they exhibit?

c. How did the infants respond to you as a stranger? What was the response? How old were the infants whose responses you observed?

d. How are parents' needs and concerns addressed?

e. How do the early childhood professionals nurture the psychosocial development of developmentally challenged infants?

4. Interview a parent to discuss how she or he juggles work and parenting. Does this person feel generally positive about his or her lifestyle? What has this parent found to be challenging? Most satisfying?

5. How might parents and/or primary caregivers ensure that infants develop a healthy sense of trust? Develop a list of dos and don'ts.

FURTHER READINGS

Brazelton, T. B. (2003). *Calming your fussy baby: The Brazelton way.* Cambridge, MA: Perseus.

Brazelton, T. B., & Greenspan, S. I. (2000). *The irreducible needs of children: What every child must have to grow, learn, and flourish.* Cambridge, MA: Perseus.

Greenspan, S. I. (1999). *The child with special needs: Encouraging intellectual and emotional growth.* New York: Perseus.

Gandini, L., & Edwards, C. P. (2000). *Bambini: The Italian approach to infant/toddler care.* Washington, DC: National Association for the Education of Young Children.

Herschkowitz, N., & Herschkowitz, E. C. (2002). *Understanding your child's brain and behavior.* Washington, DC: John Henry.

Honig, A. S. (2002). *Secure relationships: Nurturing infant–toddler attachment in early care settings.* Washington, DC: National Association for the Education of Young Children.

Shore, R. (2002). *What kids need: Today's best ideas for nurturing, teaching, and protecting young children.* Boston: Beacon.

Zigler, E. F., Finn-Stevenson, M., & Hall, N. W. (2002). *The first three years and beyond.* New Haven, CT: Yale University Press.

OTHER RESOURCES

Association for Childhood Education, International. *Focus on infancy.* A newsletter for members of the ACEI Professional Division for Infancy. Council on Contemporary Families. www.contemporary families.org

Gerber, M. (n.d.). *Seeing infants with new eyes* [Video]. Washington, DC: National Association for the Education of Young Children.

Harmes, T., Cryer, D., & Clifford, R. M. (2003). *Infant/toddler environment rating scale.* Washington, DC: National Association for the Education of Young Children.

Zero to Three. Bimonthly, available from Zero to Three, PO Box 960, Herndon, VA 20172.

Cognitive, Language, and Literacy Development of the Infant

Nature has plainly not entrusted the determination of our intellectual capacities to the blind fate of a gene or genes: she gave us parents, learning, language, culture and education to program ourselves with.

MATT RIDLEY

After studying this chapter, you will demonstrate comprehension by:

▶ Recognizing theoretical perspectives on cognitive, language, and literacy development.

▶ Describing cognitive development during the infant's first year.

▶ Describing language development during the infant's first year.

▶ Describing earliest literacy behaviors.

▶ Relating cognitive, language, and literacy development to other developmental domains.

▶ Identifying major factors influencing cognitive, language, and literacy development during infancy.

▶ Suggesting strategies for promoting and enhancing cognitive, language, and literacy development in infancy.

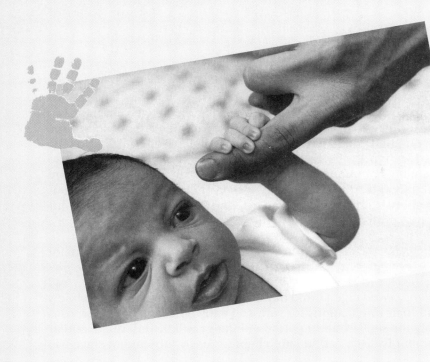

COGNITIVE DEVELOPMENT IN INFANCY

Cognitive development is the aspect of development that deals with thinking, problem solving, intelligence, and language. Infants come into the world with a remarkable capacity to process all kinds of information, from the look and scent of their birth mother and the sound of her voice to sensations of warmth and security or of pain and overstimulation. Over the first few months, the infant will demonstrate quite a repertoire of emerging capabilities and interaction patterns, becoming engaged and curious, communicative and social, and a motoric and active explorer.

cognitive development: the aspect of development that involves thinking, problem solving, intelligence, and language

THEORETICAL PERSPECTIVES ON COGNITIVE DEVELOPMENT IN INFANCY

As with all other developmental domains, changes in behaviors and abilities over time can be interpreted by reviewing theories advanced by scholars and practitioners in the various disciplines concerned with human growth and development. Chief among the theories of cognitive development are the cognitive/developmental, information processing, social/interactionist, and ecological systems theories. Many aspects of these theories are supported by information from the neurosciences. Neurobiology is shedding light on the neurological processes that are involved in learning, memory, and the complex activities associated with a child's ability to integrate and make sense of internal and external sensory experiences. Let's take a look at these points of view as we begin an intriguing exploration of the developing intellect.

Piaget's Theory of Cognitive Development

The most familiar theory of cognitive development is that of Jean Piaget (1952). Piaget's studies of cognitive development have dominated the fields of child study, psychology, philosophy, and education since the 1920s. He is perhaps the best known and most widely quoted of the contemporary cognitive theorists. As we will see later in the chapter, other theorists have challenged or modified Piaget's theory; nevertheless, his theory continues to influence knowledge and practice in early childhood education. Foremost among Piaget's contributions to early childhood education is the recognition that the thinking processes and problem-solving abilities of infants and young children are quite different from those of older children and adults. This difference in thinking processes has implications for how parents and caregivers can respond to and interact with infants and young children to promote optimal cognitive development.

Four Stages of Cognitive Development.   Piaget's theory proposes four major stages of cognitive development: the *sensorimotor period* (birth to age 2), the *preoperational period* (ages 2 to 7), the *concrete operations period* (ages 7 to 11), and the *formal operations period* (age 11 and beyond). Table 7.1 provides an overview of these stages and their implications for care and early education. For purposes of this chapter, only the sensorimotor period of infancy will be described, and as cognitive development is discussed in later chapters, each subsequent stage will be summarized.

According to Piaget, all children proceed through a stage-related sequence of cognitive development, each stage building on the accomplishments of the previous one. Piaget viewed these stages as invariant; that is, one stage always follows another in a predictable sequence. All individuals are said to proceed through the invariant sequence, but they do so at their own rates of development. Differences in rates of entering and exiting the stages are attributed to differences in individual genetic timetables and to cultural and environmental influences.

The sensorimotor period extends from birth to the onset of gestures and language at around age two. During this period, the infant's cognitive development depends on direct sensory experiences and motor actions; hence the term **sensorimotor learning**. Recall the reflexive activities of the newborn described in Chapter 5. These genetically preprogrammed reflexes provide a basis for later cognitive development. Piaget believed that all mental processes are rooted in and are a continuation of the earliest reflexive and motor activities. As the infant gains control over his or her reflexes, movement (or motor) behaviors become more purposeful. Purposeful motor activities facilitate the infant's explorations and hence the infant's awareness of and interactions with objects and people.

From birth on, through interactions with the environment, the infant begins to form mental structures, which Piaget termed *schemata*. These schemata help the infant to mentally organize and interpret experiences. Each additional experience brings new schemata or perhaps modifies existing schemata. The infant's knowledge of the environment grows through direct actions on objects and experiences with others. Piaget described the infant at this stage as egocentric, or able to perceive only from his or her own needs, experience, and perspective, not from the perspective of others.

Assimilation, Accommodation, and Equilibration.   According to Piaget, **adaptation** to environmental demands involves two complementary processes: assimilation and accommodation. As infants attempt to fit new ideas and concepts into existing ones, they must assimilate new schemata. At first, the infant visually gazes and tracks, and the infant's hands and arms respond to environmental

sensorimotor learning:
learning that occurs through the senses and motor activities

adaptation:
the process by which one adjusts to changes in the environment

TABLE 7.1   Piaget's Stages of Cognitive Development

Stages/Ages	Characteristics	Implications for Interactions and Education
I. 0–2 years Sensorimotor stage		
1. Reflexive (0–1 month)	Innate reflex responses	Interact in ways that stimulate the infant's sense of touch, taste, sight, sound, and smell
2. Primary circular reactions (1–4 months)	Repeats actions that previously happened by chance; reflexes become more coordinated	Provide sensory-stimulating toys and objects such as rattles, mobiles, baby books, recorded familiar voices or pleasing music
3. Secondary circular reactions (4–10 months)	Intentionally repeats behaviors or pleasurable actions; the notion of object permanence emerges	Provide clean, safe objects and toys; play hide and seek; continue to talk or sing when moving out of the child's auditory or visual field; play repetitive games
4. Coordination of secondary schemes (10–12 months)	Applies previously learned behaviors and activities to new situations; imitative behaviors emerge	Provide familiar toys, dolls, stuffed animals, blankets, and clothing; encourage imitation, provide encouraging verbal feedback
5. Tertiary circular reactions (12–18 months)	Cause-and-effect discoveries; seeks proximity and playful interactions with persons to whom attachments have been formed; repeats novel experiences	Respond positively to interaction overtures; provide toys that stack, nest, roll, open, close, push, pull, and are easily manipulated; talk, label, and pretend with child
6. Symbolic representation (18 months–2 years)	Applies learned skills to new situations; begins to think before acting; experiments with new uses for familiar objects; represents objects or events through imagery	Provide verbal labels for objects and events; encourage and provide props for pretend play; provide social interaction with other children; encourage and provide props and safe equipment for large motor activity
II. 2–7 years Preoperational thought	Egocentric, perception-bound thinking; more sophisticated language system, rich imagination; performs simple mental operations, but has difficulty explaining them	Provide props and toys for imaginative play and exploration, materials for constructions (e.g., crayons, clay, blocks), and a variety of talk, story, music, and pretend opportunities; encourage choices and decision making; engage in extended meaningful dialogue; encourage new experiences
III. 7–11 years Concrete operational thinking	Can solve concrete problems with physical objects; thought is reversible; thinking is based on prior experience; the ability to mentally conserve emerges, as does simple logic	Provide opportunity to pursue areas of interest; help to obtain materials and resources for exploring and learning; encourage and show interest in school and other activities and accomplishments; engage in meaningful dialogue; use questions to extend understanding
IV. 11 years–adulthood Formal operational thinking	Formulates and tests hypotheses; abstract thinking; deductive reasoning; thinking is no longer perception bound and employs logic	Challenge with hypothetical problems to solve; discuss ethical issues; encourage and support educational and hobby interests and abilities; encourage appropriate and enjoyable social interactions

stimuli through reflex activity. Later, these reflexive movements become more integrated into whole activities such as looking and grasping simultaneously or coordinated eye–hand movements. These more integrated responses and movements facilitate the infant's interactions with the objects and people around him or her, which in turn increase the number and character of the infant's schemata. Each new experience changes the infant's schemata and leads to new learning. New learning builds on previous actions, events, or experiences.

Accommodation is a process by which a previous schema (experience or concept[s]) is modified to include or adapt to a new experience. For example, the breast-fed infant who is changed from breast-feeding (existing schema) to bottle-feeding (new experience) must alter sucking behaviors to succeed with the new experience, the bottle. This altered sucking behavior is an example of accommodation to a new environmental demand. Each assimilation of an experience is complemented by accommodation to that experience, and this leads to adaptation. Adaptation to an event or experience brings about equilibrium between the individual and her or his environment.

Equilibrium is said to occur when assimilation and accommodation are in balance with each other, that is, when the infant has adapted to the demands of the environment. However, this state is usually shortlived, as the infant is constantly being confronted with new information, which requires additional assimilations and accommodations.

Development during the Sensorimotor Stage.   The sensorimotor period of cognitive development is divided into six substages as listed in Table 7.1. Development through these substages is both rapid and dramatic. During the first year, the infant proceeds through the first four of these substages.

1. *Reflexive stage* (birth to 1 month). During this period, reflexes that have been dominant since birth are modified as the infant experiences an increasing variety of sensory stimuli and interactions with the environment. Piaget believed that the infant constructs schemata from the numerous sensory experiences of these first weeks. The human face or voice, the positioning in the mother's arms before breast-feeding, and the sounds and rhythms of the household are sources of early schemata.

primary circular reactions:
simple, pleasurable, repetitive acts centered on the infant's body

2. *Primary circular reactions* (1 to 4 months). At this time, infant reactions center on bodily responses. For example, the infant can now purposefully bring the thumb to the mouth to suck. Previous thumb sucking occurred as a result of accidental and uncoordinated reflex activity. During this stage, the infant engages in other purposeful motor activity. This period is called primary because of its focus on bodily responses; it is called circular because the infant repeats the activities over and over again. This repetition may be the first indication of infant memory.

secondary circular reactions:
simple, pleasurable, repetitive responses centered on objects and events in the environment

3. *Secondary circular reactions* (4 to 8 months). This period is characterized by the infant's enlarging focus on objects and events in the environment. It is called secondary circular because it involves the infant's growing awareness of objects and events outside his or her body. Through chance events, the infant learns that he or she can make things happen to external objects. For example, the infant hits the bath water, and a big splash results. This novel experience generates interest and a desire to repeat it; and repeat it the infant does,

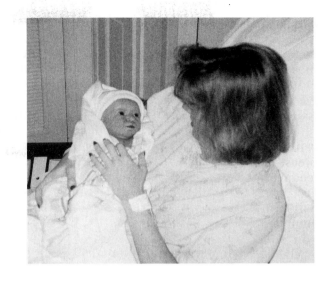

The infant's sensory capabilities are remarkably operative at birth.

motivated by both curiosity and pleasure. These behaviors represent early experimentation and become means/ends behaviors. During this substage, infants imitate sounds and actions that they have previously produced and currently hold in their own repertoires. Infants now search for a hidden object, which before this point in development was not pursued if it was not seen. Piaget believed that in the infant's mind, an object not seen did not exist.

4. *Coordination of secondary schemata* (8 to 12 months). This is the period in which the infant's intentional behaviors are clearly evident. Imitative behaviors signal the infant's growing ability to learn through observing the behavior of others. Play becomes more clearly differentiated from other means/end activities and is enjoyed for its own sake. **Object permanence**, the realization that an object exists even though it cannot be touched or seen, is beginning to emerge.

Criticisms of the Piagetian Perspective

Some contemporary scholars of cognitive theory (neo-Piagetians, as they are often called) have challenged a number of Piaget's cognitive development assumptions. For instance, Bower (1982) and Wishart and Bower (1985) challenges the notion of object permanence in the infant at 6 to 8 months. Whereas Piaget proposed that an infant will not search for an object hidden behind a screen because the infant believes that the object no longer exists, Bower believes immature space perception may explain the infant's failure to search. He suggested that from the infant's point of view, the screen has replaced the hidden object, and two objects cannot occupy the same space. Bower believes that Piaget underestimated what infants come to know about objects and that their failure to search for or locate a hidden object may represent a lack of spatial knowledge rather than a lack of knowledge of object permanence. Bower suggests that infants as young as 5 months old will not only anticipate the reappearance of an object that has been moved to a position behind the screen, but will attempt to look for it when a different object or no object appears when the screen is removed.

object permanence: the realization that objects and people continue to exist even through they may not be visible or detected through other senses

Other researchers challenged Piaget's notion that infants must do something to or with objects or people in their environment for cognitive development to occur. These scholars suggested that there may be other pathways through which cognition emerges. Studying infants and young children with impaired vision, hearing, and/or motor abilities, they demonstrated that cognitive development proceeds nonetheless (Bebko, Burke, Craven, & Sarlo, 1992; Furth, 1992a, 1992b, 1992c; Mandler, 1990, 1992). The belief is that infants, through their perceptual abilities and mental imagery, are able to form concepts with and without direct interaction with objects or people and can do so earlier than Piaget proposed.

While Piaget's theory is characterized by abstract language and ideas that are often hard to translate and to verify through research, his theory remains important to caregivers and educators for several reasons. Piaget's cognitive developmental theory

- focuses attention on the sequential aspects of growth and development in the cognitive domain;
- emphasizes the fact that thinking processes in young children are significantly different than thinking processes in older children and adults;
- emphasizes the importance of firsthand, direct, interactional experiences with objects and people;
- provides insight into numerous aspects of cognitive development, such as the development of cause-and-effect relationships; time, space, and number concepts; classification strategies; logic; morality; and language

Information Processing Theory

The information processing theory (Case, 1987, 1992; Klahr & Wallace, 1976; Sternberg, 1985) likens cognitive development to the computer's *inputs*, *throughputs*, and *outputs*. Input refers to the individual's gathering of information from sensory stimuli: vision, hearing, tasting, smelling, tactile sensations, and sensorimotor activity. Input information is then acknowledged, compared to other data already stored in memory, categorized, and stored for future use. This process represents throughput. Subsequent verbal and/or nonverbal responses represent output. Information processing theorists have been variously concerned about how the mind operates during memory, attention, and problem-solving activities. Findings from studies of these cognitive attributes suggest that information processing improves as individuals get older and can develop certain cognitive strategies that assist memory, attention, and problem solving. Nevertheless, information processing theory represents cognitive development as a continuous process in which there are age differences in children's cognitive abilities.

So far, studies have not demonstrated that cognitive strategies for remembering, paying attention, and solving problems are evident in infants. In an attempt to explain the adaptive nature of cognitive development, however, Siegler (1998) proposed that "All current theories recognize that people are biologically prepared to perceive the world in certain ways, that many important perceptual capabilities are present at birth, and that others emerge in the first few months of infancy given all but the most abnormal experience" (p. 92). Siegler further asserted that we all perceive the world through our senses, yet learning in infancy inevitably depends on three functions:

Attending: Determining what object, event, or action will be mentally processed

Identifying: Establishing what a perception is through relating a current perception to perceptions already held in memory

Locating: Determining where the object of perception exists and in what location relative to the observer

Social Interactionist Theory

Social interactionist theories emphasize the importance of social contexts and role models for learning. Many of these theories have their origins in the behaviorist point of view, in which less importance is given to developmental progressions and more importance to environmental influences. Recall from earlier discussions that behaviorists (Bijou & Baer, 1961; Skinner, 1938; Watson, 1924) believe that external factors such as reward and punishment have a greater impact on individual learning than do innate abilities or biological processes. Social learning theory (Bandura, 1977, 1997; Bandura & Walters, 1963), which is an outgrowth of the behaviorist philosophy, emphasizes the role of imitation in cognitive development. Many behaviors are learned simply by watching others, and much learning occurs in social situations. It is believed that very young infants can imitate the facial expressions of others (Meltzoff, 1989, 1995) and that infants may have an innate ability to compare information received through different modalities, such as vision, hearing, and their body movements. They then use this information to coordinate imitative behaviors on the basis of actions observed in others.

Contextualistic Theory

Still another theoretical perspective that is important in the discussion of cognitive, language, and literacy development is one in which development and social interaction are viewed as reciprocal influences on one another. Stated quite simply, this theory supposes that the growing and developing child influences and is influenced by his or her environmental context. Contextualistic theories (or ecological systems theory) (Bronfenbrenner, 1977, 1986; Bronfenbrenner & Ceci, 1994) describe cognitive (and language and literacy) development as being integral to the social and cultural context in which an individual grows and develops. Development in all domains (physical/motor, psychosocial, and cognitive, language, and literacy) is viewed as an interactive process between the individual and a variety of social and cultural influences. Cognition continually changes as contexts in which learning occurs change. Cognition, language, and literacy, then, are determined by many factors, including observation and imitation, but also opportunities to explore and discover in a variety of situations, both independently and in the company of others, and through coaching and direct instruction. From this perspective, development proceeds to some degree in all domains simultaneously. The degree of influence and rate of development in specific developmental domains depend on the context and nature of the environmental input and the nature and responses of the learner at a given point in time. The following vignettes illustrate this interactive process.

As infants gain greater mobility through crawling, standing, and walking, their actions are more means/end oriented.

Jeremy, lying in his crib, is intently watching a yellow soft-sculpture airplane dangling from the mobile above him. He kicks and squeals with glee, then stops and stares at the object bouncing above his crib. Lying still, he seems to notice that the object stopped swinging; when he kicks some more, the object begins to swing again. The entertainment is quite exhilarating and is repeated several times.

Phyllis, Jeremy's baby-sitter, noticing his playfulness and his interest in the mobile, recognizes that Jeremy has discovered the link between his own bodily movements and the subsequent jiggling of the colorful airplane. She approaches, detaches the airplane from the mobile, and holds it within Jeremy's reach while saying to him, "Do you want to hold the airplane? I think you like this bright toy, Jeremy."

Distracted from his previous activity, Jeremy's kicking subsides. He stares at the soft toy, looks at Phyllis (a bit puzzled), then back again at the toy. His eyes then travel to the mobile above where the airplane had been, then back to Phyllis and the toy in her hand. He reaches for the airplane, grasps it and brings it to his mouth momentarily, then drops it, only to return to the original activity of kicking and watching the mobile. Somehow it isn't the same, and he immediately tires of the effort and begins to fret.

Which of Piaget's sensorimotor substages does Jeremy's behavior exhibit? Approximately how old is Jeremy? If your answer is substage 3, secondary circular reactions, you are correct. If you recalled the approximate age range for this substage, you guessed Jeremy's age to be somewhere between 4 and 8 months. Jeremy is now 6 months old. His motor activity that caused the mobile to bounce and swing were entertaining in and of themselves. Jeremy was discovering that his actions could make the airplane wiggle.

However, playful infants attract their caregivers' attention. Phyllis could not resist getting in on the action, but when she did, Jeremy was presented with a choice that was perhaps difficult for him to make: reach for and hold the toy airplane, interact with Phyllis, or continue the pleasurable activity of kicking and watching the mobile move.

While her timing and assumption about what would please Jeremy at that moment missed the mark, Phyllis was supporting Jeremy's cognitive development by noticing what held his attention, naming the object, and bringing it within his reach. Observant adults soon learn to synchronize their interactions with the infant's, recognizing when to enter an activity and when to leave the infant to her or his own explorations.

Angela, now 8 months old, is in her high chair. She still has some difficulty sitting alone and slides under the tray, only to be restrained by the high-chair safety strap between her legs. Cracker crumbs are in her hair, on her eyebrows, between her fingers, clinging to her clothing, and sprinkled about on the floor on both sides of her chair. James and Cheryl, seated at the table nearby, have just finished their take-out burgers and are arguing over James's dating activities. It seems that James is seeing some other girls now, and Cheryl is very unhappy about it.

Angela slides under the high-chair tray and frets in discomfort. James offhandedly pulls her back into a seated position and continues his emotional discussion with Cheryl. Angela begins to cry intermittently. Cheryl places another cracker on the high-chair tray while continuing her emotional conversation with James. Quieted momentarily, Angela bangs the cracker on the tray, holds what is left of it over the floor, then releases her grasp and watches the cracker fall to the floor. Sliding under her tray again, she begins to cry, this time more forcefully. She is pulled back to a seated position by Cheryl, but this does not comfort or quiet her. James, tired of arguing and a bit distracted by the baby's crying, decides to leave.

Frustrated and angry, Cheryl picks up Angela, scolds her about the mess, takes her to the sink to wash her face and hands, then puts her in her playpen, even though Angela is fretful. Unable to respond to Angela's needs—her own are overwhelming at this time—Cheryl turns on the TV, props her feet up on the coffee table, and lapses into sadness.

Unable to elicit her mother's attention, Angela cries awhile longer. Defeated and tired, she picks up her blanket, puts her thumb in her mouth, watches her mother, and listens to the sounds of the television set until she finally falls asleep.

Angela's predicament involves psychosocial, physical/motor, and cognitive aspects. At 8 months old, what are Angela's cognitive needs? How would you characterize the psychosocial dynamics in this setting between Angela and her caregivers? What does her behavior suggest about her physical/motor development and needs?

Are any apparent constraints to her cognitive development illustrated in this vignette? What alternative activities might be provided for Angela that might engage her attention and contribute to her cognitive development while the adults continue their discussion? What theoretical perspectives can you apply to each of these two scenarios? Let's continue to explore these and other facets of cognitive development.

THE NEUROBIOLOGY OF COGNITIVE, LANGUAGE, AND LITERACY DEVELOPMENT

Chapter 5 described the rapid brain growth and neurological development in very young children. This growth and development are so dramatic that during the first 10 years, the child's brain will form literally trillions of connections or synapses. This growth includes a process known as myelination in which fatty tissue forms around the nerve cells, facilitating the transportation of impulses along the neurons. Rapid growth and myelination in the brain coincide with the development of the auditory system, rapid language development, and increased processing of visual, spatial, and temporal (or time) information. Simultaneously, these increased connections promote better processing of information, and their presence in the speech center of the brain facilitates the development of symbolization and communication. Gains in short-term memory and small motor skills are also attributed to the rapid myelination occurring at the ages of 4 and 5.

Also, as we discussed in earlier chapters, the structure and functions of the neurological system are determined by the interplay of experience and an individual's genetically programmed growth and development. In terms of cognitive, language, and literacy development, of particular importance in earliest brain growth and neurological development is the nature or quality of the child's first interpersonal relationships. As Siegel (1999) so aptly stated, "human connections shape the neural connections from which the mind emerges" (p. 2).

These earliest interpersonal relationships shape the neurological structures that establish mental representations of experience in the child's mind. Hence, patterns of relationships and emotional communication, particularly the character of early attachment relationships, influence the brain's biochemistry and subsequent wiring, thus laying down neurological patterns through which the child mentally constructs a view of the world (Siegel, 1999). Further, scholars are now placing significant importance on the role of emotions in the child's attempts to glean meaning from experience. It is believed that the circuits that represent social/emotional experiences are closely linked to those that create representations of meaning. These social/emotional experiences provide a range of stimuli derived from touch and the manner in which the infant is held and handled, voice tone and quality, verbal interactions, facial expressions, eye contact, and the predictability and timing of adult responses to the infant's cues. From these experiences, infants construct their first subjective representations of others, and their neurological systems establish patterns of arousal, appraisal, and response—mental activities that are essential to learning. In this regard, it becomes very difficult to separate emotions and cognition because to a great extent, from the neurological perspective, they are one and the same (Siegel, 1999). Learning does not occur without emotion.

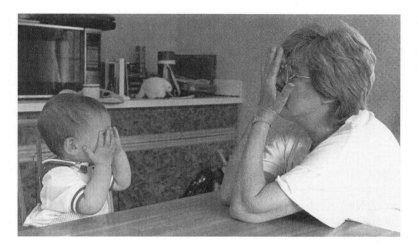

Playful interactions contribute to early cognitive development.

Another important concept associated with early brain growth and neurological development that enlightens our discussion of cognitive development has to do with the importance of timing and types of experiences during infancy and early childhood. It appears that one of the tasks of parenting and teaching is the selection of the "right experiences at the right time" (Diamond & Hopson, 1998, p. 3). Recall from Chapter 5 (Figure 5.1) that there are windows of opportunity, or critical periods, in which the brain is especially vulnerable to certain types of experience (or lack thereof). Much of what is known about sensitive periods in brain growth have been extrapolated from animal studies. One of the first studies of this nature took place in the 1960s by a group of researchers at the University of California at Berkeley and published under the title, "The Effects of an Enriched Environment on the Histology of the Rat Cerebral Cortex" (Diamond, Krech, & Rosenzweig, 1964). This research involved the examination of brain size and density in rats that had been raised in two kinds of cages: an enriched cage, which provided toys and a social environment of other rats, and a small cage with little to engage the rat's attention and no playmates. The experiments revealed that the rats raised in the enriched cage were more competent in navigating mazes than the rats raised in the impoverished cage. Microscopic examination of the rats' dissected brains showed that the enriched rats had a thicker cerebral cortex than the impoverished rats. This experiment demonstrated an actual structural change in the rats' brains based on qualitative differences in their early life experiences. This study opened the door to new ways of thinking about the brain that would emphasize the effects of environment on the biological character of the brain. Researchers over the ensuing decades continued to refine their research techniques and strategies, leading them to project a series of basic principles of brain enrichment such as the following (Diamond & Hopson, 1998):

- The impact of a stimulating or boring environment affects regions throughout the brains of the experimental rats.
- An enriched environment for pregnant female rats results in newborn pups with thicker cerebral cortex than pups born to impoverished females.
- A boring environment had a more thinning effect on the young and adolescent rat cortex than an exciting environment had on cortex thickening.

How do these and similar studies influence our thinking about the human brain? Obviously, ethics and common sense prevent the types of environmental controls and anatomical examinations of humans that are possible with laboratory rats. Nevertheless, scientific examination of donated human brain specimens during the early decades of brain research corroborated findings such as those described above; contemporary technological techniques for examining neurological activity support these early findings (Scheibel, Conrad, Perdue, Tomiyasu, & Wechsler, 1990). In short, scholars can now assert that enriched and mentally stimulating environments increase the growth and branching of dendrites and thicken the human cortex. Further, scientists can trace the emergence of various types of development, vision, hearing, motor controls, language, and so on through periods of sensitive and rapid growth, delineating certain periods in growth and development when selected experiences have their greater impact. While brain enrichment is possible throughout the life span, childhood and adolescence appear to be the optimal period for neural development—a time when neural connectivity and pruning and refining are most prolific.

SENSORY AND PERCEPTUAL ABILITIES IN INFANCY

Initially, infants learn through sensations derived from their sensory capabilities: touch, taste, smell, vision, hearing, and kinesthesis. Sensations are transmitted to the central nervous system, where interpretation and response take place. Perception is a process by which information gathered through the senses is organized. Recall from Chapter 5 the sensory capabilities of infants. For most infants, vision is reasonably acute, with an ability to visually track an object or a person moving within the infant's visual field. Infants (sometimes within the first few weeks) recognize and respond to the sight, sound, and smell of their mothers. Hearing, taste, and touch are also quite functional. Infants may distinguish their own mothers' voices from other female voices (DeCasper & Fifer, 1980) and can respond differently to infant-directed vocal affect, that is, approving and disapproving tonal qualities and other emotional expressions. It is believed that the infant can make these distinctions in infant-directed speech of several languages (Fernald, 1993). Tactile and kinesthetic sensations complete the sensory repertoire. Thus, the sensory capabilities of infants facilitate reception of environmental stimuli from which perceptions are formed. Perceptions dominate learning in the earliest stages of cognitive, language, and literacy development.

Specific perceptions such as size, shape, weight, distance, and depth, if present at all in early infancy, are imperfect. In efforts to determine specific perceptual abilities of infants, researchers have studied infant responses to facial patterns, geometric patterns, targets that approach and recede from their visual field, and looming objects, and depth awareness when placed on an elevated platform. Generally, these perceptions develop over the course of the first year and remain dependent on maturation and integration of all sensory modalities. Experience also contributes to perceptions. One can imagine, however, the potential for accidents and mishaps during infancy due to faulty perceptions.

While perceptions dominate infant learning in the first months, infant responses to the same stimuli become less noticeable over time as the events occur repeatedly and become familiar to the infant. This is referred to as an **orienting response**, in which the infant is observed to suppress body movements, exhibit

orienting response:
a reduction in the level of response to a stimulus previously experienced

alertness, and turn the head toward the stimulus (Kliegman, Jenson, & Behrman, 2003). (Recall Jeremy and the yellow soft-sculpture mobile.) Heartbeat accelerates during this orienting response, and as the stimulus becomes repetitive and familiar, the orienting response habituates; that is, the infant's responses become less and less acute to that particular stimulus. Additional new stimuli elicit new orienting responses.

During the first year, infants become aware of their own bodies, noticing and gazing at their hands, clasping them together, sucking on fists and fingers, and playing with feet, toes, and genitalia. Emerging coordination of motor skills leads infants to use their bodies and their abilities to explore, experience, and discover. Now there are infinite avenues for learning. The ability to grasp and let go leads to handling, mouthing, and experimenting with a variety of playthings. As the infant manipulates a variety of objects, information about his or her surroundings is being mentally constructed. The ability to sit, pull to a standing position, cruise around furniture, and return to a seated position provides variety to the infant's sensory experiences and increases the sources of information. The mobility provided by crawling and walking further extends the infant's explorations, experiences, and discoveries.

LANGUAGE DEVELOPMENT

One of the most remarkable cognitive achievements of early childhood is the acquisition of language. From beginnings characterized by communication through crying to a variety of interpretable vocal utterances, the infant begins to cognitively construct a very complex communicative system. This system includes focusing attention on another person, gazing and gesturing at sources of sounds, associating certain sounds and voices with particular events and people, developing reciprocity in verbal interactions (as when adult and infant coo back and forth to each other), and learning to use communicative systems to convey needs, feelings, and new learning. In addition, parents around the world seem to adjust their speech styles when talking to infants, using the simplest words and exaggerating certain vocal sounds and expressions, thus coaxing language along (Fernald & Morikawa, 1993). This altered speech is often referred to as **motherese** or **fatherese**. This manner of speaking is also referred to as **child-directed speech** and includes others who adapt their speech patterns when interacting with infants and young children (Cooper & Anslin, 1990).

From the moment of birth, infants seem to be preprogrammed to communicate. They respond readily to the sound of the human voice and have been shown to distinguish the voices of their mothers from other female voices (Mehler, 1985). Infant crying communicates a variety of messages—hunger, discomfort, distress, anger, or boredom—and does so through different intonations and patterns, which become recognizable to the infant's parents and other caregivers. Infants are intensely social, fixing their gaze on the faces of those who talk and sing to them, and are sensitive to the emotional tone of their caregivers. Quite interestingly, in the absence of speech, infants demonstrate remarkable communicative competence.

Indeed, contemporary studies of early brain growth and neurological development suggest that a sensitive period exists for the development of language, during which exposure to language is necessary for optimal development (Krasnegor, Lyon, & Goldman-Rakic, 1998). This period appears to occur during

motherese: modifications in the mother's speech when talking with infants and young children

fatherese: modifications in the father's speech when talking with infants and young children; can differ from motherese

child-directed speech: speech that has qualities of elevated pitch, conspicuous inflections, long pauses, and exaggerated stress on syllables

the first few months (Velichkovsky & Rumbaugh, 1996). During this period, opportunities to hear the language of others and observe its use in daily interactions as well as being gently talked and sung to bring about comprehension long before the physiological structures that produce speech are mature. Hence, we see language comprehension evolve when infants begin to understand what is said to them, but, as yet, are unable to speak.

Theoretical Perspectives on Language Development

As with cognitive development, a number of theoretical approaches have attempted to explain language development. A prominent theory proposes an inborn capacity for learning language called the **language acquisition device (LAD)** (Chomsky, 1968, 1980, 1993). The LAD is described as a set of innate skills that enable children to infer phoneme patterns, word meanings, and syntax from the language they hear. This skill facilitates the child's attempts to communicate. The recent work of Steven Pinker (1994) is supportive of this nativistic point of view:

> Language is not a cultural artifact that we learn the way we learn to tell time or how the federal government works. Instead, it is a distinct piece of the biological makeup of our brains. Language is a complex, specialized skill, which develops in the child spontaneously, without conscious effort or formal instruction, is deployed without awareness of its underlying logic, is qualitatively the same in every individual, and is distinct from more general abilities to process information or behave intelligently. (Pinker, 1994, p. 18)

In short, Pinker believes that the development of language is an instinctual process.

The nativist and instinctual perspectives assume a biological basis for human language, one that supposes that language emerges because there are specialized structures in the brain and neurological systems of humans. Studies of language development in children with hearing loss, of children who have suffered brain injury to the left brain hemisphere, and of people who attempt to acquire a new language after early childhood have demonstrated that there is a critical period or window of opportunity for language development. For example, when infants who are deaf are raised by parents who communicate through signing, the infants learn sign language in the same manner and with the same ease as hearing infants learn spoken language, and come to use this form of communication quite competently as they get older. Deprived of opportunities to learn sign language from infancy onward, deaf children struggle as they get older to gain skill in signing and seldom truly master this form of communication (Pinker, 1994). Because of the plasticity of the language-learning circuitry in the brain, children with left brain hemispheric injury or removal recover language to a greater extent than do adults with comparable injury. By the same token, younger immigrants acquire a new language, including accents and inflections, more completely and accurately than do their teenage or adult relatives. Between birth and age 6 years appears to be a biological prime time for the acquisition of language.

A behaviorist point of view, in contrast, holds that infants gradually learn languages through imitation of the sounds and speech they hear. When the infant spontaneously and, often accidentally, creates or repeats a sound and the parents respond with joy and encouragement, vocal productions become pleasurable experiences worth repeating (Skinner, 1957). Language is believed to be taught through reinforcement in the form of attention, repetition, and approval.

language acquisition device (LAD): an innate mental mechanism some theorists believe makes language development possible

The social interactionist point of view emphasizes the importance of the infant's interactions with caregivers in which vocal exchanges occur (Bruner, 1983; Golinkoff, 1983). These researchers recognize the communicative aspects of these early vocal exchanges and the emotional satisfaction that accrues from successful exchanges between caregiver and child. Indeed, language in humans is dependent on having other humans with whom to communicate.

A social interactionist view of language development takes into consideration the interplay of many factors, including the biological underpinnings of language, maturational patterns, cognitive development and the role of imitation, teaching and learning, and the necessity of social interaction. Through an interactive process, these factors play off one another in ways that encourage or impede language development.

Language Development in the First Year

The development of speech in the first year of life varies from child to child. A few children speak in sentences by the end of the first year. Others use only one-word "sentences" that can be understood only by those who participate consistently in the infant's everyday care. Piaget (1926) thought that cognition influences language. Since he viewed infants and young children as egocentric, Piaget therefore concluded that earliest speech is egocentric. He observed that the speech of infants and young children appears to be addressed to no one in particular. Vygotsky (1962) believed that language influences cognition and that the speech of infants and young children is not egocentric, but is communication with the self.

Under normal circumstances, infants follow similar, predictable sequences in the development of language. This seems to be true regardless of geography or culture. As with other areas of development, most children follow a predictable pattern, but not all children proceed through the sequences at the same rate. The sequence for language development during the first year is illustrated in Table 7.2.

As noted earlier, crying conveys a variety of messages, and caregivers soon learn to interpret the sounds and intensities of the infant's cries and respond appropriately. Around age 4 weeks, infants make small, throaty noises that are perhaps precursors to the vowel sounds that will begin to appear around 8 weeks. Infants discover their own voices around 12 weeks and enjoy gurgling and cooing, repeating the same vowel sound over and over, with perhaps some variation in tone. The infant is content to play with his or her voice alone or in concert with a parent or caregiver. Laughing aloud also occurs about this time. Infants are thought to view this exchange as a noise-making activity in which infant and others "speak" at the same time (Rosenthal, 1982).

Around six months of age, babbling begins to occur in which the vowel sounds are combined with the consonants m, p, b, k, and g. Babbles such as "bababa" are repeated over and over in succession, producing **echolalia.** Some scholars believe that regardless of culture or locale, children all over the world produce similar babbles (Olney & Scholnick, 1976). As infants get older, linguists are able, through the use of tape recordings of infant vocalizations, to distinguish subtle differences in the babbles of children in different environments (DeBoysson-Bardies, Sagart, & Durand, 1984). This is possible at around 6 to 7 months, when babbling becomes more varied in intonation, loudness, and rhythm and additional consonants are produced. Infants at this age begin to take turns in their vocalizations with a parent or caregiver (Rosenthal, 1982).

echolalia: replication in repetitive fashion of the sounds of another speaker in an infant–other turn-taking "conversation"

TABLE 7.2   The Language of Infancy (Birth to One Year): Prelinguistic Speech and Communication Strategies

From birth to 4 months
    Communicates through crying, fretting, and other reflexive vocalizations: coughing, burping, sneezing
    Gazes into the eyes of the caregiver
    Searches and attends to voices
    Begins to distinguish speech sounds
    Sensitive to the emotional tone of voices
    Produces some vowel sounds when cooing/gooing
    Smiles and chuckles

From 4 to 8 months
    "Plays" with voice and sound making
    Appears to experiment with contrasts in loud and soft sounds; low- and high-pitched sounds
    Produces "raspberries" (**bilabial trills**)
    Sustains some vowel sounds
    Combines some vowel and consonant sounds and begins to babble
    Produces strings of the same sounds: "mamamama," "babababa," "dadadadada"
    Produces strings of two or three different sounds, such as "dabagiba"
      Replicates in repetitive fashion the sounds of another speaker in an infant–other turn-taking
        "conversation" (echolalia)
    Points and gestures

From 8 to 12 months
    Babbling takes on the tone and inflections of "real talk" (referred to as jargon or conversational babble)
    Jargon may be accompanied by body language cues, such as nodding, tilting, or shaking head, making eye
      contact, gesturing, and exaggerated intonations
    Jargon can take the form of communicating, conveying a need or desire, e.g., request for the bottle,
      rejection of interaction, request to be picked up
    Jargon can represent engagement in vocal sound play enjoyed in and of itself
    Early words emerge from jargon
    Understands and imitates communicative gestures (bye-bye, throw a kiss, "applause" clapping)
    Babbles and early words coexist for a time

---

bilabial trills:
the production of sounds such as [m], [b], and [p] that are formed in the front of the mouth with the lips closed and move from the lips toward the back of the mouth (other structures for the articulation of sounds include the lips, teeth, roof of the mouth, and tongue)

During the latter half of the first year, infants are learning about the sounds of their native language and begin to make distinctions between their native language and other languages (Juscyzk, Cutler, & Redanz, 1993). Around 8 to 10 months, the infant may vocalize with toys, as though talking to them. Streams of babbles that sound like a conversation occur, yet no meaningful words emerge in this rich array of sounds. The infant may use sounds that approximate words or that are his or her own creation to represent objects or events. These sounds are called **vocables** (Ferguson, 1977). Later in this period, the infant may have learned a few isolated words. These words may or may not have true meaning for the infant and probably are not associated with actual objects or people. Sometimes, the streams of babble include the interjection of an occasional word, creating a kind of pseudolanguage.

By the end of the first year, the infant may use one or two words correctly and comprehend simple commands and phrases, such as "no-no" and "bye-bye," and some nonverbal language in the form of gestures, such as "come to

Daddy" and "peek-a-boo." Infants respond to their own names and know the names of a few objects, though they may not speak these names. **Holophrases**, in which one word or syllable represents a whole sentence, may emerge (e.g., "baba" means "I want my bottle").

Of interest to researchers and parents alike is the emergence of first words. Katherine Nelson refers to the infant's growing awareness of two different worlds: objects and people (Nelson, 1996; Nelson & Lucariello, 1985). During the latter half of the first year, infants begin to realize that these different entities provide different experiences. Nelson argues that coordination of these two worlds is essential for the development of language. First words, **overgeneralized speech**, represent one or the other category; for instance, "ball" may come to represent all toys, not just the child's ball. "Mama," on the other hand, may come to imply a full message to someone about the infant's need. Nelson places some emphasis on the interactive experiences infants have with adults who are aware of and in tune with emerging language. Parents and caregivers who engage in focused "conversations" with their infants and continually provide names and descriptions of objects and events around them support and enhance language development during this important period.

vocables:
early sound patterns used by infants that approximate words

holophrase:
the use of one word to convey a phrase or a sentence

overgeneralized speech:
the use of a single word or label to represent an entire category of objects similar in use or appearance

LITERACY DEVELOPMENT

Literacy has its origins in a variety of infant experiences and sensations. Listening to and engaging in vocal interactions with others, tuning into the sounds and rhythms of the voices and language surrounding them, observing the facial expressions of their caregivers, and visually fixating on objects of interest begin the journey toward literacy. On the basis of the belief that the origins of literacy occur in infancy, researchers in language and literacy development suggest that infants benefit from and enjoy sharing chants, rhymes, songs, playful games of peek-a-boo and pat-a-cake, and baby books with their parents and caregivers. Hearing softly spoken language with the rich intonations that accompany stories and

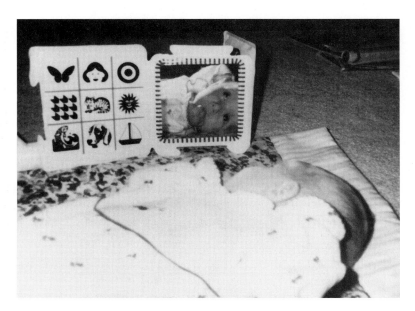

Infants enjoy and benefit from visually engaging baby books and pictures.

BOX 7.1   Types of Books Recommended for Infants

Format for very young infants

> Board books that can stand in the corner of the crib or on the floor in view range
>
> Colorful or black-and-white illustrations
>
> Lead-free and nontoxic construction materials (including inks, adhesives, and paper or cardboard content)
>
> Rounded edges (no staples, spirals, or other sharp or detachable parts)

Content and illustrations of baby books

> Image of one simple object per page (point-and-say books)
>
> Familiar objects such as baby bottle, soft stuffed toy, ball, cup, sweater, cap
>
> Enlarged photographs (bound into a board book) of familiar faces: mother, father, sibling, grandparent
>
> Enlarged photographs (bound into a board book) of familiar objects unique to the child's environment (crib, table lamp, stuffed toy, rocking chair, high chair)
>
> No print message necessary; spoken labels provide important auditory engagement

Format for older infants when books can be grasped, mouthed, and held

> Washable cloth books
>
> Washable soft plastic or vinyl books
>
> Lead-free and nontoxic construction
>
> No small removable parts
>
> Rounded or soft edges

Content and illustrations of books for older infants

> More point-and-say books with expanding "vocabulary" of familiar objects or "story" content
>
> Touch-and-smell books
>
> Simple illustrations (avoiding too many items per illustration and per page)
>
> Simple one-word print labels accompanying illustrations
>
> Simple one-, two-, or three-line story, increasing the story length and complexity only slightly as the infants get older and engagement is revealed
>
> Simple one-to-one correspondence books (one item, two items, three items per page in successive pages to no more than five items)

songs is an enriching and enjoyable auditory and cognitive experience for infants, which leads to heightened interest in both the spoken word and books.

Further, infants can be provided appropriate baby books to view and handle, beginning with heavy cardboard baby books using very simple pictures of single familiar items. The board book (as this type of book is called) can be stood in the corner of the crib or within the infant's view to provide an engaging visual experience. As the infant gains motor controls and can reach and bring items to his or her mouth, a different type of book is preferable, one that is made of fabric or another soft, washable material. Gradually, as infants become less physical and more visual in their relationships with books, their interest in the pictures and stories of books increases. Using baby books to engage older infants in very simple point-and-name activities ("This is a ball," "See the kitten?") engages the infant, enhances interest and curiosity, and begins a process whereby infants begin to form visual symbolic representations in their minds. Types of books that are recommended for infants during the first year of growth and development are described in Box 7.1.

FACTORS INFLUENCING COGNITION, LANGUAGE, AND LITERACY DEVELOPMENT

Think again about Jeremy and Angela. From the descriptions of their lives so far, several factors influencing development in all areas are becoming evident. Compare the lives of Jeremy and Angela in terms of the factors that influence cognition, language, and literacy.

1. Full-term infants get off to a healthier, less vulnerable start in life. Optimal health from the beginning facilitates all development—physical and motor, psychosocial, cognitive, language, and literacy.

2. The integrity of the sensory mechanisms, particularly hearing and vision, influences the extent to which these modalities can support and enhance learning and the extent to which compensating mechanisms come into play.

3. Proper nutrition is essential to good health and supports optimal brain and neurological development. There is evidence that appropriate and adequate nutrition during the earliest months is critical for brain growth and neurological development; in severe cases of malnutrition during the first six months, the deleterious effects can be irreversible.

4. Environments that support the infant's cognitive, language, and literacy development with engaging social interaction, enriching sensory stimuli, opportunities for motor exploration, and appropriate playthings and baby books promote optimal development.

5. Interactions with others who are responsive, supportive, and stimulating enhance not only the psychosocial development of the infant, but cognition, language, and literacy development as well.

Adults may facilitate and enhance infant cognition, language development, and emerging literacy in a number of ways. Development cannot be hurried, and any efforts should first take cues from the behaviors of the infant. Bombarding the infant with too many stimuli, inappropriate toys, visually and auditorially over-stimulating environments, and expectations that exceed their current capabilities is confusing to an infant and can impede optimal psychosocial and cognitive development. In confusing and overstimulating circumstances, infants become irritable and stressed, sometimes become depressed, and may exhibit problems with eating, sleeping, attending, and playing. An appreciation of the infant's own developmental timetable guides parents and caregivers.

ROLE OF THE EARLY CHILDHOOD PROFESSIONAL

Promoting Cognitive, Language, and Literacy Development in Infants

1. Engage readily in social interaction with the infant, responding to the infant's cues for social and emotional support.

2. Provide an enriched social environment that includes opportunities for the infant to watch, interact with, and feel and be a part of the family or child care group.

3. Provide a safe, supportive, and nurturing environment that encourages exploration beyond the crib or playpen.

4. Provide a sensory-rich environment, including vocal and verbal interactions with the infant, soft singing, shared baby books, story reading, bright and cheerful surroundings, visual access to windows, simple, uncluttered pictures on the wall, and other visual attractions.

5. Provide appropriate auditory stimuli, including talk and laughter, singing, chanting, reading, taped music, and other sources of interesting sounds, such as wind chimes.

6. Vary tactile stimuli with appropriate stuffed toys and soft sculptured items made from a variety of textures.

7. Periodically alter the child's scenery: Move the crib to another side of the room, move the high chair to another side of the table, occasionally change the visuals on the wall around the crib or play areas.

8. Provide safe, simple, engaging, age-appropriate toys and crib items, and replace them when the infant's interest in them wanes.

9. Explore the surroundings with the infant, carrying him or her about, gazing into the mirror, pointing to a photograph on the wall, looking through the window, finding the lowest kitchen drawer and examining its safe and intriguing contents, and so on.

10. Take older infants on brief outings with you. Talk about where you are going, what you are doing, and what you are seeing. Name objects, places, and people as you go.

11. Place an older infant's toys on low, open shelves for easy access and clean-up.

12. Respond with focused interest and enthusiasm to the infant's attempts to initiate playfulness and interaction.

KEY TERMS

adaptation

bilabial trills

child-directed speech

cognitive development

echolalia

fatherese

holophrase

language acquisition device (LAD)

motherese

object permanence

orienting response

overgeneralized speech

primary circular reactions

secondary circular reactions

sensorimotor learning

vocables

REVIEW STRATEGIES AND ACTIVITIES

1. Review the key terms individually or with a classmate.

2. This and other chapters have introduced a variety of theories associated with growth and development in young children. Angela and Jeremy have provided examples of development during the first year. Reread the stories of Angela and Jeremy appearing in previous chapters. On the basis of what you have learned so far about child development, make a list of your observations about Angela's and Jeremy's development and reflect on their potential. Discuss and compare your lists and reflections with those of your classmates.

3. Visit an infant care program that offers age-appropriate opportunities for cognitive, language, and literacy development. What types of interactions take place in these settings? How is cognitive, language, and literacy development supported through the activities and materials provided for infants?

FURTHER READINGS

Bredekamp, S., & Copple, C. (Eds.). (1997). *Developmentally appropriate practices in early childhood programs* (rev. ed.). Washington, DC: National Association for the Education of Young Children.

Byrnes, J. P. (2001). *Minds, brains, and learning: Understanding the psychological and educational relevance of neuroscientific research.* New York: Guilford Press.

Cryer, D., & Harms, T. (2000). *Infants and toddlers in out-of-home care.* Baltimore: Brookes.

Gopnik, A., Meltzoff, A. N., & Kuhl, P. K. (1999). *The scientist in the crib.* New York: William Morrow.

Greenspan, S. I. (1997). *The growth of the mind and the endangered origins of intelligence.* Reading, MA: Addison-Wesley.

Greenspan, S. I., & Lewis, D., (2002). *The affect-based language curriculum (ABLC): An intensive program for families, therapists, and teachers.* Bethesda, MD: Interdisciplinary Council on Developmental and Learning Disorders.

Hast, R., & Hollyfield, A. (2001). *More infant and toddler experiences.* St. Paul, MN: Redleaf Press.

Marcus, G. (2003). *The birth of the mind: How a tiny number of genes creates the complexities of human thought.* New York: Perseus.

Neuman, S. B., Copple, C., & Bredekamp, S. (2000). *Learning to read and write: Developmentally appropriate practices for young children.* Washington, DC: National Association for the Education of Young Children.

Schickedanz, J. A. (1999). *Much more than the ABCs: The early stages of reading and writing.* Washington, DC: National Association for the Education of Young Children.

Other Resources

Administration for Children and Families of the U.S. Department of Health and Human Services.
Links to Child Care, Head Start, and Early Head Start sites
    http://www.acf.dhhs.gov

Association for Childhood Education International
Focus on Infants and Toddlers (Quarterly newsletter relating to educational practices for children from birth through three years of age)
    http://acei.org

Early Head Start National Resource Center
    http://www.ehsnrc.org

National Association for the Education of Young Children
Sample publications:
    A caring place for your infant
    Developmentally appropriate practice in early childhood programs serving infants: A position statement of the National Association for the Education of Young Children
    Finding the best care for your infant or toddler
        http://naeyc.org

Zero to Three
    Journal *(Zero to Three)*, research reports, and other resources. Sample publications:
    Creating welcoming library environments for infants, toddlers and their families [Theme Issue]. *Zero to Three, 21* (December 2000/January 2001).
    The musical lives of babies and families [Theme Issue]. *Zero to Three, 23* (September 2003).
        http://zerotothree.org

PART FOUR

The Young Child: Ages One Through Three

CHAPTER EIGHT

Little children are not logical—they are motor. To give a child joy, give him something to do.

LUCY GAGE

Physical and Motor Development: Ages One Through Three

After studying this chapter, you will demonstrate comprehension by:

► Outlining expected patterns of physical and motor development from ages one through three.

► Identifying developmental landmarks in large and small muscle development.

► Identifying developmental landmarks in perceptual motor development.

► Describing the beginnings of body and gender awareness.

► Discussing factors that influence physical and motor development.

► Discussing health and well-being issues that are relevant from ages 1 through 3

► Suggesting strategies for enhancing physical and motor development from ages one through three.

PHYSICAL AND MOTOR COMPETENCE IN THE ONE- TO THREE-YEAR-OLD

By the end of the 1st year, the infant has made dramatic developmental strides in all areas of development: sensory, physical/motor, social, emotional, cognitive, and language. Of special interest to parents and child development observers are the physical growth that proceeds quite rapidly and its accompanying repertoire of motor skills. Indeed, some of the first large motor skills—pulling up, standing alone, and taking the first steps—evoke excitement, praise, and celebration. These milestones signal the beginning of a new period in child development, typically referred to as the *toddler period*. This period extends from age 1 through age 2 and into the 3rd year.

General Physical Characteristics

The rapid growth rate of infancy decelerates somewhat during the 2nd year. For example, whereas the infant's birth weight typically triples during the 1st year, the toddler gains around 5 to 6 pounds during the 2nd year. Similarly, the infant's length, which increased by about 10 to 12 inches during the 1st year, is followed by growth of about 5 inches during the 2nd year.

Body proportions begin to change from the short, rounded characteristics of the 1-year-old to a leaner, more muscular build by age 3. However, the head is still large in proportion to the rest of the body (making up one fifth of the total body length at age 1) and gives the toddler a top-heavy appearance. The toddler's early attempts to walk result in posture characterized by a protruding abdomen,

217

arms held upward and feet spread wide apart for balance (not always successfully), and a leading forehead. Awkward and unsure locomotion, body proportions, and characteristic posture make the term *toddler* quite appropriate for this period in child growth and development. By age 3, changes in body build and proportions lower the center of gravity from the upper regions of the body to the midsection, facilitating more coordinated locomotion and a leaner, more upright body profile.

Recall that brain growth and neurological development during the first 3 years are quite rapid, as neurological connections proliferate in an extensive and profoundly complex manner. When examining infants and toddlers, pediatricians often measure the circumference of the child's head, though this measure is not taken routinely after age 3. Head circumference during these first 3 years is significant in physical examinations because it assists the physician in assessing ossification of the cranial bones as the fontanelles close and in evaluating brain growth and the status of the central nervous system. Whereas the head circumference at birth is greater than that of the chest, it is about equal to the chest circumference when the child is about 1 year old.

Facial proportions are also changing. The infant and young child have rather high, rounded, and prominent foreheads, resulting from early and rapid brain and cranial growth. Because of this early growth pattern, facial features make up a smaller portion of the facial area than they will as the child gets older. The face is round with a small jaw and a small, flat nose. The eyes are set close together, and the lips are thin. Over the course of the next few years, facial proportions will change, and the child will lose the "baby face" appearance.

deciduous teeth:
the first set of teeth, which erupts during infancy; also called temporary or baby teeth; later replaced by a set of 36 permanent teeth

The eruption of teeth contributes to changes in facial proportions. By age one, 6 to 8 teeth may have appeared, though in some children, teeth appear at a much slower rate, and some have no more than 3 or 4 teeth by their first birthday. By age 2½ to 3, most children have all 20 of their **deciduous teeth** ("baby teeth"), as illustrated in Figure 8.1. Deciduous teeth, also called *primary* teeth, tend to appear

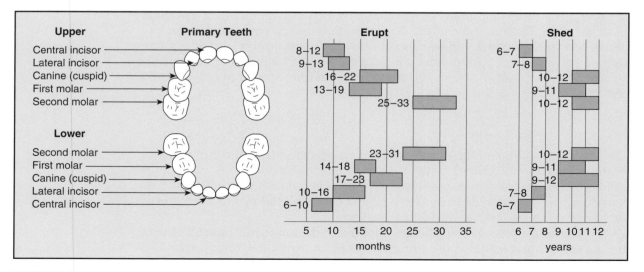

FIGURE 8.1
Typical Sequence of Eruption of Primary Teeth

sooner in boys than in girls. However, girls, who are generally thought to progress toward maturity more rapidly than boys in most areas of development, will be slightly ahead of boys in the eruption of permanent teeth.

Changes in other body proportions are also evident. Look again at Figure 5.1, and notice the changes in body proportions from fetal development to adulthood. Notice that the arms of the newborn seem long and the legs quite short in proportion to the trunk. Then compare the arm and leg lengths with those of the 2-year-old. As the legs grow longer, the arms appear shorter, and the head accounts for a much smaller proportion of the body length.

Skeletal development is characterized not only by an increase in size, but also by changes in the number and the composition of bones. Beginning in the fetal period with soft, pliable cartilage, which begins to ossify around the 5th prenatal month, bones gradually harden as calcium and other minerals are absorbed. Not all bones grow and develop at the same rate. The cranial bones and long bones of the arms and spine are among the first to ossify. The bones of the hands and wrists tend to mature early and serve as valuable indicators of general growth progress in the child (Tanner, 1989).

The amount of **adipose** (fatty tissue) children have depends on a number of factors, including heredity, body type, nutrition and eating habits, activity levels, and exercise opportunities. During infancy, adipose tissue develops more rapidly than muscle. However, children tend to lose adipose tissue toward the end of the 1st year and continue to do so during the next few years as they become upright and more mobile. The decrease will continue until about age 5, when increases in weight will result from skeletal and muscle growth.

adipose: tissue in which there is an accumulation of connective tissue cells, each containing a relatively large deposit of fat

Development of **locomotion** refers to the growing ability to move independently from place to place. Like other areas of development, motor development follows the law of developmental direction, that is, a head-to-foot direction with control over muscles of the upper regions of the body preceding control over muscles in the lower regions. This development parallels neural development, which also proceeds in a head-downward pattern. Brain development, particularly of the cerebellum, which is involved in posture and balance, is rather rapid between 6 and 18 months of age. Thus, neural and muscular development in tandem with changing body proportions facilitates locomotion and does so in a fairly predictable sequence.

locomotion: the ability to move independently from place to place

Expected Growth Patterns and Developmental Milestones

By the end of the 1st year, the child has mastered such motor skills as rolling over, sitting unassisted, crawling, pulling up, and perhaps standing alone. Between the ages of 10 and 15 months, the child may walk when held by one hand or may pull to a standing position and "cruise" by holding onto furniture. These activities are referred to as *large motor* activities because they enlist the use and coordination of the large muscles of the arms, trunk, and legs. Because these muscles generally mature earliest, children master large muscle skills sooner than small muscle skills such as handling a spoon, a crayon, or buttons.

Large Motor Development.   Large motor development follows predictable patterns. Table 8.1 identifies **developmental milestones** of the period from ages 1 to 3. Review Table 5.3, and notice how motor development progresses

developmental milestones: significant events during the course of growth and development

TABLE 8.1   Developmental Milestones in Large Motor Controls from Ages One Through Four

Age	Motor Development
12–18 months	Pulls to standing position holding onto furniture Throws objects from crib Walks with two hands held Crawls up steps Rolls a large ball, nondirected, using both hands and arms Attempts to slide from lap or high chair Begins to make shift from crawling to walking Stands alone Climbs onto a chair Takes two or three steps without support with legs widespread and arms held forward for balance Gets into a standing position unassisted Squats to pick up an object Reverts to crawling when in a hurry rather than attempting to walk Cannot yet make sudden stops or turns "Dances" in place to music
18–24 months	Bends to pick up objects Walks without falling Pulls, drags toys Seats self in a child's chair Walks up and down stairs assisted Walks backward "Dances" to music moving about Mimics household activities: bathing baby, sweeping, dusting, talking on telephone
24–36 months	Runs Walks on toes Jumps in place Kicks a large ball Imitates rhythms and animal movements; e.g., gallops like a horse, waddles like a duck Throws a ball, nondirected Catches a rolling ball Jumps in place Rides a tricycle Walks stairs one step at a time Jumps from lowest step Attempts to balance standing on one foot
36–48 months	Balances on one foot Hops, gallops, runs with ease Avoids obstacles Stops readily Walks on a line Jumps over low objects Throws a ball, directed Enjoys simple dances and rhythms

Large motor development is facilitated when infants can safely explore their surroundings.

from birth to age 1 and from ages 1 through 3. Notice the impressive array of large motor coordinations and skills that emerges during this first 36 months. However, there are individual differences in rates and sometimes sequences of development in all aspects of child growth and development. Any such sequence of developmental events can provide only approximations with which to observe and understand emerging abilities. Awareness of expected sequences is generally more helpful to us than ascertaining when a particular trait emerges.

Small Motor Development.   Equally dramatic, but probably not always as obvious, is the emergence of small motor development. Small muscle development and motor skills also follow the law of developmental direction, proceeding from the head downward and from the central axis of the body outward. This means that the coordination of the smaller muscles of the wrists, hands, and fingers is preceded by, and for the most part dependent on, the coordination of the large muscles of the upper trunk, shoulders, and upper arms.

The abilities to reach, grasp, manipulate, and let go of objects become more precise during the second year. Coordination of eyes and hands improves rapidly during the toddler period, and with ever-increasing locomotor skills, exploratory behaviors expand. Thus, locomotion, in tandem with improving eye–hand coordination, facilitates learning. Successful exploration depends on coordination of large muscles, small muscles, vision, and hearing.

Prehension, the ability to use thumb and fingers to grasp small objects, emerges during the first year. This ability is both an asset and a hazard.

prehension:
the coordination of fingers and thumb to permit grasping

flexors:
muscles that act to bend a joint

extensors:
muscles that act to stretch or extend a limb

By age 1, **prehension**, the ability to use the thumb and fingers in opposition to each other, has become reasonably efficient. Recall that during the 1st year of development, the grasping muscles (**flexors**) are stronger than the releasing muscles (**extensors**). During the toddler period, grasping and letting go become more efficient. The activities of pouring objects from a container and then putting them back into the container one by one can be an absorbing activity, requiring both grasping and releasing. This development is illustrated in Figure 8.2.

Vision and Hearing

Growth and development are influenced by the integrity and functioning of the sensory mechanisms. Of particular interest is the normal functioning of vision and hearing. While a normal adult's visual acuity (how well one sees) is 20/20, a newborn's is about 20/600, which means that something 20 feet away is seen by the newborn with the clarity of what an adult would see if the object were 600 feet away. This improves rapidly over the first 6 months to about 20/100, and by age 3 years, visual acuity has reached about 20/30. It is not until around age 5 that children reach 20/20 visual acuity (Boothe, Dobson, & Teller, 1985).

Because of rapid development during the first years, regular eye examinations are recommended to ensure early detection of any problems with the eyes that could result in visual impairment. Children who received oxygen at birth, were premature or had a low birth weight, or have congenital anomalies are at high risk for eye abnormalities. Their vision should be regularly monitored during infancy and early childhood. Behaviors and physical characteristics

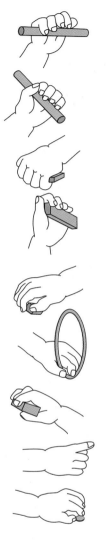

12 weeks: reflexive; ulnar side dominant

16 weeks: mouthing of fingers and mutual fingering; holds object placed in hand

20 weeks: primitive squeeze; raking with fingers only, no palm or thumb involvement

24 weeks: palmar or squeeze grasp; still no thumb involvement; eyes and hands combine for grasp

28 weeks: radial-palmar or whole-hand grasp; radial side stronger, thumb begins to adduct, unilateral approach (one hand); transfers from one hand to the other

32 weeks: inferior scissors grasp, thumb is adducted, not opposed

36 weeks: radial-digital grasp; fingers on radial side provide pressure to object, thumb begins to move forward in opposition

40 weeks: inferior-pincer grasp; thumb begins to move toward forefinger; beginning of voluntary release

44 weeks: neat pincer grasp with slight extension of the wrist

52 weeks: opposition or superior-forefinger grasp; wrist extended and deviated to ulnar side for efficient grasp; smooth release for large objects and awkward for small objects

FIGURE 8.2

Sequential Development of Grasp

Source: Assessing Infants and Preschoolers with Handicaps, by D. B. Bailey and M. Wolery, 1989; Upper Saddle River, NJ: Prentice Hall, Copyright 1989 by Prentice Hall, Inc. Reprinted with permission.

suggestive of visual problems observed in infancy and very young children are listed in Box 8.1. These symptoms indicate a need for professional evaluation and intervention.

Like vision, hearing influences the course of growth and development of young children, and, as with vision, early diagnosis and intervention is critical.

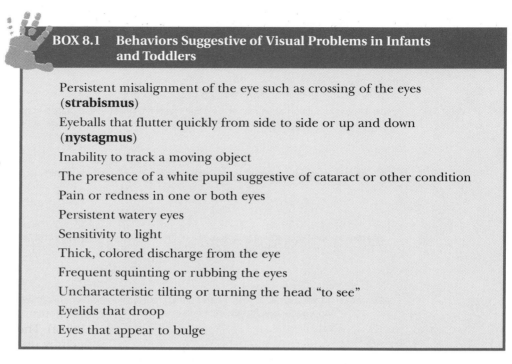

strabismus:
a condition referred to as *crossed eyes*, in which one or both eyes turn in, out, up, or down

nystagmus:
involuntary and jerky repetitive movement of the eyeballs

BOX 8.1   **Behaviors Suggestive of Visual Problems in Infants and Toddlers**

Persistent misalignment of the eye such as crossing of the eyes (**strabismus**)

Eyeballs that flutter quickly from side to side or up and down (**nystagmus**)

Inability to track a moving object

The presence of a white pupil suggestive of cataract or other condition

Pain or redness in one or both eyes

Persistent watery eyes

Sensitivity to light

Thick, colored discharge from the eye

Frequent squinting or rubbing the eyes

Uncharacteristic tilting or turning the head "to see"

Eyelids that droop

Eyes that appear to bulge

cochlear implant:
an electronic device placed in the skull, which, with help from an external hearing aid, enhances the detection of sound

Hearing impairment is classified according to its physiological basis. Conductive hearing impairment is due to some barrier in the outer or middle ear that prevents sound waves from traveling to the inner ear, as when there is fluid in the ear, wax build-up, or middle ear infection (e.g., otitis media); sometimes the structures of the ear did not develop properly or were injured. Conductive hearing impairment interferes with the child's ability to understand speech sounds and, if prolonged, can delay speech and language development. If left undetected and untreated, conductive impairments can lead to permanent hearing loss, but most can be corrected through antibiotics or surgery (Deiner, 1997). Hearing impairment may also be a result of sensorineural injury to the inner ear and/or the nerve to the brainstem, as can occur with tumors, brain injury, prenatal infections, anoxia, some genetic anomalies, and some childhood diseases such as bacterial meningitis, chicken pox, measles, and mumps. Contemporary surgical procedures such as the **cochlear implant** help some profoundly impaired children to hear. Other amplification devices may be prescribed for children with hearing impairments, and language development may include learning sign language and lip-reading techniques.

It is difficult to detect hearing loss in infants through observation. In the absence of newborn screening, hearing loss may not be detected before the child is 1 or 2 years old, an age at which important opportunities for intervention have been missed. Newborn screening through the American Academy of Pediatrics Early Hearing Detection and Intervention program helps to identify infants in need of intervention. Failure to identify hearing loss before 6 months of age is associated with delayed speech and language development. However, where regular physical examinations provide hearing evaluations, interventions can be

> **BOX 8.2   Behaviors Suggestive of Hearing Problems in Infants and Toddlers**
>
> Failure to turn in the direction of sounds
>
> Pulling or rubbing ears
>
> Turning or tilting the head toward the source of a sound
>
> Staring at a speaker's mouth
>
> Easily startled by sound
>
> Inattentiveness
>
> Failure to follow directions
>
> Delayed speech and language development
>
> Frequent ear aches, colds, or allergies

prescribed with the goal of helping infants to develop language commensurate with their cognitive development (American Academy of Pediatrics, 2002a). The more severe the hearing impairment, the more likely it is to be noticed by untrained observers. Children with hearing impairments may display any or a combination of the behaviors listed in Box 8.2. When children are old enough to indicate that they do or do not hear a sound, assessment by an **audiologist** is generally recommended.

audiologist: a trained professional who uses specialized techniques and equipment to diagnose hearing loss

Perceptual–Motor Development

Perception is a neurological process by which sensory input is organized. It involves all of the senses. For instance, visual perception involves the ability to recognize and discriminate faces, patterns, sizes, shapes, depth, distance, and so on. Auditory perception involves the use of auditory clues to identify people, objects, and events and to discern such qualities as distance, speed, and space. Tactile–kinesthetic perception provides information relating to touch, textures, temperature, weight, pressure, and one's own body position, presence, or movements. Olfactory (smell) and taste perceptions provide additional information for the recognition, discrimination, identification, and location of experienced events and objects.

Perceptual–motor development refers to the interrelationships between a child's perceptions and motor responses. Since perceptions derive from the senses and provoke awareness, motor development and perception are interdependent, and each influences learning. Space, depth, and weight perceptions, for example, depend heavily on locomotor experiences for their development. Expecting a large, hollow block to be heavier than it actually is, a child may brace himself or herself to lift it, only to discover that the block did not require such muscular readiness. Such an experience enhances weight perception. Child development observers are interested in the effective integration of perceptual and motor development. When perceptual and motor abilities are integrated, the child uses visual, auditory, tactile, or other sensory data to plan and carry out motor

perceptual–motor: interrelationship between sensory information and motor responses

activities more efficiently. By the same token, perceptions are modified as a result of motoric experiences. Imitating another child's scribbles is an example of visual–motor integration. Responding to the rhythms of music is an example of audio–motor integration. Curling into one's own cubby at the child care center is an example of kinesthetic–motor integration.

Jeremy is now 13 months old. He is aware of his parents' delight in watching him attempt his first steps. Feet widespread, arms bent at the elbows, reaching upward for balance, he lifts one foot to step, loses his balance, and tumbles sideways. On the next attempt, he is able to toddle two or three steps before falling. His new skill is thrilling but also somewhat frightening. His parents clap, laugh, coax, and praise him profusely with every attempt. Tiring, he reverts to a more expedient mode of locomotion and crawls easily to his mother's outstretched arms.

Jeremy's parents have attempted to provide space for Jeremy's increasing mobility. Furnishings are arranged to provide obstacle-free movement and to eliminate sharp edges or items over which he might trip. Jeremy especially enjoys climbing the three steps to the front door on returning from an excursion, and now that he is learning to walk, his mother experiments with his stair-climbing skills.

Holding both hands from behind him, mother and Jeremy walk toward the three steps to descend. At first, Jeremy thrusts one foot forward into the air, bringing it back to the level of the first step, as though he were walking on a level plane. Consequently, his mother must rescue him, or he will tumble down the steps. Not too happy with this effort, Jeremy returns to a crawling position and proceeds to back his way down the steps.

Jeremy's motor behaviors illustrate some aspects of perceptual–motor development. Jeremy's parents are aware that his space and speed perceptions are faulty, so they have arranged their living spaces to accommodate his poorly coordinated movements and lack of space perception. Also, Jeremy's mother's experiment reveals Jeremy's lack of depth perception. Jeremy's visual, kinesthetic, and/or depth perceptions have not yet become coordinated. In such cases, one would assert that 13-month-old Jeremy needs more time for visual–motor abilities to become integrated. It will be some time before he masters descending steps in an upright-forward position (typically, children do not descend stairs smoothly and unassisted until around age 4).

Visual–motor development is enhanced through opportunities to use developing locomotor abilities and small motor skills. Body awareness, balance, rhythm, space, and temporal awareness increase as toddlers explore their surroundings and experience their body movements and abilities.

Angela is also 13 months old. Her motor development is somewhat, though not dramatically, delayed. (Recall that Angela experienced a premature delivery, complicated by anoxia.) Measured against the usual age ranges for emergence of motor skills, Angela has performed approximately four to six months behind expectations for full-term infants. Nevertheless, her development appears to be quite normal, though she exhibits more excitability, restlessness, and frustration, which is not unusual for preterm infants. Her excursions about the house are far-reaching when she is allowed to explore beyond the playpen or crib.

Cheryl, now 16 years old, has had a happy and successful year in her new school. With help from the child care center on her high school campus, Cheryl is learning to juggle parenting and education. She is taking a child development course and is thrilled to learn about the different stages and abilities Angela is exhibiting. She is learning to provide an environment at home in which Angela can explore—though with older children around, the places Angela wants to explore are often hazardous. Consequently, Angela is often relegated to the playpen, sometimes for lengthy periods. She cruises around the playpen, watches the other children, listens to the television, and cuddles her soft toys. She enjoys dropping small blocks into a bucket and then dumping them out. The older children bring her other items to play with, and when she gets fussy, they increase their verbal interactions with her, playing games such as peek-a-boo or "which hand is the toy in?" Angela's environment is verbally rich and interactive, though often overstimulating.

The limited visual and tactile–kinesthetic environment of the playpen, however, has further delayed Angela's perceptual–motor integration. Limited opportunities to develop perceptual–motor integration could place Angela at risk for learning difficulties later on.

Tables 8.1 and 8.2 illustrate expected patterns and developmental milestones from ages 1 through 3. Keep in mind that multiple biological and environmental influences affect both the sequence and timing of motor abilities. These influences have origins in prenatal and infant developmental histories, cultural expectations, nutritional status, general health and well-being, and opportunities and encouragement to use emerging capabilities.

Opportunities to play "catch" and "kick-the-ball" challenge and encourage motor confidence.

TABLE 8.2	Developmental Milestones in Small Motor Development from Ages One Through Four

Age	Motor Development
12–18 months	Picks up small objects with pincer movement
	Drops and picks up toys
	Releases a toy into a container
	Knocks over a tower with a wave of the hand
	Throws objects to the floor
	Finger-feeds efficiently
	Uses a spoon awkwardly
	Stacks two cubes after demonstration
	Pours objects from a container
	Builds a tower of three or four cubes
	Holds two cubes in one hand
	Takes off shoes, socks
	Points to things
	Uses a cup for drinking
	Feeds self efficiently
18–24 months	Manages a spoon and a cup awkwardly
	Turns pages of a book, two and three pages at a time
	Places large pegs in a peg board
	Holds a crayon in a fist
	Scribbles
	Squeezes a soft squeak toy
24–36 months	Builds a tower of five to seven cubes
	Strings three or four large beads
	Turns the pages of a book one page at a time
	Imitates demonstrated vertical and circular scribbles
	Manages a spoon and a cup with increasing efficiency
	Lines up objects in a "train" sequence
36–48 months	Builds a tower of eight to ten cubes
	Approximates a variety of shapes in drawings
	Feeds self with few spills
	Unbuttons front clothing
	Zips, handles various simple fasteners
	Works puzzles of three to six pieces
	Handles books efficiently
	Exhibits hand preference
	Spreads butter and jam on toast
	Dresses and undresses with assistance

Toddlers with Special Needs

Children with special needs often experience diverse health and developmental problems, including chronic illnesses, disabilities and developmental delays, abuse (sexual abuse, substance abuse, neglect, or abandonment), homelessness, malnutrition, and psychological disturbances. Some key physical and motor concerns for toddlers in these categories are related to early identification, assessment, and appropriate treatment of the following:

1. General health and nutritional needs
2. Ongoing assessment of physical and motor abilities, with special attention to movement competence and emerging large and small motor abilities, including but not limited to
   * Posture
   * Reflexive reactions
   * Equilibrium
   * Flexibility
   * Voluntary movements
   * Transitional movements as in moving from sitting to standing
   * Mobility preference patterns
   * Eye–hand, eye–foot, and hand–mouth coordination
   * Prehensor and grasping/releasing abilities
   * Chewing and swallowing efficiency
3. Avoiding muscle contractures and structural deformities resulting from prolonged use of abnormal movement patterns
4. Providing appropriate physical and occupational intervention and therapies
5. Providing ongoing assessment, guidance, instruction, and, where needed, adaptive equipment to assist and facilitate emerging motor and self-help abilities
6. Providing purposeful activities and daily routines to facilitate and enhance physical and motor development
7. Providing high-quality, inclusive early childhood education programs and skilled professionals to ensure optimal developmental progress (Sexton, 1990).

Many disabling conditions, when recognized and identified early in the child's development, can be treated and often ameliorated. Regular physical examinations and ongoing observations of growth and developmental trends in individual children help to ensure that any unusual developmental events are not overlooked and are responded to in an appropriate and timely way.

Many types of intervention programs and services are available for children and families with special needs. Research in genetics and the neurosciences provides guarded hope for the amelioration and perhaps the alleviation of some disabling conditions in children who were heretofore believed to be untreatable. As new strategies are designed to identify and examine the molecular origins of specific heritable and congenital anomalies, the scientific community will be better able to direct efforts toward prevention as well as intervention and correction of many disabling conditions. The potential exists to identify the specific points during growth and development from conception through the early years when specific risk factors influence a particular growth trajectory. The potential for intervening with gene and/or drug therapy, neurological development intervention through timely environmental and social interaction adjustments, and other strategies soon to be formulated holds enormous promise for the field of child development. However, the state of our knowledge is in progress, and the hope that such new possibilities engender must be tempered with cautious optimism (Puckett, Marshall, & Davis, 1999).

Intervention programs for toddlers with special needs involve meeting the child's immediate physical, health, and psychological requirements, helping parents adjust their parenting skills to meet the needs of their special child, providing support systems for parents, adapting environments (home and out-of-home child care arrangements), providing ongoing assessments and therapies as required, providing assistive technologies as needed to facilitate self-help efforts, and coordinating services needed by the child and the family.

RELATIONSHIP BETWEEN PHYSICAL/MOTOR AND PSYCHOSOCIAL DEVELOPMENT

self-efficacy:
the feeling that one's efforts are effective; the perception that one can succeed

In Chapter 5, we pointed out that physical/motor development and psychosocial development are interrelated. Each new motor skill contributes to the child's emerging self-concept and sense of **self-efficacy**. The toddler's early definitions of self are based on his or her interactive experiences with parents, primary caregivers, and important others. These relationships and the toddler's increasing awareness of his or her own capabilities form the basis for body awareness and an emerging self-concept. Self-concept development is a gradual process, which continues throughout childhood and is subject to positive and negative changes as experiences and relationships expand.

Older infants and toddlers demonstrate an emerging self-concept by focusing on certain aspects of their bodies and emerging abilities. Pointing to and naming their body parts, telling their names, holding the appropriate number of fingers to convey their ages, saying "Look at me!" as they demonstrate a new skill, and insisting on doing things for themselves such as pulling off socks and shoes, holding their spoon or cup, and preferring to walk rather than being carried are all indications of the child's emerging body and self-awareness. Important aspects of self-concept development are the child's increasing efforts to be self-sufficient, his or her growing awareness of gender differences, and the self-governance that comes with bladder and bowel control.

Self-Help Efforts

The desire to do things for themselves emerges early when infants choose to hold their bottles, use their hands and fingers to feed themselves, retrieve and relinquish toys and other belongings, and efficiently (vocally, verbally, or through body language) communicate their needs to others. The toddler's increasing sense of self parallels a growing desire for independence or autonomy (self-governance).

Mobility, aided by refinement of large motor abilities and increasingly skilled use and coordination of eyes and hands through small motor development, facilitates the child's emerging self-help skills. Awkward yet determined attempts at dressing and undressing (usually starting with the removal of shoes and socks or perhaps a diaper), following simple directions, enjoying fetch-and-carry activities, using a washcloth to wash the face after meals, washing hands, bathing, brushing teeth, and reporting simple events ("I broke it") are examples of early self-help abilities. Spills, accidents, and delays are common.

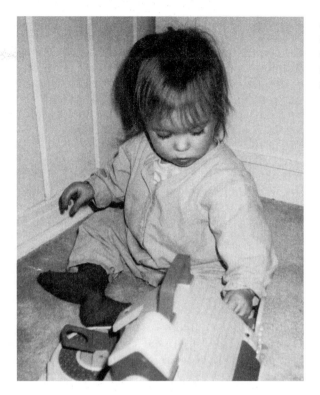

Eye–hand coordination improves as young children manipulate age-appropriate toys.

Patience, support, and encouragement are needed during these often tedious, time-consuming, and sometimes frustrating early efforts. As toddlers become more successful in their attempts at self-help, their sense of pride and positive self-regard grows, and they are motivated to continue their efforts, becoming more and more efficient with practice and experience. As we discuss in the next chapter, the child's growing sense of independence needs support if healthy psychosocial development is to emerge. Mishandling of these early self-help efforts by reprimanding, cajoling, punishing, or offering other negative responses discourages young children and can lead to dependent, defiant, and other negative behavioral outcomes. Recognizing this as an important aspect of growth and development, adults can anticipate the time it takes for young children to manage self-help tasks and allow for it as much as possible. When time is an issue, determine what the child can do while other tasks are being performed by the adult—for example, "I'll pack the diaper bag, while you pull on your socks, then I'll put on one shoe and you put on the other. You go and get your blanky, while I get your sweater; then we will be ready to go to Grandma's house."

Body and Gender Awareness

Body awareness emerges with the acquisition and repetition of each new motor skill. Motor abilities, once discovered, are repeated over and over. Throwing an object from the crib, pulling to a standing position beside furniture and dropping back to a seated one, dumping toys from a container, climbing a staircase, and

body awareness: cognizance of one's body, its parts, its functions, and what it can be willed to do

opening a drawer are some of a myriad of activities for which repetition is, in and of itself, quite pleasurable for the toddler. The intrinsic thrust toward growth and development and the ever-present desire to do more mature things drive toddlers to repeat and repeat actions until new challenges command their attention. Encouragement and praise from their caregivers forward this development. Mastering skills gives toddlers a sense of control or empowerment and an enhanced awareness of their capabilities. For the toddler, this is an exhilarating time. It is also a time for close adult supervision.

Body awareness is also an outgrowth of child's increasing ability to name body parts. Toddlers enjoy learning the names of their body parts: eyes, ears, nose, mouth, feet, toes, stomach, ribs, and so on. Naming body parts and demonstrating what they can be willed to do often become a game, with the adult asking for identification and delighting in the toddler's answers. These early body awareness experiences are precursors to a sense of identity that includes an awareness of gender and gender-related behaviors.

Discriminations between male and female emerge during the first year (Brooks-Gunn & Lewis, 1982). **Gender awareness** (the realization that men and women, girls and boys are different) and **gender identity** (the realization of being either male or female) is usually established by age 2½ to 3 years. Gender awareness involves labeling oneself and others according to gender, an assessment that is usually derived from external characteristics such as the clothing people wear, the toys they own or choose to play with, the way they wear their hair, and so on. Very young children often assume that simply by changing such external characteristics as these, they can become a different gender. Gender role stereotypes have their origins in these early attributions (Wellhousen, 1996).

Toddlers may demonstrate emerging gender awareness through curiosity about their and others' anatomies. Curiosity about body parts of others is unabashed and straightforward. The toddler may touch mother's breasts, watch intently as father urinates, become intrigued by the body parts of siblings, and explore their own genitalia. These behaviors reflect normal curiosity, are harmless, and represent the child's growing body awareness and the early stages of **sexuality** (Chrisman & Couchenour, 2002).

Sexuality develops in stages from infancy through adulthood, just as other aspects of human functioning do, and distinct differences exist between childhood sexuality and adult sexuality.

Childhood sexuality is marked by curiosity and play, spontaneity and openness, and sensuality and excitement. Adult sexuality is characterized by knowing and consequential behavior, self-consciousness and privacy, and passion and eroticism (Rothbaum, Grauer, & Rubin, 1997). Hence, the meanings that young children attach to gender differences and sexual behaviors are distinctly different from those of adults. Children's sexuality is characterized by interest in the body and its functions, labels for body parts, and experiments with adult language associated with the body and its functions. Young children are usually quite comfortable in their own skin and are not always as concerned about privacy (which is learned behavior). Hence, they are open and direct with their curiosities, questions, and sexuality behaviors. These behaviors are often unsettling to adults, particularly if the adults attach adult meanings and their own feelings and values to the behaviors and fail to recognize that young children's sexuality behaviors are

gender awareness:
the realization that men and women, girls and boys, are different

gender identity:
the cognizance of being male or female

sexuality:
the relational, biological, and procreational aspects of gender

not accompanied by the hormonal underpinnings and eroticism that character-ize adolescent and adult sexuality.

Parents and adults who work with young children should respond in a man-ner that does not convey shock, embarrassment, or reprimand. Sometimes, sim-ply naming the body parts is all that is required. It is appropriate to use correct anatomical terms such as *urinate, bowel movement, breasts,* and *penis,* as this as-sists the toddler's understanding and helps to prevent the development of mis-conceptions. Further, it is appropriate to talk about and set clear limits about pub-lic and personal behaviors, modesty and privacy, and appropriate language to use and in what contexts. Such discussion should be matter-of-fact, respectful, and free of accusation or shame.

Questions that often accompany the toddler's curiosity about gender should be answered in simple, sensitive, and nonjudgmental ways. Toddlers have many questions about why girls and boys are different, why they use the toilet in dif-ferent ways, how babies get in a mommy's tummy, why girls don't have a penis, and the like. Matter-of-fact answers that are simple enough for the child to un-derstand are all that is required at this age. What is most important is that chil-dren feel psychologically safe in asking questions. Shock, embarrassment, or reprimand stifles healthy communication between adult and child and conveys negative messages about the human body—the child's and those of others. Rather, adults need to be approachable on topics relating to human anatomy, gender, and sexuality and should refrain from elaborate technical or value-laden discussion. Answering questions as they arise is always preferable to postponement to a later time (or age), deferring to the other parent or another adult, or arranging a certain time for a formal discussion. Such strategies con-vey confusing messages to children who have asked what to them are reason-able questions.

Toilet Learning

In infancy, the elimination of body wastes occurs involuntarily as a reflexive ac-tivity when the bladder or bowels needs emptying. During the first year or so, the infant must develop a conscious awareness of the feelings of bowel and bladder fullness and develop some control over anal and urethral sphincters. Such control cannot occur until certain nerve pathways have developed and matured. The in-fant must have developed some language and locomotor skills to signal a need to caregivers, get to the toilet in due time, manage clothing, and then manage toilet-ing itself. This is not a small order.

Toilet learning is a gradual maturational process that extends over a period of several years. It is not, as the term *toilet training* implies, something that can be taught at some predetermined age. Instead, parents and caregivers learn to re-spond to the child's readiness cues. Toilet learning depends on complex neuro-logical development. Usually, bowel control precedes bladder control. A number of physiological events must have occurred before bowel and bladder controls develop. Neurological development brings consciousness of bladder and bowel discomfort. Certain large motor skills that are required for getting to and using toilet facilities must be in place, along with the fine motor skills necessary for handling clothing. Verbal skills (or, in the beginning, body language cues) are necessary to express the need for assistance, and the conscious ability to control

toilet learning: a gradual matura-tional process in which the child gains control over elimination

the sphincters that hold and let go must be present. These developments emerge over an extended time, and toileting remains a relatively unskilled activity well into the preschool years.

Between the ages of 18 and 20 months, the toddler begins to indicate an awareness of soiled diapers, may attempt to remove the diaper, and may employ idiosyncratic words to describe the need to urinate or defecate. These are early signals that toilet learning is in progress. Overresponding to these cues with expectations that control is imminent can yield disappointing results. Certainly, attempts to impose rigid toileting schedules are doomed, though being aware of the times of day when toileting seems to occur with regularity—for example, on waking from a nap, soon after breakfast, or first thing in the morning—helps adults to begin a system of inquiries or reminders that help the child to notice the need and willingly proceed to the toilet. Insistence is counterproductive, as is reprimand, shaming, or punishing. Indeed, undue pressure from adults only prolongs the process by creating stress, anxiety, or power control situations that have negative effects on both child and adult and on the adult-child relationship. The child needs to experience adult patience, assistance, encouragement, and praise for efforts as toilet learning proceeds. Toileting accidents should be treated respectfully, for many will occur before mastery is achieved; again, embarrassment or punishment do little to enhance this complex developmental process.

Some children may achieve control over their toileting needs by age 2, others may lack such control until age 3 or 4, and still others may not be free of occasional toileting accidents before age 5 or 6. Once control seems to be established, children will have relapses for a variety of reasons: impending illness, diarrhea, bladder infections, sound sleep, being too busy to notice the need, excitement, anxiety, or psychological trauma, to mention some. Toddlers sometimes revert to precontrol stages when family life is altered in some manner: a family move, a new baby, hospitalization of a family member, a death or divorce in the family, or even an unusually exciting and happy event such as a birthday party or holiday celebration. Adults should expect uneven development in toilet learning and should not show disappointment when the toddler is unsuccessful. The positive and supportive manner in which adults handle toilet learning will be instrumental in ensuring continued control and healthy attitudes toward the human body and elimination.

Theorists have related body and gender awareness experiences and toilet learning to psychosocial development. Erikson, for instance, related toilet learning to the child's developing sense of autonomy (self-governance) or feelings of shame and doubt, and suggested that its healthy management has far-reaching effects on psychosocial development.

RELATIONSHIP BETWEEN PHYSICAL/MOTOR AND COGNITIVE DEVELOPMENT

Recall earlier discussions of rapid neurological development and brain growth during the prenatal period and the first three years. The human brain is made up of billions of nerve cells, or neurons, which began developing during the embryonic period. Unlike other cells in the body, the neurons are not packed closely, but have spaces between them that allow axons and dendrites to connect or communicate with one another through the contact process known as synapsing. During infancy and the toddler period, growth of these neural fibers and synapses increases rapidly.

As neurons develop, their continued growth and survival depend on environmental stimulation. Input from the child's environment prompts new synapses. Neurons that are not stimulated tend to die. The quality and quantity of early stimulation thus have long-term implications for cognitive development. Environments that are rich in sensory stimulation—visual, auditory, olfactory, tactile, taste, and kinesthetic—enhance brain growth in this manner.

It is important to recognize this early neurological development to appreciate the influence of early stimulation and enriching experiences. Early brain growth influences first motor abilities, then sensory perceptions (Volpe, 1987). Thus, one can expect that healthy large and small motor development and sensory experiences promote cognitive development. The adult's role, then, is to provide spaces and opportunities for the toddler to explore, enriching sensory experiences, engaging language and conversations about objects and events surrounding the child, and satisfying social interactions. The toddler's increasing mobility—walking, running, climbing, reaching—and insatiable curiosity propel the child into an ever-enlarging world of explorations, manipulations, experimentations, and discoveries. The richer the experiences that are scaffolded through engaging social and verbal interactions, the more positive and promising are the effects on neurological development, brain growth, and cognitive performance.

FACTORS INFLUENCING PHYSICAL AND MOTOR DEVELOPMENT: AGES ONE THROUGH THREE

This section elaborates on topics that were introduced in Chapter 5 and includes some additional topics. You may wish to review the relevant section in Chapter 5 before reading the following.

Nutrition

The visible effects of prolonged malnutrition on young children are seen almost daily in television newscasts and philanthropic solicitations for help for children in underdeveloped countries. Hollow eyes, protruding abdomens, and skeletal bodies are disturbing features of seriously malnourished children. Nutrition-related health problems exist not only in third world countries, but in all cultures around the world. Indeed, a recent study by the Centers for Disease Control and Prevention reported the identification of nutritional rickets, a condition that causes weak or deformed bones, among some children in the United States, although the disease is rare in this country. The children who were identified as having rickets were breast fed as infants and toddlers, but did not receive recommended vitamin D supplements (Centers for Disease Control and Prevention, 2001). Poor nutrition is associated with impaired neurological and physical development, poor cognitive outcomes, numerous health and disease issues, compromised immune systems and vulnerability to environmental toxins.

Food provides the nutrients young children need to grow and develop strong minds and bodies, and the energy required to play, think, and learn. Helping toddlers to learn to eat and enjoy the types of foods that ensure proper nutrition involves (1) wise selection of nutritious foods, (2) appealing preparation and presentation of new foods, (3) mealtime social/emotional climates that are conducive to food enjoyment and digestion, and (4) respect for the child's satiety and food preferences.

Wise Selection of Nutritious Foods.   The toddler's daily dietary plan should consist of food selected from the following food groups: (1) breads, cereals, rice, and pasta; (2) vegetables and fruit; (3) milk, yogurt, and cheese; (4) meat, poultry, fish, beans, and eggs; and (5) fats, oils, and sweets (sparingly). The recommended dietary plan is illustrated by the U.S. Department of Agriculture Food Guide Pyramid in Figure 8.3. Fatty foods and sweets need not be eliminated from the toddler's diet, but should be included judiciously. Recall from Chapter 5 that

FIGURE 8.3
Food Guide Pyramid for Children from Ages 2 to 6 Years of Age

Source: U.S. Department of Agriculture Center for Nutrition Policy and Promotion

U.S. DEPARTMENT OF AGRICULTURE
CENTER FOR NUTRITION POLICY AND PROMOTION

USDA is an equal opportunity provider and employer.

young children should not be placed on low-fat diets except on the advice and guidance of a pediatrician or health care professional. However, many foods that are marketed to young children are inappropriately high in sugars and fats and should be selected only on the basis of their contribution to the overall dietary needs of the young child. Furthermore, overreliance on any of the food groups deprives the growing child of other vital nutrients. Because different foods contain different combinations of nutrients and other substances necessary for growth and health, a variety of food choices is necessary. No single food or meal plan can supply all of the essential nutrients.

Appealing Preparation and Presentation of New Foods.   Toddlers are just beginning to get acquainted with many solid foods and beverages other than milk. They are being introduced to a variety of food tastes, textures, colors, consistencies, and temperatures. Acceptance of new food experiences depends on the *v*isual, *o*lfactory, *t*exture, and *t*aste (VOTT) appeal of the food. As with older children and adults, foods that fail the "VOTT test" have a high rejection rate. New foods are best introduced in very small portions with another, familiar food that the child has an established taste for and likes. To engage interest, the food can be named in a manner that informs and responds to the child's curiosity: "You have never had spinach before; this is spinach." If it is at first rejected, the food can be reintroduced from time to time until a taste is acquired. Encouraging children to taste new foods but not insisting on their eating the whole serving gives them an opportunity to learn about the food in a positive context.

Because the young child's immune system is immature, protection from foodborne illnesses is crucial. The child's eating surfaces and utensils must be scrupulously clean, and toddlers can be taught to wash their hands and faces before and after eating. Food should be properly cleaned, cooked, and prepared and served at the appropriate temperature. It should be served in manageable portions. Finger foods should be peeled (when appropriate) and cut into small, manageable pieces. All food served to toddlers should be a size and consistency that the young child can mouth, chew, and swallow. Foods that can cause choking should be avoided. Foods that are likely to be aspirated include hot dogs, meat (beef, pork, chicken) in chunks that are too large and too tough to chew and swallow easily, peanuts and other nuts, popcorn, grapes, carrots, round hard candies, stiff chewy candies (taffy, caramels), and chewing gum.

Mealtime Social/Emotional Climates Conducive to Food Enjoyment and Digestion.   Toddlers are gaining independence in feeding themselves: finger feeding, using a spoon, and drinking from a cup—all of which involve the development of chewing and swallowing and eye–hand and hand–mouth coordinations. It takes focus and concentration to do these things well. Playful distractions and negative interactions interfere with this process. Laughing, talking, or crying with food in the mouth increases the risk of choking. Pleasant conversation and positive role models during mealtime help toddlers to focus on eating and to eat enough to satisfy their hunger. Mealtimes should never be a time to reprimand or discipline, nor should food be used to reward or punish. Using food in this manner attaches the wrong meaning to it and leads to the individual's use of food to satisfy psychological instead of physiological needs (e.g., eating when feeling unhappy, bored, angry, or self-defeated or rejecting food to self-punish or to rebel against frustrating situations).

Respect for the Child's Satiety and Food Preferences.   Toddlers' appetites vary from meal to meal and day to day and are not quite as commanding as during infancy, when growth was so rapid. Nevertheless, toddlers should be offered three nutritious meals and two nutritious snacks each day. Serving sizes should be small yet sufficient to satisfy the child's hunger. Large serving sizes can discourage the young child. Tastes and food preferences also vary from day to day, often according to temporary whims. Whims are no cause for concern as long as, over the course of two or three days, children are offered a variety of nutrient-rich foods from which to choose. Because of the toddler's short attention span, mealtimes should not be too prolonged. Taking cues from the child, the adult can end the meal when it is clear that the child is no longer hungry. Minimal intake at one or two meals is no need for concern. Healthy children generally eat sufficient amounts of food to satisfy them. Avoiding nonnutritious sugary or fatty between-meal snacks increases the child's enjoyment of mealtime and enhances his or her intake of essential nutrients provided by well-balanced meals and snacks. However, if the timing or content of a meal is such that the child is hungry at a later time, providing a nutritious snack helps to fill his or her nutritive needs and sustains the child until the next meal. Finally, it is important to note that it is the adult who purchases, prepares, and offers nutritious foods to children. However, it is the child who knows when he or she has had enough to eat and when a particular food holds no appeal.

General Health and Freedom from Disease

Rapid growth during the preschool years makes regular health assessment checkups imperative. In general, children need to be examined two or three times during the 2nd year and one or two times per year thereafter. This schedule helps to ensure that immunizations are kept current and that emerging developmental and health care needs are addressed as they arise. In addition to the general developmental and health examinations, children may be tested for anemia, lead levels in the blood, and any other unusual symptoms.

Because infectious diseases can spread rapidly among children in groups, child care and early education programs adopt attendance and participation policies. These policies address conditions or symptoms that require isolation, exclusion, or dismissal. The American Public Health Association and the American Academy of Pediatrics (2002) published recommended guidelines in *Caring for Our Children: National Health and Safety Performance Standards: Guidelines for Out-of-Home Child Care Programs.* For information on this and other health and safety topics relating to children in groups, the reader is referred to this thorough and comprehensive set of standards. Some obvious signs require immediate attention such as fever, uncharacteristic lethargy, irritability, crying, difficulty breathing, diarrhea, vomiting, mouth sores, rash, infestations such as head lice, scabies, or symptoms of any of the communicable diseases. Individuals who care for children on a daily basis are better prepared to address these health issues when they are armed with knowledge of common symptoms and behaviors and how to respond to children who are ill or injured, as well as how to prevent the spread of illness among children.

A growing concern for scientists is the increasing prevalence of bacteria that are antibiotic resistant, that is, the antibiotics used to combat some infections are no longer effective. Antibiotics can be powerful allies in the treatment of infectious diseases, but are designed to cure *bacterial* infections. Antibiotics are ineffective in treating *viral* infections. The more often a child is treated with antibiotics, particularly when the illness is caused by a virus, or when the entire course of antibiotic treatment is not taken, the higher the risk becomes for untreatable bacterial infections. This is explained by the fact that each time an antibiotic is prescribed, sensitive bacteria are killed, but resistant bacteria are left to grow and multiply. These resistant bacteria do not respond to the antibiotic, so the illness is unaffected and persists, and may increase in severity. These antibiotic-resistant bacteria may be spread to others as well.

The need for antibiotics for infections and illnesses such as ear infections, sinus infections, cough, bronchitis, sore throat, and colds is best determined by the child's physician, who may advise a parent or caregiver to allow a particular ailment to run its course without medication. A related concern under investigation is the use of antibiotics in agriculture, which creates drug-resistant strains in the food supply (Shea, 2003).

Sleep Patterns

Adequate amounts of sleep and rest contribute to general health and a sense of well-being. The need for sleep decreases as children get older. Toddlers may take one or two short naps or one long nap during the day and sleep anywhere from 8 to 12 hours at night. Many toddlers are ready to give up the crib in favor of a bed, preferably one with sturdy side rails to prevent falls. Insisting on continued use of the crib may complicate naptimes and bedtimes if the child feels that she or he has outgrown that sleeping arrangement. Regular and predictable routines (bath, bedtime story, brushing teeth, saying "good night" to family members, a few moments of quiet with a parent, and finally lights out or nightlight on) help toddlers to accept the separation and to meet their sleep needs more effectively.

Toddlers are social beings, and resistance to bedtime may well arise. Ages one through three are marked by an emerging sense of autonomy and a lingering fear of separation. These psychological issues complicate bedtime and naptime rituals. Bedtime difficulties may arise from a low sensory threshold, which causes the young child to be easily distracted by environmental noise, motion, and light; the parent's overconcern or difficulty in separating from the child; inappropriate expectations that a child can separate and fall asleep on demand; ambivalence over regular versus child-initiated routines; and a variety of physiological problems associated with growth (e.g., outgrowing the crib, wakefulness associated with toileting needs), impending illness, fatigue, overstimulation, hunger, and thirst.

Dental Health

As mentioned earlier, all of the child's primary teeth have usually appeared by age 3. Primary teeth usually follow a predictable sequence of eruption, with the lower incisors appearing first. During the 2nd and 3rd years, a total of 20 primary teeth will erupt. The American Academy of Pediatric Dentists recommends a visit to the dentist by the time a child is 1 year old and thereafter every 6 months. In addition

TABLE 8.3 Important Accident Prevention Measures for Families to Observe During the Toddler Period

Potential Accident Situations	Prevention Measures for Health Teaching
Motor vehicles	Maintain child in car seat, not just seat belt; do not be distracted from safe driving by a child in a car. Do not allow child to play outside unsupervised. Do not allow a child to operate electronic garage doors. Supervise toddler too young to be left alone on a tricycle. Teach safety with pedaling toys (look before crossing driveways; do not cross streets).
Falls	Keep house windows closed or keep secure screens in place. Place gates at top and bottom of stairs. Supervise at playgrounds. Do not allow child to walk with sharp objects in hand or mouth. Raise crib rails and check to make sure they are locked before walking away from crib.
Aspiration	Examine toys for small parts that could be aspirated, remove those that appear dangerous. Do not feed a toddler popcorn, peanuts, etc.; urge children not to eat while running. Do not leave a toddler alone with a balloon.
Drowning	Do not leave toddler alone in a bathtub or near water (including buckets of cleaning water).
Animal bites	Do not allow the toddler to approach strange dogs. Supervise child's play with family pets.
Poisoning	Never present medication as candy. Buy medication with child-proof safety caps; put away immediately after use. Never take medication in front of a child. Place all medications and poisons in locked cabinets or overhead shelves where child cannot reach. Never leave medication in parents' purse or pocket, where child can reach. Always store food or substances in their original containers. Use non-lead-based paint throughout the house. Hang plants or set them on high surfaces beyond toddler's grasp. Post telephone number of nearest poison control center by the telephone. In all first-aid boxes, maintain supply of syrup of ipecac, an emetic, with proper instructions for administering if poisoning should occur.
Burns	Buy flame-retardant clothing. Turn handles of pots toward back of stove to prevent toddler from reaching up and pulling them down. Use cool-mist vaporizer or remain in room when vaporizer is operating so that child is not tempted to play with it. Keep screen in front of fireplace or heater. Monitor toddlers carefully when they are near lit candles. Do not leave toddlers unsupervised near hot-water faucets. Do not allow toddlers to blow out matches (teach that fire is not fun); store matches out of reach. Keep electric wires and cords out of toddler's reach; cover electrical outlets with safety plugs.
General	Know whereabouts of toddlers at all times. Toddlers can climb onto chairs, stools, etc., that they could not manage before, and can turn door knobs and go places they could not go before. Be aware that the frequency of accidents increases when the family is under stress and therefore less attentive to children. Special precautions must be taken at these times. Some children are more active, curious, and impulsive and therefore more vulnerable to accidents than others.

Source: Maternal and Child Health Nursing, (p. 889), by A. Pillitteri, 1992, Philadelphia: Lippincott. Reprinted with permission of the author.

to examining for cavities, the dentist can determine the health of the child's teeth and gums and estimate when new teeth will erupt. The dentist will also counsel parents about nutritional needs, foods to avoid, and the need for fluoride or vitamin supplements to ensure healthy teeth. The dentist will monitor the effects of pacifier use or thumbsucking on the developing oral structures and recommend appropriate handling of these important self-comforting behaviors. Generally, as toddlers get older, begin to talk, and become engaged with a variety of hands-on toys and activities, there is less need or desire for the thumb or pacifier, though during times of boredom, stress, fatigue, or illness, they may rely on these self-comforting behaviors.

Dental health begins in infancy. Regular cleaning of the infant's gums and new teeth after meals with a soft, damp gauze pad begins the process of instilling good oral cleaning habits and avoiding cavities in primary teeth. Avoiding use of the bottle as a pacifier is also necessary to prevent "baby bottle caries." With increasing eye–hand and hand–mouth coordination, the toddler can soon learn to use a brush and a small amount of toothpaste. Encouraging brushing after meals and before bedtime begins an essential self-help habit.

Safety

Toddlers are particularly vulnerable to mishaps. Their impulsive behaviors, lack of experience and judgment, curiosity, and quest for independence place them at risk for accident and injury. Adult expectations also place toddlers at risk for accident and injury when adults assume that toddlers are capable of tasks or judgments that are beyond their years. Table 8.3 outlines important measures for adults to take during the toddler period to prevent accidents and injury.

Opportunities to Interact, Explore, and Play

Opportunities to interact with caring, supportive adults and compatible playmates, to explore safe and inviting environments, and to do what children do so well—play—provide motivation to use emerging skills and play behaviors in growth-enhancing ways. Toddlers need environments, toys, and materials that encourage and facilitate the following:

- *Large motor coordination* (e.g., wheeled toys; low crawling and climbing equipment; large balls to roll, kick, throw, and bounce; large blocks and construction-type toys; tricycles, wagons)
- *Small motor coordination* (e.g., fill-and-pour toys; connecting blocks and manipulative items; stacking toys; items that snap, button, zip)
- *Perceptual–motor development* (e.g., graduated stacking toys; puzzles with four to five parts; shape-sorting boxes; color-matching games; sound-identification games; texture-matching games; beanbag toss; rhythm and dance; obstacle course games; follow-the-leader games)
- *Imitative behaviors and pretend play* (e.g., dolls; trucks, cars, airplanes; household items such as plastic dishes; dress-up clothes and costumes of familiar characters)
- *Language and literacy* (e.g., books and pictures; shared-book experiences; puppets, dolls, audio- and video-recorded sounds, tunes, songs, poems, stories; conversation; field trips; drawing and writing materials)

Toddlers need safe environments and adult protection to enjoy health-promoting, stress-free play.

Appropriate and Inappropriate Expectations

As infants grow into toddlers and toddlers become preschoolers, their rapid growth and development often suggest greater maturity and capability than are actually present. This can lead to inappropriate expectations. Such expectations place young children at both physical and psychological risk. Knowledge of expected patterns and sequences of physical and motor development helps adults to appreciate each child's unique capabilities and interest and gives direction to the provision of growth-enhancing experiences for children. Further, it is important to acknowledge that young children behave in impulsive and unpredictable ways, and are a long way from being able to precede their actions with thoughtful restraint and good judgment. Nor are young children capable of protecting themselves in dangerous situations.

A case in point is the misguided assumption that teaching infants to swim will make them safer in and around swimming pools or other bodies of water. According to health and safety statistics, drowning ranks among the leading causes of unintentional injury and death in children, and is highest among children ages 1 through 2 years old (National Center for Injury Prevention and Control, Centers for Disease Control and Prevention, 2003). While aquatic programs have gained popularity in the United States in recent years, their enticements should not suggest to parents that their children can become good swimmers or be able to survive independently in the water—an age-*in*appropriate expectation.

There can be no assurance that infants and toddlers will understand water hazards, use appropriate avoidance and safety strategies, or internalize safety rules. Claims to the contrary mislead parents and give them a false sense of security about their child's safety in the water (American Academy of Pediatrics, 2000). Neither safety skills nor swimming skills are appreciably enhanced when lessons begin in infant or toddler ages. Further, there is no evidence that infant/toddler swimming lessons assure more rapid mastery of swimming skills. Depth perception, cognizance of risk levels, and judgment are still immature, and it has been noted that the complex motor skills required in swimming can be acquired more readily when fundamental motor skills are coordinated and controlled around age

5 years (American Academy of Pediatrics, 2000). As with all expectations, developmental readiness and individual interest should influence the choice of activities and experiences provided for children.

Expecting small children to use writing tools or scissors, to color within the lines, and to manage complicated clothing before they have the fine motor control to do so; expecting young children to remember safety rules and precautions; and assuming that behaviors demonstrated in one situation (e.g., managing toileting at home) will be manifest routinely in other situations (managing toileting at preschool) are examples of inappropriate expectations. Observing toddlers closely; assessing where they focus their energies and interests; and noting the questions they ask, how they manage various large and small motor tasks, express their needs, and understand, remember, and follow requests, help adults to gauge expectations and ensure that the opportunities provided for children are in sync with their developmental capabilities and needs.

Sadly, inappropriate expectations have sometimes led to child abuse when parents have become frustrated over a child's "failure" to perform as expected. Indeed, abuse of infants and toddlers has been associated with infant crying, toileting accidents, food spills, inability to verbalize needs or articulate words so as to be understood, sleep/waking patterns, curiosity and handling of objects in the environment, and many other typical and age-expected behaviors. Inappropriate expectations undermine healthy growth and development and subvert the relationship between children and the adults on whom they depend. The characteristics of healthy environments for young children are listed in Figure 8.4.

FIGURE 8.4
Healthy Environments for Young Children

Healthy home and child care environments for young children are characterized by:

1. **Adequate space.** Toddlers need sufficient space in which to try out their emerging and uncoordinated motor skills. Tumbles and collisions with furniture are minimized when adequate space is provided.

2. **Clean, sanitary surroundings.** Toddlers put their hands, toys, and other objects into their mouths. All necessary precautions must be taken to protect toddlers from infections and disease.

3. **Safe space and play materials.** Reaching, grasping, and mobility skills tempt toddlers to satisfy their natural curiosity. The toddler's environment must be kept free from obstacles, poisons, sharp edges, small objects, unstable furnishings and play equipment, exposed electrical cords and outlets, and so on.

4. **Developmentally appropriate play items and equipment.** Developmentally appropriate play items help to ensure safety and provide satisfying and engaging experiences that enhance physical, motor, and perceptual development and enrich play activities.

5. **Unrelenting supervision.** While toddler mobility and curiosity enhance physical, motor, and perceptual growth and cognitive development, constant vigilance is essential. Safety concerns are paramount at this age.

6. **Supervised health care.** To maintain healthy bodies, health care must be supervised by appropriate medical and dental professionals. Proper diet, immunizations, rest and exercise, and specialized medical attention as needed enhance chances for optimal growth and development.

HEALTH AND WELL-BEING ISSUES IN TODDLER DEVELOPMENT

Poverty

The extent to which childhood needs for food, clothing, health care, and shelter have been met determines the integrity of overall growth and development. Poverty represents a major impediment to sound growth and development. Children who live in poverty are more likely than other children to die from infections and parasitic diseases, drowning or suffocation, car accidents, or fires. Children who live in poverty are more likely to suffer deleterious outcomes associated with prematurity and low birth weight and to exhibit low weight for their height, which in turn affects brain growth and development and, concurrently, cognitive and psychosocial development. These children are also more likely to live in polluted or toxic environments, drink water that is contaminated with lead or breathe lead-contaminated paint dust, and have parents and other family members who are struggling to meet family survival needs. Families living in these circumstances are less effective in meeting the special needs of infants and children. Families living in poverty have limited resources for safe and stimulating toys, learning materials, and socially and cognitively enriching experiences; are often less able to access high-quality child care; are more likely to live in high-crime neighborhoods; and are less able to access and afford regular, ongoing health care.

Early childhood professionals are sensitive to the needs of children and families living in poverty. This includes helping families to access assistance through various community, state, and federal agencies and early childhood intervention programs, such as home visiting programs, Early Head Start, Head Start, community health care and immunization programs, family counseling services, community child safety initiatives, and other resources. Families living in poverty respond best to assistance from professionals who are nonjudgmental, supportive, and helpful. Physically and psychologically vulnerable children need adults who plan for and support their growth needs, accept and respect them, provide developmentally appropriate programs and expectations, and help to connect them and their families with appropriate intervention and support services.

Nutritional Deficiencies

food security:
the ability of the family to meet the nutritional needs of its members

food insecurity:
the inability of the family to meet the nutritional needs of all of its members

Food security is a term that refers to the ability of the family to provide for its members' nutritional needs. Studies of **food insecurity** include families in which one or more members have experienced hunger during a specified period of time. Often in food-insecure families, children's food needs take precedence over those of adults, though their nutritional needs may not be adequately met due to poverty, lack of nutritional knowledge, or lack of professional health care guidance.

Nutritional deficiencies exist among families living at all socioeconomic levels. Child hunger in the United States and the effects of malnutrition are topics seldom addressed in the media. However, the prevalence of hunger among children in the United States and around the world represents a serious child development issue. More than 250,000 children were served through soup kitchen lines in the United States during 2001 (Second Harvest, 2001). As we discuss in later chapters, hunger and malnutrition have immediate and long-term effects on both the physical and mental health of children and are particularly problematic during the very rapid growth of infants and toddlers.

Out-of-home child care settings are generally required by state licensure to provide daily diets that meet one third or more of a child's daily dietary requirements and to pay particular attention to the special dietary needs of individual children. Where child care takes place in unlicensed child care arrangements, caregivers have a responsibility to provide appropriate formula, foods, and snacks to meet the children's daily nutritional needs. In either setting, caregivers can help to meet these nutritional requirements by becoming knowledgeable about child nutrition, and communicating with parents about specific dietary needs, food preferences, or food allergies.

Immunization Benefits and Risks*

Immunizations are the world's best defense against many debilitating and life-threatening diseases. Before vaccinations became widely used, infectious diseases killed thousands of children and adults each year in the United States and around the world. Indeed, even today in parts of the world where vaccinations are not widely administered, children and adults still suffer the devastating effects of many of the diseases that have been virtually eradicated in the United States. Table 8.4 lists vaccine preventable diseases and their risk characteristics.

Because infants are particularly vulnerable to infections, it is important to begin immunizations during infancy. A precise immunization schedule is designed to provide immunizations at appropriate age intervals and doses for each preventable disease. While breast-feeding supplies some protection against some infections, such as colds, ear infections, and diarrhea, it does not stimulate the infant's immune system to fight infection against specific diseases. Therefore, breast-feeding, for all of its benefits, is not effective in preventing contagious, vaccine-preventable diseases.

In recent years, concern about the safety of some vaccinations has arisen. Reports of risks associated with various vaccines has resulted in the reluctance of some parents to have their children immunized. Modern-day vaccines are extremely safe and getting safer and more effective with continuing research and ongoing review by physicians, researchers, and public health officials. Vaccines are required to meet very strict safety standards of the U.S. Food and Drug Administration (FDA) before they are approved. Further, every vaccine is closely monitored by the FDA and the U.S. Centers for Disease Control and Prevention (CDC) as long as it is in use. In 1990, the FDA and the CDC established the Vaccine Adverse Events Reporting System (VAERS) to collect and analyze all reports (from anyone who wishes to submit one, including parents) of possible adverse reactions. Such reporting has led to a database from which analysis and large-scale research studies can be generated to determine whether a reaction is vaccine associated or has origins that are unrelated to the vaccine.

Though it is true that serious adverse effects from vaccines have occurred, the incidence of these events is extremely rare. Hence, scientists must weigh the *benefits* against the *risks* of a particular vaccine. Generally, scientists conclude that the chance of serious complications (including death) from the disease itself is many times higher than is the chance of vaccine-related complications.

*Note: Information for this section has been obtained from the Allied Vaccine Group website, accessed 26 September 2003 at www.vaccine.org. Other websites from which further information about immunizations can be obtained are included at the end of this chapter.

TABLE 8.4   Vaccine-Preventable Diseases

Disease	Characteristics and Risks
Chicken pox (varicella)	Characterized by fever, blistery, itchy rash; can cause pneumonia or death
Diphtheria	Characterized by a thick coating in nose or throat, which can lead to breathing obstruction, heart failure, paralysis, or death
Haemophilus influenzae type B (Hib) infection	Causes meningitis; swelling of the membranes surrounding the brain and/or spinal cord; also causes pneumonia and other diseases
Hepatitis B	Causes severe liver disease, liver cancer; can lead to death
Measles	Characterized by a rash, cough, and fever; can lead to pneumonia, seizures, brain damage, or death
Mumps	Characterized by fever, headaches, and swollen glands under the jaw; can lead to hearing loss and/or meningitis
Polio	Characterized by fever, stiffness in the neck and shoulders, headache, muscle spasms; can result in paralysis and death
Rubella (3-day measles)	Characterized by rash and fever; particularly dangerous for pregnant woman, who could miscarry or give birth to an infant with serious problems including brain damage, heart disease, and other anomalies
Smallpox	Characterized by high fever, headache, backache, pustular blisters that form pockmarks; high risk of death; *note:* this disease has been considered eradicated and vaccinations for it were halted in the United States in 1972; however, the threat of bioterrorism around the world suggests that there could be a time when this vaccination should be reinstituted for some populations
Tetanus (lockjaw)	Characterized by severe muscle spasms; high risk of death

During the last decade, the prestigious Institute of Medicine (IOM) has conducted extensive reviews of the scientific studies and medical literature on health problems occurring after vaccination. The IOM provides the health care community its findings from these objective and thorough reviews. A list of these reports is available through the website of the Allied Vaccine Group, a linked group of organizations committed to providing valid scientific information about vaccines (see Other Resources).

Immunizations are required when children are enrolled in child care settings and schools. All 50 states have immunization laws. Each state determines which vaccines are required by state law. Most states rely on the vaccination schedules recommended by the Committee on Infectious Diseases of the American Academy of Pediatrics, the Advisory Committee on Immunization Practices of the Centers for Disease Control and Prevention, and the American Academy of Family Physicians. Child care and school vaccination laws are designed to prevent outbreaks of contagious diseases. Unvaccinated children are at high risk of contracting and spreading a preventable disease.

As of August 2003, all 50 states have passed laws allowing for certain exemptions. States may exempt children from the immunization requirements on the basis of medical, religious, or philosophical reasons. However, to be enrolled in child care programs and schools, families must present state-required documentation to support their request for exemption. Should an outbreak of a disease occur in a school or child care setting, children who have not been immunized may be prevented by law from attending until the outbreak is over.

Nonparental Child Care

Because the toddler period is one of rapid neurological, physical/motor, psychosocial, language, and cognitive development, early childhood professionals are particularly concerned that nonparental child care be of the highest quality possible and provide surroundings, interactions, education, and care that best meet toddlers' unique needs. Research over the last decade has consistently identified certain essential qualities that ensure positive developmental outcomes for children (Blau, 1999; Helburn, 1995; National Center for Education Statistics, 1998; National Institute of Child Health and Human Development, 1999; Peisner-Feinberg et al., 1999; Phillips, 1993; Reynolds, Temple, Robertson, & Mann, 2001; U.S. Department of Health and Human Services, 2001):

- Small group size (the younger the child, the smaller the group should be)
- High adult–child ratios (as shown in Table 8.5, the younger the child, the higher this ratio should be)
- Educated, well-trained caregivers
- Stability in child–caregiver relationships over time
- Developmentally appropriate curriculum and expectations
- Family-centered care and support services

TABLE 8.5   Recommended Adult-to-Child Ratios

Age	Children per adult	Maximum group size
Birth–12 months	3	6
13–30 months	4	8
31–35 months	5	10
3 years	7	14
4 years	8	16
5 years	8	16
6–8 years	10	20
9–12 years	12	24

Note: Professional organizations such as the National Association for the Education of Young Children (2004) and the American Academy of Pediatrics with the American Public Health Association (2002) and the Federal Head Start Bureau set recommended adult-to-children ratios and maximum group sizes, as do other accrediting and regulatory organizations and agencies. While there are subtle variations among these standards that depend on age divisions and group sizes, they all emphasize small groups and low adult to children ratios such as those listed here.

High-quality child care has been shown to have long-term benefits for children. In a study of 1,300 children in 10 sites, researchers found significant positive effects on school readiness and language skills in children who had attended high-quality child care programs (McCartney & Clarke-Stewart, 1999; Peth-Pierce, 1998). Other studies have found that children in high-quality child care programs exhibit greater receptive language ability and pre-math skills, higher self-esteem, more advanced social skills, and warmer relationships with their teachers (Bowman, Donavan, & Burns, 2001; Clarke-Stewart, Vandell, Burchinal, O'Brien, & McCartney, 2002; Helburn, 1995). Yet many infants and young children are being cared for in settings that are poor to mediocre, and some are in settings that are potentially harmful because of poor sanitary conditions in diapering and feeding; unsafe surroundings; lack of supportive, warm, and nurturing interactions from the adults who care for them; and lack of appropriate toys and stimulation (Helburn, 1995).

Helping parents to make wise choices for their nonparental child care is an ongoing effort of professionals in many fields, such as early childhood education, pediatrics, sociology, psychology, and public policy. The emergence in recent years of child care resource and referral systems is helping to connect families with child care providers and other community resources that meet local, state, and national requirements for licensing, accreditation, and quality.

Resource and referral agencies exist in all states but may not be available in all communities. Resource and referral programs provide information to parents about child care that is available in their communities and referrals to other programs in response to family needs. They develop and maintain databases on child care programs. In addition, they attempt to enhance the supply of qualified providers through training and technical assistance to new and existing providers.

Other Communicable Diseases and Health Issues

There are a number of additional health issues associated with very young children. Among the more prominent ones are the rising incidence of childhood asthma, the control of HIV/AIDS disease, and the reappearance of diseases once thought to be eradicated in the United States.

Asthma.   Childhood asthma is a chronic disease that makes airways (bronchial tubes) sensitive to irritants. It affects approximately 1.3 million U.S. children younger than age 5. While most current data indicate that the incidence of asthma may have plateaued since the dramatic increases during the 1990s, children from infancy to 4 years old have had the largest increase in prevalence and require more health care supervision. Asthma appears to be a particular health issue for African American children. One study found that hospitalization and mortality rates among African American children in 1998 through 1999 were 3 times that of white children, and African American children were 4 times as likely to die from asthma (Akinbami & Schoendorf, 2002).

Because this disease can slow growth and development and can be potentially life-threatening, it is important to determine the types of triggers to an asthma episode and, where possible, control or eliminate exposure. Some common irritants and risk factors are cigarette smoke; pet dander; household dust, particularly dusty bedding, pillows, or stuffed toys; strong odors; certain foods; cockroaches; hay; dry leaves and pollen; emotional disturbances; overexertion; and seasonal and weather changes. The family's health care professional can provide appropriate therapies, medication, and guidance regarding control of triggers to asthma. Parents have a responsibility to communicate with their children's nonparental caregivers about their child's particular health care needs. Personnel in child care settings and schools may need to assess their environments for potential asthma triggers, and be clear about how to respond to a particular child's asthma episode.

HIV/AIDS.   The human immunodeficiency virus (HIV), which causes acquired immunodeficiency syndrome (AIDS), does not affect only homosexual men, as is widely believed, but is a disease that has risen rapidly in prevalence among heterosexual men and women, including adolescents. The HIV virus attacks the immune system, rendering it ineffective in fighting infectious diseases. It is spread through sexual contact, intravenous drug use, and, in very rare cases, blood transfusions and organ transplants. This disease can be transmitted to the fetus during prenatal development, labor, and delivery and through breast-feeding. However, certain medications during pregnancy can reduce the chance of a mother passing HIV to an infant. For this reason, the American College of Obstetricians and Gynecologists (2003) recommends that all pregnant women be tested for HIV so treatment can be initiated if needed.

Diagnosis of HIV in infants is possible by 1 month of age, but more definitively by 6 months of age. Nevertheless, it is recommended that infants be tested before they are 48 hours old so that treatment can begin for those who test positive (Working Group on Antiretroviral Therapy and Medical Management of Infants, Children, and Adolescents with HIV Infection, 1998). It has been estimated that half of the cases of HIV-infected infants occur because of missed opportunities for perinatal HIV prevention, which includes prenatal care and HIV testing before delivery (Peters et al., 2003). Guidelines for the care of children with AIDS in child care setting, stress protection of both the child who has AIDS and other children and adults (American Public Health Association & American Academy of Pediatrics, 2002). Of critical importance is the strictest regime to prevent infants and toddlers from consuming milk or juice from bottles or cups used by another infant. Expressed human milk from an infected mother exposes the child to a potential HIV-containing body. Further, when **standard precautions** are used in responding to incidents that involve exposure to blood or blood-containing body fluids and tissue discharges, the potential spread of disease is reduced.

Resurgence of Communicable Diseases.   Resurgence of diseases thought to be under control within a given population is always a concern to health care professionals, who diligently strive to prevent the spread of disease particularly among children. Due to state laws that allow for certain exemptions for religious or philosophical reasons, unimmunized children who contract a disease can spread it to others, both adults and other unimmunized children. The increase in cases of measles, whooping cough, and polio in recent years in the United States has been attributed to failure to fully immunize; immigrants and vacation travelers who have or carry the disease from locations around the world where the disease exists; diseases such as HIV that compromise a person's immune system; and the fading of immunity provided by vaccination to a disease as a person enters adulthood. Whooping cough is an example of this latter phenomenon, which results in a large population of teenagers and adults who are potential targets for the pertussis infection (American Medical Association, 2003).

standard precautions: procedures involving the use of protective barriers such as nonporous gloves, aprons, disposable diapers and diaper table paper, and disposable towels, and surfaces that can be sanitized to reduce the risk of exposure to pathogens

In recent years, tuberculosis (TB), generally thought of as a disease of the past, has reemerged as a serious public health problem (National Institute of Allergy and Infectious Diseases, National Institutes of Health [NIAID/NIH], 2002). It is estimated that 10 to 15 million people in the United States are infected with Mycobacterium tuberculosis (or latent TB) and are at risk at a rate of 1 in 10 of developing active TB at some time in their lives. The incidence of TB is greater among minorities; 54% of active TB cases in 1999 were among African Americans and Hispanics, and an additional 20% were in Asians (NIAID/NIH, 2002). Children who are most likely at risk for TB are those who

- are immigrants;
- have had a tuberculosis contact;
- live in cities with populations of 250,000 or more;
- are or have been homeless;
- have been exposed to an HIV-positive person;
- have contact with someone who has spent time in jail;
- live in indigent areas.

With appropriate medical diagnosis and treatment, TB can be cured in most cases. Treatment involves drug therapy over a 6- to 12-month period. Early diagnosis and treatment of M. tuberculosis is a necessary step in preventing the spread of the disease.

Environmental Toxins

Lead Poisoning.   Lead is a toxin that is known to cause brain and nervous system disorders, learning disabilities, behavior problems, kidney damage, and growth retardation. Its prevalence is quite widespread, particularly in large urban areas. Infants and toddlers are more likely than adults to ingest lead, because of their inclination to handle and put things in their mouths, and they are more likely to suffer its effects owing to their immature digestive and nervous systems.

Lead is found in certain paints, soil, sometimes food, water from old plumbing, batteries, colored newsprint, toys (particularly antique toys), antique furniture, some ceramic dishes, hobby materials (paints, solders), fishing weights, buckshot, folk remedies, cosmetics, jewelry, workplace dust particles (transported on clothing), petroleum products, and miniblinds manufactured outside the United States before 1996. Children who have elevated lead levels might not exhibit any symptoms for a time. It is possible that high lead levels in the mother's blood can result in placental transmission to the fetus. Prevention of lead poisoning in children requires thorough and careful evaluation of and modifications in the environment, avoiding lead-contaminated objects and places, and screening for blood lead levels through blood tests.

Certain nutrients have been found to aid in the prevention of lead poisoning, especially in young children. A well-balanced diet of grains; fruits; vegetables; dairy products; meat, poultry, or fish; dry beans; and eggs can help decrease the child's susceptibility to lead. It is particularly important for the diet to include adequate amounts of calcium and iron. However, since dietary fat may enhance lead absorption in the body, it should be limited to only recommended amounts. Tap water in older homes and buildings may contain lead from older pipes, and reducing the risk of ingesting lead from this source requires running the cold water faucet for at least 1 minute before using it for drinking, cooking or cleaning food. This is a particularly important precaution when infants are bottle fed formula mixed with water (Pearse & Mitchell, 2003).

Environmental Tobacco Smoke.   There are more than 4,000 compounds in environmental tobacco smoke, and it is estimated that more than 50 of them are known to cause cancer. There are two different kinds of tobacco smoke; one (sidestream smoke) is the smoke that is emitted from a burning cigarette, cigar, or pipe between puffs, and the other (mainstream smoke) is smoke that is exhaled by a smoker. Sidestream smoke appears to contain higher concentrations of toxic elements (Canadian Council on Smoking and Health, National Clearinghouse on Tobacco and Health, 1995).

Children who are exposed to environmental tobacco smoke are at greater risk for SIDS and are more prone to respiratory irritations and infections, chronic coughing, bronchitis, pneumonia, asthma, ear infections, and tonsillitis than other children. Children of parents who smoke are more likely to smoke during adolescence. Because of its harmful effects on children, courts in Canada, the United States, and Australia have begun to consider parental smoking as one of the factors to be considered in assessing the best interest of the child in custody proceedings (Canadian Council on Smoking and Health, National Clearinghouse on Tobacco and Health, 1995).

Other Toxins

There are other environmental toxins that affect the health and growth of children. They include carbon monoxide, radon, molds, asbestos, pesticides, and air pollution. Local and regional health officials provide health alerts and information to the public on how to avoid or reduce the effects of these toxins.

ROLE OF THE EARLY CHILDHOOD PROFESSIONAL

Promoting Physical and Motor Development in Children Ages One Through Three

1. Create and maintain a safe, hygienic, and healthy environment.
2. Provide for proper nutrition and for ongoing health oversight.
3. Know and use developmentally appropriate activities and expectations.
4. Encourage exploration, discovery, and independence.
5. Provide positive, supportive, and protective guidance.
6. Encourage positive body and gender awareness.
7. Provide a variety of materials to encourage both large and small motor development.
8. Provide toys and experiences that facilitate perceptual–motor development.
9. Observe children for signs or symptoms of special needs or illness.
10. Model good health and hygiene behaviors.

KEY TERMS

audiologist	flexors	perceptual–motor
adipose	food security	prehension
body awareness	food insecurity	self-efficacy
cochlear implant	gender awareness	sexuality
deciduous teeth	gender identity	standard precautions
developmental milestones	locomotion	strabismus
extensors	nystagmus	toilet learning

REVIEW STRATEGIES AND ACTIVITIES

1. Review the key terms individually or with a classmate.

2. Observe two children in a child care setting for approximately one hour during outdoor and indoor activity times. Using the physical and motor milestone lists in this chapter, record all motor behaviors that you observe. Record both large and small motor observations. Compare your lists with those of a classmate. How are the children the same? How do they differ? To what might the differences in motor abilities be attributed?

3. Invite a nutritionist to talk with your class. What dietary plan would she or he recommend for a 1-year-old? A 2-year-old? A 3-year-old? How and why do these diets change as the child gets older?

4. Discuss with a classmate safe ways to encourage toddler exploration, discovery, and independence. List your suggestions. What physical/motor or perceptual development will your suggestions enhance?

5. Visit a nursery school in which toddlers (ages 1 to 3) are enrolled. How are children's health and physical well-being protected or enhanced? What precautions are taken to prevent the spread of infection or disease?

6. Throughout this course, compile a folder of child health and safety alerts provided through the media, parenting literature, fliers from physicians, reports of the U.S. Product Safety Commission, and other sources. Discuss prevention strategies with your classmates.

7. Given what you now know about physical and motor development in toddlers, what suggestions would you make to parents and caregivers to protect children from unintentional injury and threats to their health or safety?

FURTHER READINGS

American Academy of Pediatrics. (1994). *Handbook of common poisonings in children.* Elk Grove Village, IL: Author.

American Public Health Association & American Academy of Pediatrics (2002). *Caring for our children: National health and safety performance standards: Guidelines for out-of-home child care programs.* Washington, DC, & Elk Grove Village, IL: Authors.

Chrisman, K., & Couchenour, D. (2002). *Healthy sexuality development: A guide for early childhood educators and families.* Washington, DC: National Association for the Education of Young Children.

National Safety Council. *First aid and CPR: Infants and children.* Boston: Jones & Bartlett.

Schiff, D., & Shelov, S. P. (Eds.). (1999). *American Academy of Pediatrics official complete home reference: Guide to your child's symptoms.* New York: Random House.

Wolraich, M. I. (Ed.). (2003). *American Academy of Pediatrics guide to toilet training.* New York: Bantam.

OTHER RESOURCES

Allied Vaccine Group
    http://www.vaccine.org
American Dental Association
    http://www.ada.org
Centers for Disease Control and Prevention, National Vaccine Program
    http://www.cdc.gov/od/nvpo/main.htm
Child Care Aware
    http://www.childcareaware.org
Food and Drug Administration
    http://www.fda.gov
Food Research and Action Center
    http://www.frac.org
Healthy Child Care America Campaign (HCCA)
    http://nccic.org/hcca/index.html
Lead Hotline 1-800-LEAD-FYI
National Center for Clinical Infant Programs *Zero to Three*. Bimonthly, available from Zero
    to Three, PO Box 960, Herndon, VA 20172.
National Institute of Child Health and Human Development (NICHD)
    http://www.nichd.nih.gov
National Network for Immunization Information
    http://www.immunizationinfo.org
National Safety Council
    http://www.nsc.org
Second Harvest (2001)
    http://www.secondharvest.org
National Association of Child Care Resource and Referral Agencies
    1319 F Street, NW, Suite 810, Washington, DC 20004
    202/395-5501

CHAPTER NINE

Psychosocial Development: Ages One Through Three

Our words should be like a magic canvas upon which a child cannot help but paint a positive picture of himself.

HAIM G. GINOTT

It is also clear that one of the best ways to enrich an infant or toddler is through unstinting amounts of affection, to build security and self-esteem that will influence all the child's other experiences, and all further enrichments, throughout life.

MARIAN DIAMOND AND JANET HOPSON

After studying this chapter, you will demonstrate comprehension by:

▶ Relating selected theories to the study of psychosocial development during the toddler period.

▶ Discussing selected psychosocial experiences associated with brain growth and neurological development during the toddler period.

▶ Identifying major social and emotional milestones during the toddler period.

▶ Describing factors that influence psychosocial development in toddlers.

▶ Describing the role of adults in facilitating healthy psychosocial development in toddlers.

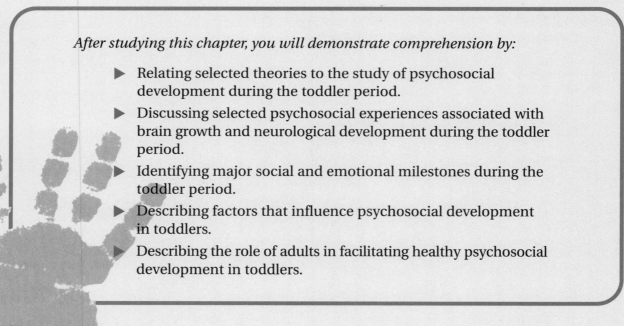

The toddler period of growth and development presents new challenges for parents and caregivers. The formerly dependent, compliant infant now strives for independence and for ever-widening opportunities to interact, explore, and learn. Increasingly, refined motor capabilities and communication skills are emerging, leading to new and unexpected behaviors. These new behaviors can, at the same time, thrill, perplex, frustrate, and intrigue parents and caregivers. The period is also a challenging one for the toddler, for the restraints of those who would guide and protect the child present obstacles and frustrations difficult for the child to understand.

THEORETICAL PERSPECTIVES ON PSYCHOSOCIAL DEVELOPMENT OF CHILDREN AGES ONE THROUGH THREE

Psychosocial Theory: Autonomy Versus Shame and Doubt

As toddlers come to trust their environments, the people within the environments, and themselves, they begin to grow in independence and a sense of autonomy (Erikson, 1963). The toddler's efforts to buckle a seat belt, turn a light switch on or off, open a door, and take off socks, shoes, or other clothing are intensely and personally important and can result in tears and tantrums when thwarted by an unsuspecting or impatient adult. Previously dependent behaviors are now being eclipsed by the toddler's efforts to gain independence. Locomotion and emerging fine motor controls encourage this independence as the toddler gains confidence in walking, climbing, running, moving, and manipulating. Language and self-awareness reveal a striving for independence as the toddler asserts, "Me do it!," "No," and "Mine." While these behaviors can tax adult patience, they are viewed as indications of positive and healthy psychosocial development.

255

According to Erik Erikson's (1963) stage theory of psychosocial development, the toddler is entering a period in which the psychological "conflict" to be resolved is that of autonomy versus shame and doubt. **Autonomy** means self-government or independence. Its development extends from about 15 months to 3 years as depicted in Figure 9.1.

During infancy, from birth to about 18 months, developing a sense of trust (versus mistrust) is a critical psychosocial task. Achieving a healthy sense of trust, derived from consistent and predictable nurturing, is perhaps the most important stage in psychosocial development. Its healthy development paves the way for successful resolution of subsequent stages.

A sense of autonomy is facilitated and enhanced by the development of a strong sense of trust during infancy. Erikson's theory proposes that the psychosocial opposite of autonomy is shame or doubt. Adults support autonomy when they recognize that the toddler needs to feel self-sufficient and capable. Lack of support for autonomy leads to a sense of shame or doubt. A sense of shame or doubt brings with it a range of negative feelings and inappropriate behaviors, including feelings of guilt or penitence, self-consciousness, negative self-regard, reluctance to try new things, increased resistance to adult guidance, and, for some children, overdependence on adults.

The challenge for those who care for the toddler is to find a balance between meeting the toddler's contradictory needs for dependence and independence, freedom and control. On one hand, toddlers need and want to do things for themselves. On the other hand, they want and need the security-building presence, protection, and guidance of a nurturing and supportive adult. Successes in locomotion and manipulative skills, the feeding process, toileting, choice making,

FIGURE 9.1
Erikson's Stages of Psychosocial Development

Development of a healthy sense of trust paves the way for successful resolution of the next stage of psychosocial development: autonomy versus shame and doubt.

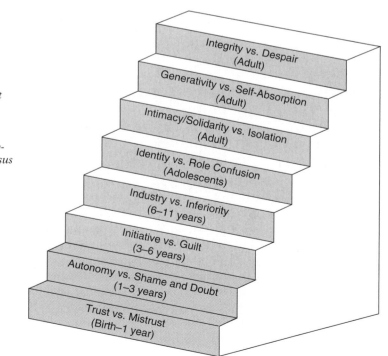

Integrity vs. Despair
(Adult)

Generativity vs. Self-Absorption
(Adult)

Intimacy/Solidarity vs. Isolation
(Adult)

Identity vs. Role Confusion
(Adolescents)

Industry vs. Inferiority
(6–11 years)

Initiative vs. Guilt
(3–6 years)

Autonomy vs. Shame and Doubt
(1–3 years)

Trust vs. Mistrust
(Birth–1 year)

Meeting the toddler's contradictory needs for dependence and independence is often a challenge.

playful interactions, and imitating more mature behaviors and activities, and increasing communicative competence, all contribute to and facilitate a growing sense of autonomy. Adults facilitate a growing sense of autonomy by observing development and assisting toddlers in their struggles, for example, providing a small step stool to reach the faucet to wash hands, handing over socks in their upright position to facilitate self-dressing, placing toys on low, open shelves for easy retrieval and clean-up, and offering choices: "Do you want to wear your jacket or your sweater today?"

As with other areas of development, adult responses to the toddler's efforts to be autonomous enhance or inhibit its emergence. Relationships and interactions that are overrestrictive or overprotective, or on the other hand, relationships that are too permissive or that expect behavior or performance that is beyond the toddler's developmental capacities, interfere with the developing sense of autonomy.

Sharing control with the toddler can be difficult for some adults. Yet determining when and how to provide choices is key to helping toddlers gain a sense of autonomy. Guidance and discipline techniques that fail to offer choices and acceptable alternatives or deteriorate into power struggles contribute to negative feelings and oppositional behaviors. These feelings and behaviors can persist into later ages, undermining the successful resolution of subsequent psychosocial issues. When the sense of autonomy outweighs feelings of shame and doubt, the child more readily develops feelings of adequacy, competence, security, worthiness, and healthy self-acceptance. With these attributes, the child is better equipped to cooperate and to learn socially acceptable behaviors.

Because toilet learning is a developmental milestone during this period, Erikson included it in his discussion of the developing sense of autonomy. With maturing biological and neurological development, the toddler begins to recognize sensations of fullness and to acquire the skills of holding and letting go in bowel and bladder control. For the toddler, this ability imparts a sense of self-government and pride. However, since bowel and bladder control depends on biological development as well as cognitive awareness, success with bowel and bladder control is uneven. Yet the toddler's desire to please caregivers is genuine. Adults who shame the child or exhibit frustration or anger at the child's inabilities or relapses undermine both the processes of toilet learning and the developing sense of autonomy. The slow process of toilet learning is facilitated through encouragement, praise, and following and responding helpfully to the child's cues.

Attachment Behaviors

From about ages 6 months to 3 years, the toddler, having grown through phase 1 of Bowlby's attachment sequence, indiscriminate responsiveness, and phase 2, focusing on familiar people, is now exhibiting the characteristics of phase 3: active **proximity seeking** (Bowlby, 1969/2000). During this phase, the child becomes very aware of and monitors the presence or absence of his or her attachment person, usually his or her mother. The child actively seeks to be near and to be held and cries on separation. When the attachment person is present, the toddler will at first remain quite close, perhaps in the adult's lap, then will tenuously venture forth and away, but will return periodically to the attachment person for assurance. As a sense of trust and self-confidence grows, these ventures will be sustained over longer periods of time. As we learned in Chapter 6, the success of these ventures is thought to relate to the quality of infant–caregiver attachments, particularly the mother's sensitivity and responsiveness to infant/toddler cues (Isabella, 1993).

proximity seeking: the child's attempts to maintain nearness and contact with the attachment person

As autonomy emerges, toddlers begin to resist assistance from others.

As toddlers get older, the ability to visually and auditorally remain attached, even though the attachment person may not be near, emerges. The toddler learns to feel attached from a distance by looking, listening, and vocally communicating. The child becomes more exploratory as feelings of security with the attachment person and with the environment increase. The toddler begins to rely on self-comforting behaviors such as thumb sucking or fondling a soft toy or blanket, and may begin to find comfort through interactions with people other than the one with whom the child has formed an attachment.

Forming secure attachments and trusting relationships with parents and family members is among the first and most important psychosocial tasks of the infant/toddler period. As the toddler gets older, forming attachments to others beyond the family begins to occur. The success of these **extrafamiliar relationships** is thought to be an outgrowth of earliest secure attachments and trusting relationships (Stroufe, 1996). Extrafamilial relationships include people outside the immediate or extended family—neighbors, family friends, or babysitters and other caregivers. Infants and toddlers can and do develop strong feelings for and attachments to others outside the family. Positive interactions and successful experiences with extrafamilial relationships enhance the child's psychosocial development (Pianta, 1999). Children whose initial attachments have been insecure learn to view adults as unresponsive and unreliable. With these disturbing perceptions, the ability to form mutually positive and supportive relationships with others is compromised (Lyons-Ruth & Jacobvitz, 1999).

extrafamilial relationships: relationships with people outside the immediate or extended family

---

Angela's high school–based child care center is, by most standards, state of the art. Situated in its own separate building on the high school campus, it is readily accessible to the young mothers whose children are enrolled. Its program and management are guided by a director with skills and knowledge in early child care and education. The center exceeds local and state licensing requirements and is accredited by the National Association for the Education of Young Children. Child caregivers are educated in child development and early education and are warm, nurturing, and effective teachers. The setting is aesthetically appealing and rich with developmentally appropriate materials and activities. The daily pace is unhurried, comfortable, yet appropriately stimulating.

Two-year-old Angela is active, alert, and eager to explore and has become reasonably secure in the child care center. She has developed a strong attachment to her primary caregiver, Ms. Ruiz, who has equally strong feelings for Angela.

On arrival today, Angela scans the playroom for the sight and sounds of Ms. Ruiz. Her facial expression shows both anticipation and anxiety. Having located Ms. Ruiz, she runs eagerly toward her, reaching up for Ms. Ruiz to acknowledge her presence with a hug. Ms. Ruiz greets Angela with a wide smile and obliges with a hug, then offers to help Angela with her coat. Angela resists, however, wanting to do this herself. Ms. Ruiz reminds Angela to say good-bye to her departing mother, as Cheryl must leave to attend her algebra class. While removing her wraps, Angela stops and watches tentatively as Cheryl leaves. Rushing to the door, she calls to her mother, who returns, kisses her good-bye, tells her to have a good time, and then goes on to class. Perhaps Angela still feels some separation anxiety, for her facial expression shows signs of impending tears.

However, Ms. Ruiz, sensitive and reassuring, directs Angela's attention to the large classroom aquarium, points to the fish, and begins to name the items in the aquarium: *gravel, light, water*. She talks with Angela about the fish: "Yes, that is a fish, Angela. This one is an angelfish. Let's put some food in the aquarium for the fish." This interaction has become somewhat routine each morning and, though quite brief, helps Angela to make the transition from home to center and from mother to caregiver.

Once at ease, Angela asserts, "No more fish," and proceeds to another part of the room to play. Very soon, she will approach her friend Leah, and a different interaction will ensue as the girls proceed to the sand table.

The child care center that Jeremy attends is also judged to be of high quality. Jeremy's parents visited a number of child care centers and preschool programs, asked many questions, and discussed their options before making their final selection.

Jeremy enjoys attending the child care center. However, in recent weeks, separation has become a particular problem for him and for his parents and caregivers. The parents' inquiry to the center director reveals an unusual amount of staff turnover in recent months, and as a consequence, Jeremy has encountered three different primary child caregivers in less than 6 months.

Unable to comprehend where the caregivers go and why they are not present, Jeremy demonstrates his confusion and anxiety by clinging to his mother and crying. On this day, he has created quite a scene with an angry and fearful tantrum. He vigorously resists Ms. Bell's attempts to comfort him.

Soon, his special friend Josh arrives and, noticing Jeremy crying, makes his way to where Jeremy and Ann are standing. Josh stares with some concern, as though he sympathizes but isn't sure what to do. Ann coaxes Jeremy: "Hi, Josh. Jeremy, here is Josh. Josh wants to play with you." Jeremy soon stops crying and, reluctantly and slowly, reaches toward his mother in a quest for a hug. Thus, he signals that he will kiss her good-bye. Mother and child hug and kiss, and Ann begins to lead Jeremy and Josh toward the block center. Once the two are involved, Jeremy's mother says a reassuring good-bye and departs without further incident.

These examples show that attachments can be formed with individuals, both adults and children, beyond the home and family. These attachments can be quite strong and can provide another source of security for the toddler. It is clear that both Angela and Jeremy have found a sense of security and well-being in their child care center relationships. For Angela, the adult caregiver has become a reliable and trusted source of security in the absence of her mother. For Jeremy, his young friend and playmate Josh has become a trusted friend, a stable presence in the absence of a continuous relationship with a dependable child caregiver.

Wisely selected child care arrangements offer an expanded circle of friends and healthy, supportive relationships for young children. However, as in Jeremy's situation, we can see that staff changes create stress for some children, returning them to earlier and less mature forms of coping and reduced social competence with peers (Howes, 1997; Howes & Hamilton, 1993). Howes cautioned that continuity of caregiving is related to the development of secure attachments in out-of-home settings. This continuity helps the child to make a smooth transition between the home and the child care setting. Howes also asserted that the child who experiences many different caregivers may fail to become attached to any of them.

Social Learning and Social Cognition

The ability to understand the perspectives and needs of others is faulty in toddlers. Egocentrism characterizes both the cognitive abilities of toddlers (Piaget, 1952) and their psychosocial development (Erikson, 1963). Piaget theorized that during the preoperational period of cognitive development, children can view the world only from their own perspectives and are unable to appreciate another person's point of view.

The toddler's behavior is punctuated with assumptions that others feel, see, and hear the same things he or she does. Inability to share is related to this thinking and is expected behavior at this stage. A coveted toy possessed by another child may be proclaimed "Mine!" The toddler who says to his mother, when observing her nursing a younger sibling, "Does her have a mommy?," is demonstrating a lack of perspective beyond his own experiences. The 3-year-old who attempts to console a crying nursery school friend with her own fuzzy blanket assumes that her friend can be comforted as she is by this particular object. And the child talking on the phone to Grandmother who asks, "Do you like this new dress I have on?," does not yet understand that Grandmother cannot see through the telephone.

Although it is true that egocentrism characterizes the toddler's way of thinking, a growing body of evidence suggests that young children may be less egocentric than was once believed (Black, 1981). Studies of **prosocial behaviors** and empathy in young children have begun to modify our thinking about egocentrism.

prosocial behavior: behavior that benefits others, such as helping, sharing, comforting, and defending

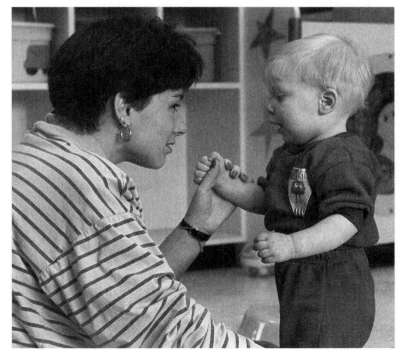

Empathic adults help toddlers to learn and accept behavior limits.

Prosocial Learning and Behaviors

Children younger than age 3 have been observed demonstrating prosocial behaviors through sharing, helping, and cooperating (Leung & Rheingold, 1981; Zahn-Waxler & Radke-Yarrow, 1990). These scholars have studied comforting, defending, and protective behaviors in preschool children (Zahn-Waxler & Radke-Yarrow, 1990). Their studies have led psychologists to believe that very young children are more capable of perceiving the perspectives of others than Piaget's theory suggests.

Kindness, sympathy, generosity, helpfulness, and distress at injustice or cruelty are fairly typical behaviors in young children. Psychologists refer to them as prosocial behaviors, since they are intended to benefit or help others without expectation of reward. Prosocial behaviors in toddlers are most likely to occur during pretend play (Rubin, Lynch, Coplan, Rose-Kresnor, & Booth, 1994) and occur with greater frequency as the child's opportunities for interactions with others increase (Rubin & Everett, 1982; Rubin, Bukowski, & Parker, 1998). Growing cognitive abilities contribute to the child's ability to view situations from the perspectives of others. More mature levels of thinking enhance perspective-taking abilities and **empathy**.

empathy:
experiencing the feelings or emotions that someone else is experiencing

Prosocial behaviors are influenced by behaviors modeled by others. Parents and caregivers who demonstrate helpfulness, altruism, cooperation, sympathy, and other prosocial attributes provide powerful examples for the toddler. Guidance and discipline strategies with young children also affect the development of prosocial behaviors. Guidance that is empathic, supportive, reasonable, and explained to the child assists toddlers in their understanding of social expectations.

Jeremy's teacher asked him to sit by her and talk about the unfortunate encounter he had just had with a playmate over the use of a puzzle. Both children wanted to work the puzzle but not together. The teacher asked Jeremy how he thought his friend felt when he hit her. She also asked him to think about what he might do about the situation now that his friend was crying and hurt. His response was not exactly what the teacher sought but was revealing nonetheless: "I think you better watch me, 'cause I think I'm going to hit her again."

Like Jeremy, toddlers need adults to help them control their impulses. An adult who says, "I can't let you hit Shannon; hitting hurts people," helps the still egocentric toddler to think about the other person. This guidance should be supportive of each child in the encounter. Blaming and punishing only serve to reinforce negative behaviors, and neither provides the child with alternative prosocial options or assists in the development of perspective taking and empathy.

To facilitate the development of prosocial behaviors, toddlers' spontaneous attempts to share, help, or cooperate should be reinforced through positive recognition and responses: "Bobby *feels better* now that you are friends again." "That was *kind* of you to get Tamara a puzzle like yours." "That was very *helpful* of you to put the blocks away with Josh." Such verbal responses, while providing positive feedback and reinforcement, also provide labels for expected prosocial behaviors. With these labels, the child's understanding and appreciation of the views and needs of others increase.

Moral Development

Moral behavior is most often described as the ability to consider the needs and well-being of others. People who are thought to be moral exhibit such behaviors as honesty, dependability, helpfulness, and fairness. These individuals do not steal from others or physically hurt or emotionally abuse others. They do not betray trusts and are loyal to their family, friends, and commitments. In short, these people have a personal morality that guides their behaviors. These behaviors represent moral values, reasoning, judgments, and actions.

Cognitive and social development and experiences are necessary for the development of moral reasoning and judgment. The conscience also plays a role in moral development. Moral values, reasoning, judgment, and conscience rely on certain levels of maturity and experience for their realization.

Piaget (1965) and Kohlberg (1968) proposed developmental sequences for moral reasoning and judgment. These theorists based their conclusions on studies of children beyond the infant/toddler period, but their theories can offer insight into this period. These theories are described more fully in Chapters 12 and 15.

Moral development has origins in (1) intellectual development; (2) social cognition, or the manner in which children perceive the behaviors of others and their own interactions with others; (3) adult socialization efforts, whereby adult values, standards, and expectations are modeled and taught to the child; and (4) the positive by-products of a child's prosocial behaviors (positive feedback and feelings of pride in having done the good or right thing). Piaget (1965) emphasized both cognitive development and social experiences as precursors to moral thinking, reasoning, and judgments. Piaget associated moral development in children with emerging abilities to interpret rules.

For very young children, notions of right or wrong are just being formulated, and most rules are first being introduced. Since moral values are learned through a personal history of experiences and social learning opportunities, infants and toddlers are said to be **premoral**. The premoral child is guided by external rules and expectations of obedience rather than by an internal system of values, beliefs, or understandings. The premoral child comes to think of "good" or "bad" in terms of doing what one is told to do. Moral behaviors (obedience) are motivated by the expectation of rewards (praise and attention) or the avoidance of punishment (having a toy or privilege taken away).

premoral: the period in early childhood when the child is unaware of moral rules or values

Hoffman (1988) advanced a theory that provides further insights into the beginnings of moral behavior. Hoffman's theory suggests that motivation to behave in moral ways is prompted by empathic feelings, particularly "empathic distress." Hoffman defined *empathy* as "a vicarious affective response that is more appropriate to someone else's situation than to one's own" (p. 509). Empathy includes both affective and cognitive aspects, the level of empathy depending to some extent on the child's level of cognition. Toddlers, as in the above example of Josh and Jeremy, may respond empathically to another's distress, but lack sufficient knowledge and experience to fully grasp the source or cause of the distress or to accurately determine what might alleviate the distress.

Hoffman (1988) described four developmental levels of empathic distress: global empathy, egocentric empathy, empathy for another's feelings, and empathy for another's life condition. The first three levels have implications for the study of infant and toddler behaviors.

Global empathic distress is observed in infants during the first year. Because of the infant's inadequate self–other distinction, the child will respond to distress cues from others, such as another child's crying, as though the discomfort were his or her own. Self-comforting strategies such as seeking mother or thumb sucking are employed; such behaviors would have been employed anyway had the distress truly been the child's own.

Egocentric empathy occurs in the 2nd year, during which a sense of the other emerges as distinct from the self. At this level, the toddler is aware that the other person is in distress but is not capable of understanding the person's internal states. The toddler inaccurately assumes that the distressed person's feelings and needs are his or her own. Hoffman cited the case of an 18-month-old boy who fetched his mother to comfort a crying friend, though the friend's mother was present.

Around age 2 or 3, the child becomes aware that others' feelings differ from his or her own and thus exhibits the third level of Hoffman's scheme: empathy for another's feelings. The fourth level, empathy for another's life condition, does not occur until later in childhood. At this level, the child can appreciate the larger life contexts in which distress occurs.

This sequence seems particularly helpful in understanding psychosocial origins of moral development. The adult's role in the socialization process should be to recognize the egocentric perspective of the toddler as she or he attempts to grasp concepts of right and wrong and to learn about the needs of others. During infancy and into the toddler period, the premoral child is incapable of evaluating the morality of her or his own actions or those of others. However, once toddlers become aware that there are expected standards for behaving, they appear to be intrinsically motivated to meet them (Kagan, 1998). When adult expectations are in conflict with the toddler's goals, the toddler tests the limits to learn which behaviors elicit which adult responses (a behavior that adults often mistakenly

The social interactions of toddlers are awkward and tend to be more physical than verbal.

perceive as mischievous rather than information seeking). By age two, children are fairly aware of their parent's do's and don'ts and generally behave according to them in the parent's presence. The presence of a parent provides a social referent. However, the ability to maintain this referent and act according to it in a parent's absence does not emerge until around age three (Crockenberg & Litman, 1990; Emde & Buchsbaum, 1990), at which point toddlers have begun to internalize the rules they have experienced.

The socialization process must be instructive and timely. Alert adults teach appropriate behaviors when opportunities arise, as when the toddler grabs a toy from another child, bites to defend herself or himself, and engages in other unacceptable behaviors. Guidance that punishes rather than provides intelligent, logical instruction fails to recognize that moral behaviors take root in cognition (understanding) and prosocial learning (perspective taking, empathy, altruism, and so on). Embarrassing, demeaning, or power-assertive discipline does little to help the toddler learn and internalize appropriate behaviors. Indeed, many negative and socially unacceptable behaviors accompanied by low self-esteem accrue from inappropriate discipline techniques. Further, moral development is a continuous process throughout life. Social learning experiences in many contexts and involving many others (siblings, babysitters, teachers, family members) accumulate over time to build an internalized sense of morality, or a moral way of behaving governed from within rather than by external rules and constraints.

Psychosocial Development of the Toddler: A Neurological Development Perspective

As pointed out in earlier chapters, the early years are critical, particularly for the neurological development that is associated with attachment, control of emotions, and an ability to cope with stress. As described in Chapter 5, the human brain becomes organized and functional from the lower, more primitive parts (brainstem and midbrain) to its higher regions (limbic and cortical regions) (review Figure 5.5). As the brain grows and develops in this hierarchical fashion, the limbic, subcortical, and cortical areas begin to influence or control the more primitive behaviors emanating from the lower regions of the brain. The manner in which toddlers, school-age children, and adults react to frustration should be quite different because the structures of their brains are quite different. In the toddler, frustration may be characterized by a reactive tantrum (deriving from lower brain regions); the school-age child may self-restrain the lower brain–driven impulse to act out in some manner, instead using words to express needs and emotions (cortical functions) or perhaps seeking the assistance of another child or adult. The older child and adult are both capable of cognitively assessing the frustrating situation (again, a cortical function). The difference in their behaviors is attributed to the growth of cortical structures that modify or control the more primitive or reactive lower regions of the brain. As the upper regions of the brain become organized, inhibitory capabilities emerge to modulate or modify such lower brain activity as arousal, impulsivity, motor hyperactivity, and aggression. When a young child's experiences fail to support this development, as when children are physically or emotionally abused, the brain fails to develop its impulse-mediating capabilities. The child's behavior reflects this failure to develop impulse control (Perry, Pollard, Blakley, Baker, & Vigilante, 1995).

The brain's impulse-mediating capacity is hampered by environments and experiences that increase the reactivity of the brainstem (as with persistent maltreatment and stress, in which the brain must persist in a state of heightened arousal and fight-or-flight preparedness) or decrease the capacity of the limbic or cortical structures to moderate aggression and impulsivity as with failure to provide warm, nurturing relationships that assure and protect (Perry et al., 1995). Disruption of the normal sequential development process during infancy and early childhood changes the structures and functions of various regions of the brain, altering the characteristic behaviors of the individual. Aggression and violence have their origins in these disruptions (Chugani, 1997; Perry, 1993a, 1993b; Perry et al., 1995).

The structure and function of the developing brain are determined by experiences, particularly early interpersonal relationships. As Siegel (1999) stated, "human connections shape the neural connections from which the mind emerges" (p. 2). As toddlers repeatedly interact with the individuals to whom they are attached, their brains are forming important neurological structures that will function in positive or negative ways according to the types and persistence of the experiences they have with others, particularly attachment people and early caregivers.

DIMENSIONS OF PSYCHOSOCIAL DEVELOPMENT DURING AGES ONE THROUGH THREE

Temperament

As with other aspects of growth and development, the individual toddler's temperament also influences the outcomes of psychosocial development. As we saw in Chapter 6, each child has a unique way of feeling, thinking, and interacting with others. *Temperament* is the term that is generally used to reflect this uniqueness. Although temperament is probably genetically determined, it nevertheless influences and is influenced by the environment (Carey & Jablow, 1997; Chess & Thomas, 1996). Think of your brothers, sisters, cousins, or other relatives. What are the similarities and differences in their temperaments? Differences in temperament among individual children within the same family are often noted with surprise and wonder. Yet mothers and fathers exhibit unique temperaments, which influence the manner in which they respond to and interact with individual children (Maccoby, 2000).

Not only parents, but all other family members expose children to a variety of interactions that reflect individual temperaments. In addition to temperament, each family member brings different age- and stage-related needs and behaviors that influence the manner in which members respond to one another and to the unique temperaments of the infant and toddler (Collins, Maccoby, Steinberg, Hetherington, & Bornstein, 2000; Maccoby, 2000). Earlier chapters describe the backgrounds of experience that the parents of Angela and Jeremy bring to the parent–child relationship. The quality of their childhood experiences, the relationships with their parents and other family members, and the role models that were available to them influence the perceptions they have of themselves and of their roles as parents. Knowledge of child growth and development plays a critical role in this regard. The interplay of all of these factors influences the interactions of parents and children.

Cheryl—young, single, and still an adolescent—is experiencing her own developmental needs, which are typical of most adolescent girls. In addition to her need to obtain and maintain support networks to assist her in nurturing Angela, she has needs relating to learning about and gaining satisfaction in the role of mother and single teen parent, completing her education, participating in the social life of her agemates, and working through Erikson's 5th psychosocial stage, that of developing a sense of identity versus role confusion (Erikson, 1963). Participating in an extended family and projecting a future beyond high school are also tasks before her.

Members of Jeremy's family also have their needs. His parents, now in their 30s, are striving for success in demanding careers. They seek social and economic upward mobility, which is a demanding quest in terms of time, energy, and allocation of family resources. Their needs at this age stage relate to maintaining an intellectually, emotionally, and physically satisfying relationship with one another; meshing career, civic, religious, and social desires and responsibilities; relating to extended family members; providing for an economically stable existence; and integrating all of this with their plans for Jeremy and perhaps additional children.

James, low-key and affectionate, enjoys holding Angela on his lap and talking and reading books to her. His manner has an enjoyably calming effect on Angela, and she responds by seeking to be held by him the moment he arrives for his visits. Knowing that he enjoys reading to her, Angela scurries off to obtain a book—any book—to offer to him. Sometimes James greets her with, "Go get a book," whereupon she promptly and happily obliges.

Angela is outgoing, affectionate, observant, and quite verbal; she names many objects and people in her environment. Though unable to focus her attention for more than a few minutes, she seems to need and enjoy the sustained interactions with James and with the books they share. In anticipating her interest, James encourages Angela's autonomy by sending her to fetch a book. Angela has learned how to seek and hold James's attention. Thus, her developing sense of autonomy, along with her temperament, is becoming enmeshed with the temperament and personality of her father.

Cheryl is more inclined to engage in physically active interactions with Angela. She may chase Angela about the house, play hide and seek, take her on outings, walk around the neighborhood with her, and dance and sing with her. They especially enjoy playing copycat games with each other. Angela has learned when and how to engage her mother in these playful moments, which are quite emotionally satisfying to both of them. James and Cheryl relate to Angela in different ways, each bringing to the interactions their unique personalities and skills. Yet, while quite different in their interactions with Angela, they are complementary.

Social Interactions and Play Behaviors

Studies of toddler friendships and play behaviors characterized the toddler as engaging in onlooker and/or **parallel play** (Parten, 1933). In parallel play, the toddler enjoys being near and playing beside other children but pursuing her or his own

parallel play: activities in which two or more children play near one another while engaged in independent activities

play interest. In parallel play, little if any interaction occurs between children. It was previously thought that onlooker and parallel play characterized the least mature levels of social interaction. More recent studies of toddler interactions suggest that while parallel play is quite evident during the toddler period, it is not limited to that period and changes in form with increasing cognition and more effective social skills.

Young children today spend more time in out-of-home child care situations than did children of past generations. Therefore, many modern-day infants and toddlers have encountered other children from a very early age. Studies have demonstrated that genuine friendships can develop between children in toddler play groups (Greenspan & Greenspan, 1985; Rubin, Bukowski, & Parker, 1998). Although first attempts at interaction are clumsy and even antagonistic on occasion, they nevertheless can be a source of pleasure and represent the earliest attempts to initiate friendships.

A typical sequence of attempts at interaction, as described by Greenspan and Greenspan (1985), begins with the toddler first noticing something about another toddler that attracts him or her—the color of clothing, long, curly hair, or a pretty ribbon, for example. This is followed by mutual explorations between the two children in which the child touches or pulls at the attraction—the ribbon, pretty hair, or whatever caught the child's attention. Usually, the other child passively allows the explorations to take place—the ribbon to be pulled, for instance. Following this level of interaction, the toddlers may seek a nearby adult, who then becomes an assistant to the interaction. The toddler hands an object to the adult, and the adult in turn hands it to the other toddler, who hands it back to the adult to begin the sequence again. Greenspan and Greenspan called these exchanges *collaborative interactions,* as the toddlers use the adult as a conduit for the sharing of objects, toys, or food. They further described toddlers as exhibiting humor in these encounters, laughing together as a block tower collapses or another playful event ensues. Then the toddlers go off to play together, during which time they continue to interact through facial expressions and gestures.

Toddler friends imitate one another, laugh with and at one another, follow one another around, and share activities such as looking at books together or filling and dumping objects from a container (Press & Greenspan, 1985). These friendships may be transitory and short lived, yet their importance to early social development is an obvious first step in learning to make and maintain friendships. As we saw in an earlier discussion, very young children can become attached to one another, and play is more focused and successful with friends with whom they play on a frequent basis (Howes, 1996). One study of separation of nursery school infants and toddlers when they were being promoted to new classrooms found that when the children were moved to new classrooms with a close friend, they adapted more readily (Field, Vega-Lahr, & Jagadish, 1984). Today, many programs have staffing patterns that move the caregiver/teacher to the next age/grade level with a class of children, maintaining continuity and security of relationships as children move to more advanced program needs.

The types and availability of toys also influence the quality of play and the success of toddler interactions. Developmentally appropriate toys ensure reasonably successful toddler play. A truck with a missing wheel cannot be successfully rolled back and forth. A room with one pull-toy instead of two creates frustration and tears, whereas pulling toys about the room together can be a joyous social encounter.

Toddler Emotions

In addition to enjoying and finding comfort in attachments and friendships, toddlers are increasingly engaged in a range of emotional transactions. They continue to express stranger and separation anxiety along with a full range of emotions, yet they are learning a lot about **display rules** (type, time, place, and acceptability) of emotions, and they are experiencing and learning about their emotional states and that others also express emotion and can be mad, sad, happy, silly, and angry. With help from sensitive adults, they are learning to label and give words to emotions.

display rules: social rules determining how and when certain emotions should or should not be expressed

Fears and Anxieties During the Toddler Period

As we discussed, separation and stranger anxiety is a normal and expected outcome of increasing cognitive ability and parallels the development of attachments, influencing and being influenced by the quality of the attachment relationships. These anxieties begin to wane around age 2½ to 3 years. However, around 18 months, additional fears begin to emerge. This is indicative of social/emotional and cognitive development. Because all development is interrelated, a discussion of fears must recognize the interrelated role of cognition. As the child can manipulate mental images and mentally elaborate on past events and experiences, new understandings and concepts—and misunderstandings and misconceptions—can bring about new fears. As the toddler begins to imagine, fantasy and reality are not separated.

Fears are normal. Fears are quite real to the child, can be very disturbing, and can be difficult to allay. In addition to separation and stranger fears, common toddler fears include fear of the dark, the bathtub drain, animals, some storybook or media characters, monsters and ghosts, lightning and thunder, and vacuum cleaners or other noisy equipment.

Toddlers may acquire some of their fears through social referencing and other social interactions. Parents who become fearful during a thunderstorm or who discuss frightening or painful experiences relating to accidents or illnesses, visits to the physician or hospital, or other adult fears may inadvertently instill these fears in their young children. When fear tactics are used to discipline, they create unhealthy and inappropriate fears in the child. For instance, imploring the toddler to "be quiet or Aunt Marti will get you" creates an unfortunate wariness of Aunt Marti and hampers her efforts to establish a positive relationship with the toddler.

Helping the toddler to understand and cope with fears requires sensitivity and patience. Because fears can be quite real to the child, adults should neither laugh at, ridicule, nor minimize them. Very young children will not understand logical explanations; instead, toddlers need adults to help them find ways to deal with their fears. A child who is afraid of the bathtub drain, for instance, can be given "control" over it by being the one who opens or closes the drain or by getting out of the tub before the drain is opened.

Fears are necessary for survival, since they signal dangers to be avoided. However, the toddler may not yet have the necessary survival fears for most potentially dangerous situations. The toddler has neither the judgment nor the background of experiences and understanding to avoid such hazards as the street, friendly strangers, fire, poisons, heights, guns, and a host of other potential dangers in their environments. Toddlers lack the space, speed, depth, and other types of perception that are needed to perceive risks accurately. Toddlers need to be protected through close supervision and must be taught in ways that instill knowledge, caution, and skills but do not unduly frighten them. Adults cannot assume that toddlers are aware of dangerous situations. In the event of the child's self-endangerment, adults should not react with physical punishment, but must recognize the child's lack of experience and knowledge. It is the adult's responsibility to monitor and maintain the child's safety and to teach the child about unsafe objects and situations. Adults set limits and rules that both protect and instruct, and recognize that with toddlers, frequent and repetitive reminders are required.

Self-Comforting Behaviors

Infants and toddlers employ idiosyncratic self-comforting behaviors when they are feeling lonely, frightened, sad, tired, bored, or overly excited. These behaviors include thumb sucking and attachment to a particular toy, piece of clothing, or blanket. Self-comforting behaviors help children to cope with their own emotional states and to self-regulate their emotions.

Thumb Sucking.   Most infants find their fists and thumbs sooner or later and derive pleasure and solace from sucking on them. Brazelton (1992) suggested that parents should expect their infants to suck their thumbs, fingers, or fists and attributes few consequences to this behavior. Thumb sucking can be the child's source of self-comfort when she or he is tense or frightened or simply trying to relax or fall asleep. Brazelton advises adults to expect a great deal of thumb or finger sucking in the 1st year, somewhat less in the active 2nd year, and even less after the 3rd and 4th years.

While infants are sometimes given pacifiers to satisfy the sucking need, pacifiers are most often provided to calm a fussy child. For some infants and toddlers, the pacifier becomes their self-comforting device; other infants reject it or find little pleasure in it. Whether thumb or pacifier has provided the source of self-comfort, either is usually given up at about the same age. Children may fall back on one or the other during periods of illness, stress, or fear.

Transitional Objects.   Another self-comforting strategy the toddler uses is the **transitional object**, so named because it assists the child in making the transition from the dependency and protection of infancy to the independence and uncertainty of the toddler period. Attachment to an object such as a teddy bear, special blanket, swatch of soft fabric, doll, or favorite piece of clothing is common and begins in the latter part of the 1st year, usually around 8 or 9 months. Because these objects have been invested with certain meanings and comforting associations, the child forms an emotional tie to them (Winnicott, 1953, 1971, 1977). The child's attachment to the object can last to age seven or eight and sometimes beyond.

Adults and children give "soft names" to these objects, such as "cuddlies," "banky," and "bear-bear." These attachments are usually quite strong and extremely important to the child. Children often perceive these objects as extensions of themselves.

Transitional objects serve a variety of comforting roles. Some observers believe that they provide a security link with the home, mother, or other attachment

transitional object: an object, usually a soft, cuddly item, to which a child becomes attached

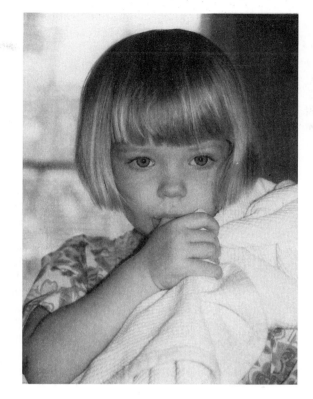

Infants and toddlers employ idiosyncratic self-comforting behaviors when they feel tired, bored, sad, frightened, or lonely.

person during times of separation. In this sense, they serve to ease separation anxiety and other fears. The transitional object provides a sense of security in new, strange, frightening, or stressful situations. Children often treat their transitional objects with love and caring, exhibiting their own abilities to express affection. Sometimes, these objects are the child's substitution for the thumb or pacifier and replace these earlier forms of self-comfort. Other children use the transitional object and the thumb or pacifier in combination as a self-comforting strategy. Interference with these attachments is strongly discouraged; rather, adults are encouraged to expect, accept, acknowledge, and appreciate the child's attachment.

Self-Concept and Self-Esteem

The self-concept is the summary definition that one devises of oneself; it represents an awareness of oneself as a separate and unique individual. The self-concept derives from interactions with others, the child's interpretation of those interactions, and the child's ability to accept or negate positive or negative feedback from interactions with others. For the most part, the manner in which others respond to and relate to the child determines the self-concept the child will devise.

The self-concept is dynamic in that it changes over time with additional experiences and increasing physical/motor, social, and cognitive abilities. Generally, the development of the self-concept is composed of four accomplishments: (1) self-awareness, (2) self-recognition, (3) self-definition, and (4) self-esteem.

Self-awareness occurs as infants begin to realize that they are distinct and separate from others and that an object is not an extension of themselves.

self-awareness: an individual's perceptions of himself or herself as distinct and separate from other people and objects

self-recognition:
the child's ability to recognize his or her image in a mirror, photograph, or other representation

self-definition:
the use of criteria to define the self, such as age, size, and physical and mental abilities

self-esteem:
the overall sense of worth as a person that the child derives from the qualities that are associated with the self-concept

Self-recognition refers to infants' ability to recognize themselves in a mirror, photograph, or other form of representation (Lewis & Brooks, 1978). This ability seems to parallel the cognitive achievement of object permanence, when the child can form and hold mental images. It is usually evident by age 18 months, and most children can distinguish their own photograph from someone else's by age 2 (Lewis & Brooks-Gunn, 1979).

Self-definition emerges as children begin to use language to describe themselves. The toddler's growing awareness of his or her age, size, gender, and skills assists the child in this definition. This development is observed when young children take pride in telling you how old they are. Holding up two, three, or four fingers and exclaiming, "I am 3" is an attempt to define oneself. Also, when children invite attention by saying, "Watch me!," they are demonstrating the skills by which they define themselves. "I can reach it," "Watch me jump," and "I am big," are verbal indications of an emerging self-concept. The responses of adults and playmates to these self-identifiers convey acceptance or rejection, respect or disrespect.

Around age 3, children begin to mentally construct an "autobiographical" memory that facilitates a continuous identity carried throughout life (Nelson, 1993). This autobiographical memory is quite dependent on the types of interactions and relationships infants and toddlers have had with their early caregivers, and determines the extent to which the child develops positive self-esteem. **Self-esteem** emerges from the feedback young children receive from others and their perceptions of that feedback. Children who perceive themselves as loved, valued, worthy, and competent develop healthy self-esteem. An interesting aspect of self-definition arises when children begin to self-correct. Rejecting a drawing, coloring over it to "cover it up," throwing an art effort into the trash because "it doesn't look right," starting over on simple tasks, and other similar behaviors indicate that the child is beginning to self-monitor and represent the child's desire to succeed (Cicchetti & Beeghly, 1990). In these events, the emotions of pride, shame, embarrassment, or guilt find expression. Healthy self-esteem ensures that these evaluations weigh more heavily on the positive than on the negative side.

Gender Awareness

Most children are able to proclaim that they are a boy or a girl by age 2½ to 3, having constructed what psychologists call *gender schemata* (Liben & Signorella, 1980). Gender identity has both biological and sociological origins. Biology determines whether the child will be male or female, and the images, hopes, and child-rearing practices of mothers, fathers, and other relatives set the stage for gender identity and gender role expectations. Studies have found that the more sex-stereotyped adult roles are in a society, the more gender specific the child-rearing practices are (Coll & Meyer, 1993).

During the 2nd year, observations of play behaviors begin to reveal differences between boys and girls, much of which is stereotypical and perhaps derived from gender-specific experiences provided by the parents. Parents may tend to be more gentle and cuddling with girls and more rough and tumble with boys; parents may talk more softly and tenderly to girls and more directly to boys. Toy preferences are particularly indicative by 18 to 20 months, as boys tend to play with transportation toys, blocks, and manipulatives and girls tend to choose soft toys and dolls and enjoy dressing up and dancing (Fagot, 1988; Goldstein, 1994). Perhaps these play choices reflect the types of toys parents have provided for their boys or girls, as well as the child's increasing gender schemata.

It is not unusual for toddlers to assume that their biological sex can change, that is, that boys can grow up to become mothers and girls can grow up to be fathers. This thinking demonstrates a lack of **gender constancy**. Gender constancy is the realization that one's sex does not change over time or as a result of changes in hairstyle, clothing, or other outward characteristics. Gender constancy is not expected to occur until ages 5 to 7 (Kohlberg, 1966).

Toddlers tend to imitate the parent of the same sex, and when gender role behaviors are deemed to be appropriate, parents provide positive feedback. On the other hand, when the behavior is deemed to be gender inappropriate, parents tend to intervene. It is not unusual for a parent to express concern about their son's interest in dolls in the nursery school sociodramatic play center. Interestingly, few if any, inquire about their daughters' play with trucks in the block center. From a developmental perspective, either play choice is sound and in no way threatens the child's gender identity.

The fact that boys are often allowed to be more active and aggressive than girls has both environmental and possibly biological antecedents. Are boys just naturally more active and aggressive than girls? Or do standards for and expectations of certain behaviors vary for boys and girls, resulting in different treatment? Again, studies suggest that gender may influence the manner in which adults respond to aggressive behaviors in boys or girls (Golombok & Fivush, 1994). Yet there seems to be some indication that assertiveness and aggressiveness in boys and girls at ages 2 to 2½ may be related to constitutional and temperamental differences in boys and girls at that age (Forman, Hetznecker, & Dunn, 1983).

Psychologists and educators are encouraging less gender stereotyping in the child's early experiences with children's books, toys, entertainment media, and adult expectations. Boys can certainly be allowed to show feelings, to nurture and be nurtured, and to participate in a range of activities from gentle to rough. Girls can be encouraged to pursue physical activities and to assert themselves in constructive and positive ways. Neither of these efforts need be viewed as endangering gender role behaviors at later ages. Congruence, though never absolute between gender identity and gender role expectations, occurs as children experience a broad range of both "feminine" and "masculine" situations and as role models provide healthy and satisfying gender acceptance.

gender constancy: the realization that one's gender remains the same, regardless of age or changes in clothing, hairstyles, or other outward characteristics

Psychosexual Development

Psychosexual development is evident in the toddler's awareness of anatomical differences between girls and boys, and their curiosity about body parts and their functions. While they have learned to name many body parts, they may have been taught substitute terms for genitals and their posterior. Such terms convey positive or negative connotations and do or do not facilitate the development of a healthy body image. Additionally, toddlers explore their bodies and may find pleasurable sensations when touching their genitals. Occasional masturbation is not unusual. These behaviors are normal and often occur when the child is tired, stressed, or perhaps trying to self-calm, as when required to sit quietly for an activity such as listening to a story. In these instances, adults use redirection and explanation regarding appropriate time and place (Honig, 2000). Shock and shame confuse children and interfere with learning and developing healthy attitudes toward their bodies and bodily functions.

It is important to understand that early childhood sexuality differs from adult sexuality (Chrisman & Couchenour, 2002). Whereas adults attribute eroticism and value systems associated with modesty, marriage, and procreation to human sexuality, young children are just learning about body parts and functions, learning about the social contexts in which certain topics or behaviors are appropriate or inappropriate, observing the expressions of affection displayed by those around them, and gaining knowledge and experiences associated with gender roles. Adults contribute to this learning in either positive or negative ways, depending on their ability to respond in an unembarrassed manner with age-appropriate, accurate, helpful, nonjudgmental information.

Awareness of Diversity and Individual Differences

A number of processes are examined in the study of how children become aware of and respond to racial differences. Ramsey (1998) identified these processes as perceptual awareness, valuative concepts, racial identification, racial preferences, behaviors toward other races, and knowledge of racial differences.

This range of processes illustrates that the development of racial awareness, understanding, and acceptance is complex. Researchers have attempted to address racial awareness from these various perspectives, though research on infant and toddler racial awareness is limited. There is evidence that racial awareness has its origins before age 3 (Helms, 1990; Katz, 1982; Small, 2001). Further evidence exists that earliest experiences with and learnings about race result in attitudes that persist into later years (Katz, 1982).

During the toddler period, racial awareness is dominated by perceptions of outward features. Young children attend with interest to facial features; skin color; hair color, texture, and style; clothing; and voice and speech patterns. However, racial group–referenced identities do not develop until between ages three and eight (Ramsey, 1998). Mature forms of racial awareness, which do not rely on superficial features but depend on deeper understandings of ethnicity, do not emerge until age nine or ten (Aboud, 1988).

The toddler's primary source of information about race is the family. Within the family, racial attitudes are transmitted and racial pride is fostered. Children learn about similarities and differences among people through their experiences with others beyond the immediate family as well as through their toys, books, and the media. In recent years, there have been improvements in the accuracy with which diverse races and cultural groups are portrayed in children's books, toys, school curricula, and the media, yet there is still a need to monitor these sources of information to ensure accurate, positive, and nonbiased portrayals. The toddler's racial identity and valuative and preferential behaviors depend on accurate information and sensitive guidance.

Development of Self-Control

An important psychosocial goal in early childhood is the development of self-control. This is a long-term goal, for self-control develops over a period of many years. For the most part, self-control is learned behavior. It is dependent on external

> **BOX 9.1   Helping Young Children to Develop Self-Control**
>
> 1. Provide an environment in which the child's growing sense of autonomy can flourish; this includes the following:
>
>   - Play items and experiences that are engaging and enriching
>   - Low, open shelves for personal and play items
>   - Adequate space for use, storage, and retrieval of personal and play items
>   - Safe and sturdy furnishings and toys
>   - Placement of dangerous and off-limit items out of sight and reach (or under lock and key as appropriate)
>
> 2. Provide an atmosphere that encourages the toddler to make choices, explore, and discover but that is in keeping with the child's developmental capacities and is free of inappropriate expectations and pressures to perform.
>
> 3. Provide a daily schedule that is predictable so that the toddler can sense the day's rhythms and anticipate and respond appropriately to regular events: mealtime, bathtime, naptime, storytime, and so on.
>
> 4. Set logical, reasonable, and fair limits for behavior, then consistently and predictably expect compliance. Use words and explanation rather than punishment to help toddlers understand the limits that are imposed on them.
>
> 5. Meet the toddler's needs for food, clothing, rest, and attention expeditiously. Adults who impose undue delays on toddlers fail to recognize their inability to delay gratification and tolerate frustration.

controls at first; then the individual gradually assumes more and more responsibility for his or her own behaviors. In very young children, this process is not a smooth one; self-control emerges haltingly. Marion (2003) listed the following indicators of self-control in children: (1) control of impulses, (2) tolerance of frustration, (3) the ability to postpone immediate gratification, and (4) the initiation of a plan that is carried out over a period of time. As with other areas of psychosocial development, cognition and social experiences both play a role in the development of self-control. Toddlers can be assisted in their development of self-control if adults use developmentally appropriate teaching and guidance techniques. Suggestions for maximizing self-control in very young children are provided in Box 9.1.

FACTORS INFLUENCING PSYCHOSOCIAL DEVELOPMENT IN CHILDREN AGES ONE THROUGH THREE

Recognizing the factors that influence psychosocial development during the toddler period helps adults to provide essential and appropriate experiences for them. Optimal psychosocial development depends on these earliest experiences.

Quality of Attachments

Across all cultures, children form attachments to their caregivers. This serves their basic needs for comfort and protection. As discussed in earlier chapters, there are variations in the levels of nurturing and security that children derive from their attachment relationships. Scholars believe that the infant's first attachments influence for the long term his or her physical well-being, personality development, mental health, social relationships, and moral behaviors (Cassidy & Shaver, 1999; Shonkoff & Phillips, 2000). Toddlers continue to need the proximity, protection, emotional support, and social interaction that a loving and caring attachment person provides.

Support and Encouragement of a Sense of Autonomy

The manner in which parents and caregivers respond to the toddler's need for autonomy is critical. The toddler's striving for independence, accompanied by contradictory feelings and needs for a secure relationship that allows for dependence, requires that adults understand the positive outcomes for children when this developmental crisis is successfully resolved.

Temperament

The child's unique temperament and personality affect and are affected by others. The quality and quantity of these early interactions affirm or discredit the child's emerging sense of self and self-esteem.

Guidance and Discipline Techniques

Guidance and discipline techniques that are consistent, predictable, logical, and supportive help toddlers begin to develop self-control, perspective-taking ability, and increasing competence in social interactions. Toddlers need the security of a guidance system that nurtures their growing independence while recognizing their continuing need for reasonable rules, clear limits, and constant protection. Through positive, instructive, and supportive interactions with adults, toddlers begin to learn to express and perceive emotions.

Opportunities to Learn Through Social Interactions

Interactions with siblings and agemates provide social experiences that lead to social understandings and a grasp of the feelings and intentions of others. Although agemate friendships between toddlers are awkward, short lived, and transitory, they provide experiences for the development of self–other distinctions.

Quality of Play Experiences

Appropriate and satisfying play interactions and developmentally appropriate toys and games enhance psychosocial development in a myriad of ways, overlapping and supporting development in all other domains: physical–motor, cognitive, language, literacy, and social and moral competence. Through play, the toddler tries out a variety of social roles and emerging social skills. The toddler also uses language with increasing facility to communicate needs and play themes and to acquire and understand new concepts and problem-solving strategies. Play enables toddlers to grow in their sense of competence and to resolve a number of fears and anxieties. Through play, toddlers continue to learn emotional display rules. Play introduces toddlers to other social convention rules from which later behaviors may be self-regulated.

Social Learning in Many Contexts

Experiences both within the family and in a variety of sociocultural contexts help children to learn to appreciate their and others' uniqueness. Racial awareness has its origins in these very early years. Self-esteem, family pride, acceptance, and respect for others are fostered in the home and in sensitive, responsive child care settings where nonbiased curriculums are provided.

Support for Special Developmental Needs

Although we have not specifically discussed children with disabilities in this chapter, it is important to note that children with delayed development, chronic disease, or disabilities are especially in need of sound, supportive emotional and social interactions. Because these children can be especially vulnerable to prolonged attachment behaviors, fears, anxieties, frustrations, and disappointments, their developing sense of autonomy, social competence, self-concept development, and healthy self-esteem can be at risk. Adults must be particularly sensitive to the child's needs for assistance and encouragement in social situations and for opportunities to develop autonomy. Adults may need to coach as well as model effective social interaction strategies.

Toddler Mental Health

Ongoing and rapid developmental processes during the toddler period bring about dramatic changes in physiological, emotional, social, and cognitive characteristics. The interplay of these growth-related changes is evident in the types of behaviors that perplex and frustrate the toddler's caregivers, for example, mood reversals, negativism, oppositional behaviors, tantrums, power struggles, rejection of affection, aggression, and eating and sleeping difficulties. Most of these types of behaviors are perfectly normal; indeed, many of them signal a maturing and healthy child. Concern arises when the primary caregivers' personalities and needs (parents, family members, nonparental caregivers) and the toddler's capabilities and needs are severely at odds and unresponsive to professional efforts to correct them. Difficult behaviors become prolonged and exacerbated; additional behavioral maladaptations (e.g., undue and unresponsive sadness, depression, withdrawal, hostility, and others) may appear. The risk factors for mental disorders in children are discussed in Chapter 6 and remain the same for toddlers and young children. As with all childhood anomalies, early diagnosis, professional intervention, and ongoing professional oversight are required.

ROLE OF THE EARLY CHILDHOOD PROFESSIONAL

Enhancing Psychosocial Development in Children Ages One Through Three

1. Recognize the importance of the adult model in directing the course of psychosocial development in young children.
2. Understand the toddler's egocentric perspective.
3. Facilitate autonomy by providing safe surroundings, reasonable limits, opportunities to make choices, and judicious assistance as needed.
4. Provide positive, predictable, supportive, and instructive guidance.
5. Understand the toddler's continuing dependency and need for security and protection.
6. Encourage and facilitate play opportunities with other children.
7. Provide labels for emotions and help the toddler to learn about display rules.
8. Promote self-esteem through positive, affirming interactions and sensitive, accurate responses to questions about race and gender.
9. Provide developmentally appropriate and age-appropriate books, toys, and electronic media that enhance the child's understanding of self and others.
10. Learn to observe and respond to the child's cues and clues.

KEY TERMS

autonomy	parallel play	self-definition
display rules	premoral	self-esteem
empathy	prosocial behavior	self-recognition
extrafamilial relationships	proximity seeking	transitional object
gender constancy	self-awareness	

REVIEW STRATEGIES AND ACTIVITIES

1. Review the key terms individually or with a classmate.
2. Ask your classmates about the transitional objects they had as young children. How many recall ever having a transitional object? What was the object? For how long did the attachment to the transitional object persist? What does this survey illustrate about transitional objects?
3. Volunteer to assist in a program for toddlers for at least 1 day. In a journal, describe instances of prosocial behaviors. What preceded the prosocial response? How did the recipient respond? What followed the prosocial encounter?
4. Engage a 3-year-old in conversation. What clues does the child give about his or her self-perceptions regarding age, size, abilities, gender, race, friends, family, and so on? Be careful not to prompt or suggest expected answers.

5. Observe arrival and departure times at a child care center. How do toddlers respond to their parents when the parents drop them off and arrive to take them home? How do parents respond? How do caregivers or teachers respond? Ask the instructor to discuss what these behaviors mean in terms of attachment and separation anxiety.

FURTHER READINGS

Bronson, M. B. (2000). *Self-regulation in early childhood: Nature and nurture.* New York: Guilford Press.

Denham, S. A. (1998). *Emotional development in young children.* New York: Guilford Press.

Fenchel, E. (Ed.). (2001). Babies, toddlers, and the media [Theme Issue]. *Zero to Three, 22*(2).

Goulet, M. (1999). *How caring relationships support self-regulation.* Washington, DC: National Association for the Education of Young Children.

Koplow, L. (1996). *Unsmiling faces: How preschools can heal.* New York: Teachers College Press.

Marion, M. (2003). *Guidance of young children* (6th ed.). Columbus, OH: Merrill/Prentice Hall.

Nakazawa, D. J. (2003). *Does anybody else look like me?: A parents' guide to raising multiracial children.* New York: Perseus.

Siegel, D. J. (1999) *The developing mind: Toward a neurobiology of interpersonal experience.* New York: Guilford Press.

OTHER RESOURCES

American Academy of Pediatrics brochures:
> *Toilet training: Guidelines for parents*
> *Discipline and your child: Guidelines for parents*
> *Temper tantrums: A normal part of growing up*

National Association for the Education of Young Children brochures:
> *Helping children learn self-control: A guide to discipline*
> *Love and learn: Discipline for young children*
> *A caring place for your infants*
> *A caring place for your toddler*
> *A good preschool for your child*
> *So many goodbyes: Ways to ease the transition between home and groups for young children*

CHAPTER TEN

Cognitive, Language, and Literacy Development: Ages One Through Three

Using their sensorimotor capacities and their abilities to master first-order symbol systems, young children develop a vast array of intuitive understandings even before they enter school. Specifically they develop robust and functional theories of matter, life, the minds of other individuals and their own minds and selves. They are aided in this task of theory construction by various constraints, some built into the genome, others a function of the particular circumstances of their culture, and still others a reflection of their own, more idiosyncratic styles and inclinations.

HOWARD GARDNER

After studying this chapter, you will demonstrate comprehension by:

▶ Recognizing theoretical perspectives on cognitive, language, and literacy development in children ages 1 through 3.

▶ Describing the cognitive development of children ages 1 through 3.

▶ Describing the language development of children ages 1 through 3.

▶ Describing the development of literacy of children ages 1 through 3.

▶ Relating cognitive, language, and literacy development to other developmental domains

▶ Identifying major factors influencing cognitive, language, and literacy development of children ages 1 through 3.

▶ Suggesting strategies for promoting cognitive, language, and literacy development in children ages 1 through 3.

COGNITIVE DEVELOPMENT IN CHILDREN AGES ONE THROUGH THREE

Cognitive development—the aspect of growth and development that involves perception, thinking, attention, memory, problem solving, creativity, language, and literacy—proceeds rapidly during the toddler period. As with other developmental domains, cognitive development during this age period is explained and described through a variety of contrasting and often complementary theories.

Theoretical Perspectives on Cognitive Development During Ages One Through Three

You have been introduced to the Piagetian and neo-Piagetian perspectives on cognitive development. Our discussion of theoretical perspectives and descriptions of cognitive, language, and literacy development during ages 1 through 3 years necessarily begins with a continuation of the description of Piaget's stages of cognitive development begun in Chapter 7. As the child moves from infancy into the toddler period, some rather dramatic transitions in cognitive abilities begin to take place as the child moves from sensorimotor activity as the guiding force behind cognitive development to mental representations and verbal interactions.

As Table 7.1 in Chapter 7 illustrates, between ages 1 and 2, children are still in the sensorimotor period of cognitive development. Around the end of the 2nd year, children move into the last two sensorimotor substages: substage 5, **tertiary circular reactions** (from about 12 to 18 months), and substage 6, the beginning of thought (from about 18 months to 2 years), and then begin to make the transition to what Piaget calls the **preoperational stage**.

Substage 5 is characterized by toddlers' use of tertiary circular reactions, or attempts to use novel ways to achieve goals. It is marked by curiosity and

tertiary circular reactions: an exploratory schema in which children devise new ways of acting on objects in their environment and from which they can derive meaning

preoperational stage: the second of Piaget's stages of cognitive development, in which children develop the ability to internally represent sensorimotor actions but do not engage in operational or logical thinking

281

experimentation, more systematic imitation, and further development of object permanence. At this stage, children are beginning to recognize cause and effect and to solve problems in their minds without the aid of sensorimotor trial and error. They are beginning to try new means of acting on objects. The following vignette illustrates how Jeremy uses both old means and new means for achieving his goal:

Jeremy tries to place a triangular shape into its corresponding opening in a three-dimensional puzzle. The puzzle slips, and Jeremy misses the opening. He immediately sets the puzzle upright and holds it with one hand while using the other hand to insert the piece into the opening. Jeremy's ability to set the puzzle upright and secure it with one hand indicates that through his actions on objects during the sensorimotor stage, he internalized information about what to do in various situations. He uses this representational intelligence to help him complete his goal of putting the puzzle piece through the opening.

Substage 6 is characterized by the development of a sense of confidence in the permanence of objects, which also includes person permanence and representational intelligence. True object permanence indicates that toddlers can search for objects that they did not see being hidden. According to Piaget, children in this stage of cognitive development realize that objects and people have an identity of their own and continue to exist even when they cannot be seen or heard.

During substage 6, children imitate not just events and behaviors in their immediate experiencing, but also behavior that they have observed at another time. Piaget called this ability **deferred imitation** (Piaget, 1952, 1962). For example, Angela, now 18 months old, picks up the remote control for the TV and pretends that she is talking on the phone. She does this when no one has been talking on the phone in her presence for several hours.

By the end of the sensorimotor period, children generally understand that objects, people, and events have certain basic characteristics, and can hold complex

deferred imitation: the ability to imitate behaviors that were observed at a prior time or another place

Through interactions with other children, toddlers are confronted with another's point of view.

schemata (or images) of people, objects, and events in their minds. This development sets the stage for learning more advanced concepts about their social and physical world. These abilities, coupled with the increasing use of symbols through gestures, language, and play, facilitate the child's transition into Piaget's next period of cognitive development: that of preoperational intelligence. The preoperational stage of cognitive development extends from age 2 to approximately 8 years of age.

According to Piaget (1952), preoperational children are not capable of operational, or logical, thinking. Logical operational thinking involves the ability to reverse a mental action. For example, the process of addition is reversible through subtraction. Although most older children and adults understand this process, preoperational children do not. However, this inability to reverse thought suggests not that young children are deficient in their thinking, but that their thought processes are simply different.

Piaget's studies suggest that young children's thinking cannot be explained as immature or based on lack of experience. He proposed that the young child's thought patterns or cognitive processes are uniquely different from those of older children and adults. Recall how Piaget became intrigued with young children's answers while he was helping Binet norm his intelligence test. Piaget noticed that young children gave markedly similar incorrect answers to the questions. This behavior motivated Piaget to research the idea that young children's thinking is not just immature adult thinking, but is qualitatively different. His and others' research has substantiated this hypothesis.

Young preoperational children continue to develop the ability to use **mental symbols** in the form of gestures, language, play, and dreams (Piaget, 1962). Notice how Jeremy uses mental imagery, or symbols, in his imitative play:

mental symbols: the behaviors that occur at the beginning of the preoperational stage, including speech, imitation, and using one object to represent another

---

Jeremy has observed city sanitation workers collecting trash around his neighborhood on his walks with Phyllis. One day, after observing this activity for several weeks, he begins to dump all his toys on his bunk bed. Between loads, he presses the bolts at the end of his bed to "grind up the trash." Through his play, he imitates the adult behaviors of the sanitation workers and uses the bolts on his bed to represent the buttons the sanitation workers use on their truck.

Preoperational thinkers hold idiosyncratic concepts and egocentric perspectives (Piaget, 1952). Maybe you can think of some comments young children have made that illustrate their unique reasoning. Often, these remarks are described as "cute," "humorous," or "off the wall." Their **transductive reasoning** can be described as thinking with illogical and incomplete concepts (or **preconcepts**). Preconcepts result from the young child's inability to focus attention on any but a few aspects of an object or experience, sometimes the most inconsequential aspect. Transductive reasoning uses these preconcepts, thus limiting the child's reasoning and problem-solving abilities.

transductive reasoning: the reasoning process of very young children, which relies on preconcepts

preconcepts: the very young child's disorganized and illogical representations of experience

---

When Angela, age 2½, was asked, "What do you want to be when you grow up?," she answered, "Nothing." "Nothing?," her inquisitor asked. "Why do you say nothing? Isn't there something you have thought you might be when you grow up?" Angela answered, "No, because I can't drive. You have to drive to go to work."

Angela has focused her attention on the fact that grown-ups drive cars to work. Therefore, she cannot imagine what she can be or do when she is grown, since her current inability to drive a car would pose insurmountable limitations. Jeremy also demonstrates transductive reasoning through his problem in understanding how gifts are selected and distributed.

Jeremy and his parents visit Bill's relatives for the holidays. Bill's brother's family is also there. After dinner, Aunt Sarah gives the children their gifts. Jeremy's 3-year-old cousin Matthew receives several presents, while Jeremy is given only one. Aunt Sarah has spent approximately equal amounts of money on both children, thinking that she was being careful to show no partiality to either child. As is typical of the young preoperational child, Jeremy attends to the specifics and the number of presents, because the more general concept of the cost is not within his range of experience or conceptual development. Jeremy becomes upset because cousin Matthew "gots more presents." Aunt Sarah tells Bill and Ann that next year she will get the boys the same number of presents and make the presents the same or very similar.

An awareness of young children's thought processes can prevent the travail that accompanies these typical misperceptions. Children's thinking is strongly influenced by their perceptions, which are dominated by how things appear.

Another characteristic of preoperational thinking is that of **idiosyncratic concepts**, or personal experiences that are overgeneralized to other situations or experiences.

idiosyncratic concepts: ideas of the preoperational child that are based on personal experience and overgeneralized to other situations

---

Jeremy was awakening at night with dreams of ghosts and monsters. In her training to become a child caregiver, Phyllis had learned that young children blend fantasy with reality. She knew that Jeremy's dreams were real to him. For this reason, she did not say, "Jeremy, there are no ghosts or monsters. They are pretend." Instead, she comforted him and reassured him that she and his parents were there at night to keep him safe. Phyllis told Jeremy that they would not let the ghosts and monsters hurt him. After these disturbing dreams continued for several more weeks, Phyllis had another idea. She asked Jeremy what he thought could be done to keep the ghosts and monsters out of his room. Jeremy thought for a moment and then said, "Get a sign that says, 'Stop. All ghosts and monsters keep out.'" Phyllis got some paper and crayons and drew a sign with that message. She and Jeremy then posted the sign on his door.

Jeremy used his past experience with signs in other contexts and overgeneralized its use to meet his personal experiences. Phyllis did not impose adult problem solving and reasoning on Jeremy, but allowed him to solve his problem at his cognitive level. As Jeremy prepares for sleep, Bill, Ann, and Phyllis remind him that they are there to keep him safe and that there is a sign on his door telling the monsters and ghosts to keep out. During the next few weeks, Jeremy's sleep is more peaceful and less filled with nightmares.

From the Piagetian perspective, the term *egocentrism* is not used to mean that a child is selfish, but rather to indicate that children are not yet able to view objects or situations from the perspective of others. Their perspectives are based on their own limited experiences. From their limited perspectives, young children are unable to consider the thoughts and feelings of others. Piaget suggested that through interactions with other children and adults, egocentric thought becomes more socialized. Piaget also believed that childhood conflicts can be beneficial when children are challenged to attend to another child's point of view.

Angela's teacher takes the 3-year-olds outdoors to play. Angela and two other children begin to play in the sand pile. Angela grabs a sifter from one of the children. This child stares at Angela and then leaves the sand area. After several minutes, Angela tries to take a large bucket from another child, Cedrick. He firmly grasps the bucket and refuses to let her have it. Angela then begins hitting Cedrick, who runs crying to the teacher. The teacher calmly asks Cedrick what happened. Cedrick takes her hand and leads her to the sand pile, telling her that Angela took his bucket and hit him. Angela's teacher asks Cedrick to tell Angela why he was crying, and the teacher repeats what Cedrick tells her. Calmly and objectively, the teacher describes the consequences of Angela's behavior. "Angela hit Cedrick. Hitting hurts. Cedrick feels bad and is crying. He said he had the bucket first. Here is another big bucket for you, Angela. We have lots of big buckets in our sand pile."

Angela's teacher understands that egocentric behavior is normal for three-year-olds. Therefore, she does not convey to Angela that she is "a bad girl" for hitting Cedrick. Rather, she repeats what Cedrick said, describing Angela's behavior and the consequences of her actions. The teachers have organized the environment so that there are duplicate materials, including several big buckets in the sand pile. They know that children at this age can become easily frustrated if they see and want something another child has. Multiple materials can prevent the interruption in children's concrete activity and can promote problem-solving skills. When it is not possible to duplicate materials, teachers can promote more socialized behavior by reinforcing children's concerns. "Cedrick said he had the big bucket first. He still wants to use it. When he is done, Cedrick will give it to you." The teacher then observes carefully to make sure Cedrick eventually shares the bucket with Angela.

Beyond Piaget's Theory

Angela is playing in the sociodramatic center of her child care center classroom. She dumps plastic fruit out of a wooden bowl. As she turns the bowl over, its inverted shape suggests that it could become a hat. Angela takes the bowl and, with considerable force, places it on Maria's head, causing Maria to cry. Angela looks very surprised at Maria's reaction. She pats Maria and tries to comfort her. Angela's teacher observes this interaction and tells Maria that Angela did not mean to hurt her. Ms. Ruiz puts Maria on her lap and attempts to calm her. Angela observes Maria and then goes to her cubbyhole, pulls out her "blanky," and gives it to Maria.

Similar behaviors by other young preoperational children have caused observant teachers, parents, and researchers to question Piaget's notion of egocentrism. Angela's behavior appears to indicate that she empathized with Maria. She tried to comfort her through gentle patting and bringing her the blanket. A number of studies have documented that under certain conditions, young children have demonstrated they are not completely egocentric. One of the earliest studies examining Piaget's notion of egocentrism in very young children was that of Yarrow and Zahn-Waxler (1977). After examining 1,500 incidents, these scholars determined that children as young as 1 year of age demonstrate compassion and other types of prosocial behavior. Other researchers have modified Piaget's well-known mountain experiment (Piaget & Inhelder, 1969) as a basis for demonstrating that young children are not completely egocentric. Piaget's mountain experiment used a three-dimensional model of three mountains. These three mountains differed in appearance. One had snow on it, the second had a house, and the third had a red cross. Children were seated at a table in front of the model. The experimenter then positioned a doll at various locations on the mountains. Children were then asked to select a picture that showed the doll's perspective. Most children usually selected a card that showed their own perspectives rather than the doll's. Piaget reasoned that these behaviors indicated these young children were egocentric because they could not take on the perspective of someone else.

Several experiments (Borke, 1983; Donaldson, 1979, 1983; Hughes & Donaldson, 1983) determined that if tasks are more appropriate and familiar to young children, children are capable of taking the perspectives of other people. Using such familiar props as a toy police officer, Grover from *Sesame Street,* a car, boats, and animals, the children were able to take the viewpoint of another. Eighty-eight percent of 3-year-olds (Hughes & Donaldson, 1983) and 80% of 3- and 4-year-olds (Borke, 1983) were able to see another's point of view.

In a study involving a "magic task," Gelman and Gallistel (1983) explored young children's conservation of number. Piaget's experiments indicated that if two rows contain the same number of objects and one row is lengthened, the pre-operational child will say that there are more objects in the longer row. In the "magic task," children were not asked to distinguish between *more* and *less,* which are abstract concepts and more difficult for young children. Rather, the children were asked to choose a winner or a loser in a number of conservation experiments. Ninety-one percent of the 3-year-olds were able to conserve when presented with various arrays. Figure 10.1, for example, illustrates how appearances fool the child's concepts of amount or number.

Hughes and Grieve (1983) also suggested that the nature of children's answers to bizarre questions often asked in Piaget's experiments demonstrates their attempt to make sense of all situations. They suggest that researchers need to re-examine the underlying assumptions about children's responses, for it appears that if experiments are made more relevant to the real-life experiences of young children, children demonstrate that they are not as egocentric as Piaget believed. In some contexts, if children are given appropriate materials with which they can identify, if the tasks involve basic human purposes to which children can relate, and if the questions asked take into account young children's understanding of

FIGURE 10.1
Piaget's experiments indicated that the preoperational child will say there are more objects in the wider array

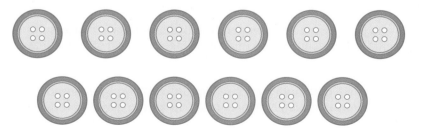

language and their motivations in answering questions, they can and do demonstrate somewhat different outcomes than Piaget proposed (Black, 1981; Bowman & Stott, 1994; Flavel, 1985; Sternberg & Berg, 1995; Sugarman, 1987). These findings do not negate Piaget's theory, but refine and focus our observations and subsequent research.

Multiple Intelligences Theory

Another view of intelligence is that proposed by a contemporary scholar, Howard Gardner (1983, 1991a, 1991b, 1993, 1999), who suggests that intelligence is the ability to solve problems or create a product that is valued by one's culture or community. As the quotation at the beginning of this chapter reveals, Gardner characterizes the learning of very young children as "intuitive." He characterizes early learning as natural, naive, and universal, wherein the young child is "superbly equipped to learn language and other symbolic systems and who evolves serviceable theories of the physical world and of the world of other people during the opening years of life" (Gardner, 1991b, p. 6).

Gardner contrasts the intuitive learner with the "traditional student" (between the ages of 7 and 20 years), who attempts to master the traditional "literacies, concepts, and disciplinary forms" of the school, and the "disciplinary expert" (at any age), who is able to use the knowledge of one discipline to inform new encounters. These are learners whose knowledge serves them at the application level of thinking and acting.

Gardner proposes that there are many different kinds of minds and that individuals learn, remember, understand, and perform in many different ways. He suggests that human beings are capable of a number of different ways of knowing. His point of view is referred to as a multiple intelligences theory. Gardner proposed that there are at least seven intelligences, and in more recent work proposed at least three additional candidate intelligences (Gardner, 1999). These intelligences include the following:

1. *Intrapersonal intelligence:* the ability to "detect and symbolize complex and highly differentiated sets of feelings"
2. *Interpersonal intelligence:* the capacity to recognize distinctions among other people's moods, temperaments, motivations, and intentions
3. *Spatial intelligence:* the ability to accurately perceive the visual–spatial world
4. *Bodily-kinesthetic intelligence:* the capacity to direct one's bodily motions and manipulate objects in a skillful fashion
5. *Musical intelligence:* exceptional awareness of pitch, rhythm, and timbre
6. *Linguistic intelligence:* sensitivity to meaning, order, sounds, rhythms, and inflections of words
7. *Logical–mathematical intelligence:* the ability to attend to patterns, categories, and relationships

The additional candidate intelligences Gardner describes are as follows:

1. *Naturalist intelligence:* the ability to recognize important distinctions in the natural world among plants and animals, natural phenomena, and changes over time

2. *Spiritual intelligence:* the ability to relate to the mysteries of life and death, and the "why" questions of human existence, the supernatural, and altered states of consciousness

3. *Existential intelligence:* a strand of spiritual intelligence, which includes the ability to locate oneself within the cosmos—the infinite—while dealing with such intellectual issues as the meaning of life and death and the ultimate fate of the physical and psychological worlds, and relating to, and perhaps explaining, the depth and breadth of experiences such as profound love, an absorbing response to a work of art or music, or other mysterious or potent life experiences

Individuals are thought to possess these intelligences in various combinations and to greater or lesser degrees. Rather than pursuing such constructs as the "IQ" (intelligence quotient), which attempts to define intellectual potential, Gardner's multiple intelligences (MI) theory suggests an approach to studying children that asks not, "How smart are you?," but "How are you smart?" Such an approach emphasizes individual strengths and idiosyncrasies, and provides a broader profile of individual capabilities than has been derived historically through traditional intelligence tests.

Information-Processing Perspectives

From the information-processing point of view, young children have a limited capacity to pay attention and to remember. Teachers of toddlers will be quick to affirm that holding their attention for any appreciable length of time is quite a task, and reminders of routines and rules are a constant necessity. As we get older, attention and memory help us to gain and retain information from our experiences. However, young children lack many of the processing skills that older children and adults use. For example, young children are unsystematic in their attentional behaviors, often fail to focus on essentials, and are easily distracted. Inability to engage in focused attention often leads to faulty and incomplete information, as illustrated above. Couple this with limited memory functions, and one can see why young children naturally form many incomplete concepts and misperceptions and are unpredictable in their behaviors, sometimes remembering behavioral expectations and at other times not.

Alert, active, and curious, young children confront and are bombarded with far more stimuli and information than they can adequately process. Most information travels through short-term memory storage but is readily lost unless the child has employed some strategy to move it to long-term memory storage. Strategies such as memorization, rehearsal (i.e., repeating something to themselves over and over), or using class and categories or associations to assist memory assist this process, but young children have limited ability to do these things. Young children remember best the activities that they have experienced a number of times, activities that were in some way novel or unusual to them, such as a friend's birthday party last week, or an event that evoked emotion, such as when a sibling got injured or they participated in a joyous family occasion, such as a family or holiday celebration. However, some scholars believe that events that evoke overwhelming emotion may alter or inhibit memory processes at the biological level, causing certain structures in the brain to inadequately process the

Young children remember best what they themselves experience.

information, leading to faulty or no memory of an event (Siegel, 1999). Memory in young children then depends on the child's ability to make meaningful and relevant sense of the event to be remembered. As children get older, they can be helped to use the strategies that move short-term memories into long-term memory storage.

Social-Interactionist Perspective

As during infancy, young children continue to learn best and most readily from the social interactions that they experience with important people in their lives. Through these interactions, self-knowledge emerges; curiosity, autonomy, and initiative are encouraged; concepts are imparted; language development is supported and enhanced; and, in the broad sense, cultural values and modes are inculcated. In a major way, cognition, language, and literacy development depend on social contexts to support and enhance them. The toddler is particularly receptive to the learning that occurs in a social context.

Recall from previous social interactionist discussions the importance of role models in the lives of young children. Observation of toddlers' imitative behaviors suggests that cognitive, language, and literacy behaviors are often profoundly influenced by the individuals they choose to imitate. Interactions with other toddlers and older children provide additional models of behavior, language, concepts, and misconcepts.

Contextualistic Perspectives

Many toddlers today participate in brief or extended preschool activities, expanding their spheres of influence beyond the microsystem of the immediate family into a mesosystem of interacting influences that include staff and teachers in part- or whole-day child care arrangements and part- or whole-week preschool programs. The philosophy of the programs, the knowledge and training of the adults who care for the children, and the relationships of parents and other family members to the people and entities in the mesosystem all influence the types of experiences the toddler will have and the learning that will accrue from those experiences. In the best circumstances, cognitive, language, and literacy development are supported through informed, family-centered programs and age-appropriate and developmentally appropriate activities, materials, and expectations for toddlers.

The Neurobiology of Cognitive, Language, and Literacy Development

receptive language: language that is comprehended, but not necessarily produced

The toddler period is a particularly important period for the development of language and vocabulary. Talking, singing, and reading to toddlers appear to enhance dendritic growth in the left hemisphere of the brain, the portion of the brain that controls most, though not all, language functions. While the subsystems of language, sound discrimination, and meaning develop gradually during childhood, with increasing language facility, both **receptive language** (understanding what is heard) and **expressive language** (communicating through language) become tools for the processing of thoughts.

expressive language: spoken language; oral communication

From these many theoretical perspectives on cognitive development, it is clear that the thinking of infants and young children differs appreciably from that of older children and adults. A description of the expected cognitive behaviors of young children is provided in Table 10.1.

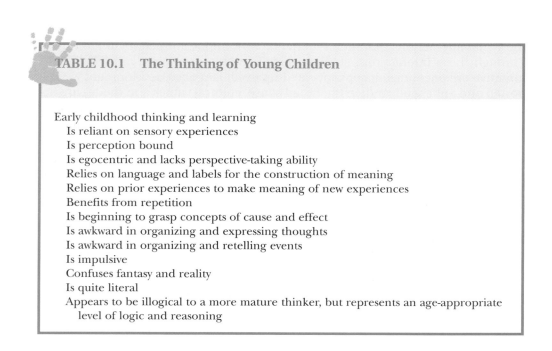

TABLE 10.1   The Thinking of Young Children

Early childhood thinking and learning
   Is reliant on sensory experiences
   Is perception bound
   Is egocentric and lacks perspective-taking ability
   Relies on language and labels for the construction of meaning
   Relies on prior experiences to make meaning of new experiences
   Benefits from repetition
   Is beginning to grasp concepts of cause and effect
   Is awkward in organizing and expressing thoughts
   Is awkward in organizing and retelling events
   Is impulsive
   Confuses fantasy and reality
   Is quite literal
   Appears to be illogical to a more mature thinker, but represents an age-appropriate
     level of logic and reasoning

LANGUAGE DEVELOPMENT

Angela awakens from her nap at the child care center. She sits up, rubs her eyes, and says, "Waa-waa." Ms. Ruiz fills a cup of water and brings it to her. Angela quickly drinks the water. Ms. Ruiz then allows Angela to play with the empty cup as she changes her diaper and says, "Water all gone, water all gone. Angela drank it all up. Is Angela still thirsty?"

This vignette demonstrates that Angela is learning about **semantics**, or the way in which language carries meaning. She indicates that she knows language is used to communicate—to mean something. She vocalizes to Ms. Ruiz that she wants "Waa-waa." Ms. Ruiz responds, reinforcing for Angela the notion that Angela is a meaning maker, that she communicates her needs to others through language. Ms. Ruiz facilitates this idea for Angela as she changes her diaper and talks with her about the cup, the water, and being thirsty.

As children attend to the language used in such meaningful interactions, they absorb the speech sounds, or **phonology**, of the language system. Jeremy and Angela internalize the basic sounds of the English language system used in the United States, just as French children learn the sounds of the French language. As Jeremy's phonological development continues, he will begin to produce the language sounds that are typical of his sociocultural context (family, community, and geographic region). Angela will also produce sounds that are typical of her sociocultural context.

As Angela and Jeremy begin to form their first sentences, they demonstrate that they are learning the **syntax**, or structure, of their language system.

It is Saturday, and Bill takes Jeremy with him to run errands. When they return, Ann asks Jeremy, "Where did you eat lunch?" Jeremy replies, "We eated at McDonald's."

Jeremy's response indicates that he has learned how to put words together in a sentence to convey meaning. In addition, his use of *eated* reflects that he had processed the rule of grammar that past tense words end in *-ed*. This ability to form such generalizations is an example of young children's amazing cognitive ability. As Jeremy matures and learns more about the language system, he will come to realize that there are some exceptions to the general patterns of language and will begin to use *ate* instead of *eated*.

Thus, in the first few years of life, young children learn (1) that language conveys meaning, (2) the sound system of the language, and (3) the structure of the language system. In addition to this linguistic or grammatical competence, they begin to learn a repertoire of behaviors that are often called interactional or **communicative competence**, as illustrated in Figure 10.2. Communicative competence is the ability to adapt language to meet the communicative needs of varying situations.

Young children acquire communicative competence in the same manner in which they acquire linguistic competence: by participating with others in

semantics:
knowledge of how language carries meaning

phonology:
the speech sounds of a particular language system

syntax:
the grammar or structure of a particular language system

communicative competence:
the repertoire of behaviors that help young children to communicate effectively with others

FIGURE 10.2
Grammatical and interactional competence interact to form the child's communicative competence

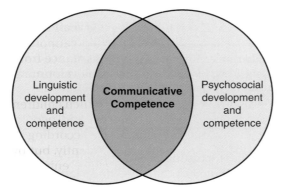

meaningful interactions, conversations, and shared experiences. Nonverbal behaviors and conversational techniques are also acquired through these interactions. These behaviors can vary according to the interactive rule structures of the child's sociolinguistic context. For example, in a number of traditional Native American cultures, children are expected to listen while adults speak. Rather than providing occasions for children to speak, adults create opportunities for children to listen (Williams, 1994). Thus, children from some cultural groups view silence as comfortable and expected behavior. Interrupting or speaking too soon after another person has spoken is viewed as rude in some cultural situations (Little Soldier, 1992; Paul, 1992). These interactive behaviors are in contrast to those of other cultural groups in which children and adults engage in simultaneous overlapping conversation, and interruption is viewed as acceptable behavior (Au & Kowakami, 1991). A sociocultural perspective on language development takes into account that while grammatical and interactional competence interact to form the child's communicative competence, communicative competence is culturally specific and develops in the context of individual interactions within a cultural context.

Interaction Between Thought and Language

Piaget believed that young children's thought influences their language. He observed that many children under age 7 frequently talked to themselves, engaging in monologues and egocentric speech. Piaget viewed this behavior as indicative of young children's egocentric thought. In addition, he viewed this behavior as the child's way of verbalizing random thinking. Piaget thought that as children mature in their cognitive development, egocentric speech eventually disappears and socialized speech develops.

Vygotsky (1962, 1978), by contrast, believed that young children talk to themselves for the purpose of solving problems or guiding behavior. He believed that talking to one's self is communication with the self. It was also his belief that over time and as children get older, this private speech internalizes as **inner speech**, or thinking in words or sentences.

Vygotsky theorized that language and talking to oneself originate in one's early interactions with others. In fact, Vygotsky (1978) thought that all cognitive functioning first evolves in social contexts with others. He believed that adults and

inner speech:
a form of speech associated with the process of internalizing spoken words or sentences

more cognitively astute children help less mature children learn by providing verbal suggestions or information, a form of assistance that he termed **scaffolding**. Vygotsky called the level of concept development at which the child cannot accomplish tasks or understand concepts alone, but can do so with assistance from adults or more cognitively mature children, the **zone of proximal development** (Vygotsky, 1978).

Whereas Piaget viewed cognitive development as a process by which children mentally construct meaning out of their interactions with objects and people, Vygotsky asserted that language and thought were interdependent. According to this view, in the beginning, language and thought develop independently, but by around age 2, they begin to mutually influence each other. Language enhances understanding and thought, and the child uses language to interpret information and express understanding. Cultural contexts and social interaction are important contributors to this process.

Research during the last several decades has tended to support Vygotsky's theory about the importance of young children's interactions with both adults and older children in the development of cognition and the relationship between thought and language (Hart & Risely, 1995; Kerwin & Day, 1985). As a result of these findings, what Piaget called *egocentric speech* and Vygotsky called *inner speech* are now referred to as **private speech**. Some scholars suggest that, contrary to Piaget's ideas, very young children who use private speech have higher rates of social participation and are more socially competent than children who do less talking to themselves. In addition, research suggests that cognitively mature children use private speech at earlier ages (Berk, 1986). These findings demonstrate the importance of social interaction and communication in the development of language and cognition in young children. This information provides one of the most important implications for promoting the

scaffolding: a process by which adults or more skilled children facilitate the acquisition of knowledge or skills in the learner through coaching or supplying needed information

zone of proximal development: the level of concept development that is too difficult for the child to accomplish alone, but can be achieved with the help of adults or more skilled children through scaffolding

private speech: speech to oneself that helps direct one's behavior, thinking, or communication

Scaffolding is a process by which helpful information and suggestions are provided as children explore their own capabilities.

cognitive development of young children: providing opportunities for children and adults to interact and communicate with each other.

Vocabulary Development

fast mapping: children's rapid learning of language by relating a word to an internalized concept and remembering it after only one encounter with that word

Young children's rapid vocabulary development is explained by a process called **fast mapping** (Carey, 1978). Fast mapping refers to the way in which young children learn and remember an average of 9 words per day from the onset of speech until age 6 (Clark, 1983). By that time, young children have acquired approximately 14,000 words (Templin, 1957).

Children's initial understanding of a word during the fast-mapping process is often expanded and refined as children continue to learn about the world. The following vignette demonstrates this clarification of vocabulary:

One of Jeremy's favorite early books was Eric Carle's (1979) *The Very Hungry Caterpillar.* Jeremy's first referent for a caterpillar was the tube-shaped animal that crawls. He was somewhat puzzled later on when he had his first encounter with another type of Caterpillar, a toy replica of the earth-moving machine. As children refine and extend their vocabulary, they discover that there are words that sound the same but have different meanings.

First Sentences

telegraphic speech: children's early speech, which, like a telegram, includes only the essential words needed to convey meaning

rich interpretation: acknowledging that young children know more than they can verbally express and use nonverbal behaviors to communicate

When children are around age 18 to 20 months, they usually have a vocabulary of about 40 to 50 words. At this time, they begin to form their first sentences, consisting of two words. Two-word sentences are often called **telegraphic speech** because only the most necessary words are used (Brown & Fraser, 1963). Prepositions, articles, auxiliary verbs, conjunctions, plurals, possessives, and past endings are usually left out of telegraphic speech. **Rich interpretation** of this sentence structure acknowledges that children know more than they can express. They are, however, capable of using nonverbal behaviors to further communicate their meaning. Bloom's (1970) classic example of "Mommy, sock" indicated that these two words could convey a variety of meanings: "Mommy's sock," "Mommy, put on my sock," or "Mommy, give me my sock." Context becomes essential to understanding the child's true meaning in these earliest sentences.

Rich interpretation allows us to recognize that sentences usually entail many elements of communication, questions, descriptions, recurrences, possessions, locations, agent actions, negations, and wishes. Bloom (1970) found that children's first use of *no* conveys nonexistence—for example, "no juice." Next, *no* is used as a negative, as in "no go home." Then *no* is used to convey what the child believes to be not true.

Between ages 2 and 3, simple sentences begin to replace telegraphic expressions, and the structures of these simple sentences reflect the linguistic nuances (e.g., word order) spoken by members of the child's cultural and linguistic community (Maratsos, 1983). Gradually, children between 1½ and 3½ years of age begin to acquire grammatical **morphemes**, which expand the mean length utterance or "sentence." Morphemes are meaningful units of language, including words and grammatical markers such as prefixes and suffixes (e.g., -ed for past tense, -s for plural). Generally, English-speaking children in these age groups acquire grammatical morphemes in a fairly predictable order (Shonkoff & Phillips, 2000).

morpheme:
the smallest unit of meaning in oral or written language

Oral Language Approximations

As children begin to acquire language, their approximations, or attempts to replicate conventional adult language, are replete with overextensions, underextensions, creative vocabulary, and overregularization. Frequently, adults misinterpret young children's developing language as incorrect and believe that it should be corrected. However, these early language approximations represent necessary cognitive processing and evolve into more mature forms of language through maturation and language-rich experiences.

Overextension involves young children's use of a word to refer to a similar but different object, situation, or category. When a child points to an airplane and says, "Truck," the child is overextending the word *truck* to refer to other objects. Young children's efforts at cognitive processing are evident in their use of overextensions. Overextensions always apply to a class of similar referents. Airplanes remind the child of the "bigness" and/or the mobility of trucks.

overextension:
the use of a word to refer to a similar but different object, situation, or category

Overextensions are thought to be a strategy that young children use when they cannot remember the appropriate word or have not had an opportunity to learn it. For example, a child who has never seen an airplane before may attach the label *truck* to it. The child has no knowledge of the word *airplane* or to what it refers. In addition, given the correct names in a comprehension task, children can point out specific objects even though they overextend. This illustrates how comprehension of language precedes production of language.

The opposite of overextension is **underextension**, in which the child uses a general or word to refer to a limited range for its use. For example, the child thinks that the name *Hannah* applies only to her sister Hannah, and no other person can have that name; or the word *dog* applies to collies but not to other types of dogs.

underextension:
the use of a general term to refer to a more specific object, situation, or category

Young children use **creative vocabulary** when they create new words to meet the need for a word that they have not learned or cannot remember, or for which no actual word exists in the language system. For example, one young child referred to a calculator as a "countulator." Another example occurred when several children in an early childhood classroom were playing restaurant. They decided that Justin would be the "cooker."

creative vocabulary:
the creation of new words to meet the need for a word that has not been learned or that has been forgotten, or for which no word exists

Overregularization occurs when young children generalize a grammatical rule to apply to all situations. As children begin to unconsciously internalize the general rules for making plurals or past tense, they overgeneralize the rules. For example, the general rule for making past tense is to add *-ed* to a word. In applying this principle, children create *goed, runned, breaked,* and so on. Remember when Jeremy told his mother that they had "eated at McDonald's"? Again, these language behaviors reflect the young child's remarkable cognitive processing of language.

overregularization:
the tendency to overgeneralize a rule of grammar

Sociocultural Aspects of Language

When we speak of *cultures* or *cultural diversity*, we are referring to the amalgam of beliefs, value systems, attitudes, traditions, and family practices that are held by different groups of people. Ethnicity refers to a particular group's shared heritage, including the group's common history, language, distinctive traditions and celebrations, and often a common religion. Young children develop language in the context of individual cultural and ethnic group membership.

Gollnick and Chinn (1990) provided a cultural definition of language: "a shared system of vocal sounds and/or nonverbal behavior by which members of a group communicate with one another" (p. 211). Language is expressed differently in different cultural groups and is characterized by both verbal and nonverbal communicative elements. Consequently, the expression of language is unique and often idiosyncratic between and among members of different cultural groups.

Dialects

dialects:
different forms of language used by different ethnic groups or by people who live in different geographic regions

Linguists say that there are many dialects throughout the United States. Consider the variations in sounds and pronunciations of the New England area, the South, and the Midwest. The state of Texas, for example, is said to have five regional dialects. Linguists define **dialects** as speech differences that are unique to various ethnic populations or geographic regions. Dialects vary in word pronunciation, verb tenses, and sound omissions. According to linguists, dialects are not inferior forms of language but are simply different forms. Dialects are rule governed just as standard English is rule governed. All young children learn the dialect of the home and community in which they live.

Many young children come from families in which a dialect such as Black English (Ebonics) is routinely spoken. If a dialect has syntactic, semantic, and phonological differences from standard English, children can have difficulty adjusting to standard English in contexts in which standard English is expected.

Bilingualism and Multilingualism

simultaneous bilingualism:
the process of learning two languages at the same time, beginning at birth

successive bilingualism:
the process of learning a second language after acquiring proficiency in a first language

metalinguistic awareness:
the ability to think about the forms and meanings of language

From birth, some children learn two languages simultaneously. This is referred to as **simultaneous bilingualism**, and these children truly have two first languages. Other children learn a second language after acquiring proficiency in a first language. This process is known as **successive bilingualism**, and these children often encounter the second language in an intensive context, such as when being cared for by an adult who speaks a language different from that of the family or when enrolled in a preschool in which the language is different from that of the home.

Increasing numbers of children in the United States come from homes in which English is not the first language. Many young children are in home, child care, and preschool environments in which different languages are spoken. Scholars who are interested in the language development of bilingual and multilingual children suggest that second-language acquisition facilitates both cognitive and linguistic skills (Bialystok, 1986; Handscombe, 1994). When matched with children who are monolingual, children who are bilingual outperform them in areas of verbal and nonverbal intellectual measures, analytic reasoning, concept formation, **metalinguistic awareness**, and creativity (Ricciardelli, 1993).

The patterns of second-language development parallel those of first-language development. Second-language acquisition, like first-language acquisition as described earlier in this chapter, is creative (deHouwer, 1995). Further, children learning two languages simultaneously do so at a rapid pace, much as if they were learning only one language. Language development in all cultures is a developmentally robust process, and is not slowed among young children who are learning more than one language (deHouwer, 1995; National Research Council & National Institute of Medicine, 1997). Children of all cultures benefit from environments that provide enriching linguistic input.

Input or social interaction with other children and adults is necessary to second-language acquisition just as it is to first-language acquisition. Some scholars believe that while younger language learners are more likely to speak a second language with minimum accent, older language learners appear to be more efficient language learners (Samway & McKeon, 1999).

LITERACY DEVELOPMENT

Cheryl has been doing her homework in front of the TV. She takes a break and walks to the kitchen to get something to eat. As she walks back to the living room, she discovers Angela (now 26 months of age) scribbling on her notebook. "Angela, that's my homework!," shouts Cheryl. Angela looks up at Cheryl and says, "Angela, homework."

It is Saturday. Ann's father has come to visit, and the family decides to go to the mall. As they enter the mall, 2-year-old Jeremy says, "There's Sears." Ann's father cannot believe his ears. "Jeremy is only 2, and he can read *Sears*," the proud grandfather remarks.

These vignettes demonstrate that very young children are learning not only about oral language but also about written language. The idea that very young children are aware of and learning about print is relatively recent.

Interaction Among Thought, Language, and Literacy

In the past, it was thought that children need to spend approximately the first five years of their lives developing a good foundation in oral language before learning to read. When children reached age 6½, they were perceived as generally possessing the maturity and perceptual development required to learn how to read (Morphett & Washburne, 1931). After learning the basic rudiments of reading, children were then ready to begin to learn how to write—to communicate with others via written symbols. This writing for the purpose of communicating with others, as opposed to the perceptual–motor task of handwriting, usually received attention somewhere around the end of the first grade or the beginning of the second. Once introduced to writing, young children were expected to produce interesting stories, with conventional spelling, appropriate grammar, good handwriting, and correct punctuation on their first attempt. If they were not successful, their papers and stories were returned to be corrected.

*Language devel-
opment is quite
rapid during the
toddler period.*

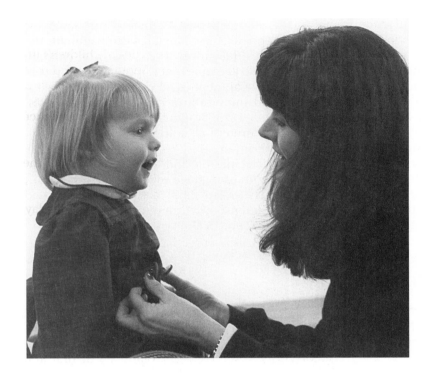

In the 1960s and 1970s, a number of researchers began to question this sequence of literacy development. Their research provided new information about how young children grow into literacy.

As oral language researchers analyzed tapes of young children's verbalizations, they noticed that many young children talked about and were very much interested in print (Snow, Burns, & Griffin, 1998). The vignettes about Jeremy and Angela illustrate children's awareness of and interest in print.

Reading researchers also recognized that some children entered first grade already knowing how to read. While some suspected that these children's parents had formally taught them to read, Durkin (1966) undertook a study of early readers and their families to determine exactly how these young children had learned to read. The study found that the parents did not formally teach their young children how to read. However, these parents displayed a number of other behaviors that seemed to facilitate early reading behaviors. Specifically, they (1) read to their children on a consistent and regular basis when the children were quite young, (2) provided their children with access to a wide range of printed materials in the home, (3) read and interacted with printed materials, (4) responded to their children's questions about printed materials, and (5) made writing and drawing tools and paper available to their children.

Further, scholars now recognize that children are sensitive to precise differences in sounds in spoken language. By the age of 6 months, infants recognize sound units in their native language and distinguish between consonants and vowels used in any language, but readily recognize the unique sounds of their own (Kuhl, 2001). The manner in which parents talk with infants (i.e., motherese and fatherese) furthers this development. This capacity is referred to as **phonological**

sensitivity. Phonological sensitivity progresses rapidly during the preschool years when children engage in word play and conversations with others and are frequently exposed to rhythm, dance, rhyme, song, and many types of children's literature. Phonological sensitivity is primarily an auditory phenomenon, and thus can develop without exposure to print. It must be noted that phonological sensitivity, while it is related to learning to read, is a different concept than "phonics," which refers to a teaching strategy that emphasizes letter/sound correspondence (Whitehurst, 2001).

Much of the literacy research has focused on the process by which young children grow into literacy. Several general ideas describe current thinking about the development of literacy in young children:

- Learning about print begins quite early in life, as early as the first year (Barclay, Benelli, & Curtis, 1995; Teale, 1986).
- Young children learn about literacy (reading and writing) by interacting with others in meaningful situations relating to print material (Neuman, Copple, & Bredekamp, 2000; Teale, 1986).
- Young children's learning about print differs from the knowledge older children and adults have about it (Ferrerio & Teberosky, 1982).
- Young children develop an awareness of oral and written language in a holistic and interrelated way rather than in a sequential stage process. In other words, very young children develop simultaneous notions about oral and written language while they are involved with significant others in meaningful situations (Goodman, 1986; Neuman, Copple, & Bredekamp, 2000).
- Virtually all children, regardless of socioeconomic background, learn about literacy early in life (Burns, Griffin, & Snow, 1999; Heath, 1983). Only in the few cultural groups that do not use written language do children lack an awareness of print.

The interaction of meaningful experiences with oral and written language is a very important contributor to the development of literacy. Such an awareness suggests it is important that young children have active, meaningful experiences with others involving both oral and written language. These experiences facilitate the child's competence in the development of thought and oral and written communication.

Developing Awareness of Print as a Form of Communication

A major concept that children acquire is that print conveys meaning. Many young children begin to develop this idea as their parents read stories to them (Neuman, Copple, & Bredekamp, 2000). Indeed, it is believed that reading aloud to children is the single most important activity for building the understanding and skills that are essential for later reading success (Bus, van Ijzendoorn, & Pelligrini, 1995). Other contexts also help children to understand that print conveys messages. Situations that demand attention to environmental printing, such as consulting written directions, writing checks, and using a TV guide to select TV programs, help children to develop the understanding that print communicates. The two primary sources of young children's learning about the communicative nature of print are environmental print and book print.

phonological sensitivity: the ability to detect and manipulate the sounds of spoken language

Environmental Print

In the vignette about Jeremy and Sears, how did Jeremy come to associate the large building at the mall with the letters *S-E-A-R-S* on the facade? The answer is through a variety of meaningful experiences that involved both oral and written language. Jeremy had been in the Sears store on numerous occasions. He was with Bill and Ann when they purchased a new washer and dryer. He watched as the Sears truck arrived and the washer and dryer were delivered and installed. Almost every time Bill and Ann are in Sears, they take Jeremy to the toy department to look around. Jeremy has also heard and seen advertisements for Sears on TV. Participating in these meaningful experiences with the accompanying oral and written language helped Jeremy to internalize the printed symbols that represent Sears.

As children use and/or observe objects in meaningful contexts, they pay attention to the objects' appearance. Seeing the box of Cheerios every morning on the breakfast table or the tube of Crest toothpaste on the sink, as well as at the grocery store or on TV, helps children to become familiar with and internalize certain features about print encountered in the environment. Studies indicate that while young children around age 2 recognize environmental print such as "Coke," "McDonald's," and "Wal-mart," they attend to this print in a very global manner (Goodman, 1980). That is, they pay attention to the whole context and not just the print. For example, very young children attend to the shape of the object, its color, and the design of the print and logo. As their print awareness develops, they begin to focus more directly on the print. Thus, experiences with environmental print are important in facilitating beginning print awareness.

Book Print

For the most part, book print differs from environmental print in that it usually consists of more than just one or two words and is organized into one or more lines. Its purpose differs somewhat from that of environmental print, and it requires a more extended focus. Knowledge of book print and how it works is critical for later success in a school context.

Learning about book print begins at home when parents share books with their children. Many parents introduce their children to books during the first year of life. Often, these experiences involve pointing to pictures or talking about pictures. During the second or third year, parents usually begin to read the book text to their children. As children hear these stories, they begin to develop the idea that books can bring them information, pleasure, and comfort. This idea can begin to foster a love of books and independent reading in children. Family book reading provides many opportunities for young children to learn a number of important concepts (Schickedanz, 1999). Specifically, they learn the following:

New information about the world around them

New vocabulary

Conversational turn taking (when parents ask questions and children respond)

The features of print and how to handle books

The concept of *story*

Literacy development finds expression as toddlers gain book handling skills and the concept of story.

The parent plays a critical role in helping young children to develop book print awareness. Parents serve as scaffolders. Recall Vygotsky's zone of proximal development. By responding to their children's interests in pictures and print, engaging in point-and-name activities, asking them questions, and commenting, parents remain in the child's zone of proximal development and thus facilitate young children's understanding and challenge their thinking. Talking with children about stories that have been read encourages reflective thinking.

Finally, intimate encounters with books provide time for parent–child communication. Time spent with books not only facilitates literacy development, but also can promote positive parent–child interactions. Parental behaviors in children's acquisition of literacy have important implications for the role of early childhood professionals in promoting literacy in their classrooms.

Factors Influencing Cognitive, Language, and Literacy Development in Children Ages One Through Three

Biological Origins of Thinking and Language

Howard Gardner's multiple intelligences theory suggests that there may be genetic predispositions for different intelligences. Nelson (1981) identified differences in young children in the early stages of oral language development that may be a function of brain hemisphere dominance as well as environmental factors. Referential speakers rely mostly on nouns, a few verbs, proper nouns, and adjectives, and they frequently label objects. Expressive speakers use varying forms of speech combinations and frequently use pronouns and compressed one- or two-word sentences. Dyson's (1993) research in the area of young children's writing also documents variation in writing strategies. These differences could be related to individual genetic predisposition as well as to environmental influences.

The interplay of rapid brain growth and neurological development during the first three years and the young child's environment influences the extent to which optimal brain growth and neurological development can occur during this period. Enriched environments have been shown to stimulate and fine tune neurological connections.

All learning is enhanced when the learner is in a state of good health. However, situations in which children are poorly nourished, obtain inadequate amounts of sleep, live with stress and lack of wholesome and protected play time, or endure family discord or other life issues interfere with optimal learning in any context. Further, undiagnosed illnesses, developmental delay, emotional disorders or disabilities such as vision, hearing, or other sensory impairments interfere with learning, and certainly present specific and sometimes profound challenges to the learner.

Again, early diagnosis and intervention is critical particularly during this time when growth, development, and learning are occurring so rapidly. Complementing regular and ongoing professional health care are programs such as the federally funded and comprehensive Early Head Start and Head Start programs for low-income families and children, which provide physical and dental, psychological, and other assessments as well as enriching age-appropriate learning opportunities. Additionally, local and state early intervention and early childhood special education programs provide diagnostic services and care and education programs for children and families. Further, some child care programs and most public schools serving very young children are able to link families to community resources such as the public health department, family services, or other specialized agencies.

Essential to cognitive and language development at all ages is the opportunity to interact in meaningful and engaging ways with others. Interactions that are positive, helpful, affirming, and supportive encourage self-esteem and self-confidence. Interactions that are thoughtful and logical help children gain intellectual clarity about their experiences. Interactions that are playful and appropriately humorous relieve stress and free the child's mind to think creatively. Probably at no other time in life is the nature and quality of one's interactions with others as important as it is during early childhood development. This is particularly true for cognitive, language, and literacy development.

Studies have revealed that the manner in which adults respond to the emerging language of toddlers is associated with the rate at which oral language develops and with reading achievement measured at age 7 (Wells, 1985). The importance of talking, singing, story telling, and reading to and with children has long been associated with positive outcomes in cognitive, language, and literacy development. Further, for children whose early experiences have been less than optimal, shared book reading experiences in which adults or older children engage in dialogue and extend the conversation about a story have been found to increase vocabulary and enhance both receptive and expressive language (Hargrave & Senechal, 2000). When adults encourage the child to continue talking about a story (or conversation) topic, ask questions, interject new information, and substitute new words for familiar ones (e.g., "scamper" for the more familiar word "run"), language development is enhanced and comprehension is strengthened.

extensions:
responses to children's language that extend the meaning of their language

Related to this process is the use of extensions and expansions in verbal interactions with children. **Extensions** are responses that include the essence of children's verbalizations and extend the meaning, while **expansions** provide children with the opportunity to hear the conventional forms of language. Jeremy said, "Get ball." Bill replied, "Oh, you need me to help you get your ball. It rolled under the table." Through this extension, Bill conveys to Jeremy that he understood what Jeremy was verbalizing. Bill also adds more information about the context through his verbalization. Adults use expansions to provide feedback to young children about their use of overregularizations. Jeremy tells Ann, "We eated at McDonald's." She replies, "Oh, you ate at McDonald's. What did you have to eat?" She does not directly correct Jeremy's *eated,* but uses the appropriate form in a conversational context and also extends by asking what Jeremy had to eat. Evidence suggests that adults who use these techniques help children to progress more rapidly in their language development and produce more complex sentences than children who are around adults who do not use extensions and expansions (Senechal, Le Fevre, Thomas, & Daley, 1998; White, 1985).

There are wide variations in the types and quantity of the language input experiences of children. Most white, middle-class infants and young children in the United States experience child-directed speech during routine and playtime activities. However, in some cultures, there is less child-directed speech, and children experience language vicariously from the skilled conversations of the people around them (Rogoff, Mistry, Goncii, & Mosier, 1991). The extent to which cultures influence qualitatively the language outcomes of children within them is not fully understood (Shonkoff & Phillips, 2000). Nevertheless, evidence of the importance of verbal input during infancy and early childhood is mounting. A particularly telling longitudinal study found that the receptive vocabularies of 5-year-old children tested on kindergarten entry ranged from the level of a child 1.9 years old to that of a 10.8-year-old child (Morrison et al., 1998; Morrison, Griffith, & Alberts, 1997). These scores appear to be predictive of (1) how teachers perceive and respond to the early learner and (2) how children will fare academically during the early grades.

Variety of Print Contexts

The nature of adult–child interactions in a variety of print contexts influences the child's awareness of various literacy contexts. Children whose parents actively involve them in reading environmental print and book print, provide them with age-appropriate drawing and writing tools so that they can explore print, and respond to the children's questions about print facilitate greater awareness of print than parents who do not respond to children's print interests (Whitehurst, 2001).

Parents as first teachers promote cognitive, language, and literacy development through the many ways that they bring their very young children into awareness of words, concepts, stories, print, and literacy behaviors. Print awareness and literacy development are dependent on the child's experiences, which importantly include adults who

- talk and converse with infants and toddlers, sharing everyday events and experiences;
- verbally label objects, provide names of people familiar to the child, and describe and label events and experiences as they occur;
- look at picture books together, and share stories and print experiences;
- include sounds, rhythms, rhymes, word play, jingles, and songs in daily interactions;

expansions:
responses to young children's use of overregularizations by using the conventional form in the conversational context

- provide opportunities to listen to recorded sounds, voices, and music;
- model literacy and daily-life print-related experiences (reading books, recipes, new publications; making grocery lists; writing checks, writing thank you notes; noticing environmental print; and labeling storage containers);
- select and read a variety of age-appropriate story and information books;
- retell in sequence (as nearly as possible) "stories" of a recent experience: the trip to the zoo, Daddy washing the car, buying cupcakes for a birthday party, spending the night with grandparents, and so on;
- label children's drawings and take dictation from them, printing the message(s) the children wish to convey.

readiness:
a term that has many different meanings depending on the context in which it is used, but generally refers to a set of prerequisite developmental expectations

Much is written today about children's **readiness** "to learn," for prekindergarten, kindergarten, first grade, or formal instruction. The term readiness has many meanings depending on the context in which it is used. This topic is discussed more fully in Chapter 13. However, related to our discussion of literacy development during ages 1 through 3, it is perhaps helpful to identify the types of knowledge and skills that can reasonably be expected to have occurred prior to the actual act of reading, which entails visually, auditorally, and cognitively decoding abstract print symbols and making meaning from the written word. Table 10.2 lists these necessary child development accomplishments during the infant and toddler period. Additional developmental accomplishments during ages 4 through 5 necessarily precede formal reading instruction.

**TABLE 10.2   Early Literacy Development
(Birth Through Age Three)**

Acquire a beginner's facility with language and nonverbal communication forms
Recognize that words represent the names of objects, people, and events
Listen with interest to the spoken word
Demonstrate facility with both receptive and expressive language
Continue vocabulary development
Demonstrate an interest in and awareness of sounds and rhythms in speech and music
Make subtle distinctions associated with sounds, rhymes, and rhythms in speech and music
Enjoy and experiment with spoken sounds and rhythms
Have an interest in and curiosity about books and book illustrations
Understand that books have both illustrations and print
Understand that print represents spoken language
Understand that print can be used to label, tell a story, and convey a message
Understand the function of books
Demonstrate book handling skills (top/bottom, left/right, front/back orientations, page turning, care, storage, and retrieval)
Demonstrate awareness of, interest in, and curiosity about environmental print
Imitate the literacy behaviors of others: look at books, "read" pictures, retell stories; draw and label, imitate writing, attempt letter/numeral formation, point to print sequences on objects and in books, ask "What does that say?"
Initiate story-reading and book-sharing activities

Types and Quality of Cognitive, Language, and Literacy Experiences

The types and quality of experiences young children have, the extent to which their caregivers are responsive to their cues and to opportunities to scaffold their learning, and the opportunities for social interaction all influence the young child's cognitive, language, and literacy development. Around age three, children begin to demonstrate that they know certain procedures and events, or **scripts**. Scripts are events that are organized in a sequential manner (Becker, 1994; Nelson, 1996; Nelson & Gruendel, 1986). Knowledge of scripts is demonstrated through verbal and nonverbal behaviors. Once children have internalized a script, they can organize their behavior and language. Jeremy's experiences in observing and participating in the collection of trash around his neighborhood have provided him with the script about what happens during this event. His knowledge of this script is reflected in his play when he collects his toys, dumps them on his bed (garbage truck), and presses the bolts (buttons) to grind up the "trash." Children whose parents provide a variety of experiences and opportunities for their children to reexperience events generally develop a greater number of scripts and more elaborate and detailed scripts than those whose parents do not (Fivush, 1984; Nelson, 1986, 1996).

Children also internalize scripts when hearing or telling stories. Studies indicate that young children can remember more details from stories that are based on familiar events. This information suggests that background experience is a critical factor when young children are involved in literacy or print settings (Neuman, Copple, & Bredekamp, 2000).

Background experiences and subsequent script formation appear to facilitate "category of concept" formation (Lucariello & Nelson, 1985). It appears that after children have developed a number of scripts involving similar objects, sequences, and functions, they can combine elements of these scripts into larger categories, thus promoting cognitive development.

scripts:
sets of social procedures or events, which include sequences of events and/or roles, often observed in young children's play

Diversity in Play and Concrete Activity

Most child development experts perceive opportunities for play or concrete, first hand activity and the quality of play as important factors in facilitating the young child's cognitive, language, and literacy development. Most experts on play suggest that sensorimotor play with or without objects facilitates the young child's beginning cognitive development (Piaget, 1962; Sutton-Smith, 1997). Garvey (1977) noted that object play often involves a four-step sequence: exploration, manipulation, practice, and repetition. Repetitive play with objects facilitates the development of **physical knowledge** and the development of **logicomathematical knowledge** (Piaget, 1969). Children between ages one and three often play with sounds, syllables, and words. Young children's play with language encourages language development.

During the child's 3rd year, sociodramatic play begins. Three-year-olds' sociodramatic play usually has no organized theme or plot. Their enactments of play roles are often one dimensional and change frequently, owing to the lack of a general theme. Play at this age often involves collecting, hauling, carrying, and dumping objects. Children tend to repeat play over and over. Jeremy's playing garbage collection is an example. In spite of these characteristics of toddler play, children at this age act out the basics or essentials of certain scripts—such as eating a meal,

physical knowledge:
knowledge of physical characteristics of objects and events gained through sensorimotor play

logicomathematical knowledge:
knowledge constructed primarily from children's actions on and interpretations of objects and events

visiting the doctor, or picking up the trash—which support the types of thinking involved in story reading and story creation.

Solitary play or play with others is essential to child development. Play with playthings that are open ended allow the child to mentally construct concepts, meaning, and ideas that are far more engaging and provide essential supports for early cognitive, language, and literacy development. Unlike toys that have limited use or can be played with in only one way, open-ended toys and playthings can be used in diverse ways and with different levels of proficiency. Blocks, for example, can be used to stack, load in a wagon, build a tower, clap to music, or symbolically represent a person, vehicle, animal, or railroad track. Blocks are enjoyed differently at different ages as play behaviors and capabilities change over time. Blocks have an enduring quality essential to play that supports cognitive and language development at all ages. Think about it: Architects and engineers use blocks to create models of their proposed structures. By contrast, a wind-up mechanical or electronic toy is of little value if all one can do with it is watch it "perform," or if its use requires adult assistance. While the social interaction skills of toddlers are awkward and unrefined, older toddlers benefit from opportunities to interact with other children in spontaneous and unstructured pretend play. Through these opportunities, children gain language and social interaction skills. A rich play life in infancy and early childhood builds the bridge to language, learning, literacy, and later academic success.

ROLE OF THE EARLY CHILDHOOD PROFESSIONAL

Promoting Cognitive, Language, and Literacy Development in Children Ages One Through Three

1. Acknowledge that each child is unique in his or her cognitive, language, and literacy development.
2. Respect sociocultural, linguistic, and socioeconomic differences among young children and their families.
3. Identify cognitive, language, and literacy needs in young children that may require special attention, services, or programs.
4. Understand that young children process information differently than older children and adults.
5. Provide safe and enriched environments so that young children can explore freely.
6. Provide a variety of interesting materials to promote thinking, talking, drawing, reading, and writing.
7. Provide opportunities for young children to interact, talk, read, draw, and write with other children and adults.
8. Demonstrate interest in and curiosity about the world.
9. Use engaging oral language with children and role model the uses of writing and print in many meaningful contexts.
10. Respond in a timely manner to children's need for scaffolding to help them grasp a concept or engage in a new skill.

KEY TERMS

creative vocabulary
communicative
   competence
deferred imitation
dialects
expansions
expressive language
extensions
fast mapping
idiosyncratic concepts
inner speech
logicomathematical
   knowledge

mental symbols
metalinguistic awareness
morpheme
overextension
overregularization
phonological sensitivity
phonology
physical knowledge
preconcepts
preoperational stage
private speech
readiness
receptive language

rich interpretation
scaffolding
scripts
semantics
simultaneous bilingualism
successive bilingualism
syntax
telegraphic speech
tertiary circular reactions
transductive reasoning
underextension
zone of proximal
   development

REVIEW STRATEGIES AND ACTIVITIES

1. Review the key terms individually or with a classmate.

2. Observe caregivers in an accredited and inclusive classroom for 1-, 2-, and 3-year-olds.

   a. Explain how developmental differences and cultural tendencies and dispositions are addressed.

   b. Describe how the environment is organized to promote cognitive, language, and literacy development.

   c. List the materials available and describe how they promote cognitive, language, and literacy development.

   d. Describe how the day is organized. Is the schedule conducive to cognitive, language, and literacy development?

   e. Observe the role of the teacher. List and describe the behaviors that facilitate cognitive, language, and literacy development.

3. Engage in a shared story-reading time with a toddler. What cognitive, language, and/or literacy behaviors does the child demonstrate?

FURTHER READINGS

Beaty, J. J. (2001). *Observing development of the young child* (5th ed.). Columbus, OH: Merrill/Prentice Hall.

Brazelton, T. B., & Greenspan, M. D. (2000). *The irreducible needs of children: What every child must have to grow, learn, and flourish.* Cambridge, MA: Perseus.

Gardner, H. (1999). *Intelligence reframed: Multiple intelligences for the 21st century.* New York: Basic Books.

Greenspan, S. I., & Wieder, S. (1997). *The child with special needs: Encouraging intellectual and emotional growth.* New York: Perseus.

Howard, V. R., Williams, B. F., Port, P. D., & Pepper, C. (2001). *Very young children with special needs: A formative approach for the 21st century.* (2nd ed.). Columbus, OH: Merrill/Prentice Hall.

McMullen, M. B. (1999). Research in review: Achieving best practices in infant and toddler care and education. *Young Children, 54*(4), 69–76

O'Brian, M. (2001). *Watch me grow: I'm two.* New York: Morrow/HarperCollins.

Rideout, V. I., Vanderwater, E. A., & Wartella, E. A. (2003). *Zero to six: Electronic media in the lives of infants, toddlers, and preschoolers.* Menlo Park, CA: Henry J. Kaiser Family Foundation.

Samway, K. D., & McKeon, D. (1999). *Myths and realities: Best practices for language minority students.* Portsmouth, NH: Heinemann.

Singer, D. G., & Singer, J. L. (2001). *Make-believe games and activities for imaginative play: A book for parents, teachers, and the young children in their lives.* Washington, DC: American Psychological Association.

OTHER RESOURCES

First Book National Book Bank
> http://nationalbookbank.org
> or
> http://www.firstbook.org

Individuals with Disabilities Education Act (IDEA)
> http://childfindidea.org/

International Society on Early Intervention
> http://www.Depts.washington.edu/isei/

National Center for Children in Poverty (NCCP)
> *Promoting the well-being of infants, toddlers, and their families: Innovative community and state strategies* (2002).
>> http://nccp.org

National Head Start Association
> http://nhsa.org

PART FIVE

The Young Child: Ages Four Through Five

CHAPTER ELEVEN

Physical and Motor Development: Ages Four Through Five

The first and foremost thing you can expect of a child is that he is a child.

ARMIN GRAMS

A secure, healthful and nourishing environment is a child's basic right.

CONVENTION ON THE RIGHTS OF THE CHILD

After studying this chapter, you will demonstrate comprehension by:

▶ Outlining expected patterns of physical and motor development in children ages 4 through 5.

▶ Identifying developmental landmarks in large and small muscle development.

▶ Describing perceptual–motor development in children ages 4 through 5.

▶ Describing body and gender awareness in children ages 4 through 5.

▶ Identifying major factors influencing physical and motor development.

▶ Identifying and describing health and well-being issues related to children ages 4 through 5.

▶ Suggesting strategies for enhancing physical and motor and perceptual–motor development in children ages 4 through 5.

Physical and Motor Competence of Children Ages Four Through Five

General Physical Characteristics

Physical growth in children seems to follow four stages. From conception to 6 months, growth is dramatically rapid. During the toddler/preschool period, growth rates tend to level off and proceed at a steady pace until puberty. Then growth rates are again strikingly rapid, followed by slower growth into adulthood. In children ages 4 through 5, growth rates are steady, with gains of 2½ to 3½ inches in height and four to five pounds in weight each year until around age 6. Children grow at individual rates that are influenced by their own genetic makeup and environment. However, sequences of growth are fairly (though not absolutely) predictable among all children. How tall, heavy, or well coordinated a child is (or will become) depends on genetics, health history, nutrition, psychosocial well-being, and opportunities for physical and motor activity.

Body proportions change from the chunky, top-heavy build of the toddler to a leaner, more upright figure. The child's head, which at age 2 was one-fourth of the total body length, at age 5 to 5½ is about one-sixth of the total body length. The brain reaches 90 percent of its adult weight by age 5, and myelination of axons and dendrites is fairly complete, making more complex motor abilities possible.

Boys and girls during this age period have similar physiques, as baby fat is being replaced with more bone and muscle. However, boys tend to gain more muscle at this age, while girls tend to retain more fat. The extent to which this difference is due primarily to cultural expectations of gender-related activities (e.g., more rough-and-tumble play versus less active pursuits) is not fully known. Changing body proportions result in a larger chest circumference and a flatter stomach, longer arms and legs, and feet that have lost the fatty arch pad characteristic of baby feet.

311

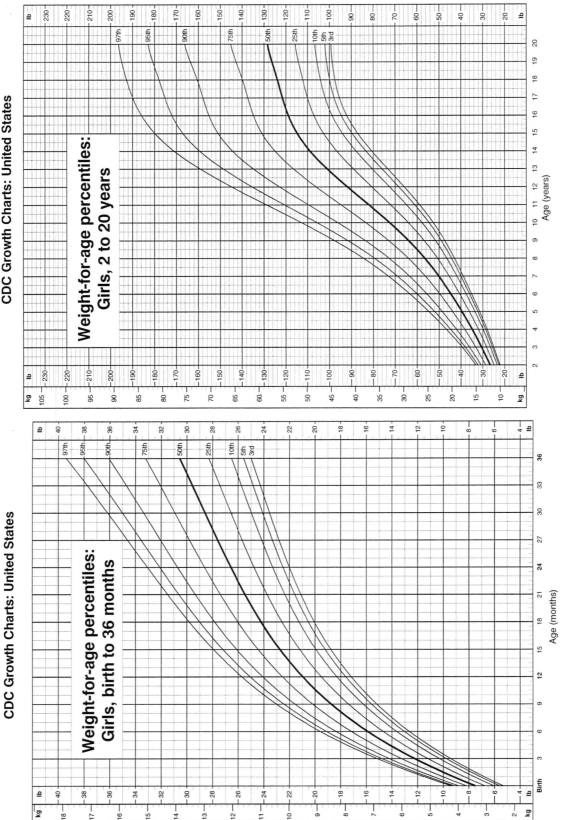

FIGURE 11.1

Growth Charts for Girls

National Center for Health Statistics, Centers for Disease Control and Prevention. (2000). CDC Growth Charts: United States. Hyattsville, MD: Author.

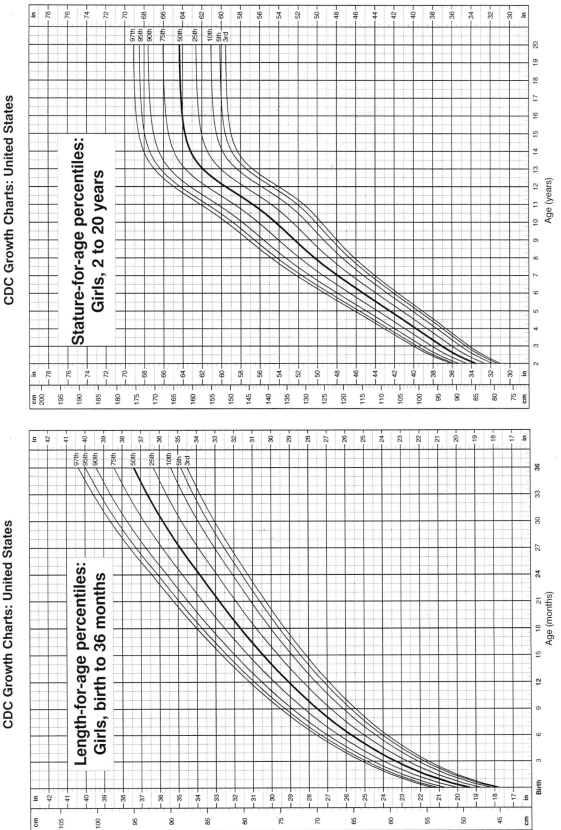

CDC Growth Charts: United States

Stature-for-age percentiles:
Girls, 2 to 20 years

CDC Growth Charts: United States

Length-for-age percentiles:
Girls, birth to 36 months

(continued)

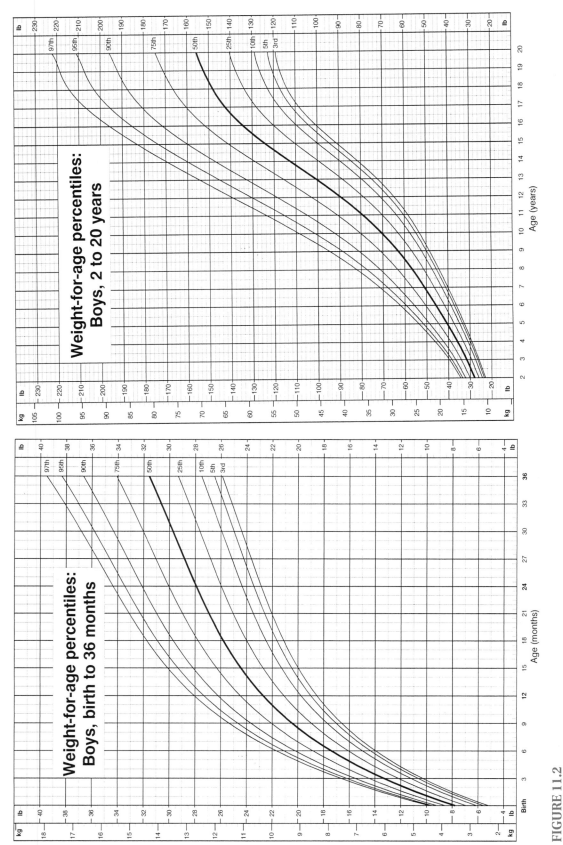

CDC Growth Charts: United States

Weight-for-age percentiles:
Boys, 2 to 20 years

CDC Growth Charts: United States

Weight-for-age percentiles:
Boys, birth to 36 months

FIGURE 11.2
Growth Charts for Boys

National Center for Health Statistics, Centers for Disease Control and Prevention. (2000). CDC Growth Charts: United States. Hyattsville, MD: Author.

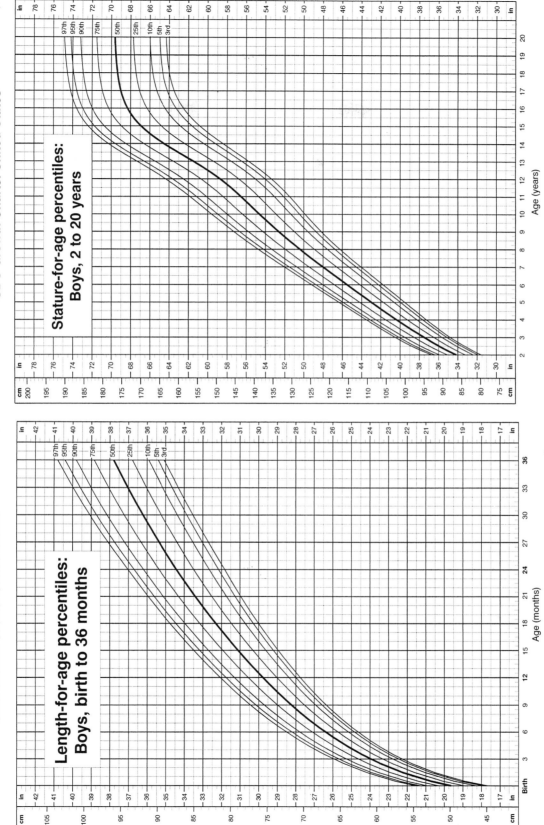

CDC Growth Charts: United States

**Stature-for-age percentiles:
Boys, 2 to 20 years**

CDC Growth Charts: United States

**Length-for-age percentiles:
Boys, birth to 36 months**

(continued)

315

Health assessments of children during these growing years regularly monitor height and weight gains, providing preliminary information about a child's overall health and nutritional status. Plotting height and weight on growth charts that compare the measurements with standardized norms helps professionals recognize individual questionable growth trends as they arise. In the United States, the most commonly used growth charts are those developed by the National Center for Health Statistics (NCHS) (Figures 11.1 and 11.2). The most recently revised growth charts also include a body mass index (BMI), which is a calculation used to judge whether a child's weight is appropriate for his or her height. Growth charts allow comparison with norms for age and sex in the general population and identify percentile rankings for each measurement of weight and height for age. Hence, percentiles tell how an individual child's height and weight compare with those of the general population of children of the same age and sex. An 80th percentile ranking means that a child's weight or height is equal to or greater than that of 80 percent of children of his or her same age and sex. Children whose measurements fall above the 95th percentile or below the 5th or whose measurements show marked change from one measure to the next may have health or nutrition anomalies that require further evaluation. However, in some cases, growth spurts occur. For instance, after a prolonged illness, the body's growth catch-up mechanisms come into play and speed the growth process for a period of time until it reaches where it would have been had the illness not occurred. (This catch-up mechanism is seen in premature and low-birth-weight infants until about age 2, when their measurements begin to follow a more normal growth curve.) Unusual growth patterns can indicate possible health problems: overnutrition or undernutrition, endocrine disorders such as hyperthyroid or hypothyroid functioning, growth hormone imbalance, disease, dehydration, fluid retention, and others.

Large Motor Development

By ages 4 through 5, children are quite motoric. Now that they have mastered walking and running, their movements are expansive and include large muscle coordinations that facilitate balancing, hopping, jumping, climbing, sliding, galloping, skipping, and many others. Their large motor skills generally include the following:

Age 4	Age 5
Rides tricycle	Rides bicycle (may need training wheels)
Climbs stairs alternating feet	Descends stairs alternating feet
Balances on one foot for a short period	Balances on one foot to a count of 5 to 10
Climbs playground equipment with agility	Experiments with playground climbing equipment
Enjoys creative responses to music	Enjoys learning simple rhythms and movement routines
Skips on one foot	Skips with both feet
Jumps easily in place	Hops on one foot in place
Throws a ball	Catches a ball
Likes to chase	Enjoys follow-the-leader
Walks a straight taped line on floor	Walks a low, wide kindergarten balance beam
Enjoys noncompetitive games	Enjoys noncompetitive games

Facility in large motor control and coordination enhances the child's development in all other developmental domains. Overall health and vitality depend on it. Independence and self-sufficiency are encouraged by it; and cognitive development is furthered through increasing ability to explore an ever-enlarging world. Mastery over body movements enhances self-image and self-confidence. As we will see in later chapters, children with positive self-images and self-confidence enjoy more successful interactions with others.

For growing children, opportunities to use, expand, and refine large motor coordination should make up a significant portion of the day. Regularly engaging in large motor activities leads to physical fitness, which, according to Gallahue (1998), has two very important components: health-related fitness and performance-related fitness. **Health-related fitness** includes muscular strength, muscular endurance, flexibility, cardiovascular endurance, and body composition. **Performance-related fitness** includes balance, coordination, agility, speed, and power. Both health-related fitness and performance-related fitness are essential to healthy, sturdy, well-coordinated bodies, which in turn contribute to perceptual–motor development and learning as sensorimotor mechanisms become increasingly refined.

The importance of health- and performance-related fitness is supported through studies of the effects of physical activity on bone growth in young children. A study of the association between physical activity and bone measures in preschool children ranging in age from 4 to 6 years old examined children's usual physical activity as reported by their parents, including the amount of time engaged in sedentary activities such as daily television viewing, and measured bone mineral content and density. The researchers concluded that physical activity is essential to optimal bone development (Janz et al., 2001).

health-related fitness: a physical state in which muscular strength, endurance, flexibility, and the circulatory–respiratory systems are all in optimal condition

performance-related fitness: a physical state in which motor coordination facilitates speed, agility, power, and balance

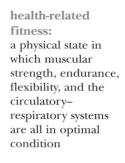

Health-related fitness characterizes sturdy, well-coordinated bodies.

Small Motor Development

Because motor development generally follows a head-downward direction, small motor development can lag behind large motor controls and coordination. As large motor controls become more refined and coordinated, the muscles of the extremities come under more precise control, and children generally become better equipped to perform a variety of small motor tasks. The ability to perform these small motor tasks becomes possible through the maturation and emergence of **prehension** and **dexterity**.

prehension:
the coordination of fingers and thumb to permit grasping

dexterity:
quick, precise movement and coordination of the hands and fingers

Age 4	Age 5
Exhibits self-help skills in dressing: some difficulty with zippers, small buttons, tying shoes	Dresses with ease
	Ties shoes
Works a puzzle of several pieces	Enjoys puzzles with many pieces
Exhibits right- or left-handedness; occasional ambidextrous behaviors	Exhibits right- or left-handedness
Enjoys crayons, paint, clay, and other art media	Enjoys drawing, painting, and using a variety of writing tools
Uses beads and strings, snap blocks, and various manipulative toys	Enjoys a variety of manipulative and construction-type toys

Prehension is the ability to grasp or grip an object and to let go of it. By age 5, grasping and prehension abilities are used to handle crayons, paintbrushes, beads and strings, pegs and pegboards, and other small manipulatives and to manage dressing and undressing with efficiency. Prehension follows a fairly predictable pattern of development, beginning in infancy and becoming more refined as the child gets older.

Dexterity refers to quick, precise movement and coordination of the hands and fingers. Though less refined at ages 4 and 5, dexterity is exhibited in the child's ability to maneuver small puzzle pieces into place; manage small buttons, fasteners, and zippers; sort playing cards; and write legible letters and numerals.

Age appropriate manipulative activities facilitate fine motor coordination.

Dexterity depends on a neurological process in which certain abilities become localized in the left and right hemispheres of the brain. Handedness is an outgrowth of this developmental process. It is believed to begin prenatally, but is apparent during infancy when a preference for a left- or right-face sleeping position and a preferred reaching hand are observed. Other behaviors, such as foot, eye, and head turning preferences depend on very complex neurological development during the early months and years. Foot preference is fairly well established from ages 3 to 5 years, though it sometimes takes longer to emerge. Handedness, however, may not be fully dominant until 6, 7, or 8 years of age (Gabbard, Dean, & Haensly, 1991; Hellige, 1993).

Handedness, whether right or left, facilitates the use of small motor abilities, leading to more refined coordination and hence dexterity. Some children ages 4 and 5 whose handedness is not clearly established use both hands with facility; some use one hand for one activity, such as eating, and the other for another activity, such as throwing or reaching. There is no reason to encourage the use of one hand over the other, as this process is governed by intricate neurological connections in the brain.

Perceptual–Motor Development

Angela has just awakened from her afternoon nap. Hearing the voice of her grandmother chatting with her teacher across the room, she is further aroused. She sits up, rubs her eyes, clumsily retrieves her shoes, and makes her way toward the area from which she heard grandmother's voice. There she is greeted with hugs and questions about her day.

Angela has just demonstrated a simple perceptual–motor sequence, which involved hearing a sound (auditory sensation), recognizing and identifying the sound as that of her grandmother's voice (perception), and making a decision to walk to the source of the sound (locomotion).

We come into the world equipped with sensory abilities: touch, vision, hearing, smell, taste, and kinesthesis. The sense organs provide information about what is going on around us and within us. The ability to make sense of these sensations—to interpret them—is called *perception*.

Perception depends on the sense organs and kinesthetic sensitivity (the sensation of body presence, position, and movement), combined with cognitive development and experience. Once a sensation is perceived, one must decide cognitively what to do with that information. Actions that follow are often motoric—for example, turning toward a sound, placing hands over eyes to shield them from a bright light, or reaching for an object. Perceptual–motor skills facilitate cognitive abilities, body awareness, spatial and directional awareness, and time–space orientation.

Perceptual–motor skills are fostered through activities that encourage the child to explore, experiment, and manipulate. Early childhood classrooms, for instance, include a variety of sensory activities: matching fragrance containers (olfactory), mixing and matching fabric patterns (visual) or textures (tactile), and cooking (taste). Musical and rhythmic activities integrate auditory and motor abilities as children respond to such elements as space, tempo, volume, and pitch (kinesthetic).

Children who do not master early sensory, perceptual, and motor skills can have difficulty with more sophisticated cognitive tasks in later school years.

Perceiving shapes necessary for forming letters and numbers later on, attending to context cues in picture books, responding adequately to tone of voice as a clue to another's message, and interpreting facial and body language cues of others are tasks that rely on sensory, motor, and perceptual abilities.

Body Awareness, Movement, and Simple Games

During the process of mastering basic locomotor skills, children develop an awareness of their bodies. This awareness includes not just the names and locations of body parts and what they can be willed to do, but also a growing sense that all body parts are interconnected and that their bodies have both abilities and limitations. Body awareness is an outgrowth of the child's visual, auditory, tactile, and kinesthetic perceptions. Body awareness includes the child's positive or negative perceptions and feelings about his or her physical characteristics and capabilities. Particularly important to body awareness are the child's kinesthetic perceptual abilities, that is, the awareness of the body as a whole that occupies space and how one's body fits into space, functions within it, and adjusts to it. The ability to move from place to place without running into people or stumbling over objects depends on vision, hearing, touch, and kinesthetic perception. Kinesthetic perception includes **laterality** (an internal sense of direction), **directionality** (the motoric expression of laterality), **left/right dominance**, and **balance**.

Body awareness is a powerful driving force in all aspects of the child's development: perceptual–motor, psychosocial, and cognitive. Body awareness is incorporated into the child's emerging sense of self and feelings of competence. Body awareness and confidence give the child a sense of control and motivate the child to attempt increasingly complex physical/motor activities.

Movement activities and simple games help to coordinate and refine fundamental body movements; establish laterality, directionality, balance, and left/right orientation; and enhance the development of more complex motor abilities. Four- and 5-year-olds especially enjoy movement activities and simple games as they continue to discover what their bodies can do. They enjoy responding to music in spontaneous and creative ways, pantomiming, playing follow-the-leader, and throwing and catching balls and bean bags. Balancing or hopping on one foot, jumping over obstacles, reaching the highest point, and walking a balance beam forward, sideways, and backward become challenging, self-affirming activities.

Jeremy and his friends, Caitlin, DeLisa, Jared, and Mac, have decided to play a racing game to see how fast they can run to the "faraway" tree on their kindergarten playground. They decide that Jeremy will tell them when to go. After he counts to three ("1 . . . 2 . . . 3 . . .") and shouts, "Go!," the five of them take off. DeLisa, who is slightly taller and heavier than her agemates and is quick of mind and movement, is the first off, followed by Caitlin, who has previously demonstrated well-coordinated large muscle control, though she is somewhat shorter than the rest of her agemates. Caitlin is followed by Mac, who is in the 80th percentile for height for boys of his age, though he is in the 40th percentile for weight. Mac is followed in the race by Jared and Jeremy, who are both in the 50th percentile for height and weight and have demonstrated average motor coordinations and abilities. (Without reading further, can you predict from these developmental descriptions how each child will perform in this game?)

laterality:
an awareness of an ability to use both sides of the body; a recognition of the distinction between left and right

directionality:
the application of the internal awareness of right and left to objects and movement

left/right dominance:
a neuromaturational preference for one or the other side of the body, as in handedness

balance:
a body awareness component in which postural adjustments prevent one from falling

The five run with energy and power. However, Jared stumbles and falls, skinning his knees; he leaves the race crying, to find his teacher. Jeremy continues his mighty effort to catch up with the others. DeLisa steps out of the race, panting and out of breath. Caitlin, short and fast, and Mac, tall with his long stride, arrive at the tree at the same time. Each believes that she or he got there first. An argument ensues, unfriendly words are exchanged, and Caitlin announces that she is going to "tell the teacher." Jeremy, in the meantime, fights back his tears. The game was his idea after all, and he fully expected to win the race. Disappointed at losing, he joins DeLisa, and the two determine that they are not going to play with Mac and Caitlin any more.

The wide ranges in physical/motor ability, sizes and body builds, and prior experiences place children variously at an advantage and a disadvantage, depending on the required skill. While physically active games for young children are most enjoyable when they are simple and, at least for the most part, child created, young children generally find competition frustrating, defeating, and unrewarding. Nevertheless, play that entails large motor challenges and activities are growth promoting and should be guided by sensitive adults toward outcomes that are enjoyable for every participant.

Child-created games characteristically entail the spontaneous establishment of rules, an important contribution to social and moral development, as we will see in later chapters. Hence, games serve important psychosocial functions in child development as well as encouraging and enhancing the physical and motor well-being of children.

Children with Special Needs

Many types of disabling conditions affect young children and with varying degrees of severity. The special needs of children generally fall into three categories:

1. *Developmental delay:* children who demonstrate delays in one or more of the following developmental domains:
   - Physical/motor: such as growth curves dramatically different from the norm for age; anomalies in gross, fine, and/or oral motor controls
   - Self-help skills: such as difficulties or inabilities to dress, feed, or use a toilet without assistance
   - Social–emotional behaviors: such as attachment problems, difficulty modulating emotions, and social interaction problems
   - Communication: such as limited use of language to communicate and inability to understand or respond to communications with others
   - Cognitive development: such as limited curiosity and interest in learning, lack of focus, difficulty learning, or unusual play behaviors or play themes
2. *Atypical development:* children whose patterns of development are different from their agemates, which include the following:
   - Sensorimotor anomalies: such as poor muscle tone, abnormal reflex activity, and sensory impairments
   - Atypical emotional/social patterns: such as atypical attachment behaviors, unusual social responses and expressions of emotions, or inappropriate self-targeted behaviors

- Atypical cognitive and language development: such as inability to focus and attend (attention span), learning and memory difficulties, difficulties associated with acquisition and use of language, and information-processing difficulties

3. *Medically diagnosed conditions:* children with numerous possible diagnoses, such as aphasia (profound lack of language), cerebral palsy, congenital muscular dystrophy, Down syndrome, drug withdrawal syndrome, failure to thrive, fetal alcohol syndrome, seizure disorders, and spinal cord injury.

RELATIONSHIP BETWEEN PHYSICAL/MOTOR DEVELOPMENT AND PSYCHOSOCIAL DEVELOPMENT

At ages 4 to 5 years, the child's self-concept is intimately associated with an awareness of his or her physical characteristics (hair, eye, and skin color; physical abilities; sex; etc.). The young child's physical characteristics and emerging capabilities also influence the child's interactions with others. These interactions provide positive and/or negative feedback, which plays a role in the formation of the self-concept. A child who is viewed as physically (or psychosocially) attractive may receive different feedback than a child who is viewed as unattractive or difficult. By the same token, a child who is viewed by others as having unusual features, such as certain hair, eye, or skin color, freckles, dimples, physical grace and poise, or other particularly noticeable features, often receives attention that may or may not be welcome to the child (even when the attention is meant to be complimentary, kind, or positive) and can influence the child's self-image and interactions with others. The child's responses to others vary along positive and negative lines. These interactions influence in both subtle and overt ways subsequent responses and interactions and, ultimately, the child's self-image, self-regard, and self-confidence.

This point is particularly poignant in the case of young children with disabilities, who sometimes have difficulty accepting and being accepted by others. Helping these children to develop their physical and motor attributes and self-help skills to the greatest extent possible builds self-confidence, which motivates further efforts and practice. This increased use of physical and motor abilities builds confidence and positive self-regard. When children feel accepted, appreciated, and self-confident and enjoy control over their bodies, their interpersonal relationships are enhanced.

RELATIONSHIP BETWEEN PHYSICAL/MOTOR DEVELOPMENT AND COGNITIVE DEVELOPMENT

As at earlier ages, children's emerging physical and motor capabilities expand their horizons and afford them new opportunities to learn about the world around them. The 4- to 5-year-old's interest and participation in real-world events that invite the use of motor abilities further cognitive development. A trip to a farm for a pony ride; assisting with selected household chores; responding to music with movement and dance; manipulating books to explore the world of print; performing a broad array of small motor tasks; taking some responsibility for

Movement activities and simple games help to coordinate and refine fundamental motor abilities.

one's own hygiene, health, and safety; and participating in the establishment of safety and health maintenance rules and procedures are some of the events that relate physical and motor development to cognitive development.

Learning to Be Responsible for One's Own Health and Safety

Children at age 4 and 5 years are beginning to understand the importance of such health and safety considerations as eating, sleeping, resting, and exercise and can now be taught to assume some responsibility for themselves. Of course, young children cannot be expected to protect themselves without adult supervision, teaching, and encouragement. Nevertheless, their cooperation can be elicited in these health and safety areas:

- Regular teeth brushing, frequent hand washing, and other hygienic practices
- Predictable naptime and bedtime routines
- Understanding the need for nutritious food rather than junk food
- Appreciating the need for regular medical and dental check-ups and immunizations
- Recognizing potential hazards (e.g., hot items, strangers, electrical items, poisons, unsafe toys, playground and other environmental hazards, streets, driveways, and other traffic hazards)
- Abiding by household and family rules (e.g., television usage and acceptable program content, guided choice of computer activities and electronic games, appropriate time and place for certain behaviors and activities)
- Consistently using transportation safety seats or restraints
- Answering the phone or door as instructed

- Understanding where to safely play with certain items, such as tricycles or other wheeled toys, and which toys or equipment require adult assistance
- Learning full name, address (with zip code), phone numbers (with area code), parent's name(s) and where to find their work phone numbers; how to call for help; and so on

Responsibility for one's own health and safety emerges slowly and sporadically over a course of many years. Children's emerging capabilities and growing sense of responsibility, however, never absolve the adult of responsibility for providing continuing and conscientious supervision and protection. It is easy to assume that young children are more capable in this area than they actually are, but their behaviors are at best inconsistent, owing to their limited long-term memory, limited or inconsistent opportunities to practice, adult inconsistencies in routines and expectations, distraction of more exciting things to do, and eagerness to explore and learn about other things. The major responsibility to provide safe, hygienic environments and developmentally appropriate experiences and expectations remains with adults. Adults continue to be the child's most powerful role models.

Gender Awareness and Gender Constancy

By age 3, children demonstrate gender awareness and identity by accurately labeling themselves and others as boys or girls. However, gender constancy, the realization that one's gender remains the same regardless of changes in appearance, age, clothing, hairstyles, or individual wishes, begins to emerge between the ages of 5 and 7 (Kohlberg, 1966). Development of gender constancy seems to follow a pattern, with children attributing gender constancy to themselves before others (Eaton & Von Bargen, 1981). The most frequently observed pattern is (1) gender constancy for self, (2) gender constancy for same-sex others, and (3) gender constancy for individuals of the opposite sex.

The emergence of gender constancy brings with it a growing awareness that boys and girls, and men and women, differ in a number of ways, not the least of which is anatomy. As children begin to realize that anatomy rather than other factors defines gender, they become interested in the human body. Young children are curious about the physiological differences between boys and girls and between men and women. They observe and compare the anatomies and behaviors of each, forming ideas, some stereotypical, about male and female anatomy, roles, and behaviors. They imitate male/female behaviors in their sociodramatic play, experimenting with "being" either male or female. Some of their behaviors evoke chagrin or consternation on the part of adults: asking direct questions about body parts and their functions, giggling about and teasing or ridiculing members of the opposite sex, engaging in "bathroom talk," and playing "doctor." These normal behaviors indicate a growing awareness of the differences between the sexes and are indicative of the earliest stages of sexuality (Chrisman & Couchenour, 2002). Responses to these behaviors should be positive and age-appropriately informing and should guide children toward acceptance and satisfaction in their gender identity.

Adult responses to these behaviors influence the outcomes of positive or negative gender identity and gender role acquisition. A frank, matter-of-fact approach is certainly preferable to shock, embarrassment, or avoidance. Children need adults to help them to learn about the differences between boys and girls and to do so with honest, straightforward answers to their questions. Providing accurate labels, discussing gender roles and behaviors, setting examples, and modeling healthy gender identity and self-acceptance are necessary to building accurate and positive concepts in children. Children must feel comfortable and safe asking questions as they arise. Adults must keep in mind that as children establish gender constancy, they are intensely interested in gender-role behaviors and are particularly interested in and attentive to gender-role models.

FACTORS INFLUENCING PHYSICAL AND MOTOR DEVELOPMENT

Genetic Makeup Revisited

Genes control the child's rate of development, dictating when motor abilities will emerge, growth spurts will occur, teeth will erupt, and the outer limits of height range will be achieved. Each individual has inherited a genetic blueprint from his or her parents. This blueprint determines such characteristics as sex, blood type, skin color, hair color and texture, eye color, potential mature height, temperament, sociability, and a host of other characteristics that make each person unique and explain the enormous array of differences among people. Optimal development relies on healthy genetic traits and supportive, healthy environments.

Because each child grows at her or his own pace, comparisons with siblings or agemates can be very misleading. Each child's growth occurs according to the child's biological blueprint and unique sets of experiences and interactions with the environment. Adults should be aware of their expectations and their reactions to individual developmental accomplishments. For instance, a parent or teacher who conveys disappointment when a child fails to achieve mastery over some valued task (e.g., using scissors, catching a ball, writing letters correctly) may impose unfair expectations on the child when the requisite biological maturity for such mastery is yet to emerge. Undue pride in developmental accomplishments over which the child has no control is equally misleading; the child is simply exhibiting observable manifestations of an inner developmental plan over which she or he has no conscious control.

In the emergence of attributes and skills, the interactions of heredity and environment undoubtedly play a role. Height and weight, for instance, depend on nutrition and other health factors. Motor coordination relies on opportunities to move about, explore, discover, and practice emerging abilities. Certain personality characteristics, such as activity level, fearfulness, and sociability, which seem to be inheritable traits, are influenced by interactions with others. Adequate health care, proper nutrition, avoidance of accidents and stress, appropriate expectations, and sociocultural factors all contribute to the full realization of a person's genetic potential. So we are reminded that while individuals bring blueprints for development with them, the development that emerges is intertwined with and dependent on environmental influences.

Sociocultural Influences Revisited

Cross-cultural studies have revealed that people from different ethnic groups vary in expected height, weight, and motor skills development. Although there are always exceptions, children of North American and European ancestry are generally shorter than children of African ancestry. Children of Asian ancestry are usually shorter than North American and European children. Differences in body proportions also reflect differences among racial and geographic groups. For instance, children of African descent develop relatively long legs and arms and narrow hips. In contrast, Asian children usually develop shorter legs and arms and broader hips.

Adults who are aware of individual differences among children are more accurate in their developmental observations and assessments. Opportunities for enhanced growth and development can be provided when adults are aware of individual and cultural attributes.

Inclusive Practices

With laws in place that mandate early screening and identification of children with disabilities, early diagnosis has resulted in timely intervention practices. Intervention services for young children with special needs include access to some or all of the following:

- Early identification
- Screening and assessment
- Assistive technology
- Vision and hearing evaluation and follow-up services
- Family counseling
- Medical and health care services
- Home visits
- Nutrition supervision
- Physical therapy
- Psychological services
- Speech and language therapy
- Transportation

As screening for at-risk children has become widespread, the potential for its abuse has become a concern. Professionals in child development and early childhood education stress the importance of standards in the selection of screening instruments and in the qualifications of individuals who screen and diagnose. Programs to which children are assigned must meet professional standards of quality and developmental appropriateness and must be judged to serve the best long-term interest of the child. Assessment for assignment to special programs is best achieved from a multifaceted approach that includes the use of standardized screening tests and medical examinations along with informal strategies that include focused observation in many contexts over extended periods of time, interviews and consultations with the child and family, and assessment of the *products* of children's work, the manner in which a child engages in work and play (*processes*), and the extent to which the child accomplishes expected goals or outcomes (*performance*). This type of assessment of young children yields comprehensive information about a child that can lead to more accurate diagnoses and can assist adults in planning growth-enhancing experiences for children (Puckett & Black, 2000; Puckett & Diffily, 2004).

During the assessment and placement process, children must be coached and prepared for their services assignments. If they are to attend an inclusive classroom, they, their families, and their teachers (and other resource personnel) need to collaborate in the preparation of the classroom and curricula to support the child's inclusion process. To prevent unwanted complications, such as poor adjustment and unsuccessful experiences, DeHaas-Warner (1994) suggested the following considerations:

1. The child's individual characteristics and needs
2. The parent's attitudes and concerns about the placement of their child in an inclusive setting
3. The program's physical and affective characteristics

General Health and Freedom from Disease or Injury

Children ages 4 and 5 are more likely to attend prekindergarten and kindergarten programs, and some are enrolled in before- and after-school programs in which they spend a considerable amount of time in the company of other children. Children in groups expose one another to a variety of illnesses—conjunctivitis (pink eye), lice, scabies, impetigo, ear infections, colds, flu, and an assortment of upper respiratory ailments. Children in preschool programs are at greater risk for contracting gastrointestinal infections with diarrhea.

To ensure continuing good health and freedom from diseases, homes, schools, and child care programs must follow a regimen of frequent and thorough cleaning and systematic observation of all children for signs of illness or infection. Providing children with regular, nutritious meals and snacks, predictable rest and sleep schedules, opportunities for vigorous play and exercise, and instruction in hygiene, and reducing stress-producing activities in children's lives, facilitate the maintenance of good health and growth-enhancing environments.

Healthy Routines

Predictable routines are essential to good health and a psychological sense of well-being. Daily schedules for children are best planned to include regular meal, snack, rest, and activity times, and opportunities to self-select what one wants to do. A general rule applied in early childhood programs and certainly applicable in the home is that of alternating quiet and active times throughout the child's day to avoid fatigue and overstimulation. Young children, in spite of their apparent excess energy, do fatigue quickly; they also tend to recover readily when provided brief rest periods. Intermittent rest times (quiet conversation, story reading, short naps, or simply dawdling) assure a healthier, happier day.

The *overscheduled* child is a phenomenon of modern-day child rearing. It is characterized by a daily schedule loaded with child care, preschool and/ or school attendance, academic requirements, homework, school-sponsored events, extracurricular lessons, sports, social activities, family commitments, appointments, parents' employer's requirements, and week-end family and faith-based obligations. Overscheduled children spend an inordinate amount of time in vehicles being transported to a plethora of places and activities. The physiological demands of overscheduling are enormous, and the psychological effects of stress associated with keeping a steady pace of activities and interactions with many different groups of people are not to be doubted. The effects of stress on brain growth and neurological development have been studied, and deleterious effects are possible (Perry, 1996, 1999). Some experts are expressing concern about the cumulative effect of years of this type of feverish activity, noting sleep disturbances, irritability, inattention, moodiness, and inability to "turn down" one's emotions after stressful or exciting events (Dahl, 1998). Many children lose interest and joy in their daily activities and exhibit signs of burnout at very early ages; their self-esteem, when measured against how well they think they are expected to perform in each of the activities, is diminished, and some experts believe that school dropout and teenage depression, substance abuse, and sexual activity are long-term consequences of overscheduling. Both school achievements and social and family interactions are at risk when daily schedules and expectations are excessive.

Nutrition

Children's diets must supply enough nutrients to meet the needs of growing bones and muscles, promote healthy formation and eruption of permanent teeth, and sustain continued growth and development of all body tissues and organs. Much energy is needed to sustain the high activity levels that are typical of 4- and 5-year-old children. More active children may need more food than less active ones of the same age and size.

Because preschool children have decreased their intake of milk, iron-fortified cereals, and nutrients such as calcium, phosphorus, iron, and vitamins A and C from levels consumed during the infant/toddler period and have not developed a taste for a wide variety of foods, particularly vegetables, there may be a need to expand the variety of foods available to them, with particular emphasis on nutrient-dense foods.

Appetites begin to wane as children get older, and food preferences and aversions begin to emerge (see Box 11.1). Parents and adults, anxious to provide adequate and nutritious meals and snacks for preschool children, are often perplexed when children show little interest in, or even distaste for, some foods. There are developmental explanations for these behaviors.

The eating behaviors of young children reflect their changing growth patterns and physiological and psychological needs. Children at ages 4 and 5 are growing less rapidly than they were in previous years and therefore require less nourishment to support their growth needs. At the same time, food preferences are emerging that reflect the child's growing ability to recognize and differentiate tastes, a desire to make choices, and a growing sense of autonomy and initiative, both at home and in other settings. The ability to help oneself to available foods and snacks at ages 4 and 5 fosters a sense of independence and control.

Children ages 4 through 5 are becoming more verbal, conversational, and social, and enjoy their interactions with others. For them, mealtimes can be particularly enjoyable, especially when parents and siblings convene to eat together or small groups of children share a meal or snack with one another and an adult in their center or school settings. The social context of eating can improve or impede the nutritional intake of young children, influencing attitudes toward eating and mealtimes and food acceptance patterns. Mealtimes that are hurried, stressful, or coercive or that are marked by negative interactions, threat, or punishment interfere with food intake, digestion, and the development of healthy attitudes toward foods and mealtimes. On the other hand, when young children experience mealtimes that are relaxed and conducive to pleasant conversation and free of coercion, their intake of nutritious foods is enhanced. In her extensive research on eating behaviors in young children, Birch and her colleagues demonstrated a number of childhood experiences that influence what and how much children choose to eat and the impact of various approaches to child feeding and nutrition on food acceptance patterns and childhood nutritional status (Birch & Fisher, 1998; Birch,

> ### BOX 11.1   Childhood Food Preferences
>
> Childhood food preferences reflect
>
> - Cultural practices and preferences
> - Peer and sibling influences
> - Television and other media advertising
> - Naturally occurring fluctuations in the child's interest in certain foods
> - Transitory "food jags"
> - The child's ability to manage the food—ease in self-feeding, chewing, swallowing
> - Food allergy
> - A temporary aversion to certain foods associated with an unpleasant experience (e.g., being reprimanded or embarrassed at a time when the food was being consumed; an illness associated with a particular food; same food served too often)
> - Associating food with a particularly pleasant memory (e.g., eating at grandparents' or a friend's house; a special occasion; a holiday dinner)
> - Appeal of the food based on temperature, texture, color, aroma, size of serving; compatibility with other foods on the plate; cleanliness of eating utensils, dishes, and eating surfaces; aesthetics associated with the table or eating surroundings
> - The child's level of cognition and accompanying ability to associate certain foods with good health and feeling good while recognizing food of little nutritional value and learning to reject such foods
> - Parental pressure to eat certain foods or "everything on your plate"

Johnson, Andersen, Peters, & Schulte, 1991; Birch, Johnson, & Fisher, 1995; Johnson & Birch, 1994). The following are examples of some of the research findings:

- Food preferences result from responses to a complex combination of stimulation involving taste, smell, appearance, and tactile characteristics, and change over time with increasing experience with foods.
- Learning and experiences within a child's cultural environment shape his or her food acceptance patterns.
- Generally, infants and young children do not readily accept new foods unless they are sweet.
- As exposure to a new food increases, the child's preference for it also increases; however, the child must at some point taste the food and sometimes must be exposed to the food as many as ten times before acceptance is achieved.
- When foods are given to children in positive social contexts, preferences for those foods are enhanced; however, when children are forced to eat nutritious foods to obtain rewards, liking for the food is reduced.
- Children appear to be innately biased to learn to prefer high-energy foods.

- Children may possess the ability to regulate how much to eat on the basis of the caloric content of the foods they eat over a number of meals, relying more on physiological sensitivity to caloric intake than adults do.
- While the amount of food consumed at individual meals can be highly variable from meal to meal at ages 2 to 5 years, children's daily overall calorie intake is fairly constant.
- Meager consumption of food at one meal is offset by greater consumption at later meals; these findings suggest that children tend to adjust their calorie needs over a 24-hour period.
- There are wide variations among children in their ability to regulate energy intake.
- Parents who are more controlling in their child-feeding strategies not only negatively affect their children's food acceptance patterns, but also negatively affect their children's ability to self-regulate energy intake, which leads to increases in body fat in these children.
- In the absence of adult coercion, young children meet their satiety needs.

Safety

The primary causes of injury to children ages 4 through 5 are automobile accidents, falls, burns, choking, poisoning, drowning, and firearms. Automobile accidents are the leading cause; more children are killed by automobiles as passengers or pedestrians than by any other hazard.

Transportation Safety.   Auto accidents are also the leading cause of brain damage, spinal cord injury, and mental retardation (Aronson, 1991). Many automobile injuries are preventable through proper use of approved car seats and seat restraints for children. Children with disabilities may need special, crashworthy devices and equipment to be safely transported.

Playground Safety.   Playground safety is another concern during the early years. Playgrounds are coming under serious scrutiny as the number and seriousness of playground accidents continue to rise. Joe Frost, a nationally recognized expert on playground design and safety, states, "American public playgrounds are perhaps the worst in the world. They are hazardous. In addition, most playgrounds are designed as though children's play needs are limited to swinging from bars and running across open spaces, as though children cannot think, symbolize, construct, and create" (Frost, 1992, p. 6).

Indeed, safe playgrounds for children can be designed to encourage productive, constructive play that engages physical/motor and cognitive abilities and encourages social interactions. However, playground designs have traditionally included equipment that encourages only parallel play and have been characterized by equipment that poses maintenance problems and injury hazards. Older playgrounds often have equipment designed for older children. Contemporary playground designers are paying closer attention to construction materials and designs that facilitate constructive types of play for different age groups, provide safe surfaces underneath playground equipment, and take into account maintenance and repair considerations and the types of injuries that occur on playgrounds and their frequencies.

Some guidelines offered by experts on playground safety include the following (Frost, Wortham, & Reifel, 2001; Rivkin, 1995; U.S. Consumer Product Safety Commission, 1997):

- Children should always be supervised on playgrounds and encouraged to use the equipment that is most suited to their age and size and should be assisted with the equipment as needed.
- Playgrounds and equipment should be regularly inspected and conscientiously maintained.
- Soft surfaces should be provided underneath playground equipment to reduce the risk of injury from falls (sand, 10 inches deep; wood chips, 12 inches deep; rubber outdoor mats).
- Guardrails at least 38 inches high should surround platforms.
- Platforms should be no higher than 6 feet above the ground.
- There should be no vertical or horizontal spaces less than 3½ inches wide or more than 9 inches wide, which would allow a small child's head to become entrapped.
- Moving parts should be enclosed to protect children or their clothing from entanglement.
- Construction materials should be chosen with regional climate conditions in mind (metal slides, for instance, can become hot enough to burn in warmer climates; painted metal surfaces chip and rust in wet climates).
- Construction materials should be chosen with safety in mind: swing seats, for example, are safer if constructed of rubber or canvas than of wood or metal.

Outdoor play is an essential part of the child's day.

• Placement of equipment should also be considered (a sufficient distance from vehicular and pedestrian traffic areas; a sufficient distance from other equipment to prevent collisions; 6 feet or more from walls or fences).

Toys, Play Equipment, and Household Safety.   In addition to playground design and equipment, reports of injuries from toys, home exercise equipment, children's trampolines, garage doors, and electric garage door openers are on the increase. Box 11.2 describes the wise choice of toys, play equipment, and safety gear. Most common sources of injury from home exercise equipment are entrapment of fingers or toes in stationary bicycle chains or wheel spokes. Eighty-three percent of extremity amputations in children were reported to have resulted from the children's touching moving parts of various home exercise equipment (American Academy of Pediatrics, 1995).

BOX 11.2   Wise Selection of Toys, Play Equipment, and Safety Gear

1. Know the age, capabilities, and interests of the individual child for whom the item is intended.

2. Scrutinize the toy, play equipment, or safety gear thoroughly, and read labels and instructions carefully.

   a. For what age child is the item intended?
   b. Are special skills or knowledge needed to use the item?
   c. Is the item appropriate given the child's large and/or small motor abilities, cognitive abilities, and interests?
   d. Is it made of nontoxic materials (avoid items that carry wording such as "harmful if swallowed," "avoid inhalation," "avoid skin contact," and "use with adequate ventilation").
   e. Is it motorized, electrical, or battery operated?
   f. Is it manufactured by a reputable firm? (Check Consumer Products Safety Commission reports or child health alerts and other publications for recall and safety histories of toys and play equipment.)
   g. Does the item do what the manufacturer claims it will do?
   h. Is the item durable?

3. Examine the item for hazards such as lead-based paint, sharp or protruding points or edges, weak construction, small parts that can be swallowed or cause choking (watch for eyes, buttons, bells, and other features on dolls and stuffed toys), and flammable materials.

4. Determine what aspect of development is enhanced through use of the item.

   a. Physical development: large motor; small motor; prehension; pincer movements; eye–hand, hand–mouth, and eye–foot coordination
   b. Cognitive: exploration, curiosity, questions, solving problems, forming concepts, connecting ideas or actions, cause-and-effect understanding, making associations, further inquiry and new ideas
   c. Language and literacy: conversation; labels; new concepts; questions; interest in symbols (signs, letters, numerals); vocabulary and creative use of language through rhymes, storytelling, role playing, songs, and poetry
   d. Psychosocial: pure enjoyment, catharsis and therapy, symbolic play, sociodramatic play, interactions with others, expression of feelings, sense of self-sufficiency and self-confidence, fantasy, imagination, prosocial understandings

5. Determine whether the item can be used in a variety of ways and whether it will sustain interest over an extended period of time.

There were 83,400 trampoline-related injuries in 1996, prompting the American Academy of Pediatrics to reissue its earlier statement that trampolines should never be used in the home environment (inside or out), in routine gym classes, or on outdoor playgrounds. Sixty-six percent of injured children were ages 5 through 14 years old, and 10 percent were 4 years old or younger (U.S. Consumer Product Safety Commission, National Electronic Injury Surveillance System [NEISS], 1996). Data from the NEISS (1991 to 1996) reveal that trampoline injuries occur in spite of warning labels, public education, and adult supervision, and occur with the following frequencies: 45 percent of trampoline injuries involve the lower extremities (legs, feet) in the form of strains or sprains; 30 percent affect the upper extremities (usually fractures of the arms and hands); and 14 percent involve head and face injuries, lacerations, concussions, and neck and spinal cord injuries. Deaths from trampoline injuries usually result from cervical spinal cord injury (American Academy of Pediatrics, 1999a; Smith, 1998; U.S. Consumer Product Safety Commission, National Electronic Injury Surveillance System, 1996).

Garage doors are the largest piece of moving equipment in a home and should be treated as a potential hazard to child safety. Most accidents involving garage doors occur when children have access to electronic door openers, activating the door and becoming entrapped under it or getting fingers or hands injured by moving door parts. Although many types of garage-door-opening devices are in use, garage doors manufactured since 1991 are required to have a reversing mechanism that causes the door to automatically back up if it touches an object in its path. Doors installed after 1993 are required to have photo eyes connected to the bottom of the track that will cause the door to reverse when its invisible beam is broken. Nothing has to physically touch these photo-beamed doors before they reverse. Guidelines for garage door safety include the following:

- Garage doors and door-opening mechanisms are best installed by professionals who are well acquainted with the product and its installation and use and can advise on proper use and safety precautions.
- The wall control panel for garage doors should be installed out of a child's reach (at least five feet above the ground).
- Remote controls should not be handled by young children.
- Children should be instructed not to play underneath the area where garage doors close.
- Users should stay in full view of a moving door until it is completely closed or open.
- Never race to beat the door as it is closing.
- As with all mechanized equipment, adults should model appropriate use and safety precautions.

Another common injury to young children is burns. Many young children are burned by tipped containers of hot food or drink, scalding bath water, microwave-heated foods (which often have hot spots), heating equipment, candles, matches, and cigarette lighters. All of these injuries are preventable. Children generally should not be in a food preparation area unless they are involved in a preparation-related activity that is being very closely supervised. Because serious burns have resulted from undetected hot spots in microwaved foods, both infant formula manufacturers and pediatricians advise against heating foods for infants, toddlers, and young children in the microwave (American Public Health Association & American Academy of Pediatrics, 2002). When a microwave is used, food should be stirred, then tested for hot spots, then cooled to a safe temperature before serving. Bathwater temperatures can be regulated by setting hot water heaters on lower temperatures. Heating equipment should be placed safely behind guards or out of child use areas.

Choking in young children can be prevented by making careful decisions about what food to serve and how to serve it. Infants and toddlers are generally at higher risk for choking because of their tendency to put things into their mouths, their immature chewing and swallowing mechanisms, and their distractibility. Four- and 5-year-olds are also prone to choking, however. The foods and objects that are most often associated with choking in young children are any small item less than half an inch in diameter, nuts, seeds, spherical or cylinder-shaped foods and objects, buttons, small toys, rocks, grapes, pieces of hot dog, round hard candies, and items of unusual or unfamiliar consistencies such as chewing gum, popcorn, corn or potato chips, some uncooked vegetables and fruits, sticky foods (peanut butter, caramel candy, dried fruits, raisins), and hard-to-chew meats. The following suggestions can lower the risk of choking:

- Cook foods to a softness that is pierceable by a fork.
- Substitute thinly sliced meats and well-cooked hamburger for hot dogs.
- Cut foods into manageable, bite-size pieces; avoid slippery round shapes.
- Be sure to remove all packaging from foods, such as bits of clinging cellophane and paper.
- Remove bones in chicken, meats, and fish.
- Remove seeds and pits from fruits.
- Avoid the snacks and foods listed in the preceding paragraph.

In addition to careful selection and preparation of foods, supervision at mealtimes and snack times is a must. Children should be seated when eating, be encouraged to eat slowly, and avoid talking and laughing with food in their mouths. Children should not eat while traveling in a car, since sudden jolts and stops can catapult food into the back of the mouth. Moreover, maneuvering a car out of traffic to tend to a choking child compounds the risk. Every adult should become familiar with the American Red Cross first aid procedures for handling a choking incident.

Poisoning is another major safety hazard for young children. Children can breathe toxins from polluted air, ingest some toxins by mouth, or absorb some poisons through the skin. Hazards exist in many forms: medicines, pesticides, aerosol sprays, gases, dusts, paints and solvents, commercial dyes, various art materials (inks, solvent-based glues, chalk dust, tempera paint dust, some crayons, paints, and clay powders). Toxins are also found in building materials (asbestos, formaldehyde, lead-based paint), lead-containing dishes and ceramics, tobacco smoke, and radon gas in soil.

Prevention of childhood poisoning involves both keeping toxic substances away from children and keeping children away from places where environmental toxins pose a hazard. At home, in child care centers, and at school, medicines, cleaning supplies, fertilizers, pesticides, and other toxins must be kept well beyond the child's reach and stored in locked cabinets. Child care center and school licensing and accreditation standards, city ordinances, and state and federal regulations must be followed, and all potentially poisonous products must be used in strict accordance with physicians', pharmacists', or manufacturers' instructions.

Young children and water create an additional safety concern. Beginning quite early in the toddler period, children must be taught to respect water. Infants, toddlers, and young children should never be left unattended in bathtubs, wading pools, or swimming areas. Basic water safety instruction for young children includes precautions such as wearing appropriate water safety devices, proper use of water toys such as floats, going into water only when an adult is present, avoiding breakable toys and dishes around bodies of water, and walking carefully on wet surfaces. Adults must establish, demonstrate, model, and enforce water safety rules with children, know rescue techniques and cardiopulmonary resuscitation, and be especially vigilant around bodies of water. Providing swimming lessons for young children at ages 4 and 5 becomes controversial when adults develop a false sense of confidence in their children's abilities. For young children, the ability to swim is not accompanied by mature judgments about when and where to swim and what to do in an emergency.

Opportunities to Interact, Explore, and Play

Another factor influencing growth and development is the opportunity to interact with others, explore, and play. Children have a natural impulse to be active—to run, climb, jump, hop, skip, shout, and ride wheeled toys. Opportunities to develop and use these abilities occur when children are provided with the space and developmentally appropriate equipment with which to do so. Opportunities to use and coordinate small muscles also occur through experiences with a variety of manipulative materials and self-help activities. Because children need to be physically active, efforts to restrain and keep them quiet for long periods of time not only are difficult, but are actually unhealthy for children. Preschool and kindergarten programs that require children to sit for long periods of time, to work at tables or desks, or to listen to teacher-directed lessons for extended periods of time are developmentally inappropriate because they curtail opportunities for more active and beneficial pursuits. Programs that promote physical and motor development provide activities that meet children's need for movement, for manipulation, and for social interactions and pretend play. For optimal health and physical development, each child's day should include opportunities for movement about the classroom and the learning centers; for singing, creative movement, and dance; and for use of equipment requiring large motor coordination. Outdoor play should be a daily event in every child's life in which running, jumping, skipping, and other large motor activities and games can build the type of physical fitness that includes both health- and performance-related components (Gallahue & Ozmun, 1998).

HEALTH AND WELL-BEING ISSUES RELATED TO CHILDREN AGES FOUR THROUGH FIVE

Nutrition Issues

As mentioned earlier, adults are responsible for providing nutritious and adequate diets for children. On the other hand, since hunger can be felt only by the child and children can be trusted to regulate their own food intake, the child should exercise control over how much to eat (Birch & Fisher, 1998). Helping children to establish regular eating times, avoiding unnecessary snacks that are high in calories but low in nutrients, and encouraging adequate amounts of exercise and activity assist children in developing sound nutritional habits and food acceptance patterns that will support their growth and ensure long-term healthy outcomes.

A number of nutrition-related issues have surfaced in recent years, including the widely publicized increase in obesity among Americans and its prevalence among younger and younger children; the changing American meal plan characterized by speedily prepared foods that can be eaten on the run; the overabundance and availability of calorie-rich, nutrient-poor snacks; and the increase in nutrition-related illnesses among children, including elevated cholesterol levels, diabetes, high blood pressure, and food-related allergies. Additionally, there are health issues associated with undernutrition, which include compromised growth and development, higher susceptibility to disease, accident proneness, and emotional and learning disabilities (Weinreb, et al., 2002).

Obesity could be an issue of concern among 4- and 5-year-old children, and the need for a well-balanced diet rich in protein, vitamins, and minerals and low in fats and sugars is recommended. As this age is one in which growth is still rapid (though not as rapid as in previous years), immediate professional attention to unusual weight, height, and growth progress is necessary so that intervention, prevention, or corrective measures can be initiated to assure adequate nutrients to sustain growth while teaching and promoting other behaviors, such as physical activity and exercise to maintain healthy bodies. Learning how to make good food choices and to avoid high-fat, high-sugar, and low-nutrient foods can begin at this age, as can learning to recognize that many foods and snacks advertised in magazines, junk mail, billboards, and television do not make people healthier. Children can be taught about the Food Guide Pyramid and engaged in planning meals and snacks based on it. When young children participate in this manner, they begin to understand the importance of good nutrition, and begin to develop more nutritious food preferences. Becoming nutrient savvy at an early age is a powerful defense against risky food behaviors (which often become habitual) and later food-related illnesses. A further discussion of obesity is given in Chapter 14.

Types and Quality of Early Care and Education

Most children enter some type of formal schooling around age 5. Many now begin the process of schooling at age 4. Some children enter nursery school and Head Start programs at age 3, and others are introduced to child care and education programs when only a few weeks old. Many children 3 years old and less are enrolled in public schools through special education programs designed to ameliorate developmental issues. All states now provide public school kindergartens for 5-year-old children, and most states offer prekindergarten programs for 4-year-olds. While still costly and not readily available to all who need it, child care programs have also been on the rise. Child care has become a basic necessity for many families along with food, clothing, shelter, and health care. It is estimated that 13 million children in the United States spend some or all of their day being cared for by someone other than their parents (Carnegie Corporation of New York, 1996).

Although excellent child care and early childhood programs exist around the country in both private and public settings, studies about low-quality programs and their effects on child development are disturbing. High-quality child care is defined as providing "a nurturing, safe, and stimulating environment for children that promotes their healthy growth and development" (Child Welfare League of America, 1997). Yet one extensive study reported that "Child care at most centers in the United States is poor to mediocre," failing to meet state or professional guidelines for quality (Helburn, 1995). This study, in which four states (California, Colorado, Connecticut, and North Carolina) collaborated to study the relationship between cost, quality, and child outcomes, found that across the United States, one in seven centers provides a level of care that promotes healthy development, seven in ten centers provide mediocre care, and one in eight provides care that is so poor that it threatens the health and safety of children.

Although this series of studies focused on child care arrangements, concern for the appropriateness of experiences that children have in more formal settings such as kindergartens and prekindergartens is also relevant. With test-driven curricula designed to meet political agendas for school improvement and accountability, younger and younger children are being subjected to experiences that are beyond widely held expectations for their age. As prekindergarten and kindergarten curriculums mimic upper-grade paradigms, young children are deprived of essential growth-promoting experiences, not the least of which are opportunities for physical and motor activity, an essential for neurological development and overall health and well-being.

Length of Child Care Day and Multiple Caregivers

Some public school programs for young children are half-day (2½ to 3½ hours), some are all-day (5½ or 6 to 7½ hours), and some range from 9 to 11 hours. Child care programs (center-based day care and family day homes) range from hourly care to 24 hours. The number of hours per setting per child each day varies. Many children of working parents are enrolled in before- and after-school programs, resulting in as many as three different sets of nonparental caregivers (before, during, and after school). For some of these children, transportation from one setting to another requires additional hours.

The psychosocial impact of these multiple relationships is discussed in later chapters. Concerns for physical and motor development center on stress and fatigue associated with long days, multiple settings, various adult personalities and expectations, changing groups of children, and varying standards and group rules for protecting health and safety. Preventing fatigue and reducing stress entail the following:

- Regularly scheduled and nutritious meals and snacks and ready access to toilet facilities and to fresh drinking water
- Regularly scheduled rest and naptimes, as well as rest periods as needed
- Teachers and staff who have knowledge of and training in child development and understand the effects of multiple settings and caregivers and long days on children
- Provision of outdoor playtimes for children to provide stress-relieving fresh air, sunshine, exercise, and spontaneous play
- Allowing children to make as many choices throughout the day as is reasonable and possible—choices about learning centers, materials and activities, playmates, snacks, and so on

- Opportunities and safe spaces to play alone without pressures to interact with others
- Allowing children to participate in classroom and group rule making to decrease the stress of dealing with multiple sets of rules and standards
- Careful observation of and attention to general health characteristics of individual children and prompt attention to signs of stress, fatigue, and/or impending illness

The complexities involved in providing multiple services through multiple settings and programs create a need for collaboration, coordination, and cooperation among all overlapping programs and services for children and their families. In recent years, many states have begun such initiatives to bring comprehensive services to children and their families (Kagan & Cohen, 1997; National Governors' Association, 1997). Changing patterns of length of day and length of school year in public schools will necessitate serious efforts to establish linkages among Head Start programs, child care providers, public schools, health and social services, and families.

Meeting the Needs of Children with Disabilities

Including children with disabilities is both an opportunity and a challenge for early childhood programs and professionals. Planning for the safety of all children and preparing to meet the health-supporting requirements of children with special needs is integral to successful inclusion practices. There is always the need for early childhood professionals to establish effective and ongoing communication with parents and other professionals who are involved in the care and education of children with special needs. Classroom layouts and other arrangements may need to be altered to facilitate the use and enjoyment of materials and activities. Special dietary requirements need to be met and considered in classroom food and nutrition lessons, snacks, parties, and other food-related events. Children with visual or hearing difficulties require appropriate adjustments in seating and in the design and placement of classroom visual materials (bulletin boards, charts, art displays, and so on). Toileting areas need to be reassessed, as does shelving and space for personal belongings. Furniture arrangements and pathways need to be configured to accommodate crutches, walkers, wheelchairs, or other assistive equipment.

Special attention must be given to daily health routines—medications, meals and snacks, access to drinking water, toileting, rest and exercise, personal hygiene, and classroom cleanliness and order. The social and intellectual climate of the classroom must be accepting, comfortable, and psychologically safe. The teacher and other adults play an important role in modeling and teaching good health habits, as well as acceptance and respect for all individuals.

Preventing Accidents and Spread of Disease Among Children in Groups

In the quest for higher performance standards at all levels of child care and education, cognitive and academic issues have come to overshadow both the teaching of nutrition, health, and safety and the importance of professional planning to meet the nutrition, health, and safety needs of children in group settings. It is thus quite enlightening that in ordering early childhood professional competency goals, the

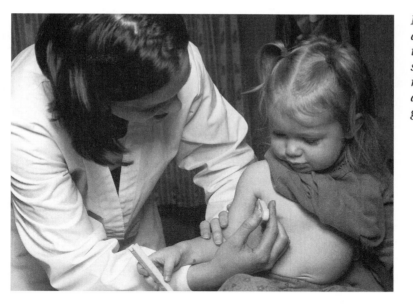

Monitoring children's health helps to prevent the spread of communicable diseases among children in groups.

Child Development Associate (CDA) credentialing program places child health and safety first of six major competency categories (Council for Early Childhood Professional Recognition, 1992): "To establish and maintain a safe, healthy learning environment." This competency is demonstrated by a CDA candidate's ability to

- provide a safe environment to prevent and reduce injury;
- promote good health and nutrition and provide an environment that contributes to the prevention of illness;
- use space, relationships, materials, and routines as resources for constructing an interesting, secure, and enjoyable environment that encourages play, exploration, and learning (Council for Early Childhood Professional Recognition, 1992, p. 5).

Standards for safety and health protection of children in group care have existed since the beginning of the twentieth century through governmental bodies and professional organizations. Concern over the spread of disease in early childhood settings in recent years has prompted considerable attention and renewed efforts of professional and medical groups to encourage policies and practices that ensure the health and safety of all children in group settings. Standards articulated by the American Public Health Association and the American Academy of Pediatrics are comprehensive and exemplary (American Public Health Association & American Academy of Pediatrics, 2002).

Because children in groups share environmental surfaces, such as tabletops, shelving and other furnishings, toys, sinks, and toileting areas, and are inclined to share food with unwashed hands, the spread of disease is inevitable if precautions are not taken. Further, young children are still inconsistent in health and hygiene habits, such as washing face and hands, using and then discarding facial tissue to contain a sneeze or cough or clear a runny nose, and using toilet tissue. Bandages also present problems, as young children love to display this symbol of injury and bravery. Taking the bandage off, examining the wound beneath it, and attempting to replace the bandage or carelessly leaving it about where others might handle it are common occurrences. To prevent the spread of infectious disease, it is necessary to establish routines and behavior habits that include

- frequent and thorough handwashing with soap and warm water;
- teaching children proper handwashing techniques and requiring handwashing after toileting, before and after eating, after coughing or sneezing, and at other appropriate times;
- cleaning toys, clothing/diaper-changing tables, and play surfaces with a disinfecting solution (commercial, or a mixture of one-fourth cup of bleach to one gallon of water);
- wearing barrier gloves when cleaning areas contaminated with blood, vomit, or other bodily fluids;
- observing children for signs or symptoms of illness and isolating an ill child until a parent can be summoned;
- providing nutritious foods, snacks, beverages, and fresh drinking water;
- maintaining healthy, predictable schedules of meals, snacks, rest, and play;
- maintaining clean and hygienic surroundings.

ROLE OF THE EARLY CHILDHOOD PROFESSIONAL

Enhancing Physical and Motor Development in Children Ages Four through Five

1. Provide safe and healthy surroundings for the child.
2. Provide for the child's nutritional needs.
3. Oversee protection of the child's health through immunizations and other protections from disease.
4. Encourage regular dental examinations.
5. Establish healthy routines for rest, sleep, play, and activity.
6. Control the stress-producing events in the child's life.
7. Provide encouragement for emerging large and small motor abilities and body awareness.
8. Provide age-appropriate and developmentally appropriate toys, equipment, and materials for the child.
9. Ensure the child's safety through adequate supervision, monitoring the types and condition of toys, materials, and equipment, and removing environmental hazards.
10. Provide opportunities for satisfying and supportive psychosocial interactions with parents, other adults, and other children.
11. Facilitate the child's awareness of health and safety practices.
12. Encourage a sense of responsibility for one's own health maintenance and safety.

KEY TERMS

balance	health-related fitness	performance-related fitness
dexterity	laterality	prehension
directionality	left/right dominance	

REVIEW STRATEGIES AND ACTIVITIES

1. Review the key terms in this chapter individually or with a classmate.

2. Visit a school playground during recess for kindergarten and for second or third grade. Compare the types of activities and games in each group, including those used by children who are physically challenged. How do the activities differ? How do the children's large motor abilities in the older, younger, and physically challenged groups compare? How might recess be used to enhance physical and motor fitness in all children?

3. Plan a week of nutritious snacks for young children using a calorie and nutrient guide. What nutrients will children derive from these snacks? How many calories will be supplied?

4. Visit a toy store. Using the information in Box 11.2, make a list of acceptable and unacceptable toys or equipment for 4- and 5-year-old children. Consider culture, gender, and challenges faced by children with special needs.

5. With your classmates, develop a home safety checklist. Inspect your home for health and safety hazards for your children or children who may visit in your home. What changes will you need to make?

6. You have interviewed for a teaching position at three different child care centers. What characteristics of each center and its expectations will influence your choice?

7. Invite a pediatrician or pediatric nurse to speak to the class. Ask about his or her perceptions of the health status of today's children. What are this professional's greatest concerns about child health today? How might parents promote optimal growth and development in their children?

FURTHER READINGS

American Public Health Association & American Academy of Pediatrics. (2002). *Caring for our children: National health and safety performance standards: Guidelines for out-of-home child care programs.* Washington, DC, and Elk Grove Village, IL: Authors.

Aronson, S. (2003). *Healthy young children: A manual for programs* (4th ed.). Washington, DC: National Association for the Education of Young Children.

Brown, W. H., & Conroy, M. A. (1997). *Including and supporting preschool children with developmental delays in early childhood classrooms.* Little Rock, AR: Southern Early Childhood Association.

Greenman, J. (1999). *Places for childhoods: Making quality happen in the real world.* Redman, WA: Child Care Information Exchange.

Kostelnick, M. J., Onaga, E., Rhode, B., & Whiren, A. (2002). *Children with special needs.* New York: Teachers College Press.

McCraken, J. B. (1999). *Playgrounds: Safe and sound.* Washington, DC: National Association for the Education of Young Children.

Perry, J. P. (2001). *Outdoor play: Teaching strategies with young children.* New York: Teachers College Press.

Sanders, S. W. (2002). *Active for life: Developmentally appropriate movement programs for young children.* Washington, DC: National Association for the Education of Young Children.

OTHER RESOURCES

Alliance to End Childhood Lead Poisoning
 www.aeclp.org
American Academy of Pediatrics
 Brochures (guidelines for parents) on numerous topics are available through local pediatricians' offices. Some example titles are as follows:
 Ear infections and children
 Your child's eyes
 Anemia and your young child
 Choking prevention and first aid for infants and children
 Common childhood infections
 Your child and the environment
 Know the facts about HIV and AIDS
 Allergies in children: Guidelines for parents
American Academy of Pediatrics
 Healthy Child Care America
 www.healthychildcare.org
American Academy of Pediatrics
 Child passenger safety
 www.aap.org/family/cps.htm
Americans with Disabilities Act Accessibility Guidelines to Play Areas
 www.access-board.gov/play/Finalrule.htm
International Food Information Council
 www.ific.org
NAEYC
 1509 16 Street, NW
 Washington, DC 20036-1426
 800-424-2460; Fax: 202-328-1846; e-mail: resource—sales@naeyc.org
National Association for the Education of Young Children
 Poster: *Rx for Keeping Healthy in Group Programs*
 (Inquire about price and related materials)
National Highway Traffic Safety Administration
 Child passenger safety resources
 www.nhtsa.dot.gov/people/injury/childps/
National Institute of Child Health and Human Development
 http://www.nichd.nih.gov/default.htm
National Resource Center for Health and Safety in Child Care
 http://nrc.uchsc.edu
National Safety Council
 http://www.nsc.org
Play Safe, Be Safe
 www.playsafe@fireproofchildren.com
 www.plasafebesafe.com
U.S. Consumer Product Safety Commission
 Childproofing your home:
 12 safety devices to protect your children (item 618F) (1999). Free brochure.
 Consumer Information Center
 Department 618F
 Pueblo, CO 81009
 Phone: (888) 8-PUEBLO

CHAPTER TWELVE

Psychosocial Development: Ages Four Through Five

And the first step, as you know, is always what matters most, particularly when we are dealing with those who are young and tender. That is the time when they are taking shape and when any impression we choose to make leaves a permanent mark.

PLATO

After studying this chapter, you will demonstrate comprehension by:

▶ Relating selected theories to the study of psychosocial development during ages 4 through 5

▶ Discussing selected psychosocial experiences associated with brain growth and neurological development during the preschool years.

▶ Describing major social and emotional milestones in psychosocial development during this period.

▶ Identifying factors that influence earliest psychosocial development.

▶ Describing the role of adults in healthy psychosocial development of 4- and 5-year-old children.

344

In contrast to children during the turbulent toddler period, 4- and 5-year-olds are composed. Refinements in motor abilities have facilitated self-help and autonomy. Advances in cognitive development have sharpened perceptions and enhanced the ability to understand. Language development has opened new and more effective communications, and an increasing ability to delay gratification of needs and desires is evident in more patient and negotiable interactions with others. The desire for and enjoyment of agemates has expanded the child's social circle beyond attachment persons, and play behaviors are more focused, purposeful, and cooperative. These developments result in a period during which the child is socially more amiable and compliant and emotionally more controlled and predictable.

THEORETICAL PERSPECTIVES ON PSYCHOSOCIAL DEVELOPMENT: AGES FOUR THROUGH FIVE

Effects of Earlier Experiences on Four- and Five-Year-Old Children

By the time a child is 4 or 5 years old, he or she has amassed a range of experiences that have influenced the course of development in a myriad of ways. Most child development theorists place a great deal of importance on the types and quality of experiences children have from birth through the first 3 to 4 years.

As the quotation by Plato suggests, for centuries philosophers and psychologists have hypothesized that events in the earliest years of a child's life influence later development, often in critical ways. Centuries after Plato's admonitions, philosophers, theorists, and scientists continue to study the relationship between early experiences during infancy and childhood and later development and

345

behavior. Sigmund Freud's (1905/1930) psychoanalytic theory, for instance, proposed that experiences and conflicts occurring during early psychosexual stages of development have lasting effects on later personality development and interpersonal relationships. Freud placed considerable importance on the mother–infant relationship in influencing a person's ability to relate to others throughout life.

Building on Freud's work, Erik Erikson's theory of psychosocial development (1963) supported an early experience/later development hypothesis. Successful outcomes at each of Erikson's eight stages of personality development are thought to prepare the child for subsequent stages culminating in a personality that is characterized as having ego integrity, or, as Erikson put it, knowing "how to be a follower of image bearers in religion and in politics, in the economic order and in technology, in aristocratic living and in the arts and sciences. Ego integrity, therefore, implies an emotional integration which permits participation by followership as well as acceptance of the responsibility of leadership" (Erikson, 1963, p. 269). Certainly, a goal of early childhood development is to provide the essential experiences that can lead to a well-integrated personality.

ethology: the scientific study of behavior

Studies by Bowlby, Ainsworth, and other theorists in **ethology** have examined the effects of early attachments on later psychosocial development (Zeanah, 1999). It is apparent that secure attachments can be interrupted by withdrawal of the attachment person from the relationship through such events as maternal or paternal debilitating physical or psychological illness, marital discord, multiple foster care assignments, reversal of adoption decisions, and a host of other disruptive circumstances. Such circumstances are often associated with attachment disorders that interfere with optimal psychosocial development. Contemporary efforts to diagnose and classify attachment disorders have noted various types of behaviors that are associated with disturbed attachment processes during infancy. The following are some of the behaviors outlined by Zeanah, Mammen, and Lieberman (1993, p. 346):

- Atypical expressions of affection in two extremes: lack of warm and affectionate interactions with potential attachment persons and/or promiscuous or nondiscriminate expressions of affection involving unfamiliar people
- Atypical comfort-seeking behaviors when hurt, frightened, or ill, either failing to seek help from a trusted attachment person or doing so in an ambivalent manner
- Excessive dependency behaviors or an inability to seek and use adult support when needed
- Poor compliance behaviors or compulsive compliance
- Failure to ascertain a caregiver's presence and/or support in unfamiliar situations
- Oversolicitous or punitive and controlling responses to caregivers
- Detached behaviors upon reunion following a separation, engaging in avoidant behaviors or anger outbursts, or not showing affection

In studies of healthy attachments, securely attached infants have been shown to be more socially competent on entering preschool and more responsive to their agemates in kindergarten (Stroufe, Carlson, & Schulman, 1993; Thompson, 1999). In other studies, securely attached children were found to be less dependent on adults and more curious than were children who had been insecurely attached (Stroufe, Fox, & Pancake, 1983), managed stress more competently (Gumar et al., 1996), and were more competent in problem-solving and memory tasks in preschool (Belsky, Spritz, & Crnic, 1996). Such studies of early attachment successes and failures support the theories that early attachment experiences influence long-term outcomes in psychosocial development.

Again, early therapeutic intervention with at-risk parents and their infants may redirect the interactional dynamics between mother and infant to foster positive outcomes. In nonparental caregiving situations, stable, predictable, supportive relationships with caregivers who are emotionally available are crucial. But we must not paint a picture that is too bleak. It is important to know that over the long term, the outcomes of both secure and insecure attachments are subject to a number of intervening influences. Children who are insecurely attached to one parent may find security and support through a strong attachment to the other or perhaps to a member of the extended family or some other important adult in their lives (Denham & Weissberg, 2003; Rosen & Rothbaum, 1993). It is also comforting to note that an insecure attachment need not inevitably lead to negative outcomes if an intervening secure attachment takes place. The extent to which the attachment experience (secure or insecure) has long-term consequences depends on the length of time the child experiences a particular quality of attachment (Lamb, 1987) and the nuturing quality of the caregiver (Dozier, Albus, Stovall, & Bates, 2002). Secure attachments during the infant and toddler periods pave the way for a smoother transition into Bowlby's phase 4 of the attachment process.

Around age 3, according to Bowlby's theory of attachment, children have entered phase 4, which is characterized by *partnership behaviors,* in which they are gaining understanding of others' intentions and can accommodate more cooperatively with the needs and wishes of others. Parent and child interactions can be more mutually goal oriented. While 4- and 5-year-olds still rely on parents for security and comfort, they are beginning to focus on peers and will often rely on friends for social and emotional support (Furman & Buhrmester, 1992).

Life Span Perspectives on Psychosocial Development of Young Children

The foregoing discussion suggests that while it is essential to pay special attention to the types and quality of infant and early childhood experiences, it is also helpful to look at growth and development from a life span perspective. A life span perspective emphasizes that development is continuous and cumulative from birth to death and that individual developmental pathways are influenced in positive and negative directions by individual biology, adaptibility, and experience (Lewis, 1997). Sociocultural contexts and family interaction patterns have an ongoing influence on the course that psychosocial development takes (Rizzo, Corsaro, & Bates, 1992). An individual's overall health and wellness influence not only growth patterns, but also personality and social interaction behaviors. Guidance and discipline techniques; adult expectations; unusual or stressful events; individual or family life joys and successes, disappointments, and traumas; and various role models influence the course of development over time.

While scholars in child development place a great deal of emphasis on the "formative" early months and years, a life span view of growth and development assures us that in most cases, single events in early childhood growth and development do not result in behaviors that cannot be modified by later growth and development, subsequent life experiences, or the individual's resilience and adaptability (Lewis, 1997). So, while certain early experiences are considered essential to optimal development, cumulative life course experiences can influence developmental outcomes in positive or negative ways. This knowledge explains and affirms the contemporary emphasis on the earliest possible medical, social, and educational intervention when healthy growth and development are at risk.

Psychosocial Theory: Initiative Versus Guilt

The 4- to 5-year-old has entered Erikson's third stage of psychosocial development as depicted in Figure 12.1. Building on the previous stages of trust and autonomy, the child is now struggling between a sense of initiative and a sense of guilt. Of this stage, Erikson (1963) wrote,

> There is in every child at every stage a new miracle of vigorous unfolding, which constitutes a new hope and a new responsibility for all. Such is the sense and the pervading quality of initiative. The criteria for all of these senses and qualities are the same: a crisis, more or less beset with fumbling and fear, is resolved in that the child suddenly seems to "grow together," both in his person and in his body. He appears "more himself," more loving, relaxed and brighter in his judgment,

FIGURE 12.1
Erikson's Stages of Psychosocial Development

The child whose sense of initiative is emerging is eager to master new skills.

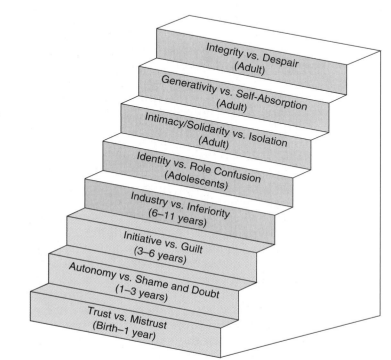

more activated and activating. He is in free possession of a surplus of energy which permits him to forget failures quickly and to approach what seems desirable (even if it also seems uncertain and even dangerous) with undiminished and more accurate direction. Initiative adds to autonomy the quality of undertaking, planning, and "attacking" a task for the sake of being active and on the move, where before self-will, more often than not, inspired acts of defiance or, at any rate, protested independence. (p. 255)

The child whose sense of **initiative** is emerging is eager to master new skills, use language to ask questions to seek new meanings, and enlist others in work and play interactions. The child's social circle is expanding rapidly, and interactions with others are actively sought. Mastery of motor skills frees the child to try new feats, such as climbing on playground structures with greater agility or riding the bicycle without training wheels. The child is eager to learn and genuinely enjoys the events that enlarge and enrich understandings of an ever-widening world. This is a time when planning and anticipating coming events or activities and being engaged in cooperative efforts with others are particularly enjoyable. Activities such as participating in planning a family outing or preparing the classroom for a special visitor provide an exhilarating sense of shared purpose.

initiative: the third of Erikson's psychosocial stages, in which the child pursues ideas, individual interests, and activities; when thwarted, the child becomes self-critical and experiences guilt

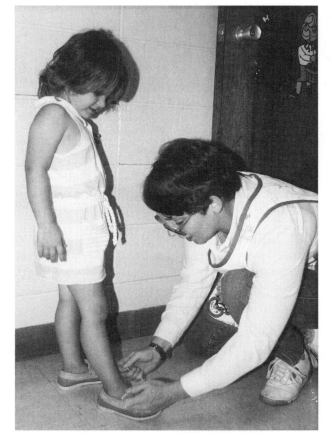

Seeking and receiving needed assistance is a form of initiative.

Initiative is used to engage others in conversation and to enlist playmates. Play becomes more social and elaborate. Imitation, imagination, and fantasy lead to complex and fluid sociodramatic enacting. Extended sociodramatic scenarios, alone or with playmates, evolve. Sociodramatic scenarios extend, digress, and diverge with new fantasies, plots, and characters as playmates enter and exit the play group.

The developing sense of initiative is not always characterized by positive behaviors, however. Sometimes, initiative gets out of bounds. Misdirected initiative is evident in some physical and verbal aggression. Pushing a playmate aside to be next on the balance beam and using words to cajole or intimidate are examples of coercive and negative interactions in which the child initiates an attempt to control others. Threats such as "I won't be your best friend" or "You can't come to my birthday party" are examples of misdirected initiative. In addition, growing facility with language increases the child's use of language to shock or perhaps to deceive, another form of misdirected initiative.

Out-of-bounds initiative can produce feelings of anxiety, embarrassment, and guilt as the child becomes aware that his or her behaviors are unacceptable to others. The unsure and socially unskilled child's emerging sense of initiative is placed at risk unless appropriate intervention occurs and alternative behaviors are suggested. Adult guidance is needed to redirect initiative toward positive, more constructive outcomes. However, guidance must provide a balance between control and freedom for the child. Both failure to guide (undercontrolling) and the opposite—persistent overriding guidance (overcontrolling)—fail to teach alternatives and thus undermine the child's opportunities to learn appropriate behaviors and to develop a healthy balance between a sense of initiative and its psychosocial opposite, a sense of guilt.

When a sense of guilt exceeds a sense of initiative, children tend to seek undue assurances and permission from adults and peers. They are more vulnerable to the suggestions of others and may tend to follow others indiscriminately, sometimes gravitating toward the wrong leaders. They are often the target of bullies. They are reluctant to take personal risks, try new activities, reach out to others for interactions, or assert their own will and often fail to fully enjoy their emerging capabilities.

Both undercontrolling and overcontrolling guidance techniques contribute to the development of a sense of guilt. Thwarted in efforts to express feelings and initiate ideas, interests, and activities, children may develop a lack of self-confidence that persists through later ages. Interactions that thwart an emerging sense of initiative and a sense of self-confidence that can arise from successful development of a sense of initiative include power-assertive discipline techniques; excessive criticism, corrections, or reprimands; teasing or ridiculing; and treating the child as though his or her questions are annoying or pretend play is needless or silly. Such interactions have potentially damaging consequences and should be avoided.

Egocentric Behaviors

Few kindergarten teachers would disagree that 4- and 5-year-old children exhibit egocentric behaviors. Fifteen 4- or 5-year-olds in a group often present 15 or more competing requests for the teachers' attention:

- In the middle of a finger-play, Justin discovers a hangnail on one of his fingers, leaves his seated position, and climbs over the group to show his injured finger to the teacher.

- On arrival at kindergarten, Beth tempts her teacher with, "Do you want to see what I brought in my lunch today?"
- During the school nurse's demonstration of handwashing, Kari interjects, "You know what? My daddy washed his new car last night."
- Deon shouts from across the room, "Teacher, Shannon is sitting in *my* chair!"

Egocentrism in 4- and 5-year-olds is characterized by the belief that others are experiencing the world as they themselves are. However, through social interactions in preschool groups, children experience the needs and wishes of others and are exposed to a variety of points of view. Peer group interactions provided by preschools and kindergartens offer unlimited opportunities for children to experience the perspectives of others. As children become more capable of perspective-taking, they become less egocentric.

Social Learning and Social Cognition

A great deal of social learning has taken place by the time a child reaches 4 and 5 years of age as a result of opportunities to observe role models and experience a variety of interactions with others (Bandura, 1997). Social cognitive theory places a great deal of importance on the influence of role models, as we shall see in discussions of the development of social competence.

Social Perspective-Taking

At age 4 to 5 years, social cognition is becoming evident in the ability to make social judgments on the basis of prior experience, observations of others, and the child's viewpoints and expectations of others. This social cognition is characterized in part by a growing awareness of the effects of one's behaviors on others and increasing (though still imperfect) perspective-taking ability. Thus, aggressive behavior may be self-controlled through an awareness of how aggression hurts others. On the other hand, through experience (and perhaps coaching), a child can learn that empathic behaviors evoke warm and friendly responses from others.

In their review of research on social perspective-taking in young children, Rubin and Everett (1982) identified three forms of perspective-taking: (1) cognitive perspective-taking, which includes the ability to consider others' thoughts and intentions; (2) affective perspective-taking, or the ability to take into account the feelings and emotions of others; and (3) spatial perspective-taking, or the ability to consider the other person's physical view of the world. A child who attempts to organize a game may be exhibiting cognitive perspective-taking. A child who attempts to comfort a crying playmate may be exhibiting affective perspective-taking, an awareness of the other child's distress or its cause. A child who removes an obstacle from the path of another, thus preventing an accident, is demonstrating spatial perspective-taking.

During sociodramatic play, pretending promotes perspective-taking. As the child engages in a variety of role-taking experiences ("You be the nurse, and I'll be sick"), awareness of others' roles emerges. In attempting to play out a sociodramatic scenario, the child becomes aware of discrepancies between her or his intentions and those of playmates. In adjusting the sociodrama to the wishes of others, the child's perspective-taking abilities are enlisted.

Adults help children to develop perspective-taking abilities by inviting them to think about the feelings and experiences of others during social encounters: "How do you think Tony felt when you knocked over his block tower?" "Let's let Tony tell us what he thinks about what happened." "Did you notice how Ms. Jones smiled when you helped open the door for her?" "Did you notice how your baby sister stopped crying and listened when you were singing to her?" "What kinds of things make us happy? . . . angry? . . . sad?" "If you will stand over here, you will see what LaToya is describing." "You helped to prevent an accident by moving that tricycle out of the pathway." There are numerous opportunities to help young children develop perspective-taking abilities during their play and interactions with others.

Theory of Mind

theory of mind:
attributing mental
states to oneself and
to others

In addition to understanding the effects of one's behaviors on others, in a complementary development, children around age 4 begin to understand the existence of mental states in themselves and others. They are growing in their awareness that feelings, desires, intentions, beliefs, and unique perceptions can exist in the mind. Contemporary theorists refer to this development as a child's **"theory of mind,"** also referred to as "mind sight" (Siegel, 1999), or an understanding of others' minds or mental states (Astington, 1993). A theory of mind

Both perspective-taking and theory of mind are gained through pretend play.

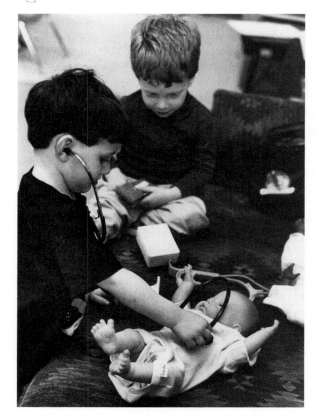

supports perspective-taking ability. A theory of mind proposes that the individual understands that others' thinking is influenced by their perceptions, feelings, desires, and beliefs. The ability to think about and reflect on what others are thinking or feeling is an important part of all interpersonal relationships. The study of children's theory of mind includes children's understanding of how the senses provide information to individuals; children's understanding and recognition of emotions in others; and their understanding that others have feelings, desires, and beliefs that are uniquely theirs (Lillard & Curenton, 1999). Researchers believe that as children develop a theory of mind, they begin to enjoy more socially satisfying interactions with others (Lalonde & Chandler, 1995).

Both perspective-taking and theory of mind are facilitated through pretend play as children assume pretend roles and encounter others' unique ways of interpreting and representing their particular role assignments. The give-and-take required to successfully and cooperatively carry out a sociodrama requires the child's attention to the minds of others (Youngblade & Dunn, 1995). These social cognitions are also facilitated through children's literature, in which dialogue can be used to draw attention to the feelings and experiences of the characters. Parallels can be drawn between characters in stories and individual experiences. The give-and-take of sibling relationships also influences this development, particularly in younger siblings (Lewis, Freeman, Kyriakidou, Maridaki-Kassotaki, & Berridge, 1996).

Prosocial Development

An outgrowth of social cognition is the development of prosocial behaviors. Prosocial behaviors include empathy and altruism. Empathy is the ability to recognize the feelings of others, such as distress, anxiety, or delight, and to vicariously experience those feelings. **Altruism** is defined as behavior that is intended to help another without expectation of reward. In young children, a number of factors influence prosocial behaviors. Among these factors are age, level of cognitive functioning, perspective-taking abilities, individual personality, family interactions, guidance strategies, and role models.

Studies have shown that when children observe prosocial models, they generally become more prosocial themselves (Bandura, 1997; Radke-Yarrow, Zahn-Waxler, & Chapman, 1983). This is particularly true when the child and the model have had a warm relationship and the child has experienced nurturing from the model.

altruism: intentions to help others without the expectation of reward

---

Jeremy's friend Shaun has just recovered from an upper respiratory infection and is finally able to visit. Ann greets Shaun on his arrival and hustles the two children off to Jeremy's room to play. Jeremy's delight in seeing his absent friend is somewhat overshadowed by his observation of his mother's greeting. Nevertheless, he leads Shaun to his room, and the two become involved in a new and rather difficult puzzle. Stumped in putting the puzzle together, Jeremy runs to another room to summon his mother's assistance. As they walk back to his room together, Jeremy engages his mother in his concern: "You didn't tell Shaun you were sorry." Confused, his mother inquires, "Sorry? About what, Jeremy?" "About he's been sick," Jeremy responds.

Jeremy's previous experiences with being sick were accompanied by expressions of concern such as "I am so sorry you are not feeling well" and "I am really glad you feel better today." He had also observed his parents convey similar concern with others. Thus, through observation, Jeremy has learned to verbally express concern for others and felt some incongruence when such concern wasn't made evident on this happy occasion with Shaun—an unintentional oversight on his mother's part.

Studies of parenting styles, guidance techniques, and the influence of role models demonstrate that when positive and instructive strategies are employed, prosocial behaviors are more likely to emerge (Baumrind, 1986, 1998; Marion, 2003). Instructive guidance is characterized by logical limits, reason, respect, warmth, affection, and clear expectations.

In addition to role models and guidance techniques, prosocial development is fostered by the following:

1. Experiences that promote positive self-concepts. There is evidence that positive feelings about oneself are related to higher frequencies of cooperative and positive behaviors among 4- and 5-year-old children (Cauley & Tyler, 1989; Honig & Wittmer, 1996).

2. Assignment of age-appropriate responsibilities whereby children come to feel that they are a contributing part of the family, class, or group (DeVries & Zan, 1994)

3. Opportunities to interact with other children and to engage in sociodramatic play that enhance role taking and perspective-taking (Rubin, Bukowski, & Parker, 1998; Rubin & Everett, 1982; Youngblade & Dunn, 1995)

4. Opportunities to participate in noncompetitive, cooperative games and group activities (Orlick, 1981; Slavin, 1990)

5. Exposure to literature, television programs, toys, and computer and video games that project prosocial themes (Donnerstein, Slaby, & Eron, 1994; Rosenkoetter, 1999)

Moral Development

moral realism: a morality that focuses on rules and the seriousness of the consequences of an act rather than on the intentions behind the act

Piaget's (1965) studies of moral development focused on how children develop a respect for rules and a sense of justice. He studied the former by quizzing children about rules as he engaged them in marble play. To assess childhood conceptions of social justice, he used moral dilemma stories with children, followed by questions concerning punishment or appropriateness of certain behaviors. From these studies, Piaget proposed a stage sequence of moral development consisting of (1) a premoral stage, (2) a stage of **moral realism**, and (3) a stage of **moral relativism**.

moral relativism: a morality that focuses on the judgment of situations and intentions underlying individual behavior rather than solely on the consequences of an act

Children below age 6 are thought to be in a premoral stage of morality because of an absent or limited concern for rules. For instance, play groups exhibit an assortment of rules and behavior expectations, making up rules as play proceeds and altering them arbitrarily and unilaterally. Awareness of the use of or reasons for rules is minimal.

Toward the end of this stage, around age 6, children begin to exhibit characteristics of Piaget's second stage, moral realism. During this stage, children become quite rule bound, believing that rules are unalterable and set forth by all-knowing authority figures (God, parent, teacher). They believe that one's behavior is judged to be "right" or "wrong" on the basis of having followed the rules or the seriousness of the consequences. This stage is often referred to as a **heteronomous** stage of morality in that the child's behaviors are governed by others rather than by the self, as would be true of autonomous behaviors.

heteronomous morality: a morality that is governed by others rather than by onself

Because of the characteristic egocentrism of this age, the child believes that others are subject to the same rules and perceive rules in the same way. In addition, the magnitude of the consequences of a deed determines for the child whether the deed is right or wrong. For instance, the child might view breaking a large but very inexpensive item as more serious than breaking a small but expensive one. Moreover, any deed that is punished is deemed wrong.

At this stage of morality, children perceive punishment as it relates to breaking the rule, usually without regard for the rule breaker's intentions. For these young moralists, punishment should be quickly forthcoming when rules are broken. Their suggestions for punishment do not necessarily relate to the misdeed. Some children at this stage may believe that injury or misfortune following their misdeeds is deserved punishment for having broken a rule. Sometimes, unable to control the rule conformity of playmates, older preschoolers seek the assistance of an adult through tattling. One should view this behavior as a natural part of the child's emerging sense of rules and rule infringement and not necessarily as an attempt to be unkind to a playmate. In this regard, tattling might be viewed as a positive aspect of moral development.

Kohlberg's Developmental Sequence of Moral Thinking

Lawrence Kohlberg (1968, 1984) expanded and modified Piaget's theory by proposing an invariant developmental sequence consisting of three levels of moral thinking: premoral (or preconventional), conventional, and postconventional, the outcome of which is a sense of justice. Children are believed to pass through each of the stages, though perhaps at different rates. Each stage incorporates the developments of the preceding stage and builds on them. The premoral and conventional levels are characteristic of young and school-age children*:

Premoral Level

Stage 1: Punishment and obedience orientation—The child's moral behaviors are oriented toward punishment and exhibit unquestioning deference to superior power. The physical consequences of action, regardless of their human meaning or value, determine goodness or badness.

Stage 2: Naive instrumental hedonism—The child views right actions as those that instrumentally satisfy his or her needs and occasionally the needs of others. Elements of fairness, reciprocity, and equal sharing are present, but they are always interpreted in a physical, pragmatic way. Reciprocity is a matter of "you scratch my back and I'll scratch yours," not of loyalty, gratitude, or justice.

*The following rules are adapted from Stages of Moral Development, from *Essays on Moral Development: The Psychology of Moral Development* (vol. II) by Lawrence Kohlberg. Copyright © 1984 by Lawrence Kohlberg. Reprinted by permission of HarperCollins Publishers Inc.

Conventional Level

Stage 3: Morality of conventional role conformity—At this level, we see a good boy/good girl orientation. Good behavior is that which pleases or helps others and is approved by them. There is much conformity to stereotypical images of what is majority or "natural" behavior. Behavior is often judged by intention; the phrase "He [or she] means well" becomes important for the first time and is often overused. One seeks approval by being "nice."

Stage 4: Authority-maintaining morality—The child's behaviors are oriented toward authority, fixed rules, and the maintenance of the social order. Right behavior consists of doing one's duty, showing respect for authority, and maintaining the social order for its own sake. One earns respect by performing dutifully.

Kohlberg's third level, *postconventional moral thinking,* is characterized by "a major thrust toward autonomous moral principles which have validity and application apart from authority of the groups or persons who hold them and apart from the individual's identification with those persons or groups" (Kohlberg, 1968, p. 63). As children are better able to ascertain intentions, take another person's perspective, and understand reciprocity, they make the transition from premoral thinking and behaving to the more mature and reasoned conventional level of morality.

PSYCHOSOCIAL DEVELOPMENT OF THE FOUR- THROUGH FIVE-YEAR-OLD: A NEUROLOGICAL DEVELOPMENT PERSPECTIVE

As young children continue to grow and to encounter wider circles of influence, their brain chemistry and neurological wiring (which continues to proliferate) activate and regulate emotional responses to new experiences. It is important to note that far more neural fibers emanate from the brain's limbic (or emotional) center than from the larger logical/rational cortical centers. For this reason, emotions can be very powerful determinants of behavior, often superseding intelligent or rational thought (Diamond & Hopson, 1998; Krasnegor, Lyon, Goldman-Rakic, 1998). For example, the need to share and take turns may be a rational concept and one that the four- or five-year-old child can intellectually understand. But the emotionally driven desire to possess and enjoy a particular play item often overrides this understanding. It may be some time before understanding can effectively govern the child's willingness to delay gratification in favor of more effective responses such as sharing. We know that the inabilities to delay gratification, to apply reason over emotion, and to exercise self-control have origins in the developing neurological wiring and chemistry in the child's brain (Diamond and Hopson, 1998; Siegel, 1999).

When an emotion stimulus is particularly strong, the nervous system assumes a fight-or-flight stress mode, which engages many biological systems, including the endocrine, circulatory, muscular, digestive, and immune systems. This fight-or-flight response can be both lifesaving and troublesome. On one hand, it alerts the individual to impending danger and allows for a quick response. On the other hand, prior experiences such as abuse, neglect, and unduly stressful events often result in neurological developments that predispose children to a state of heightened alertness in which their responses are easily triggered by their initial perceptions before they have processed what is happening. Road rage in adults is a profound and frightening example of the power of emotions (anger) over reason. Fortunately, most people develop the ability to think before acting, or, as the neuroscientist might say, to allow their brains time to communicate across the emotional and rational thought structures, leading to more intelligent and appropriate responses. Positive emotions (smiling, laughing, joyful anticipation, satisfactions in success) trigger the release of selected chemicals in the brain, such as serotonin and endorphins, that contribute to a sense of well-being and enhance social and emotional interactions. Although the brain's chemical and electrical processes of transmitting impulses and information are quite complex, it is important to know that the proliferation of certain chemicals that influence mood and reactivity depends on experiences such as opportunities to express and receive positive emotional and social interactions. As scientists continue to document the deleterious effects on the developing brain of harsh, negative, abusive, and neglecting experiences contrasted against more joyful and positive ones, the types and timing of specific experiences and/or treatment strategies will be more specifically described (Delcomyn, 1998; Perry, Pollard, Blakley, Baker, & Vigilante, 1995). Suffice it to say that parents and professionals are summoned to provide essential psychological nourishment through warm, affectionate, empathic, and instructive interactions.

DIMENSIONS OF PSYCHOSOCIAL DEVELOPMENT DURING AGES FOUR THROUGH FIVE

Emotional Development

Young children, like adults, experience a range of emotions, from joy and elation to grief and despair. They express feelings of love, acceptance, frustration, anger, hostility, jealousy, shame, embarrassment, guilt, anxiety, fear, distress, depression, pride, humor, astonishment, yearning, and many more emotions. Expressions of emotion are exhibited in numerous ways: talking about emotional events or feelings, crying, shouting, withdrawing, expressing irritability, pouting, displaying distraction or inattentiveness, engaging in verbal exchanges, being silly, showing aggression toward self and others, making self-deprecating comments, rejecting others and efforts to console, exhibiting destructive behaviors, seeking and offering affection, and many others.

An immensely important developmental task of early childhood is learning about emotions and how to express them. This learning includes *labeling, understanding,* and *modulating* emotions. Aspects of this learning include the child's ability to cognitively grasp the concept of emotion, to take into account the types of situations that cause certain emotional reactions, and to understand how her or his expressions of emotion affect others (Denham, 1998; Saarni, 1999).

Labeling occurs as children are given names for emotions in specific situations or descriptors for emotion-evoking events. ("You are really *angry.*" "Do you feel *unhappy* when your Dad and Mom are away at work?" "It makes all of us *sad* when someone dies." "When you feel *mad* at someone, let's talk about it." "I can tell that you are very *proud* of yourself." "We are all having such a *joyous* time today.") Such labeling is an important first step in young children's understanding of emotions.

Labels can go only so far, however. As suggested in the discussions above, dialogue with children about feelings is important: what feelings mean about our shared humanness; what kinds of situations evoke certain behaviors in all of us; how individuals respond in different contexts; appropriate and inappropriate, effective and ineffective, healthy and unhealthy ways to express and deal with feelings; and how the manner in which we express emotions affects others. These dialogues can explore positive and healthy ways to cope with emotional events and the feelings they create. Helping children to define and cope with their various emotions is essential to their overall mental health and their social development, including their ability to relate to and empathize with others.

By the time children are 4 or 5 years old, they have some understanding of their own emotions and the emotions of others. They have the capacity to reflect on their feelings and some idea that emotions persist for a time after the event that caused them. At this point, though self-control of emotions is far from established, children are learning and beginning to apply display rules, demonstrating knowledge of when and where certain expressions of emotion are acceptable. They are beginning to modulate their expressions of emotion in ways that serve their best interests and are becoming aware of the effects of their expressions of emotion on others.

Fear and Anxiety.   Early studies of fear attributed its evolution to maturation and increasing cognitive development (Gesell, 1930; Jersild & Holmes, 1935a, 1935b; Jones & Jones, 1928). In one of the earliest studies of childhood fears, Jones and Jones (1928) wrote, "Fear arises when we know enough to recognize the potential danger in the situation but have not advanced to the point of complete comprehension and control of the changing situation" (p. 143).

Maturation and learning contribute to changes in fear behaviors from the infant/toddler period to ages 4 through 5. The 4- through 5-year-old child experiences a variety of fears due to insufficient experience, incomplete information or knowledge, and an assortment of misconceptions. For example, after her parents' divorce, Josie feared her own impulses and behaviors lest she "cause" the other parent to leave her.

Some fears are due to the child's inability to separate fantasy and reality. In role playing the *Three Billy Goats Gruff*, Emma became so immersed in the drama that she began to cry and cling to the teacher in fear that the troll would harm her. Her mother reported that for a time thereafter, Emma had nightmares, feared the dark, and resisted retelling of the fairy tale.

Still other fears are learned through observation of fears modeled by parents, siblings, relatives, and friends. For example, Franky's mother always referred to rain, regardless of the amount of precipitation or accompanying elements, as a "storm." Her own childhood experience in a tornado had left a lingering fear of storms and a generalization that all rain is a potential deadly storm. Thus, she modeled fear of all rainy weather. Fears are also learned through one's own experience. For example, a child who is bitten by a dog may fear all dogs, or perhaps all small animals, for a time.

The sources of fear and anxiety are numerous. All children experience fear and anxiety from time to time and in varying degrees of intensity. Yet not all childhood fears are the same. Some children fear the dark; others do not. Also, there are individual differences in the way children respond to fear stimuli. One child may quietly withdraw or hover unobtrusively near a trusted adult; another may cry loudly, cling desperately, and resist being consoled. Still others may enter a flight mode and attempt to escape the feared object or event by running away from it.

Many fears or anxieties serve important adaptive or self-preservation functions and, as such, are considered healthy fears. Fear of traffic, strange animals, motorized tools and equipment, fires, dangerous elevations, and firearms are healthy because they prompt appropriate avoidance behaviors. Some children do not develop a healthy fear of danger and require guidance and supervision to protect them from mishaps. Such guidance should be informative without arousing curiosity, which can lead the child into dangerous explorations. A statement such as, "The gun is locked away because guns are very dangerous and can injure and kill," is better than, "Don't dare touch that gun," which for some children simply arouses their interest and virtually ensures that they will explore the forbidden item. On the other hand, explanations should not exaggerate the danger or alarm the child. "Fasten your seat belt, sit still, and tell me about your day at kindergarten" is better than "People get killed in car wrecks everyday; if you don't sit still, you're going to make me have a wreck, and we will all be killed."

Helping young children to understand and cope with their fears is a matter of providing appropriate experiences, explanations, and encouragement. Children need age-appropriate dialogue and explanations that provide labels and insights. When adults are calm, encouraging, and knowledgeable, children are reassured. In time, some fears subside and disappear, new fears emerge, and new coping strategies become a part of the child's behavior repertoire.

Self-Comforting Behaviors.   At ages 4 and 5, children rely on previously acquired self-comforting strategies to help them cope with uncomfortable or disturbing emotional events. They may regress to thumb sucking, withdraw to a more secure or comfortable place, find comfort in their transitional object, seek the proximity of a trusted playmate or caregiver, or divert their own attention and conversations to other topics. All of these strategies assist children in modulating their emotions, decreasing the intensity and sometimes the frequency of emotions. As children get older, they learn, as many adults have, to mask their emotions; some may deny that they are feeling certain emotions. Learning to recognize and acknowledge one's emotions and to handle them in psychologically healthy, socially constructive, and self-affirming ways is a critical part of the socializing process. This process is referred to as *emotional intelligence* (Goleman, 1995), an aspect of human growth and development that has lifelong implications for good mental health and personally satisfying social interactions.

Transitional Objects.   Although the importance of transitional objects varies from child to child, transitional objects continue to represent an important part of the psychosocial development of children ages 4 through 5. The duration of attachments to transitional objects also varies. For some children, the attachment is long lived; for others, the attachment may be brief, perhaps even being transferred from one object to another for varying periods of time. Affection for the transitional object(s) can be quite deep and openly expressed. At the same time, the object(s) can become the target of aggressive and serious mistreatment as children fantasize or work through emotional and social conflicts.

The need for the transitional object recedes as children shift their energies and attentions from themselves to others and from fantasy to real-life tasks. The child may then choose to carry the object in the car en route to school but leave it there for reunion when the school day is over. Or the child may wish to carry the object into the classroom, where it may be put in a cubbyhole to be visited on occasion during the day. Sometimes, symbolic substitutes signal a more mature approach. A symbolic substitute can take the form of a photograph of the child with the transitional object or a family photograph carried in the child's book bag or lunch box. Classroom teachers often provide bulletin board space for children's photographs of themselves and their families to help children through the transition process.

Children themselves must make the decision to give up the transitional object. Coercion, ridicule, disparaging remarks, or other attempts to separate the child from the transitional object only serve to intensify the child's resolve to cling to it (Jalongo, 1987). Hence, adults should accept the child's right to refuse to share the transitional object with others. Sometimes, the child's maturity in other areas leads adults to believe that the child should have outgrown the need for the transitional object, but this does not necessarily signal a readiness to abandon it. It is always best to take cues from the child in determining when a transitional object will be relinquished or abandoned in favor of a different self-comforting approach.

Jeremy's interest in astronomy has found support in books provided for him by his parents and teachers. Though they are beyond the expected reading abilities for a child his age, Jeremy reads his astronomy books with some facility. Each morning, his backpack is carefully prepared for school with one or two of his current favorite astronomy books *and* his well-worn teddy bear. For the duration of kindergarten, Jeremy carries his teddy bear to school with him, carefully tucked into his backpack. Wisely, neither his parents nor his teachers discourage this practice.

Self-Concept Development and Self-Esteem.   According to Erikson (1963), autonomy facilitates new discoveries and the acquisition of new skills and leads to an *activity-based self-concept* that is appropriate to the emergence of a sense of initiative. With autonomy in place, the 4- to 5-year-old describes herself or himself according to skills being mastered. At this age, the self-concept has emerged from self-awareness and self-recognition during the infancy and toddler periods to a more attribute-focused self-definition. Now the self-concept is based mostly on the child's perceptions of his or her physical attributes and possessions. It will be a while before the child's self-definition includes inner qualities or character traits (Harter, 2001). A self-description based on perceptions of physical attributes is evident in statements such as "I am bigger," "I can tie my shoes," and "Watch me skip." The child also uses self-descriptions related to age and possessions to affirm the sense of self, for example, "I'm going to be four on my birthday" or "I have a new bicycle with training wheels." A positive self-concept provides the sustenance for self-confidence and one's expectations that mastering life's challenges is possible. A well-established sense of one's worth as an individual is protective in that frustrating obstacles and failures are less likely to be followed by the perception of oneself as incapable (Stipek, Recchia, & McClintic, 1992).

Children develop positive self-concepts and self-esteem from their experiences with and the attitudes of people who are important to them: their parents, siblings, other family members, caregivers, and teachers. From the manner in which others respond to them, children form opinions of themselves. Over time, repetition of response behaviors of others reinforces these opinions, and the child begins to build cognitive structures that match important others' attitudes toward her or him. When responses are positive, respectful, and affirming, the self-concept that the child formulates is positive and self-affirming. On the other hand, when their interactions with important others are negative, demeaning, humiliating, disengaged, mollifying, or nonsupportive, children construct a concept of self that is distorted and negative. These interactions encourage or impede a critical aspect of healthy psychosocial development, that of self-esteem. High or low self-esteem is reflected in the child's emotional responses and social interactions. A recursive cycle of feedback occurs when children relate to others according to their positive or negative self-concepts and those with whom they interact respond accordingly in positive or negative ways. Thus, the self-concept (positive or negative) is reinforced in the child, and the behaviors repeat themselves in subsequent interactions. Obviously, it is critical that this recursive cycle be broken when the child exhibits low self-regard and its accompanying negative interactions with others. This takes sensitive and helpful responses on the part of adults to affirm the child's worth and competence while coaching or facilitating more positive interactions with others and setting logical and fair limits to promote appropriate behaviors.

Children can have difficulty forming positive self-concepts and self-esteem for a variety of reasons, including parenting and child care methods that hinder this development. Developmentally inappropriate expectations, limited opportunities to use and enhance emerging physical and motor abilities, lack of affection and appropriate attention and guidance, harsh or punitive discipline, unstable or insecure relationships with individuals on whom they depend, excessive negative responses to the child, undue teasing or ridicule, insufficient opportunities to play with other children, excessive or demeaning sibling rivalry, and family stress are examples of experiences that hinder healthy development of self-awareness, self-concept, and self-esteem.

On the other hand, it is believed that when young children experience supportive bonds with, and unconditional love and acceptance from, those on whom they depend and when parents and teachers use positive authoritative forms of discipline, children develop a more balanced self-concept, more positive self-regard, and higher levels of self-esteem than children who have not experienced these affirming interactions (Lamborn, Mounts, Steinberg, & Dornbusch, 1991; Verschueren, Marcoen, & Schoefs, 1996). Relationships that are marked by unconditional acceptance, genuine interest and concern, and positive guidance techniques should not be confused with permissive discipline that fails to communicate expected behaviors and value systems. Unconditional acceptance is conveyed when adults acknowledge the child's feelings and perspectives and affirm the child's competence and worth when placing limits on inappropriate behaviors.

Anger.   Anger is an emotion that ranges in expression and intensity from irritability to aggression to hostility and rage. In young children, anger is provoked by frustration in getting needs met or obstacles to goal attainment. Inability to obtain another's attention, a toy that doesn't function as desired, inability to handle clothing (e.g., a zipper that gets stuck or buttonholes that are too large), a playmate who doesn't respond appropriately to play requests, arbitrary or confusing disciplinary restrictions, and an interruption to an enjoyable playtime activity are some examples. Anger is aroused when children experience physical or verbal assault—being hit or pushed, teased, or berated. Feelings of rejection may also arouse anger. Anger arousal thresholds and the manner in which anger is expressed differ among individuals, owing to individual differences in temperament, cognitive abilities, and family and cultural expectations and role models. Some scholars have suggested a biological basis for extreme anger responses that readily escalate into violent behaviors, suggesting birth injuries (Le Doux, 1996; Panskepp, 1998; Yager, 1995) and/or prenatal or postnatal abuse or neglect, resulting in abnormal brain growth and neurological development (Perry et al., 1995).

Aggression. Aggression is behavior that is directed at another with intentions to threaten, harm, or hurt them in some manner. Aggression is also directed at animals and objects. Aggression is generally described as *instrumental* or *hostile* (Hartup, 1974) and *accidental* (Feshbach, 1970). Dodge (1994) and his colleagues designated three similar categories: *instrumental, reactive,* and *bullying* aggression. Instrumental aggression is provoked through goal blockage that prevents the person from obtaining and retaining something he or she wants (a toy, a privilege, play space). Most aggressive behaviors in young children are of this nature and are seldom accompanied by hostility (Marion, 2003). Often, children's behaviors result in injury or insult to another but are accidental rather than intentional. This, too, is common in young children owing to limitations associated with their young age, such as poor motor control (accidentally running into another block construction, knocking it over), frank and often tactless comments resulting from poor perspective-taking ability or immature theory of mind ("Why is your hair ugly today?"), and taking over a play space or play item presumed abandoned by another whose intentions to return were not apparent or noticed. When a child retaliates for the offense, the aggression could be referred to as reactive. Hostile or bullying aggression, on the other hand, is generally (though not always) unprovoked and is characterized by intent to threaten, thwart, or hurt. Hostile aggression is less common among young children but tends to increase with age (Ross, 1996).

As with anger and other emotions, the frequency, intensity, and character of aggressive behaviors are influenced by the child's individual temperament and level of cognition; the extent to which the child's basic needs for food, clothing, shelter, social interaction, emotional support, and nurturing have been predictably and successfully met; and the teaching and role models to whom the child has been most frequently exposed. The consequences of aggressive behaviors also contribute to its incidence. For instance, when an aggressive child succeeds in hurting, intimidating, or causing another to retreat, the victory increases the likelihood that the aggressive behavior will be repeated. Failure on the part of adults to intervene in aggressive acts can be perceived by the child as condoning the behavior, again increasing the likelihood of repeated occurrences. When adults (parents or teachers) directly or indirectly encourage aggression by praising children who use aggression to get what they want, coaching them to do so, or urging them to "stand up for themselves," or by laughing at, teasing, or shaming the child who has been victimized by an aggressor, the adults reinforce aggressive attitudes and behaviors.

As with other social skills, children learn aggressive behaviors from a variety of role models. Parents and teachers who use discipline techniques that are power assertive, punitive, and/or physically punishing program children to be more aggressive. Dodge (1994) and his colleagues discovered a disturbing outcome for children who had been severely punished. These scholars found that such children failed to learn to read intent in the behaviors of others; instead, they were more reactive to other children's accidental aggressions, viewing them as intentional or hostile and thus deserving an aggressive response. These scholars believe that severely punished children acquire chronic patterns of misperceiving the deeds of others in which they interpret any unpleasant interaction with others as hostile and directed at them. If this pattern is allowed to persist, the children enter a recursive cycle in which their hostile manner evokes hostility in others, which in turn confirms their misguided notions about themselves and the intentions of others toward them. The result can be the development of chronic aggression. Other antecedents of aggressive behaviors include some children's television programs, video and computer games, theme toys associated with violent media program characters, advertising, news stories, and the behaviors and expectations of older children and admired adults. There may also be a neurobiological basis for some forms of aggression and violent behaviors, as indicated in the discussion earlier in this chapter. These topics and bullying behaviors are discussed further in Chapter 15.

At this point, it is important to point out that adults in the lives of young children need to be conscientiously proactive in mediating the causes of anger and aggression in children. Identifying the antecedents—family life patterns, sibling relationships, discipline techniques, stress, physical precursors (hunger, fatigue, illness, effects of medications), role models, playmates, play themes, toy preferences, or media influences—is an important first step. Help children to identify and utilize ways to manage anger (e.g., seeking adult help in resolving conflicts, learning techniques for resolving conflicts in the absence of adult assistance, learning to accept and talk about anger and what makes them and others angry, learning the display rules for anger, learning constructive outlets for anger management). Adults can acknowledge and accept anger in children, recognizing that they, too, get angry from time to time. Adults can be role models for children by exhibiting healthy ways of handling anger, by focusing on prosocial responses rather than simply blaming or venting. Recognizing the pervasive influence of the media and the toy industry, adults have a responsibility to help children become discerning consumers. Young children can be engaged in evaluative dialogue about what they have seen or heard through the media, how advertising entices to get money for the advertisers, and how what people do in some television programs and media games is dangerous and harmful, unrealistic, and not true for real people. Providing the props for prosocial play and avoiding toys that promote aggressive and violent play are critical if children are to practice and develop prosocial perspectives and constructive interaction patterns. Again, instructive guidance techniques influence how children learn to handle anger and curtail aggression.

Gender Identity and Gender-Role Development

Children ages 4 through 5 continue to learn gender-role behaviors through the manner in which their masculine or feminine behaviors are encouraged and rewarded or punished. But they also learn gender-role expectations from their own observations (Bandura, 1986, 1997). Peers, the media, children's literature, and

Androgynous behaviors are common among young children as they grow in awareness of the various roles each gender might assume.

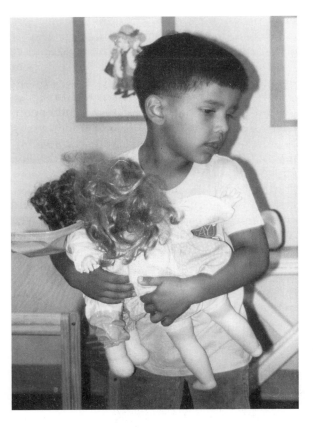

preschool classroom practices all influence a child's gender-role development, as they often apply stereotypes about "girl" or "boy" behaviors and capabilities (Alexander & Hines, 1994; Maccoby, 1990).

Kohlberg (1966) proposed a cognitive stage sequence for the development of gender roles:

1. Gender identity, when the child can provide a label for himself or herself as either a boy or a girl. This is usually achieved by age 3.
2. Gender stability, when the child realizes that boys grow up to be men and girls grow up to be women.
3. Gender constancy, when the child realizes that changes in hairstyle or clothing do not alter a person's gender. Gender constancy emerges between ages 5 and 7.

Before achievement of gender stability, children's pretend play is quite androgynous; boys can be mothers, and girls can be fathers. Child development researchers find little cause for concern in these play behaviors of young children, for these behaviors represent opportunities for children to affirm their own gender identities and gender roles. Honig (1983) advises that children need role models who encourage a wide spectrum of expressions of feelings and behaviors. Role models who are comfortable with their own gender assist children in developing healthy gender identities and gender-role behaviors.

Psychosexual Development

Children ages 4 and 5 continue to have a strong interest in their bodies, and are curious about the differences between girls and boys, adults and children. They want to know how babies get here and why girls and boys are anatomically different. When at play, they may imitate the affectional behaviors they have observed within the family, and attempt to reenact sexual behaviors observed in other contexts and in the media. "Bathroom talk" ("I see your pee pee." "Your underwear is showing!" "This is my butt.") is used to evoke shock and entertainment.

The developmental goal during this period is to help children to develop healthy attitudes toward their anatomy and the concept of personal privacy; caregivers should provide accurate terms for anatomy, age-appropriate information, and simple but accurate answers to questions. As these behaviors are typical and represent normal growth and development, it is important that children be given guidance regarding the appropriate time and place for conversations about sexual topics, and redirection toward meaningful and constructive play. It is important for adults to respond to each situation in a respectful and matter-of-fact manner. This is not a time for punishment and reprimand, which sends a distorted message about human sexuality. Rather, limits regarding appropriate language, sexual play, nudity, touching, and being touched by others need to be clearly stated and consistently monitored.

It is not uncommon for children who have been sexually abused to act out in provocative ways. They may use explicit language, be more intrusive with playmates, and fondle or attempt penetration or oral contact. Certainly, even these extreme behaviors can represent curiosity, and there are additional symptomatic behaviors associated with child abuse (e.g., visible physical signs, posttraumatic stress disorder, distorted perceptions of self and others, anger, anxiety, depression, avoidance, impaired sense of self, disassociative behaviors, and others) (Briere & Elliott, 1994). If child sexual abuse is suspected, measures must be taken to protect the child from further abuse. It is the law in all states that suspected child abuse be reported to appropriate local and state officials. Child care settings and schools have policies and procedures for child abuse reporting.

Awareness of Diversity and Individual Differences

As noted earlier, self-concept emerges as children become aware of their distinguishing physical characteristics, gender, and abilities. Between ages 3 and 5, children become aware of racial categories but do not always accurately classify themselves (Spencer & Markstrom-Adams, 1990). Sometimes, when young children discover racial differences, the disturbance in their own tenuous self-identification may cause them to respond with rejection toward others with different racial characteristics. Children at this point are not forming generalized negative attitudes toward other races, but are dealing with their own developing self-concepts and racial identities. There are now discrepancies between self-perceptions and what the child is seeing in others.

With this discovery, young children behave toward one another in a variety of ways—curious, friendly, unfriendly, apprehensive. They feel one another's hair, compare skin colors, and ask questions. There is some evidence that children from minority groups develop racial awareness earlier than other children

(Katz, 1982). Further, young children seem to be particularly vulnerable to racial stereotyping (Thurman & Lewis, 1979). Because children's perceptions of others is based on their own experiences with people in limited contexts—pediatrician, dentist, babysitters, teachers, neighbors, playmates, and television and other media personalities—they tend to generalize their experiences with individuals who are members of a particular racial group to new acquaintances of the same group. Their experiences are reinforced or mediated by the attitudes conveyed by members of their family and their caregivers and teachers. Linn and Poussaint (1999) pointed out that

> They may learn denigrating stereotypes from listening to their parents, or others, talking in overtly negative tones about people whose race or ethnicity is different from their own. They may notice that white people, with some exceptions, are dominant in advertisements, book illustrations, stories, and television programs. They observe who is present and who is absent from their schools, churches, or synagogues. Children exposed to television news will note the color of the criminals being arrested in handcuffs and the color of the police officers. All of these images, distorted or not, affect their perceptions of a wide range of people and their place in the world. (p. 50)

The point to be made is that from birth onward, child rearing occurs in a cultural context that instills in the child concepts and attitudes about race, cultural identities, values, and expectations (Derman-Sparks & Phillips, 1997). Cultural contexts encompass the language spoken in the home, modes of expression, celebrations, holidays, family traditions, family cohesion, disciplinary techniques and authority relationships, food and clothing preferences, family goals and values, achievement orientations, and choices and opportunities in education, work, and recreation and pastime activities. Children's concepts, understandings, and attitudes about race—their own and those of others—derive first from the cultural contexts of home and family.

Early child care, preschool, and kindergarten experiences play a role in supporting or negating children's perceptions of race—their own and that of others. These programs can extend and affirm a child's growing sense of membership in a particular cultural or racial group. Early childhood programs support positive racial and cultural perspectives by

- enhancing self-concept development and cultural identity;
- helping children to develop the social skills of perspective-taking, communicating, cooperating, and conflict resolution;
- broadening children's awareness of varying lifestyles, languages, points of view, and ways of doing things through enriched multicultural curriculums (Ramsey, 1998).

In addition, curriculums that are *culturally responsive* acknowledge the racial and cultural representation in a given class or group of children and provide experiences and content that respect diverse beliefs and value systems, traditions, family practices, and cultural histories. The provision of antibias curriculums and experiences recognizes cultural affiliations and other forms of diversity—language, socioeconomic, gender, and childhood ableness and special needs.

Interaction Patterns and Play Behaviors

Play provides an essential medium for the establishment of friendships and for the development of social knowledge, skills, and competence. According to Parten's (1933) early descriptions of play patterns and similar contemporary descriptions (Creasey, Jarvis, & Berk, 1998; Frost, Wortham, & Reifel, 2001; Howes, 1992, 1996), 4- and 5-year-olds should exhibit increasing skill in *associative* and/or *cooperative* play behaviors (Table 12.1). This play is characterized by greater desire to interact with playmates and participate in collaborative play activities. The onlooker, solitary/independent, and parallel/proximal forms of play that are observed in early stages of play development continue, however, and remain useful and productive play modes throughout life.

In **associative play**, children share and converse about materials and activities, but each player explores and uses the materials in individual ways. Associative play may involve following another child around, imitating or taking cues from other children's play behaviors, and engaging in conversation and nonverbal communication, yet one's own play preferences prevail over those of others. There is little or no bid for shared or focused play activities.

associative play: a loosely organized form of social play, characterized by overt social behaviors indicating common activities, shared interests, and interpersonal associations

---

TABLE 12.1   Interaction Patterns in Play

Parten (1933)	Howes (1980, 1992)	Winter (1985)
Onlooker play: Enjoys observing others		
Solitary play: Is content to play alone in same or different activity		*Independent play:* Plays alone or away from others
Parallel play: Plays beside or among others in similar activity without interacting	*Parallel play:* Plays in close proximity in similar activity; no attention to the play of others	*Proximal play:* Plays near others, engaged in own activity with no attempts to interact
Associative play: Plays with others, talking about the activity, but own play goals take precedence	*Mutual regard:* Shows awareness of others but no verbal interaction or attempt to engage in shared activity	*Relational play:* Communicates with others verbally or nonverbally but follows an activity choice without involving others
Cooperative play: Plays in an organized and cooperative way, with assigned roles and mutually agreed-upon play themes or goals	*Simple social play:* Plays in similar activity with social bids such as smiling or offering a toy	*Interactive play:* Is engaged with peers in a common activity
	Complementary play: Plays in same activity with some collaboration but no bids for shared engagement	
	Complementary reciprocal play: Involves social bids for shared engagement and collaborative activities	

cooperative play: a well-organized form of social play, characterized by well-defined social roles within play groups, influential peer leaders, and shared materials and equipment used to pursue a well-understood group play goal or theme

Cooperative play, by contrast, signals the child's growing ability to acknowledge the ideas of others and to incorporate those ideas into his or her play behaviors. This play is characterized by shared planning and organizing of play scenarios around goals or play themes. Who gets to play and who doesn't is decided by certain members of the group and can be inclusive or quite restrictive. Cooperative play, also referred to as complementary reciprocal play (Howes, 1992, 1996) and interactive play (Winter, 1985), involves higher levels of social interaction skills including interpersonal problem-solving skills and cooperation, acceptance of leadership or followership roles, perspective-taking, flexibility, language, and shared creativity and responsibilities.

Friendships and Play

In Miriam Cohen's (1967) sensitive children's book *Will I Have a Friend?*, Jim asks his father on the way to his first day at preschool, "Will I have a friend?" His father answers, "I think you will." This worried question is quite typical for children entering preschool or new play groups. It signals a very important aspect of psychosocial development: establishing and maintaining friendships.

Relating effectively with others is an important aspect of social competence, which we elaborate upon later in this chapter. Becoming socially competent with peers involves the development of certain social skills: (1) initiating interactions, (2) maintaining ongoing relations, and (3) resolving interpersonal conflicts (Asher, Renshaw, & Hymel, 1982).

Some children are more adept than others at initiating interactions, for example, the newcomer who seems to intuitively know how to integrate himself or herself into an unfamiliar group of children or an ongoing play activity. Children who tend to be popular with their peers initiate interactions by suggesting

Play provides an essential medium for the development of social knowledge, skills, and competence.

a joint activity or engaging others in talk (Asher et al., 1982; Hughes, 1999). These children seem to have a better sense of timing, waiting for an opportunity to join in, perhaps during a natural break in an ongoing activity. These children are also less obtrusive and create fewer disruptions in the play in progress. In contrast, unpopular children are more uncertain about how to initiate interactions and use offensive or vague strategies such as smiling or tactics that call attention to themselves rather than integrating themselves into the ongoing activity.

Friendships in 4- and 5-year-old children have their own characteristics, which are indicative of increasing cognitive and social development. Friendships in early childhood tend to be transient; that is, today's best friend may not be so tomorrow or perhaps even this afternoon. As children reach ages 4 and 5, friendships become more durable. During play sequences, however, conflict may arise over the use of a toy or how a shared activity should proceed, and a friendship can be promptly terminated, only to be reinstated soon thereafter.

As a rule, friendships at this age are dependent on proximity, shared activities or toys, and physical attributes (Epstein, 1989). This differs from the friendships of a later age, which are more often based on shared values, perceived virtues, and common interests (Rubin, Lynch, Coplan, Rose-Krasnor, & Booth, 1994). In young children, bartering for friendships ("I'll be your friend if you'll let me hold your doll") and threatening ("If you don't give me one of those trucks, I won't ever, ever be your friend!") are not uncommon. Once successfully initiated, social interactions teeter precariously on the edge of conflict. Young children lack the social behavior strategies, facility with language, and social knowledge needed to manage friendships well. Conflicts are frequent and can be quite intense.

For friendship maintenance and conflict resolution skills to emerge, young children need to experience peers in a variety of contexts: as visitors in their homes, in preschool settings, in neighborhood play groups, in family gatherings, and so on. There is some evidence that while parents and teachers provide very important guidance for children's developing social skills, children also benefit cognitively and socially from opportunities to interact with peers with minimum adult interaction (Kontos & Wilcox-Herzog, 1997). In the classroom context, these findings imply that activities and materials should be chosen to encourage and facilitate both children's cognitive engagement *and* social interaction.

Self-Control and Compliance

Studies of child-rearing practices have provided insights into the kinds of adult–child interactions that are most likely to result in child behaviors that are cooperative, self-controlled, and compliant. Infant attachment studies emphasize the importance of the infant–mother attachment in later development of compliance and social competence (Shonkoff & Phillips, 2000). When infants and toddlers have developed a warm, mutually affectionate relationship with their caregivers, they are more inclined to obey requests. Toddlers whose mothers are affectionate, verbally stimulating, and responsive and use positive methods of control are more compliant (Olson, Bates, & Bayles, 1984).

inductive discipline: a positive, nonpunitive form of discipline that relies on reasons and rationales to help children control their behaviors

power-assertive discipline: a form of discipline in which the power of the adult is used to coerce, deprive of privileges or material goods, or apply physical punishment to modify a child's behavior

permissive discipline: a noncontrolling, nondemanding form of discipline in which the child, for the most part, is allowed to regulate his or her behavior

authoritative discipline a child-rearing style in which child behavior is directed through rational and reasoned guidance from the adult

authoritarian discipline a child-rearing style in which parents apply rigid standards of conduct and expect unquestioning obedience from the child

Conversely, children whose parents have used arbitrary commands, physical control, or coercive strategies to bring children into compliance are less inclined to cooperate with other adults, regardless of how gentle or friendly those adults are (Londerville & Main, 1981; Main & Weston, 1981). The implications for these children as they enter preschool and kindergarten are clear. Caregivers and early childhood teachers may encounter challenges with such children in establishing rapport and in engendering a spirit of cooperation and compliance within the group.

Guidance techniques are often classified into three types: inductive, power assertive, and permissive. **Inductive discipline** uses a teaching mode in which children are provided reasons and rationales for expectations imposed on them. Inductive discipline sets logical limits for behavior and includes reasonable and logical consequences for noncompliance.

Power-assertive discipline, by contrast, uses coercion in the form of unreasonable and illogical threats (e.g., banishment from the group, withdrawal of love), deprivation of material objects and privileges, belittling remarks, and physical force or punishment. **Permissive discipline** tends to ignore inappropriate behaviors and generally fails to teach appropriate ones.

The consequences of guidance techniques have been the subject of numerous studies since the early research of Diana Baumrind (1967, 1971, 1972), in which parenting behaviors were described and classified as authoritative, authoritarian, permissive, or neglecting, each of which has its corresponding pattern of child behavior.

It is instructive to make a distinction between **authoritative** and **authoritarian** approaches to discipline. Authoritative guidance is inductive in that it provides reasoned and logical limits in a respectful, instructive, consistent, and predictable manner. Baumrind found that children of authoritative parents exhibited greater self-reliance and self-control, and friendlier and more cooperative behaviors. They tended to be more curious and optimistic, and better able to handle stress than other children. Subsequent studies have also found that inductive forms of discipline result in more cooperative, compliant, and self-controlled behaviors and are associated with more positive relationships and popularity with peers (Hart, DeWolf, Royston, Burts, & Thomasson, 1990; Hart, Ladd, & Burleson, 1990; Kontos & Wilcox-Herzog, 1997). Further, inductive forms of guidance have been associated with advanced moral development (Hoffman, 1988). More recent studies by Baumrind found that children who experienced authoritative parenting engaged in fewer risk-related behaviors during adolescence and were less inclined to experiment with or abuse drugs (Baumrind, 1991a, 1991b).

Authoritarian approaches, on the other hand, are power assertive and controlling. This style is often born out of a sensed need to maintain some preconceived order or a set standard of conduct regardless of context or extenuating circumstances. Obedience is expected, usually without benefit of explanation or logical rationale. Authoritarian adults may use coercive, punitive, forceful, or other negative means to maintain their rules or limits. Baumrind's studies found that children who experienced authoritarian guidance exhibited more moodiness, unhappiness, and annoyance, were inclined to show passive aggression or hostility, were less friendly, and were more vulnerable to stress.

Studies of children clinically referred for behavior problems find that they have often experienced parenting characterized by low tolerance levels and maturity demands on children that exceed age-related capabilities. These parents often have limited knowledge of development and therefore are insensitive to the guidance and instructional needs appropriate in different behavioral situations (Campbell, 2002).

Where permissive discipline is employed, guidelines, limits, and instruction are for the most part absent. Baumrind's studies found that children who experienced little or no guidance were the least self-controlled and self-reliant. Their behaviors were more inclined to be impulsive, aggressive, and rebellious. They were lower achievers than children who experienced more positive and instructive forms of guidance (Figure 12.2).

Clearly, guidance techniques have both short-term and long-term goals and consequences. Meeting short-term goals may require quick thinking and action on the part of an adult to protect the child and others. On the other hand, to learn from experiences and guidance, short-term strategies need to cognitively engage the child on topics of prevention, restitution, and limits and why they exist. It is important to realize that short-term "fixes" (e.g, the toy truck put away to stop the possession argument; time-out chair used for one who uttered inappropriate words; chatty friends separated; candy provided for putting toys where they belong) seldom provide the cognitive or social tools children need in order to self-control. Nor do these events help children acquire the insights needed to interact appropriately with one another or behave as expected in a variety of contexts.

Short-term goals

    Protect children from endangering themselves or others, which includes

        Curtailing risky behaviors

        Preventing or defusing anger

        Preventing and resolving conflicts

    Reduce behaviors that are disruptive or disturbing to others, which includes

        Respecting the privacy of others

        Respecting the personal space (including the visual and auditory space) of others

    Prevent the destruction of property, the child's or that of others

Long-term goals

    Establish positive self-concept and self-confidence

    Develop self-direction and self-regulation

    Develop prosocial perspectives and behaviors, which includes

        Strengthening problem-solving skills

        Learning to take another's point of view

        Increasing the capacity for empathy and altruism

    Acquire characteristics of character and morality

    Gain autonomy in choices and decision making

FIGURE 12.2
Guidance Goals for Young Children

Inductive approaches take time and repetition, and better serve long-term social and moral goals (Figure 12.3).

Social and Moral Competence

Jeremy has brought to kindergarten a large, multiple-color water painting set that was purchased for him yesterday. He proudly shows it to some of his classmates. Many of them offer to play with him if he will share the water paints. Since the water paints are still new to him, Jeremy emphatically replies, "No, not now! No one can use my paint set." He then retreats to a table to work alone with his paints. One or two persistent classmates follow him to the table and continue to beg and prod. Finally, Jeremy capitulates, "OK, Madeline, you can paint with me, but Joey, you can't paint with us. Maybe tomorrow I will let you paint."

Toys from the sociodramatic center are frequently finding their way into the restroom and remaining there until the teacher retrieves them. In addition to becoming soiled, the toys are "lost" and unavailable to others who want to play with them. Angela's teacher convenes a class meeting to discuss the situation. After explaining her concerns about the availability and cleanliness of the toys, she asks the class to help her find a solution to this problem.

Thomas asserts that whoever is doing that should "get a spanking." Geraldo insists that if the toys are really lost or too dirty to play with, his daddy will buy new toys. Katie suggests that if they get dirty, her mommy can wash them. Rashid implores the teacher to throw the toys away, as they might be "really, really, really dirty!"

Sensing the direction in which the discussion is going, the teacher attempts to bring the children back to the central issue: responsibility for the care of classroom materials. "You have made some interesting suggestions and have been very thoughtful; we all appreciate that. However, I am still wondering if there is something we ourselves can do right here in our classroom and not involve people who are not here with us every day."

Carson suggests, "We could wash our own toys in the sand–water table."

Then Angela, after moments of musing and listening and with a look of earnest contemplation, suggests, "We can put a sign on the toilet door that says 'No toys allowed' to remind everybody not to take toys in there." Her classmates agree and talk about who will make the sign.

The teacher further enlists the children: "Is there anything else we can do?"

Angela, her problem-solving abilities taxed to the limit, asserts, "They will just have to remember not to do that."

Each of these vignettes illustrates different levels of social competence. How would you characterize a socially competent person? Does that person demonstrate any of these characteristics: positive self-regard, self-confidence, curiosity, spontaneity, humor, warmth, reliability, sense of right and wrong, self-discipline, morally responsible behaviors, awareness of the needs of others, positive interactions with others, genuineness, friendliness, cooperation, problem-solving ability, adaptability, helpfulness, and/or ability to give and receive praise? Which of these or other descriptors did Jeremy display? What characteristics describe Angela's social competence?

1. Provide an environment in which the child's growing sense of initiative can flourish. Such an environment includes
   - Adequate space for the child to use and pursue toys, equipment, creative materials, and realia
   - Developmentally appropriate and culturally inclusive play items and activities through which children can experience success and enhanced self-confidence and self-esteem
   - Low, open shelves for personal work and play materials
   - Engaging, enriching play items that encourage decision making, sharing, and cooperating
   - Safe and sturdy furnishing, play items, and surroundings

2. Provide an atmosphere in which it is not only physically but also psychologically safe to explore, experiment, and ask questions. Such an atmosphere includes
   - Rich interactional opportunities that encourage dialogue
   - Answers to questions and encouragement of further curiosities

3. Provide opportunities to interact with other children and to participate in peer groups. This allows children to
   - Share and problem solve with agemates
   - Engage in sustained sociodramatic play with other children

4. Establish a predictable daily schedule to help children develop a sense of time and anticipate and respond appropriately to regular events. Such a schedule
   - Meets the child's physiological needs for food, water, rest, and exercise
   - Adjusts activities and expectations to the child's short but expanding attention span
   - Provides advance notice of a need to change from one event to another
   - Allows time for the completion of tasks once started
   - Avoids long waiting times

5. Involve children in the setting of rules, limits, and standards for behavior:
   - Set simple rules that are few in number, truly necessary, and focused on the most crucial behaviors first. Perhaps the three *D*s of discipline is a good starting point: Set rules that help children recognize things that are Dangerous, Destructive, and/or Disturbing or hurtful to others. However, rules should always be stated in a positive way, telling children *what* to do rather than *what not* to do.
   - Explain the reasons behind rules, and engage children in conversations about logical consequences and the need for reciprocity.
   - Assign age-appropriate chores and responsibilities with adult assistance if needed. Chores can include returning personal items to assigned places, tidying room or toy shelves, watering certain houseplants, or caring for a pet.

FIGURE 12.3
Supporting Compliance and Self-Control in 4- and 5-Year-Old Children

While we can describe social competence and certainly appreciate its value in social interactions, a concrete definition has been difficult for theorists to construct, particularly in terms of measuring social competence achievement (Katz & McClellan, 1997). However, for the most part, experts agree on the antecedents of social competence:

1. Social competence emerges from *social development,* in which the child exhibits a growing awareness of others and chooses to interact or not to interact with them. Social development includes establishing a repertoire of strategies for initiating interactions and ways to sustain them. Feelings and responses evoked by social interactions determine the extent to which the child is motivated to pursue further social interactions.

2. The *socialization processes* and *sociocultural contexts* in which children grow and learn impose values, beliefs, customs, and social skills that have been transmitted from one generation to the next. Through sociocultural contexts, children learn the expectations of their families and cultural groups. Children in various cultural groups develop social perspectives and social abilities that allow them to succeed in a particular sociocultural context. Parents are generally the primary socializing agents; other socializing agents include siblings and other extended family members, family friends, and neighbors. The socialization of young children is also influenced by experiences in child care and preschool settings, faith-based affiliations, and other groups. Children also develop social concepts and behaviors through their observations of and interactions with many people in many different places and contexts and through their television and other media experiences. Prosocial development (including perspective-taking ability and a theory of mind), positive self-regard, gender understandings, self-control, moral development, and awareness of diversity and individual differences all influence the development of social competence and the child's emerging abilities to make and sustain friendships and to share mutual benefits from positive interactions with others.

Given these antecedents, we find the summary definition proposed by Katz and McClellan (1997) particularly helpful: "the competent individual is a person who can use environmental and personal resources to achieve a good developmental outcome—an outcome that makes possible satisfying and competent participation in and contributions to the groups, communities, and larger society to which one belongs" (p. 1). According to these scholars, social competence is characterized by several attributes, including the following:

- The ability to regulate emotions
- Social knowledge and understanding sufficient to form friendships
- The ability to recognize and respond appropriately to social cues in others and use language to interact effectively
- Certain social skills such as social approach techniques, giving positive attention to others, contributing to ongoing discussion among peers, and turn taking
- The dispositions or habits of mind that are conducive to effective social relationships, such as cooperativeness, responsibleness, and empathy.

FACTORS INFLUENCING PSYCHOSOCIAL DEVELOPMENT IN CHILDREN AGES FOUR THROUGH FIVE

Psychosocial development can be attributed to a number of factors. Among them are the child's personality and unique developmental pathways, support for the developing sense of initiative, support for special and developmental needs, the nature of familial and extrafamilial interactions and caregiving strategies, sibling and peer relationships, and television and other media. Let's look briefly at each of these factors in turn.

Individual Temperament and Personality

In previous chapters, we explored the role of individual temperaments, which children seem to innately possess, and the effects of the goodness-of-fit relationships proposed by Chess and Thomas (1987). Additional studies of the reciprocal relationship between the personalities of children and their caregivers expand on this theory.

In their studies, Bell and Chapman (1986) proposed a control system model of how parents and children regulate each other's behaviors. The model suggests that both parent and child have behavioral repertoires that elicit predictable responses in each other. Both parent and child are said to have upper and lower limits of tolerance for the intensity, frequency, and situational appropriateness of behaviors exhibited by the other.

In addition to temperament and control systems, other characteristics of children influence the types of responses they get from others. Physical appearance, and notions of attractiveness or unattractiveness, health, vitality, cleanliness, and grooming produce behaviors that can be either positive and prosocial or negative and difficult. A study by Langlois and Down (1980) found that social behaviors of "attractive" and "unattractive" children at age 3 did not differ appreciably, but by age 5, "unattractive" children exhibited more aggression toward their peers, suggesting a behavior response to being perceived as unattractive. The manner in which others respond to a child determines, to a great extent, the child's reciprocal responses (Bierman, 2003).

Support and Encouragement for a Sense of Initiative

Initiative is fostered through opportunities to explore and engage in new and challenging activities. Four- and 5-year-old children benefit from opportunities for social interactions, cooperative endeavors, and mind-engaging projects.

Raw materials from which to create, and space and props for imaginative play, support the developing sense of initiative by providing media through which children manage their ideas. Adults support childhood initiative through dialogue and conversations with children whereby they may provide meaningful answers to *how* and *why* questions. Provision of age-appropriate toys, learning materials, and social interactions helps children to experience the products of their efforts and to begin to trust their ideas. Allowing children to make choices, helping children to reflect on the decisions they make, and anticipating ways in which children can share or take full responsibility for an activity or event also support the developing sense of initiative. Observing and acknowledging a child's particular interests and skills helps adults to select the types of activities and interactions best suited for that child. As children experience success in their particular interest or skill areas, they gain awareness of the unique ways in which they can participate and contribute to an activity or event. Setting reasoned limits and offering guidance for behavior assist children in learning the boundaries of initiative.

Support for Special Developmental Needs

Children with special needs are at heightened risk for socialization problems. Self-concept, self-esteem, prosocial behaviors, and the development of friendships may be particularly vulnerable areas of development. Socialization problems that children with development challenges, chronic disease, or disabilities may experience include problems in learning how to initiate friendships and activities, shyness and withdrawal, and the accompanying difficulty with reciprocal interactions. Hearing-impaired children tend to have difficulties in this area and are often misinterpreted by others as unfriendly. A lack of social comprehension skills is not uncommon in children with learning disabilities (Howard, Williams, Port, & Lepper, 2001), who frequently misread the social cues of others and consequently use inappropriate means of initiating contacts and making friends. These children may also have difficulty in perspective-taking, preventing them from taking others' feelings and views into consideration (Bryan & Bryan, 1986). Visually impaired children may fail to provide facial cues of friendliness and other nonverbal cues that encourage interactions with others (Van Hasselt, 1983). Children with physical impairments such as cerebral palsy may not provide the postural and gestural communications that successfully convey their feelings and needs.

Children with special needs may benefit from direct instruction in the social behaviors they need to interact successfully with others. Dialogue, role playing, peer mentoring, and role models (both adult and children) can be used to coach and enhance social skills.

Helping other children to accept and interact with children with special needs provides an essential learning experience for them. Because young children are curious and often quite frank, teachers will want to provide reassuring and accurate information about the child and the child's disabilities but should avoid labeling or an otherwise embarrassing discussion. The teacher should provide opportunities for all children to interact and should monitor play and work behaviors for opportunities to assist and to promote prosocial interactions.

Nature of Family and Extrafamilial Interactions

Although 4- through 5-year-olds are becoming more independent, self-sufficient, and eager for social interactions with their peers, they continue to depend on adults for support and guidance as they explore an ever-widening social world. As during infancy and the toddler period, children ages 4 through 5 continue to seek intimacy and affection, communication and companionship, encouragement and assistance, and assurances and affirmation from those who care for them. Children also look to adults to protect them from harm, provide reasoned guidance and leadership, and teach them or help them to discover acceptable and effective social behaviors and emotional outlets. As children attempt to understand their feelings and desires and strive to govern their behaviors and interactions, they take many of their cues from the behaviors of those around them.

Angela is setting the table in the home-living center at kindergarten. Her friend Jason joins her and proceeds to pour water in the cups for "hot chocolate." The two seat themselves and begin to sip, when Angela interrupts and reprimands Jason, "You have to put your napkin in your lap first." To which Jason queries, "Why?" Angela responds, "Because that's the way my Mama does it."

Young children carefully observe the interactions and responses, both verbal and nonverbal, of adults who care for them. Young children are particularly cognizant of the words and actions of those with whom they have close and warm relationships (Bandura, 1977, 1997; Kontos & Wilcox-Herzog, 1997). These observations often become incorporated into the child's behavior and have the potential to become internalized and lasting.

In addition to the impact of the adult model on psychosocial development, adults (parents, caregivers, preschool teachers) influence psychosocial development through the quality of the support system they provide for the child's emerging sense of self, self-esteem, and self-confidence. The nurturing dimensions of their relationships with children are critical. Guidance and disciplinary strategies, developmentally appropriate (or inappropriate) expectations, and the degree to which adults attempt to coach children in social skills are all determinants of positive or negative outcomes for psychosocial development.

Sibling Relationships

Siblings influence one another's psychosocial development in reciprocal ways. Though the quality of sibling relationships varies from family to family and depends on a variety of factors, including the number and ages of siblings in the family, children learn from interactions with their siblings. From siblings, children learn family rules and values and how to play with others of different ages. They learn to share family time, space, and resources. They learn about gender and gender-role behaviors. They learn to communicate their needs and to respond to the needs of others. They learn to disagree and to resolve disagreements. They learn about individual differences and individual rights and about loyalty and mutual caring.

Older siblings may be called on to care for younger ones. In this role, the older sibling becomes playmate, teacher, and disciplinarian. Children sometimes form attachment relationships with their older siblings. While older siblings may focus on the parent as the role model, younger ones focus on the older sibling (Baskett, 1984). In times of family grief or trauma, siblings may rely on one another for support and comfort (Banks & Kahn, 2003; Chess & Thomas, 1987), or they may suffer deteriorated peer relationships (Hetherington, Cox, & Cox, 1982).

Sibling rivalry, a common occurrence in families, receives considerable attention in both popular and scholarly literature. Studies have shown, however, that kindness and affection are more common in sibling relationships than are the antagonistic and rivalrous behaviors that are so often discussed (Abramovitch, Corter, Pepler, & Stanhope, 1986; Baskett & Johnson, 1982).

Sibling rivalry is generally a response to feelings of jealousy or loss of attention or nurturing. Changes in family structure due to divorce, remarriage, blended or reconstituted families, a new baby, or the illness of a family member may give rise to these feelings. Rivalry can occur when perceived favoritism, inconsistent child-rearing practices, birth-order attributions, or gender stereotyping within the family causes the allocation of affection, assignment of chores, and expectations of certain behaviors and achievements to differ from one child to another.

It is important to recognize the positive and supportive nature of sibling relationships for children. Four- and 5-year-olds want to talk about their younger and older siblings. They also enjoy having siblings visit their classroom, showing them around, and introducing them to friends. In school and child care settings where siblings may be attending in other classrooms, sensitive adults allow brothers and sisters to visit with one another when possible. It is particularly comforting for younger siblings to locate the older one's classroom to have a mental picture of where a brother or sister is while they are separated. This is often true for the older sibling as well. In times of illness or distress at school, siblings can provide a measure of security until parents can be summoned.

Sibling relationships are generally more positive than negative and are mutually supportive.

Peer Relationships

Young children enjoy the company of their peers. The amount and types of peer interactions that children have experienced by 4 or 5 years of age vary widely. Some children have experienced agemates from infancy through child care arrangements; others may have had few peer group interactions before enrollment in kindergarten at age 5.

From peers, children learn both appropriate and inappropriate behaviors. As models, peers often serve as frames of reference for self-evaluation. Experience with prosocial peer models may encourage prosocial imitative behaviors. Aggressive models encourage experimentation with aggressive forms of behavior. Peer groups may be viewed as a testing ground for the child to explore and experience social interactions. While peers serve to enhance and enlarge the child's social awareness at ages 4 and 5, adults remain the source of greatest influence. Later, peers will become increasingly influential in the social lives of children.

Television and Technology

Today's children enjoy the products of an ever-changing and expanding electronics industry. Although personal computers are running a close second, television remains the most universally accessed electronic medium and has been a topic of concern and research for decades. Much of the literature relating to television's influence on children's minds and behaviors has addressed violence and aggression, inadequate and inappropriate gender and cultural role models, and the effects of advertising directed at young consumers. Other studies have attempted to identify the positive influences of television on such aspects of development as language, literacy, knowledge, and prosocial behaviors. The more recent technologies of computers, video equipment, and electronic toys and devices are finding their way into more and more U.S. homes and, like television, are coming under the scrutiny of child development and early education researchers.

The effects of television, video games, assorted electronic toys, and other devices on psychosocial development depend on a number of factors, including the amount of time spent using them, the amount of time spent on other healthy and productive activities, the content and quality of the programs and games, and the attitudes and values surrounding the use of these technologies. Time spent watching television precludes physical activities needed to enhance motor development and physical fitness. The reduction in opportunities to engage in focused interactions with playmates, parents, and others interferes with healthy psychosocial development.

Because it is believed that children learn best through interactive processes, excessive solitary screen time use of electronic media can be deleterious to cognitive as well as social development. Because children seek authentic feedback from others to help them make sense of their experiences, excessive use of electronic media disrupts human input and interaction. Moreover, the child's limited abilities to separate fantasy from reality and the emerging sense of rules and their applications often make the content of television, video games, and other electronic media confusing and misleading.

Concern over bias, violence, aggression, vulgarity, and explicit sex in media programs and video games has prompted numerous studies on their long-term effects and child advocacy efforts to curtail programming known to result in imitative and desensitized behaviors (Levin, 2003). One study in 1992 estimated that by the time children finish elementary school, they will have seen 8,000 murders and 100,000 other acts of violence (American Psychological Association, 1993), and this trend has not abated as this text goes to press (Levin, 2003). Responding to increasing concern over violence in the media, the Governing Board of the National Association for the Education of Young Children (NAEYC) has published a position statement and a teachers' guide (NAEYC, 1995) condemning violent television programming, movies, videotapes, computer games, and other forms of media to which young children are exposed.

Bronfenbrenner (1970) expressed concern about the effects of television (and we would add other electronic media) on family interactions when he suggested that "[it is] not so much in the behavior it produces as the behavior it prevents" (p. 170). Family interactions, including talking, arguing, playing games, and taking part in family festivities, are among the forgone opportunities that Bronfrenbrenner (1970, 1986) saw as essential for learning and the formation of character.

On the other hand, a number of programs do promote prosocial behaviors and understandings, and child and family viewing can be guided toward them. Regular exposure to such programming has been shown to positively influence children's behavior (Coates, Pusser, & Goodman, 1976; Freidrich & Stein, 1975). However, viewing alone does not ensure positive behaviors. Children need adults to help them verbalize their understandings (and misunderstandings) of program topics and role models and to encourage them to role-play and use prosocial behaviors of admired characters in their daily interactions.

ROLE OF THE EARLY CHILDHOOD PROFESSIONAL

Enhancing Psychosocial Development of Children Ages Four through Five

1. Support the child's continuing need for nurturance and security.
2. Support the child's emerging sense of self and provide experiences and interactions that promote self-esteem.
3. Model and coach prosocial behaviors.
4. Facilitate initiative while providing safe, reasonable limits.
5. Help children to understand and cope with their fears, anger, and other emotions.
6. Facilitate perspective-taking in children through dialogue and role playing.
7. Provide authoritative and instructive discipline.
8. Facilitate engaged, productive play and interactions with other children.
9. Facilitate positive sibling relationships by minimizing comparisons and competition, and encouraging individuality.
10. Respond respectfully to the child's questions about gender, race, and diversity with focused interest and nonbiased and helpful answers.

KEY TERMS

altruism	ethology	moral relativism
associative play	heteronomous morality	permissive discipline
authoritarian discipline	inductive discipline	power-assertive discipline
authoritative discipline	initiative	theory of mind
cooperative play	moral realism	

REVIEW STRATEGIES AND ACTIVITIES

1. Review the key terms in this chapter individually or with a classmate.

2. Visit an exemplary prekindergarten or kindergarten classroom in your local public school.

   a. Observe and record teacher behaviors that model social skills for children, including empathy and altruism, initiating conversations and friendships, accepting and understanding others, perspective-taking, prosocial behaviors, and the cultural perspectives of teachers and parents.

   b. Observe and record attempts to teach or coach social skills.

3. At another time in this same classroom, observe and record anecdotal accounts of associative and cooperative play behaviors among the children. What types of activities promote cooperative play behaviors?

4. Interview several parents of 4- and 5-year-old children. Ask what kinds of limits they set for their children. Which ones do they emphasize most often? Why? How do they enforce these limits at home? What did you learn about the behavior priorities of parents?

5. Interview several prekindergarten or kindergarten teachers. What kinds of limits do they set for children in the classroom? Why? How do they enforce these limits? What did you learn about the behavior priorities of teachers? In what ways are teachers and parents the same or different in this respect?

6. Watch three popular children's television shows several times over a period of three weeks. Record the prosocial and/or aggressive or violent events that take place in each. Compare the different programs. Were there differences in the specific prosocial or aggressive behaviors emphasized by the different programs? How engaging were the role models? How did the commercials communicate with young viewers? What messages do the commercials convey to children?

7. With your classmates, develop a list of television programs and/or video games that might be considered developmentally sound for 4- and 5-year-old children. Make a list of their redeeming features.

8. Discuss with your classmates the role of adults in helping children to use technology in ways that can enhance psychosocial development.

FURTHER READINGS

Bell, S. H., Carr, V. W., Denno, D., Johnson, L. J., & Phillips, L. R. (2004). *Challenging behaviors in early childhood settings: Creating a place for all children.* Baltimore: Brookes.

Derman-Sparks, L., & Phillips, C. B. (1997). *Teaching/learning anti-racism: A developmental approach.* New York: Teachers College Press.

DeVries, R., & Zan, B. (1994). *Moral classrooms, moral children: Creating a constructivist atmosphere in early education.* New York: Teachers College Press.

Elkind, D. (2001). *The hurried child: Growing up too fast too soon.* New York: Perseus Books Group.

Hopkins, S. (1999). *Hearing everyone's voice: Educating young children for peace and democratic community.* Redmond, WA: Child Care Information Exchange.

Kaiser, B., & Rasminsky, J. S. (1999). *Meeting the challenge: Effective strategies for challenging behaviours in early childhood environments.* Ottawa: Canadian Child Care Federation.

Katz, L. G., & McClellan, D. E. (1997). *Fostering children's social competence: The teacher's role.* Washington, DC: National Association for the Education of Young Children.

Kemple, K. M. (2004). *Let's be friends: Peer competence and social inclusion in early childhood programs.* New York: Teachers College Press.

Levin, D. E. (1998). *Remote control childhood?: Combating the hazards of media culture.* Washington, DC: National Association for the Education of Young Children.

Levin, D. E. (2003). *Teaching young children in violent times* (2nd ed.). Washington, DC: National Association for the Education of Young Children.

Lowenthal, B. (2001). *Abuse and neglect: The educator's guide to the identification and prevention of child maltreatment.* Baltimore: Brookes.

Sexuality Information and Education Council of the United States. (1998). *Right from the start: Guidelines for sexuality issues birth to five years.* New York: Author.

OTHER RESOURCES

AARP Grandparent Information Center
    601 E. Street, NW
    Washington, DC 20049
    www.arp.org/grandparents

American Academy of Child and Adolescent Psychiatry Facts for Families (Fact sheets)
    http://www.aacap.org/publications/factsfam/

ERIC: Clearinghouse on Elementary and Early Childhood Education
    University of Illinois
    51 Gerty Drive
    Champaign, IL 61820-7469

ERIC digests (concise one-page articles and reports on timely issues) include the following:
    Darling, N. (1999). *Parenting style and its correlates* (EDO-PS-99-3)
    Marion, M. (1999). *Helping young children deal with anger* (EDO-PS-97-24)
    McClellan, D. E., & Katz, L. G. (1993). *Young children's social development: A checklist* (EDO-PS-93-6)
    Ramsburg, D. (1997). *The debate over spanking* (EDO-PS-97-13)

CHAPTER THIRTEEN

Cognitive, Language, and Literacy Development: Ages Four Through Five

Was it not then that I acquired all that now sustains me? And I gained so much and so quickly that during the rest of my life I did not acquire a hundredth part of it. From myself as a five-year-old to myself as I now am there is only one step. The distance between myself as an infant and myself at five years is tremendous.

LEO TOLSTOY

After studying this chapter, you will demonstrate comprehension by:

▶ Recognizing theoretical perspectives on cognitive, language, and literacy development in children ages 4 through 5.

▶ Describing cognitive development in children ages 4 through 5.

▶ Describing language development in children ages 4 through 5.

▶ Describing literacy development in children ages 4 through 5.

▶ Relating cognitive, language, and literacy development to other developmental domains.

▶ Identifying major factors influencing cognitive, language, and literacy development in children ages 4 through 5.

▶ Suggesting strategies for promoting cognitive, language, and literacy development in children ages 4 through 5.

From previous chapters, we have learned that cognitive development has both biological and environmental origins, is quite rapid in the preschool years from birth through age 8, is at first dominated by the child's sensory and motor capabilities, and influences and is influenced by growth and development in all other domains—physical, emotional, social, language, and literacy. What are we now learning about the cognitive development of children in the 4th through 5th years? Let's begin this discussion as we usually do, with a look at theoretical perspectives on cognitive, language, and literacy development.

THEORETICAL PERSPECTIVES ON COGNITIVE DEVELOPMENT DURING AGES FOUR THROUGH FIVE

Piaget and the Four- Through Five-Year-Old Child

Piaget's research indicated that children under age 6 or 7 are not capable of sophisticated mental operations or logical reasoning—hence the term *preoperational*. From Piaget's perspective, this means that young children cannot yet form accurate internal representations of actions because thought is still dependent on perceptions (Piaget & Inhelder, 1969).

Piaget came to his conclusions about the preoperational stage in children's thinking after conducting a number of conservation experiments, as when an amount of liquid is poured from a tall, slender container into a short, wider one, or when a ball of clay is rolled into a long, thin rope. To the preoperational thinker, the original amount changes depending on the size and shape of the container or the shaping of the ball of clay. Such children do not yet apply **conservation**, and judge the amount of the liquid and the clay by its appearance (tall is more; long is more), and do so even when they have seen the liquid poured from one container

conservation:
the understanding that physical attributes (e.g., mass and weight) stay the same even if appearance changes

385

centration:
the tendency to attend to a limited number of features of an object or event

transformation:
attending to all the states of an event from the beginning, to in-between, to the final stage

irreversibility:
the inability of preoperational children to reverse their thinking and to return to their original point of thought

class inclusion:
understanding the relationship between class and subclass, which occurs during the period of concrete operational thought

transivity:
the ability to seriate, or order, according to some attribute, such as height or size

to the other and back, or the clay rolled from a ball into a rope and back to its original shape. The process of **transformation** eludes them. Children generally do not apply the concept of conservation until they reach the stage of concrete operations. Conservation is the understanding that the physical attributes of an object or substance remain the same even if its appearance changes.

Piaget's explanation of this lack of ability to conserve was based on young children's behaviors in a number of his experiments. For example, he noted that preoperational children tended to focus on specific events (a thought process that he called **centration**) rather than on the process of transformation, or attending to all states or stages of an event from beginning to end. For example, preoperational children had difficulty representing the in-between successive stages of a pencil falling. Recall from Chapter 10 that Piaget described a transductive way of thinking that centers on specific parts of an event rather than on a more complete perception and the relationship among all the parts. Piaget indicated that young children lack the ability to reason inductively (to proceed in their thinking from the specific to the general) nor do they readily reason deductively (move from the general to the specifics of a situation) (Flavell, 1963). Preoperational thought is perception bound; that is, concepts are based on how things are sensed—how they appear, sound, and feel.

In addition to the perception-bound thinking of preoperational children (Table 10.1), **irreversibility** is another characteristic of their cognitive processes. It is the most distinguishing difference between the thinking of preoperational children and the thinking of older children and adults. Irreversibility refers to the inability of young children to reverse their thinking and return to the beginning point of their thought. This characteristic of preoperational thinking is illustrated by the following example: The same number of objects is placed in two parallel rows of the same length. Then, as children watch, the objects in one row are spread out so that they appear in a wider array than the other row (as in Figure 10.1). When asked which row has more objects, preoperational children point to the longer row. The children's inability to reverse their thinking to the beginning of the experiment, when there were two rows of the same length with the same number of objects, prevents them from understanding that both rows contain the same number of objects even though they watched the transformation of a short row of objects into a longer one.

If children ages 2 to 3 are asked to group objects that belong together, they are generally unable to do so. Some time between age 4 and age 6, children begin to group and classify objects on the basis of their attributes, such as color, shape, size, and function. However, their efforts are not systematic, and they often forget the attribute to which they were originally attending. Late in the preoperational period, children can systematically classify objects on the basis of attributes. However, they cannot deal with **class inclusion**, or the hierarchies of classification. This behavior is illustrated by the flower experiment (Flavell, 1985). Children are presented with an array of flowers, most of them red and a few white. The children are asked whether there are "more red flowers or more flowers." The usual response of the preoperational child is that there are more red flowers. This experiment illustrates the preoperational child's inability to focus on the whole class—flowers—and the tendency to center on certain aspects of a situation—color.

A distinguishing feature between the thought of early and later preoperational children is **transivity**, or the ability to seriate (order) according to relational order, such as size, height, and color brightness. Children ages 2 to 3 generally cannot arrange a series of objects from shortest to longest. Older preoperational children can succeed with this task. However, they cannot seriate representationally, that is, mentally place objects or ideas in some relational order, but must use concrete objects to do so (Kamii, 2000, 2003; Piaget & Inhelder, 1956).

Still another feature of thought processes that develops during the preoperational stage is **identity constancy**. Identity constancy is the understanding that the characteristics of a person or species remain the same even though its appearance can be altered through the use of masks or costumes. Younger preoperational children do not demonstrate identity constancy.

identity constancy:
the understanding
that a person or
species remains the
same, even though
appearance is
changed through
masks, costumes, or
other transforma-
tions

Angela, age 4, visited a toy store with her grandmother, where their friend and neighbor, a salesperson at the store, was dressed as the storybook character Madeline. Angela hid behind her grandmother and peeked out in fear of the costumed person. Even though the voice behind the mask was quite familiar, her fear did not abate until she and her grandmother had left the store to return home.

By the time children are around ages 5 and 6, they begin to understand that identity remains constant even though physical appearance is changed (DeVries, 1969). The development of identity constancy can be observed in Jeremy's behavior in the following vignette:

Shortly after Jeremy turned three, Ann's mother came to visit for several weeks. It was close to Halloween, and Grandma wanted to help make Jeremy's costume. Jeremy decided that he wanted to be a ghost. Ann found an old white sheet, and Grandma began to make Jeremy's costume. At first, Jeremy seemed quite enthusiastic about being a ghost for Halloween. However, as time went on, he seemed increasingly reluctant to be fitted for his costume. When Ann and her mother picked up Jeremy at school on the day of the Halloween party, they asked Jeremy's teacher whether he had worn his costume during the parade. Ms. Buckley said that he had. Ann then described the change in Jeremy's behavior while the costume was being made. Jeremy's teacher then explained that at this age, reality and fantasy are not clearly defined in the young child's mind. Jeremy was probably fearful that he might actually become a ghost if he wore the costume. The ghost costume was put in a toy box, but Jeremy did not play with it. Shortly after Jeremy's 4th birthday, he was taking all the toys out of his toy box. He discovered the ghost costume, put it on, and ran around the house shouting, "Boo!" From then on, Jeremy would play "ghost" occasionally. Ann thought about what Ms. Buckley had said. She also noted that when they were reading, Jeremy was beginning to talk about whether the story could "really happen." These behaviors seemed to indicate that Jeremy was achieving identity constancy and was becoming increasingly able to differentiate between reality and fantasy.

In summary, younger preoperational children may be perceptually bound in their approach to conservation problems. However, as children move through the preoperational stage, their reliance on perceptual strategies to solve problems decreases. Gradually, they begin to solve conservation problems through manipulation and experimentation with concrete objects, then counting, measuring, and

As children move through the pre-operational stage, their reliance on perception to solve problems decreases.

applying other logical strategies. Later in the elementary school years, they do not have to rely as often on concrete experiences to solve conservation problems; however, this process continues to facilitate understanding throughout the schooling years. Indeed, even adults sometimes rely on concrete, firsthand experiences to learn some things.

Neo-Piagetian studies during the last two decades have yielded evidence that young children's thought is more sophisticated and evolving than Piaget indicated. However, Piaget's notion that true understanding of conservation of number, length, liquid, and mass is not possible until age 6 and after is probably accurate (Flavell, 1985).

Information-Processing Theory

While Piaget's theory provides a sense of how a child thinks at different points in growth and development, the information-processing model of child cognition represents a systematic approach to cognitive development that differs from Piaget's invariant stage-sequence theory. As this model suggests, an individual receives information from the environment through the senses (vision, hearing, touch, taste, and smell). This information then enters short-term memory storage, the STM file, a place where the mind can work on this information. How does one cognitively "work" on this initial information? According to the information-processing model, certain cognitive events occur that result in either placing this information in long-term memory storage, the LTM, or discarding it. Unlike younger children, as children get older, they begin to employ memory, association, and other strategies to process input information. Such mental strategies include attending, rehearsing (repeating a thought or concept over and over until it can be remembered or understood), retrieving information stored in long-term memory, coding features of a concept to form mental images or representations, making decisions about certain features of the input that make it worth remembering, and employing problem-solving strategies.

Certain processes flow from these cognitive activities (or mental strategies); drawing further information from the environment to process and/or drawing further information from long-term memory storage to assist in interpreting, classifying, and modifying new information so that one can use the information, respond to it, and/or simply store it in the LTM.

In the past, children's cognitive development and thinking processes were explored in terms of their lack of sustained attention. The child's limited ability to store information in long-term and short-term memory and to apply it was viewed as problematic. However, many parents and early childhood professionals have observed that young children can indeed hold information in short-term and long-term memory and, in certain contexts, can demonstrate extended attention spans. Consider the number of 4- and 5-year-olds who show long-term memory and extended attention spans when dealing with a high-interest subject such as dinosaurs. Indeed, investigation has demonstrated that both short- and long-term memory appear to vary more widely than was previously thought (Gauvain, 2000; Siegler, 1998). Consequently, some researchers have modified the memory-store, information-processing approach by proposing a **levels-of-processing theory.** This idea suggests that one's attention is not limited by memory constraints, but is influenced by the following:

- The child's increasingly effective use of strategies in logical, meaningful circumstances that are easier to process than global or general situations
- The child's interests
- The extent of the child's background knowledge and experience
- The amount of freedom and time to mentally combine and consolidate previous ideas or generate new ones
- The manner in which information is presented

When information is presented appropriately, levels of attention and cognitive performance increase—and at times surpass—the performance of less knowledgeable adults and older children (Beddard & Chi, 1992; Vygotsky, 1987). Information that is processed meaningfully and linked with other background information is retained and can be demonstrated by the young child. Information that is presented in a superficial way is soon forgotten and cannot be used by the child. Early childhood professionals facilitate information processing in young children by engaging them in observing and attending to environmental stimuli and by providing interesting and meaningful experiences that develop background information from which children can draw when confronted with new information.

Case (1992) attempted to portray a model of cognitive development that integrates stage-sequence theory with recent research relating to specific tasks, developmental domains, and sociocultural dimensions of cognitive development. His theory is an attempt to unite Piagetian and information-processing theories. Case asserted that research data support the concept of general stages in cognitive development; however, he suggested that this concept does not go far enough. Other groups of neo-Piagetians continue to maintain that differences in cognitive development among and within same-age groups of children are the rule rather than the exception (Kuhn, 1992). It is believed that while children do

levels-of-processing theory: an information-processing model that focuses on the depth of attention rather than on aspects of memory in explaining levels of cognitive performance

indeed learn through assimilation and accommodation, there is no global stage for all learning; rather, each learning domain—social conventions, language, mathematics, and so on—has different and distinct stages or sequences of development. Table 13.1, given later in this chapter, provides examples of developmental sequences.

While Piaget's theory has formed the cornerstone for thinking, research, and practice for more than 50 years, more contemporary research identifying weaknesses in Piaget's theory has provided additional ways to view childhood thinking and learning. Information-processing models and information levels-of-processing models continue to be formulated. As with child study in general, this research process is a continuous one and promises further enlightenment with each new revelation.

Multiple Intelligences Perspective

Howard Gardner's (1983, 1993, 1999) theory of multiple intelligences (MI) provides another way of looking at cognitive, language, and literacy development in individuals. This multiple intelligences theory is culturally neutral in that Gardner associates differences between and among categories of people (i.e., gender, race, socioeconomic background) with variations in individual experiences and needs and the types of intelligences that are required and/or expected for survival within a particular culture or context. Gardner illustrates how intelligence is closely aligned with cultural contexts, needs, and experience by citing, as an example, findings that women in Western cultures ostensibly perform less successfully on spatial tasks than do men. In an environment where spatial orientation is important for survival, however, as among the Eskimos, for example, women and men perform equally well on spatial tasks (Gardner, 1999). From this point of view one must assume that experience, survival needs, gender, and cultural expectations all play roles in the types of intelligences that evolve within an individual and among and between culturally and geographically diverse groups of people.

In the South Sea Islands, the Puluwat culture places a high value on spatial intelligence for the purpose of navigating to and from several hundred islands. Children are taught from an early age to identify the constellations, the islands on the horizon, and textural differences on the surface of the water that pinpoint geographic information. In this society, individuals with major navigational responsibilities have more prestige than the political leaders.

Other cultures prize highly musical intelligence. For example, children of the Anang tribe in Nigeria know hundreds of dances and songs by the time they are five years of age. In Hungary, children are expected to learn and read musical notation, owing to the influence of the educator and composer Zoltán Kodály. All cultures have and use combinations of intelligences. Stereotypical references to perceived or alleged racial or ethnic attributes such as athleticism, musical or rhythmic ability, or mathematical or other academic exceptionality fail to acknowledge this fact.

In the United States, the heaviest emphasis in the schooling of children is placed on linguistic intelligence and logical–mathematical intelligence. In many school settings, this has detrimental effects on children whose strengths are found in other types of intelligence(s). The outcomes are better for children whose parents and teachers recognize and facilitate MI development allowing growth and development to proceed along lines of strength in individual children.

Social Interactionist Perspective

Another explanation for children's differences in cognitive development relates the influence of the sociocultural experiences within the family, community, and society to the formation of scripts. Recall from Chapter 10 that as young children repeatedly participate in routine events with adults over a period of time, they develop ideas about the roles people play in certain situations, the objects or materials used, and the order of various events. These ideas are called *scripts*. At first, scripts are sketchy and incomplete and contain misperceptions and mistaken concepts. As children experience similar events and contexts over time, they develop more complete scripts.

Children at 4 and 5 years of age generally demonstrate more knowledge of certain scripts than do most 3-year-olds (Nelson, 1986; Nelson & Gruendel, 1981). When playing restaurant, they take time to decide on the roles: who will be the cook, the server, and the diners. Then children enact these various roles, demonstrating knowledge of behaviors and sequences of events such as entering the restaurant, ordering, eating, paying for the food, and leaving the restaurant. Four- and 5-year-old children often use appropriate materials to facilitate script enactment. They may use real or pretend menus, ordering pads, pencils, dishes, pots and pans, tables, chairs, and cash registers. They may wear aprons and chef's hats. Thus, as children mature, their increased cognitive awareness of the culture is reflected in their scripts.

The idea of scripts can also help to explain some of the differences in young children's cultural behaviors (Childs & Greenfield, 1980). For example, children in some Asian cultures become very skilled at eating with chopsticks, origami (the art of paper folding), and other small motor tasks because adults in the culture provide many opportunities for them to practice these skills. These skills may not be important to the scripts or contexts of other cultures. Therefore, children from other cultures do not have the opportunity to repeatedly practice the same small motor tasks and so are potentially less advanced in their small motor development than children from some Asian cultures.

No one of the various types of theories adequately or singularly explains human cognitive development. Cognitive science is an emerging field in which many theories appear to fill in pieces of a larger puzzle. Nevertheless, we can draw some helpful assumptions from these theories:

- Infants and children are neurologically "wired to learn," and are innately motivated to do so.
- From infancy onward, as brain growth and neurological development proceeds, cognitive abilities undergo qualitative and quantitative changes, and do so in a somewhat predictable fashion.
- Cognitive development encompasses many mental processes including perception, attention, thinking, memory, problem solving, creativity, and communicating.
- Cognition is influenced by sensory input and the individual's increasingly more complex communicative and social interactions.
- Cognition is influenced by the individual's increasingly more complex experiences and interactions with objects and events in the environment.
- Increasing facility with language supports cognition.

- Acquisition of the tools of learning—drawing, writing, spelling, reading, and fundamental math and science thinking—support cognition as it emerges over time.

- Individuals possess unique cognitive styles and intellectual profiles (i.e., multiple intelligences of different degrees of prowess) that often defy traditional methods of description or measurement.

- Later educational and academic outcomes can be traced to the cognitive and social/emotional skills that preschoolers exhibit upon school entry and to the types of early childhood experiences that fostered these capabilities.

Shortly after Jeremy turned 3, Ann asked him to tell her about his drawing. Jeremy said that it was a cricket. Jeremy's scribbled picture was not at all representational of a cricket. He probably did not plan to draw a cricket and lacked the motor control needed to draw an identifiable cricket. Yet he is beginning to understand that marks he makes can be named and that he is expected to produce in his drawings objects that can be named. Children at 4 and 5 years of age gradually come to understand adults' requests to "draw a picture."

LANGUAGE DEVELOPMENT

In all cultures, language development proceeds at a robust pace throughout the childhood years. Failure or inability to learn language stems from (1) environments that fail to provide adequate quantity and quality of linguistic input, (2) auditory impairments, and (3) physiological limits on learning and communicative skills, such as with Down syndrome or autism (Shonkoff & Phillips, 2000).

The importance of language development and communicative competence to all aspects of child development—social interactions, cognitive development, emotional intelligence, and cultural competence—is worth noting. Facility with language and communicative competence enhances one's relationships with others, facilitates learning, and supports academic performance. Hence, children with language delay or other developmental challenges benefit from early interventions that provide specialized treatments, assistive technology, coaching, and enrichment opportunities. As a case in point, consider that deaf children who experience conventional sign language such as American Sign Language (ASL) since birth acquire that language quite readily and follow the same developmental progression as do children learning spoken language (Newport & Meier, 1985). Exposure to ASL from birth appears to be key, as the timing of language inputs, whether signed or spoken, is related to the level of proficiency children will be able to attain (Shonkoff & Phillips, 2000). It is also interesting to note that in spite of challenges or handicapping conditions, most children develop some form of communication system (Shonkoff & Phillips, 2000). Children with language-deterring challenges are best served when diagnosis and intervention procedures begin as soon as possible. With all children, a background of enriching experiences and satisfying interactions with others promotes language and communication skills.

As children get older, the ability to remember more information seems to facilitate language development. In addition, as children have more experiences, they internalize more scripts and more language that is appropriate to those scripts. Scripts and the emerging ability to sequence events lead to a more sophisticated level of language development: sustained dialogue between children (Nelson & Gruendel, 1981). This sustained dialogue is often observed as children play out the scripts with which they have become familiar, such as "going to the doctor," "eating out," or "grocery shopping."

Despite this developing competence, young children at 4 and 5 years of age still have a great deal to sort out in terms of language and exactly what it means.

One evening, as Ann helped Jeremy out of the tub and was drying his feet, she noticed how much his feet were shaped like Bill's. She said, "Jeremy, you sure have your daddy's feet." Jeremy replied, "I do not have Daddy's feet. These are *my* feet!"

Jeremy did not comprehend Ann's **indirect speech**, or speech that implies more than the actual utterance. Children begin to understand indirect speech around ages 4 and 5. At first, all young children take others' speech literally. Humor and lying are two indirect speech acts that appear during the early childhood years. Children around 5 years of age begin to be interested in riddles and jokes. They often create "jokes" that have no humorous element to older children and adults. Yet when young children provide the punch line, they laugh uproariously. They have the notion of the form of jokes or riddles, and they know that it is appropriate to laugh. However, most young children around age 5 have yet to internalize the idea that words can have double meanings. Young children also gradually become aware of lying. They are usually not very proficient at lying because they cannot take into account all the attributes of the addressee, the relationship between the addressor and the addressee, and the context (Menyuk, 1988).

indirect speech: speech that implies more than the actual words uttered

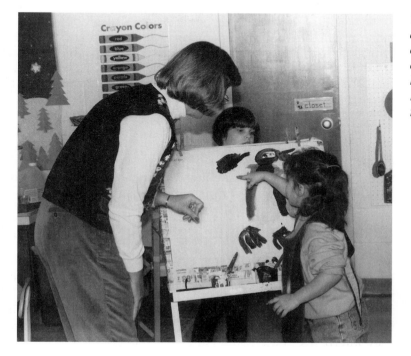

Talking about and sharing their experiences with others facilitates both thinking and language development.

Vocabulary Development

From 12 to 18 months of age, children begin to acquire an amazing number of words. Some studies indicate that young children learn and remember an average of 9 words a day from the onset of speech until age 6. If this is so, by the time a child is 6 or 7 years old, he or she will have acquired a vocabulary of approximately 14,000 words (Clark, 1983; Templin, 1957).

While many factors contribute to the child's acquisition and use of words, as the various theoretical perspectives illustrate, perhaps the most important have to do with the interactions children have with their parents and caregivers. One ambitious study of language development in young children determined that language development was overwhelmingly a function of the quantity and quality of the interactions between parents and children. Hart and Risley (1995) studied these interactions in 42 families with young children over a period of 2½ years, spending one hour per month with each family in the home and recording every word spoken between parents and children. From the transcripts of these interactions, these researchers coded and analyzed the words that were used throughout the parent–child interactions. They compared a cross section of families consisting of professional, working-class, and welfare families. They found an astounding difference of almost 300 words per hour between the professional and welfare parents. By compounding their figures over a year's time, these researchers established that the children in professional families heard approximately 11 million words per year, while the children in working-class families heard 6 million words per year and the children in welfare families heard 3 million words per year.

These scholars attributed vocabulary growth not only to the number of words that children hear, but also to certain interactional characteristic (or quality indicators): vocabulary used, sentence structure, providing choices to children, the nature of responsiveness to children's speech, and the emotional quality of the interactions. Hart and Risely found that these indicators were associated not only with vocabulary development, but also with IQ scores measured at age 3 and were better predictors of variation among children than race, gender, or birth order. A critical finding, not only from a cognitive, language point of view, but from a psychosocial one as well, was the finding that children in welfare families more often than others received disproportionate amounts of negative feedback in their language interactions with parents.

Other contributions to vocabulary growth include the manner and frequency in which adults (parents, teachers, caregivers) label objects, events, and feelings and define words; incidental encounters with words, as when hearing the conversations of others; watching or hearing the spoken word on television, movies, videos, and other media; listening to stories; interacting with older siblings and playmates; and, modestly, through direct instruction in school.

Development of Syntax

As children enter their 4th year, conjunctions with *and* begin to appear (e.g., "I want cookies *and* milk"). Later connectives such as *then, because, so, if, or,* and *but* appear. Use of *when, then, before,* and *after* develops still later. Embedded sentences, tag questions, indirect object–direct object constructions, and passive sentence forms also begin to appear during ages 4 and 5. Examples of these forms of language are illustrated in Figure 13.1. By the end of the 5th year, most children

1. **Conjunctions**
   a. Using *and* to connect whole sentences:
      "My daddy picked me up at school *and* we went to the store."
      "We ate breakfast *and* we ate doughnuts, too!"
   b. Later expressing relations between clauses using *because* and *if*:
      "I can't hold my cup *because* I'm just too little."
      "I'll play with my new truck *if* my daddy will bring it."

2. **Embedded Sentences**
   "I *want to hold it* myself!"
   "I *want to go to sleep* in my big boy bed."
   "My mommy said *she could fix it.*"

3. **Tag Questions**
   "I can do it myself, can't I?"
   "Caitlin is crying, isn't she, Mommy?"
   "Mommy, this shoe is too small, isn't it, Daddy?"

4. **Indirect Object–Direct Object Constructions**
   "My Mommy showed Daddy her new briefcase."
   "I gave Nikki my new toy just to share."
   "Mrs. Gray called me on her telephone!"

5. **Passive Sentence Forms**
   "The car was chased by the dog."
   "My toy was broken by the hammer."
   "The page was ripped by a ghost, Daddy!"

FIGURE 13.1
The Emergence of Grammatical Forms and Usage During Ages Four, Five, and Six

also have a broader understanding of pronouns. For example, they know that a pronoun does not always refer to the name of another person in the sentence, as in "*She* said Sally was sick." During the 5th year and into the 6th year, children begin to incorporate irregular inflections into their speech. At this time, they may include both the irregular form and the overregularized form within the same sentence (e.g., "We goed/we went/we wented to my grandma's house last night"). These behaviors indicate that children are becoming aware that there are some exceptions to the regularities of inflectional endings and are trying to incorporate these irregularities into their speech (Gleason, 2000).

Sound Production

Many children become considerably more proficient in the production of various sounds between ages 4 and 5. However, a number of children are still learning to produce some sounds even into the elementary school years. Some children can hear contrasting sounds but cannot produce them (Ingram, 1986). Awareness of the relative ages for the development of various sounds helps adults to detect delays and provide timely intervention. In addition, this knowledge provides assurance to parents that speech development is proceeding as expected.

Young children who since birth have been learning two languages *simultaneously* follow similar sequences in development as their monolingual agemates but with some variation. The age of appearance of first words is somewhat later.

They may also blend parts of words from both languages into the same word. Additionally, they may mix words of the different languages in phrases or sentences. By ages 4 or 5, these characteristics are replaced with language use that distinguishes the separate language systems (Fierro-Cobas & Chan, 2001). The use of the different language systems for distinct purposes also emerges as children learn to associate each language with a person (their teacher), group (classmates), or situation (home or school).

Children who since birth have been learning two languages *sequentially* also follow similar patterns in language development as their monolingual agemates and also exhibit unique language development characteristics. They often make syntactic errors in their first language and apply grammatical rules of the first language to the second language. They may go through a silent period, sometimes referred to as *selective mutism*, for a brief period of time as they mentally process or assimilate one or the other language.

When children experience equal exposure and use of both languages, their development is virtually indistinguishable from that of monolingual language learners. However, most bilingual and monolingual children are more intimately exposed to one language over the other. Most bi- and multilingual children develop a preference for one of their languages, perhaps because they feel more comfortable with it or find its use to be more effective in the contexts in which they find themselves (Fierro-Cobas & Chan, 2001).

Ann was concerned about Jeremy's inability to pronounce the *th* sound. Ann asked about Jeremy's speech at the spring conference with Ms. Buckley. Ms. Buckley showed Bill and Ann a chart indicating that the production of *th* is expected to develop in the 7th year. Ms. Buckley reassured Bill and Ann that at this stage of Jeremy's language development, there was no need to be concerned.

Communicative Competence

While young children are expanding their vocabularies and learning how to express their thoughts through oral language, they are also gaining interactional and communicative competence. Communicative competence refers to the child's knowledge of the uses of language and appropriate nonverbal behavior, and awareness of conversational conditions and constraints. Grammatical and interactional competence interact to create the child's communicative competence. There are sociocultural considerations in studying communicative competence, for there are unique communication styles within various cultures. Trawick-Smith (1994, pp. 317–322) cited examples of communication behaviors in various cultural groups:

- Some Mexican American children tend to use touch and physical cues in their interactions.
- Some Western Apache children may be somewhat less verbal than other children in their interactions.
- Some Chinese American children often use silence to avoid conflict or threatening situations.
- Brazilian and Peruvian children frequently acknowledge guests with silence (respect).

- Arab children may use silence to indicate a wish for privacy.
- Some Japanese American children may use a smile to hide embarrassment, anger, or sorrow.
- African American, Puerto Rican, and Mexican American children may avoid direct eye contact to demonstrate respect for persons in authority.
- Japanese American children and their families may seldom touch others, particularly those of a different gender.
- Puerto Rican and African American children generally stand close to conversation partners and touch one another in their interactions.
- Some African American, Hawaiian, Puerto Rican, and Jewish families engage in simultaneous talk rather than turn taking in conversation.

Communication between and among people is facilitated to the extent that different communicative styles are acknowledged and understood. Children acquire unique communicative styles in sociocultural contexts.

LITERACY DEVELOPMENT

Reading and writing are tools that can help people (1) achieve goals and meet needs, (2) communicate with others, and (3) increase knowledge and understanding. These tools are essential in a literate society. Literacy is defined as "The ability and the willingness to use reading and writing to construct meaning from printed text, in ways which meet the requirements of a particular social context" (Au, 1993, p. 20).

Adults serve as scaffolders in children's literacy development by answering their questions about print and engaging them in dialogue about the story.

TABLE 13.1   Early Literacy Development (Ages Four Through Five)

Vocabulary and comprehension

Increases vocabulary, which facilitates comprehension

Acquires greater proficiency in both receptive and expressive language

Enjoys conversation and dialogue with others

Learns conversational turn-taking skills

Enjoys rhymes, rhythms, chants, songs, and word play

Initiates story-reading and book-sharing activities

Can "fill in" missing words or phrases during shared book-reading activity

Can talk about and retell a story when provided prompts verbally or from storybook illustrations

Role plays story characters and themes

Incorporates story characters and themes into pretend play

Incorporates story characters and themes into drawings and early writing

Can answer *who, what,* and *where* questions about a story

Print awareness and writing behaviors

Demonstrates interest and increasing prowess in reading environmental print

Recites or sings the alphabet

Combines linear cursive-like scribbles and letter-like marks with drawings

Attempts to draw or copy letters from a prompt

Attempts first pseudo-letters and letters, which occupy various positions in space and may be reversed or upside down

Writes in a way that lacks conventional direction—horizontal and left to right

Recognizes and names most letters

Writes words in a string without spaces between them

Attempts to write letters; letter reversals are common

Attempts to write letters and numerals in order

Pretends to read

Writes familiar letters mixing upper and lower cases

Recognizes that groups of letters can form words

Makes first attempts at writing name, including both upper and lower cases

Starts to make distinctions between upper and lower case letters

Learns to write name using appropriate cases

Dictates labels and stories for art and other projects

Writes own labels and stories using developmental (or phonemic) spellings

May not follow left to right/top to bottom progression in early writing

Phonemic awareness and alphabetic principle

Appreciates the fact that information and entertainment can be derived from print experiences

Conveys knowledge and shares information gained from literacy experiences

Develops a disposition to read, and self-selects literature of diverse genres

Unlike language development, which seems to just explode during early childhood and develops naturally without formal instruction, learning to read and write evolves over a longer period of time. It occurs quite easily for some children and is quite elusive for others. For most children, learning to read and write requires some form of instruction, though there is no instructional methodology that works the same with all learners. Learning to read and write is not just a cognitive ability, but involves development in other domains as well: physical (vision, hearing, fine motor development, perceptual motor coordinations), emotional (desire, interest, curiosity, motivation, confidence, enjoyment, perseverance), and social (encouragement, instruction, scaffolding, support, feedback), as Table 13.1 implies.

Individual children come into literacy in unique ways, depending on the quality and quantity of their early language and literacy experiences and their individual methods for attending to and processing information. Indeed, there are wide ranges in literacy-related skills and functioning when children enter education programs at ages 4 and 5 years. For instance, in a group of 5-year-old children in kindergarten, some may exhibit literacy behaviors that are typical of 3-year-olds, while others may exhibit literacy behaviors that are more typical of an 8-year-old (Riley, 1996). As with all other developmental domains, there is considerable variation in rates of literacy development among children of the same age. And as with all other developmental domains, wide variations in rate of literacy development are explained by genetic makeup, infinite variations in experiences, and sociocultural expectations. That having been said, there appear to be some universal patterns in the manner in which children come into literacy.

Awareness of Print as a Form of Communication

One of the first steps in literacy development is the realization that marks on a page can convey a message. Children at ages 4 and 5 are very observant of the literacy behaviors of those around them and demonstrate increasing awareness that drawing and writing communicate thought. As 4- and 5-year-olds encounter drawings and print in many forms and contexts, they become increasingly aware that the thoughts they have and share with others can be drawn or written down and read by others. This realization evolves over a period of time. Concurrently, small motor skills such as eye–hand coordination are developing and facilitating the child's drawing and writing activities, and language development is providing labels and ways of thinking about what she or he wants to draw or write.

Access to paper and drawing or writing tools encourages this process. Young children usually begin to draw about experiences that are meaningful to them. As they think about these experiences and represent them in their drawings, they often talk to themselves or with others who are nearby about their thoughts and drawings (Dyson, 1997). They incorporate these thoughts into their drawings by either dictating to an adult what they want written on or about their drawing or using their own limited knowledge of print to write their ideas. An adult may say, "Tell me about your picture" or "Let me write down what you said." As children observe adults writing what they dictate, they begin to understand that thoughts can be expressed not only through words and pictures, but also through print.

James, **Cheryl, and Angela** decide to celebrate James's pay raise by going out to eat. Some friends join the celebration. Angela becomes restless while they wait for their food. One of Cheryl's friends gives Angela a pencil, and she begins to write lines imitating adult cursive writing on her paper placemat. Suddenly, she tugs at Cheryl's arm, points to her writing, and says, "This says 'double cheeseburger.' This says 'Coke.' This says 'fries.'" Angela's behavior indicates an awareness of how print is used to make a request. She has observed and has been thinking and deciding what she and others want to eat. These decisions were discussed and then given to the server, who wrote down what they said about the food they wanted to eat. Thought, oral language, and written language were all used in an interactive way to get what they wanted: food.

Ann and Jeremy are at the greeting card store in the mall. Five-year-old Jeremy knows that it is close to Ann's birthday and tells her that he wants to get her a card. Ann asks Jeremy how much money he has in his Mickey Mouse billfold. He tells her, "Four dollars." Ann shows Jeremy how the price is marked on the back of the card and helps him to decide whether he has enough money. Jeremy begins looking at cards and selects one that has pretty flowers on it. Ann looks at it and tells him that it is a get-well card. She then directs Jeremy to the birthday cards for mothers. Jeremy finds one he likes and checks with Ann to see whether he has enough money. Finding that he has enough money, he takes the card to the cash register and pays for it. As soon as they get home, Jeremy goes to a basket on his toy shelf, which holds pencils and felt pens. He selects a red pen and writes "4 U" on the envelope. Inside the card he writes, "I ♥ U JEREMY." Jeremy's behavior indicates that he knows about cards and how thoughts are written on cards to help celebrate birthdays. He uses thought, drawing, and written language to convey his birthday greeting to his mother.

The two vignettes indicate the varied contexts in which young children learn how to talk about and write their thoughts. These examples also demonstrate how adults serve as scaffolders in promoting literacy development. Adults help children to write their thoughts, provide experiences for them to participate in literacy events (e.g., sharing correspondence, making lists, labeling, locating addresses and phone numbers), and provide the tools (paper and writing implements) for them to practice their developing literacy awareness. Thus, there are specific behaviors on the part of adults that ensure the continuation of print awareness in young children.

The first behavior is alertness to opportunities for literacy development in the home, school, and community (Schickedanz, 1999). Second, appropriate scaffolding and providing answers to children's literacy-related questions help children to become more aware of print. Third, adults provide time and tools for children to engage in the act of writing. Fourth, adults continuously provide opportunities for children to experience many forms of literature through books, storytelling, poetry and rhymes, songs, and drama. Just as children need to hear oral language to learn to talk, they need experiences with spoken and written language to learn to read and write.

Early Writing Behavior

At some point during the 4th or 5th year, most children begin to realize that drawings represent objects and people and that writing represents words for objects, people, or thoughts. However, some young children in the primary grades continue to incorporate drawings into their writing to help them convey meaning

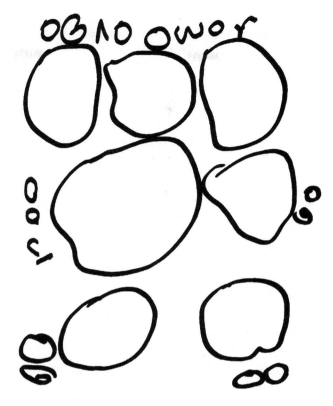

FIGURE 13.2
Four-year-old Jon has "labeled" the rocks in his drawing. He has used various letter-like shapes and configurations of the letters in his name, such as Os and inverted or partial Js and Ns.

(Davis, 1990; Dyson, 1993, 1997). Jeremy's "I ♥ U" is such an example. Occasionally, letters and numerals are also combined to express thought, as in "I 8 ic krem" ("I ate ice cream").

Children's first attempts at writing may include imitation of adult cursive writing as they attempt to write their names or various configurations of the letters in their names and other letters of the alphabet that they recognize and can reproduce (Clay, 1993). Just as young children experiment with blocks and paint, they play and experiment with letters, as is illustrated in Figure 13.2. Through this experimentation and opportunities to explore writing, children begin to learn about the characteristics of written language. This, too, is a complex process that takes time and adult support.

Another characteristic of early writing is its lack of conventional direction. It is not always horizontal, nor does it always follow a left-to-right sequence. Gradually, young writers learn that print proceeds from left to right; over time, through reading and writing experiences, they will come to internalize this aspect of reading and writing (Clay, 1993). At times, letters are inverted, sideways, or in some other nonconventional position. An important concept that the child learns about print is **constancy of position in space**. For example, a shoe is a shoe regardless of what position it is in. The same is true for a hamburger, a glass, a towel, and most other objects in the environment. This is not so for letters of our alphabet. Change the orientation of *b*, and it is no longer a *b*. It can become a *d*, a *p*, or a *q*.

In addition, young children may reverse certain letters, words, or phrases. These **reversals** are normal developmental behavior. Only if the behavior is still

constancy of position in space: the notion that letters of the alphabet must have fixed positions to maintain their identity

reversals: printing letters or words in reverse

frequent by the end of first grade should concern arise. As children cognitively and physiologically internalize left/right and top/bottom orientations their ability to perceive the differences between similar letters such as *p, d, b,* and *q* is enhanced. Physical activities such as rhythms and dance that promote left/right concepts and games that entail the use of top/bottom, in front/behind, over/under, and other positional orientations help children to internalize these directional concepts on a physiological level as well as a cognitive one. When they are faced with confusingly similar letters, talking about the placement of the curved lines on the straight lines—for instance, on the *p, b, d*—clears up the confusion.

Another explanation for reversals, or mirror writing, is found in the nature of various letters of the alphabet. Certain letters—for example, *J* and *S*—end in a right-to-left orientation. Occasionally, children who have names beginning with these letters continue writing from right to left rather than left to right. As children use these letters in their writing and begin to understand the principles of directionality, reversals of these letters also appear. Jeremy signed his name on Ann's card by reversing the *J.* This behavior suggests that he is working on the left-to-right principle of print but has not yet sorted out letters that end in the opposite direction. Sorting out these irregularities of written language can be compared to young children's sorting out irregularities in oral language ("We goed to Grandma's" rather than "We went to Grandma's").

Another common writing behavior in young children is the omission of spaces between words. They may run out of space and finish part of a word by starting another line of print below the first. Or a picture may take up most of the space, and the word is written in a vertical or other unconventional position, illustrating that the child does not yet have the concept that a word is a group of letters printed in close proximity. Children may not yet realize that there are supposed to be spaces between words. (At least this is true for English. However, some language systems use no spacing between words. Laotian print, for example, has spacing between sentences but not between words.) A third explanation is that children may not think about the needs of their reader, that is, that using spaces between words is a convention that makes it easier for others to read what we write. Finally, since writing is a complex task, it is difficult for young children to think about what they want to write, how to make the letters represent the sounds in the words, and at the same time remember to leave spaces between words. Some children may use their own markers, such as a dash between words, when they realize a need to separate words.

The Alphabetic Principle and Phonemic Awareness

alphabetic:
a writing system that associates the phonemes of oral language with letters of the alphabet

Through instruction, children learn the **alphabetic** principle, or the fact that there is a relationship between letters and sounds. Children become aware of letters, their unique shapes, and their associated sounds through the use of alphabet books, alphabet songs, alphabet puzzles, and games. They gain experience attending to the sounds of language through rhymes, songs, and storybooks. In this regard, the traditional nursery rhymes and other poetry have been found to relate to phonological sensitivity and later phonological skills (Baker, Serpell, & Sonnenschein, 1995; Gable, 1999).

The ability to think about words as a sequence of sounds (phonemes) is considered an essential aspect of learning to read (Snow, Burns, & Griffin, 1998). The precise role that phonemic awareness plays in the earliest years of literacy development is not fully understood. Although children as young as age 5 have been shown to learn phonics through direct instruction, its value over other literacy experiences for young children is questionable (International Reading Association & National Association for the Education of Young Children, 1998). Nevertheless, children ages 4 and 5 years are beginning to hear and respond to letter sounds, and this development is supported through opportunities to listen to and participate in the sharing of predictable texts, rhymes, songs, poetry, and word play. Formal phonetic instruction that takes the form of worksheets and repetitious memorization of isolated concepts is not recommended at this age. Such instruction often precludes more mentally engaging instructional strategies and can interfere with the motivational aspects of learning to read. The nature of the young child's cognitive processes makes this type of abstract learning very difficult and potentially discouraging.

Early Spelling

As children begin to realize that each letter represents a sound or phoneme in the language system, their writing becomes more communicative. Early writing is characterized by phonemic spelling, often referred to as **invented spelling** or **developmental spelling** (e.g., *bs* for *bus, mi* for *my, snac* for *snake*). Usually, young children's invented spelling first contains consonant sounds, perhaps only the initial consonant sound, such a *b* for *bus*. Later, final and medial sounds may appear with long vowel sounds, such as *bs* for *bus* and *lik* for *like*. Short vowel sounds usually appear later and are often substituted for one another, for example, *git* for get.

> **invented/developmental spelling:** spelling that young children create based on their perceptions of sound–symbol relationships

These early attempts to convey meaning through print provide teachers an opportunity to observe and better understand the systematic thinking behind children's early spelling. By attending to the nature of the misspelling, and resisting the urge to correct the spelling, teachers can find clues to individual phonemic awareness, cognitive understandings, language facility, and other developmental indicators. Some researchers have developed spelling instructional strategies based on teachers' analysis of students' invented spelling and their levels of development (Invernizzi, Abouzeid, & Gill, 1994).

Encouraging children to use their private spelling facilitates their active involvement in the writing process. Young children can be told that there is **public spelling**, the spelling that everyone learns over a long time. There is also **private spelling**, which is their own way of spelling words. Adults can remind children that learning to spell conventionally takes time, just like learning to walk, talk, or play soccer, and they can provide the tools and assistance as appropriate to help children make distinctions between their private spelling and conventional spelling.

> **public spelling:** conventional spelling that children learn through both experience with writing and direct instruction

A print-rich environment based on usefulness and meaning in young children's lives helps them to gradually become aware of conventional spellings. Interaction with the print in favorite books, environmental print, print in the classroom such as signs, labels, charts, and stories accompanying artwork, and the placing of relevant print in various learning centers all encourage young children's growing awareness of conventional spelling (Fields & Spangler, 2000). In addition, as children begin to make comparisons between their private spelling and public spelling, opportunities for direct instruction occur. This instruction can be quite meaningful to the child, for it addresses words and spellings of immediate import to the learner and motivates interest in learning to spell other words.

> **private spelling:** phonemic spelling or invented spelling that young children create when they first begin to write their ideas and thoughts

Early Reading Behavior

As with infants and toddlers, reading to and with young children on a consistent basis is the most reliable factor in successful literacy development (Bus, van Ijendoorn, & Pellegrini, 1995; Durkin, 1993; Ferreiro & Teberosky, 1982; Whitehurst, Epstein, Angell, Smith, & Fischel, 1994). Reading to children ages 4 and 5 promotes oral language development by introducing new vocabulary words (Hart & Risley, 1995; Robbins & Ehri, 1994). Reading to young children also promotes other important behaviors that facilitate literacy development.

Young children who have many story-reading experiences learn how to use a book. They learn that a book has a front and a back and that the story does not begin on the title page. They learn about reading one page and then going to the next, page turning, and the general left-to-right progression of pages. While young children often indicate that the illustrations tell the story, the scaffolding behavior of adults can help them realize that the print actually tells the story. Discussions about the title of the book and the names of the author and illustrator, telling and showing the child, "This is where the words are that tell me what to read to you," and pointing to the words can help young children to get the notion that print conveys information about the book, the title, and the author as well as the story.

predictable books: books that have repeating patterns and predictable text

Using **predictable books**, books with repeated patterns and predictable text, facilitates print awareness. Repeated readings of these books encourage children to internalize the story lines. Because the illustrations in a good predictable book support the text on that page, young children often become aware of the text and how it works. Early on, many children think that each letter represents a word. Attempts to match the predictable text with the letters in a word may not work. Children eventually figure out that each cluster of letters represents a word. Adults can help young children to grasp the relationship of words to story line. Pointing to the text with a finger or a pointer in reading a predictable book also helps children to understand the relationship between speech and print. In this early stage of literacy development, pointing is helpful in establishing the one-to-one relationship between speech and text.

Just as young children need to hear oral language to learn to talk, they need to see and hear written language to develop ideas about how to read and write. Oral language differs from written language. Spoken language often relies on the immediate context of the situation to provide needed meaning, while written language must be more formal and complete so that the reader can comprehend the meaning. In addition, as children interact with books, they see the meanings that stories can have for them in their lives. They can see that, in one book, Alexander has "terrible, horrible, no good, very bad days" just as they do. They also can find it interesting to learn that a triceratops had three horns. They discover that books can provide information, comfort, and joy.

Studies indicate that participation in the form of interruptions, questions, and comments between adults and children while stories are being read facilitates children's comprehension of the stories and also of school dialogue patterns. For example, the questions that adults ask very young children about a story are similar to the kinds of questions teachers ask children in the more formal environment of the elementary school.

Relationship between Reading and Writing

In the past, reading was thought to develop first, followed by learning to write. It is now widely accepted that children can learn about reading and writing at the same time and at earlier stages than was previously thought. However, this does not suggest that children at ages 4 and 5 should be expected to read and write like older children and adults. Even though it is now recognized that children learn about reading and writing earlier than was previously believed, this process takes time. Furthermore, early reading and writing behaviors differ in many ways from those of older children and adults. Invented spelling and the use of fingers to match the text with verbal language are two such examples.

An awareness of the apparent interrelationship between reading and writing is important in facilitating literacy development. The importance of books and reading to young children is evident when we see young children becoming aware that words, not letters, match with the oral text of the story. If young children are also provided with opportunities to write or to have their thoughts written down, they can also begin to develop concepts about what a word is. Learning to write their names, developing their own vocabulary cards, and having adults who talk about what letters are in words, the letter sounds, and what words say all help children to learn to read as well as to write. In addition, if children have thoughts that they want to write about, this motivates them to read what they have written. Thus, experiences in writing help to provide the young child with information about reading and vice versa.

The Role of Play in Promoting Cognitive, Language, and Literacy Development

Piaget (1962) suggested that children follow a developmental pattern that depends on a unique interplay between innate human characteristics and the environment. Typically, 4- and 5-year-old children's play activities correspond to their level of cognitive development. The years from age 3 to age 6 are peak years for fantasy and sociodramatic play (Hughes, 1999). Sociodramatic play activities are characterized by a group of children assuming roles and engaging in loosely coordinated performances. These sociodramatic plays represent common events in children's lives, such as going to the store, playing house, or going to the hospital. The play scripts are based on reality, and as children engage in social play more frequently, they expect their peers to be knowledgeable about the details of particular roles or social contexts. Early in the preoperational stage, these enactments are one dimensional, easily understood, and generally simplistic by adult standards. However, these early attempts to integrate a body of social knowledge and to allow these ideas to dictate their role playing are rather remarkable for an egocentric, preoperational child. As children's cognitive abilities develop, their sociodramatic play incorporates more detailed information and more peer participants. However, children are less reliant on play objects to facilitate their activities. During the preoperational stage, children engage in fantasy play activities. Fantasy play is characterized by multifaceted characterizations and dynamic, enthusiastic physical activity. Surprisingly, with more abstract social information, more peer participants, and a heightened level of activity, older preschool children effectively perform the task of coordinating all the elements of their fantasy play. Concrete objects continue to be used to represent needed props to support the play theme. Character roles are constantly shifting and changing focus, and new characteristics are added at the whim of the participants. Fantasy play activities incorporate new themes and new participants to suit the desires of the entire play group or the play group leader.

Fantasy and sociodramatic play contribute to cognitive, language, and literacy development in a variety of ways:

Contributions to Social and Emotional Development.   Through pretend play, children are able to reenact joyful events in their lives and confront troubling ones, often playing them out in ways that give the children a sense of power and mastery over people and situations in which they have little power. They can reconstruct these scripts to achieve the goals or endings that they prefer.

Social pretend play also contributes to the development of the ability to comprehend a peer's point of view in social situations. There is then a close relationship between group sociodramatic play and perspective taking (Johnson & Yawkey, 1988). During the initiation and development of group play activities, an understanding of others' perspectives among participants is essential. Further, during dramatic play, two styles of communication occur. First, pretend communication takes place and is acted out in character in a way that is generally consistent with the social parameters of the dramatic activity. Second, **metacommunication** (communicating about their talk and scripts) occurs as children reconstruct, plan, and talk about their play scripts.

As play contributes to social and emotional development, it has been shown to promote academic success in later years. A review of studies of social–emotional and cognitive development found direct links between successful and enriching early childhood social interaction opportunities and later school performance (Kauffman Foundation, 2002). The findings support historical studies of the importance of early social and emotional development to optimal outcomes in many domains including cognitive development and school achievement.

Contributions to Cognitive Development.   As children create alternative worlds through their play scripts, they engage in hypothetical activity, manipulating reality to fit their play script goals. This activity engages what-if types of thinking that form the basis for more mature hypothetical reasoning and problem solving (Bretherton, 1986). In addition, play has been found to contribute to the development of divergent problem-solving ability and creative thinking and has been associated with later creativity (Dansky, 1980). Through sociodramatic play, decentration is evidenced by the child's ability to attend simultaneously to different features of events or objects in the environment. This ability improves children's conceptual abilities by providing more complete information than is evident to them when they can focus on only one feature.

Contributions to Language Development.   Through social play interactions, children engage in planning, dialogue, debate, and many other verbal and gestural forms of communication. They gain communicative competence as they experience the give-and-take of social interaction. Through pretend play, children can experiment with and practice a variety of forms of communication: word use, phrasing, gestures and body language, inflections, listening, and so on. In bilingual and multilingual groups, they hear and learn words and sentences in other languages, learning to accept and respond to a variety of language and communicative styles.

metacommunication:
the cognitive ability to reflect on and talk about verbal interactions

Contributions to Literacy Development.   Using a variety of literacy-related props, children engage their emerging knowledge of print, writing, book reading, and other literacy behaviors. For example, the classroom sociodramatic center may have a number of literacy-related props: telephone with phone book and individual address books, storybooks, recipe cards, grocery list pads, note cards and stationery, mailbox, toy catalogs, TV guide, notebook, message board, and so on. Literacy-related materials can be incorporated into all of the learning centers to be used in both conventional and pretend ways (Neuman, Copple, & Bredekamp, 2000; Puckett, 2002; Puckett & Black, 1985; Texas Association for the Education of Young Children, 1997). These experiences provide concrete opportunities to learn about reading, writing, and spelling in engaging and meaningful ways.

Bodrova and Leong (1998), who are scholars in the Vygotskian tradition, sum up well the importance of play:

> Play provides the optimal context for the emergence and continued growth of the most important cognitive and social processes of young children or their "developmental accomplishments" [Elkonin, 1977]. . . . play prepares the foundation for the processes yet to emerge—that will appear at a later time in the context of academic activities of the school age. For Vygotskians, play influences the most essential aspects of the development of a child as a whole. Play does not simply affect discrete skills. It promotes the restructuring of the child's psychological processes and is the source of systemic change in mental development. (p. 116)

FACTORS INFLUENCING COGNITIVE, LANGUAGE, AND LITERACY DEVELOPMENT

Neurological Integrity

As we saw in previous chapters, the brain grows in response to the individual's experiences and is particularly vulnerable to certain types of experiences during certain periods of rapid growth. As noted before, but worth mentioning again here in the context of thinking about 4- and 5-year-old children, motor development, first and second language development, math, logic, and musical learning are particularly important during the early childhood years. This is a time for adults to be especially cognizant of sensory integrity, motor skills, and speech production as indicators of development or a need for assessment and intervention. Providing rich opportunities for children to experience music and movement, thought games involving numbers, and assistance in learning a second language when that is required or desired is an important way to contribute to the growth of the brain and the neurological system.

Nutrition, Health, and Well-Being

As with infants and toddlers, 4- and 5-year-old children have continuing, yet varying needs for sleep, rest, exercise, and nourishment. Even though many 4- and 5-year-old children are enrolled in prekindergarten and kindergarten, their need for predictable routines and adequate diets remains paramount. They continue to need vigorous exercise and unstructured play time. To realize this, it helps to put their age in perspective by converting years into months: Four- and 5-year-olds

Young children are naturally motivated to read what they have written.

are 48 and 60 months old, respectively. It is important to remember that 4- and 5-year-old children, in spite of their increasing sophistication with language and learning, are still quite young.

Nature of Adult–Child Interactions

The types of cognitive, language, and literacy-promoting experiences children have had during their preschool years influence further development as they enter the later stages of preoperational thinking. When children have had limited experiences, rich preschool environments are required. For example, studies show that 4- and 5-year-old children in low-income families who have had limited home literacy experiences or different ones than those of middle-income children demonstrate continued literacy learning if they are in supportive literacy environments in the school setting (Christian, Morrison, & Bryant, 1998; Teale, 1986).

Prekindergarten and Kindergarten Programs

Many children enter prekindergarten and kindergarten programs at ages between 4 and 5 years. The demands on them are changing as public policy attempts to respond to the combined growing awareness of the importance of the early years coupled with political efforts to exact school accountability and define "school readiness" (see Box 13.1). Some demands are misguided, requiring very young children to behave and perform as though they were participants in a later grade. Expectations that fail to acknowledge the actual ages and widely held knowledge

BOX 13.1   What Is "Readiness"?

Readiness is a term that holds different meanings for different situations depending on the context in which it is used. The term first came into use in the 1930s, when the physician and psychologist Arnold Gesell, who established the Clinic of Child Development at Yale University, conducted research on the "ages and stages" of early growth and development. These studies led to norms for motor skills, adaptive behaviors, language, and personal–social behavior. Gesell's studies demonstrated that each child develops at an individual pace but according to predictable patterns that are similar for all children (Gesell, 1925; Gesell & Amatruda, 1941). His research led to the theory that development is determined primarily by genetic make-up, with environment playing a lesser role. Based on his findings, Gesell argued that children should begin school on the basis of their behavioral characteristics rather than their chronological age.

Today, the interpretation of the term readiness depends on what the interpreter intends to do *with* or *for* children. For some, readiness means that a child has attained a certain level of proficiency with certain knowledge or skills, for example, has mastered toilet learning prior to enrollment in preschool; can talk and communicate sufficiently to be understood by caregivers; has mastered a certain set of "prereading" skills; demonstrates certain behavioral attributes of compliance and self-control; and meets an assortment of other "readiness" criteria. Often these expectations are arbitrary and lack empirical evidence that they matter in terms of the child's ability to benefit from the experiences offered.

In the public policy-oriented context, readiness means that the child enters formal schooling with certain knowledge, skills, and abilities sufficient to ostensibly benefit from the curriculum provided; and, from a rather self serving point of view, that the child can do so without jeopardizing the school's ranking on state or local accountability measures. Certainly, there are capabilities that facilitate a child's successful participation in a school setting. Delineating those capabilities in such a way that they can be generalized to every child upon school entry is difficult, if not impossible. Because early growth and development is rapid and dynamic, evidence of the absence of certain knowledge or skills or the presence of problematic behaviors at some given point in time does not necessarily foretell how a child will fare, nor does prowess necessarily foretell a successful schooling experience.

Still another point of view is one that assumes that if a child can score at an acceptable level on a selected standardized test, then the child is considered "ready" for admission to a particular program or school. This practice continues to be widespread in spite of mounting evidence of the limits of standardized tests for providing a complete and accurate profile of a child's abilities.

A thorough understanding of child growth and development, and acknowledgment of the wide variations in children's experiences and accomplishments during the early years, render the term "ready" problematic. Children are born learning; that is what their brains do. The responsibility for providing opportunities to learn rests with their families and caregivers. Throughout childhood, children grow, develop, and learn; their successes are celebrated; their challenges are mediated. When measures of supposed readiness assume a deficit perspective on childhood accomplishments, the expectations and the outcomes for individual children are less than optimal.

As has been implicit throughout this text, readiness should not be defined by what a child can or cannot do, but by the goodness of fit between individual children and the expectations imposed upon them.

of age-related characteristics and capabilities place many children at risk during their very first schooling experiences. This trend must be closely monitored by parents and professionals for its potential for both physical and psychological harm. Some school schedules logistically planned to accommodate the scheduling needs of other grades can fail to provide for timely exercise, rest, refreshment, and nourishment. The fatigue and stress associated with rigorous schedules and performance expectations often lead to somatic and psychosomatic illnesses and behavioral problems. Where children are further scheduled into out-of-school time activities that leave little time for rest, refreshment, nourishment, and un-structured play, their health and psychological well-being is jeopardized.

On the other hand, early childhood programs that are sensitive to the unique characteristics and physical and psychological needs of young children play a critical and essential role in their overall growth and development. These programs strategically plan for enrichment and support of growth, development, and learning in all developmental domains and work with families to assure optimal outcomes for each child. Such programs provide linkages to professional services to meet the needs of children with special developmental or learning challenges. Assessment of growth and progress is ongoing without subjecting young children to testing situations that yield limited information while imposing undue expectations on individual children.

Quality programs for young children meet accreditation standards set by professional organizations such as the National Association for the Education of Young Children (NAEYC, 2004). Accreditation standards address teacher training and qualifications as well as educational routines, nutrition, safety requirements, curricular expectations, and family involvement issues.

In their review of research on the effects of developmentally appropriate programs for young children, Dunn and Kontos (1997) noted that studies reveal the following:

- Children in child-initiated classrooms scored higher on measures of creativity and divergent thinking than did children in academically oriented classrooms.
- In child-initiated classrooms, children demonstrated better outcomes in language development, showing better verbal skills than children in academically oriented programs.
- Where literacy environments were of high quality, children's receptive language was better.
- Children in developmentally appropriate programs demonstrated greater confidence in their cognitive abilities and described their abilities in more positive terms.
- Most studies indicate that a didactic approach to instruction with young children is less successful.
- Findings regarding reading and mathematics achievement were mixed; some found better scores among children attending developmentally appropriate programs in kindergarten through second grade, others found more achievement in academically oriented classrooms, and still others found no difference between the two models.
- Children of low socioeconomic status attending developmentally appropriate kindergarten classrooms tend to have better reading achievement scores in first grade than children attending inappropriate kindergarten programs.

- Differences between children in more or less appropriate classrooms often do not appear until a year or more later.
- There are emotional costs associated with academically oriented classrooms, particularly for children from low-socioeconomic-status and minority groups.

This review of research also examined studies relating to the effects of developmentally appropriate and inappropriate programs on children's social and emotional development. The student is encouraged to read this review of the literature for a fuller understanding of the impact of the types of expectations that are placed on young growing and developing minds.

ROLE OF THE EARLY CHILDHOOD PROFESSIONAL

Promoting Cognitive, Language, and Literacy Development in Children Ages Four Through Five

1. Provide opportunities for individual and social construction of knowledge that takes into account children's intelligences, sociocultural backgrounds, and special learning needs.

2. Provide opportunities for language development that accommodate children with special language needs and diverse sociolinguistic backgrounds. For example,
   - be aware of children's attitudes and responses to physical touch and personal space preferences;
   - show appreciation for all languages and dialects;
   - avoid criticizing or correcting children's language;
   - encourage cross-linguistic conversation;
   - facilitate second-language acquisition.

3. Provide rich and varied firsthand experiences from which children can draw experiential information and inspiration for language, writing, and reading.

4. Provide a cognitively engaging classroom that challenges but does not overwhelm children. Provide developmentally sound curriculums and materials, routines, and activities. Gauge expectations to the age and individuality of children.

5. Provide a language-rich environment in which children have opportunities to talk with one another and with the adults in the environment and where storytelling, book reading, dialogue, and discussion are valued and written communication is encouraged and supported.

6. Provide a print-rich environment in which books, writing materials, visuals, and other items encourage beginning readers.

7. Provide centers and appropriate props and play materials to promote rich pretend play.

8. Make parental participation essential, and ensure that parents play an active role in their children's learning experiences.

KEY TERMS

alphabetic	indirect speech	private spelling
centration	invented/developmental	public spelling
class inclusion	spelling	reversals
conservation	irreversibility	transformation
constancy of position	levels-of-processing theory	transivity
in space	metacommunication	
identity constancy	predictable books	

REVIEW STRATEGIES AND ACTIVITIES

1. Review the key terms in this chapter individually or with a classmate.

2. Observe children in the sociodramatic area of the classroom or in other learning areas. Provide anecdotal examples of the following:

   a. Children's knowledge of scripts

   b. Communicative competence

   c. Literacy-related behaviors

3. Collect samples of young children's writing. Analyze them for children's concepts about print, including the following:

   a. Meaning

   b. Use of space

   c. Knowledge of directionality

   d. Concept of word

   e. Invented spelling

4. Interview early childhood professionals in inclusive classroom settings. Ask them to describe how they provide cognitive, language, and literacy experiences for children with diverse developmental needs.

FURTHER READINGS

Coles, G. (2000). *Misreading reading: The bad science that hurts children.* Portsmouth, NH: Heinemann.

Gauvain, M. (2000). *The social context of cognitive development.* New York: Guilford.

Gopncu, A., & Klein, E. L. (2001). *Children in play, story, and school.* New York: Guilford.

Greenspan, S. I. (1997). *The growth of the mind and the endangered origins of intelligence.* Reading, MA: Addison-Wesley.

Klein, L. (2003). *Set for success: Building a strong foundation for school readiness based on the social–emotional development of young children.* The Kaufman Early Education Exchange; available at http://www.emfk.org/

Puckett, M. B. (Ed.). (2002). *Room to grow: How to create quality early childhood environments* (3rd ed.). Austin, TX: Texas Association for the Education of Young Children.

Neuman, S. B., Copple, C., & Bredekamp, S. (2000). *Learning to read and write: Developmentally appropriate practices for young children.* Washington, DC: National Association for the Education of Young Children.

Schickedanz, J. A. (1999). *Much more than the ABCs: The early stages of reading and writing.* Washington, DC: National Association for the Education of Young Children.

Tabor, P. O. (1997). *One child, two languages: A guide for preschool educators of children learning English as a second language.* Baltimore: Brookes.

OTHER RESOURCES

American Academy of Pediatrics Reach Out and Read Program
Reach Out and Read National Center
Boston Medical Center
One BMC Place, 5th Floor High Rise
Boston, MA 02118
http://www.reachoutandread.org
American Speech-Language-Hearing Association
www.asha.org/speech/development/
    Bilingual-children.cfm
Association for Childhood Education International
17904 Georgia Avenue, Suite 215
Olney, MD 20832
http://www.udel.edu/bateman/acei
Board on Children, Youth, and Families
Institute of Medicine and the National Research Council
http://www.national-academies.org/cbsse/bocyf
For more information on Howard Gardner's theory of multiple intelligences go to
    http://www.newhorizons.org/trm_gardner.html
National Association of Child Advocates
Making Investments in Young Children: What the Research on Early Care and Education
    Tells Us
    http://www.childadvocacy.org

PART SIX

The Young Child: Ages Six Through Eight

CHAPTER FOURTEEN

14

Physical and Motor Development: Ages Six Through Eight

Children are, after all, growing organisms whose development shows an organization, pattern, and direction that is characteristic of the species.

DAVID ELKIND

Health is a state of complete physical, mental, and social well-being and not merely the absence of disease or infirmity.

WORLD HEALTH ORGANIZATION

After studying this chapter, you will demonstrate comprehension by:

▶ Outlining expected patterns of physical and motor development in children ages 6 through 8.

▶ Identifying landmarks in large and small motor development in children ages 6 through 8.

▶ Describing perceptual–motor development in children ages 6 through 8.

▶ Describing body and gender awareness in children ages 6 through 8.

▶ Identifying major factors influencing physical and motor development in children ages 6 through 8.

▶ Discussing health and well-being issues during ages 6 through 8.

▶ Suggesting strategies for enhancing physical and motor and perceptual–motor development in children ages 6 through 8.

PHYSICAL/MOTOR COMPETENCE OF CHILDREN AGES SIX THROUGH EIGHT

General Physical Characteristics

Childhood height is closely related to the heights of a child's parents, though children today seem to top out at an average of 1 to 2 inches taller than their parents. This has been attributed to improved nutrition and health care for children over the past 50 years. It is generally believed that physical growth in school-age children proceeds at a slow but steady pace, with a slight decline in rate of growth during ages 6 to 10, followed by a growth spurt during puberty and early adolescence. The expected height of a 6-year-old is about 45 inches. Over the next 2 or 3 years, increases in height average 2 to 3 inches each year. Individual heights, however, can range from 2 to 2½ inches on either side of the average of 45 inches.

In school-age children, individual variations in height and growth rates are attributed to genes; health history, including prior or present illness, thyroid or pituitary gland function, injury, or trauma; nutrition history, which may be characterized by overnutrition or undernutrition; and the extent to which the environment has facilitated and supported growth. Through regular physical examinations, growth patterns are evaluated and growth exceptionalities are diagnosed.

Graphs of boys' and girls' weights reveal similar trends. Although boys are usually heavier than girls at birth, girls catch up with them, and by age 8, boys and girls weigh about the same. The weight of 6-year-old boys at the 50th percentile on the NCHS growth chart is around 45.5 pounds. Boys gain an average of about 5 pounds per year over the next 3 years. The weight of girls at the 50th percentile position on the NCHS growth chart is slightly less than that of boys at 6 years old (42.9 pounds), but by age 8, there is little difference in girls' and boys' weights, with girls weighing around 54.6 pounds and surpassing boys in weight by age 10 to 12.

Variations in weight are due to many of the same factors as those associated with variations in height. Differences may be attributed simply to differences in genetically predetermined body build, but may also be due to overnutrition and undernutrition, and, as discussed in Chapter 11, inappropriate feeding practices and examples set by role models. Activity levels play a critical role in weight characteristics of children. Metabolic disorders can also alter growth trajectories for some children.

Body proportions change with increases in height as slender legs and arms continue to grow longer in proportion to the trunk. Muscles of the arms and legs are small and thin; the hands and feet continue to grow more slowly than the arms and legs. The abdomen becomes flatter, the shoulders more square, and the chest broader and flatter. The trunk is slimmer and more elongated, and posture is more erect. The head is still proportionally large, but the top-heavy look of younger bodies is diminishing. Facial features are also changing. The forehead is more proportionate to the rest of the face, and the nose is growing larger. The most dramatic changes to facial features during this period are those brought on by the shedding of deciduous (baby) teeth and the eruption of permanent teeth. Figure 14.1 shows the approximate ages at which the permanent teeth erupt.

Studies of growth trends in children provide interesting new perspectives on how and when growth occurs. Growth researcher Michelle Lampl and her colleagues suggested that rather than growing at a gradual, regular pace, as is generally assumed, children may grow in short, dramatic spurts, with starts and stops (Lampl, Veldhuis, & Johnson, 1992). Lampl found that some children in the population she studied grew as much as half an inch in a day, followed by a period of no

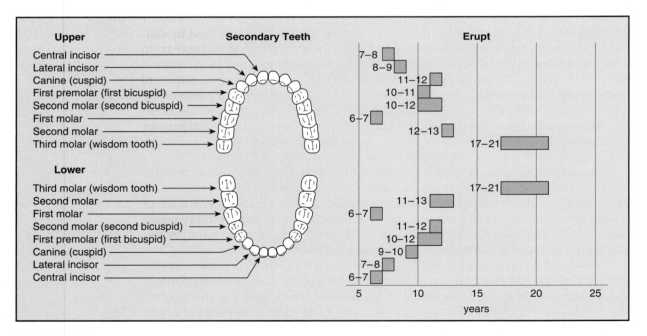

FIGURE 14.1
Eruption of Permanent Teeth

Facial features change dramatically during the period from ages 6 to 8 with the shedding of deciduous teeth and the eruption of permanent teeth.

growth at all for several days and sometimes weeks and even months. She also noted that children exhibited distinct behaviors before and during growth pulses, including being irritable, sleeping more, and having greater hunger than usual. On the basis of her findings, Lampl suggested a need for studies relating to hormonal influences on growth and the biochemical processes that trigger growth pulses. Her research, along with continuing studies of the growth hormone, which is released by the pituitary gland, may enable more accurate future treatments for children with growth disorders.

Synthetic human growth hormone treatments for children with growth deficiencies have been available since 1985, and have improved expected growth attainments in certain children. Such treatments have been used in a very limited number of cases and under strict medical supervision. Researchers caution that there is little evidence that growth hormone treatment will make a healthy short child a taller adult (Bell & Dana, 1998; Saenger, 1991).

Large Motor Development

Motor development affects all facets of a child's life. The importance of coordinated large motor abilities was stressed in earlier chapters. Such coordination facilitates **fundamental movements** of walking, running, reaching, climbing, jumping, and kicking. Facility with fundamental movements paves the way for the acquisition of more complex coordinations and movements that are involved in typical games and sports of the 6- through 8-year-old—chasing, playing dodgeball, catching, and throwing—and for small motor controls. Motor skills advance with increasing age and are enhanced by opportunities to use emerging abilities in active, unstructured play and child-initiated games.

fundamental movements: coordinations that are basic to all other movement abilities

Figure 14.2 illustrates the phases of motor development as outlined by Gallahue (1993), from reflexive movements of prenatal and infant development, to rudimentary movements of the toddler, to fundamental movements during the 3- through 7-year-old period, and then to the sports-related movement abilities of the 7- to 14-year-old. The latter two phases are important to our discussion of the 6- through 8-year-old, as a number of implications can be drawn about developmentally appropriate and inappropriate physical activities and expectations for this age group.

Organized Games and Sports

Should young children be given formal instruction in specific skill areas, such as dance, gymnastics, or swimming? Should young children participate in organized team sports? Is there a particular point in growth and development when beginning instruction and participation is advisable?

Figure 14.2 suggests that there may be optimal periods for instruction in specific skill areas. Gallahue and Ozmun (1998) maintained that fundamental movement abilities must not only be present, but also be refined before the introduction of specific skill training. Gallahue identified three main categories of fundamental movement skills (Gallahue, 1993, p. 19):

1. *Stability movement* skills, which include bending, stretching, twisting, turning, swinging, inverted supports (e.g., handstand), body rolling, landing, stopping, dodging, and balancing

FIGURE 14.2
The Phases and
Stages of Motor
Development

Source: Gallahue, D. L.,
& Ozmun, J. C. (1998).
*Understanding Motor
Development: Infants,
Children, Adolescents,
Adults* (4th ed., p. 89).
New York: Copyright
1998 McGraw-Hill
Publishing Co.
Reprinted with per-
mission.

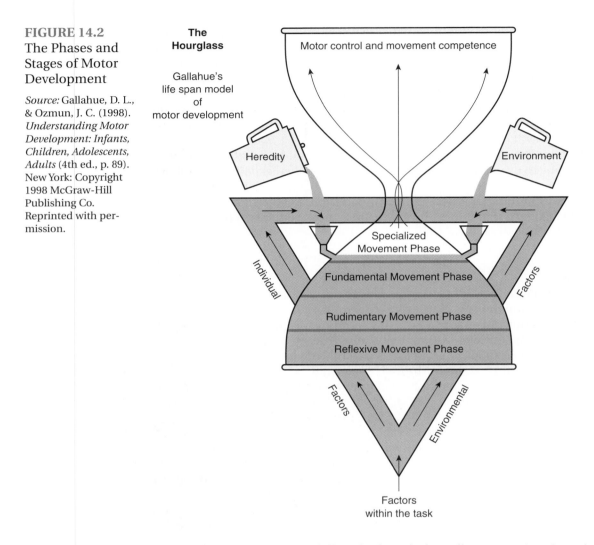

2. *Locomotor movement* skills, which include walking, running, jumping, hopping, skipping, sliding, leaping, climbing, and punting
3. *Manipulative movement* skills, which include throwing, catching, kicking,
   trapping, striking, volleying, bouncing, and ball rolling

According to Gallahue, these skills do not automatically emerge with maturation but also rely on encouragement, instruction, and practice. The goal of
early motor development is that of becoming a skillful mover. "Skillful movers
are those individuals who move with control, efficiency, and coordination in
the performance of fundamental or specialized movement tasks" (Gallahue,
1993, p. 17).

The decision to provide instruction in an activity such as gymnastics, ice skating, dance, or swimming or participation in an organized sport such as soccer,
hockey, baseball, or football should be based on the child's level of attainment of
fundamental movement skills; the sport or activity should be appropriate for the
age of the child and should be something the child has a particular interest in and

desire to pursue. Consideration must be given not only to the physiological rami-fications of early specific skill training, but also to social, emotional, and cognitive aspects. Individual children bring to any kind of formal instruction their interests, aptitudes, motivations, and perceptual–motor and cognitive abilities. In addition, as children enter the school years, peer group acceptance becomes a critical goal in their lives. Success with a particular sport in some contexts confers status on the child, while failure can be embarrassing and sometimes socially ostracizing. Parental expectations and disappointments and coaching that values winning over healthy childhood play experiences place children at both physical and psy-chological risk. Inappropriate or premature expectations for athletic performance and a competitive spirit in young children may lead to injury from lack of motor controls, distractions, and stress; diminished interest in participation; lowered self-esteem and self-confidence; and unnecessary social and emotional pres-sures. On the other hand, children who have mastered the fundamental motor skills prerequisite to a particular sport or activity may find enjoyment in partici-pation, refine large and small motor controls, benefit from adult support and guidance, and gain social skills associated with team participation and rule-governed activities.

Because preschool and primary-grade children are developing and refining fundamental movements, opportunities to use these abilities can be provided in

Creative outdoor equipment and activities encourage creative and physically active play.

both informal and guided ways through rhythm and movement activities, well-designed and well-constructed outdoor play equipment, simple games, and guided practice. Children can be assisted with such activities as aiming for a target when throwing a ball or beanbag; jumping various distances; hopping on one foot and then the other for a specified count; catching balls thrown from various distances; kicking a ball to a target; balancing on a balance beam; walking with facility on the balance beam forward, backward, and sideways; and many other motor challenges.

There is growing concern over the disproportionate amount of time children spend in sedentary pursuits as opposed to physically active ones. Computers and electronic games, television, latch key time, school days without recess, limited physical education in schools, homework, and family lifestyles characterized by low physical activity all contribute to daily schedules devoid of vigorous and growth-promoting physical activity. A lifestyle with limited physical activity is associated with a number of health-related issues, including obesity, diabetes, heart disease, and others. Physical activity, particularly running, has been associated with **neurogenesis**, the continuous creation of neurons. Vigorous exercise such as running increases heart rate and blood flow, leading to the transport of more growth factors into the brain and stimulation of neurogenesis (Gage & Jacobs, 2001). It is speculated that vigorous exercise also increases levels of serotonin, a chemical neurotransmitter that influences many brain functions including mood and simple movements. Low levels of serotonin are associated with depression. Sedentary lifestyles contribute to poor physical and mental health, which in turn interferes with normal growth and learning.

Concerns such as these have led a number of state legislatures to establish laws requiring public schools to provide daily physical education from the early childhood grades through high school. The National Association for Sport and Physical Education (2003) defines high-quality physical education as having the following components:

Opportunity to learn

- One hundred and fifty minutes per week of instruction during the elementary grades (225 minutes per week for middle and secondary school grades)
- Well-trained and qualified physical education specialists who provide developmentally appropriate programs
- Safe, age-appropriate, and adequate equipment and facilities

Meaningful physical education content

- Instruction in a variety of motor skills that are designed to enhance physical, mental, and social/emotional development
- Fitness education and assessment to help children understand, improve, and/or maintain their physical well-being
- Development of cognitive concepts about motor skills and fitness
- Opportunities to improve emerging social and cooperative skills and to gain a multicultural perspective
- Promotion of regular physical activity and the development of lifelong habits

neurogenesis:
the continuous production of neurons

Appropriate instruction

- Full inclusion of all students
- Maximum practice opportunities for class activities
- Well-designed lessons that facilitate student learning
- Out-of-school assignments that support learning and practice
- Never using physical activity for punishment

Children at a very early age begin to develop attitudes about health and physical activity. As they begin to attend physical education classes in school, they begin to experience more focused instruction on physical skills, personal responsibility for health maintenance, and the rules and joys of games and sports participation. The guidelines established for physical education by the National Association for Sport and Physical Education are instructive. These guidelines describe the physically educated person as one who

- is competent in many movement forms and proficient in a few movement forms;
- applies movement concepts and principles to understand and develop motor skills;
- leads a physically active lifestyle;
- maintains a health-enhancing level of physical fitness;
- behaves in ways that are personally and socially responsible in physical activity settings;
- understands and respects differences among people in physical activity settings;
- understands that physical activity can provide enjoyment, challenge, self-expression, and social interaction (National Association for Sport and Physical Education, 2003)

Small Motor Development

Facility in small motor development also affects many facets of a child's life, not the least of which are self-help tasks that lead to independence and self-confidence. By ages 6, 7, and 8, prehension is exhibited in the ability to hold a pencil or other writing implement, select and pick up the small pieces of a jigsaw puzzle, squeeze glue from a plastic bottle, and cut with scissors. Dexterity is revealed in assembling models and other small constructions, playing jacks with facility, shuffling and sorting playing cards, and using household tools such as a hammer or screwdriver with reasonable efficiency. Managing clothes and food packaging, unlocking a door with a key, turning the pages of a book, and folding paper along straight lines all require dexterity and are skills generally exhibited by the early primary grades.

As children enter the primary grades, handwriting becomes an important skill. Since small motor coordinations depend on fairly well-established large motor coordinations, most first-graders do not exhibit well-coordinated drawing and handwriting skills until they have mastered most fundamental movement coordinations. Skilled handwriting, drawing, painting, and cutting with scissors depend on the following:

- Facility with fundamental large motor movements
- Facility with small motor controls
- Prehension and dexterity
- Eye–hand coordination
- Ability to manage a variety of tools for writing and drawing (e.g., crayons, pencils, markers, paper, easels and paintbrushes, objects and templates for tracing)
- Ability to make basic strokes—large and sweeping, small and refined
- Perception of space, shape, and symbol (letters, numerals, and other symbols)
- Ability to draw basic shapes and intentionally make straight or curved lines
- Awareness that print conveys meaning
- Desire to communicate through drawing and writing

Since mastery of drawing and handwriting skills is dependent on both large and small motor development and other physiological and cognitive processes, children ages 6 through 8 benefit from a wide variety of motor, language, and early literacy experiences. Often, an eagerness to engage children in reading and writing activities during the primary grades results in teaching strategies that curtail the child's opportunities to refine fundamental large and small motor coordinations.

In addition to ongoing large motor activities and a variety of manipulative games and activities, opportunities to use the tools of reading and writing assist children in eye–hand coordination and visual/perceptual refinements. An assortment of writing implements such as felt markers, pencils, and ballpoint pens and paper in a variety of sizes, shapes, and textures encourage children to use their emerging drawing and handwriting skills. Experiences with print, such as story reading and environmental print, and opportunities to copy or replicate environmental print and drawings, write notes, make lists, dictate, and watch others write enhance the visual and perceptual abilities children need for later skilled drawing and handwriting.

Children benefit from curriculum materials that help to coordinate and refine small motor skills.

Perceptual–Motor Development

At ages 6, 7, and 8, children have fairly well-organized perceptual abilities. These abilities continue to be refined as children combine sensory and motor activities with cognitively challenging endeavors. Perceptual–motor development is dependent on maturation and experience.

Recall that the components of perceptual–motor development include both sensory abilities and kinesthetic sensitivity. The sensory components of perceptual–motor abilities include visual (depth, form, and figure perception), auditory (discrimination and memory), and tactile (discrimination and memory) perception. Kinesthetic abilities include body, spatial, and directional awareness and temporal awareness relating to rhythm, sequence, and synchrony.

Some important perceptual abilities during this period include recognizing and adjusting to one's and others' personal space and spatial and directional awareness needed for effective participation in games. Following directions in school (e.g., "Please walk in a single line on the right side of the hallway") requires perceptual abilities, as does the ability to focus on the dominant figure in a picture without being distracted by elements in the background, **figure–ground discrimination**. Figure–ground discrimination is dependent on size, shape, and form perceptions, which are helpful in forming letters and numbers. Visual memory assists the child in following written instructions, and auditory memory facilitates carrying out verbal instructions.

Perceptual–motor abilities at this age are fostered through both large and small motor activities. Games and activities that require visual–motor coordinations, such as tossing a beanbag to a target (large motor) and manipulating puzzle pieces (small motor), foster visual–perceptual development. Auditory–motor coordinations are fostered through rhythm and dance activities (large motor) and listening to match pairs of tone bells (small motor). Tactile discriminations occur when children attempt to tear (rather than cut) shapes from art paper. Kinesthetic awareness is fostered by such activities as rhythm and dance, pantomime, and playing games such as walking through a maze or navigating an obstacle course.

The relationship between these abilities and school success is worth noting. Refined perceptual motor abilities enhance the child's ability to meet the expectations of the school experience. Visual, auditory, tactile, and kinesthetic perceptions, integrated with refined motor coordinations, enhance all learning.

figure–ground discrimination: the ability to focus on the dominant figure in a picture without being distracted by elements in the background

Children with Special Needs

Children with special needs, developmental delay, or chronic illness may not grow and acquire physical skills at the same pace as their agemates. This, of course, depends on the nature and severity of their challenges. Although early diagnosis is essential in order to provide timely and appropriate interventions, continuing assessment and ongoing monitoring of growth and development progress are particularly important as children enter formal schooling regimes and face more rigorous performance expectations.

Monitoring the physical well-being of children with special needs includes observing and assessing growth rates with attention to height-for-age and weight-for-height, sensory integrity, food intake and nutrition status, energy and activity levels, alertness, mental engagement, emotionality, sleep/resting behaviors, self-help skills, apparent effectiveness of medicines and other treatments, and competence with adaptive equipment. Movement and motor skills, fine motor

individualized education plan (IEP):
a written plan for services for individuals of ages 3 to 21 with disabilities as defined by the Individuals with Disabilities Education Act

individualized family services plan (IFSP):
a written plan for services for birth through 2 years of age, and in some cases older, for children with disabilities under the Individuals with Disabilities Education Act

proficiency, strength, stamina, and tenacity are additional indicators of well-being. Further, skilled observation includes paying close attention to the capability, attitudinal, and/or environmental obstacles to full participation in planned activities. These observations complemented with appropriate formal assessments inform curriculums and expectations and are essential in developing an **individualized education plan (IEP)** (or, for some children, an **individualized family services plan [IFSP]**) as required by the federal Individuals with Disabilities Education Act.

The Division for Early Childhood of the Council for Exceptional Children places considerable emphasis on the appropriateness of both formal and informal assessment practices. Included in their extensive set of recommended practices in early intervention/early childhood special education is the recommendation that assessments employ "materials and procedures that accommodate the individual child's sensory, physical, responsive, and temperamental differences," and that multiple sources for assessment be used to identify individual strengths and needs across all developmental and behavior dimensions (Sandall, McLean, & Smith, 2000, p. 24). Such assessment provides insights that guide expectations and facilitate the development of curriculum and activities that challenge, but do not discourage, and promote development in all developmental areas.

Home and classroom physical activities can be adapted to increase or maintain the physical and performance fitness of individual children according to their physical, mental, and emotional challenges. Physical education programs for children with special needs are classified as adapted, remedial, and developmental (Gallahue, 1993). *Adapted* programs permit the child to function within his or her range of abilities. *Remedial* physical education programs provide corrective exercises and physical activities designed to improve body mechanics and perceptual motor development. Remedial physical education programs require specialized training and equipment, and the oversight and guidance of a health care professional. *Developmental* physical education programs serve all children (with

Children with special needs benefit from materials and activities that accommodate their individual interests and capabilities.

or without special challenges) and are concerned with individual improvement in movement, skill acquisition, fitness, cognitive, and psychosocial development.

Regardless of how the program is classified, all children should be assessed for skill and fitness levels before a specific program is implemented, provided many and varied opportunities to participate in physical/motor activities, and monitored for enjoyment and progress over time. As children gain knowledge of good health, nutrition, and hygiene practices, and as they gain confidence in their unique physical/motor abilities, they may gradually assume more responsibility for their own well-being.

RELATIONSHIP BETWEEN PHYSICAL/MOTOR DEVELOPMENT AND PSYCHOSOCIAL DEVELOPMENT

Self-concept

Whereas the younger child's self-concept is based on general physical characteristics, a more abstract, less physically based concept emerges during the early school years. Children ages 6 through 8 have the ability to compare themselves with others and are gaining a more accurate awareness of their own unique abilities and traits. As their self-concept emerges in somewhat modified form from earlier self-perceptions, they become cognizant of their relationships to others, including the roles they play within their family, their school, and various social groups. At this age, children may become self-critical, sometimes making self-deprecating remarks, and are often critical of others, engaging in putting down or teasing others. They are becoming sensitive to what others think of them and whether or not they are included in social groupings.

Self-imposed Expectations

Toward the end of the 6- through 8-year period, children may begin to assess themselves against some internalized measure relating to some self-imposed expectation. They may exaggerate or diminish their attributes and those of others. Their levels of aspiration may not be synchronized with their actual abilities or their age. Their internalized measures are expressed in interests and efforts and are verbalized in remarks such as, "I can't draw pictures," "I'm so clumsy," "You should have seen me at my recital; I didn't make one single mistake!," and "Next year, my daddy is going to teach me to ride a motorcycle!"

When these attempts at self-definition are self-critical, the child may become unwilling to take part in group games and feel self-consciousness about abilities to perform physical/motor tasks. On the other hand, attributing greater skill to themselves than exists may lead children to take physical risks such as climbing to a dangerously high tree branch, riding a bicycle at breakneck speed, attempting to lift something quite heavy, or other risky behaviors. When aspirations exceed abilities, children often experience failure, resulting in embarrassment or negative self-regard and less motivation to try new tasks. One of the goals in early childhood education is to help children accurately assess their abilities and accept their uniqueness as well as that of others. On this point, the appropriateness of competitive classroom games and sports is again called into question.

Relationships with Others

Positive and affirming interactions with others, particularly parents and teachers, assist young children in developing reasonable expectations for themselves and positive regard for their physical characteristics and abilities. Providing opportunities to enhance motor skills that are appropriate to age and capabilities facilitates individual physical and motor competence and the formulation of positive self-concepts and self-esteem (Straus, Rodzilsky, Burack, & Cole, 2001). Further, studies have found that children with high physical competence have more opportunities to develop social knowledge, which enhances their peer relationships.

From her study of the impact of physical competence on the peer relations of eight second-grade children with high and low motor skills, Barbour (1995) was able to draw these implications:

- Motor skill proficiency provides an avenue for improving social competence. Children with low physical competence who improve their physical skills relative to their peers have a better chance of group inclusion and improved social status and self-image.
- Physical education and free play programs that are developmental with a focus on increasing the physical competence of every child (as opposed to an unstructured, nonsequential activities approach or emphasis on large group competitive games) give low physically competent children opportunities to increase motor skill development, increase social knowledge, and improve peer relations.
- Participation in organized sports and games is a vehicle for popularity among boys in second grade, an age at which lack of participation can be detrimental to peer relationships among boys.
- Physical competence influences play behaviors of children. For example, low physically competent boys may choose quieter, less competitive forms of play (such as dramatic play with a domestic theme); high physically competent girls may choose more active games and sports.
- Physical competence influences cross-gender play behaviors and cross-grade and age groupings. Girls with high physical competence and boys with low physical competence may be more likely to play with peers of the opposite sex, while their same-sex counterparts may prefer same-sex groupings. When boys respond negatively to other boys who choose to play with girls, the low physically competent boys are further placed at a social disadvantage.
- Compensatory strategies may need to be taught to low physically competent children to help them to be more successful in the peer relations. Such strategies might include learning more about prosocial behaviors (cooperating, sharing, helping, having empathy, and so on), organizing play around sociodramatic scripts, and learning to use humor. Compensatory strategies may also help children to understand the effects of inappropriate behaviors, such as bossiness or withdrawal, on others (Barbour, 1995, pp. 44–45).

Gender-Related Play Behaviors

Unlike one's sex, which is biologically determined, gender is psychologically and socially constructed. Different cultures label various behaviors or expectations as *feminine* or *masculine* and may vary these labels and expectations over time relative to context- and age-expected behaviors (Wood, 1994). In most cultures in the United States, young children know their sex by ages 6 to 8 and have some understanding of society's gender expectations. This sense of gender is acquired through interactions with others: parents, siblings, peers, teachers, and other individuals. The media also play an influencing role in gender role identities. From infancy onward, children imitate the behaviors of those who are important to them and eventually internalize many of those behaviors, particularly ones that result in positive feedback and affirmation.

From a very early age, environmental cues and parental behaviors influence the play behaviors of children through role models, expectations, and the selection and provision of gender-typed toys (e.g., dolls for girls, trains for boys) (Serbin, Powlishta, & Gulko, 1993). Gender identity is influenced through the kinds of behaviors that are condoned or expected. For instance, in our culture, boys are more likely to be encouraged to be independent, aggressive, and exploratory, while girls may be protected, cuddled, and hugged (Fagot, 1988). These early gender-typed experiences influence the perceptions children form about themselves and their gender and about the gender-role expectations held by persons important to them. In turn, a child's play themes, physical activities, and choice of friends generally reflect these perceptions.

Sexuality Development

Another development in gender identity and gender-role behaviors is the child's emerging interests in topics related to sex and procreation. This interest usually begins with curiosity about the differences between boys' and girls' genitalia. Discovery of genital differences usually occurs between 16 and 19 months of age (Galenson, 1993), a time when giving appropriate names to body parts is occurring ("Where is your nose?"; "Where are your knees? your toes?"). Common in our culture, however, are substitute names for genitalia such as "pecker" or "wee-wee." To avoid misperceptions and distorted concepts and feelings about anatomy, it is better to teach the correct anatomical names of "penis" and "vagina." Think about it: Seldom is a child taught to call the eyes "peepers"; perhaps it would be cute, but hardly cognitively or developmentally helpful. Children who, beginning at this early stage, have experienced unembarrassed, frank, and accurate information about their bodies and bodily functions and the anatomical differences between boys and girls can be more forthcoming as they get older with their questions about sex-related topics. School-age children whose earlier questions about where babies come from have been answered frankly are more likely to continue such dialogue with their parents. However, television, books, and peers will augment the child's knowledge. Sometimes, the information derived from these other sources is accurate and helpful. Often, however, the information the child obtains is inaccurate and sometimes distorted. Television and other electronic media, comic books, and other print material may depict human sexuality and reproduction in sensational and perhaps sordid and frightening ways. Information shared among friends also can be misleading.

As children get older, their sexual curiosity becomes more disguised. The frank questions and unrestrained curiosity of an earlier age are less evident. Interests tend to focus on pregnancies and babies: how long the baby will be inside the mother, how the baby will get out, and the role father plays in reproduction. The 6- to 8-year-old does not, however, seek as much information as one might think. Children need simple, accurate information from adults who understand what the child is really asking and are sensitive to the child's developmental abilities to understand. At times, asking the child what she or he thinks about a question asked can provide the adults with background information about what the child is really asking, reveal possible misinformation, and give clues as to how to respond to the child's questions.

During this age period, self-consciousness associated with modesty begins to emerge. Dressing, undressing, and toileting in the presence of others are fiercely avoided. The "bathroom" talk of earlier ages decreases, though it is occasionally used to shock or insult others. Adults who provide an atmosphere of rapport and respect for children assist children in becoming comfortable with their own sexuality and accepting of their own anatomies (Chrisman & Couchenour, 2002; Honig, 2000).

RELATIONSHIP BETWEEN PHYSICAL/MOTOR DEVELOPMENT AND COGNITIVE DEVELOPMENT

From preceding chapters, you have learned that perspectives on cognitive development are changing from predominantly Piagetian to enlarged and modified neo-Piagetian models. These new perspectives have given rise to research on the influence of physical and motor development on cognition. From a Piagetian point of view, children acquire concepts and increasing knowledge as they physically interact with objects and people in their environments. Through sensorimotor activity and concrete operations, young children build on prior experience to construct new concepts and new knowledge. For many children, this process indeed occurs, but let's explore the issue from another perspective: that of the child with physical disabilities.

Neo-Piagetians have challenged the prevailing view of cognitive development by citing the cognitive development of children who are visually or hearing impaired or have motor impairments. In a review of research, Bebko, Burke, Craven, and Sarlo (1992) argued that children with various disabilities attain normal concept development despite their inability to physically and motorically explore and manipulate objects in the environment in traditional ways. These authors identified three models for describing early cognitive development and the role of physical and motor activity: the Piagetian model, the neo-Piagetian model, and the perceptual analysis model. The latter two models are supported by the fact that mental representations and concepts have been exhibited in children as young as $3\frac{1}{2}$ to $5\frac{1}{2}$ months of age, a period that precedes the onset of coordinated motor movements (Baillargeon, 1987). The perceptual analysis model, proposed by Mandler (1992), argues that children are born with a capacity to engage in perceptual analysis, a mental process by which one perception is actively compared with another. External sensorimotor activity may provide input to this analysis, but the analysis is not necessarily dependent on it. From their review of the research, Bebko et al. (1992) concluded:

> The literature on children with severe physical handicaps suggests that motor activity and the ability to handle and manipulate objects in the environment may not be necessary conditions for development. Rather, it is interaction with the environment that seems critical, but interaction defined in the broadest sense, making use of both their own direct manipulations to the extent possible and

other-mediated actions and encompassing input from any sensory system or action by any kinesthetic organ. Information from these varied sources allows for the coordination of schemes, the verification or disconfirmation of hypotheses and subsequent cognitive growth. (p. 238)

It appears that, given these different points of view, a new and more eclectic theory of cognitive development has emerged. In view of changing theoretical perspectives, the early childhood professional must not only address the needs of non-impaired children in providing physical/motor opportunities, but also consider the capabilities of children with various disabilities to formulate concepts and new knowledge by way of various physical/motor modalities. Regardless of ableness, facility to the extent possible in physical/motor controls and coordinations enhances cognitive development and learning through stimuli that utilize all of the senses.

FACTORS INFLUENCING PHYSICAL AND MOTOR DEVELOPMENT

A major goal of early childhood development is the promotion and protection of the general health and well-being of children. A number of factors influence this goal. Certainly, the child's genetic makeup sets limits on growth and development and determines the presence or absence of certain disabilities. In addition, environmental factors influence the extent to which optimal growth and development can be achieved. Proper nutrition; dental and medical care (including timely immunizations and other protections from disease); adequate rest, sleep, and physical/motor activity (see Figure 14.3); protection from accidents and injury; and emotional and social support are necessary for optimal growth and development.

Nutrition

Though the school years are often referred to as the "latent growth period," children ages 6 through 8 continue to need a well-balanced diet as depicted in the Food Guide Pyramid (Figure 8.3). Their growing bodies need adequate supplies of protein, carbohydrates, minerals, vitamins, and some fat to maintain growth, energy, and good health. A child who during the toddler and preschool years has experienced a wide variety of foods and has learned to enjoy a range of foods in all of the food groups is likely to continue to make good food choices in school and other out-of-home contexts.

Growth patterns and appetite generally parallel one another; that is, appetite generally waxes and wanes with periods of fast and slow growth. During the period of ages 6 through 8, growth has decelerated but proceeds on a relatively steady course. Food intake in school-age children depends on amount of physical activity, **basal metabolic rate**, and state of wellness or illness. Food preferences of earlier years can change as children are exposed to additional new foods and re-exposed to previously nonpreferred foods and as food is experienced in a wider variety of settings (e.g., school, camp, or the homes of friends). Learning about food and nutrition through curricular activities may also alter prior food preferences and intake patterns.

Though food patterns and habits that are modeled in the home influence a child's initial food preference behaviors, which often persist into adulthood, peers, the media, and the child's body image can also modify (for better or for worse) a child's food preferences and intake patterns. Daily routines such as

other-mediated action:
an action, originated by a child who is physically unable to act directly on objects, that is carried out by some other person or agent

basal metabolic rate:
the amount of energy required to keep the heart beating, sustain breathing, repair tissues, and keep the brain and nerves functioning

FIGURE 14.3
A Child's Physical
Activity Pyramid

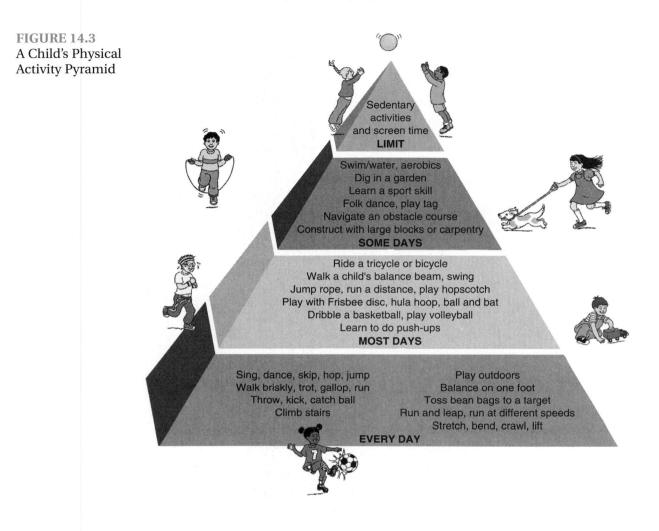

meeting a school bus, attending a school-age child care program, participating in organized sports activities, or taking lessons in music, dance, or other activity create unique schedules in which meals and snacks may occur irregularly. Unpredictable meal and snack times can change the eating patterns and food preferences of children and interfere with adequate intake of necessary nutrients. As with younger children, to the extent that the adult provides nutritious snacks and meals, the child has an opportunity to consume appropriate foods as hunger dictates. Skipping meals (as sometimes happens with early morning bus schedules) should not be an option for children, and parental control of the type and amount of between-meal snacks is necessary at this age. Also, as children and families take many of their meals at fast-food restaurants, the opportunity arises to help children learn about high-fat, high-calorie foods and how to make wise selections when eating away from home.

Undernutrition.   Undernutrition (insufficient calories to maintain energy, growth, and health) can have serious consequences for children ages 6 through 8. Children who are undernourished have difficulty in school because they tire

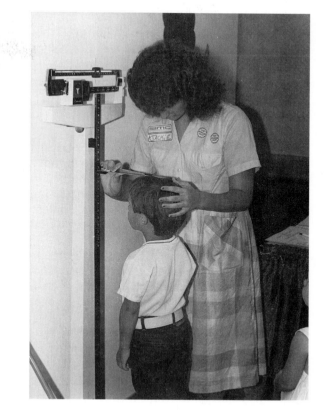

School-age children continue to need regular health check-ups.

readily, have difficulty sustaining physical and mental attention, and are more susceptible to infection, which may cause more frequent absences from school.

Evidence supports the observation that skipping breakfast affects a student's performance in school. Research on the link between children's nutrition and academic performance and behaviors indicates the following effects related to starting the day with a nutritious breakfast:

- Children who skip breakfast show impaired late-morning problem-solving ability (Pollitt, Leibel, & Greenfield, 1981)
- Children who skip breakfast have slower memory recall and make more visual perceptual mistakes (Pollitt, Cueto, & Jacoby, 1998)
- Children who skip breakfast have lower math scores and are more likely to repeat grades (Alaimo, Olson, & Frongillo, 2001)
- Children who are hungry exhibit more behavioral, emotional, and academic problems (Kleinman et al., 1998; Pollitt & Matthews, 1998)
- Children who have breakfast at the start of the school day show increased math and reading scores (Murphy, Pagano, & Bishop, 2001)
- The timing of breakfast closer to class or test-taking times enhances performance and improves standardized test scores (Vaisman, Voet, Akivis, & Vakil, 1996)

- Children who have breakfast show improved speed and memory in cognitive tests (Grantham-McGregor, Chang, & Walker, 1998)
- Children who participate in school breakfast programs have lower rates of absenteeism and tardiness (Cook, Ohri-Vachaspati, & Kelly, 1996)
- Children who eat breakfast exhibit fewer discipline problems and visit the school nurse less often (Minnesota Department of Children, Families and Learning, 1998)

Healthy Eating Index:
A U.S. Department of Agriculture measure of diet quality, which assesses the degree to which a person's diet conforms to the Food Guide Pyramid; limits saturated fat, cholesterol, and sodium; and includes a variety of foods

An important study that relates to all meals, not only breakfast, found that children who consume breakfast have higher overall **Healthy Eating Index** (HEI) scores than children who do not (Basiotis, Linn, & Anand, 1999). Healthy eating habits include eating well-balanced meals in line with the recommendations of the Food Guide Pyramid; limiting fats, cholesterol, and sodium (salt) in the diet; and consuming a variety of foods from all of the food groups. These healthy eating habits begin in childhood.

Because adequate nutrition during the growing years is essential to growth and development, health and well-being, and overall integrity of the human organism, programs serving children must be prepared to meet childhood nutritional needs. To this end, free and reduced-price meals are provided in schools and child care programs.

School Meal Programs. Begun in 1946 and expanded and modified over the years, Congress created the National School Lunch Program (NSLP) as a "measure of national security, to safeguard the health and well-being of the nation's children." Its creation was a response to a concern that arose when many young men attempting to enter the armed forces during World War II had to be rejected because of physical conditions associated with malnutrition. Today, the federal government provides additional food and nutrition programs, including the Supplemental Food Program for Women, Infants, and Children mentioned in Chapter 5, the School Breakfast Program, the Child and Adult Care Food Program, and the Summer Food Program. These supplemental food programs are made available to public and some nonprofit schools, child care programs, and residential care programs for children through the U.S. Department of Agriculture (USDA). The Food and Nutrition Service, an agency within the USDA, administers the programs, which provide cash assistance and supplemental foods to states to provide free and reduced-price meals for eligible children. State education agencies in conjunction with local school districts administer the NSLP and the School Breakfast Program at the local level. More than 97,000 schools and residential child care institutions participate in the NSLP. In addition, 75,000 schools nationwide participate in the School Breakfast Program (Food Research and Action Center, 2003).

The increase in families with both parents in the work force and the high number of single-parent families have resulted in more children attending before- and after-school programs. In addition to school lunch and breakfast programs, the Child and Adult Care Food Program subsidizes the cost of nutritious meals in licensed or registered child and adult day care facilities, and allows schools to use the NSLP as a means to serve snacks in school-sponsored and other after-school programs such as those provided by nonprofit organizations, for example, YMCAs, YWCAs, Boys and Girls Clubs, and park and recreation department programs. The USDA Summer Food Service Program provides meals for children from low-income families during the summer months, when school is not in session. Recreation programs, schools, tutoring services, and other summer programs for children living in poverty can take advantage of this program.

Parents must apply to their child's school or school district for their child to receive free or reduced-price lunch and breakfast. Household income is used to determine whether a child will pay the full price for meals or will receive a reduced-price or free meal.

Schools receiving funds from the National School Lunch or School Breakfast Programs must provide meals that meet the USDA Dietary Guidelines for Americans. These guidelines specify menu composition and serving sizes that are commensurate with the Food Guide Pyramid (Figure 8.3). Whereas school lunches in the past tended to be high in carbohydrates and fats, when meal planners follow the Food Guide Pyramid, sugars and fats are reduced and grains, fruits, and vegetables are increased. In addition to modifying menus for children, attention is being given to food service strategies that promote interest in nutritious meals, appealing presentation of foods, and educational programs that enhance knowledge of the importance of good nutrition.

Overnutrition (Obesity).   As with undernutrition, overnutrition has debilitating outcomes, and, as with pre-school-age children, there is evidence that the number of obese school-age children in the United States is increasing. The fact that children are becoming obese at earlier ages and that the tendency toward childhood obesity persists into the adult years makes this a serious concern to health care professionals as well as early childhood educators.

Long-term consequences of obesity are increasingly being identified (Slyper, 1998). Obesity is the most common cause of abnormal growth acceleration during childhood. In females, obesity has been associated with early onset of puberty and the menarche. In boys, obesity has been found to relate to both early and delayed puberty. Diabetes and glucose intolerance have been noted in obese children whose family has a history of diabetes. Hypertension and elevated cholesterol levels are also found in obese children. Obese children are more likely to experience sleep disorders such as snoring, difficulty breathing, restlessness, night waking, sweating, bed wetting, and daytime sleepiness. Overweight children are at higher risk of becoming overweight adults with accompanying high risk of debilitating chronic diseases and overall poor health (which includes diabetes, gallbladder disease, cardiovascular disease, hypertension, and breast and colon cancer).

The obese child faces both physiological and psychological penalties. School-age obesity has many possible causes, including the following:

1. Inactivity and inadequate amounts of physical exercise
2. Electronic entertainment (television, computers, and other electronic devices), which interferes with more active pursuits and may also encourage snacking
3. Food and drink advertising in the media, often for high-calorie/low-nutrient foods

4. Overeating, associated with boredom and psychological needs for self-comfort or self-reward

5. Availability of high-calorie/low-nutrient foods in the home

6. Parenting styles that use food to reward children or to relieve parental anxiety or guilt, as when adults judge their success as parents on how well their children are fed

7. Adult insistence on a "clean plate" after a meal

8. Failure to recognize and respond to one's feelings of satiety

9. Excessive daily homework requirements following a mostly sedentary school day

10. Inherited body types that predispose some children toward obesity

School-age children who are prone to obesity should be under professional health care supervision. With professional guidance, parents and teachers will need to monitor growth rates, nutrient and calorie intake, exercise and other physical activity, and psychosocial health. The family may need nutrition counseling and to modify eating and exercise habits. Responses of those who care for the child must be sensible and sensitive. Only medically approved diets should be implemented, since the child's nutritional needs remain basically the same as those for all children the same age. Failure to adequately meet the child's nutritional needs places the child at risk for complications associated with malnutrition, decreased resistance to disease, and failure to grow in height.

Sensitivity to the child's emotional and social needs is particularly important. Care must be taken to affirm the child's dignity and worth. The child may need help in finding acceptance within the peer group and realizing her or his special attributes. The child's need for acceptance and belonging, self-esteem, initiative, and industry must be supported and encouraged.

Dental Health

Around age 5 or 6 years, children begin to lose their primary teeth, and permanent teeth begin to erupt. When the primary teeth have been well cared for through professional dental supervision that includes regular check-ups and cleaning, attention to caries, fluoride treatment as needed, and monitoring for any preventive or corrective oral or dental treatments, the permanent teeth arrive in healthy form. To maintain dental and oral health, children need to consume a well-balanced diet; avoid sugary foods, which lead to tooth decay; habitually brush their teeth at least twice a day; avoid (or seek immediate dental treatment for) mouth or tooth injury; and have regular dental check-ups.

There is some evidence that untreated childhood caries can slow a child's growth (American Academy of Pediatrics, 1999b). Ostensibly, the pain and infection accompanying dental caries change a child's eating and sleeping patterns, leading to slowed growth. Findings such as this point out the importance of dental health supervision and prevention of or early attention to dental caries or gum disease.

Vision and Hearing

Jeremy's third-grade teacher has noticed that Jeremy's interest in reading has diminished. He appears stressed when called upon to read, makes mistakes, and acts silly to distract his classmates during reading times. He has also begun to make many mistakes in his math work, particularly in paper-and-pencil tasks. Upon closer observation, his teacher, Mr. Frederick, notices that Jeremy rubs his eyes frequently and holds books and papers rather close to his face. He decides that a parent conference might alert his parents to the possibility that Jeremy should have his vision checked. Indeed, an ophthalmological examination reveals that Jeremy needs corrective lenses.

When children seem to be doing poorly in school, early childhood professionals initially consider the possibility that vision or hearing problems exist. While profound vision or hearing impairments have typically been diagnosed by the time children enter school, the more subtle impairments often go undetected until children must attend to the visual and auditory tasks associated with early schooling. Tasks such as focusing on print in books and other media, copying from charts or the chalkboard, following directional signs in the school building, discriminating phonemic sounds, learning words to songs, and following verbal directions can pose challenges for children who have vision or hearing difficulties. A review of Tables 14.1 and 14.2, which lists signs and behaviors suggestive of vision and hearing problems, is instructive. Where treatment or intervention has not occurred at an earlier age, the appearance of these behaviors at ages 6 to 8 suggests a need for professional assessment.

TABLE 14.1   Behaviors Associated with Visual Impairment

Red or swollen eyelids
Tearing or drainage from one or both eyes
Unusual sensitivity to light
Squinting
Excessive blinking or grimacing
Misaligned eyes (as with strabismus)
Frequent rubbing of the eyes
Complaints of headaches, difficulty seeing, or blurred vision
Holding face unusually close to reading or table work
Unusual twisting or tilting the head to see
Closing or covering one eye to look at something
Awkward and uneven drawing and writing
Limited visual curiosity
Avoidance of tasks requiring tedious visual work
Frequent bumping into objects or people

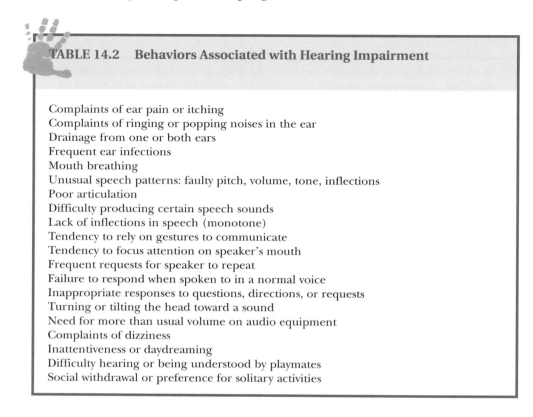

TABLE 14.2   Behaviors Associated with Hearing Impairment

Complaints of ear pain or itching
Complaints of ringing or popping noises in the ear
Drainage from one or both ears
Frequent ear infections
Mouth breathing
Unusual speech patterns: faulty pitch, volume, tone, inflections
Poor articulation
Difficulty producing certain speech sounds
Lack of inflections in speech (monotone)
Tendency to rely on gestures to communicate
Tendency to focus attention on speaker's mouth
Frequent requests for speaker to repeat
Failure to respond when spoken to in a normal voice
Inappropriate responses to questions, directions, or requests
Turning or tilting the head toward a sound
Need for more than usual volume on audio equipment
Complaints of dizziness
Inattentiveness or daydreaming
Difficulty hearing or being understood by playmates
Social withdrawal or preference for solitary activities

Safety

Children ages 6 through 8 are subject to many of the same hazards that younger children are, and some of these risks increase as they begin to expand their activities beyond the home and classroom. Their ability to explore the neighborhood, visit with friends, and play in groups or on playgrounds; their interest in physically active games and sports and spontaneous rough-and-tumble play; and their beginning use of bicycles and other sports equipment all subject them to potential hazards.

As children get older, they may be away from home more frequently and have less direct adult supervision. They are eager to do things for themselves and are often willing to go along with their friends. Common hazards for this age group are organized team sports, particularly in organizations or settings in which performance expectations are developmentally inappropriate and rules about wearing appropriate gear and using age-appropriate equipment are not enforced; inappropriate use of toys and playground equipment and inadequate supervision of children using them; traffic and pedestrian accidents; swimming pools and other bodies of water; flammable agents; tools and home appliances; toxic substances; and firearms.

Some popular recreational items are particularly dangerous. The time-honored bicycle poses very serious safety concerns. The annual number of bicycle-related deaths exceeds the number of deaths from accidental poisonings, falls, and firearm accidents combined. The use of bicycle safety helmets can reduce the risk of head trauma and brain injury by as much as 88 percent (Storo, 1993). Children must be taught the importance of bicycle helmet usage and safe bicycling practices. Safety helmets should have a sticker indicating that they meet the safety standards of the American National Standards Institute or the Snell Memorial Foundation. Helmets should fit the wearer snugly and be free of dents.

Children using in-line skates, skateboards, ice skates, and similar equipment must also wear helmets to prevent head injury. Some communities have laws and ordinances restricting or banning these activities in certain potentially dangerous locations and prescribing proper safety gear and use.

Skateboarding and in-line skating are other popular recreational activities that pose hazards to children. The U.S. Consumer Product Safety Commission recommends that children not be allowed to skate at night, when visibility is reduced, or on rough surfaces, which can cause loss of control, and not wear anything that can obstruct vision or hearing. A number of states now have laws restricting in-line skating in areas near traffic. Most injuries associated with skating are to the wrists, elbows, and knees. Appropriate gear for this sport must include helmets, wrist guards with palm protection, elbow and knee pads, and skates that are properly fitted to the user. Participants should be given lessons on proper use and safety, including how to react to road debris and defects and how to stop quickly and fall safely. "Truck-surfing" or "skitching" (skating behind or alongside a vehicle while the skater holds onto the vehicle) must be prohibited (American Academy of Pediatrics, Committee on Injury and Poison Prevention and Committee on Sports Medicine and Fitness, 1998).

Accident and injury prevention includes both setting rules and boundaries for and with children and teaching children about hazards and how to protect themselves. Adult surveillance and supervision of play, sports activities, and sports areas are a must if children are to be protected from preventable injuries. Table 14.3 lists typical hazards at this age and suggests topics to discuss with children. In addition to the safety issues addressed in Table 14.3, adults who are aware of children's play themes and cognizant of the influences of television, movies, the Internet, video games, and advertising on these themes are in a better position to intervene and guide the focus and quality of children's play. Some childhood aggressive and violent behaviors have been associated with specific media events and the behaviors of individuals children admire both at home and in the media. Mediating these impressions is an important responsibility of parents and adults who work with young children.

Exposure to Violence and Asocial Models

Violence is sadly a part of the landscape of childhood today. Children are exposed to it on many fronts, vicariously through the electronic and print media, tangentially as witnesses, directly as victims, and sometimes as perpetrators. Violence in the lives of children has become so pervasive in recent years that education and health care professionals, legislative and law enforcement agencies, and numerous faith-based and civic organizations have launched various campaigns, educational programs, and research studies in an attempt to understand and curtail it. Studies reveal that having witnessed or having been victimized by violence during childhood is strongly correlated with violence and weapon carrying in adolescents (DuRant, Getts, Cadenhead, Emans, & Woods, 1995; DuRant, Treiber, Goodman, & Woods, 1996). Further, children who have been victims of physical or emotional abuse are more prone to aggressive behaviors than children who have not had these experiences (Garbarino, 1999). Excessive viewing of violent content

TABLE 14.3   Preventing Accidents in the School-Age Child

Accident	Preventive Measure
Motor vehicle accidents	Encourage children to use seat belts in a car; role model their use. Teach street-crossing safety; stress that streets are no place for roughhousing, pushing, or shoving. Teach bicycle safety, including advice not to take "passengers" on a bicycle and to use a helmet. Teach parking lot and school bus safety (do not walk in back of parked cars, wait for crossing guard, etc.).
Community	Teach to avoid areas specifically unsafe, such as train yards, grain silos, back alleys. Teach not to go with strangers (parents can establish a code word with child; child does not leave school with anyone who does not know the word). Teach to say "no" to anyone who touches them whom they do not wish to do so, including family members (most sexual abuse is by a family member, not a stranger).
Burns	Teach safety with candles, matches, campfires—fire is not fun. Teach safety with beginning cooking skills (remember to include microwave oven safety such as closing the door firmly before turning on oven; not using metal containers). Teach not to climb electric poles.
Falls	Teach that roughhousing on fences, climbing on roofs, etc., is hazardous. Teach skateboard safety.
Sports injuries	Teach that wearing appropriate equipment for sports (face masks for hockey, knee braces for football, batting helmets for baseball) is not babyish but smart. Teach not to play to a point of exhaustion or in a sport beyond physical capability (pitching baseball or toe ballet for a grade-school child). Teach to use trampolines only with adult supervision to avoid serious neck injury.
Drowning	See to it that children learn to swim, and teach that dares and roughhousing when diving or swimming are not appropriate. Teach not to swim beyond limits of capabilities.
Drug	Teach to avoid all recreational drugs and to take a prescription medicine only as directed.
Firearms	Teach safe firearm use. Parents should keep firearms in locked cabinets with bullets separate from gun.
General	Teach school-age children to keep adults informed as to where they are and what they are doing. Be aware that the frequency of accidents increases when parents are under stress and therefore less attentive. Special precautions must be taken at these times. Some children are more active, curious, and impulsive and therefore more vulnerable to accidents than others.

Source: From Pillitteri, A. (1992). *Maternal and child health nursing: Care of the childbearing and childrearing family.* Philadelphia: J. B. Lippincott Co. Reprinted with permission by the author.

on television has been linked to depression and violence in children (Singer, 1998). A study of parents' beliefs about how children would react to finding guns revealed that most believed that their children would not touch guns that they found, often reasoning that children were "too smart" or "knew better" (Connor & Wesolowski, 2003). Yet gun accident statistics render these parental assumptions dangerously inaccurate. American children under age 15 are 12 times more likely to die from gunfire than children in 25 other industrialized countries combined (Children's Defense Fund, 2001). In 1998, 3,761 children and teens lost their lives. This computes to one child every 2½ hours, 10 children and teens every day, more than 70 young lives every week.

These and other studies of the prevalence and effects of violence in the lives of children have been widely researched and reported. The findings are disquieting. Parents and professionals can play a role in its prevention in the following ways:

1. Establish healthy routines that not only support growth and development, but build attitudes of respect and caring for one's health and well-being and that of others.

2. Promote and facilitate the development of positive attitudes toward oneself and others.

3. Provide constructive, health-promoting, enjoyable outlets for energy, interests, and talents, and encourage best efforts without undue pressure to succeed or "win."

4. Select toys, books, video games, music, movies, and other recreational activities for their prosocial qualities, avoiding those that encourage or glamorize aggressive, violent, or provocative behaviors.

5. Teach children to resist pressure from friends and the media to buy inappropriate toys or games; help them to become discerning consumers, able to resist cleverly advertised but unacceptable products or activities.

6. Set limits on television viewing (and other entertainment media: videos, video games, music), and provide substitute activities when content is inappropriate. Monitor and set limits and guidelines on the use of the computer and the Internet.

7. Provide many opportunities for children to interact and play with other children in wholesome contexts.

8. Teach children how to respond to angry, aggressive, bullying, or threatening behaviors of others.

9. Teach children how to safely care for themselves when adults are not present, including how to handle emergencies and contact parents or other supervising adults.

10. Plan for supervision, and monitor safe and productive after-school activities.

11. Model and teach anger management, conflict resolution, and negotiating skills.

12. Be available to children to engage in dialogue; answer questions; respond to concerns, fears, or anxieties; buffer daily challenges; and celebrate successes.

13. Encourage relationships with good citizen role models among peers and adults.

14. Help children to set personal goals and to prioritize the use of their time and money.

15. Encourage, facilitate, and acknowledge academic effort and success, and advocate for acceptance of individual differences and the uniqueness of each child.

Position statements and guidelines for parents have been published by various professional and civic organizations in an effort to provide information and safety precautions on subjects associated with violence: handguns and other dangerous weapons, television, video games, the Internet, music, advertising, toys and games, the need for street smart behaviors, dealing with aggression, handling stress and frustration, learning to resolve conflicts, and many other topics. In addition, efforts to provide support and education for families who are at risk for violence and abuse also have been widespread. Protecting the often fragile and vulnerable mental health of children, particularly during the years when neurological development is profound, is of critical importance. Numerous studies have documented a relationship between exposure to violence and childhood psychosocial development—a warning that cannot be dismissed.

Risky Behaviors

Children who are healthy are not just free of disease, but, importantly, are learning to make choices that promote health and well-being. They understand concepts of risk and danger, and are learning to avoid situations that place their health and safety in jeopardy or jeopardize the health and safety of others. This developmental goal takes time, guidance, and education to achieve.

Children of elementary school age do not have complete self-control, often act on impulse, are seldom good judges of character or situational potential, and have had limited life experiences. Hence, risky behaviors such as failing to follow safety precautions, testing boundaries and the limits of authority, exploring the enticements of risky friends, and succumbing to curiosities that lead them into danger are not uncommon. In the absence of guidance and education, the origins of risky behaviors such as experimentation with medicines, illicit drugs, tobacco, and alcohol and early sexual activity seen in some older children can rest in these early explorations.

Little data exist on the prevalence of these latter risky behaviors among children under age 12, although studies of the age of initiation reveal that some children engage in these behaviors at or before age 10. The 1996 Youth Risk Behavior Survey found that 11 percent of children age 16 who smoked began smoking at or before age 10 (Everett et al., 1999). Studies of other risky behaviors found that initiation of the use of alcohol occurred by fifth grade or earlier in 14 percent of the children studied, inhalants in 6.9 percent, smokeless tobacco in 4.5 percent, and marijuana in 3.2 percent (Johnson, O'Malley, & Bachman, 2001). The National Center for Health Statistics (2002) reported that, though it is rare, some girls under age 13 have given birth. In 1998, 202 girls age 12 gave birth, 23 girls age 11 gave birth, and 5 girls age 10 gave birth. Sexual activity is more prevalent among young boys than young girls, with 12.2 percent compared to 4.4 percent, respectively, reporting first intercourse before age 13 (Centers for Disease Control and Prevention, 2000). Both the short- and the long-term health and social consequences of these behaviors in children (and adolescents) have been widely publicized and are of serious concern, and include short- and long-term health problems, brain damage, early death from illness and accidents, learning disabilities, emotional problems, delinquent and criminal behaviors, social rejection, and dropping out of school.

Many factors contribute to the initiation of risky behaviors, and there are few guarantees of a "risk-free" child. However, prevention begins in early childhood and entails many of the same precautions as those listed in the discussion of violence in children's lives. Additionally, parents and other adults (teachers, caregivers, counselors, group leaders) conscientiously monitor the risky behaviors and attitudes of young and elementary age children. Without overresponding to typical age-related behaviors, it is important to note the frequency and tenacity with which children engage in risky behaviors, while setting age-appropriate expectations for behaviors (discussed in the chapters dealing with psychosocial development) and providing logical, reasonable, predictable, and consistent limits and guidelines. Teaching children, both at home and at school, the importance of good health and safety habits, the consequences of poor health, and the risks involved in certain behaviors is needed if they are to learn to protect themselves and make wise choices in the face of curiosity and temptations.

The young child who is in self-care has been referred to as the "latchkey child," so named for the house key worn on a string around the child's neck or pinned to clothing to allow entry into the home upon return from school or other activities. There is good reason to be concerned about this practice. Children in self-care, or cared for by a sibling, are at risk for accidents and injuries, social and behavior problems, and academic achievement and school adjustment problems (Vandivere, Tout, Capizzano, & Zaslow, 2003). Children in self-care are vulnerable to a host of in-home risks including exploitation, physical and sexual abuse, household accidents and exposure to toxic substances, and experimentation with unsecured medicines, drugs, alcohol, tobacco, and firearms. Telephone, television, and computer use are unsupervised. Children in self-care often experience isolation and loneliness, and miss desired opportunities to participate in non-school-related activities and interactions with friends.

Few 6- to 9-year-old children are mature enough to care for themselves on a regular basis, and they lack the experience and judgment to make quick and appropriate decisions in emergency situations. Vandivere et al. (2003) drew data from the 1999 National Survey of America's Families to determine the circumstances under which children are left in self-care. The studies determined that two groups of children may be particularly vulnerable: the youngest school-age children and low-income children. Younger school-age children are at risk for the reasons stated in the foregoing; low-income children's risks are associated with the likelihood of living in unsafe neighborhoods (Vandivere et al., 2003). Both groups of children lose opportunities to benefit from adult guidance, social interaction, and enrichment opportunities provided through high-quality child care or after-school programs. School and community planners and policy makers can assist families by encouraging and providing other options such as high-quality child care after school and also during nontraditional hours (e.g., for parents who are employed evenings or weekends), publicizing resource and referral systems where parents can locate high-quality programs and activities or qualified, trained adults, and offering specialized training for babysitters.

Children who attend high-quality after-school programs show better peer relations, emotional adjustment, grades, and conduct in school than children who do not participate in such programs.

The benefits of high-quality out-of-school time have been documented in a number of studies. Some have found that children who attend high-quality programs have better peer relations, emotional adjustment, grades, and conduct in school than their peers who do not participate in after-school programs. In high-quality programs, children spend less time watching television and enjoy more opportunities to learn and participate in enrichment activities (Baker & Witt, 1996; Posner & Vandell, 1994). Another study found that children who are supervised by adults during out-of-school time have better social skills and higher self-esteem than their peers who spend a greater deal of time unsupervised after school (Witt, 1997). In still another study, teachers and principals reported more cooperative behaviors and greater ability to handle conflicts among children who attended high-quality after-school programs. They also reported these children as having more interest in recreational reading and achieving higher grades.

Safe and healthy settings provide nutritious snacks, opportunities to rest, enriching play activities, satisfying and enjoyable interactions with other children, guidance from nurturing and supportive adults, and help with homework. Such programs can provide a wide range of opportunities and experiences for children, including library times; field trips; participation in organizations such as Cub Scouts, Boy Scouts, Girl Scouts, Camp Fire Girls and Boys, and similar groups; arts and crafts activities using community volunteers; hobby projects; pen pal activities; guided music and dance opportunities; instruction in specific games and sports, when appropriate; and many others. Such efforts to enrich out-of-school time for children provide positive experiences through which children can build social relationships and self-confidence. Caution should be exercised, however. All children need down time during the day, particularly after a day of schooling. Unstructured, unencumbered time may be more important than well-intentioned planned activities.

ROLE OF THE EARLY CHILDHOOD PROFESSIONAL

Enhancing Physical and Motor Development in Children Ages Six through Eight

1. Provide safe, hygienic, and healthy surroundings for children.
2. Provide for the child's nutritional needs.
3. Prevent the spread of childhood diseases through immunization requirements for group participation, and take all appropriate precautions to protect children from disease.
4. Insist on regular dental check-ups and appropriate vision and hearing examinations.
5. Establish healthy routines for food, drink, rest, sleep, play, and physical fitness activities.
6. Maintain a reasonably stress-free physical, emotional, social, and academic environment.
7. Provide opportunities to refine perceptual–motor abilities.
8. Provide age-appropriate and developmentally appropriate games, play equipment, and sports activities and protective sports attire.
9. Ensure the child's safety through adequate planning, rules, supervision, and education.
10. Facilitate satisfying and supportive psychosocial interactions with peers, family, and others.
11. Encourage a sense of responsibility for one's health maintenance and safety.
12. Promote high-quality, enriching out-of-school time opportunities.

KEY TERMS

basal metabolic rate
figure–ground
   discrimination
fundamental movements

Healthy Eating
   Index
individualized education
   plan (IEP)

individualized family
   services plan (IFSP)
neurogenesis
other-mediated action

REVIEW STRATEGIES AND ACTIVITIES

1. Review the key terms individually or with a classmate.
2. Select several children ages 6 to 8. Ask them what three gifts they would like to receive for their birthdays. Compare the boys' and the girls' preferences. How many of the items are gender stereotypical? How many are not gender specific? How many are opposite-gender items? Compare your survey with that of a classmate. What trends do you see in gender-related toys or gift preferences of boys and girls in this age range?

3. Visit a physical education class in which physically challenged children participate. What kinds of activities are planned for these children? What types of other-mediated activities take place? What physical and motor benefits can be realized from physical education activities? How do these activities differ from traditional physical education requirements?

4. Attend an organized sports event for children in the 6- to 8-year age range. What fundamental movement abilities are required for the sport? Are the expectations developmentally appropriate? Does each child have an opportunity to participate? Is the coach sensitive to age and individual differences? Are children's needs for rest and refreshments met? Are children required to wear and use appropriate safety gear and equipment? What appears to be the emphasis expressed by adults: winning or opportunities to learn, participation, and fun?

5. Collect a month's supply of public school breakfast and lunch menus. Compare them for child appeal, adherence to the Food Guide Pyramid, variety, and estimated calorie content.

FURTHER READINGS

American Academy of Pediatrics. (1999). *Handbook of pediatric environmental health: Reducing risk at home, school, and play.* Elk Grove Village, IL: Author.

Dietz, W. H., & Stern, L. (1999). *Guide to your child's nutrition.* Elk Grove, IL: American Academy of Pediatrics.

Halpern, R. (2003). *Making play work: The promise of after-school programs for low-income children.* New York: Teachers College Press.

Kline, F. M., Silver, L. B., & Russell, S. C. (2001). *The educator's guide to medical issues in the classroom.* Baltimore: Brookes.

Levin, D. E. (2003). *Teaching young children in violent times: Building a peaceable classroom* (2nd ed.). Washington, DC: National Association for the Education of Young Children.

Lombardi, J. (2003). *Time to care: Redesigning child care to promote education, support families, and build communities.* Washington, DC: National Association for the Education of Young Children.

Lowenthal, B. (2001). *Abuse and neglect: The educator's guide to the identification and prevention of child maltreatment.* Baltimore: Brookes.

McCracken, J. B. (1999). *Playgrounds: Safe and sound.* Washington, DC: National Association for the Education of Young Children.

Patten, P., & Robertson, A. S. (2001). *Violence prevention resource guide for parents.* Champaign, IL: National Parent Information Network of the ERIC Clearinghouse on Elementary and Early Childhood Education.

Sanders, S. (2001). *Active for life: Developmentally appropriate movement programs for young children.* Washington, DC: National Association for the Education of Young Children.

Schor, E. (Ed.). (1999). *American Academy of Pediatrics: The complete and authoritative guide: Caring for your school-age child ages 5 to 12* (rev. ed.). New York: Bantam.

OTHER RESOURCES

American Academy of Pediatrics. Brochures available through pediatricians' offices include the following:

The Internet and your family
Television and the family: Guidelines for parents

American Academy of Pediatrics TIPPS (The Injury Prevention Program) age-related safety sheets
http://www.aap.org
National Child Resources Center
National Health and Safety Performance Standards
http://www.nrc.uchsc.edu/national/index.html
National Institute on Out-of-School Time
http://www.wellesley.edu/WCW/CRW/SAC/
National Parent Information Network
http://www.npin.org
National SAFE Kids Campaign
http://www.safekids.org
Surgeon General's Call to Action to Prevent and Decrease Overweight and Obesity Fact Sheet
http://www.surgeongeneral.gov/topics/obesity/calltoaction/fact-consequences.html
U.S. Centers for Disease Control and Prevention
http://www.cdc.gov/
U.S. Department of Health and Human Services
http://www.os.dhhs.gov/
U.S. Department of Education, *A parents' guide to prevention: Growing up drug free.* Available from
National Clearinghouse for Alcohol and Drug Information
P. O. Box 2345
Rockville, MD 20852

CHAPTER FIFTEEN

Psychosocial Development: Ages Six Through Eight

If you see a child without a smile, give him yours.

TALMUD

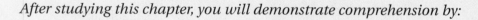

After studying this chapter, you will demonstrate comprehension by:

▶ Relating selected theories to the study of psychosocial development during ages 6 through 8.

▶ Discussing selected psychosocial experiences associated with brain growth and neurological development during ages 6 through 8.

▶ Identifying major social and emotional milestones in psychosocial development during this period.

▶ Describing factors that influence psychosocial development in young school-age children.

▶ Describing the role of adults in facilitating healthy psychosocial development of 6- through 8-year-olds.

In a popular U.S. Children's Bureau booklet from the 1960s, the 6- to 8-year-old is described as a "commuter to the wonderful outside world of middle childhood," traveling "back and forth between the outside world and the smaller more personal one of [the] family." The child's travels are said to start with short trips at age 6, becoming longer trips away from the family's "home station" with increasing age (Chilman, 1966, p. 5).

As this description implies, the psychosocial experiences of the 6- through 8-year-old are beginning to expand rapidly beyond the home and family. By age 6, children are growing less dependent on their parents and are now encountering widening circles of influence. New psychosocial challenges are emerging.

During the early part of this age period, the child is characterized as highly active, boisterous, sometimes verbally aggressive, and teasing. Boys enjoy rough-and-tumble play, and both boys and girls enjoy creative projects and playing games with rules. Children at this age are inclined to dawdle and are talkative, boastful, impatient, and competitive. They are also sensitive and affectionate and enjoy playful interactions that employ humor, jokes, and riddles. Giggling and teasing are also typical.

Around age 7, children begin to exhibit more brooding behaviors, becoming more sensitive, private, and moody. The child is growing a bit reflective and more concerned about the reactions of others. Expressions of self-confidence are not quite as verbose as before, and the child is as inclined to listen as to talk. While the 6-year-old is described as quite active and talkative, the 7-year-old is more introspective and contemplative. Helpfulness and consideration of others are more evident, and friendships are assuming prominent roles in the child's life.

By the end of this age period, behaviors that are more outgoing and interactive reappear. Curiosity and a desire to know more about the world beyond home and school spur more outward-bound interests. This includes a growing interest in the adult world, which is characterized by listening more intently to adult conversations and seeking to be included in more adult-like activities. The child is becoming more self-critical and self-conscious while struggling to gain greater self-confidence. The child reacts with both interest and hostility toward the opposite sex and is peer oriented, independent, and for the most part dependable.

What do these descriptions tell us about the 6- through 8-year-old's psychosocial development? Let us begin the discussion by revisiting several of the theories that attempt to explain psychosocial development as they apply to the development of school-age children.

Theoretical Perspectives on Psychosocial Development of Children Ages Six Through Eight

Psychosocial Theory: Industry versus Inferiority

As depicted in Figure 15.1, between ages 6 and 11, the child is in Erikson's fourth stage of psychosocial development, in which the development of a sense of industry versus inferiority is the psychosocial conflict to be resolved. The fantasy and make-believe of earlier years begin to defer to more reality-based thinking and play themes. Children at this stage are eager to learn how things work and want to master "real" tasks. Whereas process characterized the efforts of previous stages, products are now important, as children begin to take pride in their abilities to create and to produce. Art projects, blocks and other constructions, cooking, and participating in household chores become sources of pride and accomplishment. The child's activities are, in a word, *industrious*.

At this time, formal schooling takes on new importance to the child, setting goals and expectations, imposing limits on behaviors and activities, and multiplying

FIGURE 15.1

Erikson's Stages of Psychosocial Development

Supported by a healthy sense of trust, autonomy, and initiative, a sense of industry facilitates learning and enhances self-confidence.

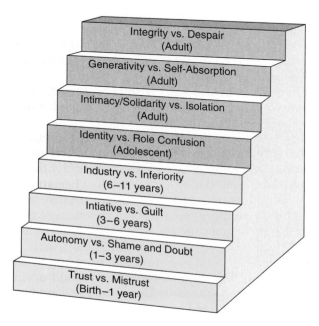

social interactions. The child is eager to learn the real skills that school can teach, and the child's sense of competence becomes vulnerable to the influences of classmates, teachers, curriculums, grades, and comparative test scores. Success with school tasks fosters a sense of competence, self-worth, and **industry**. However, for the child who experiences too many failures in school, either academic or social, the sense of industry can be intruded on or even overridden by a sense of inferiority. Confidence and feelings of self-worth begin to suffer, as do social interactions, when children develop negative self-regard.

industry:
the sense of mastery of social and academic skills necessary to feel self-assured

As children begin to develop a sense of industry (or inferiority) their individual skills and personal interests become more evident. Aspirations emerge, though levels of aspirations often outpace capabilities. Participation in a broad array of age-appropriate activities helps children to recognize and appreciate their skill areas and the products of their labors. The fifth stage of psychosocial development, developing a sense of identity (versus role confusion), has its origins in these early discoveries of skill/interests and their subsequent development.

Effects of Earlier Attachments

Decades of research document that what children learn, how they react to the events and people in their lives, and what they expect from themselves and others are significantly affected by the relationships they have with their primary caregivers and the nature of their home environments (Shonkoff & Phillips, 2000). Moreover, the quality of the relationship between infants and young children and their primary caregivers is considered of paramount importance to an individual's mental health throughout the life span (U.S. Surgeon General, 2000). Quality parent or caregiver relationships originate in the bonding and attachment success of the infancy and toddler periods. All aspects of childhood psychosocial development are affected by the nature of these caring and nurturing relationships over time. Positive, protecting, and nurturing relationships support self-concept, self-esteem, self-efficacy, and resiliency, and assist the child in acquiring social, emotional, and moral competence.

In school-age children, the nature of their earliest attachment experiences influences the manner in which they later relate to teachers. The child's sense of trust or mistrust derives from early attachment relationships. Children who have experienced secure attachments and have developed a sturdy sense of trust are more successful in their relationships with caregivers and teachers in their child care and schooling situations (Howes & Ritchie, 2002). Indeed, many children form healthy attachments to their nonparental caregivers and teachers. However, children whose earliest experiences (e.g., maltreatment, prenatal exposure to drugs, parental mental disorders, extreme poverty) resulted in insecure attachments distrust their teachers and have greater difficulty forming positive relationships with them (Lyons-Ruth, 1996; Stroufe, Egeland, & Kreutzer, 1990). According to Howes and Ritchie (2002), children with insecure, avoidant, ambivalent/resistant attachment patterns display a number of challenging behaviors such as making "preemptive strikes" in their interactions with teachers, acting out in inappropriate, even hostile ways before the teacher has an opportunity to be rejecting. Or they may avoid the adult out of fear of being rejected. They presume rejection from those on whom they depend based on their real or perceived experiences of rejection within the family. Children who experienced inconsistent care and nurturing display insecure, ambivalent/

resistant patterns and exhibit confusion over whether adults will meet their needs for protection and emotional support. Needful of comfort and security, these children may appear to seek it, but then reject the teacher's attempts to provide it. They may exhibit dependency behaviors such as proximity seeking but use inappropriate means, such as interpersonal conflict, to engage the teacher's attention.

Attachment histories also influence the child's ability to make and maintain friendships in much the same manner as just described. Children who have experienced secure attachments are more trusting of others and therefore more successful in their peer interactions. Children who have experienced insecure attachment relationships at home and at school have difficulty in their peer relationships and in their ability to focus and learn in a classroom context (Howes & Ritchie, 2002; Lyons-Ruth, Alpern, & Repacholi, 1993). The development of important social skills such as establishing rapport, trusting, cooperating, perspective-taking, sharing, negotiating, caring, and communicating effectively is often delayed and these skills are often difficult to acquire.

Self-Esteem Theory

Fully Functioning Person.   Through his work in counseling and psychotherapy, Carl Rogers (1961, Rogers & Freiberg, 1994) became interested in how the unique self evolves and what it means to be a fully functioning person. He believed that each individual is striving to become a fully functioning person. Rogers's self-theory proposes that each individual's perceptions of his or her countless experiences are subjective and private and hold special meanings for the individual. Self-concept emerges from these subjective perceptions.

In Rogers's theory, a fully functioning person is self-accepting, governed by his or her expectations rather than the expectations of others, and open to new experiences. She or he has no need to mask or repress unpleasant thoughts, feelings, or memories. The fully functioning person accepts others as separate and different individuals and can tolerate behaviors in others that he or she would not exhibit.

Adults help a child in this process of becoming a fully functioning individual when they do the following:

1. Recognize and accept their feelings and recognize the role their feelings and attitudes play in their interactions and relationships with the child
2. Establish relationships with the child that are characterized by acceptance, rapport, mutual support, and recognition
3. Recognize and accept the child's feelings (both positive and negative) and help the child to find constructive outlets for the expression of feelings
4. Assume a helping role in which genuine understanding and empathy are effectively communicated to the child
5. Support the child's growing sense of self by helping the child to recognize and build on his or her strengths and capabilities

Self-actualization.   Maslow (1968, 1970) described a hierarchy of human needs leading to self-esteem and self-actualization. Individuals are said to progress from

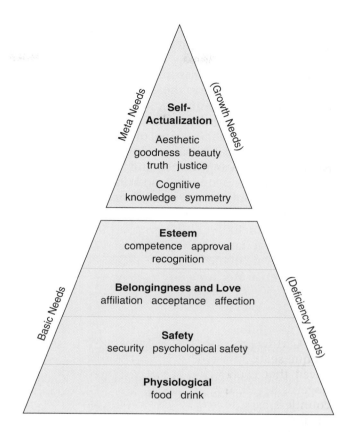

FIGURE 15.2
Maslow's Hierarchy of Needs

In Maslow's hierarchy of needs, the needs at the lowest level have the most potency—they must be fulfilled before a person is motivated to try to fulfill higher needs.

(*From Psychology of Teaching: A Bear Always Usually Sometimes Faces the Front* (3rd ed.) by Guy R. LeFrancois. © 1979 by Wadsworth Publishing Co., Inc., a division of Thomson Learning. Reprinted by permission of the publisher.)

lower needs to higher needs on the way to becoming self-actualized. Lower and higher needs differ in the degree to which they are species specific; that is, the lower physiological needs for food and water are common to all living things, and the need for love might be shared with the higher apes, but the needs for self-esteem and self-actualization are uniquely human and shared with no other animals. Figure 15.2 illustrates Maslow's hierarchy of needs.

The first and lowest, but most potent, level of the five in Maslow's hierarchy of needs is the need for physiological well-being, which includes most basically the need for food and drink. All other needs are superseded by this need. Classroom teachers are well aware that children who come to school hungry are mentally and physically sluggish and not very interested in learning. According to Maslow, their energies and innermost thoughts are directed toward satisfying this physiological need.

Level two, safety needs, includes security, stability, and dependency needs; the need for freedom from fear, anxiety, and chaos; and the need for structure, order, law, limits, protection, and strength in a protector (Maslow, 1970). As mentioned frequently throughout this text, predictable routines help children to feel safe. Unpredictable adults and routines are unsettling to children. Chaotic and uncontrolled home life or classrooms elicit anxiety and fear and the child's felt need for the adult protector (parent or teacher) to be in greater control. Children need adults who provide safe, secure surroundings and enough structure to assure them of their physical and psychological safety.

defense mechanism:
a psychological response to ego threat, frustration, or failure

At level three, belongingness and love needs are evident when the person feels the need for others. Hungering for love, affection, and acceptance, the child seeks a place in the family, play or school group, or other social entity. Parents and teachers who provide assurance to children of their place within the family or school and their value to the group help to fulfill this need.

At level four, esteem needs emerge. According to Maslow, a need for a stable and firmly based positive self-evaluation is prevalent in all individuals. The need for self-respect and the esteem of others is central to healthy personality development. Self-esteem includes feelings of self-confidence, self-worth, and efficacy and feelings of being wanted and needed. Individuals who lack self-esteem feel helpless, weak, discouraged, and unneeded. These feelings can lead to compensatory behaviors such as the **defense mechanisms** described in Table 15.1 and possibly neurotic tendencies.

TABLE 15.1   Common Defense Mechanisms

Defense Mechanism	Description	Example
Regression	Returning to earlier, less mature behaviors	Bed wetting; thumb sucking; wanting to be carried in a caregiver's arms
Repression	Inhibiting uncomfortable, frightening memories and storing them in the unconscious	Child abuse victim's inability to name abuser
Projection	Attributing to others one's thoughts, motives, and traits	Seeking a cookie for oneself; asserting that a playmate needs it
Reaction formation	Behavior opposite from true feelings	Jealous sibling's exaggerated show of affection for newborn brother or sister
Displacement	Shifting feelings or emotions from something that is threatening to a substitute	Premature weaning and adult disapproval of thumb sucking lead to nail biting or chewing on a toy
Rationalizing	Attempting to provide a logical excuse for one's disappointments, failures, or shortcomings	Person who was not invited to a party saying, "I didn't want to go to her birthday party anyway—parties are boring."
Denial	Refusing to accept or acknowledge the reality of a situation	Clinging to Santa Claus myth after learning the truth
Fixation	Serious conflict or trauma at one age or stage that arrests further development	Prolonged separation anxiety resulting from traumatic event associated with an earlier separation
Sublimation	Channeling of psychological energies (e.g., aggression) into other outlets	Overachieving in school, sports, or hobby
Escape/withdrawal	Avoiding a situation by physically or psychologically removing onself from it	Nonparticipation in classroom discussions; avoiding eye contact with others
Compensation	Finding a satisfying substitute for inadequate abilities	Pursuing hobbies or collections when social interactions are difficult

Maslow cautioned that true self-esteem derives from authentic accomplishments or deserved respect, not from contrived or trivial praise, popularity, or fame. An individual must come to base his or her self-esteem on real competence rather than on the opinions of others. This raises the question about the often overused classroom management technique in which the teacher praises inconsequential behaviors with statements such as, "I like the way Maria is sitting," ". . . holding her pencil," or ". . . using a soft voice" (Katz & McClellan, 1997; Kohn, 2001).

Moral Development Theory

Recall that Piaget's stage-sequence theory of moral development cites three stages: premoral, moral realism, and moral relativism. Earlier chapters discussed stage 1 in describing the moral behaviors of children under 6. Children in the 6 through 8 age group exhibit characteristics of Piaget's stage 2 level of moral development, that of moral realism. Moral realism is characterized by rule-bound thinking and behaving. Children at this stage of moral development believe the following:

1. Rules are rules, regardless of intentions.
2. Rules are unalterable.
3. Rules have been set by an all-knowing and powerful authority figure (God, parent, teacher).
4. The importance of a rule is in direct proportion to the severity of the punishment.
5. Obedience to rules means one is good; disobedience means one is bad.
6. Punishment is a necessary result of breaking a rule.

The term *heteronomy* describes this stage, for it implies that individuals are other-governed rather than autonomous, or self-governed. Parents, teachers, and other authoritative adults impose a variety of rules and expectations with which children must comply. Many children comply with adult rules without question, believing in the absolute authority of the adult. With the emergence of autonomy, initiative, and curiosity, the child begins to challenge adult rules.

With these developments, children begin to encounter and distinguish different kinds of rules: social conventional rules and moral rules (Turiel, 1980). *Social conventional* rules are social regulations such as those governing the modes of dress that fit the occasion, which side of the street to drive on, and how to address the classroom teacher. Such rules are arbitrary in that they do not generalize to all situations, places, cultures; they are not universal. *Moral* rules, on the other hand, are rules relating to generalized values such as honesty, fairness, and justice. According to Turiel, children as young as 6 years are able to distinguish between conventional rules and rules of morality and justice.

Children imitate the social conventions and moral values of adults who are important to them. Through these imitations during their social interactions, children become increasingly aware of moral rules and values. However, adults can be misled by some of these behaviors, believing that verbalized values and imitated social conventions indicate mature understanding and **internalization** of behaviors. Actually, children are in the process of understanding, and such behaviors

internalization: a process in which behavior standards are adopted as one's own and acted upon without explicit instruction from others

With the emergence of autonomy and initiative, children begin to challenge adult rules.

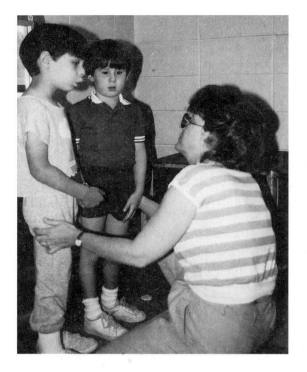

must be practiced and the consequences observed or experienced before internalized moral behavior can occur.

At this age, sociodramatic play continues to be a powerful contributor to moral understanding. Imitations of adult moral and social conventions and transgressions can be explored in the safe context of pretend play. Moreover, role-taking abilities increase through sociodramatic play, as does experiencing competing points of view. These experiences are necessary precursors to solving moral dilemmas later on.

During recess, Angela and several of her playmates get into an argument over how to manage their turn taking, which is supposed to proceed in an orderly fashion as they recite a jump-rope chant, each player jumping in on cue as the other exits. Angela is certain that her friends are not following the instructions that they learned from their student teacher and has become angry with her friends. She leaves the group to tell the teacher. She reports to her teacher, "They are not playing jump rope the right way." When Ms. Quinonez intervenes, she observes that each child has a different interpretation of the rules of the game. Rather than correcting Angela for tattling or reproving Angela's friends, Ms. Quinonez engages the participants in a discussion of how the game can be played so that each player has an equal opportunity to participate. In so doing, she helps the children come to a common perspective on the rules.

As children move from preoperational thinking to concrete operations during this period, they can compare, classify, and draw logical conclusions. These abilities assist the child in making the shift from rule-bound morality to the realization that there are many sources of rules (parents, teachers, and laws). In addition, children have become less egocentric and are gaining awareness of others' needs, intentions, feelings, and expectations and that others' needs may be more important than their own from time to time. This represents stage 3 of Kohlberg's sequence of moral development, a morality of conventional role conformity. (Revisit Chapter 12 for a discussion of Kohlberg's stages 1 and 2.)

Kohlberg refers to this stage as the "good boy/good girl" stage, during which children are quite approval seeking. They are more inclined to conform to be perceived as "good." The desire to please peers as well as adults is evident in this phase. Often, children find themselves in situations in which they must choose between family and peer group rules. They may go along with the peer group despite known prohibitions. These behaviors are not necessarily deliberate or resistive of established rules or authority; they simply preempt previous constraints. Parents who respond to these transgressions with reason and an attempt to understand the child's motivations help children to reflect on their choices, explore goals and consequences, and hone their inner controls. As the child's conscience becomes more persuasive, these exercises in reflecting provide a necessary strategy to be employed in the absence of authority figures.

Development of Conscience

The conscience is said to be a facet of the personality that comes into play when children are able to internalize adult standards and know what is expected of them. It elicits judgments of right and wrong, inhibition of behaviors that have been learned to be inappropriate, and promotion of behaviors that are deemed right or acceptable. It facilitates to some extent the development of self-control in the absence of external restraints.

Freud believed that the conscience begins to emerge around age five and results when the child has the ability to internalize the standards, rules, and expectations of their parents (Freud, 1933). Erikson's psychosocial theory suggests that the development of a conscience begins during the toddler period and is seen when children exhibit a sense of guilt when accidents or transgressions occur (Erikson, 1963). Others believe that the conscience comes forcefully into play during the elementary school years when both cognitive and social experiences provoke children's intense interest in the world around them. It is a point in development when figuring out how and why things work the way they do, and why some behaviors are acceptable and others not, is important to them.

Children are bombarded with invitations to do and behave in a myriad of ways by virtue of their experiences with peers, family friends, neighbors, increasing numbers of adult authority figures in both school and out-of-school activities, affiliations with various organized groups (e.g., faith-related groups, civic groups such as Boy and Girl Scouts, sports teams, special lessons in dance or gymnastics), computer networks, media programs and advertising, toys and games, and many others. These experiences often evoke evaluative behaviors that compare the standards of the child's home and family with those of others. The school-age child is becoming aware of individual responsibility and is concerned and vocal about what is fair, just, and ethical. Hence, during the school years, the conscience becomes a very active part of the child's personality (Cole, 1997).

As this suggests, culture plays an important role in the development of conscience by setting the parameters of behavior communicated between children and authority figures, a premise advanced by Vygotsky (1978). The conscience, then, generally emerges out of the child's identification with his or her parents (Snyder, Snyder, & Snyder, 1980) but is challenged by other influences during the school years. In its earliest stages, fear of loss of love from a parent appears to underlie the development of conscience.

Children who have internalized standards of right and wrong from their earlier family experiences fall back on these standards when confronted with discrepancies and temptations outside the family. Although self-control might not always be present in these situations, the conscience is. The conscience becomes a stand-in for the parent and attempts to guide behaviors along internalized family expectations.

It is not surprising, then, that discipline in the home that maintains supportive and affectionate relationships is more readily associated with the development of a conscience than are other forms. Inductive discipline techniques that elicit reflection, perspective taking, empathy, altruism, and other prosocial attitudes and behaviors are closely associated with the development of conscience. Power-assertive strategies, on the other hand, provide little impetus for the development of conscience.

A Neurological Development Perspective on Psychosocial Development During Ages Six Through Eight

It is important to keep in mind that while there are windows of opportunity for certain types of development, most of which occur during the early years, the brain continues to grow neurological connections and prune and refine those connections throughout life. In short, the windows do not close at age 3, 5, 8, or even 10. Child developmentalists assert that learning new ways of behaving, while perhaps becoming more difficult as we get older, does continue except in cases of extreme neglect, abuse, and trauma, particularly when the effects of these affronts to development are persistent.

That having been said, it may be interesting to examine how self-esteem becomes rooted in neuroanatomy. There are numerous developments involving the growth of neurons in the brain, the extension of neuron pathways throughout the brain and the body, and the electrical and chemical activities associated with the proliferation and pruning of these pathways. The following brief discussion of one type of neurotransmitter activity represents just one example from an encyclopedic and changing knowledge base. Nevertheless, it can be instructive.

Recent studies of neurotransmitters (the chemical agents that help neurons to communicate with one another at the point of the synapse) are finding that certain neurotransmitters play an important role in regulating individual levels of self-esteem, depression, aggression, and other mental states (Delcomyn, 1998; Sylwester, 1997). For example, studies of the effects of the neurotransmitter serotonin on levels of self-esteem can be quite instructive for those who work with young children. It appears that serotonin levels are enhanced through experiences of personal success and positive social feedback. High levels of serotonin result in higher levels of assurance accompanied by well-coordinated motor controls and positive interactions with others. On the other hand, low levels of

It is believed that enjoyable, satisfying experiences result in higher levels of certain neurotransmitters in the brain, which in turn result in higher levels of assurance and positive interactions.

serotonin have been associated with depression, irritability, impulsivity, less controlled motor activity, and—more seriously—aggression, violence, and suicidal behavior (Sylwester, 1997).

DIMENSIONS OF PSYCHOSOCIAL DEVELOPMENT DURING AGES SIX THROUGH EIGHT

Emotional Development

School age children have greater understanding of emotions in themselves and others. They are able to name the emotions they experience, and their ability to regulate their emotions is increasing and continues to be an important aspect of their psychological and social health. Emotion regulation entails moving beyond initial (heat of the moment) responses, which can interfere with the capacity to think clearly and act responsibly, to mentally organizing the perceptions and understandings of the provocation, then regulating the behaviors that respond to the provocation (Denham, 1998). Children who succeed in this development enjoy more positive social feedback. Further, there is some evidence that children who are skilled at identifying emotions and their provocations show more empathic moral thinking and behaviors (Arsenio & Lover, 1995). Again, both experience and empathic guidance help children to reflect and learn. Anticipating and role playing appropriate responses to emotion-provoking situations helps children to develop understanding and skills.

Fears and Anxieties.   The close relationship between fears and cognitive development is evidenced by the changes in causes of and responses to fears as children get older. Cognitive development results in increasing abilities to perceive meanings not previously perceived and to relate those meanings to oneself. With

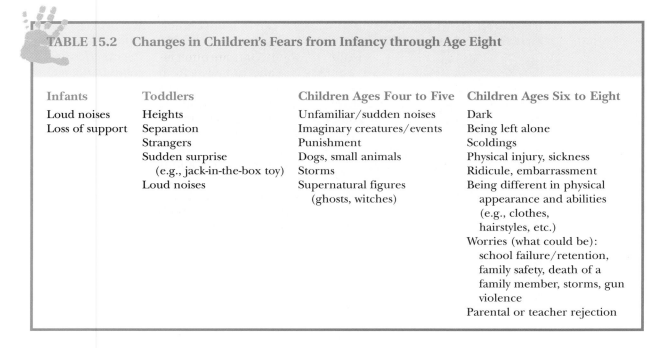

TABLE 15.2   Changes in Children's Fears from Infancy through Age Eight

Infants	Toddlers	Children Ages Four to Five	Children Ages Six to Eight
Loud noises	Heights	Unfamiliar/sudden noises	Dark
Loss of support	Separation	Imaginary creatures/events	Being left alone
	Strangers	Punishment	Scoldings
	Sudden surprise (e.g., jack-in-the-box toy)	Dogs, small animals	Physical injury, sickness
	Loud noises	Storms	Ridicule, embarrassment
		Supernatural figures (ghosts, witches)	Being different in physical appearance and abilities (e.g., clothes, hairstyles, etc.)
			Worries (what could be): school failure/retention, family safety, death of a family member, storms, gun violence
			Parental or teacher rejection

increasing experiences and understandings during the 6- to 8-year period, fear becomes less specific (e.g., fear of dogs, fear of the dark) and more general (e.g., fear of not being liked at school). The ability to imagine, empathize, and take the perspectives of others changes the nature of children's fears. Table 15.2 summarizes the way in which children's fears change as they get older.

Unlike the toddler, whose fear responses are often vociferous, the older child responds in less intense or overt ways when frightened. Older children may repress or mask their fears. Their behaviors bespeak their discomfort: nail biting, inattention or distractibility, change in eating or sleeping patterns, heightened emotionality, increased dependency, or feigned illness. They may deny that they are afraid, or they may boast of their bravery.

Previous experiences and life circumstances influence what children fear and how they respond: family life trauma, accidents and illnesses, loss of a parent to divorce or death, severe punishments, frightening movies or television programs, adult conversations not fully comprehended, and violence. School-age children typically fear being different from their peers, and in school, they fear teacher rejection and grade retention. Physical and psychological well-being also influences fear responses. As with adults, discomfort such as hunger, fatigue, illness, and stress cause children to exaggerate events, real or imagined, and respond in disproportionate ways.

Peers influence children's fears. Playmates may share frightening experiences, fabricate or exaggerate scary stories, or spread unsubstantiated rumors among other children. Peers who say that a certain teacher "never lets you go to the bathroom," that the principal "locks kids who misbehave in a closet," or that there is "a volcano under the school building" are generating fabrications that, even when unbelievable, can leave a measure of wariness in the listener. By the same token, peers often serve as models for coping with a fear. Thus, peers can influence child-hood responses to fear in both positive and negative ways.

Gender differences in fear responses are sometimes evident. Girls are often al-lowed to be more fearful; they may squeal at crawling things and run away from pretend monsters. In our society, real and pretend fear responses are socially per-missible for girls but often ridiculed in boys. Boys are expected to be stoic in the face of fearful events and are often discouraged from overtly expressing fears.

As with fears of earlier years, older children need adults to talk with them about their fears and help them to find ways to cope with and control feared situ-ations. Children learn about their fears and gain mastery over them when adults respond to childhood fears in respectful, frank, and instructive ways. Allowing children to talk about their fears as they arise gives adults clues about particular topics and misconceptions that need to be addressed. Helping children to both *feel* safe and *be* safe is how adults help children with their fears. Adults are helpful when they

- allow children to bring up subjects that concern them;
- assure children that parents and teachers are there to protect them;
- never use fear to coerce or discipline;
- explore children's topics of concern in an authoritative and unemotional way;
- provide accurate information about topics of concern, and clarify miscon-ceptions;
- help children to learn to obtain factual information about that which they fear;
- involve children in developing a plan for seeking help and protecting them-selves in specific types of situations that they may fear;
- develop together, role play, and practice family plans to meet emergencies such as a house fire, separation in a crowd, and a medical emergency;
- help children to learn important contact phone numbers (mother, father, grandparent, or other relative or neighbor) and addresses (including area phone codes and zip codes);
- assess and be prepared, should they arise, to offer appropriate advice and guidance on contemporary catastrophic subjects or events to which children are vicariously (via friends, neighbors, and news media) or directly exposed, such as gun violence, terrorism, war, child abduction, and extraordinary weather events.

Transitional Objects.   Attachment to transitional objects of earlier years may well persist into the period from ages 6 through 8 and possibly beyond. By age 7, a child who still clings to a transitional object may do so in more private and sub-tle ways, perhaps preferring its comfort only at bedtime or during times of stress or illness. Soon other sentimental objects will compete for the child's attentions, and the need for the original transitional object may wane. For some children, however, discarding the transitional object altogether is out of the question. The teddy bear may remain on the shelf well into adolescence; the worn special blan-ket may be safely tucked away in a drawer to remain there indefinitely. No attempt should be made to dispose of transitional objects, since they represent the child's continuing need to find self-comforting strategies. The affection for the transitional object continues, and only the child should decide what to do with it when it is no longer in use.

Collections and Hobbies.   Related to the transition object is an interest in collecting. During the early school years, children find enjoyment in objects to collect: popular theme cards, baseball and football cards, rocks, seashells, miniature toys or figures, insects, postcards, jewelry, doll clothes and accessories, stuffed toys, candy wrappers, comic books, and so on. Sometimes trading and bartering go along with these collections, and some children become avid collectors through this process. Children also enjoy perusing toy and electronics catalogs and thumbing through junk mail for hidden treasures. Making lists is another form of collecting: "what I want for Christmas," telephone numbers, addresses, birthdays, and other topics of interest.

Collections and hobbies enhance children's sense of self and their abilities, interests, and aspirations and expand their knowledge of certain objects or topics. Collections and hobbies engage the child in identifying, sorting, ordering, classifying, and researching tasks; they expand the child's knowledge and awareness and enhance cognitive development. They provide focus and entertainment during moments of self-imposed privacy as well as a medium for initiating contacts with others. To adults, some childhood collections may seem valueless and trivial. However, these collections and others yet to come may spark an interest that will endure and grow into other, related interests. Some represent the origins of what may some day become an occupation or a career.

Self-Concept, Self-Esteem, and Social Competence

Self-concept is more stable at ages 6 to 8, owing at least in part to gender constancy and to realizations about the permanence of racial and cultural group memberships. Self-concept during this period begins to include not only what children think about themselves, but also what they believe others think about them. This period is marked by self-criticism and comparisons of themselves with others. Self-appraisal arises from experiences in the home, school, with peers, and organized groups. Self-appraisals can be self-affirming or self-defeating.

Research on self-concept development consistently reports a relationship between a person's self-concept and his or her achievements. Since the development of a sense of industry is a major psychosocial task of this age period and feelings of competence and self-confidence are necessary for the development of a sense of industry, school plays a critical role in the child's developing sense of competence or incompetence. Children who perceive themselves as capable show little hesitation in trying new tasks and often succeed in them. On the other hand, children who feel that they are incapable often experience reduced success in new tasks. Successes at this stage, then, are paramount; failures are damaging and can lead the child to a self-perception of inadequacy and inferiority, the polar opposite of Erikson's sense of industry.

When children feel inadequate, they often employ coping strategies known to psychologists as defense mechanisms (see Table 15.1). Defense mechanisms begin to emerge during the school years. Freud was among the first to suggest that during these years, defense mechanisms emerge to protect the ego from frustration and failure. Defense mechanisms serve to relieve anxiety when a person anticipates or experiences failures, mistakes, or mishaps. If there is anything positive to say about defense mechanisms, it is that they serve to relieve distress or embarrassment, at least temporarily.

However, when defense mechanisms are relied on excessively, the individual escapes reality. When children begin to employ defense mechanisms to excess, parents and teachers must assess the expectations and stresses being placed on them. Perhaps the child is experiencing excessive teasing or ridicule from a classmate or sibling; experiences in school may be threatening in some way, as is often true when competition is used to motivate, or when expectations exceed the child's capabilities; perhaps the child fears peer or parental disappointment or disapproval over his or her inadequacies or failures. Harsh, punitive, or demeaning discipline may elicit defense mechanisms. There are many possible provocations for the employment of defense mechanisms. In any case, for the most part, the behaviors are potentially damaging to the self-concept and to interpersonal relationships.

Gender Identity and Gender Role Development

As children reach ages 6 through 8, gender identity and gender-role behaviors are evident in their mannerisms, language, play choices, and friendships. Having formed gender-role stereotypes, children now have rather inflexible ideas about girl/boy expectations, attributing to gender certain behaviors, clothing, hairstyles, play and school activities, home chores, and adult occupations.

Children's stereotypes are learned from those around them and are sometimes imposed on them by their families and cultures. School experiences particularly influence gender identity and gender-role development. There is some evidence of gender bias on the part of classroom teachers. The research of Myra Sadker and David Sadker (1985, 1994) demonstrated that teachers engage in more conversations, assistance, and praise with boys than they do with girls. They also respond to boys' questions with more precision and often answer girls' questions with bland or diffused responses.

Around the second and third grades, children tend to segregate themselves according to gender, preferring single-sex play groups. Play activities and toy preferences are indicative of the child's sense of gender identity. Peers impose gender stereotypes as well, sometimes holding rigid ideas about choice of friends, clothing, play themes, recreational activities, and behaviors (Honig, 2000).

The differences between play behaviors of girls and boys may explain the gender segregation that occurs in early childhood and the primary grades. Boys generally engage in rough-and-tumble play and enjoy play themes and electronic games that are action oriented, while girls typically show a preference for sociodramatic play centering on themes such as family, school, stage performing, and dressing up (Goodman, 2001; Honig, 2000; Maccoby, 2000). Girls tend to play in closer proximity to adults than do boys, and display more cooperative and negotiable play behaviors. Boys tend to play in larger groups than do girls and engage in more competition (Maccoby, 1990). Boys avoid feminine toys more than girls avoid masculine toys (Etaugh & Liss, 1992). All of these gender-related behaviors can become more intense in the primary grades as children sometimes find it difficult to play and work in mixed-gender groups.

Grogan and Bechtel (2003) provided suggestions for improving gender relationships in elementary school classrooms, including the following:

- Address the class as a whole: Rather than "Good morning boys and girls," use greetings such as, "Good morning everyone, . . . class, . . . children"
- Refrain from grouping or lining up children by boy/girl classifications; instead, use other classifications, such as birthdays, favorite foods, and similar interests
- Integrate boys and girls in seating arrangements
- Partner boys and girls for class projects and tasks
- Select bias-free literature and visual materials
- Engage in dialogue on gender issues with children as they arise

Stereotyping is often unconscious and subtle, though its potential for perpetuating stereotypes in children is great. Stereotypes imposed on girls and boys—such as attributing aggression, independence, and mathematical skills to boys and verbal, dependent, and passive behaviors to girls—can influence their self-perceptions well into adult life.

According to Kohlberg (1966), once the child has established gender-role constancy between ages 5 and 7, she or he becomes increasingly interested in observing and imitating the gender-role behaviors of others. Parents and teachers become powerful role models, as do other individuals the child admires, such as siblings, relatives, friends, media personalities, athletes, and other celebrities.

Studies of gender-role development emphasize gender schemata in which young children organize and internalize information about what is typical or appropriate for male and female individuals in their particular sociocultural contexts (Levy & Carter, 1989; Maccoby, 1990). According to these studies, such schemata do not necessarily depend on the emergence of gender constancy, but derive from a variety of developmental and experiential sources from infancy onward. While Kohlberg's stage descriptions emphasize the importance of the child's notion of gender constancy as a point at which the child becomes more aware of gender-related attributes, these recent theories emphasize an information-processing perspective. This point of view proposes that each person may possess internal motivations (schemata) to conform to sociocultural gender-role expectations and stereotypes.

Sexuality Development

Emerging sexuality development is evidenced, in part, by the typical gender segregation of school-age children. As they begin to find that play and work groups can include both boys and girls and friendships can be forged, their comfort level is being challenged. The gender-related play behaviors to which they have become accustomed during earlier years often interfere with their ability to relate, negotiate, and cooperate. This difficulty is often exhibited in defensive types of behaviors in which boys and girls refer to one another in derogatory terms, and ridicule or tease one another. Some of this teasing may refer to "boyfriends" and "girlfriends," "who is going to marry whom," and chasing and teasing on the playground.

According to Freudian theory, the Oedipal complex also comes into play during these years and is characterized by the child wanting to be close to and primarily interactive with the parent of the opposite sex. The child may behave in rivalrous or rejecting ways with their same-sex parent. This is an important period in which parental and other adult role models help children work through their relationships and concepts of gender roles and boy–girl relationships. Short lived, this period typically segues into admiration and imitation of the same-sex parent and an expressed desire to be like the same-sex parent.

Curiosity continues, as does using inappropriate words or provocative body language, now often accompanied with giggling and a sense of daring and enjoyment of shock effect. Children may giggle at television, magazine or billboard images of children or adults depicted in revealing clothing and provide their own names for body parts and their interpretations of the depicted poses or behaviors. Questions about sex continue to arise and often become more specific. Children may have acquired inaccurate or distorted information from siblings, playmates, the media, or other extrafamilial sources, and may have drawn conclusions that confuse or frighten them.

While most acting-out behaviors are inconsequential, some behaviors are clearly inappropriate. Responding appropriately to these behaviors requires that adults help children to learn to respect themselves and to interact with others in positive and respectful ways. Intervention is necessary when behaviors occur that tease, demean, intimidate, or make others uncomfortable. Failure to curtail and respond in instructive ways to this behavior teaches children, both boys and girls, to accept hostility and victimization (Chrisman & Couchenour, 2002).

Children's questions often perplex adults, who are not sure what or how much should be discussed with children. Responding appropriately to a child's questions requires that adults determine exactly what it is that the child is actually asking, and engage in dialogue with the child to ascertain what he or she already knows to determine if there are distortions and misinformation that need to be clarified. Age-appropriate discussion needs to be simple, frank, and unembarrassed, and should provide accurate information and terminology. There is no need for great detail, but there is need to determine whether the child has understood the information provided to avoid further confusion or distorted concepts.

Awareness of Diversity and Individual Differences

As cognitive development moves from preoperational thinking to concrete operational thinking, differences emerge in the way children view diversity. As children begin to decenter and become less egocentric, their awareness of groups emerges. Around age 5, they begin to use categories to define these groups. Children at this age are said to be **sociocentric**, that is, while they have formed a repertoire of group categories, they nevertheless are unable to take or accept the perspectives of other groups as valid. This declines after age 7, when children can focus more on individuality than on group categories and characteristics. Children's feelings about their own racial or cultural group identity are tested when they experience diverse groups of people, some of whom may exhibit stereotypes and bias.

In Aboud's (1988) theory, children at step 3 should be most susceptible to information and interventions that build positive relationships with others. At this point, children can appreciate the fact that ethnicity doesn't change, that there are individual internal qualities to be appreciated, and that differences among groups

sociocentric: the inability to take or accept as valid the perspectives of another group

are reconcilable. Aboud called this development the *focus of attentions sequence* and noted the following progression:

Step 1:

- Egocentrism

Step 2:

- Preoccupation with groups and the differences between one's own and other groups
- Exaggeration of contrasts between groups, which can lead to pro or anti perspectives
- Later increasing awareness of similarities as well as differences between one's own and other groups

Step 3:

- Focus on individuals and unique personalities
- Liking or disliking people on the basis of personal rather than ethnic group qualities
- Continuing to hold some ethnic group stereotypes

As in the development of self-concept and gender identity, the child's growing acceptance and appreciation of his or her ethnicity paves the way for acceptance of the uniqueness of others. Individuals who are comfortable with their ethnicity have little difficulty building relationships with members of other groups and do so without feelings of conflict or insecurity (Aboud, 1988).

Parents and early childhood professionals take an active role in fostering an appreciation for diversity in children. If antibias attitudes and feelings are to develop, young children need informative, positive, self-affirming, and perspective-taking experiences.

Peer Relationships

The peer group emerges as a powerful socializing force in the child's life during the early school years. The child has shifted from seeking interactions with adults more than with children to seeking interactions with children more than with adults. Peer group acceptance becomes paramount to the child.

Friendships begin to segregate along gender lines as early as the preschool years, a process that increases dramatically during the 6- through 8-year period (Powlishta, 1995). In another year or so, same-sex peer group preference will reach its peak. Boys and girls are, for all practical purposes, raised very differently; for instance, a boy's world involves participation in larger organized groups, boys are given greater access to public places and engage in more rough-and-tumble play, and boys' aggressive behaviors are more readily tolerated. Girls, by contrast, are kept closer to adults; are encouraged to be neat, tidy, and compliant; and receive less encouragement to be assertive and independent. These distinctions serve to reinforce children's gender perceptions and gender stereotyping and hence their interpersonal relationships. Many scholars believe that gender segregation and its accompanying stereotyping can result in stereotypical thinking and social patterns that persist into adult social behaviors.

Children who play and work in gender-integrated partnerships and groups have more opportunity to learn about and from each other.

On the other hand, children who play in gender-integrated partnerships and groups have greater opportunity to learn about and from each other. Indeed, studies have found that integrated play and work groups result in greater social competence (Feiring & Lewis, 1991).

Friendships among school-age children are less transient than they were in previous years. It has become somewhat more difficult to make friends, and dissolved friendships can be quite emotionally unsettling. The circle of friends is smaller than it was in previous years, as children become somewhat choosy, allowing not only gender, but culture and economic background to influence their friendship choices (Hartup, 1983). In spite of these selective behaviors, friendship choices are becoming more and more based on attributes ("She is real nice") rather than possessions or situational factors, as with younger children ("I like him because he has a Lego® set to play with") (Boggiano, Klinger, & Main, 1986). The social competence skills of initiating and maintaining friendships and resolving conflicts become important skills to have mastered by early school age.

Participation in games and activities involving rules brings children into frequent conflicts as rules become debatable and children discover that each player may perceive the rules differently. Through these conflict encounters, children's points of view compete, and their negotiating skills are tested. Lever (1976) found a difference in the amount of conflict engaged in by boys and girls. Boys' games tended to result in more conflict, while girls were more inclined to engage in turn-taking behaviors. Girls were also found to be more inclined to try to diffuse conflict situations. Boys were more likely to use heavy-handed persuasion to get what they wanted. Boys were shown to use these tactics whether in conflict with boys or with girls. Interestingly, girls tended to use heavy-handed tactics with boys but seldom with girls (Miller, Danaher, & Forbes, 1986). Some of these differences may be explained by the expectation that boys will behave more aggressively than girls (Maccoby & Jacklin, 1974/1980). There is also the expectation that girls prefer social harmony and therefore provoke less conflict (Gilligan, 1982).

Cooperation emerges through these early friendships and sustains them (Hartup, 1989). Through friendships, children derive companionship, emotional security and support, enhanced feelings of self-worth, interpersonal relationship skills, and knowledge about cultures and social conventions.

FACTORS INFLUENCING PSYCHOSOCIAL DEVELOPMENT IN CHILDREN AGES SIX THROUGH EIGHT

Sense of Industry vs Inferiority

Again, the extent to which the child's resolution of the industry versus inferiority psychosocial conflict is supported through experiences in the home, school, and extracurricular activities determines the extent to which a child will develop the subsequent healthy sense of identity that is so important during adolescence. Hence, 6- through 8-year-olds need the types of opportunities that engage their unique interests and abilities; that enlist them in mutual caring and support for the family, class, or other group to which they belong; and that provide opportunities to succeed and experience an authentic sense of accomplishment.

Individual Temperament and Personality

From previous chapters, we have seen that children have distinctive temperamental characteristics, which are genetically derived but are also influenced in a variety of ways by their environment. The manner and contexts in which temperament is expressed influence the types of reciprocal interactions the child will experience. For example, a child with a very high activity level could be viewed in positive terms ("energetic," "lively") or negative terms ("jumpy," "restless"). Such views influence the person's responses to and interactions with the child. The child, then, is subjected to a variety of responses that are based on how others perceive his or her temperament. (The frequently overused "diagnosis" of hyperactivity may actually represent adults' failure to recognize their reaction to individual temperament types.)

Differences in personality at ages 6 through 8 have their roots in these early and continuing perceptions and interactions. Recent studies have attempted to ascertain the relationship between early personality traits and later psychosocial adjustment. Some traits have been found to persist. For instance, highly aggressive children have been found to remain relatively more aggressive than others as they get older (Huesmann, Eron, Lefkowitz, & Walder, 1984). Other studies have suggested that negative emotional behaviors such as aggressiveness, being hard to please, undercompliance, and difficulties with peers are fairly stable over the course of childhood and affect later adjustment. Children who have been socially rejected during their earliest elementary school years are at greater risk for social difficulties in adolescence and early adulthood (Bierman, 2003; Hymel, Rubin, Rowden, & LeMare, 1990).

Sociocultural Experiences

The racial and ethnic composition of groups to which children belong (child care, school, out-of-school groups, and family affiliations) are increasingly more diverse and will continue to be so in the years to come (Federal Interagency Forum on Child and Family Statistics, 2003). Unlike generations of the past, today's children experience opportunities to interact with and gain knowledge of cultures beyond their own, hear and learn other languages, and practice accepting and non-biased social interactions. Children today will experience more cross-cultural friendships and shared cultural experiences than their parents experienced as children. In addition, the number of biracial families is also increasing in the United States (Chiong, 1998). The extent to which children are comfortable with and proud of their ethnicity and cultural heritage determines the extent to which all of these experiences can contribute to healthy psychosocial development.

Essential in this process is the child's growing sense of identity and family and cultural affiliation. A person's sense of identity includes perceptions of his or her physical characteristics and gender, innate and acquired abilities, socioeconomic status, and ethnic or racial group membership. Self-perceptions originate in the relationships and interactions that children persistently have with parents, family members, caregivers, teachers, and peers. Within families, children first learn racial pride and acquire attitudes of acceptance or rejection of others. Having positive and self-affirming feelings about one's race or ethnicity is a critical aspect of psychosocial development. However, equally important to successful psychosocial development is the acquisition of knowledge and attitudes conducive to non-biased relationships with others.

Nature of Adult–Child Relationships

Qualities of early experiences such as attachment, parenting styles, nonparental child care, and reactions to individual temperament are associated with psychosocial outcomes. Certain aspects of the relationship between the parent and the child have also been related to the child's psychosocial development. One study observed playful mother–child and father–child interactions and correlated them with the child's adaptation to peers (MacDonald & Parke, 1984). The findings suggest that boys who were competent with their peers had fathers who were physically playful and affectionate. The fathers of competent girls engaged their daughters in stimulating verbal exchanges. Certain maternal behaviors have been found to influence social acceptance with peers. Children whose mothers used positive verbal interactions, such as polite requests and suggestions, and were less demanding of and disagreeable with their children were found to be less abrasive and more positive in their peer interactions (Putallaz, 1987).

It is generally believed that the social skills that are necessary for later successful peer group interactions are learned through early experiences in the family (Howes & Ritchie, 2002). The quality of parent–child interactions is not the only influence on psychosocial development. By providing opportunities for peer group interaction, encouraging and facilitating friendships, and monitoring children's relationships for positive outcomes, parents provide the scaffolding that is essential to the development of social competence.

Out-of-School Time

For some school-age children, the out-of-home day may be as long as 10 to 13 hours. Long days are tiring and stressful. The daily before-school/school/after-school routine may involve two or more different settings, perhaps in two or more locations; different sets of adult authorities with different levels of education and training; different teaching and discipline styles; different behavior and performance expectations; and different modes of interacting with individual children. There may also be different peer groups with different group configurations and interactional dynamics. Clearly, children in these situations are called on to be flexible, resilient, and adaptable, not to mention physically hearty!

For some children, these demands present no problems. For others, adapting to multiple authority figures and different peer groups can be stressful and difficult. Parents, caregivers, and classroom teachers need to be sensitive to the physical and psychological demands of these routines. When a balanced schedule that includes rest, relaxation, play, self-directed activities, outdoor and indoor activities, and group and solitary moments, along with structured and adult-directed activities, is provided, the child's day can be productive and enjoyable. However, emphasis on group participation, schoolwork, and academic endeavors before, during, and after school would tax any child.

Teachers and caregivers need to provide space (both physical and psychological) for children to distance themselves from the group from time to time. Schedules in both the school and the child care program need to be sensitive to the physiological needs for nourishment, physical exercise, rest, spontaneous play, and informal interactions with friends and siblings. After-school programs need to resist the urge to "help" with schooling by insisting on additional schoolwork activities. Likewise, schools and teachers must resist the temptation to defer practice and reinforcement activities to after-school times. This, of course, opens the debate on whether homework should be regularly assigned. This topic, while critical, is beyond the intent of this discussion. The points here are as follows:

1. Long days with repeated structured activities impede school learning by causing fatigue, frustration, and burnout.
2. Children's physical and motor needs (addressed in Chapters 11 and 14) must be met for children to be physically and neurologically healthy.
3. Sound psychosocial development relies on warm, nurturing, supportive, and meaningful adult–child relationships.
4. Social competence, which includes making and maintaining friendships, social problem-solving skills, perspective-taking abilities, and prosocial abilities, depends on opportunities to interact with others in meaningful ways and be reasonably free from adult interference.

Before- and after-school child care can play a positive and supportive role in psychosocial development. When children are allowed to experience autonomy and control in the use of their time and energies and are provided with activities over which they can have a sense of mastery, adaptability to the routines of child care and school is facilitated.

Programs that provide for the safety and nurturing needs of children offer a valuable support system for families (Halpern, 2003). When parents feel secure and confident about the experiences their children are having while they are at work, family relationships are enhanced. Relieved of the worry and stress associated with unpredictable or self-care arrangements, parents can pursue their own work in a more productive manner. Emerging prescriptions for child care will include greater coordination among family, school, and child care programs and more efforts to meet a variety of family support service needs (Behrman, 1999; Vandell & Hsiu-chih, 1999).

Sibling Relationships

The sense of self derives in part from the relationships a child has with siblings. Siblings face a variety of self-concept issues relating to their close or distant relationships, their feelings of acceptance or rejection of one another, and their feelings of being similar to or different from one another (Banks & Kahn, 2003). These relationships and the perceptions that accompany them play a complex role in the child's developing sense of self as a unique and separate individual and also as part of a broader identity that includes brothers and sisters.

Rivalrous behavior at ages 6 through 8 is often an indication of the child's emerging sense of identity. Children at this age compare themselves with others in an attempt to affirm their self-worth. In families, brothers and sisters become objects for comparison as children seek to distinguish similarities and differences between themselves and others. At the same time, children begin to identify with one or more of their siblings, who are often powerful role models.

Parents who project their own unfulfilled ambitions onto one or more of the siblings place all of the children at risk on several fronts. The full realization of his or her interests and capabilities is thwarted in the child on whom these projections are imposed. The child grows to believe that success in the parent-selected pursuit will bring favor to him or her over others and failure will bring serious disappointment to the parent and perhaps lead to retribution. Siblings who are excluded from these expectations perceive themselves as being less important and/or less competent to the parent, even if they are not interested in the activities in question. The sibling relationship is undermined by feelings of rejection, envy, competition, and other negative responses to the parent's insensitive expectations. The parent–child relationship is undermined in both cases.

Teachers and others often compare one sibling to another in overt or subtle ways, attributing favorable and/or unfavorable attributes based on their prior experience. This can also impede self-concept development and undermine sibling relationships. Where sibling relationships are at risk or already strained, differential treatment by parents, teachers, or others can exacerbate the problem.

Social Interactions

As children get older, an expanding social circle, from parents and family to individuals and groups outside of the family, brings additional influences on the child's psychosocial development. Social interactions include incidental encounters (sharing the sights of the toy aisle at the supermarket with an acquaintance), informal interactions with individuals (riding bicycles with a special friend) and with loosely formed groups (neighborhood play groups), and formal or organized activities (Pee-Wee and Little League).

At this age, children establish and maintain close friendships with one or more agemates and enjoy visiting in one another's homes, sometimes overnight. Such friendships help children to grow in independence and social interaction skills. Through these friendships, children learn the importance of give-and-take and gain a sense of loyalty.

Children enlarge their friendship circles through loosely formed social groups. As a rule, these groups simply play around with one another. However, their organization may take on the elements of a club or gang, with leaders and followers, membership preferences, rules, and sometimes a name. Adults can harness the energy and enthusiasm that emerges from these friendship groups.

The peer group emerges as a powerful socializing force during the 6- through 8-year period.

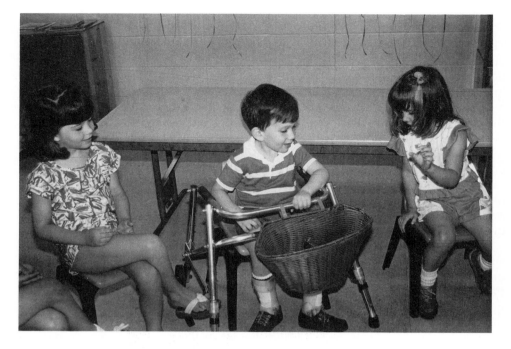

🖐 *Jeremy,* age 6, is a member of the Walla Street Club. This group includes the 7-year-old boy next door, the two brothers (ages 8 and 9) who live across the street, a 7-year-old from several houses down the street, and another 6-year-old from a block away. Girls are not admitted to the club, though two of the members have younger sisters who are allowed to participate in their games on rare occasions. The boys spend as much time together after school or on weekends as they can. They seem to have an insatiable desire to be together and boundless energy when engaged in play.

Jeremy's dad has initiated a weekend project for the boys: building a clubhouse in the backyard. The design, collection of building materials and tools (some borrowed from other members' parents), and construction of the house have been going on for about two months. The boys plan each step with energy and enthusiasm. Their wills occasionally clash: which board should go where, where the door will be, who is going to bring more nails. At home, the boys draw pictures of their clubhouse, gather items to furnish it, and brag to their siblings about their private place. They talk about the fun or complain about the conflicts with their parents. Together, they anticipate their meetings and what they will do, who will come, and who can never come into the clubhouse. It is a dynamic and ongoing avocation in their lives.

What do children gain from experiences like these? What about a child who is excluded from the play group? In these loosely formed groups, children experience leading and following, negotiating and compromising, rule setting, rule changing, and rule constraints. They become aware of the needs and wishes of others, and they practice perspective-taking and diplomacy. They experience loyalty and disloyalty, democracy, and autocracy. Their sense of industry is tapped, and their sense of belonging is reinforced. Their confidence and self-esteem are enhanced.

Despite all the positive influences of these social groupings, there can be difficulties associated with membership. Children ages six through eight measure themselves against their perceptions of others and, in so doing, are self-critical and critical of others. When group expectations are at odds with the child's abilities and desires, conflicts occur, and group membership may become detrimental. Treating others unkindly, expecting members to engage in mischief or forbidden activities, setting standards for dress, imposing undesired rivalry and competition, excluding a valued friend, and devaluing one's contribution or other activities (e.g., piano lessons, participation in scouting or a family picnic) are influences that can strain the child's abilities to negotiate. Adults need to be aware of these problems and sensitive to the child's dilemma. Guidance and support are needed, and in some instances so are intervention and coaching (Howes & Ritchie, 2002; Kim, 2003).

In addition to informally structured social groupings, children ages 6 through 8 are exposed to a variety of other extrafamilial social interactions. Now more predictable and dependable, children are included more frequently in various celebrations and recreational events—weddings, graduation ceremonies, sports events, concerts, birthday parties. Children may join their parents in religious services. These opportunities broaden the child's social awareness and provide additional role models.

Peer Rejection and Peer Neglect

Approximately 10 to 20 percent of children in early childhood classrooms are classified as popular, 10 to 22 percent as rejected, and 12 to 20 percent as neglected. The remaining children are classified as having an average status of popularity (Kim, 2003). Concern arises as psychologists are learning disturbing facts about the outcomes of persistent peer rejection, some of which are associated with (though not independently causative of) later dire behaviors that make headlines. Obviously, not all children who experience peer rejection or neglect respond in dangerous or destructive ways; many, however, suffer privately (to lesser or greater degrees) often well into their adult lives. Many forms of maladaptive emotional and social behaviors arise from continuous failure to find peer acceptance.

An important task in psychosocial development is learning to interact with others in ways that are socially desirable and appropriate and lead to competency in friendship building. Socially competent children understand the rules of social relationships (Bigelow, Tesson, & Lewko, 1996; Katz & McClellan, 1997). When children are unsuccessful in gaining social competence, they are at higher risk for interpersonal relationships problems.

Peers can be both rejecting and neglecting. Rejected children can fail to learn friendship-building behaviors of approach and integration skills, prosocial attitudes, and other interpersonal relationship requirements. Thus, they often employ behaviors that cause their peers to reject them, such as aggressive, hostile, and physically assertive behaviors (e.g., grabbing, pushing, and struggling), and they may tease, bully, or be verbally abusive (Bierman, 2003; Rubin & Clark, 1983).

Children who are neglected by their peers often display withdrawn behaviors in group situations. They may persistently play alone without demonstrating a desire to interact with others or that they can do so competently when they want to. They may exhibit shyness, anxiety, and fearfulness and convey to others more negative than positive expressions (Cassidy & Asher, 1992; Provost & LaFreniere, 1991).

Because the types of behaviors that elicit peer rejection or neglect may be indicative of serious underlying psychosocial developmental risks, early and consistent efforts to intervene are necessary. Shy, withdrawn children can be helped by providing opportunities for them to interact with one or two children with whom they can feel comfortable; coaching and scaffolding may be necessary to assist the friendship development process. It has been suggested that pairing the shy child with a younger playmate may assist him or her in gaining confidence in his or her interaction abilities (Kemple, 1992). Coaching children on approach, entry, and integration skills to help them gain acceptance into peer groups may be necessary. Teaching children to respond to the overtures of others in positive ways and helping children learn to express their enjoyments and discontents in assertive and nonaggressive ways also provide them with the tools for more satisfying peer interactions.

These informal groups, which are often based on proximity and accessibility, may also define their memberships arbitrarily along age, gender, socioeconomic, cultural, or religious lines. Children who are excluded are subjected to feelings of rejection and lowered self-esteem. Sensitive adults need to provide positive guidance for handling these situations when they arise. Adult intervention is needed to guide the group toward more prosocial goals and inclusive and antibiased behaviors. Here again, adults serve as social role models and coaches for children.

Children with Special Needs

Children with special needs face greater psychosocial challenges as they move through the elementary grades. They share needs for acceptance, belonging, and self-esteem with their agemates. The extent to which they have had opportunities to develop the social skills of initiating and maintaining friendships and resolving conflicts through inclusive programs and activities will influence their successes with interpersonal relationships and peer acceptance. By the same token, the extent to which other children have learned to understand and relate to their peers with disabilities also influences the climate for acceptance and participation.

A common challenge for children with special needs, regardless of type of disability, is the feeling of being different from other children. The self-concepts of many children with disabilities may center too heavily on their disabilities. Teachers who seek positive and successful psychosocial experiences for children with special needs will find effective ways to promote group understandings and acceptance. Teachers will structure both the physical and psychosocial environments to encourage social interactions among all children (Sandall, McLean, & Smith, 2000).

Teachers should be aware that any emphasis on competition among children can be particularly detrimental to the psychosocial development of children with special needs. Instead, arranging for more cooperative group endeavors assists all children in the development of social skills and social competence.

Stress

Children, like adults, experience stress from time to time. Unlike adults, young children lack sufficient knowledge and experience to understand their stressors and a repertoire of strategies for dealing with stress.

The causes of stress in young children are many and varied. Honig (1986) categorized stressor variables as follows:

1. *Personal,* including prematurity, sex, temperament, neurological sturdiness, age of child, and intellectual capacity
2. *Ecological,* including characteristics of living environments such as neighborhood crime, antisocial role models, unaesthetic surroundings, household density, individual privacy requirements, and inadequate play space
3. *Socioeconomical status*
4. *Catastrophes and terrors,* including hospitalization, societal disasters, threat of nuclear war and terrorism
5. *Family events,* including birth of siblings, death of parent or sibling, separation and divorce, and blended families

Obviously, a great number of potential stressors exist for young children. Pressures to perform tasks or to achieve beyond one's years and developmental capacities, changes in school or child care arrangements, and childhood social events such as birthday parties and school field trips may also be stressful. Certainly, not all of these events cause anxiety or stress in all children. Responses to stress are as varied as the stressors themselves and may be physiological (headache, stomach ache, loss of appetite, sleep disturbances) or psychological (crying, nightmares, regression, irritability, increased dependency) (Stanford & Yamamoto, 2001). See Table 15.3.

Stress can be described as either positive or negative; each type alerts us to respond or adapt in some particular way. Both types bring about physiological and psychological changes and physical and emotional responses. The impact of

---

TABLE 15.3   Stress-Related Behaviors

Physical reactions

    Physical or psychosomatic symptoms: stomach or abdominal pain, headache, sweaty palms, biting nails, hyperalertness, eating and sleep disturbances
    Regression to earlier forms of behaving: thumb sucking, toileting accidents

Emotional and social reactions

    Heightened sensitivity, irritability, low tolerance for frustration, crying
    Aggressive or oppositional behaviors, defensive outbursts
    Whining, or proximity seeking, reluctance to be alone
    Worrying, excessive concerns about what "might" or "could" happen
    Excessive shyness, avoiding interactions or challenges, fear of embarrassment

Cognitive reactions

    Inability to focus, sustain attention, think creatively
    Rationalizing undue fears and anxieties
    Poor problem-solving perspectives
    Worry about failures and consequences
    Learning difficulties

stress and the ability to cope with or adapt to stressful situations or demands depends on many interrelated factors: age, temperament, prior experience, knowledge, cognitive and metacognitive abilities, emotional intelligence, and support networks. Stressor characteristics of intensity, persistence, and duration also influence its impact.

Research indicates that children who were born premature, are boys, have limited cognitive capacity, or experienced prenatal stress are more readily affected by stressors. Further, there is a greater impact of stress for children who are younger than age 10, and have a genetic temperament that is classified as slow to warm up or difficult (Monk et al., 2000).

Characteristics that are often associated with stress-related personalities, such as competitiveness, impatience, aggressiveness, low tolerance for frustration, hostility, and high achievement orientation, have been found in very young children. The child's ability to appraise a stressful situation influences the extent to which the child will cope. Children need adults to help them to identify their stressors and to evaluate them with a goal toward eliminating the stressors when possible or finding constructive ways to deal with stress.

Jeremy's second-grade teacher invited his parents to a conference. His usual classroom performance had deteriorated since the beginning of the school year, and she was concerned. Jeremy's behaviors in school were off-task and disruptive. He teased his classmates, antagonized his project partners, and resorted to name calling when they protested. When the teacher intervened, he withdrew, became sullen, and often cried.

In conference, Ann and Bill revealed that similar behaviors were occurring at home, and they did not know what to do. Their individual work commitments, church work, and social life were consuming larger and larger amounts of their time and energies. In addition, Ann's mother had recently undergone surgery and needed Ann's assistance during her recovery.

The teacher asked them to focus on Jeremy's routines. What did he do before and after school and on the weekends? Jeremy's schedule included regular before- and after-school care at a child care center near the school. In addition, he was taking piano lessons early each Monday morning, had karate lessons on Wednesday afternoons, and played Pee-Wee League baseball on Saturday mornings.

Clearly, all members of the family had become overcommitted and overscheduled. The stress of such scheduling, the logistics of transportation and attendance, and the reduced opportunities for family interaction and mutual support were beginning to take their toll on each member. Jeremy's behavior in school was a clue to the stress he was encountering.

A reassessment of their commitments, goals, and priorities led Bill and Ann to conclude that each member of the family would benefit from a change. Jeremy was encouraged to talk about the extracurricular activities in which he was enrolled and was allowed to decide which one or ones were most important to him and most enjoyable. Ann and Bill did the same assessment of their own activities. From this exercise, each family member eliminated all but the most pressing and important activities. Jeremy chose to drop the piano and karate lessons. Maybe he will want to pursue those lessons later; for now, he feels relieved. With commitments and extracurricular activities returned to a manageable level, Jeremy and his parents have more time and energy to respond to one another and to interact with focused attention.

Television and Other Media Influences

The following research statements summarized by Levin (1998) from studies by the American Psychological Association and others are enlightening:

> By the time a child enters kindergarten he or she may have spent 4,000 hours watching television.
>
> Children average 35 hours per week of screen time with television, video and computer games, movies and videotapes.
>
> The average child sees 20,000 advertisements a year.
>
> By the end of elementary school, children will have witnessed an average of 8,000 murders and 100,000 other violent acts.
>
> Half of U.S. households with children aged 6–14 years have video game systems—and a majority of video games contain violent images.

Further, a preponderance of toys advertised and sold are linked to movies and TV programs that are characterized by aggression and violence.

Clearly, television and other electronic media play a major role in the socialization and culturalization of children. Children learn from these electronic sources, and their behaviors are influenced by what they learn. Studies of violence and aggression on television have overwhelmingly concluded that television has a measurable impact on behavior. Concern over this issue continues. Studies of gender and of racial and cultural groups on television have pointed out misrepresentations in television programming and the potentially deleterious effects of stereotyping. Studies of commercials have likewise suggested that childhood values and attitudes may be distorted and that commercials exploit children for financial gains.

Programs with prosocial themes and role models have also been shown to influence behavior, although the impact of these programs is thought to be less potent than that of programs that feature violence and aggression (Radke-Yarrow, Zahn-Waxter, & Chapman, 1983).

Contemporary studies of the impact of television on children's lives are attempting to determine the extent to which children actually attend to television when the set is on, what types of program events or program attributes attract and hold the child's attention (e.g., other children, puppets, unusual voices, animation, rhyming, laughing, and repetition), and the extent to which children comprehend what they view. Studies of the impact of other media are also emerging (Levin, 1998; 2003).

Large amounts of screen time interfere with psychosocial development in the following ways:

1. Physical activity and outdoor play are curtailed. Lack of exercise impedes physical motor development and sound physical and mental health.

2. Interaction with other children is reduced. As we have seen, children need the social experiences that peer group interaction affords. Without these experiences, they are deprived of opportunities to gain social knowledge and social competence.

3. Children who are unskilled in social interaction with peers or are unpopular and rejected by playmates find escape in screen time, further reducing their interactions with others and further impeding their psychosocial development.

4. Parent–child conversations and interactions are interrupted. Both children and parents forgo dialogue and in-depth conversations when television viewing dominates their free time. Opportunities to address issues of concern to the child and to provide needed emotional and social guidance are often irretrievably lost.

5. Opportunities for children to discover their interests and unique capabilities or talents are reduced. Children who are developing initiative, industry, self-concept and self-esteem need to explore and experience a variety of endeavors and interests on the way to self-discovery.

Adults can help children become discerning viewers of television by watching television with children and engaging them in dialogue about the programs and advertisements that they see. Family values and concepts of character, ethics, and integrity can be brought into these discussions. As with nutrition, adults control the content of children's media diets, and set standards for the amount of time that can be devoted to television viewing. It is important to remember that when the television set is on, children are receiving visual and auditory input whether they are seated in front of the set or moving about, engaged in other activities. The content of adult programs and the news may not be appropriate for them.

Television news is a case in point. The news can be delivered into our homes 24 hours a day. The news and the weather are often delivered in graphic and fear-inducing formats. News stories and footage are repeated over and over, with little amplifying explanatory background, or contextual explanation. Hence, children who hear or see only the dramatic or spectacular portrayed in the news acquire a view of local and world events that is disproportionate to their occurrences in real life. When children's attention to the news is sporadic, they obtain incomplete information, which further confuses them. Both children and adults can be unduly stressed from excessive television viewing. When children have viewed disturbing news, it is imperative to take the time to discuss the story, provide reassurances, and observe for behavioral signs of stress.

Efforts to help children to become critical consumers of television and computer fare whether formal (preprogrammed lessons or structured discussions) or informal (incidental and spontaneous) in the home or school should be focused on

- decreasing the belief that TV programs are real;
- increasing the child's tendency to compare what is seen on TV with other sources of information;
- decreasing television's credibility by teaching children about the economic and production aspects of television;
- teaching children to evaluate the content of television programming.

Parents and teachers have important roles to play in facilitating the positive effects of television for children (Table 15.4). The amount of time children spend viewing television can be curtailed in favor of more physically and mentally challenging activities and increased social interactions with others. Wise program choices can result when children are taught to evaluate the offerings. In addition, children need adults to talk with them about the content of programs they see and to help them become discerning viewers.

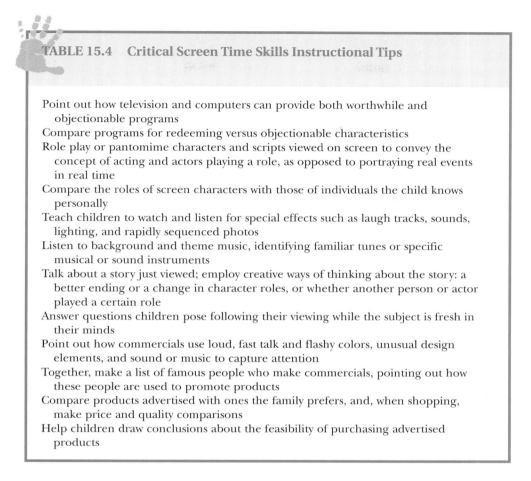

TABLE 15.4   Critical Screen Time Skills Instructional Tips

Point out how television and computers can provide both worthwhile and objectionable programs

Compare programs for redeeming versus objectionable characteristics

Role play or pantomime characters and scripts viewed on screen to convey the concept of acting and actors playing a role, as opposed to portraying real events in real time

Compare the roles of screen characters with those of individuals the child knows personally

Teach children to watch and listen for special effects such as laugh tracks, sounds, lighting, and rapidly sequenced photos

Listen to background and theme music, identifying familiar tunes or specific musical or sound instruments

Talk about a story just viewed; employ creative ways of thinking about the story: a better ending or a change in character roles, or whether another person or actor played a certain role

Answer questions children pose following their viewing while the subject is fresh in their minds

Point out how commercials use loud, fast talk and flashy colors, unusual design elements, and sound or music to capture attention

Together, make a list of famous people who make commercials, pointing out how these people are used to promote products

Compare products advertised with ones the family prefers, and, when shopping, make price and quality comparisons

Help children draw conclusions about the feasibility of purchasing advertised products

Computers and the Internet

Computers are marvelous sources of information, entertainment, and communicative expediency. They are an essential tool for learners, from preschool to senior citizens. Online services give children an endless supply of resources—encyclopedias, libraries, search capabilities, and current events coverage. However, the electronic capabilities that make all these opportunities accessible to children also pose hazards for them. Through services such as online chat rooms or news groups, children can communicate with complete strangers, some of whom may have sinister motives. Children have no way of knowing whether their contact is another child or a child predator. Further, children may access sites that have content that is inappropriate or overwhelming; that promote prejudice, violence, hate, or pornography; bombard children with advertising, which may be misleading; offer children prizes; or invite them to join a "club" and attempt to arrange a meeting.

Just as children are taught not to talk with people they do not know, open the door to their home when they are alone and do not know who is there, or give personal information on the phone, they must also be taught the concept that "strangers" exist online. Just as they monitor children's choice of friends, where they play, and what television, music, books, and magazines they read, parents (and teachers) must supervise the appropriate use of online capabilities. Children particularly need to be taught not to provide personal information (their name, family names, addresses, phone numbers, work places, schools, credit card information, computer passwords, and so on) to any online site. Certainly, children need to be taught *never* to agree to actually meet someone they meet online. Parents and teachers can take advantage of commercially available software programs that restrict access to certain sites. They need to teach children how to communicate with parents at their work sites and coach children on the etiquette of computer communications, which is the same as for face-to-face communications.

ROLE OF THE EARLY CHILDHOOD PROFESSIONAL

Enhancing Psychosocial Development in Children Ages Six through Eight

1. Support the child's continuing need for nurturing and security.
2. Enhance the child's self-esteem through positive and supportive interactions.
3. Model prosocial and moral behaviors; help children to understand the need and rationales for rules.
4. Support the child's sense of industry through opportunities to participate in meaningful activities and to experience authentic accomplishments.
5. Understand the child's increasing needs for social interactions, and encourage and facilitate a variety of social interactions.
6. Recognize the child's continuing need for boundaries and guidance.
7. Provide positive, inductive, authoritative discipline.
8. Respond to the child's changing interests in gender with acceptance and respect while guiding the child toward antibias perspectives.
9. Provide appropriate media experiences, and help the child to become a critical evaluator of media programs.
10. Monitor and guide children's use of the Internet.

KEY TERMS

defense mechanism
industry
internalization
sociocentric

REVIEW STRATEGIES AND ACTIVITIES

1. Review the key terms individually or with a classmate.

2. Develop an annotated bibliography of children's books that addresses the issues children confront in making and maintaining friendships.

3. Observe an exemplary third-grade classroom. How is social interaction encouraged? Are informal social groups evident? Observe these friendship groups on the playground at recess. What are the compositions of the groups? How do they interact with one another? Is there a leader? What rules seem to be evident? How do the children respond to nongroup members?

4. Engage in a dialogue with a member of a different ethnic background. Discuss similarities and differences in your child rearing with regard to school achievement, authority, independence, responsibilities, choice of friends, and gender and racial group membership.

5. With a partner, brainstorm ways to promote and facilitate the developing sense of industry in young school-age children.

6. Discuss with your classmates the social challenges for children with disabilities.

FURTHER READINGS

Bierman, K. L. (2003). *Peer rejection: Developmental processes and intervention strategies.* New York: Guilford.

Bullard, S. (1997). *Teaching tolerance: Raising open-minded empathetic children.* New York: Doubleday.

Derman-Sparks, L., & Phillips, C. B. (1997). *Teaching/learning anti-racism: A developmental approach.* New York: Teachers College Press.

DeVries, R., & Zan, B. (1994). *Moral classrooms, moral children: Creating a constructivist atmosphere in early education.* New York: Teachers College Press.

Gallas, K. (1998). "Sometimes I can be anything": Power, gender, and identity in a primary classroom. New York: Teachers College Press.

Greenspan, S. (2003). *The secure child: Helping our children feel safe and confident in a changing world.* New York: Perseus.

Levin, D. E. (2003). *Remote control childhood?: Combating the hazards of media culture* (2nd ed.). Washington, DC: National Association for the Education of Young Children.

National Association for the Education of Young Children (1996). *NAEYC position statement on violence in the lives of children.* Washington, DC: Author.

Paley, V. G. (1999). *The kindness of children.* Cambridge, MA: Harvard University Press.

Roffman, D. M. (2001). *Sex and sensibility: A parent's guide to talking sense about sex.* Cambridge, MA: Perseus.

Ross, D. M. (1996). *Childhood bullying and teasing: What school personnel, other professionals, and parents can do.* Alexandria, VA: American Counseling Association.

OTHER RESOURCES

Aidman, A. (1997). *Television violence: Content, context and consequences* (EDO-PS-97-26). Available from
ERIC Clearinghouse on Elementary and Early Childhood Education
University of Illinois
51 Gerty Drive
Champaign, IL 61820-7469

American Academy of Pediatrics. Brochures:
  Divorce and children
  The Internet and your family
  Television and the family
  American Academy of Pediatrics
  Division of Publications 141 Northwest Point Blvd.
  P.O. Box 747
  Elk Grove Village, IL 60009-0747
  http://www.aap.org
Children's Defense Fund (1999). *30 simple things parents can do to help keep children safe from violence.* Washington, DC: Author. Available from
  Children's Defense Fund
  25 E Street, NW
  Washington, DC 20001
  www.childrensdefense.org
New York University Child Study Center. About Our Kids. Available at
  www.aboutourkids.org
School-age notes. A bimonthy newsletter for teachers and directors of programs for school-age children. Available from
  School-Age Notes
  Box 40205
  Nashville, TN 37204
Sesame Workshop (May 30, 2001). A view from the middle: Life through the eyes of middle childhood. Available at
  http://www.sesameworkshop.org/research/0,6483, 109921,00.html
Sexuality Information and Education Council of the United States.
  www.siecus.org

CHAPTER SIXTEEN

Cognitive, Language, and Literacy Development: Ages Six Through Eight

Virtually no one argues that a given child's life course is set by the time of school entry. People are not like rockets whose trajectory is established at the moment they are launched. Indeed, it is the lifelong capacity for change and reorganization that renders human beings capable of dramatic recovery from early harm and incapable of being inoculated against later adversity. This lifelong plasticity renders us both adaptive and vulnerable.

JACK SHONKOFF AND DEBORAH PHILLIPS

Many a child's development is disrupted when family life failed to prepare him for school life, or when school life fails to sustain the promises of earlier stages.

ERIK ERIKSON

After studying this chapter, you will demonstrate comprehension by:

▶ Recognizing theoretical perspectives on cognitive, language, and literacy development in children ages 6 through 8.

▶ Describing the cognitive development of children ages 6 through 8.

▶ Describing the language development of children ages 6 through 8.

▶ Describing the literacy development of children ages 6 through 8.

▶ Relating cognitive, language, and literacy development to other developmental domains.

▶ Identifying major factors influencing cognitive, language, and literacy development in children ages 6 through 8.

▶ Suggesting strategies for promoting cognitive, language, and literacy development in children ages 6 through 8.

Cognitive development—the aspect of growth and development that deals with thinking, problem solving, intelligence, and language—is about to undergo a major shift, altering the way children perceive, respond to new information, and interact with objects and people. Perhaps it is no accident that formal schooling begins during ages 5 to 6 or 7 years. This "5 to 7 shift," as it is often called, is best described by examining theoretical perspectives.

THEORETICAL PERSPECTIVES ON COGNITIVE DEVELOPMENT IN CHILDREN AGES SIX THROUGH EIGHT

Piaget's theory describes young children's thinking during the sensorimotor and preoperational stages as having reactive, egocentric, centrated, transductive, and irreversibility characteristics. This type of thinking interferes with the child's ability to sort and classify; to understand cause and effect; to make clear distinctions between fantasy and reality; to grasp concepts of quantity, such as number, size, weight, and distance; and to conserve and understand that an amount does not change when its arrangement or appearance changes. Between ages 5 and 7, however, children gradually begin to make the transition from these unsystematic, illogical ways of thinking to the more logical thought of Piaget's **concrete operational stage**, which lasts from about age 7 to around 11.

Children in the primary grades (first, second, and third grades) are at first in the late period of the preoperational stage (ages 2 to 7), but gradually their thinking begins to shift to more concrete operational thought. The term *concrete* refers to the fact that concrete (tangible) objects are needed to help the child mentally construct concepts and understanding. The term *operational* refers to the fact that the child performs mental operations to create logical understanding of such

concrete operational stage: according to Piaget, the stage in which children around 7 to 11 years of age can use logical reasoning rather than relying on perceptions, but still use concrete objects and firsthand experiences to form concepts and reach understanding

485

formal operations:
according to Piaget,
the fourth and final
stage of cognitive
development, which
occurs during
adolescence, when
reliance on concrete
objects decreases
and abstract think-
ing begins

things as cause and effect, quantity and change, fantasy and reality, and how others perceive the same object or event. At this stage, the child is said to be mentally able to deal with functions and change in concrete objects and events but does not engage in two or more mental operations at the same time. Thinking about abstract ideas or hypothetical situations is not yet possible; this emerges during the stage of **formal operations**, beginning around age 11 or 12 years. For these reasons, the concrete operational learner does not learn well from direct instruction but must be personally and concretely involved in a learning activity.

For example, a young boy playing at the water table in his classroom is pouring water from one container into another and streaming water from a plastic pitcher down his arm. He decides to pour laundry soap into the water to make it bubbly. He discovers that soapy water feels slippery and different from water that does not have soap in it. It smells different, too. He splashes vigorously to make more bubbles and licks some bubbles off his hand. He waves some bubbles into the air and notices colors shining in the airborne bubbles. Through all of these actions, the boy is discovering and constructing his knowledge of water with soap in it; how it feels, smells, and tastes; what he can make it do; how bubbles can be stirred into the water; what they look like when they are airborne; how long bubbles can float in the air before they pop; what happens when they pop; and so on. The child cannot mentally construct this type of knowledge about soapy water unless he acts on soapy water. Adults cannot simply tell a child the facts or describe the phenomena. The act of transforming the water and experimenting with infinite possibilities itself builds concepts and understanding or mental structures.

One of the most recognizable characteristics of the stage of concrete operations is the child's emerging ability to perform the operation of conservation. Piaget and others have illustrated that conservation of number occurs first, followed by conservation of length, mass, and liquid, and finally conservation of weight and volume. The advancing ability to perform these operations helps children's thinking become more logical and flexible. Children can now return to their original point in thought (reversibility), understand transformation, or in-between events that cause change (pouring liquid from a tall, slender glass into a short, wider one), classify by more than one attribute (large red blocks versus all large or all red groupings), and think about alternative ways to solve problems.

Jeremy likes baseball. His father is also an avid baseball fan. They attend games together, and Jeremy's interest has led to quite an impressive collection of baseball cards. With his father's help when he first began to collect the cards, Jeremy enjoyed looking at them and assigning the players' names to their pictures; then he began to stack players wearing the same color of uniform together. Now his father notices that Jeremy engages in a variety of ways to sort, classify, and enjoy his collection. He classifies the cards by teams, player positions, leagues, batting averages, and other statistics. Jeremy's classification skills indicate that he can now invent a variety of ways to group objects and ideas, a characteristic of the concrete operational thinker.

According to Piaget, there are three types of knowledge: *physical knowledge, logical-mathematical knowledge,* and *social knowledge.* The young boy playing in the soapy water was constructing knowledge of the physical properties of soapy water. This type of knowledge is not acquired accurately by looking at pictures, reading about the topic, or listening to what others have to say about it. Acting on objects or events builds schemata about the objects or events. This knowledge is physical knowledge.

The second type of knowledge that Piaget described is logical–mathematical knowledge. Here the child uses the cognitive ability to perform reversible, logical, and mathematical transformations on concrete objects. The child thinks about and invents knowledge from his or her actions on objects. However, unlike physical knowledge, in this type of learning, the objects do not provide the knowledge, but serve as a medium that permits the construction of knowledge to occur. For example, a little girl stringing wooden beads places five of them on a string. She lays the string of beads on the table and counts them. Then she removes the beads from the string, places them all in a row in front of her, and counts them again. She takes another string and repeats the activity. She arranges and rearranges her set of five beads. Through this activity, she eventually constructs the concept that the number of beads in a set remains the same regardless of the arrangement: on or off of the string, in a little pile, or lined up neatly in front of her. Many experiences such as this, in which young children manipulate various objects and use them in different ways, increase conceptual development and build understanding. These processes result in mental structures that allow children to think about not only the properties of objects, but also ways in which they can be used to represent, quantify, and explain. Like physical knowledge, logical–mathematical knowledge is not acquired from being told something. It is constructed or invented in the child's mind (Kamii, 2000, 2003).

The third type of knowledge is social knowledge, or social conventional knowledge. Social knowledge includes the rules, laws, morals, values, ethics, and language systems of a cultural or social group. This knowledge is derived from the child's actions and interactions with other people. Children in the concrete operations stage of cognitive development are becoming less perception bound and less egocentric, are learning to take the perspective of others, can think about the intentions of others, and are developing the concept of rules. These cognitive abilities bring about changes in the way children relate to others. This improved ability to see the viewpoints of others results in increased proficiency in the acquisition of new knowledge and is important in facilitating cooperative learning activities. It is particularly helpful when children begin to engage in rule-based games and team sports.

Transition from the Preoperational to the Concrete Operational Stage

Piaget believed that changes in cognitive abilities are the result of a continuous developmental process, with new schemata or cognitive structures building on and incorporating preceding ones. These changes are gradual, never abrupt. Some children begin to move into the concrete operational stage at age 5 or earlier. Other children provide little evidence of concrete operational thought until around age 7. Some children in the preoperational stage demonstrate concrete operational behaviors. As with all development, there are often wide ranges in the ages at which children exhibit stage-related cognitive behaviors.

Counting experiences with concrete objects, including their fingers, help children ages 6 to 8 develop the concept of numbers.

As we shall see later in this chapter, Piaget's theory of cognitive development has important implications for instructional practices during the primary grades.

Information-Processing Theory

Rather than focusing on stages, information-processing theorists are interested in what mental representations children form, how they mentally operate on information, and how much information they can keep in mind at one time. They describe the structural characteristics of an information-processing system as having three main parts: *sensory memory*, *short-term memory*, and *long-term memory* (Siegler, 1998). Sensory memory is unanalyzed information that is remembered in unusual detail soon after an encounter or event. Short-term memory combines information from the immediate environment and information from long-term memory to make decisions about what to do with new input. Short-term memory is also referred to as *working memory*. Long-term memory includes a variety of social, emotional, and cognitive experiences. Long-term memory can hold an extremely large amount of information, and that information can reside there indefinitely. Studies of sensory memory in 5-year-old children have demonstrated sensory memory equivalent to that of an adult (Siegler, 1998). Without sustained attention, the information stored in short-term memory can remain there for only 15 to 30 seconds (Siegler, 1998). Children around ages 6, 7, and 8 are beginning to hold information in short-term memory long enough to successfully get it transferred to long-term storage. This process is facilitated by their increasing ability to use mental memory strategies such as **rehearsal**, their widening knowledge base, and their ability to think about memory. Changes in children's intellectual functioning at these ages are thought to be the result of more efficient mental processing. Rehearsal techniques and improved memory organization appear to increase children's ability to store and retrieve information in an organized and systematic manner.

Around ages 7 and 8 years, children demonstrate that they have increased knowledge about the act of remembering and can think about memory, a process called **metamemory**. They are also gaining an understanding of their cognitive processes; this is called metacognition (Sternberg & Berg, 1992/1995). This increased awareness of their memory and cognitive processes appears to facilitate other cognitive processes. As children become metacognitive, they think about what they know, what to do with what they know, and how they can use what they know to solve problems. They can be more reflective about their play and relationships, schoolwork, and learning. This ability improves over time.

rehearsal:
the mental process of repeating a thought in order to retain it in memory

metamemory:
the ability to think about memory and memory processes

Multiple Intelligence Theory

As with the Piagetian and information-processing theories, the concept that there are many different types of intelligence is one that has particular significance to understanding the cognitive development of school-age children. The theory that intelligences depend on genetically predetermined characteristics that are fixed and relatively unalterable and can be measured by standardized tests is giving way to a much broader concept of intelligence. Gardner's multiple intelligences theory challenges this long-held belief. In an interview, Gardner described this challenge as follows:

> The standard view of intelligence is that intelligence is something you are born with; you have only a certain amount of it; you cannot do much about how much of that intelligence you have; and tests exist that can tell you how smart you are. The theory of multiple intelligences challenges that view. It asks, instead, "Given what we know about the brain, evolution, and the difference in cultures, what are the sets of human abilities we all share?" (Checkley, 1997, p. 9).

According to Gardner, differences in intelligences or combinations of intelligences are evident during infancy and the preschool years. However, during the primary school years, individual intellectual strengths become more overt and observable and are vulnerable to support or inattention in the schooling process. As Gardner reports from his studies of multiple intelligences in children, a 4-year-old can exhibit distinctive cognitive profiles. For instance, some 4-year-olds approach the world through prolific use of language, others are more visually and spatially oriented, and still others are intensely interested in interacting with other people. As these proclivities play out in the ensuing years, they have profound effects on the child as a student, determining such characteristics as how the child will confront and use new information. Will the child learn best through the use of story, interaction with people, or hands-on activities (Gardner, 1991b)? In Box 16.1, we illustrate how the intelligences described by Gardner are evident in the behaviors and interests of children.

BOX 16.1   Childhood Expressions of Multiple Intelligence

Linguistic intelligence is expressed through:

Creative, expressive, and effective use of spoken and written words; listening intently to the words of others; mimicking unusual words; playing with words, enjoying one's creations, which often include rhyming, creating streams of words, attempting tongue twisters, and, in older children, using puns and riddles; forming unique word combinations, phrases, and sentences; expressing ideas in unique ways; using a broad vocabulary; having a good memory for names and places; asking many questions and enjoying extended conversations and dialogue.

Musical intelligence is expressed through:

The ability to respond to rhythm, pitch, melody, and tone qualities; sensitivity to sounds in the environment; enjoyment of singing and being sung to; the ability to remember and repeat songs and rhythms; humming, chanting, or singing to oneself; curiosity about and enjoyment of experimenting with musical instruments; a desire to master the use of one or more instruments.

Logical–mathematical intelligence is expressed through:

The ability to sort, classify, sequence, and pattern a variety of objects, events, and situations; enjoyment of counting and using numbers in many contexts to order, measure, and estimate; forming logical patterns and relationships between and among objects, events, and situations; discovering analogies; formulating hypotheses; inferring, calculating, and using numbers effectively and accurately; having a good sense of cause and effect and asking many what-if and if/then questions.

Spatial intelligence is expressed through:

Sensitivity to line, color, shape, and form; the ability to visualize spatial configurations; a good sense of direction and distance; the ability to verbalize shapes, distances, patterns, directions, and configurations; paying close attention to illustrations, pictures, and patterns; enjoying designing and constructing with blocks, carpentry, and other media.

Bodily–kinesthetic intelligence is expressed through:

The ability to direct bodily motion and manipulate objects in a skillful way; demonstrating refined large and fine motor coordinations, including balance, agility, strength, speed, and dexterity; exhibiting expressive body language and the ability to portray ideas and feelings through movement, dance, and exercise routines; an interest and skill in interpretive dance, finger play, puppetry, and mime; skilled use of various exercise and sporting equipment.

Interpersonal intelligence is expressed through:

The ability to recognize distinctions among others' feelings, moods, temperaments, motivations, and intentions; sensitivity to facial expressions, tone of voice, voice inflections, gestures, posture, and other body language cues; enjoyment of others and a desire to engage in social interactions, exceptional perspective-taking ability; skill in handling interpersonal conflicts and misunderstandings; openness to guidance and a spirit of helpfulness.

Intrapersonal intelligence is expressed through:

Awareness of one's strengths, limitations, moods, motivations, temperament, desires, and intentions and the ability to talk frankly about these characteristics; self-esteem and self-discipline; a strong sense of autonomy; the expression of aspirations that are reasonably commensurate with capabilities; enjoyment of one's own company; often, the expression of strong convictions.

Naturalistic intelligence is expressed through:

An interest in and the ability to classify natural phenomena among plants, minerals, and animals; interest and awareness of ecological, geographic, topological, and anthropological characteristics and the types of changes that affect the life and growth of plants and animals and phenomena that enhance or impede the growth and well-being of people.

Source: Puckett, M. B., & Black, J. K. (2000). *Authentic assessment of the young child: Celebrating development and learning,* 2nd ed. Upper Saddle River, NJ: Merrill/Prentice Hall. Reproduced with permission.

Social Interactionist Theory

The fact that children learn certain cognitive strategies from observing the behaviors of others is an important concept in the context of our discussions of cognitive, language, and literacy development in children ages 6 through 8. In earlier chapters, we mentioned the role of imitation during the course of cognitive development (Bandura, 1986; 1997). Deriving from the behaviorist point of view, particularly that of operant conditioning, this theory purports that children learn to imitate parents' behaviors first from the positive reinforcing feedback they get from them in imitative interactions. These behaviors, having been valued by the parents, become part of the child's repertoire and, through the value and reward associated with them, gradually become self-reinforcing (Bandura & Walters, 1963). Bandura and Walters noted that children are selective in their imitative behaviors. They tend to imitate when their behaviors have been rewarded in some manner and when the role model is someone they admire or respect and with whom they have a warm relationship. Imitations appear to occur more when models are of the same sex and less when the model is perceived by the child as different.

As children get older, certain cognitive processes come into play in observational learning, determining which events or behaviors will be observed, how much attention to give to them, what meaning can be derived from them, and what information will be retained for future retrieval and use. Children during the primary school years can observe the problem-solving skills of others. In fact, one study established that children who observe the verbalizing behaviors of another's thought processes in solving a problem perform better than children who are simply taught the rule or strategies for problem solving through direct instruction (Schunk, 1981). This has implications for such classroom teaching practices as engaging in dialogues, verbalizing processes (as opposed to simply providing answers to questions), and working in cooperative groupings in which children negotiate and share learning experiences as they proceed with their assignments.

Shared learning experiences enhance both cognitive and psychosocial development.

Bandura's social cognitive theory respects the impact of social and cultural influences on cognitive development but attempts to explain the ways in which the mind influences behaviors to be learned through attentional selectivity, the child's representational abilities, and the uses and efficacy of memory. Because older children have more sophisticated cognitive processes, they generally obtain more complete information from a learning event, store it in memory more efficiently, and recall it more completely and accurately than they did when they were younger.

Contextualistic Theory

According to Bronfenbrenner's ecological systems perspective, cognitive, language, and literacy development have multiple influences. As children enter school, influences expand, and the relative importance of each source of influence begins to take on new weighting. The mesosystem, which includes home, school, community activities, and faith-based affiliations, embodies numerous relationships: parent–child, parent–sibling, sibling–sibling, baby sitters, before- and after-school caregivers, teachers and other school personnel, leaders and instructors of extracurricular activities, religious leaders, and so on. Also emerging rapidly in importance are peer relationships. In contexts in which children are engaged in social and educational activities with other children, friendships emerge along with social aspirations and sometimes social rejection. The nature of peer relationships influences not only the social development of children, but their emotional and cognitive development as well. Peers can provide social and cognitive models, motivation, information, mutual support, and experience in collaboration, cooperation, and problem solving. Peers can also provide inappropriate role models, misinformation, distractions, and angst. Peer relationships continue to rise in importance to the individual child during the school years. However, for the great majority of children, parents remain the most important and critical influence in the child's life.

During the school years, the child begins to confront on a personal level (as opposed to vicariously or indirectly through their parents) the influences of the economy, their parents' workplace and responsibilities, the mass media, and policies set by school administrators, local school boards, and other governmental bodies. These influences come from the exosystem described by Bronfenbrenner, the larger circle of influence beyond the microsystem and the mesosystem. To some extent, but again more vicariously and embedded in child-rearing and schooling practices, the influences also come from the political, social, and cultural climate of the society at large, which originates in the macrosystem, the outermost circle (Bronfenbrenner, 1986).

Neurobiological Findings

According to Sylwester (1995),

Emotion and attention are the principal preliminary processes that our body/brain uses in its efforts to survive (and even to thrive) in the face of continual challenges. Our wary brain constantly surveys our internal and external environment to determine what's important and unimportant. Emotion provides a quick, general assessment of the situation that draws on powerful internal needs and values (to survive, eat, nurture, and mate), and attention provides the neural mechanisms that can focus on the things that seem important, while monitoring or ignoring the unimportant.

Our emotional and attentional mechanisms are ancient, quick, and powerful. They evolved to rapidly size up and respond to imminent predatory danger and fleeting feeding and mating possibilities—better to flee unnecessarily many times than to delay once for a more detailed analysis of the threat, and so die well informed. (p. 71)

As Sylwester so cleverly expressed it, the brain's emotional and attentional centers play a deciding role in what the learner perceives and addresses. As noted earlier, a greater number of neural fibers extend from the brain's limbic (emotional) center into the logical/rational cortical centers than the reverse. This means that the emotions are as important to learning as are logical/rational processes—perhaps more so. This has implications for the emotional tone of the contexts in which learning occurs.

Further neurobiological studies of the brain's attentional mechanisms reveal that there are normal cyclical patterns in our ability to attend, which are regulated by certain chemical neurotransmitters (principally dopamine and norepinephrine). According to Hobson (1989), these fluctuations occur in 90-minute cycles across the 24-hour day. For example, waking after a night's sleep is governed by an elevation in the levels of certain chemicals in the brain, which remain somewhat elevated throughout the morning. However, these levels begin to decline during the afternoon and are lowest after midnight, when most people have no choice but to respond with sleep. Of course, there are exceptions to this pattern.

Many children suffer attentional problems. Some may be due to this cyclical nature of brain chemistry; others are thought to be due to a congenital disorder of the dopamine neurotransmitter system in the brain. A small percentage of school-age children suffer from attention-deficit hyperactivity disorder (ADHD), and for about 78 percent of these children, ADHD persists into adolescence and often into adulthood (Schubiner & Robin, 1998; U.S. Surgeon General, 2000). These children have extreme difficulty focusing and sustaining their attention and display an inordinate amount of uncontrolled impulsive behaviors. Neurobiologists believe that ADHD stems from the metabolic activity and possible neurotransmitter deficiencies in the brainstem and limbic system structures. These anomalies interfere with the brain's ability to regulate motor inhibition and control and to organize and regulate attention behaviors. When properly diagnosed, ADHD can be treated with drugs that increase the availability of the appropriate neurotransmitters, making it possible for the child to select and attend to specific stimuli. Box 16.2 provides additional information on ADHD.

Memory capabilities are also evident in the structures of the brain's neurological system. When something is learned, physical changes occur at the synapse, which strengthen the neural connections that will form a memory network with repeated use. Emotion, learning, and experience strengthen useful connections in the brain's wiring and prune those that go unused or prove to be inefficient. In spite of this, the brain remains throughout the life span somewhat plastic and ready to form alternative networks when life conditions impose new challenges. The early years are immensely important for the initial neurological wiring that forms during sensitive periods (or windows of opportunity).

BOX 16.2   What Is Attention Deficit Hyperactivity Disorder?

The American Academy of Pediatrics (AAP) describes ADHD as a disorder, characterized by chronic neurological conditions, that results from persistent dysfunction within the central nervous system. ADHD is not related to gender, level of intelligence, or cultural environment. It is not a result of inappropriate parenting. The actual cause or causes of ADHD are not fully understood. A defining characteristic is that the symptoms persist over time without improvement under conditions of typical guidance and education procedures. It is estimated that 6 to 9 percent of school-age children are referred for evaluation (Reiff & Tippins, 2004).

Parents, caregivers, and teachers may notice behaviors or difficulties such as the following:

- Difficulty understanding and following through on directions, procedures, and relating to descriptions and other instructional information.
- Sequencing tasks, such as ordering or grouping items by an attribute such as height, color brightness, weight, or use
- Following procedures in a required sequence of steps
- Awkward, ungraceful large motor movement
- Difficulty with fine motor tasks
- Motoric restlessness
- Hyper- or hypoalertness (i.e., over- or underresponding to sensory stimuli)
- Difficulty bringing emotions into control
- Emotional responses that are out of proportion to the provocation, or persistent failure to exhibit expected proportionate emotions
- Uncontrolled talking, speaking out of turn, excitable communications, inappropriate voice volume
- Low tolerance for frustration
- Social interaction difficulties including failure to behave appropriately in specific contexts
- Failure to read the social cues of others

Because ADHD is often suspected in children who are outgoing, loquacious, and energetic and its symptoms are common to those of other potential problems, there are risks of misdiagnosis, which can have long-term deleterious consequences for the child. Any potential neurological disorder requires comprehensive professional evaluation for accurate diagnosis (Haber, 2000). A child with ADHD syndrome needs accurate assessment and helpful medical, psychological, and/or educational intervention. Assessment and diagnosis of ADHD require professional evaluation of the *presence* or *absence* and the *combination* of symptoms. ADHD symptoms can range from mild (almost unnoticeable) to severe (significantly interfering with daily functioning).

Treatment is determined by an evaluation team that includes the child's primary care physician, parents, licensed (certified) diagnostician, or psychologist and the child's classroom teacher. Medication may or may not be prescribed. Since ADHD represents a combination of symptoms that are found in different configurations and to greater or lesser degrees in different children, treatment programs are highly individualized. Some symptoms respond to medication, whereas others respond more readily to changes in the child's environment, such as developing a specialized and individualized education and behavioral guidance plan. All evaluations of children are legally private information and can only be shared with individuals who have a legitimate reason to have the information. Discussing or labeling the child with fellow workers, friends, other children, or parents is unethical and in some cases illegal. Professionals have a responsibility to protect the dignity of every child while assuring she or he receives timely and appropriately designed treatment and education services.

LANGUAGE DEVELOPMENT

Children at 6, 7, and 8 years of age demonstrate sophisticated language competencies. They have developed an awareness of the *phonemes* of their language and can pronounce them and hear them in the speech of others. They have acquired the knowledge that words stand for, or symbolize, things, and their knowledge of *semantics* has begun to facilitate the acquisition of words and word meanings. Using the *morphemes* of their language, they can construct and speak in meaningful phrases and sentences. Using their knowledge of *syntax*, they are able to combine words into meaningful and appropriately constructed sentences. Moreover, they have learned a great deal about the *pragmatics* of language, which is the knowledge of how language is used in different contexts—or, more simply stated, the rules of conversation. With increasing mastery of these elements of language, by the time children enter school, their language (both receptive and expressive) appears rather adultlike. However, studies indicate that there are some aspects of language development that children continue to acquire through the elementary school years, into adolescence, and throughout adult life.

Typically, figures of speech such as metaphors and similes are used to amplify meaning and are common in adult language. However, young children have difficulty with them. Their understanding of figures of speech is a gradual process that depends on cognitive development and the reduction of the constraints of literal thinking. For example, the expression "She eats like a bird" is no longer interpreted literally as a girl eating worms or pecking at food in a birdlike manner. Rather, this simile is understood as meaning that a person eats sparingly. Children understand figures of speech before they actually produce them (Green, 1985).

Understanding of figures of speech is accompanied by the awareness of puns and jokes. Children during the early school years demonstrate increasing awareness of puns and jokes because of their ability to think about the multiple meanings of words, the relationships among words, and the structure of narratives. They also become more proficient liars (should they be motivated to do so), both because they can now think about events simultaneously and because of their broader knowledge base. The use of white lies and of lying to prevent hurting another's feelings emerges as a result of children's increased social and cognitive awareness (Menyuk, 1988).

Another area of increased understanding of language is reflected in the comprehension and use of sarcasm. Adults rely on context and tone of voice when interpreting sarcasm. Young children often miss these cues. However, Ackerman (1982) found that first-graders were able to interpret sarcasm if the context was evident before the sarcastic remark was made. By third grade, children were increasingly better able to detect sarcastic remarks, using context and facial and intonation cues.

Metalinguistic awareness, or the ability to think about the meanings and forms of language, becomes more evident as children mature. The degree of metalinguistic awareness in first-graders appears to be a statistically significant predictor of reading comprehension in both third- and fifth-graders (Dreher & Zenge, 1990). Metalinguistic abilities do not develop suddenly (Menyuk, 1988). Rather, the awareness of various aspects of language develops at different times for different categories and relationships in language. However, the process by which metalinguistic awareness develops appears to have a definite pattern. First, children incorporate new structures on an unconscious level. Then they develop the ability to recognize appropriate or inappropriate uses of the structure. Finally, children become able to talk about the structures of language (deVilliers & deVilliers, 1992).

The understanding of pronominal references appears to increase with age. By second grade, children use pronouns more frequently than they did when they were younger. In addition, children during the primary grades begin to talk more about topics and ideas that are not in their immediate context.

Development of Syntax

Development of syntax continues through the primary-grade years. One grammatical development that occurs during this period is the ability to understand infinitive phrases. At age 5, children do not relate the grammatical subject with the agent role. For example, when they are presented with a blindfolded doll and asked, "Is the doll easy or hard to see," their response is "Hard to see." By age ten, the response changes to "Easy to see" (Chomsky, 1969). Understanding the passive voice ("The ball was hit by Joe" rather than "Joe hit the ball") also takes place over an extended period of time and is not achieved until the end of the elementary school years. Virtually all morphological indicators of plurals, possessives, and past tense are acquired between ages six and eight.

Vocabulary Development

Vocabulary development continues to expand, spurred onward by the child's cumulative background of experiences and social interactions, more sophisticated cognitive processes, and formal instruction. As vocabulary increases, children begin to use words in more conventional and accurate ways. Overextensions begin to disappear, and new words are used to describe existing and

Opportunities for children to talk with one another during their activities promote communicative competence.

new concepts. For example, a child might no longer just use the word *doggie*, but might talk about *poodles, German shepherds, mutts,* and *puppies,* indicating increased cognitive awareness of the various categorical labels under the general class *dogs.*

Communicative Competence

Children at ages 6, 7, and 8 are subject to an increasing number of experiences in new environments and with diverse groups of people. Upon entering first grade, children learn not only about their own teacher and classroom, but also about other teachers and classrooms; about expected behaviors in the lunchroom, in the library, and on the playground; and about special classes such as art, physical education, and music. In addition, many school-age children visit friends' homes, join sports and civics organizations such as Brownies and Cub Scouts, take lessons, and participate in faith-based activities. These experiences and interactions add to the child's repertoire of scripts, or behaviors and language appropriate to each context.

Opportunities to interact with others in various contexts help children gain knowledge of and competence in the conventions of conversational language, such as focused and respectful listening, turn taking, and other verbal courtesies. The conversational technique of **shading** is used to change the topic of a conversation. Shading requires a level of tact and finesse generally uncommon in young children, but it is beginning to appear during the 6 -to 8-year age period.

Primary-grade children also demonstrate an increasing awareness of the intent of many utterances and take cues from inflections. A second-grader knows that when mother says, "This room is a disaster area," the child had better get the room cleaned up right away. In addition, children ages 6, 7, and 8 indicate an increasing awareness of **registers**, or the speech variations needed in different social situations.

shading: gradually changing the topic of conversation

registers: variations in the style of speech according to the particular social setting

LITERACY DEVELOPMENT

By the time children enter first grade, they have had many and varied experiences with print in their preschool, kindergarten, and child care settings and in their homes. Obviously, there are wide variations in the quantity and quality of these experiences among children and in the child's responses and developmental outcomes. Nevertheless, by age 6, most children have mastered most of the concepts and skills listed in Table 13.1.

Literacy Learning in the Primary Grades: Reading

During the primary grades, children are introduced more formally to reading, writing, and spelling through both direct instruction and hands-on, concrete experiences. In first grade, children begin to read orally; by the end of first grade, they do so with some fluency; use letter–sound correspondence, word parts, and context cues to identify new words; identify an increasing number of sight words; write coherent stories on topics that are of particular interest to them; include more letters (sounds) in their private spellings; and learn about punctuation and capitalization.

sight words:
words in print that young children recognize immediately

During second grade, children begin to apply more sophisticated learning strategies (e.g., asking questions, rereading, observing others) to comprehend the written word. They use phonemic strategies more efficiently to identify unfamiliar words, can rely on an ever-increasing number of familiar **sight words**, begin to write with a specific audience in mind, demonstrate more conventional spelling in both their private and public writing, use punctuation and capitalization more often and more accurately, and can use reading for both enjoyment and to obtain information about specific topics.

By third grade, children who have become fairly fluent readers tend to enjoy reading and seek opportunities to do so. Their vocabularies, now quite large, facilitate greater comprehension. They can now use many different strategies for deriving meaning from text, can use phonics cues quite readily (if not automatically) to read unfamiliar words, and use writing in many different contexts: to correspond with others, write reports, make lists, create a story or poem, and so on.

These developments follow a rather predictable flow from book awareness and exploration experiences in infancy to relatively fluent reading by third and fourth grade. They cannot be hurried, for learning to read is one of the most challenging perceptual and cognitive tasks of early childhood. Learning to competently read, write, and spell requires a rich background of literacy-related experiences.

Literacy Instruction in the Primary Grades: Reading.   Because literacy is so important to all other school learning, our society expects its schools to provide successful reading instruction. When and how formal instruction should begin and what types of instructional strategies are thought to be the most successful are issues on which there are wide disagreements among scholars and professionals.

Literacy development is enhanced through activities that engage talking, writing, and reading.

Generally the debates fall within two camps: Those who believe that children learn best when introduced first to parts and then to wholes, and those who believe that children learn best when introduced first to wholes and then to parts. Differences in instructional strategies look something like this:

Part-to-Whole Approach	Whole-to-Part Approach
Learn letters' names, sounds	Learn familiar words in a context of specific, meaningful experiences
Use letter sounds to sound out an unfamiliar word	Identify new words using context cues
Segment words and sentences into parts	Create labels, phrases, and sentences using familiar words in writing
Use basal readers with decodable words	Use familiar children's books and literature
Encourage conventional spelling through preselected word lists and conventional spelling rules	Accept phonemic spelling as part of a learning-to-spell continuum
Use worksheets and pencil-and-paper tasks	Use first-hand experiences and concrete materials

In efforts to bring empirical data to guide the understanding of how (and when) children most successfully come into literacy and to find common points of agreement among opposing views, contemporary researchers have begun to examine research from decades of studies from many different disciplines. Recent collections of reviews of research have attempted to be helpful.

A summary of research on reading instruction published in 1990 found that there was no definitely superior method for teaching reading. Neither a whole-word approach nor a **phonics**-based (sound–letter correspondence) approach was found to be better than the other (Adams, 1990). The researcher commented,

phonics:
the sound–symbol relationship of a language system

> Much of the controversy in beginning reading centers on phonics. But like beauty, what people mean by phonics is often in the eye of the beholder. To some, phonics is irrelevant. To others, it is essential. To some, phonics instruction is a mind-numbing collection of worksheets that are assigned to keep students busy and that seem to be divorced from any real practice in reading. To others, phonics instruction is a teacher working with a group of children to initiate them directly into written language by revealing its code. Phonics can be all of these things, and even in instructional programs that claim not to teach phonics, phonics instruction can take place. It may be possible to teach reading without paying some attention to the forms of written words. On the other hand, it is possible, but not desirable, to teach only phonics and ignore the meaning of written words. (Adams, 1990, p. iii)

A full summary of the findings of this review is beyond the scope of this text, but following are some examples of Adams's (1990) review of research findings:

- Basic familiarity with letters and letter names is a strong predictor of reading success.
- Awareness that spoken language is composed of phonemes is also a predictor of success in learning to read.
- A child's general awareness of the nature and functions of print is a strong index of readiness to learn to read.

- The single most important activity for building the knowledge and skills required for learning to read appears to be reading aloud to children regularly and interactively.
- Language experience activities and the use of big books are excellent means of establishing print awareness, though they appear to be less useful as primary vehicles for reading instruction.
- Learning names of letters precedes learning about their shapes, which is then followed by learning letter sounds.
- The concept of *word* is a difficult one for young children and is learned through direct exposure to print.
- Activities that are designed to help young children develop awareness of words, syllables, and phonemes significantly increase their later success in learning to read and write.
- Approaches in which systematic code instruction is included along with reading for meaning result in superior reading achievement.
- Texts that contain decodable words (words that can be sounded out phonetically) promote independent word recognition.
- Independent writing activities are a means of developing children's appreciation of the nature of text and its comprehension.
- Children need many opportunities and encouragement to practice reading.

A more recent effort came with the convening of a representative committee of professionals in child development, early childhood education, elementary education, reading, psychology, and other related fields to examine the prevention of reading difficulties. The report of this committee was published by the National Academy of Sciences, which had been commissioned by the U.S. Department of Education and the U.S. Department of Health and Human Services to study the issue. The report was published under the title *Preventing Reading Difficulties in Young Children* (Snow, Burns, & Griffin, 1998). This document took a very strong (though not absolute) position in favor of part-to-whole instruction, with heavy emphasis beginning in kindergarten on a phonics-based, direct instruction approach:

> Beginning readers need explicit instruction and practice that lead to an appreciation that spoken words are made up of smaller units of sounds, familiarity with spelling–sound correspondences and common spelling conventions and their use in identifying printed words, "sight" recognition of frequent words, and independent reading, including reading aloud. Fluency should be promoted through practice with a wide variety of well-written and engaging texts at the child's own comfortable reading level. (Snow et al., 1998, p. 7)

The report emphasized the importance of the understanding of how sounds are represented alphabetically and encouraged more direct instruction than is commonly viewed as appropriate for young children. A few of their recommendations include practices that early childhood professionals have traditionally used, though many are at odds with widely held views of early childhood development and learning. Again, a review of all of the recommendations of this report is beyond the scope of this text. However, some of their recommendations are explicit instruction and practice that lead to phonemic awareness and letter–sound correspondence, learning to sound out words, the use of meaningful texts, the recognition and use of phonemic spelling as a beginning writing process, focused instruction on conventional spelling, curricula that build rich linguistic and conceptual knowledge, direct instruction, and providing early intervention and support for children who show signs of having difficulties acquiring early language and literacy skills.

Soon after the publication of the National Research Council's report, the National Association for the Education of Young Children (NAEYC) and the International Reading Association (IRA) published a joint statement, *Learning to Read and Write: Developmentally Appropriate Practices for Young Children* (Neuman, Copple, & Bredekamp, 1999). The authors wrote,

> Based on a thorough review of the research, this document reflects the commitment of two major professional organizations to the goal of helping children learn to read well enough by the end of third grade so that they can read to learn in all curriculum areas. IRA and NAEYC are committed not only to helping young children learn to read and write but also to fostering and sustaining their interest and disposition to read and write for their own enjoyment, information, and communication. (Neuman et al., 1999, p. 3)

While asserting that it is essential to teach children to read and write competently, the authors of this statement expressed concern about inappropriate practices: "Recognizing the early beginnings of literacy acquisition too often has resulted in use of inappropriate teaching practices suited to older children or adults perhaps but ineffective with children in preschool, kindergarten and the early grades" (Neuman et al., 1999, p. 5). Further, this statement advised, "The roots of phonemic awareness, which is related to later reading success, are found in traditional rhyming, skipping, and word games" (p. 9); and, "In the primary grades, approaches that favor some type of systematic code instruction along with meaningful connected reading promote children's superior progress in reading" (p. 12).

The NAEYC/IRA position statement has been embedded in a book that provides guidance for teachers of young children through grade three (see Further Readings at the end of this chapter). The practices are in line with the descriptions of developmentally appropriate practices discussed in earlier chapters. Instruction for literacy development is best offered in the context of these well-researched practices, keeping all developmental domains in perspective (a whole-child perspective), keeping in mind what can reasonably be expected of children at each age, and recognizing that while children benefit from both teacher-directed instruction and self-selected activities, there is an art to knowing when to do which. Teachers who are well grounded in knowledge of child growth and development soon learn the unique characteristics and needs of individual children and find that important goodness of fit between instructional strategies and the learner.

Often misinterpreted, a holistic approach to instructional strategies for young children can and does include direct instruction on specific concepts while providing for a spectrum of experiences that promote literacy. The holistic perspective on literacy development allows for the promotion of growth and development in other developmental domains. The following vignette demonstrates the holistic nature of literacy development:

Six-year-old Angela was playing with several neighborhood children in her garage. One of the children discovered a tarantula crawling across the cement floor. The children discussed what they should do and whether tarantulas were really dangerous. Finally, one of the children suggested killing the tarantula with bug spray. The tarantula was sprayed and sprayed with insecticide. Finally, it died. The children used a garden tool to turn the tarantula over and then examined it closely. Next, they scooped it up, put it in a plastic container, and went on a tour of the neighborhood, showing the tarantula to other children. The tarantula episode was the main topic at the family dinner table that evening.

The next day, Angela went to her classroom. She painted a picture and then dictated the story of the tarantula to one of the teachers in her classroom (see Figure 16.1). The spelling of *tarantula* was checked by using the dictionary. Angela's picture and story (consisting of 23 words) were hung on the classroom wall at the children's eye level. One of the teachers found some books about tarantulas to read to interested children. They discovered, among other things, that tarantulas are really not all that dangerous. Several days later, Angela and a teacher were looking at her picture and story and talking about her experience with the tarantula. The teacher asked Angela whether she could find the word *tarantula*. Without any hesitation and jumping in with pride, Joanie, a classmate, pointed accurately to the word.

FIGURE 16.1

Long words with a specific meaning, such as *tarantula*, are easier for young children to identify than shorter words without a simple meaning, such as *the* and *what*.

We had a big tarantula
We killed it by bug-spray
We had a black wasp in our house.
We were scared to death.

This vignette demonstrates the powerful relationships among thought, experience, language, and literacy. Angela had a very meaningful experience. It was talked and read about with others in several contexts: in the neighborhood, at the family dinner table, and at school. The experience was shared symbolically through Angela's painting and through oral language. It was translated into written language, which was read by Angela, her teacher, and other children. The interaction among thought, oral language, and written language in this vignette demonstrates how the wholeness of language can promote the development of literacy. Angela knew where the long word *tarantula* was located among 23 other words, as did a classmate with whom she shared her story.

Holistic approaches to language and literacy development are characterized by the following:

- Systematic planning around the assessed capabilities, prior experiences, cultural backgrounds, and special interests and needs of individual children
- The integration of language and literacy experiences in all aspects of the curriculum and daily routines
- The use of firsthand experiences to initiate learning opportunities
- The use of concrete materials to enhance concept development
- The use of children's literature to heighten interest and engage the learner
- The use of immediately available print in the learner's surroundings
- Social interaction that engages children in language, metalanguage, and broadened perspectives
- Ongoing teacher/student interactions that provide assessment, scaffolding, immediate feedback, clarification of concepts and processes, and opportunities to encourage metacognitive and metalanguage thinking
- Both structured and spontaneous literacy activities
- Encouragement of writing and reading for meaning
- Contextualized skill lessons (phonics, word order, word spacing, letter formations, spelling, and so on)

Relationship between Reading and Writing

As the vignette about Angela and the tarantula indicates, reading and writing appear to be interrelated and to facilitate the development of literacy. Children learn to read by reading what they write and by reading print that is important to them. They learn to write if they believe that they have thoughts and messages that are important enough to be shared with others in a written context (Dyson, 1993, 1997).

Both Jeremy's and Angela's first-grade teachers see the teaching of reading and writing as inseparable. They do not relegate reading and writing to separate time slots during the day; rather, both reading and writing are taught throughout the day in many contexts and in interrelated ways. Both teachers continue many of the literacy experiences that Angela and Jeremy encountered in their preprimary classrooms.

Jeremy's and Angela's primary-grade classrooms are organized to promote interaction with materials and with other children. Abundant print materials are located throughout the classroom and in learning centers. These materials include calendars, several kinds of charts (helper charts, charts with pen pal names, charts written by the children with spelling strategies, strategies for figuring out words, strategies listing the steps in the writing process, and charts of science experiment results), recipes for applesauce and pancakes, the Pledge of Allegiance, the weekly schedule, a story about the author of the week, children's artwork and written reports, learning center signs describing the learning that takes place in the center, books, and magazines. Paper and writing tools are located in each center. The class library is stocked with a wide variety of books: class-made books, individually made books, big books, and many patterned or predictable books, information books, first dictionaries, and a child's thesaurus. There are various centers in the classrooms: art, publishing/writing, computer, math, science, listening, and a display area. There are animals and plants to observe and to draw and write about. Both teachers attractively display children's writing on bulletin boards. Desks are clustered in groups of four to promote interaction, or children may work around small tables strategically placed near needed materials. Children are encouraged to talk as they engage in their learning activities. Recognizing that learning to read requires many instructional strategies, selected basal readers and other direct instruction strategies are used when they are appropriate or particularly helpful to individual students.

Literacy Instruction in the Primary Grades: Writing

The ability to write varies greatly among the children in Ms. Wood's class. The children want to write and have others read their writing. Mailboxes, pen pals, and message boards facilitate this communication process. Through writing that is meaningful to the children, they gradually learn about the forms of writing, including spelling and punctuation. They discover that the spelling of some words makes sense, but a number of words are spelled in ways that do not. Jeremy says that *egg* should have an *a* in it, not an *e*. First-graders struggle with the silent *e* and try to understand how the same letter can be used for different sounds, such as the *g* in *giant* and the *g* in *gate*.

By the end of the first-grade year, the children in Ms. Wood's room have learned much about writing. The environment has been supportive, meaningful, and rich with print experiences. Jeremy's story about dinosaurs reveals that he is confident in himself as a writer (see Figure 16.2). He organizes and presents his thoughts in a logical manner. He demonstrates no hesitancy in spelling long dinosaur names. He indicates that he has learned much about handwriting, spacing, and punctuation, and he gives evidence of moving into conventional spelling.

Both Jeremy's and Angela's first-grade teachers know that if children in their classes are to become truly literate, comprehension or understanding of the text is essential. Fields and Spangler (2000) suggested that literacy development is "a process in which reading involves *interacting* with the thoughts someone else has expressed in writing, in which writing is perceived as recording one's own thoughts, and in which thinking is basic" (p. 133). Reading aloud both high-quality fiction and nonfiction books encourages the development of critical thinking and problem solving, as well as flexibility in reading for young children (Doiron, 1994).

As children continue to develop their reading abilities in second and third grades, it is important to continue to help them to use various strategies to identify unfamiliar words (sounding out, context cues) while keeping the primary focus on the meaning of print. Third grade is usually the year in which children are expected

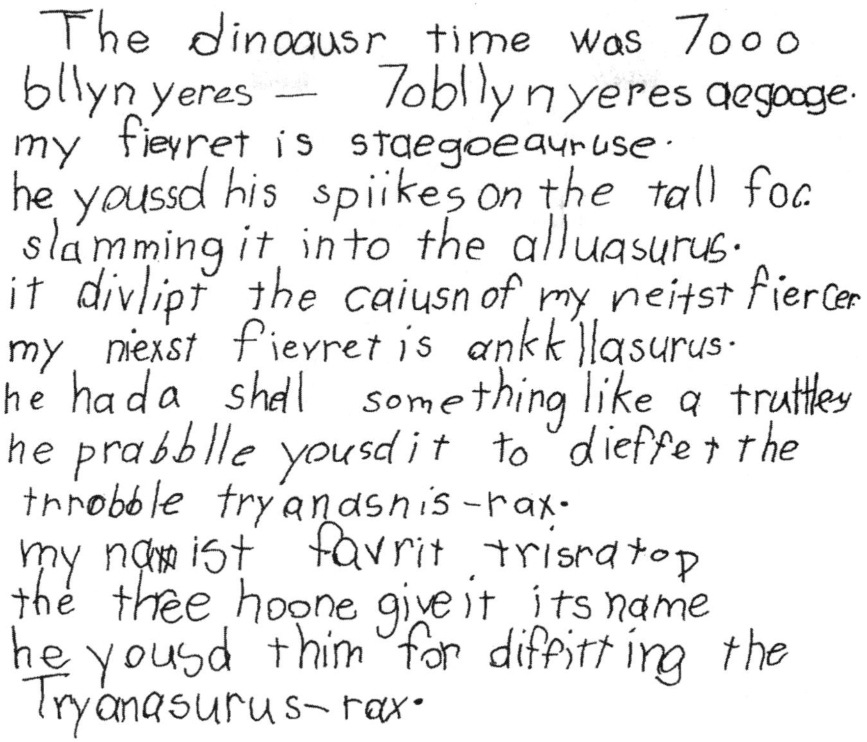

The dinoausr time was 7000
bllyn yeres — 7obllyn yeres aegooge.
my fievret is staegoeauruse.
he youssd his spiikes on the tall foc
slamming it into the alluasurus.
it divlipt the caiusn of my neitst fiercer
my niexst fievret is ankk llasurus.
he hada shdl something like a truttley
he prabblle yousd it to dieffet the
throbble tryanasnis-rax.
my nawist favrit trisratop
the three hoone give it its name
he yousd thim for diffitting the
Tryanasurus-rax.

FIGURE 16.2

Jeremy's story about
dinoausrs, written in
first grade, reveals that
he is most confident in
himself as a writer.

to deal with more content knowledge in the areas of science, health, and social studies. Specific textbooks are often introduced at this grade level, and children are expected to read for meaning and be accountable for the material through tests. If literacy experiences during the first and second grades have facilitated the development of decoding skills in ways that enhance the child's desire to read and helped children to learn that there is meaning in print, children will have the critical mindset that print has a message for them. This concept will help them as they continue to learn throughout their school years. On the other hand, if young children view reading as skill/drill activity that is focused primarily on isolated performance activity, comprehending content material and reading independently may be a problem as they progress through the elementary school grades.

Literacy Learning in the Primary Grades: Writing

Ms. Wood continues many of the writing and print experiences of Jeremy's kindergarten in her first-grade classroom. She models writing for the children and facilitates purposeful opportunities for them to write in a variety of situations, from thank-you notes to stories to lists of needed classroom supplies. Ms. Wood allows children to freely explore their writing. She provides ample time for the rehearsal stage of writing, in which the children can draw or talk about their writing. This talking and drawing help to organize children's thoughts so that they can write.

Ms. Wood also continues to read to the children. Hearing the written language helps children to learn about writing. They learn how to write fairy tales, dialogue, narratives, and other forms of literature. Ms. Wood also carefully observes children and acts as an instructor, facilitator, and scaffolder to move them into new awareness of the processes of reading and writing.

Early in the school year, the PTA at Jeremy's school invites a children's book author to visit for a day. Through this experience, children learn about the editing process and what it means to be an author. Approximately once a month, Jeremy's class publishes a class book. Ms. Wood serves as the editor and helps the children with revisions. Suggested revisions are made in pencil, and then the children recopy their stories for the published book. The final edition is read to other classes and is then placed in the school library for a period of time before becoming part of the classroom library. This experience introduces Jeremy and the other first-grade children to the editing process. Ms. Wood does little correcting of children's expressive and creative writing until (and unless) she sees a need to teach the conventional spelling of a word, as perhaps in some editing activities when children are learning the difference between their private and public writing. At this point she principally wants the children to feel competent about their writing, and she knows that invented spellings, reversals, inattention to spacing, and lack of punctuation are prevalent and developmentally appropriate behaviors at age 6. She uses her assessments of these behaviors to plan meaningful instructional strategies for individual children. Figure 16.3 illustrates a typical first-grader's attempt at writing.

Ms. Wood shares her strategies for helping children grow into conventional spellers and writers at parent orientation sessions and conferences. Showing examples (such as the one illustrated in Figures 16.3 and 16.4) of how writing develops throughout the first-grade year also enables parents to see that children will

FIGURE 16.3

A six-year-old wrote this letter to his grandparents during holiday time.

FIGURE 16.4
"The Wndrfl Fgin
A dat burds"

Children ages 6 to 8
are still developing
their physiological
ability to hear and
reproduce sounds.

make progress in their written language without those traditional red corrections. If parents want further information, Ms. Wood willingly shares articles from professional journals and books about the development of young children's writing. She also helps parents to understand that they can help their children to write at home by providing writing materials, taking advantage of opportunities to write, and being supportive of children's efforts to write at home.

Given supportive environments, children in the primary years can develop positive attitudes about writing and spelling as well as knowledge about the functions of writing. These experiences facilitate competence in reading.

If primary-grade teachers have students who do not seem to be comprehending or thinking about what they are reading, they may want to do an analysis of children's concepts about reading (Strommen & Mates, 1997). If the results indicate that these children have distorted concepts about the reading act and limited strategies for reading, teachers need to help them to learn that (1) reading is getting meaning from print; (2) good readers sometimes read quickly and sometimes read slowly, depending on the purpose for reading; and (3) good readers make mistakes in reading, but they can use a number of strategies to help them identify and correct their mistakes.

FACTORS INFLUENCING COGNITIVE, LANGUAGE, AND LITERACY DEVELOPMENT IN CHILDREN AGES SIX THROUGH EIGHT

Neurological Development

From the literature on how the brain becomes neurologically "wired" during the early years, we have learned that the brain functions most efficiently in relatively stress-free environments and in situations in which the learner is in a relaxed–alert state of mind (as opposed to fearful, anxious, or relaxed–bored, for example).

downshifting:
a psychophysiological response to perceived threat that is accompanied by a sense of helplessness or lack of self-efficacy, which affects the brain's ability to function at optimal levels

Relaxed alertness is characterized by a sense of low threat and high challenge. When learning events become overwhelming (as when expectations repeatedly exceed the learner's capabilities) or monotonous and boring, or the classroom social and emotional tone creates a psychologically unsafe environment, a phenomenon known as perceptual narrowing occurs. This perceptual narrowing has been aptly referred to as **downshifting** (Hart, 1983). As described by Caine and Caine (1997), downshifting is a psychophysiological response that affects the brain's ability to function at high levels of engagement and thwarts creative thinking and problem solving. It is provoked by perceived threat and fatigue. In downshifting, the individual's responses are limited, and he or she is less able to consider all aspects of a situation. The learner is less able to engage in complex intellectual tasks, particularly those requiring creativity and the ability to engage in open-ended thinking and questioning. Downshifting appears to affect higher-order cognitive functions of the brain. In the developing brain, situations that persistently provoke downshifting interfere with optimal brain growth and neurological development. Psychologically unsafe environments include threat of physical harm, failure, embarrassment, infringement on privacy, ridicule, retribution, and other stressors.

Nutrition, Health, and Well-Being

A theme that runs throughout this text is the importance of nutrition, health, exercise, and psychological well-being. As children get older, they are confronted with larger circles of influence and greater expectations for appropriate behaviors and achievement. As the school day can be quite long, particularly for children who attend before- and after-school programs and those engaged in extracurricular activities (sometimes more structured activities than are either helpful or healthy), the role of proper nutrition, rest, and exercise routines is quite important. The importance of breakfast in preparing the body for a day of work and learning has long been noted. A report in the *American Academy of Pediatric News* (Sears, 1998) revealed that because the biochemical messengers known as neurotransmitters help the brain to make the right connections and because the food we eat influences how neurotransmitters operate, the more balanced a person's breakfast is, the more balanced the brain's neurotransmitters function. The article lists a number of benefits of breakfast that have been determined through research. Some of the benefits are as follows (Sears, 1998, p. 30):

> Breakfast eaters are likely to make higher grades, pay closer attention, participate more in class discussions, and are able to manage more complex academic problems.
>
> Breakfast skippers are more likely to be inattentive, sluggish and make lower grades.
>
> Studies on the effects of skipping breakfast show variable results. It seems some children (such as children with attention deficit disorder or learning difficulties) are more vulnerable to the effects of missing breakfast than others.
>
> Children eating high calcium food for breakfast (e.g., yogurt and milk) show enhanced behavior and learning.
>
> Morning stress increases the levels of stress hormones in the bloodstream, which can affect behavior and learning in two ways. First, stress hormones can bother the brain. Second, stress hormones, such as cortisol, increase carbohydrate craving throughout the day, which may affect behavior and learning in children whose blood sugar levels are sensitive to fluctuations. Parents are advised to send their children off to school with a calm attitude.

Highly publicized findings of increasing obesity rates among the nation's school-age children point out the responsibilities of parents, caregivers, and educators to assure that daily schedules allocate time for physical activity. Weight control is only one reason for increasing children's opportunities for physical activity. It is easy to give classroom academic activities a high priority. However, limited attention to physiological needs for vigorous and active play, movement, and physical education negates the perceived advantages of more time on subject matter tasks. Indeed, exercise contributes to the learning process by relaxing mind and body; relieving stress; bathing the brain and its neurological structures in nature's mood- and attention-enhancing hormones; increasing physical strength, endurance, and agility; coordinating large and small motor controls; increasing cardiovascular efficiency; and improving the body's rest, thirst, and hunger rhythms.

The Nature of Prior Experiences

Studies have revealed that the effects of early child care experiences linger into the elementary school years. Children who attended child care centers with high-quality classroom practices were shown to have better language and math skills through the second grade than children who attended lower-quality programs. Quite compelling is the fact that children who had closer relationships with their child care teachers had fewer problem behaviors and better thinking skills in school. Also, it appears that warm teacher–child relationships influence children's language and math skills (Peisner-Feinberg et al., 1999). Clearly, the types of nonparental experiences that children have with other adults influence not only their psychosocial development, but their cognitive, language, and literacy development as well, and these relationships appear to have long-lasting implications.

The Nature of Instructional Strategies and Performance Expectations

As the discussions of literacy development and strategies for teaching reading and writing reveal, instructional strategies cannot be framed around a one-size-fits-all paradigm. The uniqueness of development in each child reflects multiple influences, including family and cultural backgrounds, biologically determined individual rates of growth and development, individual cognitive styles and strengths, language diversity, differences in types and quality of out-of-home child care and preschool experiences, the nature of prekindergarten and kindergarten experiences, and many, many others. The mistake that pedagogues often make is attempting to apply one teaching/learning model to all children in a particular grade or group. The decision to teach from a part-to-whole perspective, a whole-to-part perspective, or some weighted combination of the two perspectives can be based only on intimate knowledge of how best an individual learner can respond.

Because in today's society, considerable attention is directed toward the "outcomes" of children's education, schools are being required to meet stated goals and standards for student achievement and to demonstrate this achievement through accountability measures that include subjecting children to a variety of tests and measurements. The more rigorous and public the accountability measures are for a school or a school district, the less likely it is that child performance expectations will be individualized and developmentally appropriate.

Optimal learning and positive behaviors are promoted when the learner experiences the following:

- A mutually respecting, warm, and supportive relationship with teachers
- A sense of physical and psychological protection and well-being
- Recognition of his or her individuality and strengths
- Expectations that are challenging and hold the learner responsible while providing the supports necessary to accomplish assigned tasks
- Relationships that instill a sense of self-respect, self-efficacy, and shared respect for others
- A sense of belonging in this time and place with other members of the learning community

Out-of-School Time

Children ages 6, 7, and 8 years spend the larger portion of each day in school. Their out-of-school time commitments and activities either contribute to or detract from their overall health and well-being and their learning. They may attend before- and/or after-school child care programs, participate in supervised extracurricular activities, and return home to a parent or other caregiver. Some young elementary school-age children are cared for at home by an older sibling or neighbor, whereas others are in self-care at home until parents return from work or other out-of-home activities. Regardless of where the child spends time when school is out, the need for protection, supervision, and quality experiences remains.

Before- and After-School Child Care

Studies have found that children ages 5 to 9 years who have experienced quality after-school child care exhibit more positive behaviors with peers and adults, have fewer emotional and behavioral problems, develop better work habits, and perform better in school than do children in less formal child care settings, self-care, or baby-sitting situations (Vandell & Shumow, 1999). Quality before- and after-school programs provide children safe, supervised settings with opportunities to play and interact with other children and nurturing caregivers. Well-conceptualized school-age child care provides for "down time" that includes unstructured blocks of time for children to rest and renew, and private spaces where a child can distance herself or himself from the group for brief periods of time. This is necessary both from a psychological perspective and a physiological one, not unlike the adult's need for a "coffee break." Nutritious snacks (or meals) and beverages should be available, as should opportunities for vigorous physical activity (music and movement, dance, games, and outdoor play and sports). There should be time for homework and an undisturbed place for reading and study. Tutoring and special activities should be available that tap individual interests such as dance or singing; soccer, basketball, T-ball, or other sport; art; gardening; rock collecting; and singing. Props should be available for pretend play. Considering the number of hours of out-of-home time many children experience, such programs can contribute significantly to child and family well-being. The issue for consumers is the great need in contemporary society for well-designed and well-regulated school-age child care programs that are affordable and accessible to the increasing numbers of families who need them. Unfortunately, many programs fall short of these qualities. Parents need to be informed consumers who choose wisely, and who diligently monitor their children's daily care and experiences in school-age child care.

Screen Time

Both in-school and out-of-school time for most children includes time spent working at a computer, watching television or video programs, and, for some, accessing the Internet. These activities present both opportunities and challenges for children and families.

Television.   Over the last three decades, there has been extensive research on the effects of television on the minds and behaviors of growing children. From this large body of research, parents and educators can make informed decisions about how the medium can be used in ways that serve the best interest of children. Some scholars propose that children need to develop **television literacy**, or the understanding of the symbolic ways in which television conveys information, and that doing so will help children to develop critical viewing skills. While this understanding is dependent on the active participation of an adult, the nature of television programs and advertising makes it a worthwhile endeavor (Grossman et al., 1997; Levin, 2003).

television literacy: understanding the specialized symbolic codes conveyed through the medium of television

To become television literate, young children need to be able to make distinctions between reality and fantasy and between fact, opinion, and hyperbole. Research by Dorr (1983) indicates that 7- and 8-year-old children still confuse the performers in a television program and their real-life relationships and behaviors. In addition, studies have demonstrated that young children do not grasp many television production techniques before age 8. When coached, young children gradually learn to understand techniques such as fades (Anderson & Smith, 1984) and instant replays (Rice, Huston, & Wright, 1986). However, fast-paced programs that lack clearly defined continuity between scenes are still not understood by 9- and 10-year-olds (Wright et al., 1984). Children need interaction with adults who can clarify and mediate television's messages to help them understand and evaluate television programs and media techniques (Levin, 2003).

Television broadens children's knowledge base. However, there is no clear consensus about the types of formats that promote learning. Early research on such programs as *Sesame Street* appeared to confirm that children do learn from a fast-paced format (Ball & Bogatz, 1972). However, Singer and Singer (1979) found that programs with a slower pace allow children time to reflect. Thus, programs with the pace of *Mister Rogers' Neighborhood,* for example, may be more effective in stimulating thinking in young children than the faster-paced formats. There may not be one type of television programming that is best for all children (Lesser, 1979). Rather, exposure to a variety of types of programming enriches children's experiences and serves their individual interests and learning styles.

When parents or other adults coview and discuss programs with children, learning is facilitated, and the children's television literacy is enhanced. Through coviewing practices, children develop more discerning tastes regarding what they choose to watch. More learning occurs in the company of adults who share the television experience with the child than when adults are not present and no discussion takes place (Abelman, 1984; Anderson & Collins, 1988; Houston et al., 1992).

Too much television viewing takes time away from other activities that promote learning and creativity. Extensive television viewing can also deny children the opportunity to engage in reading, play, conversation, and creative endeavors that promote thinking, concentration, and an extended attention span. Further, psychologists are finding that the violence and obscenities to which young children are often exposed through television engender fear and aggressive behaviors and, over time, desensitize them to aggressive and violent acts, rendering them incapable of judging the appropriateness and inappropriateness of these behaviors (Eron, 1992). The news frequently attests to this desensitization through stories of children who have committed acts of violence similar to what they have viewed on television. Indeed, studies of television programs such as *The Mighty Morphin Power Rangers* and others have demonstrated that after viewing just one episode, children, especially boys, committed aggressive acts seven times more often than did children in the control group of the study, typically using karate chops and flying kicks against their peers (Boyatzis, 1997). This was viewed as obvious imitation of the characters in the television program. (We are reminded here of Bandura's social cognitive theory, in which children learn through imitation.) While not all children who watch violent programming on television exhibit violent behaviors, many do. These programs affect different children in different ways. However, decades of research on this topic have demonstrated unequivocally that watching violent television programs increases the likelihood that children will behave in more aggressive ways (Boyatzis, 1997).

Parents and teachers can help children to become TV literate by employing a number of strategies:

- Place children on a reduced TV diet, allowing them to watch a favorite unfavorable show only once or twice a week but with assignments such as the following:
  a. Count the number of violent acts against another person during a specified number of minutes (e.g., 10 minutes).
  b. Describe what the "good" characters did when violence occurred.
  c. Imagine a character who could prevent or settle conflicts through nonviolent means.
- Make a deal with children that if allowed to watch a show with violence, they will not imitate any of its violent behaviors.
- Watch and discuss the program with the children, pointing out its unrealistic and inappropriate features that do not (or should never) occur in real-life situations.
- Have children imagine how the story might be changed to have a different, more positive outcome (Boyatzis, 1997; Levine, 1994).
- Discuss how advertisers use television to sell products to their viewers. Have children count the number of times a program is interrupted to sell a product.
- Talk about the difference between fact, opinion, and hyperbole. Point out these elements when coviewing a program with children.

Violence is not the only aspect of television that influences the psychosocial and cognitive development of children. In addition, watching television consumes time, interfering with physical activity, exercise, sleep, homework, and other worthwhile activities; it contributes to snacking, preferences for advertised foods that are often less nutritious than desirable, and obesity; it exposes children to adult behaviors such as sex and abrasive and obscene language, and questionable role models; and it entices them with tantalizing commercials for toys, clothes, foods, drinks, sporting gear, and other items pitched to children.

Television is not all bad, however; high-quality, nonviolent children's shows can have positive effects on their psychosocial and cognitive development. Television can promote young children's cognitive, language, and literacy development if (1) programming is appropriate to young children's age and cognitive development, (2) adults are involved in the viewing process and discuss the program with children, and (3) children have opportunities to engage in other, more socially interactive and physically challenging activities that promote cognitive, language, and literacy development.

Computers and Other Media.   The explosion of computer technologies, innumerable types of software, digital technologies, the expanding Internet, and other technologies are dramatically transforming our personal lives and education. All types of activities can take place on one's personal computer, and computers in the classroom are opening its curriculums to wider and wider vistas.

Assistive technologies facilitate full participation of children with special needs

Today's children are growing up in a technological world in which the possibilities are astounding. Children are exposed to computer technology every place they go: home, school, child care programs, recreational programs, shopping malls, toy stores, sporting events, libraries, and museums. Electronic toys and video games abound. Today's child is at ease with CDs, VCRs, DVDs, floppy discs, computer keyboards, and computer mice and have experienced software that teaches them to draw, write, read, compute, research and do homework, communicate with friends and relatives through e-mail, and play all manner of games.

Computer experiences in the classroom can be highly sociable, promoting language and interaction with both adults and other children. Teachers appear to facilitate this interaction by encouraging group participation rather than individual activity and through their availability to children. In addition, teachers can encourage children to use one another as resources for learning to use the computer and software. Knowledge of developmentally appropriate software programs can help teachers to determine how much independence children can assume and when the teacher's assistance is needed.

Computer experiences also seem to facilitate divergent and creative thinking. Software is now available that can be used to interface with differences in interests and intelligences. Computer experiences allow young children to make all manner of discoveries about an almost unlimited number of topics. Software exists to teach and tutor in school skills and school subjects, and programs exist to assist in learning English and other languages as a second language. Electronic portfolios can document children's learning and achievements.

Computers can help children to develop reading, writing, spelling, and mathematics skills. Word processing can assist children in more in-depth composing by freeing them from the small motor task of handwriting. The process of revision is also facilitated, since word processing makes it easier for children to edit their compositions (Hoot & Silvern, 1989).

Yet computers, like television, offer both promise and peril. Educators are confronted with scores of catalogs of computer software and classroom computer-based technologies. The selection process can be overwhelming. Wise selection is vital to how beneficial computer use will be for learners. Just because a program is fun does not always mean that it is a developmentally appropriate or worthwhile learning activity. Drill should not be confused with thinking and learning. Teachers must evaluate software for ineffective approaches to instruction for young children, such as isolated drills and activities that resemble workbooks, which, when used at all, should be used quite sparingly.

The use of computers in the classroom is now commonplace. Yet the computer business is extremely competitive. Educators are cautioned against high-pressure sales techniques that encourage schools to spend large amounts of money on inappropriate programs. Teachers and school technology resource personnel should carefully evaluate all software programs for their developmental appropriateness for young children.

Further, because not all children have access to computers in their homes, many children will be less computer competent than others. For this reason, computers that are readily accessible within the classroom facilitate equity in technology learning. All children benefit when a computer is located where they can coordinate its use with other classroom activities (Hohmann, 1990). Both at home and in the classroom, the use of the Internet should be closely monitored.

ROLE OF THE EARLY CHILDHOOD PROFESSIONAL

Enhancing Cognitive, Language, and Literacy Development in Children Ages Six through Eight

1. Provide for continuity of learning experiences from kindergarten to first grade and through the primary grades. Include families in planning for a smooth transition.

2. Acknowledge and plan for wide variations in rate of development in cognitive, language, and literacy development among children.

3. Provide learning experiences that are concrete, whole, and integrated rather than experiences that are abstract, are isolated, or overemphasize skill/drill learning strategies.

4. Provide learning experiences that allow children to interact with materials, other children, and adults.

5. Provide opportunities for child-initiated learning.

6. Spend time in one-on-one conversation and scaffolding activities with individual learners

7. Demonstrate curiosity and interest in learning.

8. Model appropriate oral and written language and enjoyment of good literature. Read frequently to and with children, sharing engaging and stimulating literature.

9. Engage parents as partners and collaborators in the cognitive, language, and literacy development process.

10. Provide appropriate and meaningful technological and media experiences.

11. Continue to encourage and support sociodramatic play and incorporate literacy activities into it.

12. Maintain a stress-free atmosphere around literacy that encourages interest and involvement in a relaxed–alert frame of mind.

13. Control or reduce stress-provoking situations in the schooling process.

KEY TERMS

concrete operational stage	phonics	sight words
downshifting	registers	television literacy
formal operations	rehearsal	
metamemory	shading	

REVIEW STRATEGIES AND ACTIVITIES

1. Review the key terms individually or with a classmate.

2. Interview principals and kindergarten and primary-grade teachers in several school districts to determine how transitions from prekindergarten and kindergarten to the primary grades are managed.

3. Collect samples of children's writing from first, second, and third grades. Analyze them according to (a) content, (b) form, and (c) developmental progression.

4. Make a list of the many ways in which computers affect children's lives. Discuss your list with your classmates. Reflect on how children can benefit from computer technology and ways in which their development may be negatively affected by this technology.

5. Examine the teachers' manuals for several different reading programs used in the primary grades. Compare the programs for part-to-whole and whole-to-part orientations to literacy development.

FURTHER READINGS

Bergen, D., & Coscia, J. (2001). *Brain research and childhood education: Implications for educators.* Olney, MD: Association for Childhood Education International.

Brookes-Gunn, J., Fuligni, A. S., & Berlin, L. J. (2003). *Early child development in the 21st century.* New York: Teachers College Press.

Coles, G. (2000). *Misreading reading: The bad science that hurts children.* Portsmouth, NH: Heinemann.

Dyson, A. H. (1997). *Writing superheroes: Contemporary childhood, popular culture, and classroom literacy.* New York: Teachers College Press.

Fields, M. V., & Spangler, K. L. (2000). *Let's begin reading right: Developmentally appropriate beginning literacy* (4th ed.). Columbus, OH: Merrill/Prentice Hall.

Finn-Stevenson, M., & Zigler, E. (1999). *Schools of the 21st century: Linking child care and education.* New York: Perseus Books Group.

Gardner, H. (1993). *Multiple intelligences: The theory in practice.* New York: Basic Books.

Greenspan, S. I., & Benderly, B. L. (1997). *The growth of the mind: And the endangered origins of intelligence.* Reading, MA: Addison-Wesley.

Hatcher, B., & Beck, S. S. (Eds). (1997). *Learning opportunities beyond the school.* (2nd ed). Olney, MD: Association for Childhood Education International.

Healy, J. M. (1998). *Failure to connect: How computers affect our children's minds—and what we can do about it.* New York: Simon & Schuster.

Neuman, S. B., Copple, C., & Bredekamp, S. (1999). *Learning to read and write: Developmentally appropriate practices for young children.* Washington, DC: National Association for the Education of Young Children.

Puckett, M. B., & Black, J. K. (2000). *Authentic assessment of the young child: Celebrating development and learning* (2nd ed.). Upper Saddle River, NJ: Merrill/Prentice Hall.

Puckett, M. B., & Diffily, D. (2004). *Teaching young children: An introduction to the profession* (2nd ed.). Clifton Park, NY: Delmar Learning.

Reiff, M. I., & Tippins, S. (Eds.). (2004). *The American Academy of Pediatrics: ADHD: A complete and authoritative guide.* New York: HarperCollins.

Scully, P. A., Seefeldt, C., & Barbour, N. H. (2003). *Developmental continuity across preschool and primary grades* (2nd ed.). Olney, MD: Association for Childhood Education International.

Siegel, D. J. (1999). *The developing mind: Toward a neurobiology of interpersonal experience.* New York: Guilford.

OTHER RESOURCES

American Academy of Child and Adolescent Psychiatry
Brochure topics include
    Children with Learning Disabilities
    Childhood Stress

Children and Watching TV
Influence of Music and Music Videos
Children Online
Children and the News
http://www.aacap.org/publications/factsfam/
Association for Childhood Education International. Brochures include
Burris, L. L. (1998). *Safety in the cybervillage: Some guidelines for teachers and parents*
Paintal, S. (1997). *Homework: Ways parents can help*
Association for Childhood Education International
17904 Georgia Avenue, Suite 215
Olney, MD 20832
http://www.udel.edu/bateman/acei
Child Trends
www.childtrends.org
National Parent Teacher Association
http://www.npta.org
National Education Association. *Parent's guide to testing and accountability.* Available at
http://www.nea.org/parents/testingguide/
National Association of Elementary School Principals
http://www.naesp.org
National Institute for Early Education Research
http://www.NIEER.org
Southern Early Childhood Association Position Statements
Assessment of development and learning in young children.
Supporting learning with technology in the early childhood classroom.
Quality child care. Available from
Southern Early Childhood Association
P.O. Box 55930
Little Rock, AR 72215-5930

Epilogue

The universe of knowledge in the field of child growth and development is growing nearly boundless. Each textbook can touch on only a tiny segment of the scholarship on the many topics relating to how children grow and learn. Once begun, the study of child growth, development, and learning evokes a multitude of interests to explore further. The authors hope that this introductory text has drawn you in, and its content and questions have captivated your curiosity, motivating you to explore further its topics or questions that are yet unanswered for you.

We were all children once, and what we learn about child growth and development makes us reflect on our own experiences, feelings, and behaviors (after all, who isn't interested in herself or himself?). A measure of self-understanding prepares us to interact more effectively with others, and knowledge of the resilience and plasticity of childhood assures us that not all childhood experiences determine our destiny. The understanding of oneself is not the purpose of child study, however, but is only an interesting by-product of it.

The purpose of child study is to gain a level of knowledge and understanding that leads to good, enjoyable, and successful parenting; supportive and nurturing child care; enriching and challenging teaching; practical and helpful public policies; and, for every child, a protected and satisfying childhood—a childhood with every hope of reaching its potential.

Childhood and parenthood are each challenging journeys that can be supported by knowledgeable and empathic early childhood professionals.

519

Glossary

abortion: the ending of a pregnancy

accommodation: the cognitive process by which patterns of thought (schemata) and related behaviors are modified to conform to new information or experience

achievement test: a test that measures what children have learned as a result of instruction

acquired immunodeficiency syndrome (AIDS): a disease that attacks the immune system, causing death from illnesses that the immune system cannot ward off

adaptation: the process by which one adjusts to changes in the environment

adipose: tissue in which there is an accumulation of connective tissue cells, each containing a relatively large deposit of fat

adolescence: the time of rapid development between the later childhood years and adulthood

afterbirth: the placenta after it moves from the uterus and is expelled

alphabetic principle: a writing system that associates the phonemes of oral language with letters of the alphabet

alphafetoprotein test (AFP): a blood test that can identify disorders in the brain or spinal column in the fetus

altruism: intentions to help others without the expectation of reward

amniocentesis: a technique that involves extracting amniotic fluid from the uterus for the purpose of detecting all chromosomal and more than 100 biomedical disorders

anecdotal record: a type of narrative observation that describes an incident in detail

anemia: a condition caused by a lack of red blood cells

anomaly: a deviation from an expected norm

anorexia: a severe disorder, usually seen in adolescent girls, characterized by self-starvation

anoxia: a condition caused by the lack of oxygen in the brain of an infant during labor and delivery, which can cause brain damage

antibias curriculum: an active approach to challenging prejudice, stereotyping, bias and the *isms* (sexism, racism, etc.)

Apgar score: a score that rates the physical condition of newborns in the areas of *a*ppearance, *p*ulse, *g*rimace, *a*ctivity, and *r*espiration

apnea: absence of breathing for a period of up to 20 seconds

approximations: children's attempts at conventional oral or written language, which, when produced, are not quite conventional

assimilation: the process of incorporating new motor or conceptual learning into existing schemata

associative play: a loosely organized form of social play, characterized by overt social behaviors indicating common activities, shared interests, and interpersonal associations

at-risk: infants and children who are subject to any of a number of risk factors (such as poverty, drug exposure, genetic and/or developmental anomalies, and family dynamics) that make them vulnerable to compromised growth, development, and learning

atrophy: waste away, diminish in size and/or function

attachment: a strong emotional relationship between two people, characterized by mutual affection and a desire to maintain proximity

audiologist: a trained professional who uses specialized techniques and equipment to diagnose hearing loss

authentic assessment: the ongoing, continuous, context-based observation and documentation of children's learning behaviors

authoritarian discipline: a child-rearing style in which parents apply rigid standards of conduct and expect unquestioning obedience from the child

authoritative discipline: a child-rearing style in which child behavior is directed through rational and reasoned guidance from the adult

autonomy: a sense of independence or self-government

axon: a branchlike projection from the neuron that carries information away from the cell body

balance: a body awareness component in which postural adjustments prevent one from falling

basal metabolic rate: the amount of energy required to keep the heart beating, sustain breathing, repair tissues, and keep the brain and nerves functioning

behavior modification: a system of techniques employing positive and/or negative reinforcers to change behavior

behavioral theory: a theory that emphasizes that learning is the acquisition of specific responses provoked by specific stimuli

521

behaviorist perspective: the point of view that growth and development are primarily governed by external influences in the individual's environment

bilabial trills: the production of sounds such as [m], [b], and [p] that are formed in the front of the mouth with the lips closed and move from the lips toward the back of the mouth (other structures for the articulation of sounds include the lips, teeth, roof of the mouth, and tongue)

biological model: the explanation of cognitive development as influenced by biological processes of growth and development in the brain

body awareness: cognizance of one's body, its parts, its functions, and what it can be willed to do

bonding: a complex psychobiological connection between parent and infant

book-handling knowledge: knowledge of fronts and backs of books, where the story begins, left-to-right progression of pages, and differences between print and illustrations

botulism: a potentially fatal form of food poisoning

Brazelton Neonatal Behavioral Assessment Scale: an assessment of 16 reflexes, responsiveness, state changes, and ability to self-calm in the newborn

breech position delivery: a birth in which a body part other than the head presents itself for delivery first, usually the buttocks, feet, or in some cases the umbilical cord

bulimia: a severe disorder, usually seen in adolescent girls, characterized by binging and then self-induced vomiting

centration: the tendency to attend to a limited number of features of an object or event

cephalocaudal: refers to the long axis of the body from the head downward

cerebral cortex: the outer layer of the cerebral hemisphere, which is mostly responsible for higher mental functions, sensory processing, and motor control

cervix: the opening of the uterus

cesarean delivery: a surgical procedure during which an incision is made through the abdominal and uterine walls of the mother to deliver the baby

checklist: a list of developmental behaviors that the observer identifies as being present or absent

child-directed speech: speech that has qualities of elevated pitch, conspicuous inflections, long pauses, and exaggerated stress on syllables

chorionic villus test (CVT):   a test that analyzes samples of the hairlike projections (chorionic villi) of tissue in the placenta to determine chromosomal disorders (can take place earlier than amniocentesis)

chromosomes: ordered groups of genes within the nucleus of a cell

class inclusion: understanding the relationship between class and subclass, which occurs during the period of concrete operational thought

classical conditioning theory: a theory according to which, when an unconditioned neutral stimulus and an unconditioned response are paired repeatedly, a conditioned response is the result

Clostridium botulinum: the bacterium that causes botulism

cochlear implant: an electronic device placed in the skull, which, with help from an external hearing aid, enhances the detection of sound

cognitive development: the aspect of development that involves thinking, problem solving, intelligence, and language

cognitive science: the investigation of the knowledge and strategies used in the cognitive process that distinguish expert cognitive processes from novice cognitive processes

cognitive theory: a theory that explains the development of learning in terms of how children think and process information

colostrum: the first fluid secreted by the mammary glands soon after childbirth, before true milk is formed

communication competence: the repertoire of behaviors that help young children to communicate effectively with others

comprehension: understanding the meaning of something, for example, print

concept clusters: organization of the tools of the world into categories or patterns of thinking

concrete operational stage: according to Piaget, the stage in which children around 7 to 11 years of age can use logical reasoning rather than relying on perceptions, but still use concrete objects and first-hand experiences to form concepts and reach understanding

configuration: the general shape or outline of a word

congenital anomalies: skeletal or body system abnormalities caused by defective genes within the chromosomes, which usually affect the developing embryo during the first eight weeks of pregnancy

conservation: the understanding that physical attributes (e.g., mass and weight) stay the same even if appearance changes

constancy of position in space: the notion that letters of the alphabet must have fixed positions to maintain their identity

contraction: the movement of the muscles of the uterus that pushes the baby through the cervical opening and into the birth canal

cooperative play: a well-organized form of social play, characterized by well-defined social roles within play groups, influential peer leaders, and shared materials and equipment used to pursue a well-understood group play goal or theme

correlational study: research that attempts to determine a relationship between two or more sets of measurements

creative vocabulary: the creation of new words to meet the need for a word that has not been learned or that has been forgotten, or for which no word exists

critical period: a time of physiological and/or psychological sensitivity during which the normal development of a major organ or structural system is vulnerable to insult or injury

cross-sectional study: research that studies subjects of different ages at the same time

deciduous teeth: the first set of teeth, which erupts during infancy; also called temporary or baby teeth; later replaced by a set of 36 permanent teeth

defense mechanism: a psychological response to ego threat, frustration, or failure

deferred imitation: the ability to imitate behaviors that were observed at a prior time or another place

dendrites: branches from the neuron that carry information toward the cell body; a neuron can have several dendrites

descriptive study: research collected by observing and recording behavior and providing a description of the observed behavior

developmental interactionist perspective: the point of view that growth and development result from an individual's actions and interactions within and upon the environment

developmental milestones: significant events during the course of growth and development

developmental screening test: an initial procedure for identifying individuals who may need formal diagnostic tests

developmental spelling: spelling that young children create based on their perceptions of sound–symbol relationships

developmentally appropriate: pertains to (1) age appropriateness, the universal and predictable patterns of growth and development that occur in children from birth through age eight, and (2) individual appropriateness, the individual rates and patterns of physical/motor, psychosocial, cognitive, language and literacy development, personality and learning style, and family and cultural background of each child

developmentally inappropriate: expectations or practices that fail to acknowledge age and individual characteristics and needs

dexterity: quick, precise movement and coordination of the hands and fingers

diagnostic test: a process of compiling and assessing characteristics and symptoms (physiological, emotional, or social) to identify needs and establish treatment and/or intervention strategies

dialects: different forms of language used by different ethnic groups or by people who live in different geographic regions

dilation: the gradual opening of the cervix, which occurs in the first stage of labor

directionality: the application of the internal awareness of right and left to objects and movement

disequilibrium: an imbalance in thinking that leads the thinker to assimilate or accommodate

display rules: social rules determining how and when certain emotions should or should not be expressed

DNA: deoxyribonucleic acid, the molecule containing the information that causes the formation of proteins that stimulate the development of tissues and organs and affect other genes and physiological functions

doula: a Greek word for a female servant who provides assistance and support during childbirth

downshifting: a psychophysiological response to perceived threat that is accompanied by a sense of helplessness or lack of self-efficacy, which affects the brain's ability to function at optimal levels

dyslexia: a general term for the condition affecting the auditory and visual processes that causes print to be perceived with distortions

early childhood development: the study of the physical/motor, psychosocial, cognitive, language, and literacy development in children from prebirth through age 8, including those from developmentally and culturally diverse backgrounds

echolalia: replication in repetitive fashion of the sounds of another speaker in an infant–other turn-taking "conversation"

ecological systems theory: a theory that argues that a variety of social systems influence the development of children

egocentrism: the tendency to view the world from one's own perspective; the inability to see another point of view

electronic fetal monitor: a device used during labor, which is attached to the abdomen of the pregnant woman or the scalp of the fetus to determine the fetal heart rate

embryonic cell mass: the developing fertilized ovum during the first 3 months of pregnancy when cells are dividing rapidly to form the fetus

embryonic stage: weeks three through eight of pregnancy, during which the major organ systems are formed

empathy: experiencing the feelings or emotions that someone else is experiencing

environment: the experiences, conditions, objects, and people that directly or indirectly influence the development and behavior of a child

episiotomy: an incision made in the opening of the vulva to prevent it from tearing during delivery

equilibration: the attempt to restore cognitive balance by modifying existing cognitive structures when confronted with new information

essential experiences: experiences deemed critical at certain times during early growth and development, which have growth-inducing influence on the brain's neurological structures

ethics: a set of standards describing professional responsibilities in terms of behaviors and conduct

ethology: the scientific study of behavior

event sampling: a procedure in which the researcher notes the occurrences of particular behaviors or events

expansions: responses to young children's use of overgeneralizations by using the conventional form in the conversational context

experimental study: research that involves treating each of two or more groups in different ways to determine cause-and-effect relationships

expressive language: spoken language; oral communication

extensions: responses to children's language that extend the meaning of their language

extensors: muscles that act to stretch or extend a limb

extinguish: stopping a behavior or response by not reinforcing it over a period of time

extrafamilial: actions and behaviors occurring outside the immediate family

extrafamilial relationships: relationships with people outside the immediate or extended family

extrauterine: the environment outside of the uterus

failure to thrive: a condition in which an apparently healthy infant fails to grow normally

family child care home: a private residence in which child care is provided for a small number of children

fast mapping: children's rapid learning of language by relating a word to an internalized concept and remembering it after only one encounter with that word

fatherese: modifications in the father's speech when talking with infants and young children; can differ from motherese

fertility: the capability of conceiving a child

fertility rate: the number of births per 1,000 women of age 15 to 44 years

fetal alcohol syndrome (FAS): the physical and mental abnormalities found in babies whose mothers consumed alcohol during pregnancy

fetal stage: the stage that begins after the first eight weeks of pregnancy and continues until birth

fetus: the developing human from nine weeks after conception to birth

figure–ground discrimination: the ability to focus on the dominant figure in a picture without being distracted by elements in the background

fixation: in psychoanalytic theory, a point in development that becomes fixed, failing to move forward to more mature forms

flexors: muscles that act to bend a joint

fontanelles: membranous spaces between the cranial bones of the fetus and the infant

food insecurity: the inability of the family to meet the nutritional needs of all of its members

food security: the ability of the family to meet the nutritional needs of its members

forceps: a surgical instrument, similar to tongs, that is applied to the head of the fetus to facilitate delivery

formal assessment: information gathered about young children, usually through standardized tests

formal operations: according to Piaget, the fourth and final stage of cognitive development, which occurs during adolescence, when reliance on concrete objects decreases and abstract thinking begins

fraternal twins: twins whose development began by the fertilization of two ova (eggs) by two sperm, causing each twin to have a different genetic code

fundamental movements: coordinations that are basic to all other movement abilities

gavage feeding: introducing fluids or foods through a tube passed orally or through a nasal passage into the stomach

gender: the maleness or femaleness of the zygote as determined by the kind of sperm fertilizing the ovum (Y sperm: genetically male; X sperm: genetically female)

gender awareness: the realization that men and women, girls and boys, are different

gender constancy: the realization that one's gender remains the same regardless of age or changes in clothing, hairstyles, or other outward characteristics

gender identity: the cognizance of being male or female

gender role: the public expression of one's gender identity

genes: molecules of DNA that encode and transmit the characteristics of past generations

genetic counseling: information provided to parents or prospective parents regarding the possibility and nature of genetic disorders in their offspring

genome: the sum total of gene types possessed by a particular species

genotype: the combination of genes inherited from both parents and their ancestors

gestation: the length of an average pregnancy of 280 days, or 40 weeks, from the first day of the last menstrual period; can range from 37 to 42 weeks

gestational diabetes: diabetes that develops after a woman becomes pregnant

gifted: children who give evidence of high performance in various areas of development

glial cells: supporting cells, which serve to protect and insulate (as with myelin) cells in the nervous system

health-related fitness: a physical state in which muscular strength, endurance, flexibility, and the circulatory–respiratory systems are all in optimal condition

Healthy Eating Index: a U.S. Department of Agriculture measure of diet quality, which assesses the degree to which a person's diet conforms to the Food Guide Pyramid; limits saturated fat, cholesterol, and sodium; and includes a variety of foods

heredity: the inherited characteristics of humans encoded by genes

heteronomous morality: a morality that is governed by others rather than by oneself

holophrase: the use of one word to convey a phrase or a sentence

home visitor: a trained nurse or paraprofessional who provides in-home education and support services to pregnant women and families with young children

human immunodeficiency virus (HIV): the virus that causes AIDS; it can be transmitted from an infected mother to the fetus or embryo via the placenta or delivery fluids

hypertension: high blood pressure

hyperthermia: a very high body temperature

hypothermia: a below-normal body temperature

hypothesis: a hunch or supposition that one wants to verify or prove

identical twins: twins whose development began when the zygote split into two identical halves, thus ensuring that both twins have the identical genetic code

identity constancy: the understanding that a person or species remains the same, even though appearance is changed through masks, costumes, or other transformations

idiosyncratic concepts: ideas of the preoperational child that are based on personal experience and over-generalized to other situations

in utero: the environment in which the fetus grows within the uterus

inclusion: the education model that includes children with developmental challenges in general education settings

indirect speech: speech that implies more than the actual words uttered

individualized education plan (IEP): a written plan for services for individuals of ages 3 to 21 with disabilities as defined by the Individuals with Disabilities Education Act

individualized family services plan (IFSP): a written plan for services for birth through two years of age and in some cases older, for children with disabilities under the Individuals with Disabilities Education Act

inductive discipline: a positive, nonpunitive form of discipline that relies on reasons and rationales to help children control their behaviors

industry: the sense of mastery of social and academic skills necessary to feel self-assured

infant mortality: deaths during the first year of life

informal assessment: information gathered about young children through approaches other than standardized tests

information-processing theory: a theory of cognitive development that suggests that the mind is similar to the information-processing system of a computer and, unlike the theory of Piaget, emphasizes similarities in the thinking of children and adults

initiative: the third of Erikson's psychosocial stages, in which the child pursues ideas, individual interests, and activities; when thwarted, the child becomes self-critical and experiences guilt

inner speech: a form of speech associated with the process of internalizing spoken words or sentences

inservice: individuals who have completed professional training programs and are employed in the early childhood profession

intelligence test: a standardized measure used to establish an intelligence level rating (i.e., intelligence quotient [IQ]) by measuring a child's ability to perform various selected mental tasks

interactional competence: the repertoire of behaviors that help young children communicate effectively with others

interactionist perspective: derived primarily from the works of Jean Piaget, refers to the interactive influences of heredity and environment

internalization: a process in which behavior standards are adopted as one's own and acted upon without explicit instruction from others

interview: engaging in a dialogue with a child that is either free-flowing or with predetermined questions to assess understanding and feelings

intrafamilial: actions and behaviors occurring within the immediate family

invented/developmental spelling: spelling that young children create based on their perceptions of sound–symbol relationships

irreversibility: the inability of preoperational children to reverse their thinking and to return to their original point of thought

isolette: a small crib, which provides a controlled environment for newborns

kangaroo care: the practice of holding an infant next to the mother's or father's skin to comfort and nurture the child

kinesthesis: the sensation of body presence, position, and movement

labor: the three stages of the birth process: dilation, birth of the baby, and discharge of the placenta

Lamaze method: a method developed by Fernand Lamaze, which involves training the prospective mother and a partner/coach in breathing and relaxation techniques to be used during labor

language acquisition device (LAD): an innate mental mechanism some theorists believe make language development possible

later childhood: the period of development between the early childhood years and adolescence (ages 9 through 11)

laterality: an awareness of an ability to use both sides of the body; a recognition of the distinction between left and right

Leboyer method: a technique used during childbirth to help the baby in the transition from life inside to outside the uterus; characterized by warm delivery rooms, muted lighting, soothing music, a warm bath, and so on

left/right dominance: a neuromaturational preference for one or the other side of the body, as in handedness

levels-of-processing theory: an information-processing model that focuses on the depth of attention rather than aspects of memory in explaining levels of cognitive performance

locomotion: the ability to move independently from place to place

logicomathematical knowledge: knowledge constructed primarily from children's actions on and interpretations of objects and events

longitudinal study: research that collects information about the same subjects at different ages over a period of time

low birth weight: a weight at birth of less than 5½ pounds, or 2,500 grams

low-risk: infants and children whose risk factors are minimal or absent

maturational theory: a theory that holds that growth and development are predetermined by inheritance and largely unaffected by the environment

maturationist perspective: the point of view that growth and development are primarily governed by an individual's genetic makeup

mental symbols: the behaviors that occur at the beginning of the preoperational stage, including speech, imitation of others, and using one object to represent another

mentor: an experienced early childhood professional who provides support and guidance to a beginning teacher

metabolic: pertains to the body's complex chemical conversion of food into substances and energy necessary for maintenance of life

metacognition: the ability to think about one's own cognitive processes

metacommunication: the cognitive ability to reflect on and talk about verbal interactions

metalanguage: talk about language

metalinguistic awareness: the ability to think about the forms and meanings of language

metamemory: the ability to think about memory and memory processes

moral behavior: the ability to consider the needs and well-being of others and exhibit appropriate behaviors consistent with a set of standards or value orientation

moral realism: a morality that focuses on rules and the seriousness of the consequences of an act rather than on the intentions behind the act

moral relativism: a morality that focuses on the judgment of situations and intentions underlying individual behavior rather than solely on the consequences of an act

morpheme: the smallest unit of meaning in oral or written language

motherese: modifications in the mother's speech when talking with infants and young children

motor fitness: a physical state in which motor coordination facilitates speed, agility, power, and balance

multicultural education: learning experiences that help young children become more aware of and appreciate the commonalities as well as the diversity of various cultural and ethnic groups

myelin: a fatty substance surrounding the axons and dendrites of some neurons, which speeds the conduction of nerve impulses

myelinization: a process in which nerve fibers are coated with a fatty sheath (myelin) that facilitates the transmission of messages across synapses

narrative observation: a written observation of behavior

neonate: the newborn from birth to four weeks

Neonatal Behavioral Assessment Scale (NBAS or Brazelton Scale):   an assessment of 16 reflexes, responsiveness, state changes, and ability to self-calm in the newborn

neonatal period: the first four weeks of extrauterine life

neonatologist: a medical specialist concerned with care and treatment of the neonate, or newborn infant, during the first four to six weeks

neo-Piagetians: researchers who support Piaget's ideas, but update his theory according to recent findings about cognitive development

neural tube: the rudimentary beginning of the brain and spinal cord

neurobiological agents: hormones and chemicals that facilitate the transmission of information throughout the nervous system

neurogenesis: the continuous production of neurons

neuron: a type of cell that conveys information; a nerve cell

neurotransmitter: a chemical that facilitates transmission of information through the synapse

nonmaternal care: child care provided by someone other than the child's mother

nonparental care: child care provided by someone other than the child's parent

norms: the average ages of the emergence of certain behaviors or average scores on tests that are based on large representative samples of a population

nystagmus: involuntary and jerky repetitive movement of the eyeballs

object permanence: the realization that objects and people continue to exist even though they may not be visible or detected through other senses

objectivity: the ability to observe and draw inferences about child development that are free of observer bias

operant conditioning theory: a theory in which behavior is changed or modified through the positive or negative consequences that follow the behavior

orienting response: a reduction in the level of response to a stimulus previously experienced

ossification: the conversion of the softer cartilage of the skeletal system into bone

other-mediated action: an action, originated by a child who is physically unable to act directly on objects, that is carried out by some other person or agent

overextension: the use of a word to refer to a similar but different object, situation, or category

overgeneralized speech: the use of a single word or label to represent an entire category of objects similar in use or appearance

overregularization: the tendency to overgeneralize a rule of grammar

parallel play: activities in which two or more children play near one another while engaged in independent activities

participant–observer: a researcher who participates in the daily lives of the subjects of the study

peers: other children who are the same age as a particular child

percentile: a rank reflecting an individual's position relative to others, indicating the percentage of others falling at or below the noted rank or percentile

perception: the physiological process by which sensory input is interpreted

perceptually bound: young, preoperational children's explanations for certain phenomena (because it "looks" that way)

perceptual–motor: interrelationship between sensory information and motor responses

performance-related fitness: a physical state in which motor coordination facilitates speed, agility, power, and balance

perinatal: the period encompassing the weeks before a birth, the birth, and the few weeks thereafter

permissive discipline: a noncontrolling, nondemanding form of discipline in which the child, for the most part, is allowed to regulate his or her behavior

perspective-taking: the ability to understand one's own or another's viewpoint and be aware of the coordinated and interrelated sets of ideas and actions that are reflected in behavior

phonics: the sound–symbol relationship of a language system

phonological sensitivity: the ability to detect and manipulate the sounds of spoken language

phonology: the speech sounds of a particular language system

physical fitness: a physical state in which muscular strength, endurance, flexibility, and the circulatory–respiratory systems are all in optimal condition

physical knowledge: knowledge of physical characteristics of objects and events gained through sensorimotor interactions

placenta: an organ attached to the wall of the uterus, which transmits nutrients from the mother to the embryo/fetus and filters wastes from the embryo/fetus to the mother

plasticity: the ability of some parts of the nervous system to alter their functional characteristics

polymerase chain reaction (PCR): a procedure used to identify disease-causing genes in an eight-cell embryo

portfolio: an assemblage of information derived from various assessment strategies, including representative samples of the child's play creations and academic products

postpartum depression: a period of depression that affects most mothers for a few days and in some cases for weeks and months after childbirth

postpartum psychosis: a psychological condition associated with severe depression following childbirth in which there is a loss of insight, good judgment, and coping strength; sometimes there is a loss of touch with reality

power-assertive discipline: a form of discipline in which the power of the adult is used to coerce, deprive of privileges or material goods, or apply physical punishment to modify a child's behavior

preconcepts: the very young child's disorganized and illogical representations of experience

predictable books: books that have repeating patterns and predictable text

prehension: the coordination of fingers and thumb to permit grasping

prematurity: a preterm delivery that occurs prior to 37 completed weeks of gestation

premoral: the period in early childhood when the child is unaware of moral rules or values

prenatal: the time from conception until birth, an average of 266 days, or 38 weeks

preoperational stage: the second of Piaget's stages of cognitive development, in which children develop the ability to internally represent sensorimotor actions, but do not engage in the operational or logical thinking

preprimary: the time in young children's lives before they enter the primary (first, second, or third) grades

preservice: individuals who are in training to teach or serve young children

preterm: infants born several weeks before the full term (38 weeks) of pregnancy

primagravida: a woman who is pregnant for the first time

primary caregiver: the person primarily responsible for the nonparental care and nurturing of a child, who provides consistency, predictability, and the opportunity for attachments to form

primary circular reactions: simple, pleasurable, repetitive acts centered on the infant's body

primary disabilities: learning disabilities involving attention, memory, and perception

primitive reflexes: reflexes controlled by subcortical structures in the brain, which gradually disappear during the first year

private speech: speech to oneself that helps direct one's thinking, behavior, or communication

private spelling: phonemic spelling or invented spelling that young children create when they first begin to write their ideas and thoughts

professional development center: an organization, usually established within a public elementary school, in which professional development of preservice and inservice teachers is pursued collaboratively

professionals: individuals who have internalized the evolving knowledge base of their particular fields and use this knowledge to improve practices that have an impact on the lives of children and families

prosocial behavior: behavior that benefits others, such as helping, sharing, comforting, and defending

proximity seeking: the child's attempts to maintain nearness and contact with the attachment person

proximodistal: refers to the direction from the body's center outward to the extremities

psychoanalytic theory: a theory that attempts to explain the inner thoughts and feelings, at both the conscious and subconscious levels, that influence behavior

psychological state: pertains to conditions of arousal and alertness in infancy

psychosexual theory: a theory that suggests that sexual drives play an important role in personality development

psychosocial theory: a theory that argues that social interactions are more important than sexual drives in personality development

puberty: the biological developments that result in the ability to produce children

public spelling: conventional spelling that children learn through both experience with writing and direct instruction

random selection: a procedure for assigning subjects to an experimental or a control group so that each person has the same chance of being selected for either group

rating scale: a scale with various traits or categories that allows the observer to indicate the importance of the observed behaviors

readiness: a term that has many different meanings depending on the context in which it is used, but generally refers to a set of prerequisite developmental expectations

readiness test: a test that measures capabilities needed for certain new experiences or types of curriculum

receptive language: language that is comprehended, but not necessarily produced

recessive gene: a gene that carries a trait that may not appear unless a gene for the same trait is inherited from both parents

reciprocal determinism: a socialization process through which the individual both influences and is influenced by the environment

reflecting-in-action: an ongoing process in which educators think about and critically analyze their own and their students' performance to review, assess, and modify interactions, expectations, and instructional strategies

reflex: an unlearned, involuntary response to stimuli

registers: variations in the style of speech according to the particular social setting

rehearsal: the mental process of repeating a thought in order to retain it in memory

reliability: the consistency with which various research methods produce the same or similar results for each individual from one assessment to the next

replicability: the likelihood that a research procedure can be followed by another person with the same or similar results

representative sample: a sample of subjects who are representative of the larger population of individuals about whom the researcher wants to draw conclusions

resource persons: people outside the educational setting, usually from health-related fields, who can provide information about young children's development and learning

reversals: printing letters or words in reverse

Rh factor: a condition in the mother that produces antibodies that destroy the red blood cells of her second and subsequent babies

rich interpretation: acknowledging that young children know more than they can verbally express and use nonverbal behaviors to communicate

rubella: a viral disease that can cause birth disorders if the mother contracts it during the first three months of pregnancy (also known as German measles)

running record: a type of narrative observation that records all behaviors in sequential order as they occur

satiety: the feeling of having had sufficient food to satisfy hunger

scaffolding: a process by which adults or more skilled children facilitate the acquisition of knowledge or skills in the learner through coaching or supplying needed information

schemata: mental concepts or categories; plural for schema

scripts: sets of social procedures or events, which includes sequences of events and/or roles, often observed in young children's play

secondary circular reactions: simple, pleasurable, repetitive responses centered on objects and events in the environment

secondary disabilities: learning disabilities involving thinking and oral language

self-actualization: the process of having basic physical and social/emotional needs met so that outcomes for the individual lead to positive self-regard and a creative, contributing member of society

self-awareness: an individual's perceptions of himself or herself as distinct and separate from other people and objects

self-concept: one's sense of oneself as separate and unique from others

self-control: the ability to govern one's behavior

self-definition: the use of criteria to define the self, such as age, size, and physical and mental abilities

self-efficacy: the feeling that one's efforts are effective; the perception that one can succeed

self-esteem: the overall sense of worth as a person that the child derives from the qualities that are associated with the self-concept

self-recognition: the infant's ability to recognize his or her image in a mirror, photograph, or other representation

semantics: knowledge of how language carries meaning

sensorimotor learning: learning that occurs through the senses and motor activities

separation anxiety: fear of being separated from the attachment person

separation individuation: the realization in infants that others are separate entities and not extensions of themselves

service words: words that help hold a sentence together, such as *the* and *to*

sexuality: the relational, biological, and procreational aspects of gender

shading: gradually changing the topic of conversation

shaken baby syndrome: head (intracranial) or long bone injury caused by forceful shaking or jerking of an infant; may result in serious injuries (including blindness), and often death

sight words: words in print that young children recognize immediately

signs: internalized representations that are later associated with tools of the world

simultaneous bilingualism: the process of learning two languages at the same time, beginning at birth

skeletal age: a measure of physical development based on examination of skeletal X-rays

social cognition: the ability to understand the thoughts, intentions, and behaviors of oneself and of others

social learning theory: a theory that argues that learning occurs through observing others, and emphasizes the influencing role of behavioral models

social referencing: behavior in which the emotional/social reactions of others are observed and used to guide one's behavior in unfamiliar situations

socialization: the process by which individuals acquire the accepted behaviors and values of their families and society

sociocentric: the inability to take or accept as valid the perspectives of another group

sociocultural model: the explanation of cognitive development as influenced by various sociocultural experiences within the family, the community, and society

specimen record: a type of narrative observation that provides detailed information about a particular event, child, or time of day

standard precautions: procedures involving the use of protective barriers such as nonporous gloves, aprons, disposable diapers and diaper table paper, disposable towels, and surfaces that can be sanitized to reduce the risk of exposure to pathogens

standardized test: a test that is administered and scored according to set procedures and whose scores can be interpreted according to predetermined statistical measures

strabismus: a condition referred to as *crossed eyes,* in which one or both eyes turn in, out, up, or down

stranger anxiety: fear of strangers, characterized by avoidance, crying, or other distress signals

subcortical: refers to the portion of the brain just below the cerebral cortex, which is responsible for controlling unlearned and reflexive behavior

subcutaneous tissue: tissue that forms beneath the skin

successive bilingualism: the process of learning a second language after acquiring proficiency in a first language

support staff: other people within the educational setting who support the learning and development of young children, such as nurses, social workers, diagnosticians, psychologists, secretaries, and food service and housekeeping personnel

survival reflexes: reflexes essential to sustaining life

synapse: the point of contact between nerve fibers

syndrome: a group of combined symptoms that characterizes a physiological or psychological disorder

systems perspective: a point of view that emphasizes the ecological aspects of human existence and proposes that there are many layers of influence between and among the contexts in which the individual exists

syntax: the grammar or structure of a particular language system

teacher-as-learner: the process by which educators continue to learn from children, parents, other professionals, and the changing professional research and literature throughout their careers

teacher-as-researcher: the process by which early childhood professionals, through their perspective-taking and reflecting-in-action, acquire and demonstrate the behaviors of a researcher

telegraphic speech: children's early speech, which, like a telegram, includes only the essential words needed to convey meaning

television literacy: understanding the specialized symbolic codes conveyed through the medium of television

temperament: an individual's behavior style, which is both biologically and environmentally derived

teratogens: environmental factors, such as viruses and chemical substances, that can cause abnormalities in the developing embryo or fetus

tertiary circular reactions: an exploratory schema in which children devise new ways of acting on objects in their environments and from which they can derive meaning

theories: bodies of principles used to interpret a set of circumstances or facts

theory of mind: attributing mental states to oneself and to others

time sampling: a procedure for recording selected observations on a predetermined schedule

toilet learning: a gradual maturational process in which the child gains control over elimination

tools of the world: the language and objects of the external world

toxemia: a disease of unknown cause that occurs in the last trimester of pregnancy and can cause death to both mother and child

toxoplasmosis: an infection that can be transmitted from cat droppings or raw meat to the mother and from her to the fetus or embryo via the placenta, causing birth disorders

transactional model: the give-and-take model of hereditary and environmental influences on growth and development

transactional perspective: the point of view that growth and development are an outgrowth of the interplay between an individual's heredity and environment

transductive reasoning: the reasoning process of very young children, which relies on preconcepts

transformation: attending to all the states of an event from the beginning, to in-between, to the final stage

transitional object: an object, usually a soft, cuddly item, to which a child becomes attached

transivity: the ability to seriate, or order, according to some attribute, such as height or size

trimester: the first, second, or third three months of pregnancy

ultrasound: a technique using sound frequencies that can detect structural characteristics of the fetus and the approximate week of pregnancy

underextension: the use of a general term to refer to a more specific object, situation, or category

validity: the degree to which an instrument or a procedure measures what it is intended to measure

vernix caseosa: an oily covering that protects the skin of the fetus

viability: the capability of sustaining extrauterine survival

vocables: early sound patterns used by infants that approximate words

water intoxication: dangerous, potentially life-threatening physiological condition caused by over-consumption of water apart from or in overdiluted formula or juices

washout effect: the decline of gains in intelligence and achievement scores several years after the termination of an intervention program for young children

word analysis skills: the ability to analyze words using a variety of strategies, such as rhyming words

zone of proximal development: the level of concept development that is too difficult for the child to accomplish alone, but can be achieved with the help of adults or more skilled children through scaffolding

zygote: the first cell resulting from the fertilization of the ovum by the sperm

References

Abelman, R. (1984). Children and TV: The ABC's of TV literacy. *Childhood Education, 60,* 200–205.

Aboud, F. (1988). *Children and prejudice.* Cambridge, MA: Blackwell.

Abramovitch, R., Corter, C., Pepler, D. J., & Stanhope, L. (1986). Sibling and peer interaction: A final follow-up and a comparison. *Child Development, 57,* 217–229.

Abramson, R., Altfeld, S., & Tiebloom-Mishkin, J. (2000). The community-based doula: An emerging role in family support. *Zero to Three, 21*(2), 11–16.

Ackerman, B. (1982). Contextual integration and utterance interpretation: The ability of children and adults to interpret sarcastic utterances. *Child Development, 53,* 1075–1083.

Adair, R., Baucher, H., Philipp, B., Levenson, S., & Zuckerman, B. (1991). Night waking during infancy: Role of parental presence at bedtime. *Pediatrics, 87*(4), 500–504.

Adams, M. J. (1990). *Beginning to read: Thinking and learning about print: A Summary.* Urbana-Champaign: Center for the Study of Reading, University of Illinois at Urbana-Champaign.

Adams, R. J., Mauer, D., & Davis, M. (1986). Newborns' discrimination of chromatic from achromatic stimuli. *Journal of Experimental Child Psychology, 41,* 267–281.

Adamson, L. B., & Bakeman, R. (1985). Affect and attention: Infants observed with mothers and peers. *Child Development, 56,* 582–593.

Adcock, S. G., & Patton, M. M. (2001). Views of effective early childhood educators regarding systemic constraints that affect their teaching. *Journal of Research in Childhood Education, 15*(2), 194–208.

Ainsworth, M. D. S. (1962). The effects of maternal deprivation: A review of findings and controversy in the context of research strategy. In *Deprivation of maternal care: A reassessment of its effects* (Public Health Paper No. 14, pp. 97–165). Geneva: World Health Organization.

Ainsworth, M. D. S. (1967). *Infancy in Uganda: Infant care and the growth of love.* Baltimore: Johns Hopkins University Press.

Ainsworth, M. D. S. (1973). The development of infant–mother attachment. In B. M. Caldwell & H. N. Ricciuti (Eds.), *Review of child development research* (Vol. 3, pp. 1–94). Chicago: University of Chicago Press.

Ainsworth, M. D. S., Bell, S. M., & Stayton, D. J. (1974). Infant–mother attachment and social development: Socialization as a product of reciprocal responsiveness to signals. In M. P. M. Richards (Ed.), *The integration of the child into a social world* (pp. 99–135). London: Cambridge University Press.

Ainsworth, M. D. S., & Wittig, B. A. (1969). Attachment and the exploratory behavior of one-year-olds in a strange situation. In B. M. Foss (Ed.), *Determinants of infant behavior* (Vol. 4, pp. 113–136). London: Methuen.

Akinbami, L. J., & Schoendorf, K. (2002). Trends in childhood asthma: Prevalence, health care utilization, and mortality. *Pediatrics, 110,* 315–322.

Alaimo, K., Olson, C. M., & Frongillo, E. A., Jr. (2001). Food insufficiency and American school-aged children's cognitive, academic, and psychosocial development. *Pediatrics, 108,* 44–53.

Alan Guttmacher Institute. (1998, January). *Facts in brief.* Washington, DC: Author.

Alan Guttmacher Institute. (2002a, September). *Facts in brief: Sexual and reproductive health: Women and men.* New York: Author.

Alan Guttmacher Institute. (2002b). *Family planning can reduce high infant mortality levels* (Issues in Brief, 2002 Series, No. 2). New York: Author.

Alan Guttmacher Institute. (2003). *Policies to promote marriage target out-of-wedlock births but ignore unintended pregnancy among married women* (News release). Retrieved May 31, 2003, from www.agi-usa.org

Alexander, G. M., & Hines, M. (1994). Gender labels and play styles: Their relative contribution to children's selection of playmates. *Child Development, 65,* 869–879.

Allied Vaccine Group. (2003). *Vaccines: Common questions.* Retrieved September 26, 2003, from www.vaccine.org

Als, H., & Gilkerson, L. (1995). Developmentally supportive care in the neonatal intensive care unit. *Zero to Three, 15*(6), 1, 3–10.

American Academy of Family Physicians. (1996). *Recommended core educational guidelines for family practice residents.* Kansas City, MO: Author.

American Academy of Pediatrics. (1998a). *Pediatric nutrition handbook* (4th ed.). Elk Grove Village, IL: Author.

American Academy of Pediatrics. (1998b). *A woman's guide to breastfeeding.* Elk Grove Village, IL: Author.

American Academy of Pediatrics. (1998c). The role of home-visitation programs in improving health outcomes for children and families. *Pediatrics, 101*(3), 486–489.

American Academy of Pediatrics. (1998d). *A woman's guide to breastfeeding.* Elk Grove Village, IL: Author.

American Academy of Pediatrics. (1999a). Health Alert: Avoid using home trampolines, Academy says. *AAP News, 15*(5), 31.

American Academy of Pediatrics. (1999b). *Health briefs.* Elk Grove Village, IL: Author.

American Academy of Pediatrics. (2000, April). *Swimming programs for infants and toddlers: Policy statement.* Retrieved May 15, 2001, from http://www.aap.org/policy/re9940.html

American Academy of Pediatrics. (2002a). *Universal newborn hearing screening* (Parent education pamphlet). Elk Grove Village, IL: Author.

American Academy of Pediatrics. (2002b). *Take time to talk.* Retrieved March 13, 2002, from www.aap.org/bfc/bfpress.htm

American Academy of Pediatrics & American College of Obstetrics and Gynecology. (1992). *Guidelines for prenatal care.* Elk Grove Village, IL: Author.

American Academy of Pediatrics, Committee on Child Abuse and Neglect. (1994). Distinguishing sudden infant death syndrome from child abuse and fatalities. *Pediatrics, 94*(1), 124–126.

American Academy of Pediatrics, Committee on Child Abuse and Neglect. (2001). *Distinguishing sudden infant death syndrome from child abuse fatalities.* Retrieved April 10, 2003, from http://www.aap.org/policy/

American Academy of Pediatrics, Committee on Genetics. (1994). Prenatal genetic diagnosis for pediatricians. *Pediatrics, 93*(6), 1010–1015.

American Academy of Pediatrics, Committee on Injury and Poison Prevention and Committee on Sports Medicine and Fitness. (1998). In-line skating injuries in children and adolescents. *Pediatrics, 101*(4), 720–722.

American Academy of Pediatrics, Committee on Practice and Ambulatory Medicine, Section on Ophthalmology. (2002, April). *Eye examinations in infants, children and young adults by pediatricians.* Retrieved July 7, 2003, from http://www.pediatrics.aappublications.org

American Academy of Pediatrics Task Force on Infant Sleep Position and Sudden Infant Death Syndrome. (2002). Changing concepts of sudden infant death syndrome: Implications for infant sleeping environment and sleep position. *Pediatrics, 105,* 650–656.

American Academy Pediatrics Workgroup on Breastfeeding. (1997). Breastfeeding and the use of human milk. *Pediatrics, 100*(6), 1035–1039.

American Academy of Pediatrics, Working Group on Antiretroviral Therapy and Medical Management of Infants, Children and Adolescents with HIV Infection. (1998). Antiretroviral therapy and medical management of pediatric HIV infection. *Pediatrics, 102* (4; Supplement, Part 2 of 2).

American College of Obstetricians and Gynecologists. (1999). *Pregnancy: You and your baby: Prenatal care, labor and delivery, and postpartum care.* Washington, DC: Author.

American College of Obstetricians and Gynecologists. (2003). *The face of AIDS is changing.* Retrieved June 23, 2003, from http://www.acog.org

American Medical Association. (2003). *News from the AMA: Measles and pertussis risk higher for children with personal exemptions from immunizations.* Retrieved September 20, 2003, from http://www.medem.com

American Psychological Association. (1993). *Violence and youth: Psychology's response. Vol. 1: Summary report.* Washington, DC: Author.

American Psychological Association (2002). *Ethical principles of psychologists and code of conduct.* Washington, DC: Author.

American Psychological Association, Committee on Ethical Standards in Psychological Research. (1972). Ethical standards for research with human subjects. *APA Monitor, 1972* (May), I–XIX.

American Public Health Association & American Academy of Pediatrics. (2002). *Caring for our children: National health and safety performance standards: Guidelines for out-of-home child care (2nd ed.).* Washington, DC, and Elk Grove Village, IL: Author.

Americans with Disabilities Act of 1990. P.L. 101–336, 42 U.S.C. §12101.

Anastasi, A. (1958). Heredity, environment, and the question: How? *Psychological Review, 65*(4), 197–208.

Anderson, D., & Collins, P. (1988). *The impact on children's education: Television's influence on cognitive development.* Washington, DC: U.S. Department of Education, Office of Educational Research and Improvement.

Andrew, C. (1998). When to worry about infants and toddlers 'at risk.' *ACEI Focus on Infants and Toddlers, 11,* 1–3.

Anselmo, S. (1987). *Early childhood development: Prenatal through age eight.* Columbus, OH: Merrill.

Apgar, V. A. (1953). A proposal for a new method of evaluation in the newborn infant. *Current Research in Anesthesia and Analgesia, 32,* 260–267.

Arnold, L. D. W., & Tully, M. R. (Eds.). (1996). *Guidelines for the establishment and operation of a donor human milk bank.* West Hartford, CT: Human Milk Banking Association of North America.

Aronson, S. (1991). *Health and safety in child care.* New York: HarperCollins.

Arsenio, W. F., & Lover, A. (1995). Children's conceptions of sociomoral affect: Happy victimizers, mixed emotions, and other expressions. In M. Killen & D. Hart (Eds.), *Morality in everyday life: Developmental perspectives* (pp. 87–128). New York: Cambridge University Press.

Asher, S. R., Renshaw, P. D., & Hymel, S. (1982). Peer relations and the development of social skills. In S. G. Moore & C. R. Cooper (Eds.), *The young child: Reviews of research* (Vol. 3, pp. 137–158). Washington, DC: National Association for the Education of Young Children.

Astington, J. W. (1993). *The child's discovery of the mind.* Cambridge, MA: Harvard University Press.

Astington, J. W., & Olson, J. W. (1995). The cognitive revolution in children's understanding of mind. *Human Development, 38,* 179–189.

Au, K. H. (1993). *Literacy instruction in multicultural settings.* Fort Worth, TX: Harcourt Brace.

Au, K. H., & Kowakami, A. J. (1991). Culture and ownership: Schooling minority students. *Childhood Education, 67*(5), 280–284.

Baillargeon, R. (1987). Object permanence in 3½ and 4½ month old infants. *Developmental Psychology, 23*(5), 655–664.

Baker, D., & Witt, P. A. (1996). Evaluation of the impact of two after-school recreation programs. *Journal of Park and Recreation Administration, 14*(3), 23–44.

Baker, L., Serpell, R., & Sonnenschein, S. (1995). Opportunities for literacy learning in the homes of urban preschoolers. In L. M. Morrow (Ed.,). *Family literacy: Connections in schools and communities.* Newark, DE: International Reading Association.

Ball, S., & Bogatz, G. A. (1972). Summative research of Sesame Street. Implications for the study of preschool children. In A. D. Pick (Ed.). *Minnesota symposium on child psychology* (Vol. 6, pp. 3–17). Minneapolis: University of Minnesota Press.

Baltes, P. B., Dittman-Kohli, F., & Dixon, R. A. (1984). New perspectives on the development of intelligence in adulthood: Toward a dual-process conception and a model of selective optimization with compensation. In P. B. Baltes & O. G. Brim, Jr. (Eds.), *Life-span development and behavior* (Vol. 6, pp. 33–76). New York: Academic.

Bandura, A. (1965). Influence of models' reinforcement contingencies on the acquisition of imitative responses. *Journal of Personality and Social Psychology, 1,* 587–595.

Bandura, A. (1977). *Social learning theory.* Upper Saddle River, NJ: Prentice Hall.

Bandura, A. (1986). *Social foundation of thoughts and actions: A social cognitive theory.* Upper Saddle River, NJ: Prentice Hall.

Bandura, A. (1989). Social cognitive theory. In R. Vasta (Ed.), *Annals of child development, Vol. 6: Theories of child development: Revised formulations and current issues* (pp. 1–60). Greenwich, CT: JAI.

Bandura, A. (1997). *Self-efficacy: The exercise of control.* New York: Freeman.

Bandura, A., & Walters, R. (1963). *Social learning and personality development.* New York: Holt, Rinehart & Winston.

Banks, S. P., & Kahn, M. D. (2003). *The sibling bond.* New York: Basic Books.

Barbour, A. C. (1995). Physical competence and peer relations in 2nd graders: Qualitative case studies from recess play. *Journal of Research in Childhood Education, 11*(1), 35–46.

Barclay, K., Benelli, C., & Curtis, A. (1995). Literacy begins at birth: What caregivers can learn from parents of children who read early. *Young Children 50*(4), 24–28.

Barnett, W. S. (1995). Long-term effects of early childhood programs on cognitive and school outcomes.

In R. E. Behrman (Ed.), *The future of children, 5*(3), 25–50. Los Altos, CA: The Center for the Future of Children/The David and Lucile Packard Foundation.

Bar-Tal, D., Raviv, A., & Goldberg, M. (1982). Helping behavior among children: An observational study. *Child Development, 53,* 396–402.

Basiotis, P. P., Linn, M., & Anand, R. S. (1999, December). *Eating breakfast greatly improves schoolchildren's diet quality* (Nutrition Insights #15, Fact Sheet). Washington, DC: USDA Center for Nutrition Policy and Promotion.

Baskett, L. M. (1984). Ordinal position differences in children's family interactions. *Developmental Psychology, 20,* 1026–1031.

Baskett, L. M., & Johnson, S. M. (1982). The young child's interaction with parents versus siblings: A behavioral analysis. *Child Development, 53,* 643–650.

Baumrind, D. (1967). Child care practices anteceding three patterns of preschool behavior. *Genetic Psychology Monographs, 75,* 43–88.

Baumrind, D. (1971). Current patterns of parental authority. *Developmental Psychology Monographs, 4* (No. 1, Pt. 2).

Baumrind, D. (1972). Socialization and instrumental competence in young children. In W. W. Hartrup (Ed.), *The young child: Reviews of research* (Vol. 2, pp. 202–224). Washington, DC: National Association for the Education of Young Children.

Baumrind, D. (1991a). Parenting styles and adolescent development. In R. Lerner, A. C. Petersen, & J. Brooks-Gunn (Eds.). *The encyclopedia of adolescence* (pp. 746–758). New York: Garland.

Baumrind, D. (1991b). The influence of parenting style on adolescent competence and substance use. *Journal of Early Adolescence 1,* 56–95.

Baumrind, D. (1995). The discipline controversy revisited. *Family Relations 45,* 405–414.

Baumrind, D. (1998). Reflections on character and competence. In A. Colby, J. James, & D. Hart (Eds.), *Competence and character through life* (pp. 1–28). Chicago: University of Chicago Press.

Bayley, N. (1969). *Bayley scales of infant development.* New York: Psychological Corporation.

Bebko, J. M., Burke, L., Craven, J., & Sarlo, N. (1992). The importance of motor activity in sensorimotor development: A perspective from children with physical handicaps. *Human Development, 35*(4), 226–240.

Becker, J. (1994). Pragmatic socialization: Parental input to preschoolers. *Discourse Processes, 17,* 131–148.

Beddard, J. R., & Chi, M. T. H. (1992). Expertise. *Current Directions in Psychological Science, 1,* 135–139.

Behrman, R. E. (Ed.). (1997). *The future of children: Welfare to work.* Los Altos, CA: David and Lucile Packard Foundation.

Behrman, R. E. (Ed.). (1999). *The future of children: When school is out.* Los Altos, CA: David and Lucile Packard Foundation.

Beilin, H. (1980). Piaget's theory: Refinement, revision, or rejection? In R. Kluwe & H. Spada (Eds.), *Developmental models of thinking* (pp. 245–261). New York: Academic.

Bell, J. J., & Dana, K. (1998). Lack of correlation between growth hormone provocative test results and subsequent growth rates during growth hormone therapy. *Pediatrics, 102*(2; Supplement, Part 3 of 3), 518–520.

Bell, R. Q., & Chapman, M. (1986). Child effects in studies using experimental or brief longitudinal approaches to socialization. *Developmental Psychology, 22,* 1353–1354.

Bell, S. M., & Ainsworth, M. D. S. (1972). Infant crying and maternal responsiveness. *Child Development, 43,* 1171–1190.

Belsky, J. (1988). The effects of infant day care reconsidered. *Early Childhood Research Quarterly, 3,* 235–272.

Belsky, J., & Rovine, M. (1988). Non-maternal care in the first year of life and the security of infant–parent attachment. *Child Development, 59*(1), 157–167.

Belsky, J., Spritz, B., & Crnic, K. (1996). Infant attachment security and affective cognitive information processing at age three. *Psychological Science, 7,* 111–114.

Bench, J. (1978). The auditory response. In V. Stave (Ed.), *Perinatal physiology.* New York: Plenum Press.

Berk, L. E. (1984). Development of private speech among low-income Appalachian children. *Developmental Psychology, 20,* 271–286.

Berk, L. E. (1985). Why children talk to themselves. *Young children, 40*(5), 46–52.

Berk, L. E. (1986). Relationship of elementary school children's private speech to behavioral accompaniment to task, attention and performance. *Developmental Psychology, 22,* 671–680.

Berk, L. E. (1994). *Child development.* (3rd ed.). Boston: Allyn & Bacon.

Berk, L. E., & Winsler, A. (1995). *Scaffolding children's learning: Vygotsky and early childhood education.* Washington, DC: National Association for the Education of Young Children.

Berkowitz, G. S., Wolff, M. S., Janevic, T. M., Holzman, I. R., Yehuda, R., & Landrigan, P. J. (2003). The World Trade Center disaster and intrauterine growth restriction. *Journal of the American Medical Association, 290,* 595–596.

Berreuta-Clement, J. R., Schweinhart, L. J., Barnett, W. S., Epstein, A. S., & Weikart, D. P. (1984). *Changed lives: The effects of the Perry Preschool Program on youths through age 19* (Monographs of the High/Scope Educational Research Foundation, 8). Ypsilanti, MI: High/Scope Press.

Bialystok, E. (1986). Factors in the growth of linguistic awareness. *Child Development, 57,* 498–510.

Bierman, K. L. (2003). *Peer rejection: Developmental processes and intervention strategies.* New York: Guilford.

Bigelow, B. J., Tesson, G., & Lewko, J. H. (1996). *Learning the rules: The anatomy of children's relationships.* New York: Guilford.

Bijou, S., & Baer, D. (1961). *Child development. Vol. 1: A systematic and empirical theory.* Upper Saddle River, NJ: Prentice Hall.

Birch, L. L., & Fisher, J. O. (1998). Development of eating behaviors among children and adolescents. *Pediatrics, 101*(3, Supplement), 539–549.

Birch, L. L., Johnson, S. L., Andersen, G., Peters, J. C., & Schulte, M. C. (1991). The variability of young children's energy intake. *New England Journal of Medicine, 324,* 232–235.

Birch, L. L., Johnson, S. L., & Fisher, J. A. (1995). Research in review: Children's eating: The development of food-acceptance patterns. *Young Children 50*(2), 71–78.

Birch, L. L., Johnson, S. L., Graciela, A., Peters, J. C., & Schulte, M. C. (1991). The variability of young children's energy intake. *New England Journal of Medicine, 324*(4), 232–235.

Birch, L. L., McPhee, L., Shoba, B. C., Steinberg, L., & Krehbiel, R. (1987). "Clean up your plate": Effects of child feeding practices on the conditioning of meal size. *Learning and Motivation, 18,* 301–317.

Birch, L. L., Zimmerman, S., & Hind, H. (1980). The influence of social–affective context on preschool children's food preferences. *Child Development, 51,* 856–861.

Black, J. K. (1981). Are young children really egocentric? *Young Children, 36*(6), 51–55.

Black, J. K., & Puckett, M. (1987). Informing others about developmentally appropriate practice. In S. Bredekamp (Ed.), *Developmentally appropriate practice in early childhood programs serving children from birth through age 8* (pp. 83–87). Washington, DC: National Association for the Education of Young Children.

Blass, E. M., & Shah, A. (1995). Pain-reducing properties of sucrose in human newborns. *Chemical Senses, 20*(1), 29–35.

Blau, D. M. (1999). The effects of child care characteristics on child development. *Journal of Human Resources, 34,* 786–822.

Bloom, B. (1964). *Stability and change in human characteristics.* New York: Wiley.

Bloom, L. (1970). *Form and function in emerging grammars.* Cambridge, MA: MIT Press.

Blosch, N., Tabachnick, B. R., & Espinosa-Dulanto, D. (1994). Teacher perspectives on the strengths and achievements of young children: Relationship to ethnicity, language, gender and class. In B. L. Mallory & R. S. New (Eds.), *Diversity and developmentally appropriate practices* (pp. 223–249). New York: Teachers College Press.

Bodrova, E., & Leong, D. J. (1998). Development of dramatic play in young children and its effects on self-regulation: The Vygotskian approach. *Journal of Early Childhood Teacher Education, 19*(2), 115–124.

Bogin, B. (1999). *Patterns of human growth.* Cambridge, MA: Cambridge University Press.

Boggiano, A. K., Klinger, C. A., & Main, D. S. (1986). Enhancing interest in peer interaction: A developmental analysis. *Child Development, 57,* 852–861.

Boothe, R. G., Dobson, V., & Teller, D. Y. (1985). Postnatal development of vision in human and nonhuman primates. *Annual Review of Neuroscience, 8,* 495–545.

Borke, H. (1983). Piaget's mountains revisited: Changes in the egocentric landscape. In M. Donaldson, R. Grieve, & C. Pratt (Eds.), *Early childhood development and education: Readings in psychology* (pp. 254–259). New York: Guilford.

Bornstein, M. H. (1984). A descriptive taxonomy of psychological categories used by infants. In C. Sophian (Ed.), *Origins of cognitive skills. The eighteenth annual Carnegie symposium on cognition* (pp. 313–338). Hillsdale, NJ: Erlbaum.

Bornstein, M. H. (1985). Human infant color vision and color perception. *Infant Behavior and Development, 8,* 109–113.

Bornstein, M. H. (1988). Perceptual development across the life cycle. In M. H. Bornstein & M. E. Lamb (Eds.), *Developmental psychology: An advanced textbook* (2nd ed., pp. 151–204). Hillsdale, NJ: Erlbaum.

Bornstein, M. H., & Lamb, M. E. (1992). *Development in infancy: An introduction* (3rd ed.). New York: McGraw-Hill.

Bower, T. G. R. (1982). *Development in infancy* (2nd ed.). New York: Freeman.

Bowlby, J. (1969/2000). *Attachment and loss: Vol. 1. Attachment* (2nd ed.). New York: Basic Books.

Bowlby, J. (1973). *Attachment and loss: Vol. 2. Separation: Anxiety and anger.* New York: Basic Books.

Bowlby, J. (1980). *Attachment and loss: Vol. 3. Loss: Sadness and depression.* New York: Basic Books.

Bowman, B., Donovan, M. S., & Burns, S. (Eds.). (2001). *Eager to learn: Educating our preschoolers.* Washington, DC: National Academy Press.

Bowman, B. T., & Stott, F. M. (1994). Understanding development in a cultural context: The challenge for teachers. In B. L. Mallory & R. S. New (Eds.), *Diversity and developmentally appropriate practices* (pp. 119–133). New York: Teachers College Press.

Boyatzis, C. J. (1997). Of Power Rangers and V-chips. *Young Children, 52*(7), 74–79.

Brazelton, T. B. (1973). *Neonatal Behavioral Assessment Scale* (Clinics in Developmental Medicine No. 50, Spastics International Medical Publication). Philadelphia: Lippincott.

Brazelton, T. B. (1992). *Touchpoints: The essential reference: Your child's emotional and behavioral development.* Reading, MA: Addison-Wesley.

Brecht, M. C. (1989). The tragedy of infant mortality. *Nursing Outlook, 37,* 18.

Bredekamp, S. (1995). What do early childhood professionals need to know and be able to do? *Young Children, 50*(2), 67–69.

Bredekamp, S., & Copple, C. (Eds.). (1997). *Developmentally appropriate practices in early childhood programs (rev. ed.).* Washington, DC: National Association for the Education of Young Children.

Bredekamp, S., & Shepard, L. (1989). How best to protect children from inappropriate school expectations, practices, and policies. *Young Children, 44*(3), 14–24.

Bretherton, I. (1986). Representing the social world in symbolic play: Reality and fantasy. In A. S. Gottfried & C. C. Brown (Eds.), *Play interactions: The contributions of play materials and parental involvement to children's development* (pp. 119–148). Lexington, MA: Lexington.

Bretherton, I., & Walters, E. (Eds.). (1985). *Growing points in attachment theory and research* (Monographs of the Society for Research in Child Development, Vol. 50, No. 1–2, serial no. 209). Chicago: University of Chicago Press.

Briere, J. N., & Elliott, D. M. (1994). Immediate and long-term impacts of child sexual abuse. *The Future of Children, 4*(2), 54–69.

Bronfenbrenner, U. (1970, November). *Who cares for America's children?* Keynote address delivered at the Annual Conference of the National Association for the Education of Young Children, Boston.

Bronfenbrenner, U. (1977). Toward an experimental ecology of human development. *American Psychologist, 32,* 513–531.

Bronfenbrenner, U. (1979). *The ecology of human development.* Cambridge, MA: Harvard University Press.

Bronfenbrenner, U. (1986). Ecology of the family as a context for human development: Research perspectives. *Developmental Psychology, 22,* 723–742.

Bronfenbrenner, U., & Ceci, S. J. (1994). Nature–nurture reconceptualized in developmental perspective: A bioecological model. *Psychological Review, 101*(4), 568–586.

Brooks-Gunn, J., & Lewis, M. (1982). The development of self-knowledge. In C. Kropp & J. Krakow (Eds.), *The child: Development in a social context* (pp. 333–387). Reading, MA: Addison-Wesley.

Brown, R. (1973). *A first language: The early stages.* Cambridge, MA: Harvard University Press.

Brown, R., & Fraser, C. (1963). The acquisition of syntax. In C. N. Cofer & B. S. Musgrave (Eds.), *Verbal behavior and learning: Problems and processes* (pp. 158–209). New York: McGraw-Hill.

Bruner, J. (1983). The acquisition of pragmatic commitments. In R. M. Golinkoff (Ed.), *The transition from prelinguistic to linguistic communication* (pp. 27–42). Hillsdale, NJ: Erlbaum.

Bryan, J. H., Sonnefeld, J., & Greenberg, F. (1981). Children's and parents' views about integration tactics. *Learning Disability Quarterly, 4,* 170–179.

Bryan, T. H., & Bryan, J. H. (1986). *Understanding learning disabilities.* Palo Alto, CA: Mayfield.

Burchinal, M. R., Bryant, D. M., Lee, M. W., & Ramey, C. T. (1992). Early day care, infant–mother attachment, and maternal responsiveness in the infant's first year. *Early Childhood Research Quarterly, 7,* 383–396

Burns, M. S., Griffin, P., & Snow, C. (Eds.). (1999). *Starting out right: A guide to promoting children reading success.* Washington, DC: National Academy Press.

Bus, A., van Ijendoorn, M., & Pellegrini, A. D. (1995). Mothers reading to their 3-year-olds: The role of mother–child attachment security in becoming literate. *Reading Research Quarterly, 30,* 998–1015.

Buss, A. H., & Plomin, R. (1984). *Temperament: Early developing personality traits.* Hillsdale, NJ: Erlbaum.

Caine, R. N., & Caine, G. (1997). *Education on the edge of possibility.* Alexandria, VA: Association for Supervision and Curriculum Development.

Campbell, F. A., & Ramey, C. T. (1994). Effects of early intervention on intellectual and academic achievement: A follow-up study of children from low-income families. *Child Development, 65,* 684–698.

Campbell, S. B. (2002). *Behavior problems in preschool children: Clinical and developmental issues* (2nd ed.). New York: Guilford.

Campos, J. J., & Stenberg, C. R. (1981). Perception appraisal and emotion: The onset of social referencing. In M. E. Lamb & L. R. Sherrod (Eds.), *Infant social cognition: Empirical and theoretical considerations* (pp. 273–314). Hillsdale, NJ: Erlbaum.

Canadian Council on Smoking and Health, National Clearinghouse on Tobacco and Health. (1995). *Environmental tobacco smoke (ETS) in home environments.* Toronto, Canada: Author.

Cardone, I. (2002). Maternal mental health: Early identification in a hospital-based multidisciplinary setting. *Zero to Three, 22*(6), 35–36.

Carey, S. (1978). The child as word learner. In M. Halle, J. Bresnan, & G. Miller (Eds.), *Linguistic theory and psychological reality* (pp. 264–293). Cambridge, MA: MIT Press.

Carey, W. B., & Jablow, M. M. (1997). *Understanding young children's temperament.* New York: Macmillan.

Carle, E. (1979). *The very hungry caterpillar.* New York: Collins.

Carlson, M., & McLanahan, S. (2002). *Characteristics and antecedents of involvement by young unmarried fathers.* Princeton University, Center for Research on Child Well-being. Retrieved April 2002, from http:/crcw. princeton.edu/workingpapers/WP02-09-FF-Carlson-pdf

Carnegie Corporation of New York. (1996). *Years of promise: A comprehensive learning strategy for America's children.* New York: Carnegie Corporation.

Caron, A. J., Caron, R. F., & MacLean, D. (1988). Infant discrimination of naturalistic emotional expressions: The role of face and voice. *Child Development, 59,* 604–616.

Case, R. (1992). Neo-Piagetian theories of intellectual development. In H. Beilin & P. B. Pufall (Eds.), *Piaget's theory: Prospects and possibilities* (pp. 61–104). Hillsdale, NJ: Erlbaum.

Case, R. (1992). *The mind's staircase: Exploring the conceptual underpinnings of children's thought and knowledge.* Hillsdale, NJ: Erlbaum.

Casper, V. (1996). Making familiar unfamiliar and unfamiliar familiar. *Zero to Three, 16*(3), 14–20.

Casper, V., Cooper, R. M., Finn, C. D., & Stott, R. (2003). Caregiver goals and societal expectations. *Zero to Three, 23*(5), 4–6.

Cassidy, J., & Asher, S. R. (1992). Loneliness and peer relations in young children. *Child Development, 63,* 350–365.

Cassidy, J., & Berlin, L. J. (1994). The insecure/ambivalent patterns of attachments: Theory and research. *Child Development, 65*(4), 971–991.

Cassidy, J., & Shaver, P. R. (Eds.). (1999). *Handbook of attachment: Theory, research, and clinical applications.* New York: Guilford.

Cauley, K., & Tyler, B. (1989). The relationship of self-concept to prosocial behavior in children. *Early Childhood Research Quarterly, 4,* 51–60.

Centers for Disease Control and Prevention. (2000). Youth risk behavior surveillance—United States, 1999. *Mortality and Morbidity Weekly Report, 49,* SS-5.

Centers for Disease Control and Prevention. (2001). CDC identifies nutritional deficiencies among young children. *Morbidity and Mortality Weekly Report.* Retrieved April 1, 2001, from http.www.cdc.gov

Chance, N. (1984). Growing up in a Chinese village. *Natural History, 93,* 78–81.

Charlesworth, R. (1989). "Behind" before they start? Deciding how to deal with the risk of kindergarten "failure." *Young Children, 44*(3), 5–13.

Charlesworth, R. (1998). Developmentally appropriate practice is for everyone. *Childhood Education, 74,* 274–282.

Checkley, K. (1997). The first seven—and the eighth: A conversation with Howard Gardner. *Education Leadership, 55*(1), 8–13.

Chess, S. (1967). Temperament in the normal infant. In B. Straub & J. Hellmuth (Eds.), *Exceptional infant: Vol. 1. The normal infant* (pp. 143–162). Seattle, WA: Special Child.

Chess, S., & Thomas, A. (1987). *Origins and evolution of behavior disorders from infancy to early adult life.* Cambridge, MA: Harvard University Press.

Chess, S., & Thomas, A. (1996). *Temperament: Theory and practice.* New York: Brunner/Mazel.

Child Abuse Prevention and Treatment Act of 1975. 42, U.S. Code 501.

Child Trends. (2001). *Nonmarital births: Myths and realities.* Retrieved April 17, 2001, from http://www. childtrends.org/marriagepatterns.asp

Child Welfare League of America. (1997). *Guarding children's rights—Serving children's needs.* New York: Author.

Children's Defense Fund. (2001). *2001: The state of America's children.* Washington, DC: Author.

Children's Defense Fund. (2002). *The state of children in America's union, 2002.* Washington, DC: Author.

Children's Educational Television Act of 1990. United States Code 1988, Title 47, Section 394, 397, October 18, 1990 (P.L. 101–437), 104 Stat. 996 Title 2.

Childs, C. P., & Greenfield, P. M. (1980). Informal modes of learning and teaching: The case of Zinacanteco learning. In N. Warren (Ed.), *Studies in cross-cultural psychology* (Vol. 2). New York: Academic.

Chilman, C. S. (1966). *Your child from 6 to 12.* Washington, DC: Children's Bureau, U.S. Department of Health, Education, and Welfare.

Chiong, J. (1998). *Racial categorization of multiracial children in schools.* Westport, CT: Bergin and Garvey.

Chomsky, N. (1968). *Language and mind.* San Diego, CA: Harcourt Brace Jovanovich.

Chomsky, N. (1969). *The acquisition of syntax in children from five to ten.* Cambridge, MA: MIT Press.

Chomsky, N. (1980). *Rules and representations.* New York: Columbia University Press.

Chomsky, N. (1993). *Language and thought.* Kingston, RI: Moyer Bell.

Chrisman, K., & Couchenour, D. (2002). *Healthy sexuality development: A guide for early childhood educators*

and families. Washington, DC: National Association for the Education of Young Children.

Christian, K., Morrison, F. J., & Bryant, F. B. (1998). Predicting kindergarten academic skills: Interactions among child care, maternal education, and family literacy environments. *Early Childhood Research Quarterly, 13,* 501–502.

Christian, J. L., & Gregor, J. L. (1993). *Nutrition for living* (2nd ed.). Menlo Park, CA: Benjamin/Cummings.

Chugani, H. T. (1997). Neuroimaging of developmental non-linearity and developmental pathologies. In R. W. Thatcher, G. R. Lyon, J. Rumsey, & N. Krasnegor (Eds.), *Developmental neuroimaging: Mapping the development of brain and behavior* (pp. 187–195). San Diego, CA: Academic Press.

Cicchetti, D., & Beeghly, M. (Eds.). (1990). *The self in transition: Infancy to childhood.* Chicago: University of Chicago Press.

Clark, E. V. (1983). Meanings and concepts. In J. H. Flavel & E. M. Markman (Eds.), *Handbook of child psychology. Vol. 3: Cognitive development* (4th ed., pp. 787–840). New York: Wiley.

Clarke-Stewart, K. A., Vandell, D. L., Burchinal, M. R. O'Brien, M., & McCartney, K. (2002). Do regulable features of child care homes affect children's development? *Early Childhood Research Quarterly, 17,* 52–86.

Clay, M. M. (1979). *Sand—The concepts about print test.* Auckland, New Zealand: Heinemann.

Clay, M. M. (1993). *An observation survey of early literacy achievement.* Auckland, New Zealand: Heinemann.

Clyman, R. B., Emde, R. N., Kempe, J. E., & Harmon, R. J. (1986). Social referencing and social looking among 12-month-old infants. In T. B. Brazelton & M. W. Yogman (Eds.), *Affective development in infancy* (pp. 75–94). Norwood, NJ: Ablex.

Coates, B., Pusser, H. E., & Goodman, I. (1976). The influence of "Sesame Street" and "Mister Rogers' Neighborhood" on children's social behavior in the preschool. *Child Development, 47,* 138–144.

Cohen, M. (1967). *Will I have a friend?* New York: Macmillan.

Cole, R. (1997). *The moral intelligence of children: How to raise a moral child.* New York: Plume.

Coll, C. G., & Meyer, E. C. (1993). The sociocultural context of infant development. In C. H. Zeanah, Jr. (Ed.), *Handbook of infant mental health* (pp. 56–69). New York: Guilford.

Collins, W. A., Maccoby, E. E., Steinberg, L., Hetherington, E. M., & Bornstein, M. H. (2000). Contemporary research on parenting: The case for nature and nurture. *American Psychologist, 55*(2), 218.

Comer, J. P., & Poussaint, A. F. (1992). *Raising Black children.* New York: Penguin.

Connor, S. M., & Wesolowski, K. L. (2003). "They're too smart for that": Predicting what children would do in the presence of guns. *Pediatrics, 111,* e109–e114.

Cook, J. T., Ohri-Vachaspati, P., & Kelly, G. L. (1996). *Evaluation of a universally-free school breakfast program demonstration project, Central Falls, Rhode Island.* Medford, MA: Tufts University, Center on Hunger, Poverty, and Nutrition Policy.

Cooper, R. P., & Anslin, R. N. (1990). Preference for infant-directed speech in the first month after birth. *Child Development, 61,* 1584–1595.

Coopersmith, S. (1967). *The antecedents of self-esteem.* San Francisco: Freeman.

Cornell, E. H., & McDonnell, P. M. (1986). Infants' acuity at twenty feet. *Investigative Ophthalmology and Visual Science, 27,* 1417–1420.

Council for Early Childhood Professional Recognition. (1992). *Child Development Associate assessment and competency standards.* Washington, DC: Author.

Creasy, G., Jarvis, P., & Berk, L. (1998). Play and social competence. In O. Saracho & B. Spodek (Eds.), *Multiple perspectives on play in early childhood* (pp. 116–143). Albany, NY: State University of New York Press.

Crockenberg, S., & Litman, C. (1990). Autonomy as competence in two-year-olds: Maternal correlates of child compliance, defiance, and self-assertion. *Development Psychology, 26,* 961–971.

Dahl, R. (1998). Life's gracefulness lost on overstimulated, overtired children. *American Academy of Pediatrics News, 14*(5), 28.

Dansky, J. L. (1980). Make-believe: A mediator of the relationship between play and associative fluency. *Child Development, 51,* 576–579.

Darwin, C. (1859). *The origin of species.* London: Murray.

Davis, R. (1990). *A comparison of the reading and writing performance of children in a whole language pre-first grade class and a modified traditional first grade class.* Unpublished doctoral dissertation, University of North Texas, Denton.

Davis, D. W., & Bell, P. A. (1991). Infant feeding practices and occlusal outcomes: A longitudinal study. *Journal of the Canadian Dental Association, 57*(7), 593–594.

DeBoysson-Bardies, B., Sagart, L., & Durand, C. (1984). Discernible differences in the babbling of infants according to target language. *Journal of Child Language, 11,* 1–16.

DeCasper, A. J., & Fifer, W. P. (1980). Of human bonding: Newborns prefer their mothers' voices. *Science, 208,* 1174–1176.

DeCasper, A. J., & Spence, M. J. (1986). Prenatal maternal speech influences newborn's perception of speech sounds. *Infant Behavior and Development, 9,* 133–150.

DeCasper, A. J., & Spence, M. J. (1992). Auditorily mediated behavior during the perinatal period: A cognitive view. In M. J. S. Weiss & P. R. Zealazo (Eds.), *Newborn attention: Biological constraints and the influence of experience.* Norwood, NJ: Ablex.

DeHaas-Warner, S. (1994). The role of child care professionals in placement and programming decisions for preschoolers with special needs in community based settings. *Young Children, 45*(5), 76–78.

deHouwer, A. (1995). Bilingual language acquisition. In P. Fletcher & B. MacWhinney (Eds.), *The handbook of child language* (pp. 219–250). Oxford: Blackwell.

Deiner, P. L. (1997). *Infant and toddlers: Development and program planning.* Fort Worth, TX: Harcourt Brace.

Delcomyn, F. (1998). *Foundations of neurobiology.* New York: Freeman.

Denham, S. A. (1998). *Emotional development in young children.* New York: Guilford.

Denham, S., & Weissberg, R. (2003). Social–emotional learning in early childhood: What we know and where to go from here. In M. Bloom & T. P. Guillotta (Eds.), *A blueprint for the promotion of prosocial behavior in early childhood.* New York: Kluwer/Academic.

Derman-Sparks, L., & Phillips, C. B. (1997). *Teaching/learning anti-racism: A developmental approach.* New York: Teachers College Press.

deVilliers, P. A., & deVilliers, J. G. (1992). Language development. In M. E. Lamb & M. H. Bornstein (Eds.), *Developmental psychology: An advanced textbook* (3rd ed.). Hillsdale, NJ: Erlbaum.

DeVries, R. (1969). *Constancy of generic identity in the years three to six* [Monographs of the Society for Research in Child Development, 34 (3, Serial No. 127)]. Chicago: University of Chicago Press.

DeVries, R., & Zan, B. (1994). *Moral classrooms, moral children: Creating a constructivist atmosphere in early education.* New York: Teachers College Press.

Diamond, J. (1990). War babies. *Discover, 11*(12), 70–75.

Diamond, M. C., & Hopson, J. (1998). *Magic trees of the mind.* New York: Plume.

Diamond, M. C., Krech, D., & Rosenzweig, M. R. (1964). The effects of an enriched environment on the histology of the rat cerebral cortex. *Journal of Comparative Neurology, 123,* 111–120.

Dienstbier, R. A. (January). Arousal and physiological toughness: Implications for mental and physical health. *Psychological Review 96*(1), 84–100.

Dobbing, J. (1984). Infant nutrition and later achievement. *Nutrition Reviews, 42,* 1–7.

Dodge, K. A. (1994). Studying mechanism in the cycle of violence. In C. Thompson & P. Cowas (Eds.), *Violence: Basic and clinical science.* Oxford: Butterworth-Hernemas.

Doiron, R. (1994). Using nonfiction in a read-aloud program: Letting the facts speak for themselves, *Reading Teacher, 47*(8), 616–624.

Donaldson, M. (1979). *Children's minds.* New York: Norton.

Donaldson, M. (1983). Children's reasoning. In M. Donaldson, R. Grieve, & C. Pratt (Eds.), *Early childhood development and education: Readings in psychology* (pp. 231–236). New York: Guilford.

Donnerstein, E., Slaby, R. G., & Eron, L. (1994). The mass media and youth aggression. In L. D. Eron, J. H. Gentry, & P. Schlegel (Eds.), *Reason to hope: A psychosocial perspective on violence and youth.* Washington, DC: American Psychological Association.

Dorr, A. (1983). No shortcuts to judging reality. In P. E. Bryant & S. Anderson (Eds.), *Watching and understanding TV: Research on children's attention and comprehension.* New York: Academic Press.

Dorr, A., Graves, S., & Phelps, E. (1980). Television literacy for young children. *Journal of Communication, 30,* 71–83.

Dozier, M., Albus, K. E., Stovall, K. C., & Bates, B. (2002). Attachment for infants in foster care: The role of caregiver state of mind. *Child Development, 72,* 1467–1477.

Dreher, M. J., & Zenge, S. D. (1990). Using metalinguistic awareness in first grade to predict reading achievement in third and fifth grades. *Journal of Educational Research, 84*(1), 13–21.

Dresden, J., & Myers, B. K. (1989). Early childhood professionals: Toward self-definition. *Young Children, 44*(2), 62–66.

Dunn, L., & Kontos, S. (1997). Research in review: What have we learned about developmentally appropriate practice? *Young Children, 52*(5), 4–13.

DuRant, R. H., Getts, A. G., Cadenhead, C., Emans, J., & Woods, E. R. (1995). Exposuure to violence and victimization and depression, hopelessness and purpose of life among adolescents living in and around public housing. *Journal of Developmental and Behavioral Pediatrics, 16,* 233–237.

DuRant, R. H., Treiber, F., Goodman, E., & Woods, E. R. (1996). Intentions to use violence among young adolescents. *Pediatrics, 98,* 1104–1108.

Durkin, D. (1966). *Children who read early.* New York: Teachers College Press.

Durkin, D. (1993). *Teaching them to read* (6th ed.). Needham Heights, MA: Allyn & Bacon.

Dyson, A. H. (1981). *A case study examination of the role of oral language in writing processes of kindergartners.* Unpublished doctoral dissertation, University of Texas at Austin.

Dyson, A. H. (1993). *Social worlds of children learning to write in an urban primary school.* New York: Teachers College Press.

Dyson, A. H. (1997). *Writing superheroes: Contemporary childhood, popular culture, and classroom literacy.* New York: Teachers College Press.

Earls, F., & Carlson, M. (1993). Towards sustainable development for American families. *Daedalus, 122*(1), 93–121.

Easterbrooks, M. A., & Goldberg, W. A. (1990). Toddler–parent attachment: Relation to children's sociopersonality functioning during kindergarten. In M. T. Greenberg, D. Cicchetti, & E. M. Cummings (Eds.), *Attachment in the preschool years: Theory, research and intervention* (pp. 221–224). Chicago: University of Chicago Press.

Eaton, W. O., Chipperfield, J. G., & Singbell, C. E. (1989). Birth order and activity level in children. *Developmental Psychology, 25,* 668–672.

Eaton, W. O., & Von Bargen, D. (1981). Asynchronous development of gender understanding in preschool children. *Child Development, 52,* 1020–1027.

Education for All Handicapped Children Act of 1975. United States Code 1976, Title 20, 1232, 1401, 1405, 1406, 1411 to 1420, 1433, November 29, 1975 (P. L. 94–142), Stat. 773.

Education of All Handicapped Children Act Amendments of 1986. United States Code 1988, Title 20, 1401, 1471, October 6, 1986 (P. L. 99–57), 100 Stat. 1143.

Education of All Handicapped Children Act Amendments of 1990. United States Code 1988,

Title 20, 1401, 1471, October 1990 (P. L. 101–476), 104 Stat. 1103.

Elder, G. H., Jr. (1982). Historical experiences in the later years. In T. K. Hareven & K. J. Adams (Eds.), *Aging and life course transitions: An interdisciplinary perspective* (pp. 75–107). New York: Guilford.

Elkonin, D. (1977). Toward the problem of stages in the mental development of the child. In M. Cole (Ed.), *Soviet developmental psychology* (pp. 538–563). White Plains, NY: Sharpe.

Emde, R. N., & Buchsbaum, H. K. (1990). 'Didn't you hear my mommy?': Autonomy with connectedness in moral self-emergence. In D. Cicchetti & M. Beeghly (Eds.), *Infancy to Childhood* (pp. 35–60). Chicago: University of Chicago Press.

Emde, R. N., & Harmon, R. J. (1972). Endogenous and exogenous smiling systems in early infancy. *Journal of the American Academy of Child Psychiatry, 11,* 177–200.

Emory, E. K., Schlackman, L. J., & Fiano, K. (1996). Drug–hormone interactions on neurobehavioral responses in human neonates. *Infant Behavior and Development, 19*(2), 213–220.

Entwisle, D. R., & Alexander, K. L. (1987). Long term effects of cesarean delivery on parents' beliefs and children's schooling. *Developmental Psychology, 23,* 676–682.

Epperson, N. (2002). Postpartum mood changes: Are hormones to blame? *Zero to Three, 22*(6), 17–23.

Epstein, J. L. (1989). The selection of friends: Changes across the grades and in different school environments. In T. J. Berndt & G. W. Ladd (Eds.), *Peer relations in child development* (pp. 158–187). New York: Wiley.

Erikson, E. (1963). *Childhood and society* (2nd ed.). New York: Norton.

Eron, L. D. (1992). The impact of televised violence. Testimony on behalf of the American Psychological Association before the Senate Committee on Governmental Affairs, *Congressional Record, 1992* (June 18).

Etaugh, C., & Liss, M. B. (1992). Home, school, and playroom: Training grounds for adult gender roles. *Sex Roles, 26,* 639–648.

Evans, H. J., Fletcher, J., Torrance, M., & Hardgreave, T. B. (1981). Sperm abnormalities and cigarette smoking. *Lancet, 1,* 627–634.

Everett, S. A., Warren, C. W., Sharp, D., Kann, L., Husten, C. G., & Crossett, L. S. (1999). Initiation of cigarette smoking and subsequent smoking behavior among U.S. high school students. *Preventive Medicine, 29,* 337–333.

Fagot, B. I. (1988). Toddlers, play and sex stereotyping. In D. Bergen (Ed.), *Play as a medium for learning and development: A handbook of theory and practice* (pp. 133–135). Portsmouth, NH: Heinemann.

Fagot, B. I., Hagan, R., Leinback, M. D., & Kronsberg, D. (1985). Differential reactions to assertive and communication acts of toddlers boys and girls. *Child Development, 56*(6), 1499–1505.

Fagot, B. I., & Kavanagh, K. (1990). The prediction of antisocial behaviors from avoidant attachment classifications. *Child Development, 61*(3), 863–873.

Family and Medical Leave Act of 1993. Public Law No. 103, 29 USC §2601.

Fantz, R. L. (1961). The origin of form perception. *Scientific American, 204,* 66–72.

Fassler, R. (1998). Room for talk: Peer support for getting into English in an ESL kindergarten. *Early Childhood Research Quarterly, 13,* 370–409.

Federal Interagency Forum on Child and Family Statistics. (1998). *America's children: Key national indicators of well-being, 1998.* Washington, DC: U.S. Government Printing Office.

Federal Interagency Forum on Child and Family Statistics. (2003). *America's children: Key national indicators of well-being 2002.* Washington, DC: U.S. Government Printing Office.

Federal Motor Vehicle Safety Standard Act of 1980. 213 U.S. Code (1981).

Federman, J. (Ed.). (1997). *National television violence study. Vol. 2: Executive summary.* Santa Barbara: University of California Center for Communication & Social Policy.

Feeney, S., & Kipnis, K. (1992). *The National Association for the Education of Young Children code of ethical conduct and statement of commitment.* Washington, DC: National Association for the Education of Young Children.

Fein, G. (1978). *Child development.* Upper Saddle River, NJ: Prentice Hall.

Fein, G., Gariboldi, A., & Boni, R. (1993). The adjustment of infants and toddlers to group care: The first 6 months. *Early Childhood Research Quarterly, 8*(1), 1–14.

Feiring, C., & Lewis, M. (1991). The development of social networks from early to middle childhood: Gender differences and the relation to school competence. *Sex Roles, 25,* 527–253.

Feldman, R., Eidelman, A. I., Sirota, L., & Weller, A. (2002). Comparison of skin-to-skin (kangaroo) and traditional care: Parenting outcomes and preterm infant development. *Pediatrics, 110,* 16–26.

Fenichel, E. (Ed.). (2002). Perinatal mental health: Supporting new families through vulnerability and change [Theme Issue]. *Zero to Three, 22*(6).

Ferguson, C. A. (1977). Learning to pronounce: The earliest stages of phonological development in the child. In F. D. Minifie & L. L. Lloyd (Eds.), *Communicative and cognitive abilities: Early behavioral assessment* (pp. 141–155). Baltimore: University Park Press.

Fernald, A. (1993). Approval and disapproval: Infant responsiveness to vocal affect in familiar and unfamiliar languages. *Child Development, 64*(3), 657–674.

Fernald, A., & Morikawa, H. (1993). Common themes and cultural variations in Japanese and American mothers' speech to infants. *Child Development, 64*(3), 637–656.

Ferrerio, E., & Teberosky, A. (1982). *Literacy before schooling.* Exeter, NH: Heinemann.

Feshbach, S. (1970). Aggression. In P. Mussen (Ed.), *Carmichael's manual of child psychology* (Vol. 2). New York: Wiley.

Field, T. M. (1979). Differential behavioral and cardiac responses of 3-month-old infants to a mirror and a peer. *Infant Behavior and Development, 2,* 179–184.

Field, T. M., Schanberg, S. M., Scafidi, F., Bauer, C. R., Vegalahr, N., Garcia, R., Nystrom, J., & Kuhn, C. M. (1986). Effects of tactile/kinesthetic stimulation on preterm neonates. *Pediatrics, 77,* 654–658.

Field, T. M., Vega-Lahr, N., & Jagadish, S. (1984). Separation stress of nursery school infants and toddlers graduating to new classes. *Infant Behavior and Development, 7,* 277–284.

Fields, D. (1981). Can preschool children really learn to conserve? *Child Development, 52,* 326–334.

Fields, M. V., & Spangler, K. L., (2000). *Let's begin reading right: A developmental approach to emergent literacy* (4th ed.). Upper Saddle River, NJ: Merrill/Prentice Hall.

Fierro-Cobas, V., & Chan, E. (2001). Language development in bilingual children: A primer for pediatricians. *Contemporary Pediatrics, 7,* 79

Fifer, W. P., & Moon, C. M. (1995). The effects of fetal experience with sound. In J. P. Lecanuet, W. E. Fifer, N. A. Krasnegor, & W. P. Smotherman (Eds.), *Fetal development: A psychobiological perspective.* Hillsdale, NJ: Erlbaum.

Fike, R. D. (1993). Personal relationship-building between fathers and infants. *Childhood Education, 5*(4), 1–2.

Fivush, R. (1984). Learning about school: The development of kindergartners' school scripts. *Child Development, 55,* 1697–1709.

Flavell, J. H. (1963). *The developmental psychology of Jean Piaget.* New York: Van Nostrand.

Flavell, J. H. (1985). *Cognitive development* (2nd ed.). Upper Saddle River, NJ: Prentice Hall.

Fleege, P. O., Charlesworth, R., Burts, D. C., & Hart, C. H. (1992). Stress begins in kindergarten: A look at behavior during standardized testing. *Journal of Research in Childhood Education, 7*(1), 20–26.

Fogel, A. (1979). Peer vs. mother directed behavior in 1- to 3-month-old infants. *Infant Behavior and Development, 2,* 215–226.

Food Research and Action Center. (2003). *Current news and analyses.* Available at http://www.frac.org/html/news/103097.html

Forman, M. A., Hetznecker, W. H., & Dunn, J. M. (1983). Psychosocial dimensions of pediatrics: Gender identity and roles. In R. E. Behrman & V. C. Vaughn III (Eds.), *Nelson textbook of pediatrics* (12th ed., pp. 56–58). Philadelphia: Saunders.

Freel, K. S. (1996). Finding complexities and balancing perspectives: Using an ethnographic viewpoint to understand children and families. *Zero to Three, 16*(3), 3–7.

Freidrich, L. K., & Stein, A. H. (1975). Prosocial television and young children: The effect of verbal labeling and role-playing on learning and behavior. *Child Development, 46,* 27–38.

Freud, S. (1905/1930). *Three contributions to the theory of sex.* New York: Nervous and Mental Disease Publishing.

Freud, S. (1933). *New introductory lectures on psychoanalysis.* New York: Norton.

Freud, S. (1938). The history of the psychoanalytic movement. In A. A. Brill (Ed. and Trans.), *The basic writings of Sigmund Freud* (pp. 931–977). New York: Modern Library.

Frost, J. L. (1992). Reflections on research and practice in outdoor play environments. *Dimensions, 20*(4), 6–10.

Frost, J. L., Wortham, S. L., & Reifel, S. (2001). *Play and child development.* Upper Saddle River, NJ: Merrill/Prentice Hall.

Fuller, B., Eggers-Pierola, C., Holloway, S. D. Liang, X., & Rambaud, M. (1995). Rich culture, poor markets: Why do Latino parents choose to forego preschooling? In B. Fuller, R. Elmore, & G. Orfield, (Eds.), *School choice: The cultural logic of families, the political rationality of institutions.* New York: Teachers College Press.

Furman, W., & Buhmester, D. (1992). Age and sex difference in perceptions of networks of personal relationships. *Child Development, 63,* 103–115.

Furth, H. G. (1992a). The developmental origin of human societies. In H. Beilin and P. B. Pufall (Eds.), *Piaget's theory: Prospects and possibilities.* Hillsdale, NJ: Erlbaum.

Furth, H. G. (1992b). Life's essential—The story of mind over body: A review of "I raise my eyes to say yes": A memoir by Ruth Sienkiewicz-Mercer & S. B. Kaplan. *Human Development, 35*(2), 254–261.

Furth, H. G. (1992c). Commentary on Bebko, Burke, Craven & Sarlo (1992): The importance of sensorimotor development: A perspective from children with physical handicaps. *Human Development, 36*(4), 226–240.

Gabbard, C., Dean, M., & Haensly, P. (1991). Foot preference behavior during early childhood. *Journal of Applied Developmental Psychology, 12*(1), 131–137.

Gable, S. (1999). Promoting children's literacy with poetry. *Young Children, 54*(5), 12–15.

Gage, F. H. (2003). Brain: Heal thyself. *Scientific American, 2003* (September), 48–55.

Gage, F. H., & Jacob, B. (2001, July 15). Exercise and adult neurogenesis. *London News, Financial Times,* p. 11.

Gallahue, D. L. (1993). *Developmental physical education for today's children* (2nd ed.). Madison, WI: Brown & Benchmark.

Gallahue, D. L., & Ozmun, J. C. (1998) *Understanding motor development: Infants, children, adolescents, adults* (4th ed.). New York: McGraw-Hill.

Galenson, E. (1993). Sexual development in preoedipal females: Arrest versus intrapsychic conflict. In T. B. Cohen & M. Etezady (Eds.), *The vulnerable child* (Vol. 1). Madison, CT: International Universities Press.

Galler, J. R., Ramsey, F., & Solimano, G. (1984). The influence of early malnutrition on subsequent development: 3. Learning disabilities as a sequel to malnutrition. *Pediatric Research, 18,* 309.

Galler, J. R., Ramsey, F., & Solimano, G. (1985). A follow-up study of the effects of early malnutrition on subsequent development: 2. Fine motor skills in adolescence. *Pediatric Research, 19,* 524.

Garbarino, J. (1999). *Rasing children in a socially toxic environment.* San Francisco, CA: Jossey-Bass.

Garcia-Coll, C. T. (1990). Developmental outcomes of minority infants: A process-oriented look into our beginnings. *Child Development, 61*(2), 270–289.

Gardner, H. (1983). *Frames of mind: Theory of multiple intelligences.* New York: Basic Books.

Gardner, H. (1991a). Assessment in context: The alternative to standardized testing. In B. R. Gifford & M. C. O'Connor (Eds.), *Changing assessments: Alternative views of attitude, achievement and instruction.* Boston: Kluwer.

Gardner, H. (1991b). *The unschooled mind: How children think and how schools should teach.* New York: Basic Books.

Gardner, H. (1993). *Multiple intelligences: The theory in practice.* New York: Basic Books.

Gardner, H. (1999). *Intelligence reframed: Multiple intelligences for the 21st century.* New York: Basic Books.

Garrett, P., Ferron, J., Ng'Andu, N., Bryant, D., & Harbin, G. (1994). A structural model for the developmental status of young children. *Journal of Marriage and the Family, 56*(1), 147–163.

Garvey, C. (1977). *Play.* Cambridge, MA: Harvard University Press.

Gauvain, M. (2000). *The social context of cognitive development.* New York: Guilford.

Gazzaniga, M. (1988). *Mind matters; How mind and brain interact to create our conscious lives.* Boston: Houghton Mifflin, in association with MIT Press.

Gehrke, N. J. (1987). *On being a teacher.* West Lafayette, IN: Kappa Delta Pi.

Gelles, R. J., & Edfeldt, A. W. (1990). Violence toward children in the United States and Sweden. In M. A. Jensen & Z. W. Chevalier (Eds.), *Issues and advocacy in early education* (pp. 133–140). Boston: Allyn & Bacon.

Gelman, R., Bullock, M., & Meck, E. (1980). Preschooler's understanding of simple object transformation. *Child Development, 51,* 691–699.

Gelman, R., & Gallistel, C. R. (1983). The child's understanding of number. In M. Donaldson, R. Grieve, & C. Pratt (Eds.), *Early childhood development and education: Readings in psychology* (pp. 185–203). New York: Guilford.

Gergen, P. J., Fowler, J. A., Maurer, K. R., Davis, W. W., & Overpeck, M. D. (1999). The burden of environmental tobacco smoke exposure on the respiratory health of children 2 months through 5 years of age in the United States: Third national health and nutrition examination survey, 1988–1994. Electronic abstracts. Available at www.pediatrics.org

Gesell, A. (1925). *The mental growth of the preschool child: A psychological outline of normal development from birth to the sixth year.* New York: Macmillan.

Gesell, A. (1930). *Guidance of mental growth in infant and child.* New York: Macmillan.

Gesell, A., & Amatruda, C. S. (1941). *Developmental diagnosis: Normal and abnormal child development.* New York: Hoeber.

Gesell, A., & Ilg, F. L. (1949). *Child development.* New York: Harper & Row.

Gesell, A., & Thompson, H. (1929). Learning and growth in identical infant twins: An experimental study by the method of co-twin control. *Genetic Psychology Monographs, 6,* 1–125.

Ghazvini, A. S., & Readdick, C. A. (1994). Parent–caregiver communication and quality of care in diverse child care settings. *Early Childhood Research Quarterly, 9*(2), 207–222.

Gilligan, C. (1982). *In a different voice.* Cambridge, MA: Harvard University Press.

Gleason, J. B. (2000). *The development of language* (5th ed.). Boston: Allyn & Bacon.

Goffin, S. G., & Lombardi, J. (1989). *Speaking out: Early childhood advocacy.* Washington, DC: National Association for the Education of Young Children.

Goldstein, J. H. (1994). *Toys, play, and child development.* New York: Cambridge University Press.

Goleman, D. (1995). *Emotional intelligence.* New York: Bantam.

Golinkoff, R. M. (1983). The preverbal negotiation of failed messages: Insights into the transition period. In R. M. Golinkoff (Ed.), *The transition from prelinguistic to linguistic communication* (pp. 57–75). Hillsdale, NJ: Erlbaum.

Gollnick, D. M., & Chinn, P. C. (1990). *Multicultural education in a pluralistic society* (3rd ed.). Upper Saddle River, NJ: Merrill/Prentice Hall.

Golombok, S., & Fivush, R. (1994). *Gender development.* New York: Cambridge University Press.

Gomby, D. S., Culross, P. L., & Behrman, R. E. (Spring/Summer, 1999). Home visiting: Recent program evaluations—Analysis and recommendations. In R. E. Behrman (Ed.), *The future of children. Vol. 9, Number 1: Home visiting: Recent program evaluations* (pp. 4–26). Los Altos, CA: David and Lucile Packard Foundation.

Goodman, K. (1986). *What's whole in whole language?* Portsmouth, NH: Heinemann.

Goodman, R. F. (2001). *A view from the middle: Life through the eyes of middle childhood: A critique of research conducted by Sesame Workshop.* New York University Child Study Center. Retrieved 17 September 2001 from www.aboutourkids.org

Goodman, Y. (1980). The roots of literacy. In M. P. Douglass (Ed.), *Claremont Reading Conference forty-fourth yearbook.* Claremont, CA: Claremont Graduate School.

Gopnik, A., Meltzoff, A. N., & Kuhl, P. K. (1999). *The scientist in the crib: Minds, brains, and how children learn.* New York: Morrow.

Gottfried, A. (1984). Touch as an organizer of human development. In C. Brown (Ed.), *The many facets of touch* (pp. 114–120). Skillman, NJ: Johnson & Johnson.

Gottlieb, G. (1991). *Individual development and evolution: The genesis of novel behavior.* New York: Oxford University Press.

Gottlieb, G. (1995). Some conceptual deficiencies in 'developmental' behavior genetics. *Human Development 38*(3), 131–141, 165–169.

Gottman, J. M. (1983). *How children become friends* (Monographs of the Society for Research in Child Development, Vol. 48, No. 3, serial no. 291). Chicago: University of Chicago Press.

Grantham-McGregor, S., Chang, S., & Walker, S. (1998). Evaluation of school feeding programs: Some Jamaican examples. *American Journal of Clinical Nutrition, 67,* 785S–789S.

Green, J. A., Jones, L. E., & Gustafson, G. E. (1987). Perception of cries by parents and nonparents: Relation to cry acoustics. *Developmental Psychology, 23,* 370–382.

Green, M. (1985). The development of metaphoric comprehension and preference (Doctoral dissertation, Boston University). *Dissertation Abstracts International, 46,* 1264A.

Greenough, W., Gunnar, M., Emde, R. N., Massinga, R., & Shonkoff, J. P. (2001). The impact of the caregiving environment on young children's development: Different ways of knowing. *Zero to Three, 21*(5), 16–23.

Greenspan, S., & Greenspan, N. T. (1985). *First feelings.* New York: Penguin.

Gregorchik, L. A. (1992). The cocaine exposed children are here. *Phi Delta Kappan, 73*(9), 709–711.

Grogan, T., & Bechtel, L. (2003). Boys and girls together: Improving gender relationships in school. *Responsive Classroom, 15*(1), 1–2.

Grossman, D. C., Neckerman, T. D., Koepsell, P. Y., Liu, K. N, Asher, D. B., Frey, K., & Rivara, F. P. (1997). Effectiveness of a violence prevention curriculum among children in elementary school. *Journal of the American Medical Association, 277,* 1605–1611.

Grossmann, K., Grossmann, K. E., Spangler, G., Suess, G. L., & Unzner, L. (1985). Maternal sensitivity and newborns' orientation responses as related to quality of attachment in Northern Germany. In I. Bretherton & E. Waters (Eds.), *Growing points of attachment theory and research* (Monographs of the Society for Research in Child Development, Vol. 50, No. 1–2, serial no. 209, pp. 233–256). Chicago: University of Chicago Press.

Gunnar, M. R. (1996). *Quality of care and the buffering of stress physiology: Its potential in protecting the developing human brain.* Minneapolis: University of Minnesota Institute of Child Development.

Gunnar, M. R. (1998). Quality of early care and buffering of neuroendocrine stress reactions: Potential effects on the developing human brain. *Preventive Medicine, 27,* 208–211.

Gunnar, M. R., Broderson, L., Nachmias, M., Buss, K., & Rigatuso, J. (1996). Stress reactivity and attachment security. *Developmental Psychology, 29*(3), 191–204.

Haber, J. S. (2000). *The great misdiagnosis: ADHD.* Dallas, TX: Taylor.

Hack, M., Schluchter, M., Cartar, L., Rahman, M., Cuttler, L., & Borawski, E. (2003). *Pediatrics, 112*(1), e30–e38. Retrieved July 7, 2003, from http://www.pediatrics.aappublications.org/

Hack, M., Klein, N. K., & Taylor, H. G. (1995). Long-term developmental outcomes of low birth weight infants. In *The future of children: Low birth weight* (Vol. 5[1], pp. 176–196). Los Altos, CA: David and Lucile Packard Foundation.

Haith, M. M. (1966). The response of human newborns to visual movement. *Journal of Experimental Child Psychology, 3,* 235–243.

Hall, G. S. (1893). *The contents of children's minds.* New York: Kellogg.

Halpern, R. (2003). *Making play work: The promise of after-school programs for low-income children.* New York: Teachers College Press.

Handscombe, J. (1994). "Putting it all together." In F. Genesee (Ed.), *Educating second language children* (pp. 331–355). New York: Cambridge University Press.

Hargrave, A. C., & Senechal, M. (2000). A book reading intervention with preschool children who have limited vocabularies: The benefits of regular reading and dialogic reading. *Early Childhood Research Quarterly, 15* (1), 78–90.

Hart, B., & Risley, T. R. (1995). *Meaningful differences in the everyday experience of young American children.* Baltimore: Brookes.

Hart, C. H., DeWolf, D. M., Royston, K. E., Burts, D. C., & Thomasson, R. H. (1990, Spring). *Maternal and paternal disciplinary styles: Relationships to behavioral orientations and sociometric status.* Paper presented at the annual conference of the American Educational Research Association, Boston.

Hart, C. H., Ladd, G. W., & Burleson, B. R. (1990). Children's expectations of the outcomes of social strategies: Relations with sociometric status and maternal disciplinary styles. *Child Development, 61,* 127–137.

Hart, L. (1983). *Human brain, human learning.* New York: Longman.

Harter, S. (2001). *The construction of self: A developmental perspective.* New York: Guilford.

Hartup, W. W. (1974). Aggression in childhood: Developmental perspectives. *American Psychologist, 29,* 336–341.

Hartup, W. W. (1983). Peer relations. In E. M. Hetherington (Ed.), *Handbook of child psychology. Vol. 4: Socialization, personality and social development* (4th ed., pp. 103–196). New York: Wiley.

Hartup, W. W. (1989). Behavioral manifestations of children's friendships. In T. J. Berndt & G. W. Ladd (Eds.), *Peer relationships in child development* (pp. 46–70). New York: Wiley.

Havighurst, R. J. (1972). *Developmental tasks and education.* New York: McKay.

Hay, D. R., Nash, A., & Pederson, J. (1983). Interaction between six-month-old peers. *Child Development, 54,* 557–562.

Head Start Bureau. (1998). *Head Start performance measures: Second progress report.* Washington, DC: Head Start, Department of Health and Human Services.

Heath, D. C. (1977). *Maturity and competence: A transcultural view.* New York: Gardner.

Heath, S. B. (1983). *Ways with words: Language life and work in communities and classrooms.* Cambridge: Cambridge University Press.

Heck, S., & Williams, C. R. (1984). *The complex roles of the teacher: An ecological perspective.* New York: Teachers College Press.

Helburn, S. (Ed.). (1995). *Cost, quality, and child outcomes in child care centers. Technical report.* Denver: University of Colorado at Denver, Economics Department.

Helburn, S., & Bergmann, B. (2002). *America's child care problem: The way out.* New York: Palgrave for St. Martin's Press.

Hellige, J. B. (1993). *Hemispheric asymmetry: What's right and what's left.* Cambridge, MA: Harvard University Press.

Helms. J. E. (1990). *Black and white racial identity: Theory, research, and practice.* Westport, CT: Greenwood.

Heneghan, A. M., Silver, E. J., Bauman, L. J., Westbrook, L. E. & Stein, R. E. K. (1998). Depressive symptoms in inner-city mothers of young children: Who is at risk? *Pediatrics 102*(6), 1394–1400.

Henshaw, S. K. (2003). *U.S. Teenage pregnancy statistics with comparative statistics for women aged 20–24.* Alan Guttmacher Institute. Retrieved June 4, 2003, from www.guttmacher.org/

Hetherington, E. M., Cox, M., & Cox, R. (1982). Effects of divorce on parents and children. In M. E. Lamb (Ed.), *Nontraditional families* (pp. 233–288). Hillsdale, NJ: Erlbaum.

Hobson, J. (1989). *Sleep.* New York: Freeman.

Hoffman, M. L. (1988). Moral development. In M. H. Bornstein & M. E. Lamb (Eds.), *Developmental psychology: An advanced textbook* (2nd ed., pp. 497–548). Hillsdale, NJ: Erlbaum.

Hohmann, C. (1990). *Young children and computers.* Ypsilanti, MI: High/Scope Press.

Honig, A. S. (1983). Research in review: Sex role socialization in early childhood. *Young Children, 38*(6), 57–70.

Honig, A. S. (1986). Research in review: Stress and coping in children (Part I). *Young Children, 41*(4), 50–63.

Honig, A. S. (2000). Psychosexual development in infants and young children: Implications for caregivers. *Young Children, 55*(5), 70–77.

Honig, A., & Wittmer, D. (1996). Helping children become more prosocial: Ideas for classrooms, families, school, and communities (Part 2). *Young Children, 51*(2), 62–70.

Hoot, J. L., & Silvern, S. (Eds.). (1989). *Writing with computers in the early grades.* New York: Teachers College Press.

Houston, A. C., Donnerstein, E., Fairchild, H., Feshbach, N. D., Katz, P. A., Murray, J. P., Rubenstein, E. A., Wilcox, G. L., & Zuckerman, D. (1992). *Big world, small screen.* Lincoln: University of Nebraska Press.

Howard, V. F., Williams, B. F., Port, P. D., & Pepper, C. (2001). *Very young children with special needs: A formative approach for the 21st century* (2nd ed.). Upper Saddle River, NJ: Merrill/Prentice Hall.

Howes, C. (1980). Peer play scale as an index of complexity of peer interaction. *Developmental Psychology, 16,* 371–372.

Howes, C. (1987). Quality indicators in infant and toddler child care: The Los Angeles study. In D. A. Phillips (Ed.), *Quality in child care: What does research tell us?* (pp. 81–88). Washington, DC: National Association for the Education of Young Children.

Howes, C. (1992). *The collaborative construction of pretend: Social pretend play functions.* Albany: State University of New York Press.

Howes, C. (1996). The earliest friendships. In W. M. Berkowski, A. F. Newcomb, & W. W. Hartup (Eds.), *The company they keep: Friendships in childhood and adolescence.* Cambridge, MA: Cambridge University Press.

Howes, C. (1997). Children's experiences in center-based child care as a function of teacher background and adult: child ratio. *Merrill-Palmer Quarterly, 43,* 404–425.

Howes, C., & Hamilton, C. E. (1993). The changing experience of child care: Changes in teachers and in teacher–child relationships and children's social competence with peers. *Early Childhood Research Quarterly, 8*(1), 15–32.

Howes, C., & Ritchie, S. (2002). *A matter of trust: Connecting teachers and learners in the early childhood classroom.* New York: Teachers College Press.

Huesmann, L. R., Eron, L. D., Lefkowitz, M. M., & Walder, L. O. (1984). Stability over time and generations. *Developmental Psychology, 20,* 1120–1134.

Hughes, F. P. (1999). *Children, play and development* (3rd ed.). Boston: Allyn & Bacon.

Hughes, M., & Donaldson, M. (1983). The use of hiding games for studying coordination of points. In M. Donaldson, R. Grieve, & C. Pratt (Eds.), *Early childhood development and education: Readings in psychology* (pp. 245–253). New York: Guilford.

Hughes, M., & Grieve, R. (1983). On asking children bizarre questions. In M. Donaldson, R. Grieve, & C. Pratt (Eds.), *Early childhood development and education: Readings in psychology* (pp. 104–114). New York: Guilford.

Hunt, C. E., & Brouillette, R. T. (1987). Sudden infant death syndrome: 1987 perspective. *Journal of Pediatrics, 110,* 669–678.

Hunt, J. McV. (1961). *Intelligence and experience.* New York: Ronald.

Hunziker, U. A., & Barr, R. G. (1986). Increased carrying reduces infant crying: A randomized controlled trial. *Pediatrics, 77,* 641–648.

Hymel, S., Rubin, K., Rowden, L., & LeMare, L. (1990). Children's peer relationships: Longitudinal prediction of internalizing and externalizing problems from middle to late childhood. *Child Development, 61,* 2004–2021.

Iglowstein, I., Jenni, O. G., Molinari, L., & Largo, R. H. (2003). Sleep duration from infancy to adolescence: Reference values and generational trends. *Pediatrics, 111,* 302–307.

Individuals with Disabilities Education Act Amendments of 1991. United States Code 1988, Title 20, 1401, October 7, 1991 (P.L. 102–119), 105 Stat. 587.

Ingram, D. (1986). Phonological development: Production. In P. Fletcher & M. Garman (Eds.), *Language acquisition* (2nd ed., pp. 223–239). Cambridge, England: Cambridge University Press.

International Reading Association & National Association for the Education of Young Children (1998). *Learning to read and write: A joint position statement.* Newark, DE: Author.

Invernizzi, M., Abouzeid, M., & Gill, J. T. (1994). Using students' invented spellings as a guide for spelling instruction that emphasizes word study. *Elementary School Journal, 95*(2), 155–167.

Isabella, R. A. (1993). Origins of attachment: Maternal interactive behavior across the first year. *Child Development, 64*(2), 605–621.

Isabella, R. A., Belsky, J., & von Eye, A. (1989). Origins of infant–mother attachment: An examination of interaction synchrony during the infant's first year. *Developmental Psychology, 25*, 12–21.

Izard, C. E. (1991). *The psychology of emotions.* New York: Plenum.

Izard, C. E., & Buechler, S. (1986). Theoretical perspectives on emotions in developmental disabilities. In M. Lewis & L. Taft (Eds.), *Developmental disabilities: Theory, assessment, and intervention.* New York: Medical & Scientific Books.

Izard, C. E., Huebner, R., Risser, D., McGinnes, G., & Dougherty, L. (1980). The young infant's ability to produce discrete emotion expressions. *Developmental Psychology, 16*, 132–140.

Jalongo, M. R. (1987). Do security blankets belong in preschool? *Young Children, 42*(3), 3–8.

Janz, K. F., Burns, T. L., Torner, J. C., Levy, S. M., Paulos, R., Willing, M. C., & Warren, J. J. (2001). Physical activity and bone measure in young children: The Iowa bone development study. *Pediatrics, 107*, 1387–1393.

Jeffrey, H. E., Megevand, A., & Page, H. D. (1999). Why the prone position is a risk factor for sudden infant death syndrome. *Pediatrics, 104*, 263–269.

Jellinek, M., Patel, B. P., & Froehle, M. C. (2002). *Bright futures in practice: Mental Health* (Vols. I & II). Washington, DC: U.S. Department of Health and Human Services, Maternal and Child Health Bureau & National Center for Education in Maternal and Child Health.

Jensen, W. A., Heinrich, B., Wake, D. B., & Wake, M. H. (1979). *Biology.* Belmont, CA: Wadsworth.

Jersild, A. T., & Holmes, F. B. (1935a). *Children's fears.* New York: Teachers College Press.

Jersild, A. T., & Holmes, F. B. (1935b). Methods of overcoming children's fears. *Journal of Psychology, 1*, 75–104.

Johnson, B. H. (1995). Newborn intensive care units pioneer family-centered change in hospitals across the country. *Zero to Three, 15*(6), 11–17.

Johnson, J., & McCracken, J. B. (Eds.). (1994). *The early childhood career lattice: Perspectives on professional development.* Washington, DC: National Association for the Education for Young Children

Johnson, J. E., & Yawkey, T. D. (1988). Play and integration. In T. D. Yawkey & J. E. Johnson (Eds.), *Integrative processes and socialization: Early to middle childhood* (pp. 97–117). Hillsdale, NJ: Erlbaum.

Johnson, L. D., O'Malley, P. M., & Bachman, J. G. (2001). *Monitoring the future. National survey results on drug use, 1975–2000. Vol. I: Secondary school students.* (National Institute of Health Publication #01-4924). Bethesda, MD: National Institute on Drug Abuse.

Johnson, S. L., & Birch, L. L. (1994). Parents' and children's adiposity and eating style. *Pediatrics, 94*(5), 653–661.

Jones, H. E., & Jones, M. C. (1928). A study of fear. *Childhood Education, 5*, 136–143.

Jones, N. A., Field, T., Fox, N. A., Davalos, M., Lundy, B., Hart, S. (1998). Newborns of mothers with depressive symptoms are physiologically less developed. *Infant Behavior and Development, 21*(3), 537–541.

Jorgensen, M. H., Hernell, O., Lund, P., Hilmer, G., & Michaelsen, K. F. (1996). Visual acuity and erythrocyte docosahexaenoic acid status in breast-fed and formula-fed term infants during the first four months of life. *Lipids 31*(1), 99–105.

Jusczyk, P. W., Cutler, A., & Redanz, N. J. (1993). Infants' preference for the predominant stress patterns of English words. *Child Development, 64*(3), 675–687.

Kagan, J. (1971). *Change and continuity in infancy.* New York: Wiley.

Kagan, J. (1997). *Galen's prophecy: Temperament in human nature.* New York: Perseus.

Kagan, J. (1998). Biology and the child. In W. Damon (Ed.), *Handbook of child psychology: Social, emotional, and personality development* (5th ed., Vol. 3, pp. 177–235). New York: Wiley.

Kagan, J., Snidman, N., & Arcus, D. M. (1992). Initial reactions to unfamiliarity. *Current Directions in Psychological Science, 1*, 171–174.

Kagan, S. L., & Cohen, N. E. (1997). *Not by chance: Creating an early care and education system for America's children.* New Haven, CT: Bush Center in Child Development and Social Policy at Yale University.

Kagan, S. L., & Neuman, M. J. (1997). Public policy report: Highlights of the Quality 2000 Initiative: Not by chance. *Young Children, 52*(6), 54–62.

Kamii, C. K. (2000). *Young children reinvent arithmetic: Implications of Piaget's theory* (2nd ed.). New York: Teachers College Press.

Kamii, C. K. (2003). *Young children reinvent arithmetic (2nd grade): Implications of Piaget's theory* (2nd ed.). New York: Teachers College Press.

Karmel, M. (1959). *Thank you, Dr. Lamaze: Painless childbirth.* Philadelphia: Lippincott.

Karoly, L. A., Greenwood, P. W., Everingham, S. S., Hoube, J., Kilburn, M. R., Rydell, C. P., Sanders, M., & Chiesa, J. (1998). *Investing in our children: What we know and don't know about the costs and benefits of early childhood interventions.* Santa Monica, CA: RAND.

Katz, L. G. (1977). *Talks with teachers.* Washington, DC: National Association for the Education of Young Children.

Katz, L. G. (1995). *Talks with teachers of young children: A collection.* Norwood, NJ: Ablex.

Katz, L. G., & McClellan, D. E. (1997). *Fostering children's social competence: The teacher's role.* Washington, DC: National Association for the Education of Young Children.

Katz, P. A. (1982). Development of children's awareness and intergroup attitudes. In L. G. Katz (Ed.), *Current topics in early childhood education* (Vol. 4, pp. 17–54). Norwood, NJ: Ablex.

Kauffman Foundation. (2002). *New report links school success to early childhood social, emotional development.* Retrieved September 24, 2002, from http://www.emkf.org

Kemp, C. (1999). Early life social–emotional experiences affect brain development. *American Academy of Pediatric News, 15*(6), 18.

Kemp, C. (1999). Health Briefs: Tooth decay may affect growth. *American Academy of Pediatrics News, 15*(7), 2.

Kemple, K. M. (1992). *Understanding and facilitating preschool children's peer acceptance* (Report No. EDO-PS-92-5; ERIC Document Reproduction Service No. ED 345866). East Lansing, MI: National Center for Research on Teacher Learning.

Kendall, E. D., & Moukaddem, V. E. (1992). Who's vulnerable in infant child care centers? *Young Children, 47*(5), 72–78.

Kerwin, M. L. E., & Day, J. D. (1985). Peer influences on cognitive development. In J. B. Pryor & J. D. Day (Eds.), *The development of social cognition* (pp. 211–218). New York: Springer.

Kim, Y. A. (2003). Review of research: Necessary social skills related to peer acceptance. *Childhood Education, 79,* 234–238.

King, V., & Heard, H. E. (1999). Nonresident father visitation, parental conflict and mother's satisfactions: What's best for child well-being? *Journal of Marriage and the Family, 61*(2), 385–396.

Klahr, D., & Wallace, J. G. (1976). *Cognitive development: An information processing view.* Hillsdale, NJ: Erlbaum.

Klaus, M. H., & Kennell, J. H. (1982). *Parent–infant bonding* (2nd ed.). St. Louis, MO: Mosby.

Klauss, M. H., Kennell, J. H., & Klaus, P. H. (1993). *Mothering the mother.* Reading, MA: Addison-Wesley.

Klaus, M. H., Klaus, P. H., & Kennell, J. H., (2002). *The doula book: How a trained labor companion can help you have a shorter, easier, and healthier birth.* New York: Perseus.

Kleinman, R. E., Murphy, J. M., Little, M., Pagano, M. E., Wehler, C. A., Regal, K., & Jellinek, M. S. (1998). Hunger in children in the United States: Potential behavioral and emotional correlates. *Pediatrics, 101,* E3.

Kliegman, R. M., Jenson, H. B., & Behrman, R. E. (2003). *Nelson's textbook of pediatrics* (17th ed.). Philadelphia: Saunders.

Klinnert, M. D., Campos, J. J., Sorce, J. F., Emde, R. N., & Svejda, M. (1983). Emotions as behavior regulators; Social referencing in infancy. In R. Plutchik, & H. Kellerman (Eds.), *Emotion: Theory, research, and experience. Vol. 2: Emotions in early development (pp. 57–86).* New York: Academic.

Kohl, H. (1984). *Growing minds: On becoming a teacher.* New York: Harper & Row.

Kohlberg, L. (1966). A cognitive-developmental analysis of children's sex-role concepts and attitudes. In E. E. Maccoby (Ed.), *The development of sex differences* (pp. 82–173). Stanford, CA: Stanford University Press.

Kohlberg, L. (1968). The child as a moral philosopher. *Psychology Today, 1968* (September): 63–67.

Kohlberg, L. (1984). *Essays on moral development. Vol. 2: The psychology of moral development.* San Francisco: Harper & Row.

Kohlberg, L. (1987). *Child psychology and childhood education: A cognitive-developmental view.* New York: Longman.

Kohn, A. (2001). Five reasons to stop saying "good job." *Young Children, 56*(5), 24–28.

Kontos, S., & Wilcox-Herzog, A. (1997). Research in review: Teachers' interactions with children: Why are they so important? *Young Children, 52*(2), 4–12.

Korner, A. F., Zeanah, C. H., Linden, J., Berkowitz, R. I., Kraemer, H. C., & Agras, W. S. (1985). The relation between neonatal and later activity and temperament. *Child Development, 56,* 38–42.

Kraemer, H. C., Kazdin, A. E., Offord, D., Kessler, R. C., Jensen, P. S., & Kupfer, D. J. (1997). Coming to terms with the terms of risk. *Archives of General Psychiatry, 54,* 337–343.

Krasnegor, N. A., Lyon, G. R., & Goldman-Rakic, P. S. (1998). *Development of the prefrontal cortex: Evolution, neurobiology, and behavior.* Baltimore: Brookes.

Kuhl, P. K. (2001, July 27). *Born to learn: Language, reading, and the brain of the child.* Paper presented at the White House summit: Early childhood cognitive development: Ready to read; Ready to learn. Washington, DC.

Kuhn, D. (1992). Cognitive development. In M. H. Bornstein & M. E. Lamb. (Eds.), *Developmental psychology: An advanced textbook.* Hillsdale, NJ: Erlbaum.

Labov, W. (1972). *Language in the inner city: Studies in the Black English vernacular.* Philadelphia: University of Pennsylvania Press.

Ladd, G. W. (1990). Having friends, keeping friends, making friends, and being liked by peers in the classroom: Predictors of children's early school adjustment? *Child Development, 61,* 1081–1100.

Lally, J. R., Lerner, C., & Lurie-Hurvitz, E. (2001). National survey reveals gaps in the public's and parents' knowledge about early childhood development. *Young Children, 56*(2), 49–53.

Lalonde, C. E., & Chandler, M. J. (1995). False belief understanding goes to school: On the social–emotional consequences of coming early or late to a first theory of mind. *Cognition and Emotion, 9,* 167–185.

Lamb, M. E. (1978). The development of sibling relationships in infancy: A short-term longitudinal study. *Child Development, 49,* 1189–1196.

Lamb, M. E. (1987). Predictive implications of individual differences in attachment. *Journal of Consulting and Clinical Psychology, 55,* 817–824.

Lamb, M. E., Morrison, D. C., & Malkin, C. M. (1987). The development of infant social expectations in face-to-face interaction: A longitudinal study. *Merrill-Palmer Quarterly, 33,* 241–254.

Lamborn, S. D., Mounts, N. S., Steinberg, L. & Dornbusch, S. M. (1991). Patterns of competence and adjustment among adolescents from authoritative, authoritarian, indulgent and neglectful families. *Child Development 62,* 1049–1065.

Lampl, M., Veldhuis, J. D., & Johnson, M. L. (1992). Saltation and stasis: A model of human growth. *Science, 258,* 801–803.

Langlois, J. H., & Down, C. A. (1980). Mothers, fathers, and peers as socialization agents of sex-typed play behavior in young children. *Child Development, 51,* 1237–1247.

Larsen, J., & Robinson, C. (1989). Latter effects of preschool on low risk children. *Early Childhood Research Quarterly, 4*(1), 133–144.

Lazar, I., & Darlington, R. (1982). *Lasting effects of early education: A report from the Consortium for Longitudinal Studies* (Monographs of the Society for Research in Child Development, Vol. 47, No. 2-3, serial no. 195). Chicago: University of Chicago Press.

Leckman, J. F., & Mayes, L. C. (1999). Preoccupations and behaviors associated with romantic and parental love—The origin of obsessive-compulsive disorder? *Child and Adolescent Psychiatry Clinics of North America, 8,* 635–665.

LeDoux, J. (1996). *The emotional brain.* New York: Touchstone.

Le Francois, G. R. (1979). *Psychology of teaching: A bear always usually, sometimes faces the front* (3rd ed.). Belmont, CA: Wadsworth.

Lerman, E. (1997). *Teen moms: The pain and the promise.* Buena Park, CA: Morning Glory.

Lesser, G. S. (1979). Stop picking on Big Bird. *Psychology Today, 1979*(March), 57, 60.

Leung, E. H., & Rheingold, H. L. (1981). Development of pointing as a social gesture. *Developmental Psychology, 17,* 215–220.

Lever, J. (1976). Sex differences in games children play. *Social Problems, 23,* 478–487.

Levin, D. E. (1998). *Remote control childhood?: Combating the hazards of media culture.* Washington, DC: National Association for the Education of Young Children.

Levin, D. E. (2003). *Teaching young children in violent times* (2nd ed.). Washington, DC: National Association for the Education of Young Children.

Levine, S. B. (1994). Caution: Children watching. *Ms. 1994* (July/August), 23–25.

Levinson, D. J. (1986). A conception of adult development. *American Psychologist, 41,* 3–13.

Levy, G. D., & Carter, D. B. (1989). Gender schema, gender constancy, and gender role knowledge: The roles of cognitive factors in preschoolers' gender-role stereotype attributions. *Developmental Psychology, 25,* 444–449.

Lewis, C., Freeman, N., Kyriakidou, C., Maridaki-Kassotaki, K., & Berridge, D. (1996). Social influences on false belief access: Specific sibling influences or general apprenticeship? *Child Development 67,* 2930–2947.

Lewis, M. (1987). Social development in infancy and early childhood. In J. D. Osofsky (Ed.), *Handbook of infant development* (2nd ed., pp. 419–493). New York: Wiley.

Lewis, M. (1997). *Altering fate: Why the past does not predict the future.* New York: Guilford.

Lewis, M., & Brooks, J. (1978). Self-knowledge and emotional development. In M. Lewis & L. Rosenblum (Eds.), *The development of affect* (pp. 205–226). New York: Plenum.

Lewis, M., & Brooks-Gunn, J. (1979). *Social cognition and the acquisition of self.* New York: Plenum.

Liben, L. S., & Signorella, M. L. (1980). Gender-related schemata and constructive memory in children. *Child Development, 51*(1), 11–18.

Lieberman, A., & Miller, L. (1984). *Teachers, their world, and their work: Implications for school improvement.* Alexandria, VA: Association for Supervision and Curriculum Development.

Lieberman, A. F., & Zeanah, C. Y. (1995). Disorders of attachment in infancy. *Infant Psychiatry 4*(3), 571–587.

Lillard, A., & Curenton, S. M. (1999). Research in review: Do young children understand what others feel, want, and know? *Young Children, 54*(5), 52–57.

Linn, S., & Poussaint, A. F. (1999). Watching television: What are children learning about race and ethnicity? *Child Care Information Exchange, 128,* 50–52.

Little Soldier, L. (1992). Working with Native American children. *Young Children, 47*(6), 15–21.

Locust, C. (1988). Wounding the spirit: Discrimination and traditional American Indian belief systems. *Harvard Educational Review, 58*(3), 315–329.

Londerville, S., & Main, M. (1981). Security attachment, compliance, and maternal training methods in the second year of life. *Developmental Psychology, 17,* 289–299.

Lucariello, J., & Nelson, K. (1985). Slot-filler categories as memory organizers for young children. *Developmental Psychology, 21,* 272–282.

Lucas, A., Morley, R., & Coles, T. J. (1998). Randomized trial of early diet in preterm babies and later intelligence quotient. *British Medical Journal, 317,* 1481–1487.

Lyons-Ruth, K. (1996). Attachment relationships among children with aggressive behavior problems: The role of disorganized early attachment patterns. *Journal of Counseling and Clinical Psychology, 64,* 64–73.

Lyons-Ruth, K., Alpern, L., & Repacholi, B. (1993). Disorganized infant attachment classification and maternal psychosocial problems as predictors of hostile aggressive behavior in the preschool classroom. *Child Development, 64,* 572–585.

Lyons-Ruth, K., & Jacobvitz, D. (1999). Attachment disorganization: Unresolved loss, relational violence, and lapses in behavioral and attentional strategies. In J. Cassidy & P. R. Shaver (Eds.), *Handbook of attachment theory, research, and clinical applications* (pp. 520–554). New York: Guilford.

Maccoby, E. E. (1990). Gender and relationships: A developmental account. *American Psychologist, 45,* 513–520.

Maccoby, E. E. (2000). Parenting and its effects on children: On reading and misreading behavior genetics. *Annual Review of Psychology, 51*(1), 1–27.

Maccoby, E. E., & Jacklin, C. N. (1974/1980). Sex differences in aggression: A rejoinder and a reprise. *Child Development, 51,* 964–980.

MacDonald, K., & Parke, R. D. (1984). Bridging the gap. Parent–child play interaction and peer interactive competence. *Child Development, 55,* 1265–1277.

MacFarlane, A. (1977). *The psychology of childbirth.* Cambridge, MA: Harvard University Press.

MacLaughlin, B. (1978). *Second language learning in children.* Hillsdale, NJ: Erlbaum.

Maclean, M., Bryant, P., & Bradley, L. (1987). Rhymes, nursery rhymes, and reading in early childhood. *Merrill-Palmer Quarterly, 33,* 255–81.

Main, M., & Cassidy, J. (1988). Categories of response to reunion with parent at age 6: Predictable from infant attachment classification and stable over 1-month period. *Developmental Psychology, 24,* 415–426.

Main, M., & Solomon, J. (1990). Procedures for identifying infants as disorganized/disoriented during the Ainsworth strange situation. In M. Greenberg, D. Cicchetti, & E. M. Cummings (Eds.), *Attachment in the preschool years: Theory, research, and intervention* (pp. 121–160). Chicago: University of Chicago Press.

Main, M., & Weston, D. R. (1981). The quality of the toddler's relationship to mother and father: Related to conflict behavior and the readiness to establish new relationships. *Child Development, 52,* 932–940.

Maisels, M. J., & Kring, E. (1997). Early discharge from the newborn nursery: Effect on scheduling of follow-up visits by pediatricians. *Pediatrics 100,* 72–74.

Makin, J. W., & Porter, R. H. (1989). Attractiveness of lactating females' breast odors to neonates. *Child Development, 60,* 803–810.

Malloy, M. H. (1998). Effectively delivering the message on infant sleep position. *Journal of the American Medical Association, 280,* 373–374.

Mandler, J. M. (1990). A new perspective on cognitive development in infancy. *American Scientist, 78*(3), 236–243.

Mandler, J. M. (1992). Commentary on Bebko, Burke, Craven and Sarlo: The importance of sensorimotor development: A perspective from children with physical handicaps. *Human Development, 36*(4), 226–240.

Maratsos, M. (1983). Some current issues in the study of the acquisition of grammar. In J. H. Flavell & E. M. Markman (Eds.), *Handbook of child psychology. Vol. 3: Cognitive development* (4th ed., pp. 707–786). New York: Wiley.

Marion, M. (2003). *Guidance of young children* (6th ed.). Upper Saddle River, NJ: Merrill/Prentice Hall.

Maslow, A. H. (1962). Some basic propositions of a growth and self-actualization psychology. In A. W. Combs (Ed.), *Perceiving, behaving, becoming: Association for Supervision and Curriculum Development 1962 Yearbook* (pp. 34–49). Alexandria, VA: Association for Supervision and Curriculum Development.

Maslow, A. (1968). *Toward a psychology of being* (2nd ed.). Princeton, NJ: Van Nostrand.

Maslow, A. (1970). *Motivation and personality* (2nd ed.). New York: Harper & Row.

Mason, J. A., & Herrmann, K. R. (1998). Universal infant hearing screening by automated auditory brainstem response measurement. *Pediatrics, 101*(2), 221–228.

Mayes, L. C. (2002). Parental preoccupation and perinatal mental health. *Zero to Three, 22*(6), 4–9.

Mayhall, P., & Norgard, K. (1983). *Child abuse and neglect.* New York: Wiley.

McCartney, K. A., & Clarke-Stewart, A. (1999). *Does child care quality matter?* Presented at the symposium at the Biennial Meeting of the Society for Research in Child Development, Albuquerque, NM.

Meanella, J. A., Jagnow, C. P., & Beauchamp, G. K. (2001). Prenatal and postnatal flavor learning by human infants. *Pediatrics 107,* p. e88. Retrieved June 30, 2003, from http://pediatrics.aappublications.org/

Mehler, J. (1985). Language related dispositions in early infancy. In J. Mehler & R. Fox (Eds.), *Neonate cognition: Beyond the blooming buzzing confusion* (pp. 7–28). Hillsdale, NJ: Erlbaum.

Melmed, M. (1997). Public policy report: parents speak: Zero to Three's findings from research on parents' views of early childhood development. *Young Children, 52*(5), 46–49.

Meltzoff, A. N. (1989). Imitation in newborn infants: Exploring the range of gestures initiated and the underlying mechanisms. *Developmental Psychology, 25,* 954–962.

Meltzoff, A. N. (1995). Understanding the intentions of others: Re-enactment of intended acts by 18-month-old children. *Developmental Psychology 3,* 838–850.

Menyuk, P. (1988). *Language development: Knowledge and use.* Glenview, IL: Scott Foresman.

Meyerhoff, M. K. (March, 1994). Perspective on parenting: Crawling around. *Pediatrics for Parents, 1994* (March), 8, 9.

Miller, N. E., & Dollard, J. (1941). *Social learning and imitation.* New Haven, CT: Yale University Press.

Miller, P. M., Danaher, D. L., & Forbes, D. (1986). Sex-related strategies for coping with interpersonal conflict in children aged five and seven. *Developmental Psychology, 22,* 543–548.

Minnesota Department of Children, Families and Learning. (1998). *School breakfast programs energizing the classroom.* Roseville, MN: Author.

Monk, C. F., Fifer, W. P., Myers, M. M., Sloan, R. P., Trein, L., & Hurtado, A. (2000). Maternal stress responses and anxiety during pregnancy: Effects on fetal heart rate. *Developmental Psychology, 36*(1), 67–77.

Moore, B. S., & Eisenberg, N. (1984). The development of altruism. In G. Whitchurst (Ed.), *Annals of child development* (Vol. 1, pp. 107–174). Greenwich, CT: JAI.

Morphett, M. V., & Washburne, C. (1931). When should children begin to read? *Elementary School Journal, 31,* 496–503.

Morrison, F. J., Frazier, J. A., Hardway, C. L., Griffith, E. M., Williamson, G. I., & Miyazaki, Y. (1998). *Early literacy: The nature and sources of individual differences.* New York: MTA Cooperative Group.

Morrison, F. J., Griffith, E. M., & Alberts, D. M. (1997). Nature–nurture in the classroom: Entrance age, school readiness, and learning in children. *Developmental Psychology, 33*(2), 254–262.

Mortensen, E. L., Michaelsen, K. F., Sanders, S. A., & Reinisch, J. M. (2002). The association between duration of breastfeeding and adult intelligence. *Journal of the American Medical Association, 287,* 2365–2371.

Murphy, J. M., Pagano, M., & Bishop, S. J. (2001). *Impact of a universally free, in-classroom school breakfast program on achievement: Results of the ABELL*

Foundation Baltimore Breakfast Challenge Program. Boston, MA: Massachusetts General Hospital.

Murray, L., & Cooper, P. (1996). The impact of postnatal depression and associated adversity on early mother–infant interactions and later infant outcomes. *Child Development, 67,* 2512–2526.

Musick, J. S., & Householder, J. (1986). *Infant development: From theory to practice.* Belmont, CA: Wadsworth.

Myers, B. J. (1982). Early intervention using Brazelton training with middle-class mothers and fathers of newborns. *Child Development, 53,* 462–471.

National Academy of Early Childhood Programs. (1998). *Accreditation criteria and procedures* (rev. ed.). Washington, DC: National Association for the Education of Young Children.

National Association for Sport and Physical Education. (2003). *What constitutes a quality physical education program?* Retrieved October 10, 2003, from http://www.aahperd.org

National Board for Professional Teaching Standards. (1991). *Toward high and rigorous standards for the teaching profession: Initial policies and perspectives of the National Board for Professional Teaching Standards* (2nd ed.). Detroit, MI: Author.

National Association for the Education of Young Children. (1988). *Position statement on standardized testing of young children 3 through 8 years of age.* Washington, DC: Author.

National Association for the Education of Young Children. (1995). *Media violence and children: A guide for parents.* Washington, DC: Author.

National Association for the Education of Young Children. (1996). *NAEYC guidelines for preparation of early childhood professionals.* Washington, DC: Author.

National Association for the Education of Young Children. (2004). *Early childhood program standards and accreditation criteria.* Washington, DC: Author.

National Association for the Education of Young Children & National Association of Early Childhood Specialists in State Departments of Education. (1992). *Guidelines for appropriate curriculum content and assessment in programs serving children 3 through 8 years of age.* Washington, DC: National Association for the Education of Young Children.

National Association for the Education of Young Children & National Council for Accreditation of Teacher Education. (2001). *NAEYC standards for early childhood professional preparation: Initial licensure level.* Washington, DC: National Association for the Education of Young Children.

National Center for Children in Poverty, Columbia University School of Public Health. (2001). *Kith and kin—Informal child care: Highlights from recent research.* New York: Author.

National Center for Education Statistics. (1998). *Characteristics of children's early care and education programs: Data from the 1995 National household education survey.* Washington, DC: Author.

National Center for Health Statistics. (July, 1994). *Vital and health statistics* [Series 20, No. 24; DHHS Pub. No.

(PHS) (94-1852)]. Hyattsville, MD: U.S. Department of Health and Human Services.

National Center for Health Statistics. (2002). *Vital statistics of the United States, 1998. Vol. I: Natality.* Atlanta, GA: Centers for Disease Control and Prevention, National Center for Health Statistics.

National Governors' Association. (1997). *The first three years: A governor's guide to early childhood.* Washington, DC: Author.

National Governors' Association. (1998). *Early childhood activities in the states, 1996–1998.* Available at http://www.nga.org/Children/Survey1998.htm

National Institute of Allergy and Infectious Diseases, National Institutes of Health. (2002). *Tuberculosis FNIAID fact sheet.* Retrieved April 20, 2002, from http://www.niaid.nih.gov/factsheets/tb.htm

National Institute of Child Health and Human Development. (1999). Child outcomes when child care center classes meet recommended standards for quality. *American Journal of Public Health, 89,* 1072–1077.

National Research Council & National Institute of Medicine. (1997). *Improving schooling for language-minority children: A research agenda.* Washington, DC: National Academy Press.

National Safety Council. (2002). *Why child safety seats?* National Safety Belt Coalition of the National Safety Council. Retrieved December 18, 2002, from http://www.nsc.orgtraf/sbcchild.html

Nelson, C. A., & Luciana, M. (2001). *Handbook of developmental cognitive neuroscience.* Cambridge, MA: MIT Press.

Nelson, K. (1996). *Language in cognitive development: Emergence of the mediated mind.* Cambridge, England: Cambridge University Press.

Nelson, K. (1981). Individual differences in language development: Implications for development and language. *Developmental Psychology, 17,* 170–187.

Nelson, K. (1986). *Event knowledge.* Hillsdale, NJ: Erlbaum.

Nelson, K. (1993). The psychological and social origins of autobiographical memory. *Psychological Science, 4,* 7–14.

Nelson, K., & Gruendel, J. (1981). Generalized event representations: Basic building blocks of cognitive development. In M. Lamb & A. Brown (Eds.), *Advances in development psychology* (Vol. 1, pp. 131–158). Hillsdale, NJ: Erlbaum.

Nelson, K., & Gruendel, J. M. (1986). Children's scripts. In K. Nelson (Ed.), *Event knowledge: Structure and function in development.* Hillsdale, NJ: Erlbaum.

Nelson, K., & Lucariello, J. (1985). The development of meaning in first words. In M. Barrett (Ed.), *Children's single word speech.* New York: Wiley.

Neuman, S. B., Copple, C., & Bredekamp, S. (2000). *Learning to read and write: Developmentally appropriate practices for young children.* Washington, DC: National Association for the Education of Young Children.

Newport, E. L., & Meier, R. P. (1985). The acquisition of American Sign Language. In D. I. Slobin (Ed.). *The cross-linguistic study of language acquisition. Vol. 1: The data* (pp. 881–938). Hillsdale, NJ: Erlbaum.

Norton, D. G. (1996). Early linguistic interactions and school achievement: An ethnographic ecological perspective. *Zero to Three, 16*(3), 8–14.

Ogbu, J. U. (1981). Origins of human competence: A cultural ecological perspective. *Child Development, 52*(2), 413–429.

O'Hara, M. W. (1994). *Postpartum depression: Causes and consequences.* New York: Springer-Verlag.

Olney, R., & Scholnick, E. (1976). Adult judgments of age and linguistic differences in infant vocalizations. *Journal of Child Language, 3,* 145–156.

Olson, S. L., Bates, J. E., & Bayles, K. (1984). Mother–infant interaction and the development of individual differences in children's cognitive competence. *Developmental Psychology, 20,* 166–179.

Orlick, T. D. (1981). Positive socialization via cooperative games. *Developmental Psychology, 17,* 426–429.

Ost, D. H. (1989). The culture of teaching: Stability and change. *Educational Forum, 53,* 163–181.

Oster, H., & Ekman, P. (1977). Facial behavior in child development. In A. Collins (Ed.), *Minnesota Symposium on Child Psychology* (Vol. 11, pp. 231–276). New York: Crowell.

Panskepp, J. (1998). *Affective neuroscience: The foundations of human and animal emotions.* New York: Oxford University Press.

Parke, R. D., & Sawin, D. B. (1981). Father–infant interaction in the newborn period: A re-evaluation of some current myths. In E. M. Hetherington & R. D. Parke (Eds.), *Contemporary readings in child psychology* (2nd ed., pp. 229–234). New York: McGraw-Hill.

Parten, M. B. (1933). Social participation among preschool children. *Journal of Abnormal Psychology, 27,* 243–269.

Paul, A. S. (1992). American Indian (Native American) influences. In L. R. Williams & D. P. Fromberg (Eds.), *Encyclopedia of early education* (pp. 11–13). New York: Garland.

Pearse, A. J., & Mitchell, M. D. (2003). *Nutrition and childhood lead poisoning* (Ohio State University Extension Fact Sheet). Retrieved October 18, 2003, from http://ohioline.osu.edu/hyg-fact/5000/5536.html

Pederson, F. A., Zaslow, M., Cain, R., & Anderson, B. J. (1981). Cesarean childbirth: Psychological implications for mothers and fathers. *Infant Mental Health Journal, 2,* 257–263.

Peisner-Feinberg, E. S., Burchinal, M. R., Clifford, R. M., Yazejian, N., Culkin, M. L., Zelazo, J., Howes, C., Byler, P., Kagan, S. L., & Rustici, J. (1999). *The children of the Cost, Quality, and Outcomes Study go to school (Executive Summary).* Chapel Hill: University of North Carolina.

Perry, B. (1993a). Neurodevelopmental and the neurophysiology of trauma I: Conceptional considerations for clinical work with maltreated children. *The Advisor 6*(1, Spring), 1–2, 14–17.

Perry, B. (1993b). Neurodevelopmental and the neurophysiology of trauma II: Clinical work along the alarm-fear-terror continuum. *The Advisor 6*(1, Summer), 1–2, 14–18.

Perry, B. D. (1996). Incubated in terror: Neurodevelopmental factors in the 'cycle of violence'. In J. Osofsky (Ed.), *Children, youth, and violence: The search for solutions* (pp. 2–20). New York: Guilford.

Perry, B. (1998). *Brain growth and neurological development in infants.* Keynote presentation at the annual conference of the Texas Association for the Education of Young Children, Fort Worth, Texas, October 9, 1998.

Perry, B. (1999). Early life social–emotional experiences affect brain development. *American Academy of Pediatric News 15*(6), 18–19.

Perry, B. D., Pollard, R. A., Blakley, T. L., Baker, W. L., & Vigilante, D. (1995). Childhood trauma, the neurobiology of adaptation, and 'use-dependent' development of the brain: How 'states' become 'traits.' *Infant Mental Health Journal, 16*(4), 271–291.

Peters, V., Kai-Lih, L., Dominguez, K., Frederick, T., Melville, S., Ho-Wen, H., Ortiz, I., Rakusan, T., Gill, B., & Thomas, P. (2003). Missed opportunities for perinatal HIV prevention among HIV-exposed infants born 1996–2000; pediatric spectrum of HIV disease cohort. *Pediatrics, 111,* 1186–1191.

Peth-Pierce, R. (1998). *The NICHD study of early child care.* Washington, DC: National Institute of Child Health and Human Development.

Phillips, D. (Ed.). (1993). *Quality child care: What does research tell us?* Washington, DC: National Association for the Education of Young Children.

Piaget, J. (1926). *The language and thought of the child.* New York: Harcourt, Brace & World.

Piaget, J. (1952). *The origins of intelligence in children.* New York: Norton.

Piaget, J. (1954). *The construction of reality in the child.* New York: Basic Books.

Piaget, J. (1962). *Play, dreams and imitation in childhood.* New York: Norton.

Piaget, J. (1963). *The psychology of intelligence.* Paterson, NJ: Littlefield, Adams.

Piaget, J. (1965). *The moral judgment of the child.* New York: Norton.

Piaget, J. (1969). *Six psychological studies.* New York: Vintage.

Piaget, J., & Inhelder, B. (1956). *The child's conception of space.* London: Routledge & Kegan Paul.

Piaget, J., & Inhelder, B. (1969). *The psychology of the child.* New York: Basic Books.

Pianta, R. C. (1999). *Enhancing relationships between children and teachers.* Washington, DC: American Psychological Association.

Pillitteri, A. (1992). *Maternal and child health nursing: Care of the childbearing and childrearing family.* Philadelphia: Lippincott.

Pinker, S. (1994). *The language instinct: How the mind creates language.* New York: Harper Perennial.

Pipes, P. L. (1989). *Nutrition in infancy and childhood* (4th ed.). St. Louis, MO: Times Mirror/Mosby.

Plomin, R. (1987). Developmental behavioral genetics and infancy. In J. Osofsky (Ed.), *Handbook of infant development* (pp. 363–414). New York: Wiley.

Poest, C. A., Williams, J. R., Witt, D. D., & Atwood, M. E. (1989). Physical activity patterns of preschool children. *Early Childhood Research Quarterly, 4,* 367–376.

Pollitt, E., Cueto, S., & Jacoby, E. R., (1998). Fasting and cognition in well- and undernourished schoolchildren: A review of three experimental studies. *American Journal of Clinical Nutrition, 67,* 779S–784S.

Politt, E., Leibel, R. L., & Greenfield, D. (1981). Brief fasting, stress, and cognition in children. *American Journal of Clinical Nutrition, 34,* 1526–1533.

Pollitt, E., & Matthews, R. (1998). Breakfast and cognition: An integrative summary. *American Journal of Clinical Nutrition, 67,* 804S–813S.

Porter, F. L., Miller, R. H., & Marshall, R. E. (1986). Neonatal pain cries: Effect of circumcision on acoustic features and perceived urgency. *Child Development, 57,* 790–802.

Posner, J. K., & Vandell, D. L. (1994). Low-income children's after-school care: Are there beneficial effects of after-school programs? *Child Development, 65,* 440–456.

Powlishta, K. K. (1995). Research in review: Gender segregation among children: Understanding the "cootie phenomenon." *Young Children, 50*(4), 61–69.

Press, B., & Greenspan, S. (1985). Ned and Dan: The development of a toddler friendship. *Children Today, 14,* 24–29.

Province, S., & Lipton, R. C. (1962). *Infants in institutions.* New York: International Universities Press.

Provost, M. A., & LaFreniere, P. J. (1991). Social participation and peer competence in preschool children. Evidence for discriminant and convergent validity. *Child Study Journal, 21,* 57–71.

Puckett, M. B. (Ed.). (2002). *Room to grow: How to create quality early childhood environments* (3rd ed.). Austin, TX: Texas Association for the Education of Young Children.

Puckett, M. B., & Black, J. K. (1985). Learning to read. *Dimensions, 13*(3), 15–18.

Puckett, M. B., & Black, J. K. (2000). *Authentic assessment of the young child: Celebrating development and learning* (2nd ed.). Upper Saddle River, NJ: Merrill/Prentice Hall.

Puckett, M. B., & Diffily, D. (2004). *Teaching young children: An introduction to the early childhood profession* (2nd ed.). Clifton Park, NY: Delmar Learning.

Puckett, M. B., Marshall, C. S., & Davis, R. (1999). Examining the emergence of brain development research: The promises and the perils. *Childhood Education, 75*(7), 8–12.

Putallaz, M. (1987). Maternal behavior and children's sociometric status. *Child Development, 58,* 324–340.

Radke-Yarrow, M., Zahn-Waxler, C., & Chapman, M. (1983). Children's prosocial dispositions and behavior. In E. M. Hetherington (Ed.), *Handbook of child psychology. Vol. 4: Socialization, personality and social development* (4th ed., pp. 469–545). New York: Wiley.

Raikes, H. (1993). Relationship duration in infant care: Time with a high ability teacher and infant–teacher attachment. *Early Childhood Research Quarterly, 8*(3), 309–325.

Ramsay, D. S. (1980). Onset of unimanual handedness in infants. *Infant Behavior and Development, 3,* 377–385.

Ramsey, P. G. (1998). *Teaching and learning in a diverse world* (2nd ed.). New York: Teachers College Press.

Reiff, M. I., & Tippins, S. (Eds.). (2004). *The American Academy of Pediatrics: ADHD: A complete and authoritative guide.* New York: HarperCollins.

Reynolds, A. J., Temple, J. A., Robertson, D. L., & Mann, E. A. (2001). *Long-term effects of an early childhood intervention on educational attainment and juvenile arrests.* Washington, DC: U.S. Department of Health and Human Services.

Rhodes, W., & Hennessy, E. (2001). The effects of specialized training on caregivers and children in early-years settings: As evaluation of the foundation course in playgroup practice. *Early Childhood Research Quarterly, 15,* 559–576.

Ricciardelli, L. A. (1993). Creativity and bilingualism. *Journal of Creative Behavior, 26*(4), 242–254.

Rice, M. L., Huston, A. C., & Wright, J. C. (1986). Replays as repetitions: Young children's interpretation of television forms. *Journal of Applied Developmental Psychology, 7,* 61–76.

Ridely, M. (1999). *Genome: The autobiography of a species in 23 chapters.* New York: Perennial.

Riley, J. (1996). *The teaching of reading.* London: Chapman.

Rivkin, M. (1995). *The great outdoors: Restoring children's right to play outside.* Washington, DC: National Association for the Education of Young Children.

Rizzo, T., Corsaro, W., & Bates, J. E. (1992). Ethnographic methods and interpretive analysis: Expanding the methodological options of psychologists. *Developmental Review, 12,* 101–123.

Rogers, C. R. (1961). *On becoming a person.* Boston: Houghton Mifflin.

Rogers, C. (1962). Toward becoming a fully functioning person. In A. W. Combs (Ed.), *Perceiving, behaving, becoming: Association for Supervision and Curriculum Development 1962 Yearbook.* Alexandria, VA: Association for Supervision and Curriculum Development.

Rogers, C., & Freiberg, H. J. (1994). *Freedom to learn* (3rd. ed.). New York: Merrill/Macmillan.

Rogoff, B. J., Mistry, J., Goncii, A., & Mosier, C. E. (1991). Cultural variation in the role relations of toddlers and their families. In M. H. Bornstein (Ed.), *Cultural approaches to parenting* (pp. 173–183). Hillsdale, NJ: Erlbaum.

Rosen, K. S., & Rothbaum, F. (1993). Quality of parental caregiving and security of attachment. *Developmental Psychology, 29,* 358–367.

Rosenkoetter, L. (1999). The television situation comedy and children's prosocial behavior. *Journal of Applied Social Psychology, 29*(5), 979–993.

Rosenthal, M. K. (1982). Vocal dialogues in the neonatal period. *Developmental Psychology, 18,* 17–21.

Ross, D. M. (1996). *Childhood bullying and teasing: What school personnel, other professionals, and parents can do.* Alexandria, VA: American Counseling Association.

Rossi, A. S. (2002). Transition to parenthood (7th ed.). In A. S. Skolnick & J. H. Skolnick (Eds.), *Family in transition.* New York: HarperCollins.

Rothbaum, F., Grauer, A., & Rubin, D. J. (1997). Becoming sexual: Differences between child and adult sexuality. *Young Children, 52*(6), 22–28.

Rousseau, J. J. (1762). *Emile.* Amsterdam: Néaulme.

Roy, K., & Burton, L. (2003). Kinscription: Mothers keeping fathers connected to children. *Zero to Three, 23*(3), 27–32.

Rubin, K. H. (1973). Egocentrism in childhood: A unitary construct? *Child Development, 44,* 102–110.

Rubin, K. H., Bukowski, W., & Parker, J. G. (1998). Peer interactions, relationships and groups. In W. Damon (Ed.), *Handbook of child psychology. Vol. 3: Social, emotional, and personality development* (5th ed.). New York: Wiley.

Rubin, K. H., & Clark, M. L. (1983). Preschool teachers' ratings of behavioral problems: Observational, sociometric, and social-cognitive correlates. *Journal of Abnormal Child Psychology, 11,* 273–286.

Rubin, K. H., & Everett, B. (1982). Social perspective-taking in young children. In S. G. Moore & C. R. Cooper (Eds.), *The young child: Reviews of research* (Vol. 3, pp. 97–113). Washington, DC: National Association for the Education of Young Children.

Rubin, K. H., Lynch, D., Coplan, R., Rose-Krasnor, L., & Booth, C. L. (1994). "Birds of a feather . . . ": Behavioral concordance and preferential personal attraction in children. *Child Development, 64,* 1778–1785.

Ryan, C. A., & Finer, N. N. (1994). Changing attitudes and practices regarding local analgesia for newborn circumcision. *Pediatrics, 94*(2), 230–233.

Saarni, C. (1999). *The development of emotional competence.* New York: Guilford.

Sadker, M., & Sadker, D. (1985). Sexism in the schoolroom of the '80's. *Psychology Today, 1985*(March), 54–57.

Sadker, M., & Sadker, D. (1994). *Failing at fairness: How our schools cheat girls.* New York: Simon & Schuster.

Saenger, P. (1991). Use of growth hormone in the treatment of short stature: Boon or abuse? *Pediatrics in Review, 12*(12), 355–363.

Safford, P. L., & Safford, E. J. (1996). *A history of childhood and disability.* New York: Teachers College Press

Sameroff, A. J. (1983). Developmental systems: Contexts and evolution. In W. Kessen (Vol. Ed.) & P. H. Mussen (Gen. Ed.). *Handbook of child psychology. Vol. 1: History, theory, and methods* (4th ed., pp. 237–294). New York: Mosby.

Sameroff, A. J. (1995). General systems theories and developmental psychopathology. In D. Cicchetti & D. J. Cohen (Eds.), *Developmental psychopathology. Vol. 1: Theory and methods.* New York: Wiley.

Sameroff, A. J. (1999). Models of development and developmental risk. In C. H. Zeanah, Jr. (Ed.), *Handbook of infant mental health* (2nd ed., pp. 3–19). New York: Guilford.

Sameroff, A., & Chandler, M. J. (1975). Reproductive risk and the continuum of caretaking casualty. In F. D. Horowitz (Ed.), *Review of child development research* (Vol. 4, pp. 187–244). Chicago: University of Chicago Press.

Samuels, C. A. (1985). Attention to eye contact opportunity and facial motion by three-month-old infants. *Journal of Experimental Child Psychology, 40,* 105–114.

Samway, K. D., & McKeon, D. (1999). *Myths and realities: Best practices for language minority students.* Portsmouth, NH: Heinemann.

Sandall, S., McLean, M. E., & Smith, B. J. (2000). *Division for Early Childhood recommended practice in early intervention/early childhood special education.* Denver, CO: Division for Early Childhood of the Council for Exceptional Children.

Scheibel, A., Conrad, T., Perdue, S., Tomiyasu, U., & Wechsler, A. (1990). A quantitative study of dendrite complexity in selected areas of the human cerebral cortex. *Brain and Cognition, 12,* 85–101.

Schickedanz, J. A. (1999). *Much more than ABCs: The early stages of reading and writing.* Washington, DC: National Association for the Education of Young Children.

Schoendorf, K. C., & Kiely, J. L. (1992). Relationship of sudden infant death syndrome to maternal smoking during and after pregnancy. *Pediatrics, 90,* 905–908.

Schubiner, H. H., & Robin, A. L. (July, 1998). Attention-deficit/hyperactivity disorder in adolescence. *Adolescent Health Update 10,* (3), 1–8.

Schumacher, R., & Irish, K. (2003). *What's new in 2002?: A snapshot of Head Start children, families, teaching.* (May 2003, Brief No. 2). Washington, DC: Center for Law and Public Policy.

Schunk, D. H. (1981). Modeling and attributional effects on children's achievement: A self-efficacy analysis. *Journal of Educational Psychology, 73,* 93–105.

Schweinhart, L. J., Barnes, A. V., & Weikart, D. P. (1993). *Significant benefits: The High/Scope Perry Preschool Study through age 27* (Monographs of the High/Scope Educational Research Foundation, 10). Ypsilanti, MI: High/Scope Press.

Schweinhart, L. J., & Weikart, D. P. (1997). The High/Scope Preschool Curriculum Comparison Study through age 23. *Early Childhood Research Quarterly, 12,* 117–143.

Sears, W. P. (1998). Parents, patients need to know about breakfast–brain connection. *American Academy Pediatric News, 14*(9), 30.

Second Harvest (2001). *Hunger in America, 2001.* Retrieved December 4, 2001, from http://www.secondharvest.org

Seidel, J. F. (1992). Children with HIV-related difficulties. *Phi Delta Kappan, 74*(1), 38–40.

Senechal, M., LeFevre, J., Thomas, E., & Daley, K. (1998). Different effects of home literacy experiences on the development of oral and written language. *Reading Research Quarterly, 32,* 96–114.

Sepkowski, C. (1985). Maternal obstetric medication and newborn behavior. In J. W. Scanlon (Ed.), *Prenatal anesthesia.* London: Blackwell.

Serbin, L. A., Powlishta, K. K., & Gulko, J. (1993). *The development of sex typing in middle childhood* (Monographs of the Society for Research in Child Development, Vol. 58). Chicago: University of Chicago Press.

Sexton, D. (1990). Quality integrated programs for infants and toddlers with special needs. In E. Surbeck & M. F. Kelley, (Eds.), *Personalizing care of infants, toddlers and families* (pp. 41–50). Olney, MD: Association for Childhood Education International.

Shaffer, H. R. (1971). *The growth of stability*. London: Penguin.

Shea, K. M. (2003). Antibiotic resistance: What is the impact of agricultural uses of antibiotics on children's health? *Pediatrics, 112*, 253–258.

Shepard, L. A., & Smith, M. L. (1986). Synthesis of research on school readiness and kindergarten retention. *Educational Leadership, 44*(3), 78–86.

Shepard, L. A., & Smith, M. L. (1987). Effects of kindergarten retention at the end of first grade. *Psychology in the School, 24*, 346–357.

Shonkoff, J. P., & Phillips, D. A. (2000). *From neurons to neighborhoods: The science of early childhood development*. Washington, DC: National Academy Press.

Shlono, P. H., Klebanoff, M. A., Graubard, M. A., Berendes, H. W., & Rhoads, G. G. (1986). Birth weight among women of different ethnic groups. *Journal of the American Medical Association, 255*, 48–52.

Shonkoff, J. P., Phillips, D. A., & Keilty, B. (Ed.). (2000). *Early childhood intervention: Views from the field*. Washington, DC: National Academy Press.

Shore, R. (1997). *Rethinking the brain: New insights into early development*. New York: Families and Work Institute.

Siegel, D. J. (1999). *The developing mind: Toward a neurobiology of interpersonal experience*. New York: Guilford.

Siegler, R. S. (1998). Children's thinking (3rd ed.). Upper Saddle River, NJ: Prentice Hall.

Singer, J. L., & Singer, D. G. (March). Come back, Mr. Rogers, come back. *Psychology Today, 1979* (March), 56, 59–60.

Singer, J. L., & Singer, D. G. (1986). Family experiences and television viewing as predictors of children's imagination, restlessness, and aggression. *Journal of Social Issues, 42*, 107–24.

Singer, M. I., Slovak, K., Frierson, T., & York, P. (1998). Viewing preferences, symptoms of psychological trauma, and violent behaviors among children who watch television. *Journal of the American Academy of Child and Adolescent Psychiatry, 37*, 1041–1048.

Skinner, B. F. (1938). *The behavior of organisms*. Upper Saddle River, NJ: Prentice Hall.

Skinner, B. F. (1948). *Walden two*. New York: Macmillan.

Skinner, B. F. (1957). *Verbal behavior*. East Norwalk, CT: Appleton-Century-Crofts.

Skinner, B. F. (1974). *About behaviorism*. New York: Knopf.

Skinner, B. F. (1979). *The shaping of a behaviorist*. New York: Knopf.

Skolnick, A. S., & Skolnick, J. H. (1992). *Family in transition* (7th ed.). New York: HarperCollins.

Slade, A. (2002). Keeping the baby in mind: A critical factor in perinatal mental health. *Zero to Three, 22*(6), 10–11.

Slavin, R. E. (1990). *Cooperative learning: Theory, research and practice*. Upper Saddle River, NJ: Prentice Hall.

Slyper, A. H. (1998). Childhood obesity, adipose tissue distribution, and the pediatric practitioner. *Pediatrics, 102*(1) [Electronic abstracts]. Available at http://www.pediatrics.org/cgi/content/full/102/1e4

Smith, G. A. (1998). Injuries to children in the United States related to trampolines, 1990–1995: A national epidemic. *Pediatrics, 101*(3), 406–412.

Small, M. F. (2001). *Kids: How biology and culture shape the way we raise our children*. New York: Doubleday.

Snow, C. E. (1983). Literacy and language: Relationships during the preschool years. *Harvard Educational Review, 53*, 165–189.

Snow, C. E., Burns, S., & Griffin, P. (Eds.). (1998). *Preventing reading difficulties in young children*. Washington, DC: National Academy Press.

Snyder, M., Snyder, R., & Snyder, R., Jr. (1980). *The young child as person: Toward the development of healthy conscience*. New York: Human Sciences.

Society for Research in Child Development, Committee on Ethical Standards for Research with Children. (1990–1991). *Ethical standards for research with children*. Ann Arbor, MI: Author.

Solomon, J. (2003). The caregiving system in separated and divorcing parents. *Zero to Three, 23*(3), 33–37.

Solomon, J., & George, C. (1996). Defining the caregiving system: Toward a theory of caregiving. *Infant Mental Health Journal, 17*, 182–197.

Spencer, M. B., & Markstrom-Adams, C. (1990). Identity processes among racial and ethnic minority children in America. *Child Development, 61*, 290–310.

Stanford, B. H., & Yamamoto, K. (Eds.). (2001). *Children and stress: Understanding and helping*. Olney, MD: Association for Childhood Education International.

Steiner, J. E. (1979). Human facial expressions in response to taste and smell stimulation. In H. Reese & L. Lipsitt (Eds.), *Advances in child development and behavior* (Vol. 13, pp. 257–295). New York: Academic.

Sternberg, R. J. (1985). *Beyond IQ: A triarchic theory of human intelligence*. New York: Cambridge University Press.

Sternberg, R. J., & Berg, C. A. (1995). (Eds.). *Intellectual development*. New York: Cambridge University Press.

Stewart, R. B. (1983). Sibling attachment relationships: Child infant interactions in the strange situation. *Developmental Psychology, 19*, 192–199.

Stewart, R. B., Mobley, L. A., Van Tuyl, S. S., & Salvador, M. A. (1987). The firstborn's adjustment to the birth of a sibling: A longitudinal assessment. *Child Development, 58*, 341.

Stipek, D., Recchia, S., & McClintic, S. (1992). *Self-evaluation in young children* (Monographs of the Society for Research in Child Development, Vol. 57, No. 1, serial no. 226). Chicago: University of Chicago Press.

Storo, W. (1993). Role of bicycle helmet in bicycle related injury prevention. *Clinical Digest Series, 4*(3), 23. [Reprinted from *Clinical Pediatrics* (1992), 31, 421–427.]

Strauss, R. S., Rodzilsky, D., Burack, G., & Cole, M. (2001). Psychosocial correlates of physical activity in healthy children. *Archives of Pediatric and Adolescent Medicine, 155,* 897–902.

Strommen, L. T., & Mates, B. F. (1997). What readers do: Young children's ideas about the nature of reading. *Reading Teacher, 51*(2), 98–107.

Stroufe, L. A. (1996). *Emotional development: The organization of emotional life in the early years.* New York: Cambridge University Press.

Stroufe, L. A., Carlson, E., & Schulman, S. (1993). Individuals in relationships: Development from infancy through adolescence. In D. C. Funder, R. D. Parke, C.Tomlinson-Keasey, & K. Widaman, (Eds.), *Studying lives through time: Personality and development.* Washington, DC: American Psychological Association.

Stroufe, L. A., Egeland, B., & Kreutzer, T. (1990). The fate of early experience following developmental change: Longitudinal approaches to individual adaptation in childhood. *Child Development, 61,* 1363–1373.

Stroufe, L. A., Fox, N. E., & Pancake, V. R. (1983). Attachment and dependency in developmental perspective. *Child Development, 54,* 1615–1627.

Sugarman, S. (1987). *Piaget's construction of the child's reality.* Cambridge, England: Cambridge University Press.

Susman-Stillman, A., Appleyard, K., & Siebenbruner, J. (2003). For better or for worse: An ecological perspective on parents' relationships and parent–infant interaction. *Zero to Three, 23*(3), 4–12.

Sussman, J. R., & Levitt, B. B. (1989). *Before you conceive: The complete pregnancy guide.* New York: Bantam.

Sutton-Smith, B. (1997). *The ambiguity of play.* Cambridge, MA: Harvard University Press.

Swick, K., Brown, M., & Guddemi, M. (1986). *Personality dimensions of effective teachers.* Columbia: University of South Carolina.

Sylwester, R. (1995). *A celebration of neurons: An educator's guide to the human brain.* Alexandria, VA: Association for Supervision and Curriculum Development.

Sylwester, R. (1997). The neurobiology of self-esteem and aggression. *Education Leadership, 54*(5), 75–79.

Tanner, J. M. (1973). The regulation of human growth. In F. Rebelsky & L. Dorman (Eds.), *Child development and behavior.* New York: Knopf.

Tanner, J. M. (1989). *Fetus into man: Physical growth from conception to maturity* (rev. ed.). Cambridge, MA: Harvard University Press.

Teale, W. H. (1986). Home background and young children's literacy development. In W. H. Teale & E. Sulzby (Eds.), *Emergent literacy: Writing and reading* (pp. 173–206). Norwood, NJ: Ablex.

Teitler, J. O. (2001). Father involvement, child health and maternal health behavior. *Children and Youth Services Review, 23*(4/5), 403–425.

Templin, M. C. (1957). *Certain skills in children: Their development and interrelationships.* Minneapolis: University of Minnesota Institute of Child Welfare.

Texas Association for the Education of Young Children. (1997). *Early childhood literacy development: A position statement.* Austin, TX: Author.

Thomas, A., & Chess, S. (1977). *Temperament and development.* New York: Brunner/Mazel.

Thomas, A., & Chess, S. (1996). Temperament. In M. Lewis (Ed.), *Child and adolescent psychiatry: A comprehensive textbook* (2nd ed.). Baltimore: Williams & Wilkins.

Thomas, A., Chess, S., & Birch, H. G. (1968). *Temperament and behavior disorders in children.* New York: New York University Press.

Thomas, A., Chess, S., Birch, H.G., Hertzig, M. E., & Korn, S. (1963). *Behavioral individuality in early childhood.* New York: New York University Press.

Thompson, R. A. (1999). Early attachment and later development. In J. Cassidy & P. R. Shaver (Eds.), *Handbook of attachment: Theory, research, and clinical application* (pp. 265–286). New York: Guilford.

Thurman, S. K., & Lewis, M. (1979). Children's responses to differences: Some possible implications for mainstreaming. *Exceptional Children, 45,* 468–470.

Trawick-Smith, J. (1994). *Interactions in the classroom: Facilitating play in the early years.* Upper Saddle River: Merrill/Prentice Hall.

Trawick-Smith, J. (1998). A qualitative analysis of metaplay in the preschool years. *Early Childhood Research Quarterly, 13,* 433–452.

Trepanier-Street, M., Hong, S. B., & Donegan, M. M. (2001). Constructing the image of the teacher in a Reggio-inspired teacher preparation program. *Journal of Early Childhood Teacher Education, 22*(1), 47–52.

Tronick, E. Z., Cohn, J., & Shea, E. (1986). The transfer of affect between mother and infant. In T. B. Brazelton & M. W. Yogman (Eds.), *Affective development in infancy* (pp. 11–25). Norwood, NJ: Ablex.

Turiel, E. (1980). The development of social-conventional and moral concepts.In M. Windmiller, N. Lambert, & E. Turiel (Eds.), *Moral development and socialization* (pp. 69–106). Boston: Allyn & Bacon.

U.S. Consumer Product Safety Commission. (1997). *Handbook for public playground safety.* Washington, DC: Author.

U.S. Consumer Product Safety Commission, National Electronic Injury Surveillance System. (1996). *Consumer Product Safety Review, 2*(4).

U.S. Department of Education. (1991). *America 2000: Educate America* (rev. ed.). Washington, DC: Author.

U.S. Department of Health and Human Services. (1990a). *The health consequences of smoking for women: A report of the Surgeon General.* Rockville, MD: Author.

U.S. Department of Health and Human Services. (1990b). *Healthy People 2000: National health promotion and disease prevention objectives.* Washington, DC: U.S. Government Printing Office.

U.S. Department of Health and Human Services. (2001). *Child care quality: Does it matter and does it need to be improved? (Executive Summary).* Retrieved January 3, 2003, from http://www.aspe.hhs.gov/hsp/ccqualityoo/execsum.htm

U.S. General Accounting Office. (March). *Newborn screening: Characteristics of state programs.* Washington, DC: Author.

U.S. Surgeon General. (2000). *United States Public Health Service report of the Surgeon General's conference on*

children's mental health: A national action agenda. Washington, DC: Department of Health and Human Services.

Vaisman, N., Voet, H., Akivis, A., & Vakil, E. (1996). Effects of breakfast timing on the cognitive functions of elementary school students. *Archives of Pediatric and Adolescent Medicine, 150,* 1089–1092.

Vandell, D. L., & Hsiu-Chih, S. (1999). Research in review: Child care and school age children. *Young Children, 54*(6), 62–71.

Vandell, D. L., & Shumow, L. (1999). After-school child care programs. *The Future of Children, 9*(2), 64–80.

Vandivere, M. P., Tout, K., Capizzano, J., & Zaslow, M. (2003, April). *Left unsupervised: A look at the most vulnerable children.* Washington, DC: Child Trends.

Van Hasselt, V. C. (1983). Social adaptation in the blind. *Clinical Psychology Review, 3,* 87–102.

Vaughn III, V. C., & Litt, I. F. (1987). The newborn infant. In R. E. Behrman & V. C. Vaughn (Eds.), *Nelson textbook of pediatrics* (13th ed., pp. 7–17). Philadelphia: Saunders.

Velichkovsky, B., & Rumbaugh, D. M. (Eds.). (1996). *Communicating meaning.* Hillsdale, NY: Erlbaum.

Verschueren, K., Marcoen, A., & Schoefs, V. (1996). The internal working model of the self, attachment and competence in five year olds. *Child Development, 67,* 2493–2511.

Vincent, J. D. (1990). *The biology of emotions,* transl. by J. Hughes. Cambridge, MA: Blackwell.

Volpe, J. J. (1987). *Neurology of the newborn* (2nd ed.). Philadelphia: WB Saunders.

Vygotsky, L. S. (1962). *Thought and language.* Cambridge, MA: MIT Press.

Vygotsky, L. S. (1978). *Mind in society: The development of higher mental processes.* Cambridge, MA: Harvard University Press.

Vygotsky, L. S. (1987). Thinking and speech. In N. Minick (Transl.), *The collected works of L. S. Vygotsky. Vol. 1: Problems in general psychology.* New York: Plenum.

Watson, D. J. (1994). Whole language: Why bother? *Reading Teacher, 48*(8), 600–607.

Watson, J. B. (1924). *Behaviorism.* New York: Norton.

Watson, J. B. (1928). *Psychological care of infant and child.* New York: Norton.

Watson, J. B., & Rayner, R. (1920). Conditioned emotional reactions. *Journal of Experimental Psychology, 3,* 1–14.

Weber, E. (1984). *Ideas influencing early childhood education.* New York: Teachers College Press.

Weinreb, L., Wehler, C., Perloff, J., Scott, R., Hosmer, D., Sagor, L., & Gundersen, C. (2002). Hunger: Its impact on children's health and mental health. *Pediatrics 110,* ep41. Retrieved October 7, 2002, from http://www.pediatrics.org/cgi/content/full/110/4/e41

Weiss, E. (1984). Learning disabled children's understanding of social interactions with peers. *Journal of Learning Disabilities, 17,* 612–615.

Wellhousen, K. (1996). Girls can be bull riders, too! Supporting children's understanding of gender roles through children's literature. *Young Children 51*(5), 79–83.

Wells, G. (1985). *Learning through interaction: The study of language development.* Cambridge, MA: Cambridge University Press.

Werner, E. E. (1989). Children of the garden island. *Scientific American, 260,* 107–111.

Werner, E. E., & Smith, R. S. (1982). *Vulnerable but invincible: A longitudinal study of resilient children and youth.* New York: McGraw-Hill.

White, B. (1985). *The first three years of life.* Upper Saddle River, NJ: Prentice Hall.

Whitehurst, G. J. (2001). Untitled presentation on pre-reading skills. White House summit: Early childhood cognitive development: Ready to read; ready to learn. July 26, Washington, DC.

Whitehurst, G. J., Epstein, A. J., Angell, A., Smith, M., & Fischel, J. (1994). A picture book reading intervention in day care and home for children from low income families. *Developmental Psychology, 30,* 679–689.

Wilson, J. G. (1977). Current status of teratology. In J. G. Wilson & F. C. Fraser (Eds.), *Handbook of teratology* (Vol. 1). New York: Plenum.

Winnicott, D. W. (1953). Transitional objects and transitional phenomena. *International Journal of Psycho-Analysis, 34,* 1–9.

Winnicott, D. W. (1971). *Playing and reality.* London: Tavistock.

Winnicott, D. W. (1977). *The piggle.* New York: International Universities Press.

Winter, W. M. (1985). Toddler play behaviors and equipment choices in an outdoor play environment. In J. L. Frost & S. Sunderlin (Eds.), *When children play.* Olney, MD: Association for Childhood Education International.

Wishart, J. G., & Bower, T. G. R. (1985). A longitudinal study of the development of the object concept. *British Journal of Developmental Psychology, 3,* 243–258.

Witt, P. A. (1997). *Evaluation of the impact of three after-school recreation programs sponsored by the Dallas Park and Recreation Department.* Available from http://wwwrpts.tamu.edu/rpts/faculty/pubs/wittpub2.htm

Wolff, P. H. (1963). Observation on the early development of smiling. In B. Foss (Ed.), *Determinants of infant behavior* (Vol. 2, pp. 113–138). London: Methuen.

Wolff, P. H. (1966). *The causes, controls, and organization of behavior in the neonate* (Psychology Issues, Monograph 17). New York: International Universities Press.

Wood, J. T. (1994). *Gendered lives.* Belmont, CA: Wadsworth.

Working Group on Antiretroviral Therapy and Medical Management of Infants, Children, and Adolescents with HIV Infection. (1998). Antiretroviral therapy and medical management of pediatric HIV infection. *Pediatrics, 102*(4, Supplement, Part 2 of 2).

Wright, J. C., Huston, A. C., Ross, R. P., Calvert, S. L., Rolandelli, D., Weeks, L. A., Raeissi, P., & Potts, R. (1984). Pace and continuity of television programs: Effects on children's attentions and comprehension. *Developmental Psychology, 20,* 653–666.

Yager, J. (1995). Clinical manifestations of psychiatric disorders. In H. I. Kaplan & B. J. Sadock (Eds.),

Comprehensive textbook of psychiatry. (Vol. 1, 5th ed., Chapter 10). Baltimore: Williams & Wilkins.

Yarrow, L. (1961). Maternal deprivation: Toward an empirical and conceptual re-evaluation. *Psychological Bulletin, 58,* 459–490.

Yarrow, M. R., & Zahn-Waxler, C. Z. (1977). The emergence and functions of prosocial behaviors in young children. In R. C. Smart & M. S. Smart (Eds.), *Readings in child development and relationships* (2nd ed., pp. 77–81). New York: Macmillan.

Yawkey, T., & Johnson, J. E. (1988). *Integrative processes and socialization: Early to middle childhood.* Hillsdale, NJ: Erlbaum.

Youngblade, L. M., & Dunn, J. (1995). Individual differences in young children's pretend play with mother and sibling: Links to relationships and understanding of other people's feeling and beliefs. *Child Development, 66,* 1472–1492.

Zahn-Waxler, C., & Radke-Yarrow, M. (1990). The origins of empathic concern. *Motivation and Emotion, 14,* 107–130.

Zeanah, C. H., Jr. (Ed.). (1993). *Handbook of infant mental health.* New York: Guilford.

Zeanah, C. H. (Ed.). (1999). *Handbook of infant mental health* (2nd ed.). New York: Guilford.

Zeanah, C. H., Jr., Mammen, O. K., & Lieberman, A. F. (1993). Disorders of attachment. In C. H. Zeanah, Jr. (Ed.), *Handbook of infant mental health* (pp. 332–349). New York: Guilford.

Zero to Three National Center for Infants, Toddlers, and Families. (2000). *What grown-ups understand about child development: A national benchmark survey.* Washington, DC: Author.

Zero to Three National Center for Infants, Toddlers, and Families. (2002). *Perinatal mental health: Supporting new families through vulnerability and change.* Washington, DC: Author.

Appendixes

Appendix A

Acronyms Associated with Childhood-Related Terms, Agencies, and Associations

Appendix B

Centers for Disease Control and Prevention Growth Charts: United States

Appendix C

Quality Child Care: A Position Statement of the Southern Early Childhood Association

Appendix A
Acronyms Associated with Childhood-Related Terms, Agencies, and Associations

AACAP	American Academy of Child and Adolescent Psychiatry
AAP	American Academy of Pediatrics
ACEI	Association for Childhood Education International
ACOG	American College of Obstetricians and Gynecologists
ACYF	Administration for Children, Youth, and Families (US DHHS)
ADA	Americans with Disabilities Act
ADD	attention deficit disorder
ADHD	attention deficit hyperactivity disorder
AFP	alphafetoprotein test
AIDS	acquired immunodeficiency syndrome
APGAR	appearance, pulse, grimace, activity, and respiration assessment of the newborn
BMI	body mass index
BMR	basal metabolic rate
CA	chronological age
CACFP	Child and Adult Care Food Program
CAPTA	Child Abuse Prevention and Treatment Act (changed in 2003 to the Keeping Children and Families Safe Act of 2003 [P. L. 108-36])
CCDBG	Child Care and Development Block Grant
CCDF	Child Care and Development Fund (federal)

CCDP	comprehensive child development program
CDA	Child Development Associate
CDF	Children's Defense Fund
CDC	Centers for Disease Control and Prevention
CECPR	Council for Early Childhood Professional Recognition
CHIP	Children's Health Insurance Program
CNS	central nervous system
CPS	Child Protective Services
CPSC	Consumer Product Safety Commission
CSE	Child Support Enforcement
CVT	chorionic villus test
CWLA	Child Welfare League of America
DAP	developmentally appropriate practices
DB	deaf/blindness
DCTC	Dependent Care Tax Credit
DEC/CEC	Division for Early Childhood of the Council for Exceptional Children
DNA	deoxyribonucleic acid
ECCE	early childhood care and education
ECI	Early Childhood Intervention
ECS	Education Commission of the States
ECSE	Early Childhood Special Education
ED	emotional disturbance or emotionally disturbed
EHS	Early Head Start
EI	early intervention
EIIT	Early Intervention for Infants and Toddlers (Part C of IDEA)
EITC	earned income tax credit
EPA	Environmental Protection Agency
EPSDT	Early and Periodic Screening Diagnosis and Treatment (Medicaid)
ERIC/ECE	Education Research and Information Clearinghouse/Early Childhood Education
ES	Even Start
ESEA	Elementary and Secondary Education Act
ESL	English as a Second Language
FAPE	Free Appropriate Public Education (IDEA)
FAS	fetal alcohol syndrome
FDA	U.S. Food and Drug Administration
FHCC	family home child care
FMLA	Family and Medical Leave Act of 1993
FRAC	Food Research and Action Council
GAO	U.S. Government Accounting Office
HEI	Healthy Eating Index
HHS	U.S. Department of Health and Human Services
HI	hearing impaired
HIPPY	Home Instruction Program for Preschool Youngsters

HMBANA	Human Milk Banking Association of North America
HUD	U.S. Department of Housing and Urban Development
IDEA	Individuals with Disabilities Act
IDRA	Intercultural Development Research Association
IEP	Individual Education Plan (IDEA)
IFSP	Individualized Family Services Plan (IDEA)
IOM	(National) Institute of Medicine
IQ	intelligence quotient
IRA	International Reading Association
LAD	language acquisition device
LBW	low birth weight
LEP	limited English proficiency
LGA	large for gestational age
L1	Native or first language
L2	Second language
MD	multiple disabilities
MH	multiple handicaps
ML	multilingual
MMWR	*Morbidity and Mortality Weekly Report*
MR	mental retardation
NAESP	National Association of Elementary School Principals
NAEYC	National Association for the Education of Young Children
NACCP	National Association of Child Care Professionals
NACCRRA	National Association of Child Care Resource and Referral Agencies
NAFCC	National Association for Family Child Care
NBCDI	National Black Child Development Institute
NCATE	National Council for Accreditation of Teacher Education
NCCP	National Center for Children in Poverty
NCES	National Center for Educational Statistics
NCLB	No Child Left Behind Education Act of 2003
NEISS	National Electronic Injury Survey System
NICHD	National Institute of Child Health and Human Development
NIDCD	National Institute on Deafness and other Communication Disorders
NIECPD	National Institute for Early Childhood Program Development
NIH	National Institutes of Health
NIMH	National Institute of Mental Health
NRC	National Research Council
NSACA	National School Age Alliance
NTSB	National Transportation Safety Board
OHI	other health impairments
OI	orthopedic impaired
OMEP	World Organization for Early Childhood Education
PAT	Parents as First Teachers
PCR	polymerase chain reaction test
PKU	phenylketonuria

SCHIP	State Child Health Insurance Program
SECA	Southern Early Childhood Association
SGA	small for gestational age
SIDS	sudden infant death syndrome
SLI	speech or language impairment
SRCD	Society for Research in Child Development
SSA	Social Security Administration
SSI	Social Security Supplemental Security Income program
STD	sexually transmitted disease
TANF	Temporary Assistance to Needy Families
TBI	traumatic brain injury
UNCRC	United Nations Convention of the Rights of the Child
UNICEF	United Nations Children's Fund
USDA	U.S. Department of Agriculture
USDE	U.S. Department of Education
US DHHS	U.S. Department of Health and Human Services
VAERS	Vaccine adverse-event reporting system
VI	visual impairment
VLBW	very low birth weight
WHO	World Health Organization
WIC	U.S. Special Supplemental Nutrition Program for Women, Infants, and Children
ZPD	zone of proximal development

Appendix B
Centers for Disease
Control and Prevention
Growth Charts:
United States

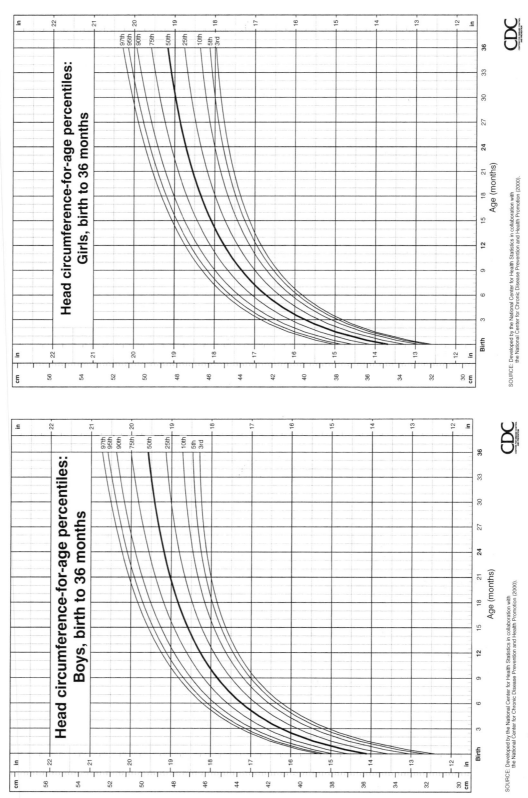

CDC Growth Charts: United States

Head circumference-for-age percentiles:
Girls, birth to 36 months

Age (months)

97th
95th
90th
75th
50th
25th
10th
5th
3rd

SOURCE: Developed by the National Center for Health Statistics in collaboration with
the National Center for Chronic Disease Prevention and Health Promotion (2000).

CDC

CDC Growth Charts: United States

Head circumference-for-age percentiles:
Boys, birth to 36 months

Age (months)

97th
95th
90th
75th
50th
25th
10th
5th
3rd

SOURCE: Developed by the National Center for Health Statistics in collaboration with
the National Center for Chronic Disease Prevention and Health Promotion (2000).

CDC

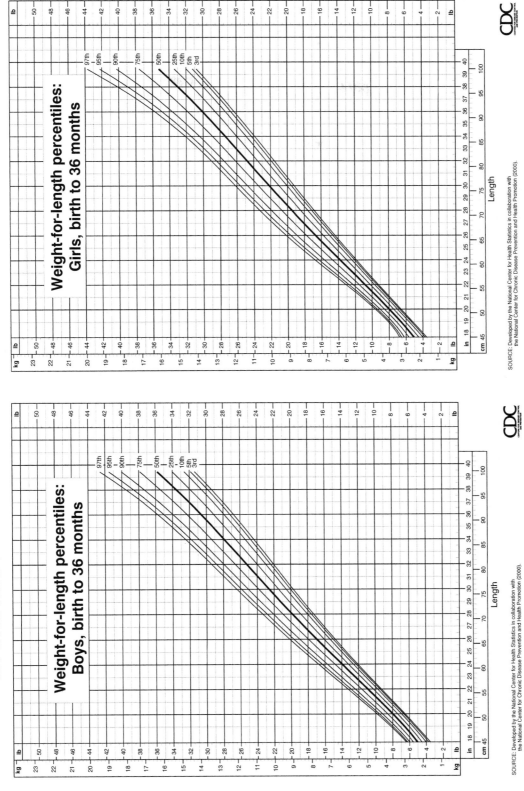

CDC Growth Charts: United States

Weight-for-length percentiles:
Boys, birth to 36 months

Length

SOURCE: Developed by the National Center for Health Statistics in collaboration with
the National Center for Chronic Disease Prevention and Health Promotion (2000).

CDC Growth Charts: United States

Weight-for-length percentiles:
Girls, birth to 36 months

Length

SOURCE: Developed by the National Center for Health Statistics in collaboration with
the National Center for Chronic Disease Prevention and Health Promotion (2000).

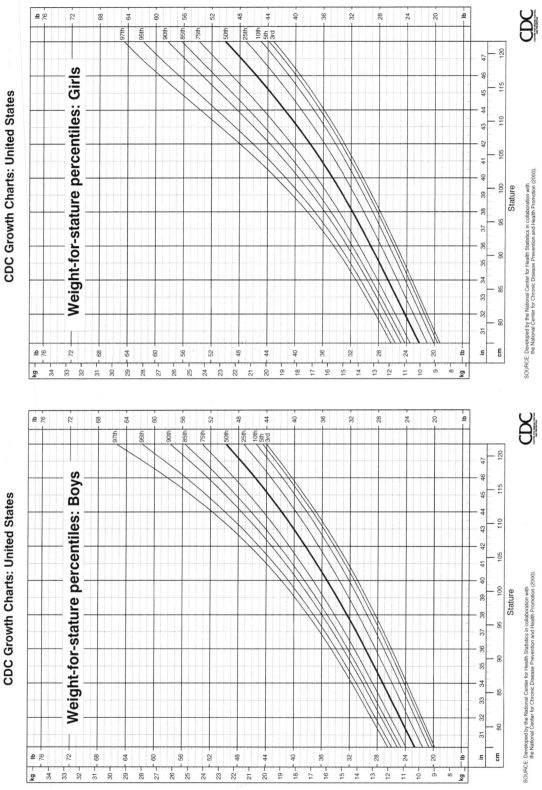

CDC Growth Charts: United States

Weight-for-stature percentiles: Boys

Weight-for-stature percentiles: Girls

Stature

SOURCE: Developed by the National Center for Health Statistics in collaboration with the National Center for Chronic Disease Prevention and Health Promotion (2000).

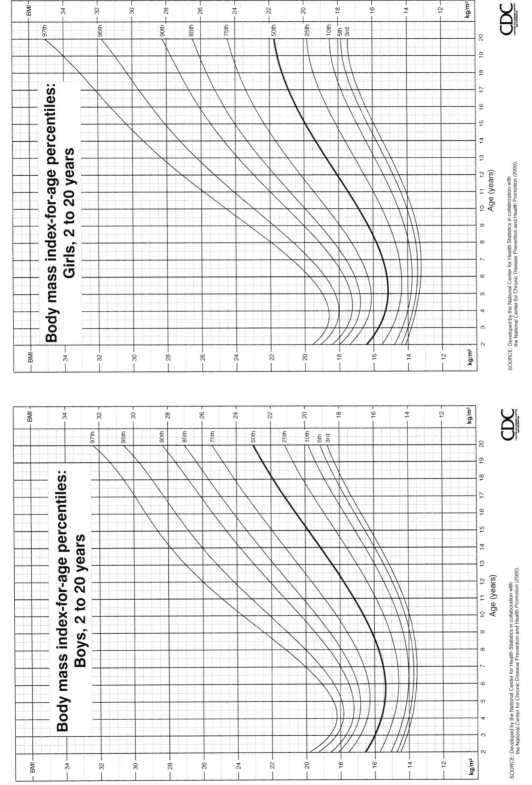

Body mass index-for-age percentiles:
Girls, 2 to 20 years

Age (years)

SOURCE: Developed by the National Center for Health Statistics in collaboration with
the National Center for Chronic Disease Prevention and Health Promotion (2000).

Body mass index-for-age percentiles:
Boys, 2 to 20 years

Age (years)

SOURCE: Developed by the National Center for Health Statistics in collaboration with
the National Center for Chronic Disease Prevention and Health Promotion (2000).

Appendix C
Quality Child Care:
A Position Statement
of the Southern Early
Childhood Association*

FAMILIES NEED CHILD CARE

The demand for child care in the United States has soared in recent years. This sharp rise has been linked to several factors: a rapid increase in the number of women working outside the home, parents' longer work hours, the growing population of children under the age of 6, and large numbers of families moving from welfare dependency.

Access to affordable, high-quality child care is critical to working parents. In 1996, 27% of families were headed by single parents. More than half of mothers with children under age 1 work outside the home, and one-third of all infants experience at least three different child care arrangements in the first year of life.

QUALITY CHILD CARE

> How we function as adults hinges to a significant extent on how our brain develops when we are young (Shore, 1997, p. 4).

High-quality care supports children's physical, emotional, social and mental development that can boost their school success in later years. "Early care and nurture have a decisive and long lasting impact on how people develop, their ability to learn, and their capacity to regulate their emotions" (Shore, 1997, p. xvii).

High-quality child care is a comprehensive service to children and families. It provides educational activities and services to support children's health, cognitive, physical, social, and emotional needs. The quality of care

*Reproduced with permission of Southern Early Childhood Association.

children receive greatly impacts their futures. Parents want their children to receive experiences that meet their needs. High-quality child care can provide those experiences. Recent brain research shows that high-quality child care and early education can enhance children's later school success. Good nutrition, pleasant surroundings, positive stimulation, and educational experiences are all elements of quality care.

Children Need:

1. To feel safe
2. To develop good self concepts
3. To participate in meaningful activities throughout the day
4. To develop social skills
5. To develop good health habits
6. To develop academic skills that will allow them to succeed in school and life

Quality Care Includes:

Experiences which:

- Are appropriate for the child's age and culture.
- Allow children to be successful and challenged.
- Include play as a child's way of learning.
- Encourage independence while meeting the child's need to feel safe.
- Provide opportunities to make choices and solve problems.
- Include opportunities for "real work," such as cleaning up after play.
- Provide materials to handle, such as puzzles and construction toys.
- Support language learning through talking, books, and songs.
- Allow self-expression through art and music.
- Extend learning through field trips and visits by adults from the community.
- Provide opportunities to develop literacy through engagement with books and writing materials.
- Promote wellness and healthy living.
- Help children learn to be civil, respectful, and responsible.

Caregivers who:

- Model appropriate manners and behavior for children.
- Enjoy children, understand development, and respond attentively to their needs.
- Demonstrate respect for individuality.
- Have reasonable expectations of the child.
- Demonstrate positive ways of guiding behavior.
- Set clear, consistent, and fair limits for behavior.
- Encourage curiosity by responding to children's questions.
- Consider that children learn through activities with people and objects.

- Help children learn to deal with feelings and develop and practice conflict resolution skills.
- Respect parents and recognize that parents are the most significant influence in a child's life.
- Provide for communication between parents and caregivers through:

  Talking at arrival and departure times.

  Holding conferences.

  Contacts by telephone and notes.

An environment that:
- Is beautiful and aesthetically pleasing.
- Is safe and developmentally appropriate for the age of the child.
- Has a low child to adult ratio and small groups of children with a teacher.
- Has caregivers who are trained in early childhood development and education.
- Provides for a smooth transition from home to the child care program.
- Lessens separation anxiety for the child as parents leave for the day.
- Provides consistency in daily activities and caregivers.
- Has a relaxed and flexible order to the day.
- Is clean and free of hazards.
- Guards against the spread of illness.
- Provides nutritious meals and snacks.
- Encourages physical activity.
- Allows time for active and quiet play, rest, and other routines.
- Supports exploration, investigation, and discovery.
- Exceeds minimum licensing standards of city and/or state.
- Has many of the elements of a high-quality home atmosphere.

SECA Supports Quality Care

Everyone concerned with children's development shares the responsibility for quality child care. This responsibility even extends beyond parents, educators, and human service professionals to our policy makers and the leaders in neighborhoods and business communities.

The Southern Early Childhood Association supports licensed, high-quality child care programs to protect the safety and welfare of all children.

References

Bredekamp, S., and Copple, D. (Eds.). (1997). *Developmentally appropriate practice in early childhood programs,* rev. ed. Washington, DC: National Association for the Education of Young Children.

Frede, E. C. (1995). The role of program quality in producing early childhood program benefits. In R. E. Behrman (Ed.), *The future of children: Long-term outcomes of early childhood programs* (pp. 115–133). Los Altos, CA: The Center for the Future of Children: The David & Lucile Packard Foundation.

Morrison, G. S. (2001). *Early childhood education today,* 8th ed. Upper Saddle River, NJ: Prentice Hall.

National Commission on Children (1993). *Just the facts.* Washington, DC: Author.

Shore, R. (1997). *Rethinking the brain: New insights into early development.* New York: Families and Work Institute.

The Cost and Quality Team. (1995). *Cost, quality, and child outcomes in child care centers: Executive summary.* Denver: University of Colorado at Denver.

Wedst, J., Wright, D., & Germino Hausken, E. (1995). *Child care and early education program participation of infants, toddlers, and preschoolers.* Washington, D.C.: U.S. Department of Education, National Center for Education Statistics.

Author Index

Subject Index